Microsoft Windows™ 3.1

Programmer's Reference

Volume 2

Functions

Microsoft
P R E S S

PUBLISHED BY
Microsoft Press
A Division of Microsoft Corporation
One Microsoft Way
Redmond, Washington 98052-6399

Library of Congress Cataloging-in-Publication Data
Microsoft Windows programmer's reference.
        p. cm.
    Includes indexes.
    Contents: v. 1. Overview -- v. 2. Functions -- v. 3. Messages,
structures, macros -- v. 4. Resources.
      ISBN 1-55615-453-4 (v. 1). -- ISBN 1-55615-463-1 (v. 2). -- ISBN
1-55615-464-X (v. 3). -- ISBN 1-55615-494-1 (v. 4)
      1. Microsoft Windows (Computer program) I. Microsoft
Corporation.
QA76.76.W56M532 1992
005.4'3--dc20   91-34199
                                                 CIP

Printed and bound in the United States of America.

1 2 3 4 5 6 7 8 9 MLML 7 6 5 4 3 2

Distributed to the book trade in Canada by Macmillan of Canada, a division of Canada Publishing Corporation.

Distributed to the book trade outside the United States and Canada by Penguin Books Ltd.

Penguin Books Ltd., Harmondsworth, Middlesex, England
Penguin Books Australia Ltd., Ringwood, Victoria, Australia
Penguin Books N.Z. Ltd., 182-190 Wairau Road, Auckland 10, New Zealand

British Cataloging-in-Publication Data available.

The Symbol fonts provided with Windows version 3.1 are based on the CG Times font, a product of AGFA Compugraphic Division of Agfa Corporation.

U.S. Patent No. 4974159

Document No. PC28916-0492

Contents

Introduction

The Microsoft® Windows™ 3.1 operating system is a single-user system for personal computers. Applications that run with this operating system use functions in the Windows applications programming interface (API). This manual describes the API functions in alphabetic order, including each function's purpose, the version of Windows in which it first appeared, and the function's syntax, parameters, and possible return values. Many function descriptions also contain additional information and simple code examples that illustrate how the function can be used to carry out simple tasks.

How to Use This Manual

For most of the functions described in this manual, the syntax is given in C-language format. In your C-language source files, the function name must be spelled exactly as given in syntax and the parameters must be used in the order given in syntax.

The Windows API uses many types, structures, and constants that are not part of standard C language. These items, designed for Windows, are defined in the Windows C-language header files. Although there are many Windows header files, the majority of API functions, structures, and messages are defined in the WINDOWS.H header file. You can use these items in your Windows application by placing an **#include** directive specifying WINDOWS.H at the beginning of your C-language source file.

In this manual, if a function is not defined in WINDOWS.H, its appropriate header file is included in the first line of syntax. If no header file is listed, you can assume the function is defined in WINDOWS.H.

Note You will find a list of the appropriate module and library for each Windows function in the *Microsoft Windows Programmer's Reference, Volume 1*. A list of the types used in the Windows API, with a brief description of each, is provided in the *Microsoft Windows Programmer's Reference, Volume 3*.

Document Conventions

The following conventions are used throughout this manual to define syntax:

Convention	Meaning
Bold text	Denotes a term or character to be typed literally, such as a resource-definition statement or function name (**MENU** or **CreateWindow**), a Microsoft MS-DOS® command, or a command-line option (**/nod**). You must type these terms exactly as shown.
Italic text	Denotes a placeholder or variable: You must provide the actual value. For example, the statement **SetCursorPos**(X, Y) requires you to substitute values for the X and Y parameters.
[ ]	Enclose optional parameters.
|	Separates an either/or choice.
...	Specifies that the preceding item may be repeated.
BEGIN . . . END	Represents an omitted portion of a sample application.

In addition, certain text conventions are used to help you understand this material:

Convention	Meaning
SMALL CAPITALS	Indicate the names of keys, key sequences, and key combinations—for example, ALT+SPACEBAR.
FULL CAPITALS	Indicate filenames and paths, most type and structure names (which are also bold), and constants.
monospace	Sets off code examples and shows syntax spacing.

AbortDoc

3.1

int AbortDoc(*hdc*)
HDC *hdc*;   /* handle of device context   */

The **AbortDoc** function terminates the current print job and erases everything drawn since the last call to the **StartDoc** function. This function replaces the ABORTDOC printer escape for Windows version 3.1.

Parameters   *hdc*
Identifies the device context for the print job.

Return Value   The return value is greater than or equal to zero if the function is successful. Otherwise, it is less than zero.

Comments   Applications should call the **AbortDoc** function to terminate a print job because of an error or if the user chooses to cancel the job. To end a successful print job, an application should use the **EndDoc** function.

If Print Manager was used to start the print job, calling the **AbortDoc** function erases the entire spool job—the printer receives nothing. If Print Manager was not used to start the print job, the data may have been sent to the printer before **Abort-Doc** was called. In this case, the printer driver would have reset the printer (when possible) and closed the print job.

See Also   **EndDoc, SetAbortProc, StartDoc**

AbortProc

3.1

BOOL CALLBACK AbortProc(*hdc*, *error*)
HDC *hdc*;   /* handle of device context   */
int *error*;   /* error value   */

The **AbortProc** function is an application-defined callback function that is called when a print job is to be canceled during spooling.

Parameters   *hdc*
Identifies the device context.

error
Specifies whether an error has occurred. This parameter is zero if no error has occurred; it is SP_OUTOFDISK if Print Manager is currently out of disk space

and more disk space will become available if the application waits. If this parameter is SP_OUTOFDISK, the application need not cancel the print job. If it does not cancel the job, it must yield to Print Manager by calling the **Peek-Message** or **GetMessage** function.

Return Value   The callback function should return TRUE to continue the print job or FALSE to cancel the print job.

Comments   An application installs this callback function by calling the **SetAbortProc** function. **AbortProc** is a placeholder for the application-defined function name. The actual name must be exported by including it in an **EXPORTS** statement in the application's module-definition file.

See Also   **GetMessage, PeekMessage, SetAbortProc**

AccessResource   2.x

int AccessResource(*hinst, hrsrc*)
HINSTANCE *hinst*;   /* handle of module with resource   */
HRSRC *hrsrc*;   /* handle of resource   */

The **AccessResource** function opens the given executable file and moves the file pointer to the beginning of the given resource.

Parameters   *hinst*
                 Identifies the instance of the module whose executable file contains the resource.

                 hrsrc
                 Identifies the desired resource. This handle should be created by using the **FindResource** function.

Return Value   The return value is the handle of the resource file if the function is successful. Otherwise, it is −1.

Comments   The **AccessResource** function supplies an MS-DOS file handle that can be used in subsequent file-read calls to load the resource. The file is opened for reading only.

                 Applications that use this function must close the resource file by calling the **_lclose** function after reading the resource. **AccessResource** can exhaust available MS-DOS file handles and cause errors if the opened file is not closed after the resource is accessed.

In general, the **LoadResource** and **LockResource** functions are preferred. These functions will access the resource more quickly if several resources are being read, because Windows maintains a file-handle cache for accessing executable files. However, each call to **AccessResource** requires that a new handle be opened to the executable file.

You should not use **AccessResource** to access executable files that are installed in ROM on a ROM-based system, since there are no disk files associated with the executable file; in such a case, a file handle cannot be returned.

See Also   **FindResource**, _**lclose**, **LoadResource**, **LockResource**

AddAtom

2.x

ATOM AddAtom(*lpszName*)
LPCSTR *lpszName*;   /* address of string to add   */

The **AddAtom** function adds a character string to the local atom table and returns a unique value identifying the string.

Parameters   *lpszName*
    Points to the null-terminated character string to be added to the table.

Return Value   The return value specifies the newly created atom if the function is successful. Otherwise, it is zero.

Comments   The **AddAtom** function stores no more than one copy of a given string in the atom table. If the string is already in the table, the function returns the existing atom value and increments (increases by one) the string's reference count.

The **MAKEINTATOM** macro can be used to convert a word value into a string that can be added to the atom table by using the **AddAtom** function.

The atom values returned by **AddAtom** are in the range 0xC000 through 0xFFFF.

Atoms are case-insensitive.

Example   The following example uses the **AddAtom** function to add the string "This is an atom" to the local atom table:

```
            ATOM at;
            char szMsg[80];

            at = AddAtom("This is an atom");

            if (at == 0)
                MessageBox(hwnd, "AddAtom failed", "", MB_ICONSTOP);
            else {
                wsprintf(szMsg, "AddAtom returned %u", at);
                MessageBox(hwnd, szMsg, "", MB_OK);
            }
```

See Also   **DeleteAtom, FindAtom, GetAtomName**

AddFontResource   2.x

int AddFontResource(*lpszFilename*)
LPCSTR *lpszFilename*;   /* address of filename   */

The **AddFontResource** function adds a font resource to the Windows font table. Any application can then use the font.

Parameters   *lpszFilename*
Points to a character string that names the font resource file or that contains a handle of a loaded module. If this parameter points to a font resource filename, it must be a valid MS-DOS filename, including an extension, and the string must be null-terminated. The system passes this string to the **LoadLibrary** function if the font resource must be loaded.

Return Value   The return value specifies the number of fonts added if the function is successful. Otherwise, it is zero.

Comments   Any application that adds or removes fonts from the Windows font table should send a WM_FONTCHANGE message to all top-level windows in the system by using the **SendMessage** function with the *hwnd* parameter set to 0xFFFF.

When font resources added by using **AddFontResource** are no longer needed, you should remove them by using the **RemoveFontResource** function.

Example   The following example uses the **AddFontResource** function to add a font resource from a file, notifies other applications by using the **SendMessage** function, then removes the font resource by using the **RemoveFontResource** function:

```
AddFontResource("fontres.fon");
SendMessage(HWND_BROADCAST, WM_FONTCHANGE, 0, 0);
        .
        . /* Work with the font. */
        .
if (RemoveFontResource("fontres.fon")) {
    SendMessage(HWND_BROADCAST, WM_FONTCHANGE, 0, 0);
    return TRUE;
}
else
    return FALSE;
```

See Also   **LoadLibrary, RemoveFontResource, SendMessage**

AdjustWindowRect   [2.x]

void AdjustWindowRect(*lprc, dwStyle, fMenu***)**
RECT FAR* *lprc*;   /* address of client-rectangle structure   */
DWORD *dwStyle*;   /* window styles   */
BOOL *fMenu*;   /* menu-present flag   */

The **AdjustWindowRect** function computes the required size of the window rectangle based on the desired client-rectangle size. The window rectangle can then be passed to the **CreateWindow** function to create a window whose client area is the desired size.

Parameters   *lprc*
Points to a **RECT** structure that contains the coordinates of the client rectangle. The **RECT** structure has the following form:

```
typedef struct tagRECT {    /* rc */
    int left;
    int top;
    int right;
    int bottom;
} RECT;
```

For a full description of this structure, see the *Microsoft Windows Programmer's Reference, Volume 3.*

dwStyle
Specifies the window styles of the window whose client rectangle is to be converted.

fMenu
Specifies whether the window has a menu.

Return Value   This function does not return a value.

Comments   A client rectangle is the smallest rectangle that completely encloses a client area. A window rectangle is the smallest rectangle that completely encloses the window.

AdjustWindowRect does not take titles and borders into account when computing the size of the client area. For window styles that include titles and borders, applications must add the title and border sizes after calling **AdjustWindowRect**. This function also does not take the extra rows into account when a menu bar wraps to two or more rows.

See Also   **AdjustWindowRectEx**, **CreateWindowEx**

AdjustWindowRectEx   3.0

void AdjustWindowRectEx(*lprc***,** *dwStyle***,** *fMenu***,** *dwExStyle***)**
RECT FAR* *lprc*;   /* address of client-rectangle structure   */
DWORD *dwStyle*;   /* window styles   */
BOOL *fMenu*;   /* menu-present flag   */
DWORD *dwExStyle*;   /* extended style   */

The **AdjustWindowRectEx** function computes the required size of the rectangle of a window with extended style based on the desired client-rectangle size. The window rectangle can then be passed to the **CreateWindowEx** function to create a window whose client area is the desired size.

Parameters   *lprc*
Points to a **RECT** structure that contains the coordinates of the client rectangle. The **RECT** structure has the following form:

```
typedef struct tagRECT {    /* rc */
    int left;
    int top;
    int right;
    int bottom;
} RECT;
```

For a full description of this structure, see the *Microsoft Windows Programmer's Reference, Volume 3*.

dwStyle
Specifies the window styles of the window whose client rectangle is to be converted.

fMenu
Specifies whether the window has a menu.

dwExStyle
Specifies the extended style of the window being created.

Return Value   This function does not return a value.

Comments   A client rectangle is the smallest rectangle that completely encloses a client area. A window rectangle is the smallest rectangle that completely encloses the window.

AdjustWindowRectEx does not take titles and borders into account when computing the size of the client area. For window styles that include titles and borders, applications must add the title and border sizes after calling **AdjustWindowRectEx**. This function also does not take the extra rows into account when a menu bar wraps to two or more rows.

See Also   **AdjustWindowRect, CreateWindowEx**

AllocDiskSpace

3.1

#include <stress.h>

int AllocDiskSpace(lLeft, uDrive**)**
long *lLeft*;   /* number of bytes left available   */
UINT *uDrive*;   /* disk partition   */

The **AllocDiskSpace** function creates a file that is large enough to ensure that the specified amount of space or less is available on the specified disk partition. The file, called STRESS.EAT, is created in the root directory of the disk partition.

If STRESS.EAT already exists when **AllocDiskSpace** is called, the function deletes it and creates a new one.

Parameters   *lLeft*
Specifies the number of bytes to leave available on the disk.

uDrive
Specifies the disk partition on which to create the STRESS.EAT file. This parameter must be one of the following values:

Value	Meaning
EDS_WIN	Creates the file on the Windows partition.
EDS_CUR	Creates the file on the current partition.
EDS_TEMP	Creates the file on the partition that contains the TEMP directory.

Return Value

The return value is greater than zero if the function is successful; it is zero if the function could not create a file; or it is −1 if at least one of the parameters is invalid.

Comments

In two situations, the amount of free space left on the disk may be less than the number of bytes specified in the *lLeft* parameter: when the amount of free space on the disk is less than the number in *lLeft* when an application calls **Alloc-DiskSpace**, or when the value of *lLeft* is not an exact multiple of the disk cluster size.

The **UnAllocDiskSpace** function deletes the file created by **AllocDiskSpace**.

See Also

UnAllocDiskSpace

AllocDStoCSAlias   3.0

UINT AllocDStoCSAlias(*uSelector***)**
UINT *uSelector*;   /* data-segment selector   */

The **AllocDStoCSAlias** function accepts a data-segment selector and returns a code-segment selector that can be used to execute code in the data segment.

Parameters

uSelector
   Specifies the data-segment selector.

Return Value

The return value is the code-segment selector corresponding to the data-segment selector if the function is successful. Otherwise, it is zero.

Comments

The application should not free the new selector by calling the **FreeSelector** function. Windows will free the selector when the application terminates.

In protected mode, attempting to execute code directly in a data segment will cause a general-protection violation. **AllocDStoCSAlias** allows an application to execute code that the application had created in its own stack segment.

Windows does not track segment movements. Consequently, the data segment must be fixed and nondiscardable; otherwise, the data segment might move, invalidating the code-segment selector.

The **PrestoChangoSelector** function provides another method of obtaining a code selector corresponding to a data selector.

An application should not use this function unless it is absolutely necessary, since its use violates preferred Windows programming practices.

See Also   **FreeSelector, PrestoChangoSelector**

AllocFileHandles   <u>3.1</u>

#include <stress.h>

int **AllocFileHandles**(*Left*)
int *Left*;   /* number of file handles to leave available   */

The **AllocFileHandles** function allocates file handles until only the specified number of file handles is available to the current instance of the application. If this or a smaller number of handles is available when an application calls **AllocFile-Handles**, the function returns immediately.

Before allocating new handles, this function frees any handles previously allocates by **AllocFileHandles**.

Parameters   *Left*
      Specifies the number of file handles to leave available.

Return Value   The return value is greater than zero if **AllocFileHandles** successfully allocates at least one file handle. The return value is zero if fewer than the specified number of file handles were available when the application called **AllocFileHandles**. The return value is −1 if the *Left* parameter is negative.

Comments   **AllocFileHandles** will not allocate more than 256 file handles, regardless of the number available to the application.

The **UnAllocFileHandles** function frees all file handles previously allocated by **AllocFileHandles**.

See Also   **UnAllocFileHandles**

AllocGDIMem

3.1

#include <stress.h>

BOOL AllocGDIMem(*uLeft*)
UINT *uLeft*;   /* number of bytes to leave available   */

The **AllocGDIMem** function allocates memory in the graphics device interface (GDI) heap until only the specified number of bytes is available. Before making any new memory allocations, this function frees memory previously allocated by **AllocGDIMem**.

Parameters   *uLeft*
                Specifies the amount of memory, in bytes, to leave available in the GDI heap.

Return Value   The return value is nonzero if the function is successful. Otherwise, it is zero.

Comments   The **FreeAllGDIMem** function frees all memory allocated by **AllocGDIMem**.

See Also   **FreeAllGDIMem**

AllocMem

3.1

#include <stress.h>

BOOL AllocMem(*dwLeft*)
DWORD *dwLeft*;   /*smallest memory allocation   */

The **AllocMem** function allocates global memory until only the specified number of bytes is available in the global heap. Before making any new memory allocations, this function frees memory previously allocated by **AllocMem**.

Parameters   *dwLeft*
                Specifies the smallest size, in bytes, of memory allocations to make.

Return Value   The return value is nonzero if the function is successful. Otherwise, it is zero.

Comments   The **FreeAllMem** function frees all memory allocated by **AllocMem**.

See Also   **FreeAllMem**

AllocResource

HGLOBAL AllocResource(*hinst, hrsrc, cbResource*)
HINSTANCE *hinst*;   /* handle of module containing resource   */
HRSRC *hrsrc*;   /* handle of resource   */
DWORD *cbResource*;   /* size to allocate, or zero   */

The **AllocResource** function allocates uninitialized memory for the given resource.

Parameters   *hinst*
Identifies the instance of the module whose executable file contains the resource.

hrsrc
Identifies the desired resource. This handle should have been created by using the **FindResource** function.

cbResource
Specifies the size, in bytes, of the memory object to allocate for the resource. If this parameter is zero, Windows allocates enough memory for the specified resource.

Return Value   The return value is the handle of the global memory object if the function is successful.

See Also   **FindResource, LoadResource**

AllocSelector

UINT AllocSelector(*uSelector*)
UINT *uSelector*;   /* selector to copy or zero   */

The **AllocSelector** function allocates a new selector.

Do not use this function in an application unless it is absolutely necessary, since its use violates preferred Windows programming practices.

Parameters   *uSelector*
Specifies the selector to return. If this parameter specifies a valid selector, the function returns a new selector that is an exact copy of the one specified here. If this parameter is zero, the function returns a new, uninitialized sector.

Return Value   The return value is a selector that is either a copy of an existing selector, or a new, uninitialized selector. Otherwise, the return value is zero.

Comments   The application must free the new selector by calling the **FreeSelector** function.

An application can call **AllocSelector** to allocate a selector that it can pass to the **PrestoChangoSelector** function.

See Also   **PrestoChangoSelector**

AllocUserMem   3.1

#include <stress.h>

BOOL AllocUserMem(*uContig*)
UINT *uContig*;   /* smallest memory allocation   */

The **AllocUserMem** function allocates memory in the USER heap until only the specified number of bytes is available. Before making any new allocations, this function frees memory previously allocated by **AllocUserMem**.

Parameters   *uContig*
     Specifies the smallest size, in bytes, of memory allocations to make.

Return Value   The return value is nonzero if the function is successful. Otherwise, it is zero.

Comments   The **FreeAllUserMem** function frees all memory allocated by **AllocUserMem**.

See Also   **FreeAllUserMem**

AnimatePalette   3.0

void AnimatePalette(*hpal*, *iStart*, *cEntries*, *lppe*)
HPALETTE *hpal*;   /* handle of palette   */
UINT *iStart*;   /* first palette entry to animate   */
UINT *cEntries*;   /* number of entries in palette   */
const PALETTEENTRY FAR* *lppe*;   /* address of color structure   */

The **AnimatePalette** function replaces entries in the specified logical palette. An application does not have to update the client area when it calls **AnimatePalette**, because Windows maps the new entries into the system palette immediately.

Parameters

hpal
Identifies the logical palette.

iStart
Specifies the first entry in the palette to be animated.

cEntries
Specifies the number of entries in the palette to be animated.

lppe
Points to the first member of an array of **PALETTEENTRY** structures. These palette entries will replace the palette entries identified by the *iStart* and *cEntries* parameters. The **PALETTEENTRY** structure has the following form:

```
typedef struct tagPALETTEENTRY {     /* pe */
    BYTE   peRed;
    BYTE   peGreen;
    BYTE   peBlue;
    BYTE   peFlags;
} PALETTEENTRY;
```

For a full description of this structure, see the *Microsoft Windows Programmer's Reference, Volume 3*.

Return Value

This function does not return a value.

Comments

The **AnimatePalette** function can change an entry in a logical palette only when the PC_RESERVED flag is set in the corresponding **palPaletteEntry** member of the **LOGPALETTE** structure that defines the current logical palette.

Example

The following example initializes a **LOGPALETTE** structure and an array of **PALETTEENTRY** structures, uses the **CreatePalette** function to retrieve a handle of a logical palette, and then uses the **AnimatePalette** function to map the entries into the system palette:

```
#define NUMENTRIES 128
HPALETTE hpal;
PALETTEENTRY ape[NUMENTRIES];

plgpl = (LOGPALETTE*) LocalAlloc(LPTR,
    sizeof(LOGPALETTE) + cColors * sizeof(PALETTEENTRY));

plgpl->palNumEntries = cColors;
plgpl->palVersion = 0x300;
```

```
                    for (i = 0, red = 0, green = 127, blue = 127; i < NUMENTRIES;
                         i++, red += 1, green += 1, blue += 1) {
                    ape[i].peRed =
                        plgpl->palPalEntry[i].peRed = LOBYTE(red);
                    ape[i].peGreen =
                        plgpl->palPalEntry[i].peGreen = LOBYTE(green);
                    ape[i].peBlue =
                        plgpl->palPalEntry[i].peBlue = LOBYTE(blue);
                    ape[i].peFlags =
                        plgpl->palPalEntry[i].peFlags = PC_RESERVED;
                    }
                    hpal = CreatePalette(plgpl);
                    LocalFree((HLOCAL) plgpl);
                    AnimatePalette(hpal, 0, NUMENTRIES, (PALETTEENTRY FAR*) &ape);
```

See Also   **CreatePalette**

AnsiLower   2.x

LPSTR AnsiLower(*lpsz***)**
LPSTR *lpsz*;   /* address of string, or specific character   */

The **AnsiLower** function converts a character string to lowercase.

Parameters   *lpsz*
                    Points to a null-terminated string or specifies a single character. If the high-
                    order word of this parameter is zero, the low-order byte of the low-order word
                    must contain a single character to be converted.

Return Value   The return value points to a converted character string if the function is successful.
                    Otherwise, the return value is a 32-bit value that contains the converted character
                    in the low-order byte of the low-order word.

Comments   The conversion is made by the language driver for the current language (the one
                    selected by the user at setup or by using Control Panel). If no language driver has
                    been selected, Windows uses an internal function.

Example   The following example uses the **AnsiLower** function to convert two strings to
                    lowercase for a non–case-sensitive comparison:

```
/*
 * Convert the target string to lowercase, and then
 * convert the subject string one character at a time.
 */
```

```
AnsiLower(pszTarget);
while (*pszTarget != '\0') {
    if (*pszTarget != (char) (DWORD) AnsiLower(
            MAKELP(0, *pszSubject)))
        return FALSE;
    pszTarget = AnsiNext(pszTarget);
    pszSubject = AnsiNext(pszSubject);
}
```

See Also   **AnsiLowerBuff, AnsiNext, AnsiUpper**

AnsiLowerBuff   3.0

UINT AnsiLowerBuff(*lpszString*, *cbString*)
LPSTR *lpszString*;   /* address of string to convert   */
UINT *cbString*;   /* length of string   */

The **AnsiLowerBuff** function converts a character string in a buffer to lowercase.

Parameters   *lpszString*
Points to a buffer containing one or more characters.

cbString
Specifies the number of bytes in the buffer identified by the *lpszString* parameter. If *cbString* is zero, the length is 64K (65,536).

Return Value   The return value specifies the length of the converted string if the function is successful. Otherwise, it is zero.

Comments   The language driver makes the conversion for the current language (the one selected by the user at setup or by using Control Panel). If no language driver has been selected, Windows uses an internal function.

Example   The following example uses the **AnsiLowerBuff** function to convert two strings to lowercase for a non–case-sensitive comparison:

```
AnsiLowerBuff(pszSubject, (UINT) lstrlen(pszSubject));
AnsiLowerBuff(pszTarget, (UINT) lstrlen(pszTarget));
```

```
while (*pszTarget != '\0') {
    if (*pszTarget != *pszSubject)
        return FALSE;
    pszTarget = AnsiNext(pszTarget);
    pszSubject = AnsiNext(pszSubject);
}
```

See Also   **AnsiLower, AnsiUpper**

AnsiNext

2.x

LPSTR AnsiNext(_lpchCurrentChar_**)**
LPCSTR _lpchCurrentChar_;   /* address of current character   */

The **AnsiNext** function moves to the next character in a string.

Parameters   _lpchCurrentChar_
    Points to a character in a null-terminated string.

Return Value   The return value points to the next character in the string or to the null character at
    the end of the string, if the function is successful.

Comments   The **AnsiNext** function can be used to move through strings where each character
    is a single byte, or through strings where each character is two or more bytes (such
    as strings that contain characters from a Japanese character set).

Example   The following example uses the **AnsiNext** function to step through the characters
    in a filename:

```
/* Find the last backslash. */

for (lpszFile = lpszTemp; *lpszTemp != '\0';
        lpszTemp = AnsiNext(lpszTemp)) {

    if (*lpszTemp == '\\')
        lpszFile = AnsiNext(lpszTemp);
}
```

See Also   **AnsiPrev**

AnsiPrev

LPSTR AnsiPrev(*lpchStart*, *lpchCurrentChar*)
LPCSTR *lpchStart*;   /* address of first character   */
LPCSTR *lpchCurrentChar*;   /* address of current character   */

The **AnsiPrev** function moves to the previous character in a string.

Parameters   *lpchStart*
                       Points to the beginning of the string.

                   lpchCurrentChar
                       Points to a character in a null-terminated string.

Return Value   The return value points to the previous character in the string, or to the first character in the string if the *lpchCurrentChar* parameter is equal to the *lpchStart* parameter.

Comments   The **AnsiPrev** function can be used to move through strings where each character is a single byte, or through strings where each character is two or more bytes (such as strings that contain characters from a Japanese character set).

                   This function can be very slow, because the string must be scanned from the beginning to determine the previous character. Wherever possible, the **AnsiNext** function should be used instead of this function.

Example   The following example uses the **AnsiNext** and **AnsiPrev** functions to change every occurrence of the characters '\&' in a string to a single newline character:

```
/* Find ampersands. */

for (lpsz = lpszTest; *lpsz != '\0'; lpsz = AnsiNext(lpsz)) {

    /* Check the previous character. */

    if (*lpsz == '&' &&
            *(lpsz2 = AnsiPrev(lpszTest, lpsz)) == '\\') {
        lstrcpy(lpsz2, lpsz);
        *lpsz2 = '\n';
    }
}
```

See Also   **AnsiNext**

AnsiToOem

void AnsiToOem(*hpszWindows*, *hpszOem*)
const char _huge* *hpszWindows*;   /* address of string to translate   */
char _huge* *hpszOem*;   /* address of buffer for string   */

The **AnsiToOem** function translates a string from the Windows character set into the specified OEM character set.

Parameters

hpszWindows
    Points to a null-terminated string of characters from the Windows character set.

hpszOem
    Points to the location where the translated string is to be copied. To translate the string in place, this parameter can be the same as *hpszWindows*.

Return Value

This function does not return a value.

Comments

The string to be translated can be greater than 64K in length.

Windows-to-OEM mappings are defined by the keyboard driver, where this function is implemented. Some keyboard drivers may have different mappings than others, depending on the machine environment, and some keyboard driver support loading different OEM character sets; for example, the standard U.S. keyboard driver for an IBM keyboard supports loadable code pages, with the default being code page 437 and the most common alternative being code page 850. (The Windows character set is sometimes referred to as code page 1007.)

The OEM character set must always be used when accessing string data created by MS-DOS or MS-DOS applications. For example, a word processor should convert OEM characters to Windows characters when importing documents from an MS-DOS word processor. When an application makes an MS-DOS call, including a C run-time function call, filenames must be in the OEM character set, whereas they must be presented to the user in Windows characters (because the Windows fonts use Windows characters).

Example

The following example is part of a dialog box in which a user would create a directory by typing a name in an edit control:

```
case IDOK:
    GetWindowText(GetDlgItem(hwndDlg, ID_EDITDIRNAME), szDirName,
        sizeof(szDirName));
    AnsiToOem(szDirName, szDirName);
    mkdir(szDirName);
    EndDialog(hwndDlg, 1);
    return TRUE;
```

See Also   AnsiToOemBuff, OemToAnsi

AnsiToOemBuff   `3.0`

void AnsiToOemBuff(*lpszWindowsStr*, *lpszOemStr*, *cbWindowsStr*)
LPCSTR *lpszWindowsStr*;   /* address of string to translate   */
LPSTR *lpszOemStr*;   /* address of buffer for translated string   */
UINT *cbWindowsStr*;   /* length of string to translate   */

The **AnsiToOemBuff** function translates a string from the Windows character set into the specified OEM character set.

Parameters   *lpszWindowsStr*
                     Points to a buffer containing one or more characters from the Windows character set.

                     lpszOemStr
                     Points to the location where the translated string is to be copied. To translate the string in place, this parameter can be the same as *lpszWindowsStr*.

                     cbWindowsStr
                     Specifies the number of bytes in the buffer identified by the *lpszWindowsStr* parameter. If *cbWindowsStr* is zero, the length is 64K (65,536).

Return Value   This function does not return a value.

See Also   AnsiToOem, OemToAnsi

AnsiUpper   `2.x`

LPSTR AnsiUpper(*lpszString*)
LPSTR *lpszString*;   /* address of string, or specific character   */

The **AnsiUpper** function converts the given character string to uppercase.

Parameters   *lpszString*
                     Points to a null-terminated string or specifies a single character. If the high-order word of this parameter is zero, the low-order byte of the low-order word must contain a single character to be converted.

Return Value   The return value points to a converted character string if the function parameter is a character string. Otherwise, the return value is a 32-bit value that contains the converted character in the low-order byte of the low-order word.

Comments   The language driver makes the conversion for the current language (the one selected by the user at setup or by using Control Panel). If no language driver is selected, Windows uses an internal function.

Example   The following example uses the **AnsiUpper** function to convert two strings to uppercase for a non–case-sensitive comparison:

```
/*
 * Convert the target string to uppercase, and then
 * convert the subject string one character at a time.
 */

AnsiUpper(pszTarget);
while (*pszTarget != '\0') {
    if (*pszTarget != (char) (DWORD) AnsiUpper(
            MAKELP(0, *pszSubject)))
        return FALSE;
    pszTarget = AnsiNext(pszTarget);
    pszSubject = AnsiNext(pszSubject);
}
```

See Also   **AnsiLower, AnsiUpperBuff**

AnsiUpperBuff   `3.0`

UINT AnsiUpperBuff(*lpszString*, *cbString*)
LPSTR *lpszString*;   /* address of string to convert   */
UINT *cbString*;   /* length of string   */

The **AnsiUpperBuff** function converts a character string in a buffer to uppercase.

Parameters   *lpszString*
                      Points to a buffer containing one or more characters.

                      cbString
                      Specifies the number of bytes in the buffer identified by the *lpszString* parameter. If *cbString* is zero, the length is 64K (65,536).

Return Value	The return value specifies the length of the converted string if the function is successful.
Comments	The language driver makes the conversion for the current language (the one selected by the user at setup or by using Control Panel). If no language driver is selected, Windows uses an internal function.
Example	The following example uses the **AnsiUpperBuff** function to convert two strings to lowercase for a non–case-sensitive comparison:

```
/*
 * Convert both the subject and target strings to uppercase before
 * comparing.
 */

AnsiUpperBuff(pszSubject, (UINT) lstrlen(pszSubject));
AnsiUpperBuff(pszTarget, (UINT) lstrlen(pszTarget));

while (*pszTarget != '\0') {
    if (*pszTarget != *pszSubject)
        return FALSE;
    pszTarget = AnsiNext(pszTarget);
    pszSubject = AnsiNext(pszSubject);
}
```

See Also	**AnsiLower, AnsiUpper**

AnyPopup
2.x

BOOL AnyPopup(void)

The **AnyPopup** function indicates whether an unowned, visible, top-level pop-up, or overlapped window exists on the screen. The function searches the entire Windows screen, not just the caller's client area.

Parameters	This function has no parameters.
Return Value	The return value is nonzero if a pop-up window exists, even if the pop-up window is completely covered by other windows. The return value is zero if no pop-up window exists.

Comments

AnyPopup is a Windows 1.*x* function and remains for compatibility reasons. It is generally not useful.

This function does not detect unowned pop-up windows or windows that do not have the WS_VISIBLE style bit set.

See Also

GetLastActivePopup, ShowOwnedPopups

AppendMenu

3.0

```
BOOL AppendMenu(hmenu, fuFlags, idNewItem, lpNewItem)
HMENU hmenu;          /* handle of menu                */
UINT fuFlags;         /* menu-item flags               */
UINT idNewItem;       /* menu-item identifier          */
LPCSTR lpNewItem;     /* specifies menu-item content   */
```

The **AppendMenu** function appends a new item to the end of a menu. The application can specify the state of the menu item by setting values in the *fuFlags* parameter.

Parameters

hmenu
   Identifies the menu to be changed.

fuFlags
   Specifies information about the state of the new menu item when it is added to the menu. This parameter consists of one or more of the values listed in the following Comments section.

idNewItem
   Specifies either the command identifier of the new menu item or, if the *fuFlags* parameter is set to MF_POPUP, the menu handle of the pop-up menu.

lpNewItem
   Specifies the content of the new menu item. The interpretation of the *lpNewItem* parameter depends on the value of the *fuFlags* parameter.

Value	Menu-item content
MF_STRING	Contains a long pointer to a null-terminated string.
MF_BITMAP	Contains a bitmap handle in its low-order word.

Value	Menu-item content
MF_OWNERDRAW	Contains an application-supplied 32-bit value that the application can use to maintain additional data associated with the menu item. An application can find this value in the **itemData** member of the structure pointed to by the *lParam* parameter of the WM_MEASUREITEM and WM_DRAWITEM messages that are sent when the menu item is changed or initially displayed.

Return Value

The return value is nonzero if the function is successful. Otherwise, it is zero.

Comments

Whenever a menu changes (whether or not the menu is in a window that is displayed), the application should call the **DrawMenuBar** function.

Each of the following groups lists flags that are mutually exclusive and cannot be used together:

- MF_DISABLED, MF_ENABLED, and MF_GRAYED
- MF_BITMAP, MF_STRING, and MF_OWNERDRAW
- MF_MENUBARBREAK and MF_MENUBREAK
- MF_CHECKED and MF_UNCHECKED

Following are the flags that can be set in the *fuFlags* parameter:

Value	Meaning
MF_BITMAP	Uses a bitmap as the item. The low-order word of the *lpNewItem* parameter contains the handle of the bitmap.
MF_CHECKED	Places a check mark next to the item. If the application has supplied check mark bitmaps (see the **SetMenuItem-Bitmaps** function), setting this flag displays the "check mark on" bitmap next to the menu item.
MF_DISABLED	Disables the menu item so that it cannot be selected, but does not gray it.
MF_ENABLED	Enables the menu item so that it can be selected, and restores it from its grayed state.
MF_GRAYED	Disables the menu item so that it cannot be selected, and grays it.
MF_MENUBARBREAK	Same as MF_MENUBREAK except that, for pop-up menus, separates the new column from the old column with a vertical line.
MF_MENUBREAK	Places the item on a new line for static menu-bar items. For pop-up menus, places the item in a new column, with no dividing line between the columns.

Value	Meaning
MF_OWNERDRAW	Specifies that the item is an owner-drawn item. The window that owns the menu receives a WM_MEASUREITEM message when the menu is displayed for the first time to retrieve the height and width of the menu item. The WM_DRAWITEM message is then sent whenever the owner window must update the visual appearance of the menu item. This option is not valid for a top-level menu item.
MF_POPUP	Specifies that the menu item has a pop-up menu associated with it. The *idNewItem* parameter specifies a handle to a pop-up menu to be associated with the item. This is used for adding either a top-level pop-up menu or adding a hierarchical pop-up menu to a pop-up menu item.
MF_SEPARATOR	Draws a horizontal dividing line. Can be used only in a pop-up menu. This line cannot be grayed, disabled, or highlighted. The *lpNewItem* and *idNewItem* parameters are ignored.
MF_STRING	Specifies that the menu item is a character string; the *lpNewItem* parameter points to the string for the menu item.
MF_UNCHECKED	Does not place a check mark next to the item (default). If the application has supplied check mark bitmaps (see **SetMenuItemBitmaps**), setting this flag displays the "check mark off" bitmap next to the menu item.

Example

The following example uses the **AppendMenu** function to append three items to a floating pop-up menu:

```
POINT ptCurrent;
HMENU hmenu;

ptCurrent = MAKEPOINT(lParam);
hmenu = CreatePopupMenu();
AppendMenu(hmenu, MF_ENABLED, IDM_ELLIPSE, "Ellipse");
AppendMenu(hmenu, MF_ENABLED, IDM_SQUARE, "Square");
AppendMenu(hmenu, MF_ENABLED, IDM_TRIANGLE, "Triangle");
ClientToScreen(hwnd, &ptCurrent);
TrackPopupMenu(hmenu, TPM_LEFTALIGN, ptCurrent.x,
    ptCurrent.y, 0, hwnd, NULL);
```

See Also   **CreateMenu, DeleteMenu, DrawMenuBar, InsertMenu, RemoveMenu, SetMenuItemBitmaps**

Arc

BOOL Arc(*hdc, nLeftRect, nTopRect, nRightRect, nBottomRect, nXStartArc, nYStartArc, nXEndArc,*
   nYEndArc)

HDC *hdc*;	/* handle of device context	*/
int *nLeftRect*;	/* x-coordinate upper-left corner bounding rectangle	*/
int *nTopRect*;	/* y-coordinate upper-left corner bounding rectangle	*/
int *nRightRect*;	/* x-coordinate lower-right corner bounding rectangle	*/
int *nBottomRect*;	/* y-coordinate lower-right corner bounding rectangle	*/
int *nXStartArc*;	/* x-coordinate arc starting point	*/
int *nYStartArc*;	/* y-coordinate arc starting point	*/
int *nXEndArc*;	/* x-coordinate arc ending point	*/
int *nYEndArc*;	/* y-coordinate arc ending point	*/

The **Arc** function draws an elliptical arc.

Parameters

hdc
Identifies the device context.

nLeftRect
Specifies the logical x-coordinate of the upper-left corner of the bounding rectangle.

nTopRect
Specifies the logical y-coordinate of the upper-left corner of the bounding rectangle.

nRightRect
Specifies the logical x-coordinate of the lower-right corner of the bounding rectangle.

nBottomRect
Specifies the logical y-coordinate of the lower-right corner of the bounding rectangle.

nXStartArc
Specifies the logical x-coordinate of the point that defines the arc's starting point. This point need not lie exactly on the arc.

nYStartArc
Specifies the logical y-coordinate of the point that defines the arc's starting point. This point need not lie exactly on the arc.

nXEndArc
Specifies the logical x-coordinate of the point that defines the arc's endpoint. This point need not lie exactly on the arc.

nYEndArc
Specifies the logical y-coordinate of the point that defines the arc's endpoint. This point need not lie exactly on the arc.

Return Value   The return value is nonzero if the function is successful. Otherwise, it is zero.

Comments   The arc drawn by using the **Arc** function is a segment of the ellipse defined by the specified bounding rectangle. The starting point of the arc is the point at which a ray drawn from the center of the bounding rectangle through the specified starting point intersects the ellipse. The end point of the arc is the point at which a ray drawn from the center of the bounding rectangle through the specified end point intersects the ellipse. The arc is drawn in a counterclockwise direction. Since an arc is not a closed figure, it is not filled.

Both the width and the height of a rectangle must be greater than 2 units and less than 32,767 units.

Example   The following example uses a **RECT** structure to store the points defining the bounding rectangle and uses **POINT** structures to store the coordinates that specify the beginning and end of the arc:

```
HDC hdc;

RECT rc = { 10, 10, 180, 140 };
POINT ptStart = {  12,  12 };
POINT ptEnd = { 128, 135 };

Arc(hdc, rc.left, rc.top, rc.right, rc.bottom,
    ptStart.x, ptStart.y, ptEnd.x, ptEnd.y);
```

See Also   **Chord**

ArrangeIconicWindows   `3.0`

UINT ArrangeIconicWindows(*hwnd***)**
HWND *hwnd*;   /* handle of parent window   */

The **ArrangeIconicWindows** function arranges all the minimized (iconic) child windows of a parent window.

Parameters   *hwnd*
                   Identifies the parent window.

Return Value   The return value is the height of one row of icons if the function is successful. Otherwise, it is zero.

Comments	An application that maintains its own minimized child windows can call **Arrange-IconicWindows** to arrange icons in a client window. This function also arranges icons on the desktop window, which covers the entire screen. The **GetDesktop-Window** function retrieves the window handle of the desktop window.
	An application sends the WM_MDIICONARRANGE message to the MDI client window to prompt the client window to arrange its minimized MDI child windows.
See Also	**GetDesktopWindow**

BeginDeferWindowPos

HDWP BeginDeferWindowPos(*cWindows*)
int *cWindows*;   /* number of windows   */

The **BeginDeferWindowPos** function returns a handle of an internal structure. The **DeferWindowPos** function fills this structure with information about the target position for a window that is about to be moved. The **EndDeferWindowPos** function accepts a handle of this structure and instantaneously repositions the windows by using the information stored in the structure.

Parameters	*cWindows*
	Specifies the initial number of windows for which to store position information in the structure. The **DeferWindowPos** function increases the size of the structure if necessary.
Return Value	The return value identifies the internal structure if the function is successful. Otherwise, it is NULL.
Comments	If Windows must increase the size of the internal structure beyond the initial size specified by the *cWindows* parameter but cannot allocate enough memory to do so, Windows fails the entire begin/defer/end window-positioning sequence. By specifying the maximum size needed, an application can detect and handle failure early in the process.
See Also	**DeferWindowPos, EndDeferWindowPos**

BeginPaint

HDC **BeginPaint**(*hwnd*, *lpps*)
HWND *hwnd*;   /* handle of window to paint   */
PAINTSTRUCT FAR* *lpps*;   /* address of structure with paint information */

The **BeginPaint** function prepares the specified window for painting and fills a **PAINTSTRUCT** structure with information about the painting.

Parameters

hwnd
Identifies the window to be repainted.

lpps
Points to the **PAINTSTRUCT** structure that will receive the painting information. The **PAINTSTRUCT** structure has the following form:

```
typedef struct tagPAINTSTRUCT {    /* ps */
    HDC   hdc;
    BOOL  fErase;
    RECT  rcPaint;
    BOOL  fRestore;
    BOOL  fIncUpdate;
    BYTE  rgbReserved[16];
} PAINTSTRUCT;
```

For a full description of this structure, see the *Microsoft Windows Programmer's Reference, Volume 3*.

Return Value

The return value is the handle of the device context for the given window if the function is successful.

Comments

The **BeginPaint** function automatically sets the clipping region of the device context to exclude any area outside the update region. The update region is set by the **InvalidateRect** or **InvalidateRgn** function and by the system after sizing, moving, creating, scrolling, or any other operation that affects the client area. If the update region is marked for erasing, **BeginPaint** sends a WM_ERASEBKGND message to the window.

An application should not call **BeginPaint** except in response to a WM_PAINT message. Each call to the **BeginPaint** function must have a corresponding call to the **EndPaint** function.

If the caret is in the area to be painted, **BeginPaint** automatically hides the caret to prevent it from being erased.

If the window's class has a background brush, **BeginPaint** will use that brush to erase the background of the update region before returning.

Example   The following example calls an application-defined function to paint a bar graph in a window's client area during the WM_PAINT message:

```
PAINTSTRUCT ps;

case WM_PAINT:
    BeginPaint(hwnd, &ps);
        .
        .
        .
    EndPaint(hwnd, &ps);
    break;
```

See Also   **EndPaint, InvalidateRect, InvalidateRgn, ValidateRect, ValidateRgn**

BitBlt

2.x

BOOL BitBlt(_hdcDest, nXDest, nYDest, nWidth, nHeight, hdcSrc, nXSrc, nYSrc, dwRop_**)**

HDC _hdcDest_;	/* handle of destination device context	*/
int _nXDest_;	/* upper-left corner destination rectangle	*/
int _nYDest_;	/* upper-left corner destination rectangle	*/
int _nWidth_;	/* bitmap width	*/
int _nHeight_;	/* bitmap height	*/
HDC _hdcSrc_;	/* handle of source device context	*/
int _nXSrc_;	/* upper-left corner source bitmap	*/
int _nYSrc_;	/* upper-left corner source bitmap	*/
DWORD _dwRop_;	/* raster operation for copy	*/

The **BitBlt** function copies a bitmap from a specified device context to a destination device context.

Parameters   _hdcDest_
Identifies the destination device context.

nXDest
Specifies the logical x-coordinate of the upper-left corner of the destination rectangle.

nYDest
Specifies the logical y-coordinate of the upper-left corner of the destination rectangle.

nWidth
Specifies the width, in logical units, of the destination rectangle and source bitmap.

nHeight
    Specifies the height, in logical units, of the destination rectangle and source bitmap.

hdcSrc
    Identifies the device context from which the bitmap will be copied. This parameter must be NULL if the *dwRop* parameter specifies a raster operation that does not include a source. This parameter can specify a memory device context.

nXSrc
    Specifies the logical x-coordinate of the upper-left corner of the source bitmap.

nYSrc
    Specifies the logical y-coordinate of the upper-left corner of the source bitmap.

dwRop
    Specifies the raster operation to be performed. Raster operation codes define how the graphics device interface (GDI) combines colors in output operations that involve a current brush, a possible source bitmap, and a destination bitmap. This parameter can be one of the following:

Code	Description
BLACKNESS	Turns all output black.
DSTINVERT	Inverts the destination bitmap.
MERGECOPY	Combines the pattern and the source bitmap by using the Boolean AND operator.
MERGEPAINT	Combines the inverted source bitmap with the destination bitmap by using the Boolean OR operator.
NOTSRCCOPY	Copies the inverted source bitmap to the destination.
NOTSRCERASE	Inverts the result of combining the destination and source bitmaps by using the Boolean OR operator.
PATCOPY	Copies the pattern to the destination bitmap.
PATINVERT	Combines the destination bitmap with the pattern by using the Boolean XOR operator.
PATPAINT	Combines the inverted source bitmap with the pattern by using the Boolean OR operator. Combines the result of this operation with the destination bitmap by using the Boolean OR operator.
SRCAND	Combines pixels of the destination and source bitmaps by using the Boolean AND operator.
SRCCOPY	Copies the source bitmap to the destination bitmap.
SRCERASE	Inverts the destination bitmap and combines the result with the source bitmap by using the Boolean AND operator.
SRCINVERT	Combines pixels of the destination and source bitmaps by using the Boolean XOR operator.

Code	Description
SRCPAINT	Combines pixels of the destination and source bitmaps by using the Boolean OR operator.
WHITENESS	Turns all output white.

Return Value

The return value is nonzero if the function is successful. Otherwise, it is zero.

Comments

An application that uses the **BitBlt** function to copy pixels from one window to another window or from a source rectangle in a window into a target rectangle in the same window should set the CS_BYTEALIGNWINDOW or CS_BYTEALIGNCLIENT flag when registering the window classes. By aligning the windows or client areas on byte boundaries, the application can ensure that the **BitBlt** operations occur on byte-aligned rectangles. **BitBlt** operations on byte-aligned rectangles are considerably faster than **BitBlt** operations on rectangles that are not byte-aligned.

GDI transforms the *nWidth* and *nHeight* parameters, once by using the destination device context, and once by using the source device context. If the resulting extents do not match, GDI uses the **StretchBlt** function to compress or stretch the source bitmap as necessary. If destination, source, and pattern bitmaps do not have the same color format, the **BitBlt** function converts the source and pattern bitmaps to match the destination. The foreground and background colors of the destination bitmap are used in the conversion.

When the **BitBlt** function converts a monochrome bitmap to color, it sets white bits (1) to the background color and black bits (0) to the foreground color. The foreground and background colors of the destination device context are used. To convert color to monochrome, **BitBlt** sets pixels that match the background color to white and sets all other pixels to black. **BitBlt** uses the foreground and background colors of the source (color) device context to convert from color to monochrome.

The foreground color is the current text color for the specified device context, and the background color is the current background color for the specified device context.

Not all devices support the **BitBlt** function. An application can determine whether a device supports **BitBlt** by calling the **GetDeviceCaps** function and specifying the **RASTERCAPS** index.

For a complete list of the raster-operation codes, see the *Microsoft Windows Programmer's Reference, Volume 4.*

Example

The following example loads a bitmap, retrieves its dimensions, and displays it in a window:

```
HDC hdc, hdcMemory;
HBITMAP hbmpMyBitmap, hbmpOld;
BITMAP bm;

hbmpMyBitmap = LoadBitmap(hinst, "MyBitmap");
GetObject(hbmpMyBitmap, sizeof(BITMAP), &bm);

hdc = GetDC(hwnd);
hdcMemory = CreateCompatibleDC(hdc);
hbmpOld = SelectObject(hdcMemory, hbmpMyBitmap);

BitBlt(hdc, 0, 0, bm.bmWidth, bm.bmHeight, hdcMemory, 0, 0, SRCCOPY);
SelectObject(hdcMemory, hbmpOld);

DeleteDC(hdcMemory);
ReleaseDC(hwnd, hdc);
```

See Also   **GetDeviceCaps, PatBlt, SetTextColor, StretchBlt, StretchDIBits**

BringWindowToTop   `2.x`

BOOL BringWindowToTop(*hwnd***)**
HWND *hwnd*;   /* handle of window   */

The **BringWindowToTop** function brings the given pop-up or child window (including an MDI child window) to the top of a stack of overlapping windows. In addition, it activates pop-up, top-level, and MDI child windows. The **Bring-WindowToTop** function should be used to uncover any window that is partially or completely obscured by any overlapping windows.

Parameters   *hwnd*
          Identifies the pop-up or child window to bring to the top.

Return Value   The return value is nonzero if the function is successful. Otherwise, it is zero.

Comments   Calling this function is similar to calling the **SetWindowPos** function to change a window's position in the Z-order. The **BringWindowToTop** function does not make a window a top-level window.

See Also   **SetWindowPos**

BuildCommDCB

int **BuildCommDCB**(*lpszDef*, *lpdcb*)
LPCSTR *lpszDef*;   /* address of device-control string   */
DCB FAR* *lpdcb*;   /* address of device-control block   */

The **BuildCommDCB** function translates a device-definition string into appropriate serial device control block (DCB) codes.

Parameters

lpszDef

Points to a null-terminated string that specifies device-control information. The string must have the same form as the parameters used in the MS-DOS **mode** command.

lpdcb

Points to a **DCB** structure that will receive the translated string. The structure defines the control settings for the serial-communications device. The **DCB** structure has the following form:

```
typedef struct tagDCB        /* dcb                            */
{
    BYTE Id;                 /* internal device identifier     */
    UINT BaudRate;           /* baud rate                      */
    BYTE ByteSize;           /* number of bits/byte, 4-8        */
    BYTE Parity;             /* 0-4=none,odd,even,mark,space    */
    BYTE StopBits;           /* 0,1,2 = 1, 1.5, 2              */
    UINT RlsTimeout;         /* timeout for RLSD to be set     */
    UINT CtsTimeout;         /* timeout for CTS to be set      */
    UINT DsrTimeout;         /* timeout for DSR to be set      */

    UINT fBinary       :1;   /* binary mode (skip EOF check)   */
    UINT fRtsDisable   :1;   /* don't assert RTS at init time  */
    UINT fParity       :1;   /* enable parity checking         */
    UINT fOutxCtsFlow  :1;   /* CTS handshaking on output      */
    UINT fOutxDsrFlow  :1;   /* DSR handshaking on output      */
    UINT fDummy        :2;   /* reserved                       */
    UINT fDtrDisable   :1;   /* don't assert DTR at init time  */

    UINT fOutX         :1;   /* enable output XON/XOFF         */
    UINT fInX          :1;   /* enable input XON/XOFF          */
    UINT fPeChar       :1;   /* enable parity err replacement  */
    UINT fNull         :1;   /* enable null stripping          */
    UINT fChEvt        :1;   /* enable Rx character event      */
    UINT fDtrflow      :1;   /* DTR handshake on input         */
    UINT fRtsflow      :1;   /* RTS handshake on input         */
    UINT fDummy2       :1;
```

```
        char XonChar;          /* Tx and Rx XON character        */
        char XoffChar;         /* Tx and Rx XOFF character       */
        UINT XonLim;           /* transmit XON threshold         */
        UINT XoffLim;          /* transmit XOFF threshold        */
        char PeChar;           /* parity error replacement char  */
        char EofChar;          /* end of Input character         */
        char EvtChar;          /* received event character       */
        UINT TxDelay;          /* amount of time between chars    */
    } DCB;
```

For a full description of this structure, see the *Microsoft Windows Programmer's Reference, Volume 3*.

Return Value   The return value is zero if the function is successful. Otherwise, it is −1.

Comments   The **BuildCommDCB** function only fills the buffer. To apply the settings to a
                      port, an application should use the **SetCommState** function.

                      By default, **BuildCommDCB** specifies XON/XOFF and hardware flow control as
                      disabled. To enable flow control, an application should set the appropriate mem-
                      bers in the **DCB** structure.

Example   The following example uses the **BuildCommDCB** and **SetCommState** functions
                      to set up COM1 to operate at 9600 baud, with no parity, 8 data bits, and 1 stop bit:

```
idComDev = OpenComm("COM1", 1024, 128);
if (idComDev < 0) {
    ShowError(idComDev, "OpenComm");
    return 0;
}

err = BuildCommDCB("COM1:9600,n,8,1", &dcb);
if (err < 0) {
    ShowError(err, "BuildCommDCB");
    return 0;
}

err = SetCommState(&dcb);
if (err < 0) {
    ShowError(err, "SetCommState");
    return 0;
}
```

See Also   **SetCommState**

CallMsgFilter

BOOL CallMsgFilter(*lpmsg*, *nCode*)
MSG FAR* *lpmsg*;   /* address of structure with message data   */
int *nCode*;   /* processing code   */

The **CallMsgFilter** function passes the given message and code to the current message-filter function. The message-filter function is an application-specified function that examines and modifies all messages. An application specifies the function by using the **SetWindowsHook** function.

Parameters

lpmsg
Points to an **MSG** structure that contains the message to be filtered. The **MSG** structure has the following form:

```
typedef struct tagMSG {        /* msg */
    HWND    hwnd;
    UINT    message;
    WPARAM  wParam;
    LPARAM  lParam;
    DWORD   time;
    POINT   pt;
} MSG;
```

For a full description of this structure, see the *Microsoft Windows Programmer's Reference, Volume 3.*

nCode
Specifies a code used by the filter function to determine how to process the message.

Return Value

The return value specifies the state of message processing. It is zero if the message should be processed or nonzero if the message should not be processed further.

Comments

The **CallMsgFilter** function is usually called by Windows to let applications examine and control the flow of messages during internal processing in menus and scroll bars or when moving or sizing a window.

Values given for the *nCode* parameter must not conflict with any of the MSGF_ and HC_ values passed by Windows to the message-filter function.

See Also

SetWindowsHook

CallNextHookEx

3.1

LRESULT CallNextHookEx(*hHook*, *nCode*, *wParam*, *lParam*)
HHOOK *hHook*;   /* handle of hook function   */
int *nCode*;   /* hook code   */
WPARAM *wParam*;   /* first message parameter   */
LPARAM *lParam*;   /* second message parameter   */

The **CallNextHookEx** function passes the hook information to the next hook function in the hook chain.

Parameters

hHook
Identifies the current hook function.

nCode
Specifies the hook code to pass to the next hook function. A hook function uses this code to determine how to process the message sent to the hook.

wParam
Specifies 16 bits of additional message-dependent information.

lParam
Specifies 32 bits of additional message-dependent information.

Return Value

The return value specifies the result of the message processing and depends on the value of the *nCode* parameter.

Comments

Calling the **CallNextHookEx** function is optional. An application can call this function either before or after completing any processing in its own hook function. If an application does not call **CallNextHookEx**, Windows will not call the hook functions that were installed before the application's hook function was installed.

See Also

SetWindowsHookEx, **UnhookWindowsHookEx**

CallWindowProc

2.x

LRESULT CallWindowProc(*wndprcPrev*, *hwnd*, *uMsg*, *wParam*, *lParam*)
WNDPROC *wndprcPrev*;   /* instance address of previous procedure   */
HWND *hwnd*;   /* handle of window   */
UINT *uMsg*;   /* message   */
WPARAM *wParam*;   /* first message parameter   */
LPARAM *lParam*;   /* second message parameter   */

The **CallWindowProc** function passes message information to the specified window procedure.

Parameters

wndprcPrev
Specifies the procedure-instance address of the previous window procedure.

hwnd
Identifies the window that will receive the message.

uMsg
Specifies the message.

wParam
Specifies 16 bits of additional message-dependent information.

lParam
Specifies 32 bits of additional message-dependent information.

Return Value

The return value specifies the result of the message processing and depends on the message sent.

Comments

The **CallWindowProc** function is used for window subclassing. Normally, all windows with the same class share the same window procedure. A subclass is a window or set of windows belonging to the same window class whose messages are intercepted and processed by another window procedure (or procedures) before being passed to the window procedure of that class.

The **SetWindowLong** function creates the subclass by changing the window procedure associated with a particular window, causing Windows to call the new window procedure instead of the previous one. Any messages not processed by the new window procedure must be passed to the previous window procedure by calling **CallWindowProc**. This allows you to create a chain of window procedures.

See Also

SetWindowLong

CallWndProc

3.1

LRESULT CALLBACK CallWndProc(*code*, *wParam*, *lParam*)
int *code*;   /* process-message flag   */
WPARAM *wParam*;   /* current-task flag   */
LPARAM *lParam*;   /* address of structure with message data   */

The **CallWndProc** function is a library-defined callback function that the system calls whenever the **SendMessage** function is called. The system passes the message to the callback function before passing the message to the destination window procedure.

Parameters

code

Specifies whether the callback function should process the message or call the **CallNextHookEx** function. If the *code* parameter is less than zero, the callback function should pass the message to **CallNextHookEx** without further processing.

wParam

Specifies whether the message is sent by the current task. This parameter is non-zero if the message is sent; otherwise, it is NULL.

lParam

Points to a structure that contains details about the message. The following shows the order, type, and description of each member of the structure:

Member	Description
lParam	Contains the *lParam* parameter of the message.
wParam	Contains the *wParam* parameter of the message.
uMsg	Specifies the message.
hWnd	Identifies the window that will receive the message.

Return Value

The callback function should return zero.

Comments

The **CallWndProc** callback function can examine or modify the message as necessary. Once the function returns control to the system, the message, with any modifications, is passed on to the window procedure.

This callback function must be in a dynamic-link library.

An application must install the callback function by specifying the WH_CALLWNDPROC filter type and the procedure-instance address of the callback function in a call to the **SetWindowsHookEx** function.

CallWndProc is a placeholder for the library-defined function name. The actual name must be exported by including it in an **EXPORTS** statement in the library's module-definition file.

See Also

CallNextHookEx, SendMessage, SetWindowsHookEx

Catch

int **Catch**(*lpCatchBuf*)
int **FAR*** *lpCatchBuf*;   /* address of buffer for array   */

The **Catch** function captures the current execution environment and copies it to a buffer. The **Throw** function can use this buffer later to restore the execution environment. The execution environment includes the state of all system registers and the instruction counter.

Parameters

lpCatchBuf
    Points to a memory buffer large enough to contain a **CATCHBUF** array.

Return Value

The **Catch** function returns immediately with a return value of zero. When the **Throw** function is called, it returns again, this time with the return value specified in the *nErrorReturn* parameter of the **Throw** function.

Comments

The **Catch** function is similar to the C run-time function **setjmp**.

Example

The following example calls the **Catch** function to save the current execution environment before calling a recursive sort function. The first return value from **Catch** is zero. If the doSort function calls the **Throw** function, execution will again return to the **Catch** function. This time, **Catch** will return the STACKOVERFLOW error passed by the doSort function. The doSort function is recursive—that is, it calls itself. It maintains a variable, wStackCheck, that is used to check to see how much stack space has been used. If more then 3K of the stack has been used, doSort calls **Throw** to drop out of all the nested function calls back into the function that called **Catch**.

```
#define STACKOVERFLOW 1

UINT uStackCheck;
CATCHBUF catchbuf;

{
    int iReturn;
    char szBuf[80];

    if ((iReturn = Catch((int FAR*) catchbuf)) != 0) {
        .
        . /* Error processing goes here. */
        .
    }
```

```
        else {
            uStackCheck = 0;        /* initializes stack-usage count */
            doSort(1, 100);         /* calls sorting function        */
        }
        break;
}

void doSort(int sLeft, int sRight)
{
    int sLast;

    /*
     * Determine whether more than 3K of the stack has been
     * used, and if so, call Throw to drop back into the
     * original calling application.
     *
     * The stack is incremented by the size of the two parameters,
     * the two local variables, and the return value (2 for a near
     * function call).
     */

    uStackCheck += (sizeof(int) * 4) + 2;

    if (uStackCheck > (3 * 1024))
        Throw((int FAR*) catchbuf, STACKOVERFLOW);

    .
    . /* A sorting algorithm goes here. */
    .

    doSort(sLeft, sLast - 1);   /* note recursive call         */
    uStackCheck -= 10;          /* updates stack-check variable */
}
```

See Also   **Throw**

CBTProc

3.1

LRESULT CALLBACK CBTProc(*code*, *wParam*, *lParam*)
int *code*;   /* CBT hook code   */
WPARAM *wParam*;   /* depends on the code parameter   */
LPARAM *lParam*;   /* depends on the code parameter   */

The **CBTProc** function is a library-defined callback function that the system calls before activating, creating, destroying, minimizing, maximizing, moving, or sizing a window; before completing a system command; before removing a mouse or keyboard event from the system message queue; before setting the input focus; or before synchronizing with the system message queue.

The value returned by the callback function determines whether to allow or prevent one of these operations.

Parameters   *code*

Specifies a computer-based-training (CBT) hook code that identifies the operation about to be carried out, or a value less than zero if the callback function should pass the *code*, *wParam*, and *lParam* parameters to the **CallNextHookEx** function. The *code* parameter can be one of the following:

Code	Meaning
HCBT_ACTIVATE	Indicates that the system is about to activate a window.
HCBT_CLICKSKIPPED	Indicates that the system has removed a mouse message from the system message queue. A CBT application that must install a journaling playback filter in response to the mouse message should do so when it receives this hook code.
HCBT_CREATEWND	Indicates that a window is about to be created. The system calls the callback function before sending the WM_CREATE or WM_NCCREATE message to the window. If the callback function returns TRUE, the system destroys the window—the **CreateWindow** function returns NULL, but the WM_DESTROY message is not sent to the window. If the callback function returns FALSE, the window is created normally.
	At the time of the HCBT_CREATEWND notification, the window has been created, but its final size and position may not have been determined, nor has its parent window been established.
	It is possible to send messages to the newly created window, although the window has not yet received WM_NCCREATE or WM_CREATE messages.
	It is possible to change the Z-order of the newly created window by modifying the **hwndInsertAfter** member of the **CBT_CREATEWND** structure.
HCBT_DESTROYWND	Indicates that a window is about to be destroyed.
HCBT_KEYSKIPPED	Indicates that the system has removed a keyboard message from the system message queue. A CBT application that must install a journaling playback filter in response to the keyboard message should do so when it receives this hook code.
HCBT_MINMAX	Indicates that a window is about to be minimized or maximized.

Code	Meaning
HCBT_MOVESIZE	Indicates that a window is about to be moved or sized.
HCBT_QS	Indicates that the system has retrieved a WM_QUEUESYNC message from the system message queue.
HCBT_SETFOCUS	Indicates that a window is about to receive the input focus.
HCBT_SYSCOMMAND	Indicates that a system command is about to be carried out. This allows a CBT application to prevent task switching by hot keys.

wParam
This parameter depends on the *code* parameter. See the following Comments section for details.

lParam
This parameter depends on the *code* parameter. See the following Comments section for details.

Return Value

For operations corresponding to the following CBT hook codes, the callback function should return zero to allow the operation, or 1 to prevent it:

HCBT_ACTIVATE
HCBT_CREATEWND
HCBT_DESTROYWND
HCBT_MINMAX
HCBT_MOVESIZE
HCBT_SYSCOMMAND

The return value is ignored for operations corresponding to the following CBT hook codes:

HCBT_CLICKSKIPPED
HCBT_KEYSKIPPED
HCBT_QS

Comments

The callback function should not install a playback hook except in the situations described in the preceding list of hook codes.

This callback function must be in a dynamic-link library.

An application must install the callback function by specifying the WH_CBT filter type and the procedure-instance address of the callback function in a call to the **SetWindowsHookEx** function.

CBTProc is a placeholder for the library-defined function name. The actual name must be exported by including it in an **EXPORTS** statement in the library's module-definition file.

The following table describes the *wParam* and *lParam* parameters for each HCBT_ constant.

Constant	*wParam*	*lParam*
HCBT_ACTIVATE	Specifies the handle of the window about to be activated.	Specifies a long pointer to a **CBT-ACTIVATESTRUCT** structure that contains the handle of the currently active window and specifies whether the activation is changing because of a mouse click.
HCBT_CLICKSKIPPED	Identifies the mouse message removed from the system message queue.	Specifies a long pointer to a **MOUSE-HOOKSTRUCT** structure that contains the hit-test code and the handle of the window for which the mouse message is intended. For a list of hit-test codes, see the description of the WM_NCHITTEST message.
HCBT_CREATEWND	Specifies the handle of the new window.	Specifies a long pointer to a **CBT_CREATEWND** data structure that contains initialization parameters for the window.
HCBT_DESTROYWND	Specifies the handle of the window about to be destroyed.	This parameter is undefined and should be set to 0L.
HCBT_KEYSKIPPED	Identifies the virtual key code.	Specifies the repeat count, scan code, key-transition code, previous key state, and context code. For more information, see the description of the WM_KEYUP or WM_KEYDOWN message.
HCBT_MINMAX	Specifies the handle of the window being minimized or maximized.	The low-order word specifies a show-window value (SW_) that specifies the operation. For a list of show-window values, see the description of the **ShowWindow** function. The high-order word is undefined.
HCBT_MOVESIZE	Specifies the handle of the window to be moved or sized.	Specifies a long pointer to a **RECT** structure that contains the coordinates of the window.
HCBT_QS	This parameter is undefined; it should be set to 0.	This parameter is undefined and should be set to 0L.
HCBT_SETFOCUS	Specifies the handle of the window gaining the input focus.	The low-order word specifies the handle of the window losing the input focus. The high-order word is undefined.

Constant	*wParam*	*lParam*
HCBT_SYSCOMMAND	Specifies a system-command value (SC_) that specifies the system command. For more information about system command values, see the description of the WM_SYSCOMMAND message.	If *wParam* is SC_HOTKEY, the low-order word of *lParam* contains the handle of the window that task switching will bring to the foreground. If *wParam* is not SC_HOTKEY and a System-menu command is chosen with the mouse, the low-order word of *lParam* contains the x-coordinate of the cursor and the high-order word contains the y-coordinate. If neither of these conditions is true, *lParam* is undefined.

See Also   **CallNextHookEx, SetWindowsHookEx**

ChangeClipboardChain

2.x

BOOL ChangeClipboardChain(*hwnd, hwndNext*)
HWND *hwnd*;   /* handle of window to remove   */
HWND *hwndNext*;   /* handle of next window   */

The **ChangeClipboardChain** function removes the window identified by the **hwnd** parameter from the chain of clipboard viewers and makes the window identified by the *hwndNext* parameter the descendant of the *hwnd* parameter's ancestor in the chain.

Parameters   *hwnd*
Identifies the window that is to be removed from the chain. The handle must have been passed to the **SetClipboardViewer** function.

hwndNext
Identifies the window that follows *hwnd* in the clipboard-viewer chain (this is the handle returned by the **SetClipboardViewer** function, unless the sequence was changed in response to a WM_CHANGECBCHAIN message).

Return Value   The return value is nonzero if the function is successful. Otherwise, it is zero.

See Also   **SetClipboardViewer**

ChangeMenu `2.x`

The Microsoft Windows 3.1 Software Development Kit (SDK) has replaced this function with five specialized functions, listed as follows:

Function	Description
AppendMenu	Appends a menu item to the end of a menu.
DeleteMenu	Deletes a menu item from a menu, destroying the menu item.
InsertMenu	Inserts a menu item into a menu.
ModifyMenu	Modifies a menu item in a menu.
RemoveMenu	Removes a menu item from a menu but does not destroy the menu item.

Applications written for Windows versions earlier than 3.0 may continue to call **ChangeMenu** as previously documented. Applications written for Windows 3.0 and 3.1 should call the new functions.

Example

The following example shows a call to **ChangeMenu** and how it would be rewritten to call **AppendMenu**:

```
ChangeMenu(hMenu,                        /* handle of menu            */
    0,                                   /* position parameter not used */
    "&White",                            /* menu-item string          */
    IDM_PATTERN1,                        /* menu-item identifier      */
    MF_APPEND | MF_STRING | MF_CHECKED); /* flags                     */

AppendMenu(hMenu,                        /* handle of menu            */
    MF_STRING | MF_CHECKED,              /* flags                     */
    IDM_PATTERN1,                        /* menu-item identifier      */
    "&White");                           /* menu-item string          */
```

See Also

AppendMenu, DeleteMenu, InsertMenu, ModifyMenu, RemoveMenu

CheckDlgButton `2.x`

void CheckDlgButton(*hwndDlg, idButton, uCheck*)
HWND *hwndDlg*;   /* handle of dialog box   */
int *idButton*;   /* button-control identifier */
UINT *uCheck*;   /* check state   */

The **CheckDlgButton** function selects (places a check mark next to) or clears (removes a check mark from) a button control, or it changes the state of a three-state button.

Parameters

hwndDlg
Identifies the dialog box that contains the button.

idButton
Identifies the button to be modified.

uCheck
Specifies the check state of the button. If this parameter is nonzero, **CheckDlgButton** selects the button; if the parameter is zero, the function clears the button. For a three-state check box, if *uCheck* is 2, the button is grayed; if *uCheck* is 1, it is selected; if *uCheck* is 0, it is cleared.

Return Value

This function does not return a value.

Comments

The **CheckDlgButton** function sends a BM_SETCHECK message to the specified button control in the given dialog box.

See Also

CheckRadioButton, IsDlgButtonChecked

CheckMenuItem

2.x

```
BOOL CheckMenuItem(hmenu, idCheckItem, uCheck)
HMENU hmenu;          /* handle of menu             */
UINT idCheckItem;     /* menu-item identifier       */
UINT uCheck;          /* check state and position   */
```

The **CheckMenuItem** function selects (places a check mark next to) or clears (removes a check mark from) a specified menu item in the given pop-up menu.

Parameters

hmenu
Identifies the menu.

idCheckItem
Identifies the menu item to be selected or cleared.

uCheck
Specifies how to determine the position of the menu item (MF_BYCOMMAND or MF_BYPOSITION) and whether the item should be selected or cleared (MF_CHECKED or MF_UNCHECKED). This parameter can be a combination of these values, which can be combined by using the bitwise OR operator. The values are described as follows:

Value	Meaning
MF_BYCOMMAND	Specifies that the *idCheckItem* parameter gives the menu-item identifier (MF_BYCOMMAND is the default).
MF_BYPOSITION	Specifies that the *idCheckItem* parameter gives the position of the menu item (the first item is at position zero).
MF_CHECKED	Selects the item (adds check mark).
MF_UNCHECKED	Clears the item (removes check mark).

Return Value   The return value specifies the previous state of the item—MF_CHECKED or MF_UNCHECKED—if the function is successful. The return value is −1 if the menu item does not exist.

Comments   The *idCheckItem* parameter may identify a pop-up menu item as well as a menu item. No special steps are required to select a pop-up menu item.

Top-level menu items cannot have a check.

A pop-up menu item should be selected by position since it does not have a menu-item identifier associated with it.

See Also   **GetMenuState, SetMenuItemBitmaps**

CheckRadioButton   2.x

void CheckRadioButton(*hwndDlg*, *idFirstButton*, *idLastButton*, *idCheckButton*)
HWND *hwndDlg*;   /* handle of dialog box   */
int *idFirstButton*;   /* identifier of first radio button in group   */
int *idLastButton*;   /* identifier of last radio button in group   */
int *idCheckButton*;   /* identifier of radio button to select   */

The **CheckRadioButton** function selects (adds a check mark to) a given radio button in a group and clears (removes a check mark from) all other radio buttons in the group.

Parameters   *hwndDlg*
Identifies the dialog box that contains the radio button.

idFirstButton
Specifies the identifier of the first radio button in the group.

idLastButton
Specifies the identifier of the last radio button in the group.

idCheckButton
>Specifies the identifier of the radio button to select.

Return Value   This function does not return a value.

Comments   The **CheckRadioButton** function sends a BM_SETCHECK message to the specified radio button control in the given dialog box.

See Also   **CheckDlgButton**, **IsDlgButtonChecked**

ChildWindowFromPoint

2.x

HWND ChildWindowFromPoint(*hwndParent, pt*)
HWND *hwndParent*;   /* handle of parent window   */
POINT *pt*;   /* structure with point coordinates   */

The **ChildWindowFromPoint** function determines which, if any, of the child windows belonging to the given parent window contains the specified point.

Parameters   *hwndParent*
>Identifies the parent window.

pt
>Specifies a **POINT** structure that defines the client coordinates of the point to be checked. The **POINT** structure has the following form:

```
typedef struct tagPOINT {    /* pt */
    int x;
    int y;
} POINT;
```

>For a full description of this structure, see the *Microsoft Windows Programmer's Reference, Volume 3*.

Return Value   The return value is the handle of the child window (hidden, disabled, or transparent) that contains the point, if the function is successful. If the given point lies outside the parent window, the return value is NULL. If the point is within the parent window but is not contained within any child window, the return value is the handle of the parent window.

Comments   More than one window may contain the given point, but Windows returns the handle only of the first window encountered that contains the point.

See Also   **WindowFromPoint**

ChooseColor

3.1

#include <commdlg.h>

BOOL ChooseColor(*lpcc***)**
CHOOSECOLOR FAR* *lpcc*;   /* address of structure with initialization data   */

The **ChooseColor** function creates a system-defined dialog box from which the user can select a color.

Parameters   *lpcc*
Points to a **CHOOSECOLOR** structure that initially contains information necessary to initialize the dialog box. When the **ChooseColor** function returns, this structure contains information about the user's color selection. The **CHOOSE-COLOR** structure has the following form:

```
#include <commdlg.h>

typedef struct tagCHOOSECOLOR {     /* cc */
    DWORD    lStructSize;
    HWND     hwndOwner;
    HWND     hInstance;
    COLORREF rgbResult;
    COLORREF FAR* lpCustColors;
    DWORD    Flags;
    LPARAM   lCustData;
    UINT     (CALLBACK* lpfnHook)(HWND, UINT, WPARAM, LPARAM);
    LPCSTR   lpTemplateName;
} CHOOSECOLOR;
```

For a full description of this structure, see the *Microsoft Windows Programmer's Reference, Volume 3.*

Return Value   The return value is nonzero if the function is successful. It is zero if an error occurs, if the user chooses the Cancel button, or if the user chooses the Close command on the System menu (often called the Control menu) to close the dialog box.

Errors   Use the **CommDlgExtendedError** function to retrieve the error value, which may be one of the following:

CDERR_FINDRESFAILURE
CDERR_INITIALIZATION
CDERR_LOCKRESFAILURE

                CDERR_LOADRESFAILURE
                CDERR_LOADSTRFAILURE
                CDERR_MEMALLOCFAILURE
                CDERR_MEMLOCKFAILURE
                CDERR_NOHINSTANCE
                CDERR_NOHOOK
                CDERR_NOTEMPLATE
                CDERR_STRUCTSIZE

Comments   The dialog box does not support color palettes. The color choices offered by the dialog box are limited to the system colors and dithered versions of those colors.

If the hook function (to which the **lpfnHook** member of the **CHOOSECOLOR** structure points) processes the WM_CTLCOLOR message, this function must return a handle for the brush that should be used to paint the control background.

Example   The following example initializes a **CHOOSECOLOR** structure and then creates a color-selection dialog box:

```
/* Color variables */

CHOOSECOLOR cc;
COLORREF clr;
COLORREF aclrCust[16];
int i;

/* Set the custom-color controls to white. */

for (i = 0; i < 16; i++)
    aclrCust[i] = RGB(255, 255, 255);

/* Initialize clr to black. */

clr = RGB(0, 0, 0);

/* Set all structure fields to zero. */

memset(&cc, 0, sizeof(CHOOSECOLOR));

/* Initialize the necessary CHOOSECOLOR members. */

cc.lStructSize = sizeof(CHOOSECOLOR);
cc.hwndOwner = hwnd;
cc.rgbResult = clr;
cc.lpCustColors = aclrCust;
cc.Flags = CC_PREVENTFULLOPEN;
```

```
if (ChooseColor(&cc))
    .
    . /* Use cc.rgbResult to select the user-requested color. */
    .
```

ChooseFont

3.1

#include <commdlg.h>

BOOL ChooseFont(*lpcf*)
CHOOSEFONT FAR*lpcf;   /* address of structure with initialization data   */

The **ChooseFont** function creates a system-defined dialog box from which the user can select a font, a font style (such as bold or italic), a point size, an effect (such as strikeout or underline), and a color.

Parameters   *lpcf*
Points to a **CHOOSEFONT** structure that initially contains information necessary to initialize the dialog box. When the **ChooseFont** function returns, this structure contains information about the user's font selection. The **CHOOSEFONT** structure has the following form:

```
#include <commdlg.h>

typedef struct tagCHOOSEFONT {  /* cf */
    DWORD           lStructSize;
    HWND            hwndOwner;
    HDC             hDC;
    LOGFONT FAR*    lpLogFont;
    int             iPointSize;
    DWORD           Flags;
    COLORREF        rgbColors;
    LPARAM          lCustData;
    UINT (CALLBACK* lpfnHook)(HWND, UINT, WPARAM, LPARAM);
    LPCSTR          lpTemplateName;
    HINSTANCE       hInstance;
    LPSTR           lpszStyle;
    UINT            nFontType;
    int             nSizeMin;
    int             nSizeMax;
} CHOOSEFONT;
```

For a full description of this structure, see the *Microsoft Windows Programmer's Reference, Volume 3.*

Return Value   The return value is nonzero if the function is successful. Otherwise, it is zero.

Errors   Use the **CommDlgExtendedError** function to retrieve the error value, which may be one of the following:

CDERR_FINDRESFAILURE
CDERR_INITIALIZATION
CDERR_LOCKRESFAILURE
CDERR_LOADRESFAILURE
CDERR_LOADSTRFAILURE
CDERR_MEMALLOCFAILURE
CDERR_MEMLOCKFAILURE
CDERR_NOHINSTANCE
CDERR_NOHOOK
CDERR_NOTEMPLATE
CDERR_STRUCTSIZE
CFERR_MAXLESSTHANMIN
CFERR_NOFONTS

Example   The following example initializes a **CHOOSEFONT** structure and then displays a font dialog box:

```
LOGFONT lf;
CHOOSEFONT cf;

/* Set all structure fields to zero. */

memset(&cf, 0, sizeof(CHOOSEFONT));

cf.lStructSize = sizeof(CHOOSEFONT);
cf.hwndOwner = hwnd;
cf.lpLogFont = &lf;
cf.Flags = CF_SCREENFONTS | CF_EFFECTS;
cf.rgbColors = RGB(0, 255, 255); /* light blue */
cf.nFontType = SCREEN_FONTTYPE;

ChooseFont(&cf);
```

Chord

BOOL Chord(*hdc, nLeftRect, nTopRect, nRightRect, nBottomRect, nXStartLine, nYStartLine, nXEndLine, nYEndLine*)

HDC *hdc*;	/* handle of device context	*/
int *nLeftRect*;	/* x-coordinate upper-left corner bounding rectangle	*/
int *nTopRect*;	/* y-coordinate upper-left corner bounding rectangle	*/
int *nRightRect*;	/* x-coordinate lower-right corner bounding rectangle	*/
int *nBottomRect*;	/* y-coordinate lower-right corner bounding rectangle	*/
int *nXStartLine*;	/* x-coordinate line-segment starting point	*/
int *nYStartLine*;	/* y-coordinate line-segment starting point	*/
int *nXEndLine*;	/* x-coordinate line-segment ending point	*/
int *nYEndLine*;	/* y-coordinate line-segment ending point	*/

The **Chord** function draws a chord (a closed figure bounded by the intersection of an ellipse and a line segment).

Parameters

hdc
Identifies the device context.

nLeftRect
Specifies the logical x-coordinate of the upper-left corner of the bounding rectangle.

nTopRect
Specifies the logical y-coordinate of the upper-left corner of the bounding rectangle.

nRightRect
Specifies the logical x-coordinate of the lower-right corner of the bounding rectangle.

nBottomRect
Specifies the logical y-coordinate of the lower-right corner of the bounding rectangle.

nXStartLine
Specifies the logical x-coordinate of the starting point of the line segment.

nYStartLine
Specifies the logical y-coordinate of the starting point of the line segment.

nXEndLine
Specifies the logical x-coordinate of the ending point of the line segment.

nYEndLine
Specifies the logical y-coordinate of the ending point of the line segment.

Return Value
The return value is nonzero if the function is successful. Otherwise, it is zero.

Comments   The (*nLeftRect, nTopRect*) and (*nRightRect, nBottomRect*) parameter combinations specify the upper-left and lower-right corners, respectively, of a rectangle bounding the ellipse that is part of the chord. The (*nXStartLine, nYStartLine*) and (*nXEndLine, nYEndLine*) parameter combinations specify the endpoints of a line that intersects the ellipse. The chord is drawn by using the selected pen and is filled by using the selected brush.

The figure the **Chord** function draws extends up to but does not include the right and bottom coordinates. This means that the height of the figure is determined as follows:

nBottomRect – nTopRect

The width of the figure is determined similarly:

nRightRect – nLeftRect

Example   The following example uses a **RECT** structure to store the points defining the bounding rectangle and uses **POINT** structures to store the coordinates that specify the beginning and end of the chord:

```
HDC hdc;

RECT rc = { 10, 10, 180, 140 };
POINT ptStart = {  12,  12 };
POINT ptEnd = { 128, 135 };

Chord(hdc, rc.left, rc.top, rc.right, rc.bottom,
    ptStart.x, ptStart.y, ptEnd.x, ptEnd.y);
```

See Also   **Arc**

ClassFirst   3.1

#include <toolhelp.h>

BOOL ClassFirst(*lpce***)**
CLASSENTRY FAR* *lpce*;   /* address of structure for class info   */

The **ClassFirst** function fills the specified structure with general information about the first class in the Windows class list.

Parameters   *lpce*

Points to a **CLASSENTRY** structure that will receive the class information. The **CLASSENTRY** structure has the following form:

```
#include <toolhelp.h>

typedef struct tagCLASSENTRY {  /* ce */
    DWORD   dwSize;
    HMODULE hInst;
    char    szClassName[MAX_CLASSNAME + 1];
    WORD    wNext;
} CLASSENTRY;
```

For a full description of this structure, see the *Microsoft Windows Programmer's Reference, Volume 3.*

Return Value   The return value is nonzero if the function is successful. Otherwise, it is zero.

Comments   The **ClassFirst** function can be used to begin a walk through the Windows class list. To examine subsequent items in the class list, an application can use the **ClassNext** function.

Before calling **ClassFirst**, an application must initialize the **CLASSENTRY** structure and specify its size, in bytes, in the **dwSize** member. An application can examine subsequent entries in the Windows class list by using the **ClassNext** function.

For more specific information about an individual class, use the **GetClassInfo** function, specifying the name of the class and instance handle from the **CLASSENTRY** structure.

See Also   **ClassNext, GetClassInfo**

ClassNext

3.1

#include <toolhelp.h>

BOOL ClassNext(*lpce***)**
CLASSENTRY FAR* *lpce*;   /* address of structure for class info   */

The **ClassNext** function fills the specified structure with general information about the next class in the Windows class list.

Parameters   *lpce*
                        Points to a **CLASSENTRY** structure that will receive the class information.
                        The **CLASSENTRY** structure has the following form:

```
#include <toolhelp.h>

typedef struct tagCLASSENTRY {  /* ce */
    DWORD   dwSize;
    HMODULE hInst;
    char    szClassName[MAX_CLASSNAME + 1];
    WORD    wNext;
} CLASSENTRY;
```

                        For a full description of this structure, see the *Microsoft Windows Program-*
                        mer's Reference, Volume 3.

Return Value   The return value is nonzero if the function is successful. Otherwise, it is zero.

Comments   The **ClassNext** function can be used to continue a walk through the Windows
                        class list started by the **ClassFirst** function.

                        For more specific information about an individual class, use the **GetClassInfo**
                        function with the name of the class and instance handle from the **CLASSENTRY**
                        structure.

See Also   **ClassFirst**

ClearCommBreak   2.x

int ClearCommBreak(*idComDev*)
int *idComDev*;   /* device to be restored   */

                        The **ClearCommBreak** function restores character transmission and places the
                        communications device in a nonbreak state.

Parameters   *idComDev*
                        Identifies the communications device to be restored. The **OpenComm** function
                        returns this value.

Return Value   The return value is zero if the function is successful, or −1 if the *idComDev* parameter does not identify a valid device.

Comments   This function clears the communications-device break state set by the **SetComm-Break** function.

See Also   **OpenComm, SetCommBreak**

ClientToScreen

2.x

void ClientToScreen(*hwnd*, *lppt*)
HWND *hwnd*;   /* window handle for source coordinates   */
POINT FAR* *lppt*;   /* address of structure with coordinates   */

The **ClientToScreen** function converts the client coordinates of a given point on the screen to screen coordinates.

Parameters   *hwnd*
    Identifies the window whose client area is used for the conversion.

lppt
    Points to a **POINT** structure that contains the client coordinates to be converted. The **POINT** structure has the following form:

```
typedef struct tagPOINT {    /* pt */
    int x;
    int y;
} POINT;
```

For a full description of this structure, see the *Microsoft Windows Programmer's Reference, Volume 3*.

Return Value   This function does not return a value.

Comments   The **ClientToScreen** function replaces the coordinates in the **POINT** structure with the screen coordinates. The screen coordinates are relative to the upper-left corner of the screen.

Example

The following example uses the **LOWORD** and **HIWORD** macros and the **ClientToScreen** function to convert the mouse position to screen coordinates:

```
POINT pt;

pt.x = LOWORD(lParam);
pt.y = HIWORD(lParam);
ClientToScreen(hwnd, &pt);
```

See Also

MapWindowPoints, ScreenToClient

ClipCursor

2.x

void ClipCursor(*lprc***)**
const RECT FAR* *lprc*;   /* address of structure with rectangle   */

The **ClipCursor** function confines the cursor to a rectangle on the screen. If a subsequent cursor position (set by the **SetCursorPos** function or by the mouse) lies outside the rectangle, Windows automatically adjusts the position to keep the cursor inside.

Parameters

lprc
Points to a **RECT** structure that contains the screen coordinates of the upper-left and lower-right corners of the confining rectangle. If this parameter is NULL, the cursor is free to move anywhere on the screen. The **RECT** structure has the following form:

```
typedef struct tagRECT {    /* rc */
    int left;
    int top;
    int right;
    int bottom;
} RECT;
```

For a full description of this structure, see the *Microsoft Windows Programmer's Reference, Volume 3*.

Return Value

This function does not return a value.

Comments

The cursor is a shared resource. An application that has confined the cursor to a given rectangle must free it before relinquishing control to another application.

See Also

GetClipCursor, GetCursorPos, SetCursorPos

CloseClipboard

2.x

BOOL CloseClipboard(void)

The **CloseClipboard** function closes the clipboard.

Parameters

This function has no parameters.

Return Value

The return value is nonzero if the function is successful. Otherwise, it is zero.

Comments

The **CloseClipboard** function should be called when a window has finished examining or changing the clipboard. This lets other applications access the clipboard.

See Also

GetOpenClipboardWindow, OpenClipboard

CloseComm

2.x

int CloseComm(*idComDev*)
int *idComDev*;   /* device to close   */

The **CloseComm** function closes the specified communications device and frees any memory allocated for the device's transmission and receiving queues. All characters in the output queue are sent before the communications device is closed.

Parameters

idComDev
Specifies the device to be closed. The **OpenComm** function returns this value.

Return Value

The return value is zero if the function is successful. Otherwise, it is less than zero.

See Also

OpenComm

CloseDriver

LRESULT CloseDriver(*hdrvr*, *lParam1*, *lParam2*)
HDRVR *hdrvr*;   /* handle of installable driver   */
LPARAM *lParam1*;   /* driver-specific data   */
LPARAM *lParam2*;   /* driver-specific data   */

The **CloseDriver** function closes an installable driver.

Parameters

hdrvr
Identifies the installable driver to be closed. This parameter must have been obtained by a previous call to the **OpenDriver** function.

lParam1
Specifies driver-specific data.

lParam2
Specifies driver-specific data.

Return Value

The return value is nonzero if the function is successful. Otherwise, it is zero.

Comments

When an application calls **CloseDriver** and the driver identified by *hdrvr* is the last instance of the driver, Windows calls the **DriverProc** function three times. On the first call, Windows sets the third **DriverProc** parameter, *wMessage*, to DRV_CLOSE; on the second call, Windows sets *wMessage* to DRV_DISABLE; and on the third call, Windows sets *wMessage* to DRV_FREE. When the driver identified by *hdrvr* is not the last instance of the driver, only DRV_CLOSE is sent. The values specified in the *lParam1* and *lParam2* parameters are passed to the *lParam1* and *lParam2* parameters of the **DriverProc** function.

See Also

DriverProc, OpenDriver

CloseMetaFile

HMETAFILE CloseMetaFile(*hdc*)
HDC *hdc*;   /* handle of device context   */

The **CloseMetaFile** function closes a metafile device context and creates a handle of a metafile. An application can use this handle to play the metafile.

Parameters

hdc
Identifies the metafile device context to be closed.

Return Value   The return value is the handle of the metafile if the function is successful. Otherwise, it is NULL.

Comments   If a metafile handle created by using the **CloseMetaFile** function is no longer needed, you should remove it (using the **DeleteMetaFile** function).

Example   The following example creates a device-context handle of a memory metafile, draws a line in the device context, retrieves a handle of the metafile, plays the metafile, and finally deletes the metafile.

```
HDC hdcMeta;
HMETAFILE hmf;

hdcMeta = CreateMetaFile(NULL);
MoveTo(hdcMeta, 10, 10);
LineTo(hdcMeta, 100, 100);
hmf = CloseMetaFile(hdcMeta);
PlayMetaFile(hdc, hmf);
DeleteMetaFile(hmf);
```

See Also   **CreateMetaFile, DeleteMetaFile, PlayMetaFile**

CloseSound   2.x

void CloseSound(void)

This function is obsolete. Use the multimedia audio functions instead. For information about these functions, see the *Microsoft Windows Multimedia Programmer's Reference.*

CloseWindow   2.x

void CloseWindow(*hwnd***)**
HWND *hwnd*;   /* handle of window to minimize   */

The **CloseWindow** function minimizes (but does not destroy) the given window. To destroy a window, an application must use the **DestroyWindow** function.

Parameters   *hwnd*
Identifies the window to be minimized.

Return Value   This function does not return a value.

Comments   This function has no effect if the *hwnd* parameter identifies a pop-up or child window.

See Also   **DestroyWindow, IsIconic, OpenIcon**

CombineRgn   `2.x`

int CombineRgn(*hrgnDest, hrgnSrc1, hrgnSrc2, fCombineMode*)
HRGN *hrgnDest*;   /* handle of region to receive combined regions   */
HRGN *hrgnSrc1*;   /* handle of first source region   */
HRGN *hrgnSrc2*;   /* handle of second source region   */
int *fCombineMode*;   /* mode for combining regions   */

The **CombineRgn** function creates a new region by combining two existing regions.

Parameters   *hrgnDest*
        Identifies an existing region that will be replaced by the new region.

        hrgnSrc1
        Identifies an existing region.

        hrgnSrc2
        Identifies an existing region.

        fCombineMode
        Specifies the operation to use when combining the two source regions. This parameter can be any one of the following values:

Value	Meaning
RGN_AND	Uses overlapping areas of both regions (intersection).
RGN_COPY	Creates a copy of region 1 (identified by the *hrgnSrc1* parameter).
RGN_DIFF	Creates a region consisting of the areas of region 1 (identified by *hrgnSrc1*) that are not part of region 2 (identified by the *hrgnSrc2* parameter).
RGN_OR	Combines all of both regions (union).
RGN_XOR	Combines both regions but removes overlapping areas.

Return Value   The return value specifies that the resulting region has overlapping borders (COMPLEXREGION), is empty (NULLREGION), or has no overlapping borders

(SIMPLEREGION), if the function is successful. Otherwise, the return value is ERROR.

Comments

The size of a region is limited to 32,000 by 32,000 logical units or 64K of memory, whichever is smaller.

The **CombineRgn** function replaces the region identified by the *hrgnDest* parameter with the combined region. To use **CombineRgn** most efficiently, *hrgnDest* should be a trivial region, as shown in the following example.

Example

The following example creates two source regions and an empty destination region, uses the **CombineRgn** function to create a complex region, selects the region into a device context, and then uses the **PaintRgn** function to display the region:

```
HDC hdc;
HRGN hrgnDest, hrgnSrc1, hrgnSrc2;

hrgnDest = CreateRectRgn(0, 0, 0, 0);
hrgnSrc1 = CreateRectRgn(10, 10, 110, 110);
hrgnSrc2 = CreateRectRgn(90, 90, 200, 150);

CombineRgn(hrgnDest, hrgnSrc1, hrgnSrc2, RGN_OR);
SelectObject(hdc, hrgnDest);
PaintRgn(hdc, hrgnDest);
```

See Also

CreateRectRgn, PaintRgn

CommDlgExtendedError

3.1

#include <commdlg.h>

DWORD CommDlgExtendedError(void)

The **CommDlgExtendedError** function identifies the cause of the most recent error to have occurred during the execution of one of the following common dialog box procedures:

- **ChooseColor**
- **ChooseFont**
- **FindText** ·
- **GetFileTitle**
- **GetOpenFileName**

- **GetSaveFileName**
- **PrintDlg**
- **ReplaceText**

Parameters   This function has no parameters.

Return Value   The return value is zero if the prior call to a common dialog box procedure was successful. The return value is CDERR_DIALOGFAILURE if the dialog box could not be created. Otherwise, the return value is a nonzero integer that identifies an error condition.

Comments   Following are the possible **CommDlgExtendedError** return values and the meaning of each:

Value	Meaning
CDERR_FINDRESFAILURE	Specifies that the common dialog box procedure failed to find a specified resource.
CDERR_INITIALIZATION	Specifies that the common dialog box procedure failed during initialization. This error often occurs when insufficient memory is available.
CDERR_LOADRESFAILURE	Specifies that the common dialog box procedure failed to load a specified resource.
CDERR_LOCKRESFAILURE	Specifies that the common dialog box procedure failed to lock a specified resource.
CDERR_LOADSTRFAILURE	Specifies that the common dialog box procedure failed to load a specified string.
CDERR_MEMALLOCFAILURE	Specifies that the common dialog box procedure was unable to allocate memory for internal structures.
CDERR_MEMLOCKFAILURE	Specifies that the common dialog box procedure was unable to lock the memory associated with a handle.
CDERR_NOHINSTANCE	Specifies that the ENABLETEMPLATE flag was set in the **Flags** member of a structure for the corresponding common dialog box but that the application failed to provide a corresponding instance handle.
CDERR_NOHOOK	Specifies that the ENABLEHOOK flag was set in the **Flags** member of a structure for the corresponding common dialog box but that the application failed to provide a pointer to a corresponding hook function.

Value	Meaning
CDERR_NOTEMPLATE	Specifies that the ENABLETEMPLATE flag was set in the **Flags** member of a structure for the corresponding common dialog box but that the application failed to provide a corresponding template.
CDERR_REGISTERMSGFAIL	Specifies that the **RegisterWindowMessage** function returned an error value when it was called by the common dialog box procedure.
CDERR_STRUCTSIZE	Specifies as invalid the **lStructSize** member of a structure for the corresponding common dialog box.
CFERR_NOFONTS	Specifies that no fonts exist.
CFERR_MAXLESSTHANMIN	Specifies that the size given in the **nSizeMax** member of the **CHOOSEFONT** structure is less than the size given in the **nSizeMin** member.
FNERR_BUFFERTOOSMALL	Specifies that the filename buffer is too small. (This buffer is pointed to by the **lpstrFile** member of the structure for a common dialog box.)
FNERR_INVALIDFILENAME	Specifies that a filename is invalid.
FNERR_SUBCLASSFAILURE	Specifies that an attempt to subclass a list box failed due to insufficient memory.
FRERR_BUFFERLENGTHZERO	Specifies that a member in a structure for the corresponding common dialog box points to an invalid buffer.
PDERR_CREATEICFAILURE	Specifies that the **PrintDlg** function failed when it attempted to create an information context.
PDERR_DEFAULTDIFFERENT	Specifies that an application has called the **PrintDlg** function with the DN_DEFAULTPRN flag set in the **wDefault** member of the **DEVNAMES** structure, but the printer described by the other structure members does not match the current default printer. (This happens when an application stores the **DEVNAMES** structure and the user changes the default printer by using Control Panel.)
	To use the printer described by the **DEVNAMES** structure, the application should clear the DN_DEFAULTPRN flag and call the **PrintDlg** function again. To use the default printer, the application should replace the **DEVNAMES** structure (and the **DEVMODE** structure, if one exists) with NULL; this selects the default printer automatically.

Value	Meaning
PDERR_DNDMMISMATCH	Specifies that the data in the **DEVMODE** and **DEVNAMES** structures describes two different printers.
PDERR_GETDEVMODEFAIL	Specifies that the printer driver failed to initialize a **DEVMODE** structure. (This error value applies only to printer drivers written for Windows versions 3.0 and later.)
PDERR_INITFAILURE	Specifies that the **PrintDlg** function failed during initialization.
PDERR_LOADDRVFAILURE	Specifies that the **PrintDlg** function failed to load the device driver for the specified printer.
PDERR_NODEFAULTPRN	Specifies that a default printer does not exist.
PDERR_NODEVICES	Specifies that no printer drivers were found.
PDERR_PARSEFAILURE	Specifies that the **PrintDlg** function failed to parse the strings in the [devices] section of the WIN.INI file.
PDERR_PRINTERNOTFOUND	Specifies that the [devices] section of the WIN.INI file did not contain an entry for the requested printer.
PDERR_RETDEFFAILURE	Specifies that the PD_RETURNDEFAULT flag was set in the **Flags** member of the **PRINTDLG** structure but that either the **hDevMode** or **hDevNames** member was nonzero.
PDERR_SETUPFAILURE	Specifies that the **PrintDlg** function failed to load the required resources.

For more information about the **CommDlgExtendedError** function, see the *Microsoft Windows Programmer's Reference, Volume 1.*

See Also   **ChooseColor, ChooseFont, FindText, GetFileTitle, GetOpenFileName, GetSaveFileName, PrintDlg, ReplaceText**

CopyCursor   3.1

HCURSOR CopyCursor(*hinst*, *hcur*)
HINSTANCE *hinst*;   /* handle of application instance   */
HCURSOR *hcur*;   /* handle of cursor to copy   */

The **CopyCursor** function copies a cursor.

Parameters   *hinst*
Identifies the instance of the module that will copy the cursor.

hcur
Identifies the cursor to be copied.

Return Value   The return value is the handle of the duplicate cursor if the function is successful. Otherwise, it is NULL.

Comments   When it no longer requires a cursor, an application must destroy the cursor, using the **DestroyCursor** function.

The **CopyCursor** function allows an application or dynamic-link library to accept a cursor from another module. Because all resources are owned by the module in which they originate, a resource cannot be shared after the module is freed. **Copy-Cursor** allows an application to create a copy that the application then owns.

See Also   **CopyIcon, DestroyCursor, GetCursor, SetCursor, ShowCursor**

CopyIcon

3.1

HICON CopyIcon(*hinst*, *hicon*)
HINSTANCE *hinst*;   /* handle of application instance   */
HICON *hicon*;   /* handle of icon to copy   */

The **CopyIcon** function copies an icon.

Parameters   *hinst*
Identifies the instance of the module that will copy the icon.

hicon
Identifies the icon to be copied.

Return Value   The return value is the handle of the duplicate icon if the function is successful. Otherwise, it is NULL.

Comments   When it no longer requires an icon, an application should destroy the icon, using the **DestroyIcon** function.

The **CopyIcon** function allows an application or dynamic-link library to accept an icon from another module. Because all resources are owned by the module in which they originate, a resource cannot be shared after the module is freed. **Copy-Icon** allows an application to create a copy that the application then owns.

See Also   **CopyCursor**, **DestroyIcon**, **DrawIcon**

CopyLZFile   3.1

#include <lzexpand.h>

LONG CopyLZFile(*hfSource*, *hfDest*)
HFILE *hfSource*;   /* handle of source file   */
HFILE *hfDest*;   /* handle of destination file   */

The **CopyLZFile** function copies a source file to a destination file. If the source file is compressed, this function creates a decompressed destination file. If the source file is not compressed, this function duplicates the original file.

Parameters   *hfSource*
                      Identifies the source file.

                      hfDest
                      Identifies the destination file.

Return Value   The return value specifies the size, in bytes, of the destination file if the function is successful. Otherwise, it is an error value less than zero; it may be one of the following:

Value	Meaning
LZERROR_BADINHANDLE	The handle identifying the source file was not valid.
LZERROR_BADOUTHANDLE	The handle identifying the destination file was not valid.
LZERROR_READ	The source file format was not valid.
LZERROR_WRITE	There is insufficient space for the output file.
LZERROR_GLOBALLOC	There is insufficient memory for the required buffers.
LZERROR_UNKNOWNALG	The file was compressed with an unrecognized compression algorithm.

Comments   This function is identical to the **LZCopy** function.

The **CopyLZFile** function is designed for copying or decompressing multiple files, or both. To allocate required buffers, an application should call the **LZStart** function prior to calling **CopyLZFile**. To free these buffers, an application should call the **LZDone** function after copying the files.

If the function is successful, the file identified by *hfDest* is decompressed.

If the source or destination file is opened by using a C run-time function (rather than by using the **_lopen** or **OpenFile** function), it must be opened in binary mode.

Example   The following example uses the **CopyLZFile** function to create copies of four text files:

```
#define STRICT

#include <windows.h>
#include <lzexpand.h>

#define NUM_FILES    4

char *szSrc[NUM_FILES] =
    {"readme.txt", "data.txt", "update.txt", "list.txt"};
char *szDest[NUM_FILES] =
    {"readme.bak", "data.bak", "update.bak", "list.bak"};
OFSTRUCT ofStrSrc;
OFSTRUCT ofStrDest;
HFILE hfSrcFile, hfDstFile;
int i;

/* Allocate internal buffers for the CopyLZFile function. */

LZStart();

/* Open, copy, and then close the files. */

for (i = 0; i < NUM_FILES; i++) {
    hfSrcFile = LZOpenFile(szSrc[i], &ofStrSrc, OF_READ);
    hfDstFile = LZOpenFile(szDest[i], &ofStrDest, OF_CREATE);
    CopyLZFile(hfSrcFile, hfDstFile);
    LZClose(hfSrcFile);
    LZClose(hfDstFile);
}

LZDone(); /* free the internal buffers */
```

See Also   **_lopen, LZCopy, LZDone, LZStart, OpenFile**

CopyMetaFile

HMETAFILE CopyMetaFile(*hmfSrc*, *lpszFile*)
HMETAFILE *hmfSrc*;   /* handle of metafile to copy   */
LPCSTR *lpszFile*;   /* address of name of copied metafile   */

The **CopyMetaFile** function copies a source metafile to a specified file and returns a handle of the new metafile.

Parameters

hmfSrc
Identifies the source metafile to be copied.

lpszFile
Points to a null-terminated string that specifies the filename of the copied metafile. If this value is NULL, the source metafile is copied to a memory metafile.

Return Value

The return value is the handle of the new metafile if the function is successful. Otherwise, it is NULL.

Example

The following example copies a metafile to a specified file, plays the copied metafile, retrieves a handle of the copied metafile, changes the position at which the metafile is played 200 logical units to the right, and then plays the metafile at the new location:

```
HANDLE hmf, hmfSource, hmfOld;
LPSTR lpszFile1 = "MFTest";

hmf = CopyMetaFile(hmfSource, lpszFile1);
PlayMetaFile(hdc, hmf);
DeleteMetaFile(hmf);

hmfOld = GetMetaFile(lpszFile1);
SetWindowOrg(hdc, -200, 0);
PlayMetaFile(hdc, hmfOld);

DeleteMetaFile(hmfSource);
DeleteMetaFile(hmfOld);
```

See Also

GetMetaFile, PlayMetaFile, SetWindowOrg

CopyRect

void CopyRect(*lprcDst*, *lprcSrc*)
RECT FAR* *lprcDst*;   /* address of struct. for destination rect.   */
const RECT FAR* *lprcSrc*;   /* address of struct. with source rect.   */

The **CopyRect** function copies the dimensions of one rectangle to another.

Parameters

lprcDst
Points to the **RECT** structure that will receive the dimensions of the source rectangle. The **RECT** structure has the following form:

```
typedef struct tagRECT {    /* rc */
    int left;
    int top;
    int right;
    int bottom;
} RECT;
```

For a full description of this structure, see the *Microsoft Windows Programmer's Reference, Volume 3*.

lprcSrc
Points to the **RECT** structure whose dimensions are to be copied.

Return Value

This function does not return a value.

See Also

SetRect

CountClipboardFormats

int CountClipboardFormats(void)

The **CountClipboardFormats** function retrieves the number of different data formats currently in the clipboard.

Parameters

This function has no parameters.

Return Value

The return value specifies the number of different data formats in the clipboard, if the function is successful.

See Also

EnumClipboardFormats

CountVoiceNotes

`2.x`

int CountVoiceNotes(*nvoice*)
int *nvoice*;   /* sound queue to be counted   */

>This function is obsolete. Use the multimedia audio functions instead. For information about these functions, see the *Microsoft Windows Multimedia Programmer's Reference*.

CPlApplet

`3.1`

LONG CALLBACK* CPlApplet(*hwndCPl, iMessage, lParam1, lParam2*)
HWND *hwndCPl*;   /* handle of Control Panel window   */
UINT *iMessage*;   /* message   */
LPARAM *lParam1*;   /* first message parameter   */
LPARAM *lParam2*;   /* second message parameter   */

>The **CPlApplet** function serves as the entry point for a Control Panel dynamic-link library (DLL). This function is supplied by the application.

Parameters

>*hwndCPl*
>>Identifies the main Control Panel window.

>*iMessage*
>>Specifies the message being sent to the DLL.

>*lParam1*
>>Specifies 32 bits of additional message-dependent information.

>*lParam2*
>>Specifies 32 bits of additional message-dependent information.

Return Value

>The return value depends on the message. For more information, see the descriptions of the individual Control Panel messages in *Microsoft Windows Programmer's Reference, Volume 3*.

Comments

>Use the *hwndCPl* parameter for dialog boxes or other windows that require a handle of a parent window.

CreateBitmap

HBITMAP CreateBitmap(*nWidth*, *nHeight*, *cbPlanes*, *cbBits*, *lpvBits*)
int *nWidth*;   /* bitmap width   */
int *nHeight*;   /* bitmap height   */
UINT *cbPlanes*;   /* number of color planes   */
UINT *cbBits*;   /* number of bits per pixel   */
const void FAR* *lpvBits*;   /* address of array with bitmap bits   */

The **CreateBitmap** function creates a device-dependent memory bitmap that has the specified width, height, and bit pattern.

Parameters

nWidth
Specifies the width, in pixels, of the bitmap.

nHeight
Specifies the height, in pixels, of the bitmap.

cbPlanes
Specifies the number of color planes in the bitmap. The number of bits per plane is the product of the plane's width, height, and bits per pixel ($nWidth \times nHeight \times cbBits$).

cbBits
Specifies the number of color bits per display pixel.

lpvBits
Points to an array of short integers that contains the initial bitmap bit values. If this parameter is NULL, the new bitmap is left uninitialized. For more information about these bit values, see the description of the **bmBits** member of the **BITMAP** structure in the *Microsoft Windows Programmer's Reference, Volume 3*.

Return Value

The return value is the handle of the bitmap if the function is successful. Otherwise, it is NULL.

Comments

The bitmap created by the **CreateBitmap** function can be selected as the current bitmap for a memory device context by using the **SelectObject** function.

For a color bitmap, either the *cbPlanes* or *cbBits* parameter should be set to 1. If both of these parameters are set to 1, **CreateBitmap** creates a monochrome bitmap.

Although a bitmap cannot be copied directly to a display device, the **BitBlt** function can copy it from a memory device context (in which it is the current bitmap) to any compatible device context, including a screen device context.

When it has finished using a bitmap created by **CreateBitmap**, an application should select the bitmap out of the device context and then remove the bitmap by using the **DeleteObject** function.

Example   The following example uses the **CreateBitmap** function to create a bitmap with a zigzag pattern and then uses the **PatBlt** function to fill the client area with that pattern:

```
HDC hdc;
HBITMAP hbmp;
HBRUSH hbr, hbrPrevious;
RECT rc;

int aZigzag[] = { 0xFF, 0xF7, 0xEB, 0xDD, 0xBE, 0x7F, 0xFF, 0xFF };

hbmp = CreateBitmap(8, 8, 1, 1, aZigzag);
hbr = CreatePatternBrush(hbmp);

hdc = GetDC(hwnd);
UnrealizeObject(hbr);
hbrPrevious = SelectObject(hdc, hbr);
GetClientRect(hwnd, &rc);

PatBlt(hdc, rc.left, rc.top,
    rc.right - rc.left, rc.bottom - rc.top, PATCOPY);
SelectObject(hdc, hbrPrevious);
ReleaseDC(hwnd, hdc);

DeleteObject(hbr);
DeleteObject(hbmp);
```

See Also   **BitBlt, CreateBitmapIndirect, CreateCompatibleBitmap, CreateDIBitmap, CreateDiscardableBitmap, DeleteObject, SelectObject**

CreateBitmapIndirect   ⎡ 2.x ⎤

HBITMAP CreateBitmapIndirect(*lpbm***)**
BITMAP FAR* *lpbm*;   /* address of structure with bitmap information   */

The **CreateBitmapIndirect** function creates a bitmap that has the width, height, and bit pattern specified in a **BITMAP** structure.

Parameters

lpbm

Points to a **BITMAP** structure that contains information about the bitmap. The **BITMAP** structure has the following form:

```
typedef struct tagBITMAP {  /* bm */
    int     bmType;
    int     bmWidth;
    int     bmHeight;
    int     bmWidthBytes;
    BYTE    bmPlanes;
    BYTE    bmBitsPixel;
    void FAR* bmBits;
} BITMAP;
```

For a full description of this structure, see the *Microsoft Windows Programmer's Reference, Volume 3*.

Return Value

The return value is the handle of the bitmap if the function is successful. Otherwise, it is NULL.

Comments

Large bitmaps cannot be displayed on a display device by copying them directly to the device context for that device. Instead, applications should create a memory device context that is compatible with the display device, select the bitmap as the current bitmap for the memory device context, and then use a function such as **BitBlt** or **StretchBlt** to copy it from the memory device context to the display device context. (The **PatBlt** function can copy the bitmap for the current brush directly to the display device context.)

When an application has finished using the bitmap created by the **Create-BitmapIndirect** function, it should select the bitmap out of the device context and then delete the bitmap by using the **DeleteObject** function.

If the **BITMAP** structure pointed to by the *lpbm* parameter has been filled in by using the **GetObject** function, the bits of the bitmap are not specified, and the bitmap is uninitialized. To initialize the bitmap, an application can use a function such as **BitBlt** or **SetDIBits** to copy the bits from the bitmap identified by the first parameter of **GetObject** to the bitmap created by **CreateBitmapIndirect**.

Example

The following example assigns values to the members of a **BITMAP** structure and then calls the **CreateBitmapIndirect** function to create a bitmap handle:

```
BITMAP bm;
HBITMAP hbm;

int aZigzag[] = { 0xFF, 0xF7, 0xEB, 0xDD, 0xBE, 0x7F, 0xFF, 0xFF };
```

```
bm.bmType = 0;
bm.bmWidth = 8;
bm.bmHeight = 8;
bm.bmWidthBytes = 2;
bm.bmPlanes = 1;
bm.bmBitsPixel = 1;
bm.bmBits = aZigzag;

hbm = CreateBitmapIndirect(&bm);
```

See Also   **BitBlt, CreateBitmap, CreateCompatibleBitmap, CreateDIBitmap, CreateDiscardableBitmap, DeleteObject, GetObject**

CreateBrushIndirect   2.x

HBRUSH CreateBrushIndirect(*lplb***)**
LOGBRUSH FAR* *lplb*;   /* address of structure with brush attributes   */

The **CreateBrushIndirect** function creates a brush that has the style, color, and pattern specified in a **LOGBRUSH** structure. The brush can subsequently be selected as the current brush for any device.

Parameters   *lplb*
Points to a **LOGBRUSH** structure that contains information about the brush. The **LOGBRUSH** structure has the following form:

```
typedef struct tagLOGBRUSH {     /* lb */
    UINT     lbStyle;
    COLORREF lbColor;
    int      lbHatch;
} LOGBRUSH;
```

For a full description of this structure, see the *Microsoft Windows Programmer's Reference, Volume 3*.

Return Value   The return value is the handle of the brush if the function is successful. Otherwise, it is NULL.

Comments   A brush created by using a monochrome (one plane, one bit per pixel) bitmap is drawn by using the current text and background colors. Pixels represented by a bit set to 0 are drawn with the current text color, and pixels represented by a bit set to 1 are drawn with the current background color.

When it has finished using a brush created by **CreateBrushIndirect**, an application should select the brush out of the device context in which it was used and then remove the brush by using the **DeleteObject** function.

Example

The following example creates a hatched brush with red diagonal hatch marks and uses that brush to fill a rectangle:

```
LOGBRUSH lb;
HBRUSH hbr, hbrOld;

lb.lbStyle = BS_HATCHED;
lb.lbColor = RGB(255, 0, 0);
lb.lbHatch = HS_BDIAGONAL;

hbr = CreateBrushIndirect(&lb);
hbrOld = SelectObject(hdc, hbr);
Rectangle(hdc, 0, 0, 100, 100);
```

See Also

CreateDIBPatternBrush, **CreatePatternBrush**, **CreateSolidBrush**, **DeleteObject**, **GetStockObject**, **SelectObject**

CreateCaret

`2.x`

void CreateCaret(_hwnd_**,** _hbmp_**,** _nWidth_**,** _nHeight_**)**
HWND _hwnd_;   /* handle of owner window   */
HBITMAP _hbmp_;   /* handle of bitmap for caret shape */
int _nWidth_;   /* caret width   */
int _nHeight_;   /* caret height   */

The **CreateCaret** function creates a new shape for the system caret and assigns ownership of the caret to the given window. The caret shape can be a line, block, or bitmap.

Parameters

hwnd
Identifies the window that owns the new caret.

hbmp
Identifies the bitmap that defines the caret shape. If this parameter is NULL, the caret is solid; if the parameter is 1, the caret is gray.

nWidth
Specifies the width of the caret in logical units. If this parameter is NULL, the width is set to the system-defined window-border width.

nHeight

Specifies the height of the caret, in logical units. If this parameter is NULL, the height is set to the system-defined window-border height.

Return Value

This function does not return a value.

Comments

If the *hbmp* parameter contains a bitmap handle, the *nWidth* and *nHeight* parameters are ignored; the bitmap defines its own width and height. (The bitmap handle must have been created by using the **CreateBitmap**, **CreateDIBitmap**, or **Load-Bitmap** function.) If *hbmp* is NULL or 1, *nWidth* and *nHeight* give the caret's width and height, in logical units; the exact width and height (in pixels) depend on the window's mapping mode.

The **CreateCaret** function automatically destroys the previous caret shape, if any, regardless of which window owns the caret. Once created, the caret is initially hidden. To show the caret, use the **ShowCaret** function.

The system caret is a shared resource. A window should create a caret only when it has the input focus or is active. It should destroy the caret before losing the input focus or becoming inactive.

The system's window-border width or height can be retrieved by using the **GetSystemMetrics** function, specifying the SM_CXBORDER and SM_CYBORDER indices. Using the window-border width or height guarantees that the caret will be visible on a high-resolution screen.

Example

The following example creates a caret, sets its initial position, and then displays the caret:

```
case WM_SETFOCUS:
    CreateCaret(hwndParent, NULL, CARET_WIDTH, CARET_HEIGHT);
    SetCaretPos(CARET_XPOS, CARET_YPOS);
    ShowCaret(hwndParent);
    break;
```

See Also

CreateBitmap, CreateDIBitmap, DestroyCaret, GetSystemMetrics, LoadBitmap, ShowCaret

CreateCompatibleBitmap

HBITMAP CreateCompatibleBitmap(*hdc*, *nWidth*, *nHeight*)
HDC *hdc*;   /* handle of device context   */
int *nWidth*;   /* bitmap width   */
int *nHeight*;   /* bitmap height   */

The **CreateCompatibleBitmap** function creates a bitmap that is compatible with the given device.

Parameters

hdc
　　Identifies the device context.

nWidth
　　Specifies the width, in bits, of the bitmap.

nHeight
　　Specifies the height, in bits, of the bitmap.

Return Value

The return value is the handle of the bitmap if the function is successful. Otherwise, it is NULL.

Comments

The bitmap created by the **CreateCompatibleBitmap** function has the same number of color planes or the same bits-per-pixel format as the given device. It can be selected as the current bitmap for any memory device that is compatible with the one identified by *hdc*.

If *hdc* identifies a memory device context, the bitmap returned has the same format as the currently selected bitmap in that device context. A memory device context is a memory object that represents a screen surface. It can be used to prepare images in memory before copying them to the screen surface of the compatible device.

When a memory device context is created, the graphics device interface (GDI) automatically selects a monochrome stock bitmap for it.

Since a color memory device context can have either color or monochrome bitmaps selected, the format of the bitmap returned by the **CreateCompatible-Bitmap** function is not always the same; however, the format of a compatible bitmap for a non–memory device context is always in the format of the device.

When it has finished using a bitmap created by **CreateCompatibleBitmap**, an application should select the bitmap out of the device context and then remove the bitmap by using the **DeleteObject** function.

Example   The following example shows a function named DuplicateBitmap that accepts the handle of a bitmap, duplicates the bitmap, and returns a handle of the duplicate. This function uses the **CreateCompatibleDC** function to create source and destination device contexts and then uses the **GetObject** function to retrieve the dimensions of the source bitmap. The **CreateCompatibleBitmap** function uses these dimensions to create a new bitmap. When each bitmap has been selected into a device context, the **BitBlt** function copies the bits from the source bitmap to the new bitmap. (Although an application could use the **GetDIBits** and **SetDIBits** functions to duplicate a bitmap, the method illustrated in this example is much faster.)

```
HBITMAP PASCAL DuplicateBitmap(HBITMAP hbmpSrc)
{
    HBITMAP hbmpOldSrc, hbmpOldDest, hbmpNew;
    HDC     hdcSrc, hdcDest;
    BITMAP  bmp;

    hdcSrc = CreateCompatibleDC(NULL);
    hdcDest = CreateCompatibleDC(hdcSrc);

    GetObject(hbmpSrc, sizeof(BITMAP), &bmp);

    hbmpOldSrc = SelectObject(hdcSrc, hbmpSrc);

    hbmpNew = CreateCompatibleBitmap(hdcSrc, bmp.bmWidth,
        bmp.bmHeight);

    hbmpOldDest = SelectObject(hdcDest, hbmpNew);

    BitBlt(hdcDest, 0, 0, bmp.bmWidth, bmp.bmHeight, hdcSrc, 0, 0,
        SRCCOPY);

    SelectObject(hdcDest, hbmpOldDest);
    SelectObject(hdcSrc, hbmpOldSrc);

    DeleteDC(hdcDest);
    DeleteDC(hdcSrc);

    return hbmpNew;
}
```

See Also   **CreateBitmap, CreateBitmapIndirect, CreateDIBitmap, DeleteObject**

CreateCompatibleDC

HDC CreateCompatibleDC(*hdc*)
HDC *hdc*;   /* handle of device context   */

The **CreateCompatibleDC** function creates a memory device context that is compatible with the given device.

An application must select a bitmap into a memory device context to represent a screen surface. The device context can then be used to prepare images in memory before copying them to the screen surface of the compatible device.

Parameters   *hdc*
Identifies the device context. If this parameter is NULL, the function creates a memory device context that is compatible with the system screen.

Return Value   The return value is the handle of the new memory device context if the function is successful. Otherwise, it is NULL.

Comments   The **CreateCompatibleDC** function can be used only to create compatible device contexts for devices that support raster operations. To determine whether a device supports raster operations, an application can call the **GetDeviceCaps** function with the RC_BITBLT index.

GDI output functions can be used with a memory device context only if a bitmap has been created and selected into that context.

When it has finished using a device context created by **CreateCompatibleDC**, an application should free the device context by calling the **DeleteDC** function. All objects selected into the device context after it was created should be selected out and replaced with the original objects before the device context is removed.

Example   The following example loads a bitmap named Dog, uses the **Create-CompatibleDC** function to create a memory device context that is compatible with the screen, selects the bitmap into the memory device context, and then uses the **BitBlt** function to move the bitmap from the memory device context to the screen device context:

```
HDC hdc, hdcMemory;
HBITMAP hbmpMyBitmap, hbmpOld;
BITMAP bm;

hbmpMyBitmap = LoadBitmap(hinst, "MyBitmap");
GetObject(hbmpMyBitmap, sizeof(BITMAP), &bm);
```

```
hdc = GetDC(hwnd);
hdcMemory = CreateCompatibleDC(hdc);
hbmpOld = SelectObject(hdcMemory, hbmpMyBitmap);

BitBlt(hdc, 0, 0, bm.bmWidth, bm.bmHeight, hdcMemory, 0, 0, SRCCOPY);
SelectObject(hdcMemory, hbmpOld);

DeleteDC(hdcMemory);
ReleaseDC(hwnd, hdc);
```

See Also   **DeleteDC**, **GetDeviceCaps**

CreateCursor   3.0

HCURSOR CreateCursor(*hinst, xHotSpot, yHotSpot, nWidth, nHeight, lpvANDplane, lpvXORplane*)
HINSTANCE *hinst*;   /* handle of application instance   */
int *xHotSpot*;   /* horizontal position of hot spot   */
int *yHotSpot*;   /* vertical position of hot spot   */
int *nWidth*;   /* cursor width   */
int *nHeight*;   /* cursor height   */
const void FAR* *lpvANDplane*;   /* address of AND mask array   */
const void FAR* *lpvXORplane*;   /* address of XOR mask array   */

The **CreateCursor** function creates a cursor that has the specified width, height, and bit patterns.

Parameters   *hinst*
              Identifies the instance of the module that will create the cursor.

              xHotSpot
              Specifies the horizontal position of the cursor hot spot.

              yHotSpot
              Specifies the vertical position of the cursor hot spot.

              nWidth
              Specifies the width, in pixels, of the cursor.

              nHeight
              Specifies the height, in pixels, of the cursor.

              lpvANDplane
              Points to an array of bytes that contains the bit values for the AND mask of the cursor. These can be the bits of a device-dependent monochrome bitmap.

lpvXORplane
Points to an array of bytes that contains the bit values for the XOR mask of the cursor. These can be the bits of a device-dependent monochrome bitmap.

Return Value   The return value is the handle of the cursor if the function is successful. Otherwise, it is NULL.

Comments   The *nWidth* and *nHeight* parameters must specify a width and height supported by the current display driver, since the system cannot create cursors of other sizes. An application can determine the width and height supported by the display driver by calling the **GetSystemMetrics** function and specifying the SM_CXCURSOR or SM_CYCURSOR value.

Before terminating, an application must call the **DestroyCursor** function to free any system resources associated with the cursor.

See Also   **CreateIcon**, **DestroyCursor**, **GetSystemMetrics**, **SetCursor**

CreateDC   2.x

#include <print.h>

HDC CreateDC(_lpszDriver_, _lpszDevice_, _lpszOutput_, _lpvInitData_**)**
LPCSTR *lpszDriver*;   /* address of driver name   */
LPCSTR *lpszDevice*;   /* address of device name   */
LPCSTR *lpszOutput*;   /* address of filename or port name */
const void FAR* *lpvInitData*;   /* address of initialization data   */

The **CreateDC** function creates a device context for the given device.

Parameters   *lpszDriver*
Points to a null-terminated string that specifies the MS-DOS filename (without extension) of the device driver (for example, Epson).

lpszDevice
Points to a null-terminated string that specifies the name of the specific device to be supported (for example, Epson FX-80). This parameter is used if the module supports more than one device.

lpszOutput
Points to a null-terminated string that specifies the MS-DOS filename or device name for the physical output medium (file or output port).

lpvInitData

Points to a **DEVMODE** structure that contains device-specific initialization in-formation for the device driver. The **ExtDeviceMode** function retrieves this structure already filled in for a given device. The *lpvInitData* parameter must be NULL if the device driver is to use the default initialization (if any) specified by the user through Windows Control Panel.

The **DEVMODE** structure has the following form:

```
#include <print.h>

typedef struct tagDEVMODE {    /* dm */
    char    dmDeviceName[CCHDEVICENAME];
    UINT    dmSpecVersion;
    UINT    dmDriverVersion;
    UINT    dmSize;
    UINT    dmDriverExtra;
    DWORD   dmFields;
    int     dmOrientation;
    int     dmPaperSize;
    int     dmPaperLength;
    int     dmPaperWidth;
    int     dmScale;
    int     dmCopies;
    int     dmDefaultSource;
    int     dmPrintQuality;
    int     dmColor;
    int     dmDuplex;
    int     dmYResolution;
    int     dmTTOption;
} DEVMODE;
```

For a full description of this structure, see the *Microsoft Windows Program-mer's Reference, Volume 3*.

Return Value

The return value is the handle of the device context for the specified device if the function is successful. Otherwise, it is NULL.

Comments

The PRINT.H header file is required if the **DEVMODE** structure is used.

Device contexts created by using the **CreateDC** function must be deleted by using the **DeleteDC** function. All objects selected into the device context after it was created should be selected out and replaced with the original objects before the device context is deleted.

MS-DOS device names follow MS-DOS conventions; an ending colon (:) is rec-ommended, but optional. Windows strips the terminating colon so that a device name ending with a colon is mapped to the same port as the same name without a colon. The driver and port names must not contain leading or trailing spaces.

Example   The following example uses the **CreateDC** function to create a device context for a printer, using information returned by the **PrintDlg** function in a **PRINTDLG** structure:

```
PRINTDLG    pd;
HDC         hdc;
LPDEVNAMES  lpDevNames;
LPSTR       lpszDriverName;
LPSTR       lpszDeviceName;
LPSTR       lpszPortName;

/*
 * PrintDlg displays the common dialog box for printing. The
 * PRINTDLG structure should be initialized with appropriate values.
 */

PrintDlg(&pd);
lpDevNames = (LPDEVNAMES) GlobalLock(pd.hDevNames);
lpszDriverName = (LPSTR) lpDevNames + lpDevNames->wDriverOffset;
lpszDeviceName = (LPSTR) lpDevNames + lpDevNames->wDeviceOffset;
lpszPortName   = (LPSTR) lpDevNames + lpDevNames->wOutputOffset;
GlobalUnlock(pd.hDevNames);
hdc = CreateDC(lpszDriverName, lpszDeviceName, lpszPortName, NULL);
```

See Also   **CreateIC, DeleteDC, ExtDeviceMode, PrintDlg**

CreateDialog   2.x

HWND CreateDialog(*hinst, lpszDlgTemp, hwndOwner, dlgprc*)
HINSTANCE *hinst*;   /* handle of application instance   */
LPCSTR *lpszDlgTemp*;   /* address of dialog box template name   */
HWND *hwndOwner*;   /* handle of owner window   */
DLGPROC *dlgprc*;   /* instance address of dialog box procedure */

The **CreateDialog** function creates a modeless dialog box from a dialog box template resource.

Parameters   *hinst*
         Identifies an instance of the module whose executable file contains the dialog box template.

    lpszDlgTemp
         Points to a null-terminated string that names the dialog box template.

    hwndOwner
         Identifies the window that owns the dialog box.

dlgprc
Specifies the procedure-instance address of the dialog box procedure. The address must be created by using the **MakeProcInstance** function. For more information about the dialog box procedure, see the description of the **Dialog-Proc** callback function.

Return Value
The return value is the handle of the dialog box that was created, if the function is successful. Otherwise, it is NULL.

Comments
The **CreateWindowEx** function is called to create the dialog box. The dialog box procedure then receives a WM_SETFONT message (if the DS_SETFONT style was specified) and a WM_INITDIALOG message, and then the dialog box is displayed.

The **CreateDialog** function returns immediately after creating the dialog box.

To make the dialog box appear in the owner window upon being created, use the WS_VISIBLE style in the dialog box template.

Use the **DestroyWindow** function to destroy a dialog box created by the **Create-Dialog** function.

A dialog box can contain up to 255 controls.

Example
The following example creates a modeless dialog box:

```
HWND hwndDlgFindBox;
DLGPROC dlgprc = (DLGPROC) MakeProcInstance(FindDlgProc, hinst);

hwndDlgFindBox = CreateDialog(hinst, "dlgFindBox", hwndParent, dlgprc);
```

See Also
CreateDialogIndirect, CreateDialogIndirectParam, CreateDialogParam, DestroyWindow, MakeProcInstance

CreateDialogIndirect

HWND **CreateDialogIndirect**(*hinst*, *lpvDlgTmp*, *hwndOwner*, *dlgprc*)
HINSTANCE *hinst*;   /* handle of application instance   */
const void FAR* *lpvDlgTmp*;   /* address of dialog box template   */
HWND *hwndOwner*;   /* handle of owner window   */
DLGPROC *dlgprc*;   /* instance address of dialog box procedure */

The **CreateDialogIndirect** function creates a modeless dialog box from a dialog box template in memory.

Parameters

hinst
Identifies the instance of the module that will create the dialog box.

lpvDlgTmp
Points to a global memory object that contains a dialog box template used to create the dialog box. This template is in the form of a **DialogBoxHeader** structure. For more information about this structure, see Chapter 7, "Resource Formats Within Executable Files," in the *Microsoft Windows Programmer's Reference, Volume 4*.

hwndOwner
Identifies the window that owns the dialog box.

dlgprc
Specifies the procedure-instance address of the dialog box procedure. The address must be created by using the **MakeProcInstance** function. For more information, see the description of the **DialogProc** callback function.

Return Value

The return value is the window handle of the dialog box if the function is successful. Otherwise, it is NULL.

Comments

The **CreateWindowEx** function is called to create the dialog box. The dialog box procedure then receives a WM_SETFONT message (if the DS_SETFONT style was specified) and a WM_INITDIALOG message, and then the dialog box is displayed.

The **CreateDialogIndirect** function returns immediately after creating the dialog box.

To make the dialog box appear in the owner window upon being created, use the WS_VISIBLE style in the dialog box template.

Use the **DestroyWindow** function to destroy a dialog box created by the **CreateDialogIndirect** function.

A dialog box can contain up to 255 controls.

Example   The following example uses the **CreateDialogIndirect** function to create a dialog box from a dialog box template in memory:

```
DLGPROC dlgprc = (DLGPROC) MakeProcInstance(DialogProc, hinst);
HWND hdlg;
BYTE FAR* lpbDlgTemp;


. /* Allocate global memory and build a dialog box template. */
.

hdlg = CreateDialogIndirect(hinst, lpbDlgTemp, hwndParent, dlgprc);
```

See Also   **CreateDialog, CreateDialogIndirectParam, CreateDialogParam, Destroy-Window, MakeProcInstance**

CreateDialogIndirectParam   3.0

HWND CreateDialogIndirectParam(*hinst, lpvDlgTmp, hwndOwner, dlgprc, lParamInit*)
HINSTANCE *hinst*;   /* handle of application instance   */
const void FAR* *lpvDlgTmp*;   /* address of dialog box template   */
HWND *hwndOwner*;   /* handle of owner window   */
DLGPROC *dlgprc*;   /* instance address of dialog box procedure */
LPARAM *lParamInit*;   /* initialization value   */

The **CreateDialogIndirectParam** function creates a modeless dialog box from a dialog box template in memory. Before displaying the dialog box, the function passes an application-defined value to the dialog box procedure as the *lParam* parameter of the WM_INITDIALOG message. An application can use this value to initialize dialog box controls.

Parameters   *hinst*
              Identifies the instance of the module that will create the dialog box.

              lpvDlgTmp
              Points to a global memory object that contains a dialog box template used to create the dialog box. This template is in the form of a **DialogBoxHeader** structure. For more information about this structure, see Chapter 7, "Resource Formats Within Executable Files," in the *Microsoft Windows Programmer's Reference, Volume 4*.

hwndOwner
Identifies the window that owns the dialog box.

dlgprc
Specifies the procedure-instance address of the dialog box procedure. The address must be created by using the **MakeProcInstance** function. For more information, see the description of the **DialogProc** callback function.

lParamInit
Specifies the value to pass to the dialog box when processing the WM_INITDIALOG message.

Return Value

The return value is the window handle of the dialog box if the function is successful. Otherwise, it is NULL.

Comments

The **CreateWindowEx** function is called to create the dialog box. The dialog box procedure then receives a WM_SETFONT message (if the DS_SETFONT style was specified) and a WM_INITDIALOG message, and then the dialog box is displayed.

The **CreateDialogIndirectParam** function returns immediately after creating the dialog box.

To make the dialog box appear in the owner window upon being created, use the WS_VISIBLE style in the dialog box template.

Use the **DestroyWindow** function to destroy a dialog box created by the **CreateDialogIndirectParam** function.

A dialog box can contain up to 255 controls.

Example

The following example calls the **CreateDialogIndirectParam** function to create a modeless dialog box from a dialog box template in memory. The example uses the *lParamInit* parameter to send two initialization parameters, wInitParm1 and wInitParm2, to the dialog box procedure when the WM_INITDIALOG message is being processed.

```
#define MEM_LENGTH  100
HGLOBAL hglbDlgTemp;
BYTE FAR* lpbDlgTemp;
DLGPROC dlgprc = (DLGPROC) MakeProcInstance(DialogProc, hinst);
HWND hwndDlg;
```

```
/* Allocate a global memory object for the dialog box template. */

hglbDlgTemp = GlobalAlloc(GHND, MEM_LENGTH);
      .
      . /* Build a DLGTEMPLATE structure in the memory object. */
      .
lpbDlgTemp = GlobalLock(hglbDlgTemp);
hwndDlg = CreateDialogIndirectParam(hinst, lpbDlgTemp,
    hwndParent, dlgprc, 0);
```

See Also   **CreateDialog, CreateDialogIndirect, CreateDialogParam, DestroyWindow,
MakeProcInstance**

CreateDialogParam   `3.0`

HWND CreateDialogParam(*hinst, lpszDlgTemp, hwndOwner, dlgprc, lParamInit*)
HINSTANCE *hinst*;   /* handle of application instance   */
LPCSTR *lpszDlgTemp*;   /* address of name of dialog box template   */
HWND *hwndOwner*;   /* handle of owner window   */
DLGPROC *dlgprc*;   /* instance address of dialog box procedure */
LPARAM *lParamInit*;   /* initialization value   */

The **CreateDialogParam** function creates a modeless dialog box from a dialog box template resource. Before displaying the dialog box, the function passes an application-defined value to the dialog box procedure as the *lParam* parameter of the WM_INITDIALOG message. An application can use this value to initialize dialog box controls.

Parameters   *hinst*
            Identifies an instance of the module whose executable file contains the dialog box template.

            lpszDlgTemp
            Points to a null-terminated string that names the dialog box template.

            hwndOwner
            Identifies the window that owns the dialog box.

            dlgprc
            Specifies the procedure-instance address of the dialog box procedure. The address must be created by using the **MakeProcInstance** function. For more information about the dialog box procedure, see the description of the **Dialog-Proc** callback function.

lParamInit
   Specifies the value to pass to the dialog box when processing the
   WM_INITDIALOG message.

Return Value   The return value is the handle of the dialog box that was created, if the function is
successful. Otherwise, it is NULL.

Comments   The **CreateWindowEx** function is called to create the dialog box. The dialog box
procedure then receives a WM_SETFONT message (if the DS_SETFONT style
was specified) and a WM_INITDIALOG message, and then the dialog box is displayed.

The **CreateDialogParam** function returns immediately after creating the dialog
box.

To make the dialog box appear in the owner window upon being created, use the
WS_VISIBLE style in the dialog box template.

A dialog box can contain up to 255 controls.

Example   The following example uses the **CreateDialogParam** function to create a modeless dialog box. The function passes the application-defined flags MIXEDCASE
and WHOLEWORD, which will be received by the dialog box as the *lParam* parameter of the WM_INITDIALOG message.

```
HWND hwndChangeBox;
DLGPROC dlgprc = (DLGPROC) MakeProcInstance(ChangeDlgProc, hinst);

hwndChangeBox = CreateDialogParam(hinst, "dlgFindBox",
    hwndParent, dlgprc, MIXEDCASE | WHOLEWORD);
```

See Also   **CreateDialog, CreateDialogIndirect, CreateDialogIndirectParam, Destroy-
Window**

CreateDIBitmap   `3.0`

HBITMAP CreateDIBitmap(*hdc, lpbmih, dwInit, lpvBits, lpbmi, fnColorUse*)
HDC *hdc*;   /* handle of device context   */
BITMAPINFOHEADER FAR* *lpbmih*;   /* address of structure with header   */
DWORD *dwInit*;   /* CBM_INIT to initialize bitmap   */
const void FAR* *lpvBits*;   /* address of array with bitmap values */
BITMAPINFO FAR* *lpbmi*;   /* address of structure with bitmap data */
UINT *fnColorUse*;   /* RGB or palette indices   */

The **CreateDIBitmap** function creates a device-specific memory bitmap from a device-independent bitmap (DIB) specification and optionally sets bits in the bitmap.

Parameters

hdc

Identifies the device context.

lpbmih

Points to a **BITMAPINFOHEADER** structure that describes the size and format of the device-independent bitmap. The **BITMAPINFOHEADER** structure has the following form:

```
typedef struct tagBITMAPINFOHEADER {     /* bmih */
    DWORD    biSize;
    LONG     biWidth;
    LONG     biHeight;
    WORD     biPlanes;
    WORD     biBitCount;
    DWORD    biCompression;
    DWORD    biSizeImage;
    LONG     biXPelsPerMeter;
    LONG     biYPelsPerMeter;
    DWORD    biClrUsed;
    DWORD    biClrImportant;
} BITMAPINFOHEADER;
```

For a full description of this structure, see the *Microsoft Windows Programmer's Reference, Volume 3*.

dwInit

Specifies whether the memory bitmap is initialized. If this value is CBM_INIT, the function initializes the bitmap with the bits specified by the *lpvBits* and *lpbmi* parameters.

lpvBits

Points to a byte array that contains the initial bitmap values. The format of the bitmap values depends on the **biBitCount** member of the **BITMAPINFO-HEADER** structure identified by the *lpbmi* parameter.

lpbmi

Points to a **BITMAPINFO** structure that describes the dimensions and color format of the *lpvBits* parameter. The **BITMAPINFO** structure contains a **BIT-MAPINFOHEADER** structure and an array of **RGBQUAD** structures specifying the colors in the bitmap. The **BITMAPINFO** structure has the following form:

```
typedef struct tagBITMAPINFO {  /* bmi */
    BITMAPINFOHEADER    bmiHeader;
    RGBQUAD             bmiColors[1];
} BITMAPINFO;
```

For a full description of the **BITMAPINFO** and **RGBQUAD** structures, see the *Microsoft Windows Programmer's Reference, Volume 3*.

fnColorUse

Specifies whether the **bmiColors** member of the **BITMAPINFO** structure contains explicit red, green, blue (RGB) values or indices into the currently realized logical palette. The *fnColorUse* parameter must be one of the following values:

Value	Meaning
DIB_PAL_COLORS	The color table consists of an array of 16-bit indices into the currently realized logical palette.
DIB_RGB_COLORS	The color table contains literal RGB values.

Return Value

The return value is the handle of the bitmap if the function is successful. Otherwise, it is NULL.

When it has finished using a bitmap created by **CreateDIBitmap**, an application should select the bitmap out of the device context and then remove the bitmap by using the **DeleteObject** function.

Example

The following example initializes an array of bits and an array of **RGBQUAD** structures, allocates memory for the bitmap header and color table, fills in the required members of a **BITMAPINFOHEADER** structure, and calls the **CreateDIBitmap** function to create a handle of the bitmap:

```
HANDLE hloc;
PBITMAPINFO pbmi;
HBITMAP hbm;

BYTE aBits[] = { 0x00, 0x00, 0x00, 0x00,     /* bottom row */
                 0x01, 0x12, 0x22, 0x11,
                 0x01, 0x12, 0x22, 0x11,
                 0x02, 0x20, 0x00, 0x22,
                 0x02, 0x20, 0x20, 0x22,
                 0x02, 0x20, 0x00, 0x22,
                 0x01, 0x12, 0x22, 0x11,
                 0x01, 0x12, 0x22, 0x11 };  /* top row    */

RGBQUAD argbq[] = {{ 255, 0, 0, 0 },         /* blue  */
                   { 0, 255, 0, 0 },         /* green */
                   { 0, 0, 255, 0 }};        /* red   */

hloc = LocalAlloc(LMEM_ZEROINIT | LMEM_MOVEABLE,
    sizeof(BITMAPINFOHEADER) + (sizeof(RGBQUAD) * 16));
pbmi = (PBITMAPINFO) LocalLock(hloc);
```

```
pbmi->bmiHeader.biSize = sizeof(BITMAPINFOHEADER);
pbmi->bmiHeader.biWidth = 8;
pbmi->bmiHeader.biHeight = 8;
pbmi->bmiHeader.biPlanes = 1;
pbmi->bmiHeader.biBitCount = 4;
pbmi->bmiHeader.biCompression = BI_RGB;

memcpy(pbmi->bmiColors, argbq, sizeof(RGBQUAD) * 3);

hbm = CreateDIBitmap(hdcLocal, (BITMAPINFOHEADER FAR*) pbmi, CBM_INIT,
    aBits, pbmi, DIB_RGB_COLORS);
LocalFree(hloc);

    .
    . /* Use the bitmap handle. */
    .
DeleteObject(hbm);
```

See Also   **CreateBitmap, CreateBitmapIndirect, CreateCompatibleBitmap, Create-
DiscardableBitmap, DeleteObject**

CreateDIBPatternBrush   3.0

HBRUSH CreateDIBPatternBrush(*hglbDIBPacked*, *fnColorSpec*)
HGLOBAL *hglbDIBPacked*;   /* handle of device-independent bitmap   */
UINT *fnColorSpec*;   /* type of color table   */

The **CreateDIBPatternBrush** function creates a brush that has the pattern
specified by a device-independent bitmap (DIB). The brush can subsequently be
selected for any device that supports raster operations.

Parameters   *hglbDIBPacked*
Identifies a global memory object containing a packed device-independent bitmap. A packed DIB consists of a **BITMAPINFO** structure immediately followed by the array of bytes that define the pixels of the bitmap. The
BITMAPINFO structure has the following form:

```
typedef struct tagBITMAPINFO {  /* bmi */
    BITMAPINFOHEADER   bmiHeader;
    RGBQUAD            bmiColors[1];
} BITMAPINFO;
```

For a full description of this structure, see the *Microsoft Windows Programmer's Reference, Volume 3.*

fnColorSpec

Specifies whether the **bmiColors** member(s) of the **BITMAPINFO** structure contain explicit red, green, blue (RGB) values or indices into the currently realized logical palette. This parameter must be one of the following values:

Value	Meaning
DIB_PAL_COLORS	The color table consists of an array of 16-bit indices into the currently realized logical palette.
DIB_RGB_COLORS	The color table contains literal RGB values.

Return Value

The return value is the handle of the brush if the function is successful. Otherwise, it is NULL.

Comments

To retrieve the handle identified by the *hglbDIBPacked* parameter, an application calls the **GlobalAlloc** function to allocate a global memory object and then fills the memory with the packed DIB.

Bitmaps used as fill patterns should be 8 pixels by 8 pixels. If such a bitmap is larger, Windows creates a fill pattern using only the bits corresponding to the first 8 rows and 8 columns of pixels in the upper-left corner of the bitmap.

When an application selects a two-color DIB pattern brush into a monochrome device context, Windows ignores the colors specified in the DIB and instead displays the pattern brush, using the current text and background colors of the device context. Pixels mapped to the first color (at offset 0 in the DIB color table) of the DIB are displayed using the text color, and pixels mapped to the second color (at offset 1 in the color table) are displayed using the background color.

When it has finished using a brush created by **CreateDIBPatternBrush**, an application should remove the brush by using the **DeleteObject** function.

Example

The following example retrieves a bitmap named DIBit from the application's resource file, uses the bitmap to create a pattern brush in a call to the **CreateDIB-PatternBrush** function, selects the brush into a device context, and fills a rectangle by using the new brush:

```
HRSRC hrsrc;
HGLOBAL hglbl;
HBRUSH hbr, hbrOld;

hrsrc = FindResource(hinst, "DIBit", RT_BITMAP);
hglbl = LoadResource(hinst, hrsrc);
LockResource(hglbl);
```

```
hbr = CreateDIBPatternBrush(hglbl, DIB_RGB_COLORS);
hbrOld = SelectObject(hdc, hbr);
Rectangle(hdc, 10, 10, 100, 100);
UnlockResource(hglbl);
```

See Also   **CreatePatternBrush, DeleteObject, FindResource, GetDeviceCaps, Global-Alloc, LoadResource, LockResource, SelectObject, SetBkColor, SetText-Color, UnlockResource**

CreateDiscardableBitmap   2.x

HBITMAP CreateDiscardableBitmap(*hdc*, *nWidth*, *nHeight*)
HDC *hdc*;   /* handle of device context   */
int *nWidth*;   /* bitmap width   */
int *nHeight*;   /* bitmap height   */

The **CreateDiscardableBitmap** function creates a discardable bitmap that is compatible with the given device. The bitmap has the same number of color planes or the same bits-per-pixel format as the device. An application can select this bitmap as the current bitmap for a memory device that is compatible with the one identified by the *hdc* parameter.

Parameters   *hdc*
                      Identifies the device context.

                      nWidth
                      Specifies the width, in bits, of the bitmap.

                      nHeight
                      Specifies the height, in bits, of the bitmap.

Return Value   The return value is the handle of the bitmap if the function is successful. Otherwise, it is NULL.

Comments   Windows can discard a bitmap created by this function only if an application has not selected it into a device context. If Windows discards the bitmap when it is not selected and the application later attempts to select it, the **SelectObject** function will return zero.

                      Applications should use the **DeleteObject** function to delete the handle returned by the **CreateDiscardableBitmap** function, even if Windows has discarded the bitmap.

See Also   **CreateBitmap, CreateBitmapIndirect, CreateDIBitmap, DeleteObject**

CreateEllipticRgn   2.x

HRGN CreateEllipticRgn(*nLeftRect*, *nTopRect*, *nRightRect*, *nBottomRect*)
int *nLeftRect*;   /* x-coordinate upper-left corner bounding rectangle   */
int *nTopRect*;   /* y-coordinate upper-left corner bounding rectangle   */
int *nRightRect*;   /* x-coordinate lower-right corner bounding rectangle   */
int *nBottomRect*;   /* y-coordinate lower-right corner bounding rectangle   */

The **CreateEllipticRgn** function creates an elliptical region.

Parameters   *nLeftRect*
Specifies the logical x-coordinate of the upper-left corner of the bounding rectangle of the ellipse.

nTopRect
Specifies the logical y-coordinate of the upper-left corner of the bounding rectangle of the ellipse.

nRightRect
Specifies the logical x-coordinate of the lower-right corner of the bounding rectangle of the ellipse.

nBottomRect
Specifies the logical y-coordinate of the lower-right corner of the bounding rectangle of the ellipse.

Return Value   The return value is the handle of the region if the function is successful. Otherwise, it is NULL.

Comments   The size of a region is limited to 32,767 by 32,767 logical units or 64K of memory, whichever is smaller.

When it has finished using a region created by using the **CreateEllipticRgn** function, an application should remove it by using the **DeleteObject** function.

See Also   **CreateEllipticRgnIndirect, DeleteObject, PaintRgn**

CreateEllipticRgnIndirect   2.x

HRGN CreateEllipticRgnIndirect(*lprc*)
const RECT FAR* *lprc*;   /* address of structure with bounding rectangle   */

The **CreateEllipticRgnIndirect** function creates an elliptical region.

Parameters

lprc

Points to a **RECT** structure that contains the logical coordinates of the upper-left and lower-right corners of the bounding rectangle of the ellipse. The **RECT** structure has the following form:

```
typedef struct tagRECT {    /* rc */
    int left;
    int top;
    int right;
    int bottom;
} RECT;
```

For a full description of this structure, see the *Microsoft Windows Programmer's Reference, Volume 3.*

Return Value

The return value is the handle of the region if the function is successful. Otherwise, it is NULL.

Comments

The size of a region is limited to 32,767 by 32,767 logical units or 64K of memory, whichever is smaller.

When it has finished using a region created by **CreateEllipticRgnIndirect**, an application should remove the region by using the **DeleteObject** function.

Example

The following example assigns values to the members of a **RECT** structure, uses the **CreateEllipticRgnIndirect** function to create an elliptical region, selects the region into a device context, and then uses the **PaintRgn** function to display the region:

```
HDC hdc;
RECT rc;
HRGN hrgn;

SetRect(&rc, 10, 10, 200, 50);

hrgn = CreateEllipticRgnIndirect(&rc);
SelectObject(hdc, hrgn);
PaintRgn(hdc, hrgn);
```

See Also

CreateEllipticRgn, DeleteObject, PaintRgn

CreateFont

HFONT CreateFont(*nHeight, nWidth, nEscapement, nOrientation, fnWeight, fbItalic, fbUnderline, fbStrikeOut, fbCharSet, fbOutputPrecision, fbClipPrecision, fbQuality, fbPitchAndFamily, lpszFace*)

int *nHeight*;	/* font height	*/
int *nWidth*;	/* character width	*/
int *nEscapement*;	/* escapement of line of text	*/
int *nOrientation*;	/* angle of base line and x-axis	*/
int *fnWeight*;	/* font weight	*/
BYTE *fbItalic*;	/* flag for italic attribute	*/
BYTE *fbUnderline*;	/* flag for underline attribute	*/
BYTE *fbStrikeOut*;	/* flag for strikeout attribute	*/
BYTE *fbCharSet*;	/* character set	*/
BYTE *fbOutputPrecision*;	/* output precision	*/
BYTE *fbClipPrecision*;	/* clipping precision	*/
BYTE *fbQuality*;	/* output quality	*/
BYTE *fbPitchAndFamily*;	/* pitch and family	*/
LPCSTR *lpszFace*;	/* address of typeface name	*/

The **CreateFont** function creates a logical font that has the specified characteristics. The logical font can subsequently be selected as the font for any device.

Parameters

nHeight
Specifies the requested height, in logical units, for the font. If this parameter is greater than zero, it specifies the cell height of the font. If it is less than zero, it specifies the character height of the font. (Character height is the cell height minus the internal leading. Applications that specify font height in points typically use a negative number for this member.) If this parameter is zero, the font mapper uses a default height. The font mapper chooses the largest physical font that does not exceed the requested size (or the smallest font, if all the fonts exceed the requested size). The absolute value of the *nHeight* parameter must not exceed 16,384 after it is converted to device units.

nWidth
Specifies the average width, in logical units, of characters in the font. If this parameter is zero, the font mapper chooses a "closest match" default width for the specified font height. (The default width is chosen by matching the aspect ratio of the device against the digitization aspect ratio of the available fonts. The closest match is determined by the absolute value of the difference.)

nEscapement
Specifies the angle, in tenths of degrees, between the escapement vector and the x-axis of the screen surface. The escapement vector is the line through the origins of the first and last characters on a line. The angle is measured counterclockwise from the x-axis.

nOrientation
Specifies the angle, in tenths of degrees, between the base line of a character and the x-axis. The angle is measured in a counterclockwise direction from the x-axis for left-handed coordinate systems (that is, MM_TEXT, in which the y-direction is down) and in a clockwise direction from the x-axis for right-handed coordinate systems (in which the y-direction is up).

fnWeight
Specifies the font weight. This parameter can be one of the following values:

Constant	Value
FW_DONTCARE	0
FW_THIN	100
FW_EXTRALIGHT	200
FW_ULTRALIGHT	200
FW_LIGHT	300
FW_NORMAL	400
FW_REGULAR	400
FW_MEDIUM	500
FW_SEMIBOLD	600
FW_DEMIBOLD	600
FW_BOLD	700
FW_EXTRABOLD	800
FW_ULTRABOLD	800
FW_BLACK	900
FW_HEAVY	900

The appearance of the font depends on the typeface. Some fonts have only FW_NORMAL, FW_REGULAR, and FW_BOLD weights. If FW_DONTCARE is specified, a default weight is used.

fbItalic
Specifies an italic font if set to nonzero.

fbUnderline
Specifies an underlined font if set to nonzero.

fbStrikeOut
Specifies a strikeout font if set to nonzero.

fbCharSet
Specifies the character set of the font. The following values are predefined:

Constant	Value
ANSI_CHARSET	0
DEFAULT_CHARSET	1
SYMBOL_CHARSET	2
SHIFTJIS_CHARSET	128
OEM_CHARSET	255

The DEFAULT_CHARSET value is not used by the font mapper. An application can use this value to allow the name and size of a font to fully describe the logical font. If the specified font name does not exist, a font from any character set can be substituted for the specified font; to avoid unexpected results, applications should use the DEFAULT_CHARSET value sparingly.

The OEM character set is system-dependent.

Fonts with other character sets may exist in the system. If an application uses a font with an unknown character set, it should not attempt to translate or interpret strings that are to be rendered with that font.

fbOutputPrecision
Specifies the requested output precision. The output precision defines how closely the output must match the requested font's height, width, character orientation, escapement, and pitch. This parameter can be one of the following values:

OUT_CHARACTER_PRECIS
OUT_DEFAULT_PRECIS
OUT_DEVICE_PRECIS
OUT_RASTER_PRECIS
OUT_STRING_PRECIS
OUT_STROKE_PRECIS
OUT_TT_PRECIS

Applications can use the OUT_DEVICE_PRECIS, OUT_RASTER_PRECIS, and OUT_TT_PRECIS values to control how the font mapper chooses a font when the system contains more than one font with a given name. For example, if a system contained a font named Symbol in raster and TrueType form, specifying OUT_TT_PRECIS would force the font mapper to choose the TrueType version. (Specifying OUT_TT_PRECIS forces the font mapper to choose a TrueType font whenever the specified font name matches a device or raster font, even when there is no TrueType font of the same name.)

fbClipPrecision
Specifies the requested clipping precision. The clipping precision defines how to clip characters that are partially outside the clipping region. This parameter can be one of the following values:

CLIP_CHARACTER_PRECIS
CLIP_DEFAULT_PRECIS
CLIP_ENCAPSULATE

CLIP_LH_ANGLES
CLIP_MASK
CLIP_STROKE_PRECIS
CLIP_TT_ALWAYS

To use an embedded read-only font, applications must specify
CLIP_ENCAPSULATE.

To achieve consistent rotation of device, TrueType, and vector fonts, an application can use the OR operator to combine the CLIP_LH_ANGLES value with any of the other *fbClipPrecision* values. If the CLIP_LH_ANGLES bit is set, the rotation for all fonts is dependent on whether the orientation of the coordinate system is left-handed or right-handed. If CLIP_LH_ANGLES is not set, device fonts always rotate counterclockwise, but the rotation of other fonts is dependent on the orientation of the coordinate system. (For more information about the orientation of coordinate systems, see the description of the *nOrientation* parameter.)

fbQuality

Specifies the output quality of the font, which defines how carefully the graphics device interface (GDI) must attempt to match the attributes of a logical font to those of a physical font. This parameter can be one of the following values:

Value	Meaning
DEFAULT_QUALITY	Appearance of the font does not matter.
DRAFT_QUALITY	Appearance of the font is less important than when the PROOF_QUALITY value is used. For GDI raster fonts, scaling is enabled. Bold, italic, underline, and strikeout fonts are synthesized if necessary.
PROOF_QUALITY	Character quality of the font is more important than exact matching of the logical-font attributes. For GDI raster fonts, scaling is disabled and the font closest in size is chosen. Bold, italic, underline, and strikeout fonts are synthesized if necessary.

fbPitchAndFamily

Specifies the pitch and family of the font. The two low-order bits specify the pitch of the font and can be one of the following values:

DEFAULT_PITCH
FIXED_PITCH
VARIABLE_PITCH

Applications can set bit 2 (0x04) of the **lfPitchAndFamily** member to choose a TrueType font.

The four high-order bits specify the font family and can be one of the following values:

Value	Meaning
FF_DECORATIVE	Novelty fonts. Old English is an example.
FF_DONTCARE	Don't care or don't know.
FF_MODERN	Fonts with constant stroke width, with or without serifs. Pica, Elite, and Courier New® are examples.
FF_ROMAN	Fonts with variable stroke width and with serifs. Times New Roman® and New Century Schoolbook® are examples.
FF_SCRIPT	Fonts designed to look like handwriting. Script and Cursive are examples.
FF_SWISS	Fonts with variable stroke width and without serifs. MS® Sans Serif is an example.

An application can specify a value for the *fbPitchAndFamily* parameter by using the Boolean OR operator to join a pitch constant with a family constant.

Font families describe the look of a font in a general way. They are intended for specifying fonts when the exact typeface requested is not available.

lpszFace
Points to a null-terminated string that specifies the typeface name of the font. The length of this string must not exceed LF_FACESIZE – 1. The **EnumFontFamilies** function can be used to enumerate the typeface names of all currently available fonts. If this parameter is NULL, GDI uses a device-dependent typeface.

Return Value

The return value is the handle of the logical font if the function is successful. Otherwise, it is NULL.

Comments

The **CreateFont** function creates the handle of a logical font. The font mapper uses this logical font to find the closest match from the fonts available in GDI's pool of physical fonts.

Applications can use the default settings for most of these parameters when creating a logical font. The parameters that should always be given specific values are *nHeight* and *lpszFace*. If *nHeight* and *lpszFace* are not set by the application, the logical font that is created is device-dependent.

Fonts created by using the **CreateFont** function must be selected out of any device context in which they were used and then removed by using the **DeleteObject** function.

Example

The following example sets the mapping mode to MM_TWIPS and then uses the **CreateFont** function to create an 18-point logical font:

```
                    HFONT hfont, hfontOld;
                    int MapModePrevious, iPtSize = 18;
                    PSTR pszFace = "MS Serif";

                    MapModePrevious = SetMapMode(hdc, MM_TWIPS);
                    hfont = CreateFont(-iPtSize * 20, 0, 0, 0, 0, /* specify pt size   */
                        0, 0, 0, 0, 0, 0, 0, 0, pszFace);       /* and face name only */

                    hfontOld = SelectObject(hdc, hfont);

                    TextOut(hdc, 100, -500, pszFace, strlen(pszFace));
                    SetMapMode(hdc, MapModePrevious);
                    SelectObject(hdc, hfontOld);
                    DeleteObject(hfont);
```

See Also   **CreateFontIndirect, DeleteObject, EnumFontFamilies**

CreateFontIndirect   2.x

HFONT CreateFontIndirect(*lplf*)
const LOGFONT FAR* *lplf*;   /* address of struct. with font attributes   */

The **CreateFontIndirect** function creates a logical font that has the characteristics given in the specified structure. The font can subsequently be selected as the current font for any device.

Parameters   *lplf*
                    Points to a **LOGFONT** structure that defines the characteristics of the logical font. The **LOGFONT** structure has the following form:

```
typedef struct tagLOGFONT {     /* lf */
    int    lfHeight;
    int    lfWidth;
    int    lfEscapement;
    int    lfOrientation;
    int    lfWeight;
    BYTE   lfItalic;
    BYTE   lfUnderline;
    BYTE   lfStrikeOut;
    BYTE   lfCharSet;
    BYTE   lfOutPrecision;
    BYTE   lfClipPrecision;
    BYTE   lfQuality;
    BYTE   lfPitchAndFamily;
    BYTE   lfFaceName[LF_FACESIZE];
} LOGFONT;
```

For a full description of this structure, see the *Microsoft Windows Programmer's Reference, Volume 3.*

Return Value

The return value is the handle of the logical font if the function is successful. Otherwise, it is NULL.

Comments

The **CreateFontIndirect** function creates a logical font that has the characteristics specified in the **LOGFONT** structure. When the font is selected by using the **SelectObject** function, the graphics device interface (GDI) font mapper attempts to match the logical font with an existing physical font. If it cannot find an exact match for the logical font, the font mapper provides an alternative whose characteristics match as many of the requested characteristics as possible.

Fonts created by using the **CreateFontIndirect** function must be selected out of any device context in which they were used and then removed by using the **DeleteObject** function.

Example

The following example uses the **CreateFontIndirect** function to retrieve the handle of a logical font. The nPtSize and pszFace parameters are passed to the function containing this code. The **MulDiv** and **GetDeviceCaps** functions are used to convert the specified point size into the correct point size for the MM_TEXT mapping mode on the current device.

```
HFONT hfont, hfontOld;

PLOGFONT plf = (PLOGFONT) LocalAlloc(LPTR, sizeof(LOGFONT));

plf->lfHeight = -MulDiv(nPtSize, GetDeviceCaps(hdc, LOGPIXELSY), 72);
strcpy(plf->lfFaceName, pszFace);

hfont = CreateFontIndirect(plf);

hfontOld = SelectObject(hdc, hfont);

TextOut(hdc, 10, 50, pszFace, strlen(pszFace));

LocalFree((HLOCAL) plf);
SelectObject(hdc, hfontOld);
DeleteObject(hfont);
```

See Also

CreateFont, DeleteObject

CreateHatchBrush

2.x

HBRUSH CreateHatchBrush(*fnStyle*, *clrref*)
int *fnStyle*;   /* hatch style of brush   */
COLORREF *clrref*;   /* color of brush   */

The **CreateHatchBrush** function creates a brush that has the specified hatched pattern and color. The brush can then be selected for any device.

Parameters

fnStyle
Specifies one of the following hatch styles for the brush:

Value	Meaning
HS_BDIAGONAL	45-degree upward hatch (left to right)
HS_CROSS	Horizontal and vertical crosshatch
HS_DIAGCROSS	45-degree crosshatch
HS_FDIAGONAL	45-degree downward hatch (left to right)
HS_HORIZONTAL	Horizontal hatch
HS_VERTICAL	Vertical hatch

clrref
Specifies the foreground color of the brush (the color of the hatches).

Return Value

The return value is the handle of the brush if the function is successful. Otherwise, it is NULL.

Comments

When an application has finished using the brush created by the **CreateHatch-Brush** function, it should select the brush out of the device context and then delete it by using the **DeleteObject** function.

The following illustration shows how the various hatch brushes appear when used to fill a rectangle:

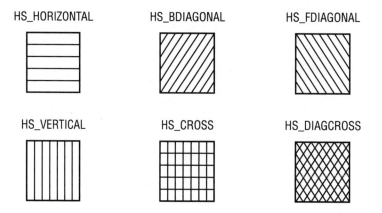

Example   The following example creates a hatched brush with green diagonal hatch marks and uses that brush to fill a rectangle:

```
HBRUSH hbr, hbrOld;

hbr = CreateHatchBrush(HS_FDIAGONAL, RGB(0, 255, 0));
hbrOld = SelectObject(hdc, hbr);
Rectangle(hdc, 0, 0, 100, 100);
```

See Also   **CreateBrushIndirect, CreateDIBPatternBrush, CreatePatternBrush, CreateSolidBrush, DeleteObject, SelectObject**

CreateIC   2.x

HDC CreateIC(*lpszDriver, lpszDevice, lpszOutput, lpvInitData*)
LPCSTR *lpszDriver*;   /* address of driver name   */
LPCSTR *lpszDevice*;   /* address of device name   */
LPCSTR *lpszOutput*;   /* address of filename or port name   */
const void FAR* *lpvInitData*;   /* address of initialization data   */

The **CreateIC** function creates an information context for the specified device. The information context provides a fast way to get information about the device without creating a device context.

Parameters   *lpszDriver*
Points to a null-terminated string that specifies the MS-DOS filename (without extension) of the device driver (for example, EPSON).

lpszDevice
Points to a null-terminated string that specifies the name of the specific device to be supported (for example, EPSON FX-80). This parameter is used if the module supports more than one device.

lpszOutput
Points to a null-terminated string that specifies the MS-DOS filename or device name for the physical output medium (file or port).

lpvInitData
Points to a **DEVMODE** structure that contains, initially, device-specific information necessary to initialize the device driver. The **ExtDeviceMode** function retrieves this structure filled in for a given device. The *lpvInitData* parameter must be NULL if the device driver is to use the default initialization information (if any) specified by the user through Windows Control Panel.

The **DEVMODE** structure has the following form:

```
#include <print.h>

typedef struct tagDEVMODE {    /* dm */
    char  dmDeviceName[CCHDEVICENAME];
    UINT  dmSpecVersion;
    UINT  dmDriverVersion;
    UINT  dmSize;
    UINT  dmDriverExtra;
    DWORD dmFields;
    int   dmOrientation;
    int   dmPaperSize;
    int   dmPaperLength;
    int   dmPaperWidth;
    int   dmScale;
    int   dmCopies;
    int   dmDefaultSource;
    int   dmPrintQuality;
    int   dmColor;
    int   dmDuplex;
    int   dmYResolution;
    int   dmTTOption;
} DEVMODE;
```

Return Value

The return value is the handle of an information context for the given device if the function is successful. Otherwise, it is NULL.

Comments

The PRINT.H header file is required if the **DEVMODE** structure is used.

MS-DOS device names follow MS-DOS conventions; an ending colon (:) is recommended, but optional. Windows strips the terminating colon so that a device name ending with a colon is mapped to the same port as would be the same name without a colon.

The driver and port names must not contain leading or trailing spaces.

GDI output functions cannot be used with information contexts.

When it has finished using an information context created by **CreateIC**, an application should remove the information context by using the **DeleteDC** function.

Example

The following example uses the **CreateIC** function to create an information context for the display and then uses the **GetDCOrg** function to retrieve the origin for the information context:

```
HDC    hdcIC;
DWORD  dwOrigin;
```

```
hdcIC = CreateIC("DISPLAY", NULL, NULL, NULL);
dwOrigin = GetDCOrg(hdcIC);

DeleteDC(hdcIC);
```

See Also   **CreateDC**, **DeleteDC**, **ExtDeviceMode**

CreateIcon   3.0

HICON CreateIcon(*hinst, nWidth, nHeight, bPlanes, bBitsPixel, lpvANDbits, lpvXORbits*)
HINSTANCE *hinst*;	/* handle of application instance	*/
int *nWidth*;	/* icon width	*/
int *nHeight*;	/* icon height	*/
BYTE *bPlanes*;	/* number of planes in XOR mask	*/
BYTE *bBitsPixel*;	/* number of bits per pixel in XOR mask	*/
const void FAR* *lpvANDbits*;	/* address of AND mask array	*/
const void FAR* *lpvXORbits*;	/* address of XOR mask array	*/

The **CreateIcon** function creates an icon that has the specified width, height, colors, and bit patterns.

Parameters

hinst
Identifies an instance of the module that will create the icon.

nWidth
Specifies the width, in pixels, of the icon.

nHeight
Specifies the height, in pixels, of the icon.

bPlanes
Specifies the number of planes in the XOR mask of the icon.

bBitsPixel
Specifies the number of bits per pixel in the XOR mask of the icon.

lpvANDbits
Points to an array of bytes that contains the bit values for the AND mask of the icon. This array must specify a monochrome mask.

lpvXORbits
Points to an array of bytes that contains the bit values for the XOR mask of the icon. These bits can be the bits of a monochrome or device-dependent color bitmap.

Return Value
The return value is the handle of the icon if the function is successful. Otherwise, it is NULL.

Comments   The *nWidth* and *nHeight* parameters must specify a width and height supported by the current display driver, since the system cannot create icons of other sizes. An application can determine the width and height supported by the display driver by calling the **GetSystemMetrics** function, specifying the SM_CXICON or SM_CYICON constant.

Before terminating, an application must call the **DestroyIcon** function to free system resources associated with the icon.

See Also   **DestroyIcon, GetSystemMetrics**

CreateMenu
$\boxed{\text{2.x}}$

HMENU CreateMenu(void)

The **CreateMenu** function creates a menu. The menu is initially empty but can be filled with menu items by using the **AppendMenu** or **InsertMenu** function.

Parameters   This function has no parameters.

Return Value   The return value is the handle of the newly created menu if the function is successful. Otherwise, it is NULL.

Comments   If the menu is not assigned to a window, an application must free system resources associated with the menu before exiting. An application frees menu resources by calling the **DestroyMenu** function. Windows automatically frees resources associated with a menu that is assigned to a window.

Example   The following example creates a main menu and a pop-up menu and associates the pop-up menu with an item in the main menu:

```
HMENU hmenu;
HMENU hmenuPopup;

/* Create the main and pop-up menu handles. */

hmenu = CreateMenu();
hmenuPopup = CreatePopupMenu();
```

```
/* Create the pop-up menu items. */

AppendMenu(hmenuPopup, MF_ENABLED | MF_STRING, IDM_NEW,
    "&New");
AppendMenu(hmenuPopup, MF_ENABLED | MF_STRING, IDM_SAVE,
    "&Save");
AppendMenu(hmenuPopup, MF_ENABLED | MF_STRING, IDM_SAVE_AS,
    "&Save As");

/* Add the pop-up menu to the main menu. */

AppendMenu(hmenu, MF_ENABLED | MF_POPUP, (UINT) hmenuPopup,
    "&File");
```

See Also   **AppendMenu**, **DestroyMenu**, **InsertMenu**, **SetMenu**

CreateMetaFile   2.x

HDC CreateMetaFile(*lpszFile*)
LPCSTR *lpszFile*;   /* address of metafile name   */

The **CreateMetaFile** function creates a metafile device context.

Parameters   *lpszFile*
    Points to a null-terminated string that specifies the MS-DOS filename of the
    metafile to create. If this parameter is NULL, a device context for a memory
    metafile is returned.

Return Value   The return value is the handle of the metafile device context if the function is
    successful. Otherwise, it is NULL.

Comments   When it has finished using a metafile device context created by **CreateMetaFile**,
    an application should close it by using the **CloseMetaFile** function.

Example   The following example uses the **CreateMetaFile** function to create the handle of a
    device context for a memory metafile, draws a line in that device context, retrieves
    a handle of the metafile by calling the **CloseMetaFile** function, plays the metafile
    by using the **PlayMetaFile** function, and finally deletes the metafile by using the
    DeleteMetaFile function:

```
HDC hdcMeta;
HMETAFILE hmf;
```

```
hdcMeta = CreateMetaFile(NULL);
MoveTo(hdcMeta, 10, 10);
LineTo(hdcMeta, 100, 100);
hmf = CloseMetaFile(hdcMeta);
PlayMetaFile(hdc, hmf);
DeleteMetaFile(hmf);
```

See Also   **DeleteMetaFile**

CreatePalette   3.0

HPALETTE CreatePalette(*lplgpl***)**
const LOGPALETTE FAR* *lplgpl*;   /* address of LOGPALETTE structure   */

The **CreatePalette** function creates a logical color palette.

Parameters   *lplgpl*
          Points to a **LOGPALETTE** structure that contains information about the
          colors in the logical palette. The **LOGPALETTE** structure has the following
          form:

```
typedef struct tagLOGPALETTE {  /* lgpl */
    WORD          palVersion;
    WORD          palNumEntries;
    PALETTEENTRY  palPalEntry[1];
} LOGPALETTE;
```

          For a full description of this structure, see the *Microsoft Windows Program-*
          mer's Reference, Volume 3.

Return Value   The return value is the handle of the logical palette if the function is successful.
          Otherwise, it is NULL.

Comments   When it has finished using a palette created by **CreatePalette**, an application
          should remove the palette by using the **DeleteObject** function.

Example   The following example initializes a **LOGPALETTE** structure and an array of
          PALETTEENTRY structures, and then uses the **CreatePalette** function to re-
          trieve a handle of a logical palette:

```
#define NUMENTRIES 128
HPALETTE hpal;
PALETTEENTRY ape[NUMENTRIES];
```

```
plgpl = (LOGPALETTE*) LocalAlloc(LPTR,
    sizeof(LOGPALETTE) + cColors * sizeof(PALETTEENTRY));

plgpl->palNumEntries = cColors;
plgpl->palVersion = 0x300;

for (i = 0, red = 0, green = 127, blue = 127; i < NUMENTRIES;
        i++, red += 1, green += 1, blue += 1) {
    ape[i].peRed =
        plgpl->palPalEntry[i].peRed = LOBYTE(red);
    ape[i].peGreen =
        plgpl->palPalEntry[i].peGreen = LOBYTE(green);
    ape[i].peBlue =
        plgpl->palPalEntry[i].peBlue = LOBYTE(blue);
    ape[i].peFlags =
        plgpl->palPalEntry[i].peFlags = PC_RESERVED;
}
hpal = CreatePalette(plgpl);
LocalFree((HLOCAL) plgpl);
.
. /* Use the palette handle. */
.
DeleteObject(hpal);
```

See Also   **DeleteObject**

CreatePatternBrush   2.x

HBRUSH CreatePatternBrush(*hbmp*)
HBITMAP *hbmp*;   /* handle of bitmap   */

The **CreatePatternBrush** function creates a brush whose pattern is specified by a bitmap. The brush can subsequently be selected for any device that supports raster operations.

Parameters   *hbmp*
                       Identifies the bitmap.

Return Value   The return value is the handle of the brush if the function is successful. Otherwise, it is NULL.

Comments   The bitmap identified by the *hbmp* parameter is typically created by using the **CreateBitmap**, **CreateBitmapIndirect**, **CreateCompatibleBitmap**, or **Load-Bitmap** function.

Bitmaps used as fill patterns should be 8 pixels by 8 pixels. If the bitmap is larger, Windows will use the bits corresponding to only the first 8 rows and 8 columns of pixels in the upper-left corner of the bitmap.

An application can use the **DeleteObject** function to remove a pattern brush. This does not affect the associated bitmap, which means the bitmap can be used to create any number of pattern brushes. In any case, when the brush is no longer needed, the application should remove it by using **DeleteObject**.

A brush created by using a monochrome bitmap (one color plane, one bit per pixel) is drawn using the current text and background colors. Pixels represented by a bit set to 0 are drawn with the current text color, and pixels represented by a bit set to 1 are drawn with the current background color.

Example

The following example loads a bitmap named Pattern, uses the bitmap to create a pattern brush in a call to the **CreatePatternBrush** function, selects the brush into a device context, and fills a rectangle by using the new brush:

```
HBITMAP hbmp;
HBRUSH hbr, hbrOld;

hbmp = LoadBitmap(hinst, "Pattern");
hbr = CreatePatternBrush(hbmp);
hbrOld = SelectObject(hdc, hbr);
Rectangle(hdc, 10, 10, 100, 100);
```

See Also

CreateBitmap, CreateBitmapIndirect, CreateCompatibleBitmap, CreateDIB-PatternBrush, DeleteObject, GetDeviceCaps, LoadBitmap, SelectObject, SetBkColor, SetTextColor

---

CreatePen

2.x

HPEN CreatePen(*fnPenStyle*, *nWidth*, *clrref*)
int *fnPenStyle*;   /* style of pen   */
int *nWidth*;   /* width of pen   */
COLORREF *clrref*;   /* color of pen   */

The **CreatePen** function creates a pen having the specified style, width, and color. The pen can subsequently be selected as the current pen for any device.

Parameters

fnPenStyle
Specifies the pen style. This parameter can be one of the following values:

Value	Meaning
PS_SOLID	Creates a solid pen.
PS_DASH	Creates a dashed pen. (Valid only when the pen width is 1.)
PS_DOT	Creates a dotted pen. (Valid only when the pen width is 1.)
PS_DASHDOT	Creates a pen with alternating dashes and dots. (Valid only when the pen width is 1.)
PS_DASHDOTDOT	Creates a pen with alternating dashes and double dots. (Valid only when the pen width is 1.)
PS_NULL	Creates a null pen.
PS_INSIDEFRAME	Creates a pen that draws a line inside the frame of closed shapes produced by graphics device interface (GDI) output functions that specify a bounding rectangle (for example, the **Ellipse**, **Rectangle**, **RoundRect**, **Pie**, and **Chord** functions). When this style is used with GDI output functions that do not specify a bounding rectangle (for example, the **LineTo** function), the drawing area of the pen is not limited by a frame.

nWidth
Specifies the width, in logical units, of the pen. If this value is zero, the width in device units is always one pixel, regardless of the mapping mode.

clrref
Specifies the color of the pen.

Return Value

The return value is the handle of the pen if the function is successful. Otherwise, it is NULL.

Comments

Pens whose width is greater than one pixel always have the PS_NULL, PS_SOLID, or PS_INSIDEFRAME style.

If a pen has the PS_INSIDEFRAME style and a color that does not match a color in the logical color table, the pen is drawn with a dithered color. The PS_SOLID pen style cannot be used to create a pen with a dithered color. The PS_INSIDEFRAME style is identical to PS_SOLID if the pen width is less than or equal to 1.

When it has finished using a pen created by **CreatePen**, an application should remove the pen by using the **DeleteObject** function.

The following illustration shows how the various system pens appear when used to draw a rectangle.

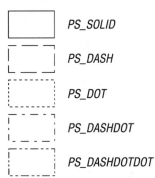

PS_SOLID

PS_DASH

PS_DOT

PS_DASHDOT

PS_DASHDOTDOT

Example

The following example uses the **CreatePen** function to create a solid blue pen 6 units wide, selects the pen into a device context, and then uses the pen to draw a rectangle:

```
HPEN hpen, hpenOld;

hpen = CreatePen(PS_SOLID, 6, RGB(0, 0, 255));
hpenOld = SelectObject(hdc, hpen);

Rectangle(hdc, 10, 10, 100, 100);

SelectObject(hdc, hpenOld);
DeleteObject(hpen);
```

See Also

CreatePenIndirect, DeleteObject, Ellipse, Rectangle, RoundRect

---

CreatePenIndirect

2.x

HPEN CreatePenIndirect(lplgpn**)**
LOGPEN FAR* lplgpn;   /* address of structure with pen data   */

The **CreatePenIndirect** function creates a pen that has the style, width, and color given in the specified structure.

Parameters

lplgpn
    Points to the **LOGPEN** structure that contains information about the pen. The **LOGPEN** structure has the following form:

```
typedef struct tagLOGPEN {   /* lgpn */
    UINT     lopnStyle;
    POINT    lopnWidth;
    COLORREF lopnColor;
} LOGPEN;
```

For a full description of this structure, see the *Microsoft Windows Programmer's Reference, Volume 3.*

Return Value

The return value is the handle of the pen if the function is successful. Otherwise, it is NULL.

Comments

Pens whose width is greater than 1 pixel always have the PS_NULL, PS_SOLID, or PS_INSIDEFRAME style.

If a pen has the PS_INSIDEFRAME style and a color that does not match a color in the logical color table, the pen is drawn with a dithered color. The PS_INSIDEFRAME style is identical to PS_SOLID if the pen width is less than or equal to 1.

When it has finished using a pen created by **CreatePenIndirect**, an application should remove the pen by using the **DeleteObject** function.

Example

The following example fills a **LOGPEN** structure with values defining a solid red pen 10 logical units wide, uses the **CreatePenIndirect** function to create this pen, selects the pen into a device context, and then uses the pen to draw a rectangle:

```
LOGPEN lp;
HPEN hpen, hpenOld;

lp.lopnStyle = PS_SOLID;
lp.lopnWidth.x = 10;
lp.lopnWidth.y = 0;                 /* y-dimension not used */
lp.lopnColor = RGB(255, 0, 0);

hpen = CreatePenIndirect(&lp);
hpenOld = SelectObject(hdc, hpen);
Rectangle(hdc, 10, 10, 100, 100);
```

See Also

CreatePen, **DeleteObject**

CreatePolygonRgn

HRGN CreatePolygonRgn(*lppt*, *cPoints*, *fnPolyFillMode*)
const POINT FAR* *lppt*;   /* address of array of points   */
int *cPoints*;   /* number of points in array   */
int *fnPolyFillMode*;   /* polygon-filling mode   */

The **CreatePolygonRgn** function creates a polygonal region. The system closes the polygon automatically, if necessary, by drawing a line from the last vertex to the first.

Parameters

lppt

Points to an array of **POINT** structures. Each structure specifies the x-coordinate and y-coordinate of one vertex of the polygon. The **POINT** structure has the following form:

```
typedef struct tagPOINT {    /* pt */
    int x;
    int y;
} POINT;
```

For a full description of this structure, see the *Microsoft Windows Programmer's Reference, Volume 3.*

cPoints

Specifies the number of **POINT** structures in the array pointed to by the *lppt* parameter.

fnPolyFillMode

Specifies the polygon-filling mode. This value may be either ALTERNATE or WINDING.

Return Value

The return value is the handle of the region if the function is successful. Otherwise, it is NULL.

Comments

The size of a region is limited to 32,767 by 32,767 logical units or 64K of memory, whichever is smaller.

When the polygon-filling mode is ALTERNATE, the system fills the area between odd-numbered and even-numbered polygon sides on each scan line. That is, the system fills the area between the first and second side, between the third and fourth side, and so on.

When the polygon-filling mode is WINDING, the system uses the direction in which a figure was drawn to determine whether to fill an area. Each line segment in a polygon is drawn in either a clockwise or a counterclockwise direction. Whenever an imaginary line drawn from an enclosed area to the outside of a figure passes through a clockwise line segment, the system increments a count (increases it by one); when the line passes through a counterclockwise line segment, the system decrements the count. The area is filled if the count is nonzero when the line reaches the outside of the figure.

When it has finished using a region created by **CreatePolygonRgn**, an application should remove the region by using the **DeleteObject** function.

Example

The following example fills an array of **POINT** structures with the coordinates of a five-pointed star, uses this array in a call to the **CreatePolygonRgn** function, selects the region into a device context, and then uses the **PaintRgn** function to display the region:

```
HDC hdc;
HRGN hrgn;
POINT apts[5] = {{ 200, 10  },
                 { 300, 200 },
                 { 100, 100 },
                 { 300, 100 },
                 { 100, 200 }};

hrgn = CreatePolygonRgn(apts,            /* array of points  */
    sizeof(apts) / sizeof(POINT),        /* number of points */
    ALTERNATE);                          /* alternate mode   */
SelectObject(hdc, hrgn);
PaintRgn(hdc, hrgn);
```

See Also

CreatePolyPolygonRgn, DeleteObject, Polygon, SetPolyFillMode

CreatePolyPolygonRgn

3.0

HRGN CreatePolyPolygonRgn(*lppt, lpnPolyCount, cIntegers, fnPolyFillMode***)**
const POINT FAR* *lppt*;   /* address of structure of points   */
const int FAR* *lpnPolyCount*;   /* address of array of vertex data   */
int *cIntegers*;   /* number of integers in array   */
int *fnPolyFillMode*;   /* polygon-filling mode   */

The **CreatePolyPolygonRgn** function creates a region consisting of a series of closed polygons. The polygons may be disjoint, or they may overlap.

Parameters

lppt

Points to an array of **POINT** structures that define the vertices of the polygons. Each polygon must be explicitly closed, because the system does not close them automatically. The polygons are specified consecutively. The **POINT** structure has the following form:

```
typedef struct tagPOINT {    /* pt */
    int x;
    int y;
} POINT;
```

For a full description of this structure, see the *Microsoft Windows Programmer's Reference, Volume 3*.

lpnPolyCount
Points to an array of integers. The first integer specifies the number of vertices in the first polygon in the array pointed to by the *lppt* parameter, the second integer specifies the number of vertices in the second polygon, and so on.

cIntegers
Specifies the total number of integers in the array pointed to by the *lpnPolyCount* parameter.

fnPolyFillMode
Specifies the polygon-filling mode. This value may be either ALTERNATE or WINDING.

Return Value   The return value is the handle of the region if the function is successful. Otherwise, it is NULL.

Comments   The size of a region is limited to 32,767 by 32,767 logical units or 64K of memory, whichever is smaller.

When the polygon-filling mode is ALTERNATE, the system fills the area between odd-numbered and even-numbered polygon sides on each scan line. That is, the system fills the area between the first and second side, between the third and fourth side, and so on.

When the polygon-filling mode is WINDING, the system uses the direction in which a figure was drawn to determine whether to fill an area. Each line segment in a polygon is drawn in either a clockwise or a counterclockwise direction. Whenever an imaginary line drawn from an enclosed area to the outside of a figure passes through a clockwise line segment, the system increments a count (increases it by one); when the line passes through a counterclockwise line segment, the system decrements the count. The area is filled if the count is nonzero when the line reaches the outside of the figure.

When it has finished using a region created by **CreatePolyPolygonRgn**, an application should remove the region by using the **DeleteObject** function.

Example   The following example fills an array of **POINT** structures with the coordinates of a five-pointed star and a rectangle, uses this array in a call to the **CreatePolyPolygonRgn** function, selects the region into a device context, and then uses the **PaintRgn** function to display the region:

```
HDC hdc;
HRGN hrgn;
int aVertices[2] = { 6, 5 };
POINT apts[11] = {{ 200, 10  },
                   { 300, 200 },
                   { 100, 100 }, /* Star figure, manually closed */
                   { 300, 100 },
                   { 100, 200 },
                   { 200, 10  },

                   {  10, 150 },
                   { 350, 150 },
                   { 350, 170 }, /* Rectangle, manually closed */
                   {  10, 170 },
                   {  10, 150 }};
hrgn = CreatePolyPolygonRgn(apts,        /* array of points         */
    aVertices,                           /* array of vertices       */
    sizeof(aVertices) / sizeof(int),     /* integers in vertex array */
    ALTERNATE);                          /* alternate mode          */
SelectObject(hdc, hrgn);
PaintRgn(hdc, hrgn);
```

See Also   **CreatePolygonRgn**, **DeleteObject**, **PolyPolygon**, **SetPolyFillMode**

CreatePopupMenu   `3.0`

HMENU CreatePopupMenu(void)

The **CreatePopupMenu** function creates an empty pop-up menu.

Parameters   This function has no parameters.

Return Value   The return value is the handle of the newly created menu if the function is successful. Otherwise, it is NULL.

Comments   An application adds items to the pop-up menu by calling the **InsertMenu** and **AppendMenu** functions. The application can add the pop-up menu to an existing menu or pop-up menu, or it can display and track selections on the pop-up menu by calling the **TrackPopupMenu** function.

Before exiting, an application must free system resources associated with a pop-up menu if the menu is not assigned to a window. An application frees a menu by calling the **DestroyMenu** function.

Example   The following example creates a main menu and a pop-up menu, and associates
                    the pop-up menu with an item in the main menu:

```
HMENU hmenu;
HMENU hmenuPopup;

/* Create the main and pop-up menu handles. */

hmenu = CreateMenu();
hmenuPopup = CreatePopupMenu();

/* Create the pop-up menu items. */

AppendMenu(hmenuPopup, MF_ENABLED | MF_STRING, IDM_NEW,
    "&New");
AppendMenu(hmenuPopup, MF_ENABLED | MF_STRING, IDM_SAVE,
    "&Save");
AppendMenu(hmenuPopup, MF_ENABLED | MF_STRING, IDM_SAVE_AS,
    "&Save As");

/* Add the pop-up menu to the main menu. */

AppendMenu(hmenu, MF_ENABLED | MF_POPUP, (UINT) hmenuPopup,
    "&File");
```

See Also   **AppendMenu, CreateMenu, InsertMenu, SetMenu, TrackPopupMenu**

CreateRectRgn   2.x

HRGN CreateRectRgn(*nLeftRect, nTopRect, nRightRect, nBottomRect*)
int *nLeftRect*;   /* x-coordinate upper-left corner of region   */
int *nTopRect*;   /* y-coordinate upper-left corner of region   */
int *nRightRect*;   /* x-coordinate lower-right corner of region   */
int *nBottomRect*;   /* y-coordinate lower-right corner of region   */

The **CreateRectRgn** function creates a rectangular region.

Parameters   *nLeftRect*
                      Specifies the logical x-coordinate of the upper-left corner of the region.

                    nTopRect
                      Specifies the logical y-coordinate of the upper-left corner of the region.

                    nRightRect
                      Specifies the logical x-coordinate of the lower-right corner of the region.

nBottomRect
Specifies the logical y-coordinate of the lower-right corner of the region.

Return Value   The return value is the handle of a rectangular region if the function is successful. Otherwise, it is NULL.

Comments   The size of a region is limited to 32,767 by 32,767 logical units or 64K of memory, whichever is smaller.

When it has finished using a region created by **CreateRectRgn**, an application should remove the region by using the **DeleteObject** function.

Example   The following example uses the **CreateRectRgn** function to create a rectangular region, selects the region into a device context, and then uses the **PaintRgn** function to display the region:

```
HDC hdc;
HRGN hrgn;

hrgn = CreateRectRgn(10, 10, 110, 110);
SelectObject(hdc, hrgn);
PaintRgn(hdc, hrgn);
```

See Also   **CreateRectRgnIndirect, CreateRoundRectRgn, DeleteObject, PaintRgn**

CreateRectRgnIndirect   2.x

HRGN CreateRectRgnIndirect(*lprc*)
const RECT FAR* *lprc*;   /* address of structure with region   */

The **CreateRectRgnIndirect** function creates a rectangular region by using a **RECT** structure.

Parameters   *lprc*
Points to a **RECT** structure that contains the logical coordinates of the upper-left and lower-right corners of the region. The **RECT** structure has the following form:

```
typedef struct tagRECT {    /* rc */
    int left;
    int top;
    int right;
    int bottom;
} RECT;
```

For a full description of this structure, see the *Microsoft Windows Programmer's Reference, Volume 3.*

Return Value   The return value is the handle of the rectangular region if the function is successful. Otherwise, it is NULL.

Comments   The size of a region is limited to 32,767 by 32,767 logical units or 64K of memory, whichever is smaller.

When it has finished using a region created by **CreateRectRgnIndirect**, an application should remove the region by using the **DeleteObject** function.

Example   The following example assigns values to the members of a **RECT** structure, uses the **CreateRectRgnIndirect** function to create a rectangular region, selects the region into a device context, and then uses the **PaintRgn** function to display the region:

```
RECT rc;
HRGN hrgn;

SetRect(&rc, 10, 10, 200, 50);

hrgn = CreateRectRgnIndirect(&rc);
SelectObject(hdc, hrgn);
PaintRgn(hdc, hrgn);
```

See Also   **CreateRectRgn, CreateRoundRectRgn, DeleteObject, PaintRgn**

CreateRoundRectRgn   3.0

HRGN CreateRoundRectRgn(*nLeftRect, nTopRect, nRightRect, nBottomRect, nWidthEllipse, nHeightEllipse***)**

int *nLeftRect*;	/* x-coordinate upper-left corner of region	*/
int *nTopRect*;	/* y-coordinate upper-left corner of region	*/
int *nRightRect*;	/* x-coordinate lower-right corner of region	*/
int *nBottomRect*;	/* y-coordinate lower-right corner of region	*/
int *nWidthEllipse*;	/* height of ellipse for rounded corners	*/
int *nHeightEllipse*;	/* width of ellipse for rounded corners	*/

The **CreateRoundRectRgn** function creates a rectangular region with rounded corners.

Parameters

nLeftRect
Specifies the logical x-coordinate of the upper-left corner of the region.

nTopRect
Specifies the logical y-coordinate of the upper-left corner of the region.

nRightRect
Specifies the logical x-coordinate of the lower-right corner of the region.

nBottomRect
Specifies the logical y-coordinate of the lower-right corner of the region.

nWidthEllipse
Specifies the width of the ellipse used to create the rounded corners.

nHeightEllipse
Specifies the height of the ellipse used to create the rounded corners.

Return Value

The return value is the handle of the region if the function is successful. Otherwise, it is NULL.

Comments

The size of a region is limited to 32,767 by 32,767 logical units or 64K of memory, whichever is smaller.

When it has finished using a region created by **CreateRoundRectRgn**, an application should remove the region by using the **DeleteObject** function.

Example

The following example uses the **CreateRoundRectRgn** function to create a region, selects the region into a device context, and then uses the **PaintRgn** function to display the region:

```
HRGN hrgn;
int nEllipWidth = 10;
int nEllipHeight = 30;

hrgn = CreateRoundRectRgn(10, 10, 110, 110,
    nEllipWidth, nEllipHeight);
SelectObject(hdc, hrgn);
PaintRgn(hdc, hrgn);
```

See Also

CreateRectRgn, CreateRectRgnIndirect, DeleteObject, PaintRgn

CreateScalableFontResource

BOOL CreateScalableFontResource(*fHidden, lpszResourceFile, lpszFontFile, lpszCurrentPath*)
UINT *fHidden*;   /* flag for read-only embedded font   */
LPCSTR *lpszResourceFile*;   /* address of filename of font resource   */
LPCSTR *lpszFontFile*;   /* address of filename of scalable font   */
LPCSTR *lpszCurrentPath*;   /* address of path to font file   */

The **CreateScalableFontResource** function creates a font resource file for the specified scalable font file.

Parameters

fHidden
Specifies whether the font is a read-only embedded font. This parameter can be one of the following values:

Value	Meaning
0	The font has read-write permission.
1	The font has read-only permission and should be hidden from other applications in the system. When this flag is set, the font is not enumerated by the **EnumFonts** or **EnumFontFamilies** function.

lpszResourceFile
Points to a null-terminated string specifying the name of the font resource file that this function creates.

lpszFontFile
Points to a null-terminated string specifying the scalable font file this function uses to create the font resource file. This parameter must specify either the filename and extension or a full path and filename, including drive and filename extension.

lpszCurrentPath
Points to a null-terminated string specifying either the path to the scalable font file specified in the *lpszFontFile* parameter or NULL, if *lpszFontFile* specifies a full path.

Return Value

The return value is nonzero if the function is successful. Otherwise, it is zero.

Comments

An application must use the **CreateScalableFontResource** function to create a font resource file before installing an embedded font. Font resource files for fonts with read-write permission should use the .FOT filename extension. Font resource files for read-only fonts should use a different extension (for example, .FOR) and should be hidden from other applications in the system by specifying 1 for the *fHidden* parameter. The font resource files can be installed by using the **Add-FontResource** function.

When the *lpszFontFile* parameter specifies only a filename and extension, the *lpszCurrentPath* parameter must specify a path. When the *lpszFontFile* parameter specifies a full path, the *lpszCurrentPath* parameter must be NULL or a pointer to NULL.

When only a filename and extension is specified in the *lpszFontFile* parameter and a path is specified in the *lpszCurrentPath* parameter, the string in *lpszFontFile* is copied into the .FOT file as the .TTF file that belongs to this resource. When the **AddFontResource** function is called, the system assumes that the .TTF file has been copied into the SYSTEM directory (or into the main Windows directory in the case of a network installation). The .TTF file need not be in this directory when the **CreateScalableFontResource** function is called, because the *lpszCurrentPath* parameter contains the directory information. A resource created in this manner does not contain absolute path information and can be used in any Windows installation.

When a path is specified in the *lpszFontFile* parameter and NULL is specified in the *lpszCurrentPath* parameter, the string in *lpszFontFile* is copied into the .FOT file. In this case, when the **AddFontResource** function is called, the .TTF file must be at the location specified in the *lpszFontFile* parameter when the **Create-ScalableFontResource** function was called; the *lpszCurrentPath* parameter is not needed. A resource created in this manner contains absolute references to paths and drives and will not work if the .TTF file is moved to a different location.

The **CreateScalableFontResource** function supports only TrueType scalable fonts.

Example

The following example shows how to create a TrueType font file in the SYSTEM directory of the Windows startup directory:

```
CreateScalableFontResource(0, "c:\\windows\\system\\font.fot",
   "font.ttr", "c:\\windows\\system");

AddFontResource("c:\\windows\\system\\font.fot");
```

The following example shows how to create a TrueType font file in a specified directory:

```
CreateScalableFontResource(0, "c:\\windows\\system\\font.fot",
   "c:\\fontdir\\font.ttr", NULL);

AddFontResource("c:\\windows\\system\\font.fot");
```

The following example shows how to work with a standard embedded font:

```
HFONT hfont;

/* Extract .TTF file into C:\MYDIR\FONT.TTR. */

CreateScalableFontResource(0, "font.fot", "c:\\mydir\\font.ttr", NULL);

AddFontResource("font.fot");

hfont = CreateFont(..., CLIP_DEFAULT_PRECIS, ..., "FONT");
   .
   . /* Use the font. */
   .
DeleteObject(hfont);

RemoveFontResource("font.fot");
   .
   . /* Delete C:\MYDIR\FONT.FOT and C:\MYDIR\FONT.TTR. */
   .
```

The following example shows how to work with a read-only embedded font:

```
HFONT hfont;

/* Extract.TTF file into C:\MYDIR\FONT.TTR. */

CreateScalableFontResource(1, "font.for", "c:\\mydir\\font.ttr", NULL);

AddFontResource("font.for");

hfont = CreateFont(..., CLIP_EMBEDDED, ..., "FONT");
   .
   . /* Use the font. */
   .
DeleteObject(hfont);

RemoveFontResource("font.for");
   .
   . /* Delete C:\MYDIR\FONT.FOR and C:\MYDIR\FONT.TTR. */
   .
```

See Also   **AddFontResource**

CreateSolidBrush

HBRUSH CreateSolidBrush(*clrref*)
COLORREF *clrref*;   /* brush color   */

The **CreateSolidBrush** function creates a brush that has a specified solid color. The brush can subsequently be selected as the current brush for any device.

Parameters

clrref
Specifies the color of the brush.

Return Value

The return value is the handle of the brush if the function is successful. Otherwise, it is NULL.

Comments

When an application has finished using the brush created by **CreateSolidBrush**, it should select the brush out of the device context and then remove it by using the **DeleteObject** function.

Example

The following example uses the **CreateSolidBrush** function to create a green brush, selects the brush into a device context, and then uses the brush to fill a rectangle:

```
HBRUSH hbrOld;
HBRUSH hbr;

hbr = CreateSolidBrush(RGB(0, 255, 0));
hbrOld = SelectObject(hdc, hbr);
Rectangle(hdc, 10, 10, 100, 100);
```

See Also

CreateBrushIndirect, CreateDIBPatternBrush, CreateHatchBrush, CreatePatternBrush, DeleteObject

CreateWindow

HWND CreateWindow(*lpszClassName*, *lpszWindowName*, *dwStyle*, *x*, *y*, *nWidth*, *nHeight*, *hwndParent*, *hmenu*, *hinst*, *lpvParam*)

LPCSTR *lpszClassName*;	/* address of registered class name	*/
LPCSTR *lpszWindowName*;	/* address of window text	*/
DWORD *dwStyle*;	/* window style	*/
int *x*;	/* horizontal position of window	*/
int *y*;	/* vertical position of window	*/
int *nWidth*;	/* window width	*/
int *nHeight*;	/* window height	*/
HWND *hwndParent*;	/* handle of parent window	*/
HMENU *hmenu*;	/* handle of menu or child-window identifier	*/
HINSTANCE *hinst*;	/* handle of application instance	*/
void FAR* *lpvParam*;	/* address of window-creation data	*/

The **CreateWindow** function creates an overlapped, pop-up, or child window. The **CreateWindow** function specifies the window class, window title, window style, and (optionally) the initial position and size of the window. The **Create-Window** function also specifies the window's parent (if any) and menu.

Parameters   *lpszClassName*

Points to a null-terminated string specifying the window class. The class name can be any name registered with the **RegisterClass** function or any of the prede-fined control-class names. (See the following Comments section for a complete list.)

lpszWindowName

Points to a null-terminated string that represents the window name.

dwStyle

Specifies the style of window being created. This parameter can be a combina-tion of the window styles and control styles given in the following Comments section.

x

Specifies the initial x-position of the window. For an overlapped or pop-up win-dow, the *x* parameter is the initial x-coordinate of the window's upper-left corner, in screen coordinates. For a child window, *x* is the x-coordinate of the upper-left corner of the window in the client area of its parent window.

If this value is CW_USEDEFAULT, Windows selects the default position for the window's upper-left corner and ignores the *y* parameter. CW_USEDEFAULT is valid only for overlapped windows. If CW_USEDEFAULT is specified for a non-overlapped window, the *x* and *y* parameters are set to 0.

y

Specifies the initial y-position of the window. For an overlapped window, the *y* parameter is the initial y-coordinate of the window's upper-left corner. For a pop-up window, *y* is the y-coordinate, in screen coordinates, of the upper-left corner of the pop-up window. For list-box controls, *y* is the y-coordinate of the upper-left corner of the control's client area. For a child window, *y* is the y-coordinate of the upper-left corner of the child window. All of these coordinates are for the window, not the window's client area.

If an overlapped window is created with the WS_VISIBLE style and the *x* parameter set to CW_USEDEFAULT, Windows ignores the *y* parameter.

nWidth

Specifies the width, in device units, of the window. For overlapped windows, the *nWidth* parameter is either the window's width (in screen coordinates) or CW_USEDEFAULT. If *nWidth* is CW_USEDEFAULT, Windows selects a default width and height for the window (the default width extends from the initial x-position to the right edge of the screen, and the default height extends from the initial y-position to the top of the icon area). CW_USEDEFAULT is valid only for overlapped windows. If CW_USEDEFAULT is specified in *nWidth* for a non-overlapped window, *nWidth* and *nHeight* are set to 0.

nHeight

Specifies the height, in device units, of the window. For overlapped windows, the *nHeight* parameter is the window's height in screen coordinates. If the *nWidth* parameter is CW_USEDEFAULT, Windows ignores *nHeight*.

hwndParent

Identifies the parent or owner window of the window being created. A valid window handle must be supplied when creating a child window or an owned window. An owned window is an overlapped window that is destroyed when its owner window is destroyed, hidden when its owner is minimized, and that is always displayed on top of its owner window. For pop-up windows, a handle can be supplied but is not required. If the window does not have a parent window or is not owned by another window, the *hwndParent* parameter must be set to HWND_DESKTOP.

hmenu

Identifies a menu or a child window. This parameter's meaning depends on the window style. For overlapped or pop-up windows, the *hmenu* parameter identifies the menu to be used with the window. It can be NULL, if the class menu is to be used. For child windows, *hmenu* identifies the child window and is an integer value that is used by a dialog box control to notify its parent of events (such as the EN_HSCROLL message). The child window identifier is determined by the application and should be unique for all child windows with the same parent window.

hinst

Identifies the instance of the module to be associated with the window.

lpvParam

Points to a value that is passed to the window through the **CREATESTRUCT** structure referenced by the *lParam* parameter of the WM_CREATE message. If an application is calling **CreateWindow** to create a multiple document interface (MDI) client window, *lpvParam* must point to a **CLIENTCREATE- STRUCT** structure. The **CREATESTRUCT** structure has the following form:

```
typedef struct tagCREATESTRUCT {     /* cs */
    void FAR* lpCreateParams;
    HINSTANCE hInstance;
    HMENU     hMenu;
    HWND      hwndParent;
    int       cy;
    int       cx;
    int       y;
    int       x;
    LONG      style;
    LPCSTR    lpszName;
    LPCSTR    lpszClass;
    DWORD     dwExStyle;
} CREATESTRUCT;
```

The **CLIENTCREATESTRUCT** structure has the following form:

```
typedef struct tagCLIENTCREATESTRUCT {  /* ccs */
    HANDLE  hWindowMenu;
    UINT    idFirstChild;
} CLIENTCREATESTRUCT;
```

For a full description of these two structures, see the *Microsoft Windows Programmer's Reference, Volume 3*.

Return Value

The return value is the handle of the new window if the function is successful. Otherwise, it is NULL.

Comments

For overlapped, pop-up, and child windows, the **CreateWindow** function sends WM_CREATE, WM_GETMINMAXINFO, and WM_NCCREATE messages to the window. If the WS_VISIBLE style is specified, **CreateWindow** sends the window all the messages required to activate and show the window.

If the window style specifies a title bar, the window title pointed to by the *lpszWindowName* parameter is displayed in the title bar. When using **Create- Window** to create controls such as buttons, check boxes, and edit controls, use the *lpszWindowName* parameter to specify the text of the control.

Before returning, the **CreateWindow** function sends a WM_CREATE message to the window procedure.

Following are the predefined control classes an application can specify in the *lpszClassName* parameter:

Class	Meaning
BUTTON	Designates a small rectangular child window that represents a button the user can turn on or off by clicking. Button controls can be used alone or in groups, and can either be labeled or appear without text. Button controls typically change appearance when the user clicks them.
COMBOBOX	Designates a control consisting of a list box and a selection field similar to an edit control. The list box may be displayed at all times or may be dropped down when the user selects a pop-up list box next to the selection field.
	Depending on the style of the combo box, the user can or cannot edit the contents of the selection field. If the list box is visible, typing characters into the selection box will cause the first list box entry that matches the characters typed to be highlighted. Conversely, selecting an item in the list box displays the selected text in the selection field.
EDIT	Designates a rectangular child window in which the user can type text from the keyboard. The user selects the control, and gives it the input focus by clicking it or moving to it by pressing the TAB key. The user can type text when the control displays a flashing caret. The mouse can be used to move the cursor and select characters to be replaced, or to position the cursor for inserting characters. The BACKSPACE key can be used to delete characters.
	Edit controls use the variable-pitch System font and display characters from the Windows character set. Applications compiled to run with earlier versions of Windows display text with a fixed-pitch System font unless they have been marked by the Windows 3.0 MARK utility (with the **MEMORY FONT** option specified). An application can also send the WM_SETFONT message to the edit control to change the default font.
	Edit controls expand tab characters into as many space characters as are required to move the cursor to the next tab stop. Tab stops are assumed to be at every eighth character position.
LISTBOX	Designates a list of character strings. This control is used whenever an application must present a list of names, such as filenames, from which the user can choose. The user can select a string by pointing to it and clicking. When a string is selected, it is highlighted and a notification message is passed to the parent window. A vertical or horizontal scroll bar can be used with a list box control to scroll lists that are too long for the control window. The list box automatically hides or shows the scroll bar as needed.

Class	Meaning
MDICLIENT	Designates an MDI client window. The MDI client window receives messages that control the MDI application's child windows. The recommended style bits are WS_CLIPCHILDREN and WS_CHILD. To create a scrollable MDI client window that allows the user to scroll MDI child windows into view, an application can also use the WS_HSCROLL and WS_VSCROLL styles.
SCROLLBAR	Designates a rectangle that contains a scroll box (also called a "thumb") and has direction arrows at both ends. The scroll bar sends a notification message to its parent window whenever the user clicks the control. The parent window is responsible for updating the position, if necessary. Scroll bar controls have the same appearance and function as scroll bars used in ordinary windows. Unlike scroll bars, however, scroll bar controls can be positioned anywhere in a window and used whenever needed to provide scrolling input for a window.

The scroll bar class also includes size box controls (Maximize and Minimize buttons). These controls are small rectangles that the user can click to change the size of the window. |
| STATIC | Designates a simple text field, box, or rectangle that can be used to label, box, or separate other controls. Static controls take no input and provide no output. |

Following are the window styles an application can specify in the *dwStyle* parameter.

Style	Meaning
MDIS_ALLCHILDSTYLES	Creates an MDI child window that can have any combination of window styles. When this style is not specified, an MDI child window has the WS_MINIMIZE, WS_MAXIMIZE, WS_HSCROLL, and WS_VSCROLL styles as default settings.
WS_BORDER	Creates a window that has a border.
WS_CAPTION	Creates a window that has a title bar (implies the WS_BORDER style). This style cannot be used with the WS_DLGFRAME style.
WS_CHILD	Creates a child window. Cannot be used with the WS_POPUP style.
WS_CHILDWINDOW	Same as the WS_CHILD style.
WS_CLIPCHILDREN	Excludes the area occupied by child windows when drawing within the parent window. Used when creating the parent window.

Style	Meaning
WS_CLIPSIBLINGS	Clips child windows relative to each other; that is, when a particular child window receives a paint message, the WS_CLIPSIBLINGS style clips all other overlapped child windows out of the region of the child window to be updated. (If WS_CLIPSIBLINGS is not specified and child windows overlap, it is possible, when drawing within the client area of a child window, to draw within the client area of a neighboring child window.) For use with the WS_CHILD style only.
WS_DISABLED	Creates a window that is initially disabled.
WS_DLGFRAME	Creates a window with a double border but no title.
WS_GROUP	Specifies the first control of a group of controls in which the user can move from one control to the next by using the arrow keys. All controls defined with the WS_GROUP style after the first control belong to the same group. The next control with the WS_GROUP style ends the style group and starts the next group (that is, one group ends where the next begins). Only dialog boxes use this style.
WS_HSCROLL	Creates a window that has a horizontal scroll bar.
WS_MAXIMIZE	Creates a window of maximum size.
WS_MAXIMIZEBOX	Creates a window that has a Maximize button.
WS_MINIMIZE	Creates a window that is initially minimized. For use with the WS_OVERLAPPED style only.
WS_MINIMIZEBOX	Creates a window that has a Minimize button.
WS_OVERLAPPED	Creates an overlapped window. An overlapped window has a title and a border.
WS_OVERLAPPEDWINDOW	Creates an overlapped window having the WS_OVERLAPPED, WS_CAPTION, WS_SYSMENU, WS_THICKFRAME, WS_MINIMIZEBOX, and WS_MAXIMIZEBOX styles.
WS_POPUP	Creates a pop-up window. Cannot be used with the WS_CHILD style.
WS_POPUPWINDOW	Creates a pop-up window that has the WS_BORDER, WS_POPUP, and WS_SYSMENU styles. The WS_CAPTION style must be combined with the WS_POPUPWINDOW style to make the System menu visible.
WS_SYSMENU	Creates a window that has a System-menu box in its title bar. Used only for windows with title bars.

Style	Meaning
WS_TABSTOP	Specifies one of any number of controls through which the user can move by using the TAB key. The TAB key moves the user to the next control specified by the WS_TABSTOP style. Only dialog boxes use this style.
WS_THICKFRAME	Creates a window with a thick frame that can be used to size the window.
WS_VISIBLE	Creates a window that is initially visible. This applies to overlapped, child, and pop-up windows. For overlapped windows, the *y* parameter is used as a **ShowWindow** function parameter.
WS_VSCROLL	Creates a window that has a vertical scroll bar.

Following are the button styles (in the BUTTON class) that an application can specify in the *dwStyle* parameter:

Value	Meaning
BS_3STATE	Creates a button that is the same as a check box, except that the box can be grayed (dimmed) as well as checked. The grayed state is used to show that the state of a check box is not determined.
BS_AUTO3STATE	Creates a button that is the same as a three-state check box, except that the box changes its state when the user selects it. The state cycles through checked, grayed, and normal.
BS_AUTOCHECKBOX	Creates a button that is the same as a check box, except that an X appears in the check box when the user selects the box; the X disappears (is cleared) the next time the user selects the box.
BS_AUTORADIOBUTTON	Creates a button that is the same as a radio button, except that when the user selects it, the button automatically highlights itself and clears (removes the selection from) any other buttons in the same group.
BS_CHECKBOX	Creates a small square that has text displayed to its right (unless this style is combined with the BS_LEFTTEXT style).
BS_DEFPUSHBUTTON	Creates a button that has a heavy black border. The user can select this button by pressing the ENTER key. This style is useful for enabling the user to quickly select the most likely option (the default option).
BS_GROUPBOX	Creates a rectangle in which other controls can be grouped. Any text associated with this style is displayed in the rectangle's upper-left corner.

Value	Meaning
BS_LEFTTEXT	Places text on the left side of the radio button or check box when combined with a radio button or check box style.
BS_OWNERDRAW	Creates an owner-drawn button. The owner window receives a WM_MEASUREITEM message when the button is created, and it receives a WM_DRAWITEM message when a visual aspect of the button has changed. The BS_OWNERDRAW style cannot be combined with any other button styles.
BS_PUSHBUTTON	Creates a push button that posts a WM_COMMAND message to the owner window when the user selects the button.
BS_RADIOBUTTON	Creates a small circle that has text displayed to its right (unless this style is combined with the BS_LEFTTEXT style). Radio buttons are usually used in groups of related but mutually exclusive choices.

Following are the combo box styles (in the COMBOBOX class) that an application can specify in the *dwStyle* parameter:

Style	Description
CBS_AUTOHSCROLL	Automatically scrolls the text in the edit control to the right when the user types a character at the end of the line. If this style is not set, only text that fits within the rectangular boundary is allowed.
CBS_DISABLENOSCROLL	Shows a disabled vertical scroll bar in the list box when the box does not contain enough items to scroll. Without this style, the scroll bar is hidden when the list box does not contain enough items.
CBS_DROPDOWN	Similar to CBS_SIMPLE, except that the list box is not displayed unless the user selects an icon next to the edit control.
CBS_DROPDOWNLIST	Similar to CBS_DROPDOWN, except that the edit control is replaced by a static text item that displays the current selection in the list box.
CBS_HASSTRINGS	Specifies that an owner-drawn combo box contains items consisting of strings. The combo box maintains the memory and pointers for the strings so the application can use the CB_GETLBTEXT message to retrieve the text for a particular item.

Style	Description
CBS_NOINTEGRALHEIGHT	Specifies that the size of the combo box is exactly the size specified by the application when it created the combo box. Normally, Windows sizes a combo box so that the combo box does not display partial items.
CBS_OEMCONVERT	Converts text entered in the combo-box edit control from the Windows character set to the OEM character set and then back to the Windows set. This ensures proper character conversion when the application calls the **AnsiToOem** function to convert a Windows string in the combo box to OEM characters. This style is most useful for combo boxes that contain filenames and applies only to combo boxes created with the CBS_SIMPLE or CBS_DROPDOWN styles.
CBS_OWNERDRAWFIXED	Specifies that the owner of the list box is responsible for drawing its contents and that the items in the list box are all the same height. The owner window receives a WM_MEASUREITEM message when the combo box is created and a WM_DRAWITEM message when a visual aspect of the combo box changes.
CBS_OWNERDRAWVARIABLE	Specifies that the owner of the list box is responsible for drawing its contents and that the items in the list box are variable in height. The owner window receives a WM_MEASURE-ITEM message for each item in the combo box when the combo box is created and a WM_DRAWITEM message when a visual aspect of the combo box changes.
CBS_SIMPLE	Displays the list box at all times. The current selection in the list box is displayed in the edit control.
CBS_SORT	Automatically sorts strings entered into the list box.

Following are the edit control styles (in the EDIT class) that an application can specify in the *dwStyle* parameter:

Style	Meaning
ES_AUTOHSCROLL	Automatically scrolls text to the right by 10 characters when the user types a character at the end of the line. When the user presses the ENTER key, the control scrolls all text back to position zero.

Style	Meaning
ES_AUTOVSCROLL	Automatically scrolls text up one page when the user presses ENTER on the last line.
ES_CENTER	Centers text in a multiline edit control.
ES_LEFT	Left aligns text.
ES_LOWERCASE	Converts all characters to lowercase as they are typed into the edit control.
ES_MULTILINE	Designates a multiline edit control. (The default is single-line edit control.)
	When a multiline edit control is in a dialog box, the default response to pressing the ENTER key is to activate the default button. To use the ENTER key as a carriage return, an application should use the ES_WANTRETURN style.
	When the multiline edit control is not in a dialog box and the ES_AUTOVSCROLL style is specified, the edit control shows as many lines as possible and scrolls vertically when the user presses the ENTER key. If ES_AUTOVSCROLL is not specified, the edit control shows as many lines as possible and beeps if the user presses ENTER when no more lines can be displayed.
	If the ES_AUTOHSCROLL style is specified, the multiline edit control automatically scrolls horizontally when the caret goes past the right edge of the control. To start a new line, the user must press ENTER. If ES_AUTOHSCROLL is not specified, the control automatically wraps words to the beginning of the next line when necessary. A new line is also started if the user presses ENTER. The position of the wordwrap is determined by the window size. If the window size changes, the wordwrap position changes and the text is redisplayed.
	Multiline edit controls can have scroll bars. An edit control with scroll bars processes its own scroll bar messages. Edit controls without scroll bars scroll as described in the previous two paragraphs and process any scroll messages sent by the parent window.
ES_NOHIDESEL	Negates the default behavior for an edit control. The default behavior is to hide the selection when the control loses the input focus and invert the selection when the control receives the input focus.
ES_OEMCONVERT	Converts text entered in the edit control from the Windows character set to the OEM character set and then back to the Windows set. This ensures proper character conversion when the application calls the **AnsiToOem** function to convert a Windows string in the edit control to OEM characters. This style is most useful for edit controls that contain filenames.

Style	Meaning
ES_PASSWORD	Displays all characters as an asterisk (*) as they are typed into the edit control. An application can use the EM_SETPASSWORDCHAR message to change the character that is displayed.
ES_READONLY	Prevents the user from typing or editing text in the edit control.
ES_RIGHT	Right aligns text in a multiline edit control.
ES_UPPERCASE	Converts all characters to uppercase as they are typed into the edit control.
ES_WANTRETURN	Specifies that a carriage return be inserted when the user presses the ENTER key while entering text into a multiline edit control in a dialog box. If this style is not specified, pressing the ENTER key has the same effect as pressing the dialog box's default push button. This style has no effect on a single-line edit control.

Following are the list box styles (in the LISTBOX class) that an application can specify in the *dwStyle* parameter:

Style	Meaning
LBS_DISABLENOSCROLL	Shows a disabled vertical scroll bar for the list box when the box does not contain enough items to scroll. If this style is not specified, the scroll bar is hidden when the list box does not contain enough items.
LBS_EXTENDEDSEL	Allows multiple items to be selected by using the SHIFT key and the mouse or special key combinations.
LBS_HASSTRINGS	Specifies that a list box contains items consisting of strings. The list box maintains the memory and pointers for the strings so the application can use the LB_GETTEXT message to retrieve the text for a particular item. By default, all list boxes except owner-drawn list boxes have this style. An application can create an owner-drawn list box either with or without this style.
LBS_MULTICOLUMN	Specifies a multicolumn list box that is scrolled horizontally. The LB_SETCOLUMNWIDTH message sets the width of the columns.
LBS_MULTIPLESEL	Turns string selection on or off each time the user clicks or double-clicks the string. Any number of strings can be selected.

Style	Meaning
LBS_NOINTEGRALHEIGHT	Specifies that the size of the list box is exactly the size specified by the application when it created the list box. Normally, Windows sizes a list box so that the list box does not display partial items.
LBS_NOREDRAW	Specifies that the list box's appearance is not updated when changes are made. This style can be changed at any time by sending a WM_SETREDRAW message.
LBS_NOTIFY	Notifies the parent window with an input message whenever the user clicks or double-clicks a string.
LBS_OWNERDRAWFIXED	Specifies that the owner of the list box is responsible for drawing its contents and that the items in the list box are the same height. The owner window receives a WM_MEASURE-ITEM message when the list box is created and a WM_DRAWITEM message when a visual aspect of the list box changes.
LBS_OWNERDRAWVARIABLE	Specifies that the owner of the list box is responsible for drawing its contents and that the items in the list box are variable in height. The owner window receives a WM_MEASUREITEM message for each item in the list box when the list box is created and a WM_DRAWITEM message whenever the visual aspect of the list box changes.
LBS_SORT	Sorts strings in the list box alphabetically.
LBS_STANDARD	Sorts strings in the list box alphabetically. The parent window receives an input message whenever the user clicks or double-clicks a string. The list box has borders on all sides.
LBS_USETABSTOPS	Allows a list box to recognize and expand tab characters when drawing its strings. The default tab positions are 32 dialog box units. (A dialog box unit is a horizontal or vertical distance. One horizontal dialog box unit is equal to one-fourth of the current dialog box base width unit. The dialog box base units are computed based on the height and width of the current system font. The **GetDialogBaseUnits** function returns the current dialog box base units in pixels.)

Style	Meaning
LBS_WANTKEYBOARDINPUT	Specifies that the owner of the list box receives WM_VKEYTOITEM or WM_CHARTOITEM messages whenever the user presses a key and the list box has the input focus. This allows an application to perform special processing on the keyboard input. If a list box has the LBS_HASSTRINGS style, the list box can receive WM_VKEYTOITEM messages but not WM_CHARTOITEM messages. If a list box does not have the LBS_HASSTRINGS style, the list box can receive WM_CHARTOITEM messages but not WM_VKEYTOITEM messages.

Following are the scroll bar styles (in the SCROLLBAR class) that an application can specify in the *dwStyle* parameter:

Style	Meaning
SBS_BOTTOMALIGN	Aligns the bottom edge of the scroll bar with the bottom edge of the rectangle defined by the following **CreateWindow** parameters: *x*, *y*, *nWidth*, and *nHeight*. The scroll bar has the default height for system scroll bars. Used with the SBS_HORZ style.
SBS_HORZ	Designates a horizontal scroll bar. If neither the SBS_BOTTOMALIGN nor SBS_TOPALIGN style is specified, the scroll bar has the height, width, and position specified by the **CreateWindow** parameters.
SBS_LEFTALIGN	Aligns the left edge of the scroll bar with the left edge of the rectangle defined by the **CreateWindow** parameters. The scroll bar has the default width for system scroll bars. Used with the SBS_VERT style.

Style	Meaning
SBS_RIGHTALIGN	Aligns the right edge of the scroll bar with the right edge of the rectangle defined by the **CreateWindow** parameters. The scroll bar has the default width for system scroll bars. Used with the SBS_VERT style.
SBS_SIZEBOX	Designates a size box. If neither the SBS_SIZEBOXBOTTOMRIGHTALIGN nor SBS_SIZEBOXTOPLEFTALIGN style is specified, the size box has the height, width, and position specified by the **CreateWindow** parameters.
SBS_SIZEBOXBOTTOMRIGHTALIGN	Aligns the lower-right corner of the size box with the lower-right corner of the rectangle specified by the **CreateWindow** parameters. The size box has the default size for system size boxes. Used with the SBS_SIZEBOX style.
SBS_SIZEBOXTOPLEFTALIGN	Aligns the upper-left corner of the size box with the upper-left corner of the rectangle specified by the following **CreateWindow** parameters: x, y, *nWidth*, and *nHeight*. The size box has the default size for system size boxes. Used with the SBS_SIZEBOX style.
SBS_TOPALIGN	Aligns the top edge of the scroll bar with the top edge of the rectangle defined by the **CreateWindow** parameters. The scroll bar has the default height for system scroll bars. Used with the SBS_HORZ style.
SBS_VERT	Designates a vertical scroll bar. If neither the SBS_RIGHTALIGN nor SBS_LEFTALIGN style is specified, the scroll bar has the height, width, and position specified by the **CreateWindow** parameters.

Following are the static control styles (in the STATIC class) that an application can specify in the *dwStyle* parameter. A static control can have only one of these styles.

Style	Meaning
SS_BLACKFRAME	Specifies a box with a frame drawn in the same color as window frames. This color is black in the default Windows color scheme.
SS_BLACKRECT	Specifies a rectangle filled with the color used to draw window frames. This color is black in the default Windows color scheme.
SS_CENTER	Designates a simple rectangle and displays the given text centered in the rectangle. The text is formatted before it is displayed. Words that would extend past the end of a line are automatically wrapped to the beginning of the next centered line.
SS_GRAYFRAME	Specifies a box with a frame drawn with the same color as the screen background (desktop). This color is gray in the default Windows color scheme.
SS_GRAYRECT	Specifies a rectangle filled with the color used to fill the screen background. This color is gray in the default Windows color scheme.
SS_ICON	Designates an icon displayed in the dialog box. The given text is the name of an icon (not a filename) defined elsewhere in the resource file. The *nWidth* and *nHeight* parameters are ignored; the icon automatically sizes itself.
SS_LEFT	Designates a simple rectangle and displays the given text left-aligned in the rectangle. The text is formatted before it is displayed. Words that would extend past the end of a line are automatically wrapped to the beginning of the next left-aligned line.
SS_LEFTNOWORDWRAP	Designates a simple rectangle and displays the given text left-aligned in the rectangle. Tabs are expanded but words are not wrapped. Text that extends past the end of a line is clipped.
SS_NOPREFIX	Prevents interpretation of any & characters in the control's text as accelerator prefix characters (which are displayed with the & removed and the next character in the string underlined). This static control style may be included with any of the defined static controls.
	You can combine SS_NOPREFIX with other styles by using the bitwise OR operator. This is most often used when filenames or other strings that may contain an & need to be displayed in a static control in a dialog box.

Style	Meaning
SS_RIGHT	Designates a simple rectangle and displays the given text right-aligned in the rectangle. The text is formatted before it is displayed. Words that would extend past the end of a line are automatically wrapped to the beginning of the next right-aligned line.
SS_SIMPLE	Designates a simple rectangle and displays a single line of text left-aligned in the rectangle. The line of text cannot be shortened or altered in any way. (The control's parent window or dialog box must not process the WM_CTLCOLOR message.)
SS_WHITEFRAME	Specifies a box with a frame drawn in the same color as window backgrounds. This color is white in the default Windows color scheme.
SS_WHITERECT	Specifies a rectangle filled with the color used to fill window backgrounds. This color is white in the default Windows color scheme.

Following are the dialog box styles an application can specify in the *dwStyle* parameter:

Style	Meaning
DS_LOCALEDIT	Specifies that edit controls in the dialog box will use memory in the application's data segment. By default, all edit controls in dialog boxes use memory outside the application's data segment. This feature may be suppressed by adding the DS_LOCALEDIT flag to the Style command for the dialog box. If this flag is not used, EM_GETHANDLE and EM_SETHANDLE messages must not be used, because the storage for the control is not in the application's data segment. This feature does not affect edit controls created outside of dialog boxes.
DS_MODALFRAME	Creates a dialog box with a modal dialog box frame that can be combined with a title bar and System menu by specifying the WS_CAPTION and WS_SYSMENU styles.
DS_NOIDLEMSG	Suppresses WM_ENTERIDLE messages that Windows would otherwise send to the owner of the dialog box while the dialog box is displayed.
DS_SYSMODAL	Creates a system-modal dialog box.

See Also   **AnsiToOem, GetDialogBaseUnits, ShowWindow**

CreateWindowEx

HWND CreateWindowEx(*dwExStyle, lpszClassName, lpszWindowName, dwStyle, x, y, nWidth,*
  nHeight, hwndParent, hmenu, hinst, lpvCreateParams)
DWORD *dwExStyle*;	/* extended window style	*/
LPCSTR *lpszClassName*;	/* address of registered class name	*/
LPCSTR *lpszWindowName*;	/* address of window text	*/
DWORD *dwStyle*;	/* window style	*/
int *x*;	/* horizontal position of the window	*/
int *y*;	/* vertical position of the window	*/
int *nWidth*;	/* window width	*/
int *nHeight*;	/* window height	*/
HWND *hwndParent*;	/* handle of parent window	*/
HMENU *hmenu*;	/* handle of menu or child-window identifier	*/
HINSTANCE *hinst*;	/* handle of application instance	*/
void FAR* *lpvCreateParams*;	/* address of window-creation data	*/

The **CreateWindowEx** function creates an overlapped, pop-up, or child window with an extended style; otherwise, this function is identical to the **CreateWindow** function. For more information about creating a window and for full descriptions of the other parameters of **CreateWindowEx**, see the preceding description of the **CreateWindow** function.

Parameters   *dwExStyle*
Specifies the extended style of the window. This parameter can be one of the following values:

Style	Meaning
WS_EX_ACCEPTFILES	Specifies that a window created with this style accepts drag-drop files.
WS_EX_DLGMODALFRAME	Designates a window with a double border that may (optionally) be created with a title bar by specifying the WS_CAPTION style flag in the *dwStyle* parameter.
WS_EX_NOPARENTNOTIFY	Specifies that a child window created by using this style will not send the WM_PARENTNOTIFY message to its parent window when the child window is created or destroyed.
WS_EX_TOPMOST	Specifies that a window created with this style should be placed above all non-topmost windows and stay above them even when the window is deactivated. An application can use the **SetWindowPos** function to add or remove this attribute.

Style	Meaning
WS_EX_TRANSPARENT	Specifies that a window created with this style is to be transparent. That is, any windows that are beneath the window are not obscured by the window. A window created with this style receives WM_PAINT messages only after all sibling windows beneath it have been updated.

lpszClassName
Points to a null-terminated string containing the name of the window class.

lpszWindowName
Points to a null-terminated string containing the name of the window.

dwStyle
Specifies the style of the window. For a list of the window styles that can be specified in this parameter, see the preceding description of the **CreateWindow** function.

x
Specifies the initial left-side position of the window.

y
Specifies the initial top position of the window.

nWidth
Specifies the width, in device units, of the window.

nHeight
Specifies the height, in device units, of the window.

hwndParent
Identifies the parent or owner window of the window to be created.

hmenu
Identifies a menu or a child window. The meaning depends on the window style.

hinst
Identifies the instance of the module to be associated with the window.

lpvCreateParams
Contains any application-specific creation parameters. The window being created may access this data when the **CREATESTRUCT** structure is passed to the window by the WM_NCCREATE and WM_CREATE messages.

The **CREATESTRUCT** structure has the following form:

```
typedef struct tagCREATESTRUCT {      /* cs */
    void FAR* lpCreateParams;
    HINSTANCE hInstance;
    HMENU     hMenu;
    HWND      hwndParent;
    int       cy;
    int       cx;
    int       y;
    int       x;
    LONG      style;
    LPCSTR    lpszName;
    LPCSTR    lpszClass;
    DWORD     dwExStyle;
} CREATESTRUCT;
```

For a full description of this structure, see the *Microsoft Windows Programmer's Reference, Volume 3.*

Return Value   The return value identifies the new window if the function is successful. Otherwise, it is NULL.

Comments   The **CreateWindowEx** function sends the following messages to the window being created:

WM_NCCREATE
WM_NCCALCSIZE
WM_CREATE

Example   The following example creates a main window that has the WS_EX_TOPMOST extended style, makes the window visible, and updates the window's client area:

```
char szClassName[] = "MyClass";

/* Create the main window. */

hwnd = CreateWindowEx(WS_EX_TOPMOST, szClassName, "Grouper",
    WS_OVERLAPPEDWINDOW, CW_USEDEFAULT, CW_USEDEFAULT,
    CW_USEDEFAULT, CW_USEDEFAULT, NULL, NULL,
    hinst, NULL);

/* Make the window visible and update its client area. */

ShowWindow(hwnd, SW_SHOW);    /* always show the window */
UpdateWindow(hwnd);
```

See Also   **CreateWindow, SetWindowPos**

DdeAbandonTransaction

$\boxed{3.1}$

#include <ddeml.h>

BOOL DdeAbandonTransaction(*idInst*, *hConv*, *idTransaction*)
DWORD *idInst*;   /* instance identifier   */
HCONV *hConv*;   /* handle of conversation   */
DWORD *idTransaction*; /* transaction identifier   */

The **DdeAbandonTransaction** function abandons the specified asynchronous transaction and releases all resources associated with the transaction.

Parameters

idInst
Specifies the application-instance identifier obtained by a previous call to the **DdeInitialize** function.

hConv
Identifies the conversation in which the transaction was initiated. If this parameter is NULL, all transactions are abandoned (the *idTransaction* parameter is ignored).

idTransaction
Identifies the transaction to terminate. If this parameter is NULL, all active transactions in the specified conversation are abandoned.

Return Value

The return value is nonzero if the function is successful. Otherwise, it is zero.

Errors

Use the **DdeGetLastError** function to retrieve the error value, which may be one of the following:

DMLERR_DLL_NOT_INITIALIZED
DMLERR_INVALIDPARAMETER
DMLERR_NO_ERROR
DMLERR_UNFOUND_QUEUE_ID

Comments

Only a dynamic data exchange (DDE) client application should call the **DdeAbandonTransaction** function. If the server application responds to the transaction after the client has called **DdeAbandonTransaction**, the system discards the transaction results. This function has no effect on synchronous transactions.

See Also

DdeClientTransaction, DdeGetLastError, DdeInitialize, DdeQueryConvInfo

DdeAccessData

3.1

#include <ddeml.h>

BYTE FAR* DdeAccessData(*hData, lpcbData*)
HDDEDATA *hData*;   /* handle of global memory object   */
DWORD FAR* *lpcbData*;   /* pointer to variable that receives data length   */

The **DdeAccessData** function provides access to the data in the given global memory object. An application must call the **DdeUnaccessData** function when it is finished accessing the data in the object.

Parameters

hData
Identifies the global memory object to access.

lpcbData
Points to a variable that receives the size, in bytes, of the global memory object identified by the *hData* parameter. If this parameter is NULL, no size information is returned.

Return Value

The return value points to the first byte of data in the global memory object if the function is successful. Otherwise, the return value is NULL.

Errors

Use the **DdeGetLastError** function to retrieve the error value, which may be one of the following:

DMLERR_DLL_NOT_INITIALIZED
DMLERR_INVALIDPARAMETER
DMLERR_NO_ERROR

Comments

If the *hData* parameter has not been passed to a Dynamic Data Exchange Management Library (DDEML) function, an application can use the pointer returned by **DdeAccessData** for read-write access to the global memory object. If *hData* has already been passed to a DDEML function, the pointer can only be used for read-only access to the memory object.

Example

The following example uses the **DdeAccessData** function to obtain a pointer to a global memory object, uses the pointer to copy data from the object to a local buffer, then frees the pointer:

```
HDDEDATA hData;
LPBYTE lpszAdviseData;
DWORD cbDataLen;
DWORD i;
char szData[128];

lpszAdviseData = DdeAccessData(hData, &cbDataLen);
```

```
for (i = 0; i < cbDataLen; i++)
    szData[i] = *lpszAdviseData++;
DdeUnaccessData(hData);
```

See Also

DdeAddData, DdeCreateDataHandle, DdeFreeDataHandle, DdeGetLast-Error, DdeUnaccessData

---

DdeAddData

3.1

#include <ddeml.h>

HDDEDATA DdeAddData(*hData, lpvSrcBuf, cbAddData, offObj***)**
HDDEDATA *hData*;   /* handle of global memory object   */
void FAR* *lpvSrcBuf*;   /* address of source buffer   */
DWORD *cbAddData*;   /* length of data   */
DWORD *offObj*;   /* offset within global memory object   */

The **DdeAddData** function adds data to the given global memory object. An application can add data beginning at any offset from the beginning of the object. If new data overlaps data already in the object, the new data overwrites the old data in the bytes where the overlap occurs. The contents of locations in the object that have not been written to are undefined.

Parameters

hData
Identifies the global memory object that receives additional data.

lpvSrcBuf
Points to a buffer containing the data to add to the global memory object.

cbAddData
Specifies the length, in bytes, of the data to be added to the global memory object.

offObj
Specifies an offset, in bytes, from the beginning of the global memory object. The additional data is copied to the object beginning at this offset.

Return Value

The return value is a new handle of the global memory object if the function is successful. The new handle should be used in all references to the object. The return value is zero if an error occurs.

Errors

Use the **DdeGetLastError** function to retrieve the error value, which may be one of the following:

DMLERR_DLL_NOT_INITIALIZED
DMLERR_INVALIDPARAMETER
DMLERR_MEMORY_ERROR
DMLERR_NO_ERROR

Comments

After a data handle has been used as a parameter in another Dynamic Data Exchange Management Library (DDEML) function or returned by a DDE callback function, the handle may only be used for read access to the global memory object identified by the handle.

If the amount of global memory originally allocated is not large enough to hold the added data, the **DdeAddData** function will reallocate a global memory object of the appropriate size.

Example

The following example creates a global memory object, uses the **DdeAddData** function to add data to the object, and then passes the data to a client with an XTYP_POKE transaction:

```
DWORD idInst;          /* instance identifier    */
HDDEDATA hddeStrings;  /* data handle            */
HSZ hszMyItem;         /* item-name string handle */
DWORD offObj = 0;      /* offset in global object */
char szMyBuf[16];      /* temporary string buffer */
HCONV hconv;           /* conversation handle    */
DWORD dwResult;        /* transaction results    */
BOOL fAddAString;      /* TRUE if strings to add */

/* Create a global memory object. */

hddeStrings = DdeCreateDataHandle(idInst, NULL, 0, 0,
    hszMyItem, CF_TEXT, 0);

/*
 * If a string is available, the application-defined function
 * IsThereAString() copies it to szMyBuf and returns TRUE. Otherwise,
 * it returns FALSE.
 */

while ((fAddAString = IsThereAString())) {

    /* Add the string to the global memory object. */

    DdeAddData(hddeStrings,              /* data handle     */
        &szMyBuf,                        /* string buffer   */
        (DWORD) strlen(szMyBuf) + 1,     /* character count */
        offObj);                         /* offset in object */

    offObj = (DWORD) strlen(szMyBuf) + 1; /* adjust offset */
}
```

```
/* No more data to add, so poke it to the server. */

DdeClientTransaction((void FAR*) hddeStrings, -1L, hconv, hszMyItem,
    CF_TEXT, XTYP_POKE, 1000, &dwResult);
```

See Also   **DdeAccessData, DdeCreateDataHandle, DdeGetLastError, DdeUnaccessData**

DdeCallback

3.1

#include <ddeml.h>

HDDEDATA CALLBACK DdeCallback(*type, fmt, hconv, hsz1, hsz2, hData, dwData1, dwData2*)

UINT *type*;	/* transaction type	*/
UINT *fmt*;	/* clipboard data format	*/
HCONV *hconv*;	/* handle of conversation	*/
HSZ *hsz1*;	/* handle of string	*/
HSZ *hsz2*;	/* handle of string	*/
HDDEDATA *hData*;	/* handle of global memory object	*/
DWORD *dwData1*;	/* transaction-specific data	*/
DWORD *dwData2*;	/* transaction-specific data	*/

The **DdeCallback** function is an application-defined dynamic data exchange (DDE) callback function that processes DDE transactions sent to the function as a result of DDE Management Library (DDEML) calls by other applications.

Parameters   *type*

Specifies the type of the current transaction. This parameter consists of a combination of transaction-class flags and transaction-type flags. The following table describes each of the transaction classes and provides a list of the transaction types in each class. For information about a specific transaction type, see the individual description of that type in the *Microsoft Windows Programmer's Reference, Volume 3*.

Value	Meaning
XCLASS_BOOL	A DDE callback function should return TRUE or FALSE when it finishes processing a transaction that belongs to this class. Following are the XCLASS_BOOL transaction types: XTYP_ADVSTART XTYP_CONNECT

Value	Meaning
XCLASS_DATA	A DDE callback function should return a DDE data handle, CBR_BLOCK, or NULL when it finishes processing a transaction that belongs to this class. Following are the XCLASS_DATA transaction types: XTYP_ADVREQ XTYP_REQUEST XTYP_WILDCONNECT
XCLASS_FLAGS	A DDE callback function should return DDE_FACK, DDE_FBUSY, or DDE_FNOTPROCESSED when it finishes processing a transaction that belongs to this class. Following are the XCLASS_FLAGS transaction types: XTYP_ADVDATA XTYP_EXECUTE XTYP_POKE
XCLASS_NOTIFICATION	The transaction types that belong to this class are for notification purposes only. The return value from the callback function is ignored. Following are the XCLASS_NOTIFICATION transaction types: XTYP_ADVSTOP XTYP_CONNECT_CONFIRM XTYP_DISCONNECT XTYP_ERROR XTYP_MONITOR XTYP_REGISTER XTYP_XACT_COMPLETE XTYP_UNREGISTER

fmt

Specifies the format in which data is to be sent or received.

hconv

Identifies the conversation associated with the current transaction.

hsz1

Identifies a string. The meaning of this parameter depends on the type of the current transaction. For more information, see the description of the transaction type.

hsz2

Identifies a string. The meaning of this parameter depends on the type of the current transaction. For more information, see the description of the transaction type.

hData

Identifies DDE data. The meaning of this parameter depends on the type of the current transaction. For more information, see the description of the transaction type.

dwData1

Specifies transaction-specific data. For more information, see the description of the transaction type.

dwData2

Specifies transaction-specific data. For more information, see the description of the transaction type.

Return Value

The return value depends on the transaction class. For more information about return values, see the descriptions of the individual DDE transactions in the *Microsoft Windows Programmer's Reference, Volume 3*.

Comments

The callback function is called asynchronously for transactions that do not involve creating or terminating conversations. An application that does not frequently accept incoming messages will have reduced DDE performance because DDEML uses messages to initiate transactions.

An application must register the callback function by specifying its address in a call to the **DdeInitialize** function. **DdeCallback** is a placeholder for the application- or library-defined function name. The actual name must be exported by including it in an **EXPORTS** statement in the application's module-definition file.

See Also

DdeEnableCallback, DdeInitialize

DdeClientTransaction

3.1

#include <ddeml.h>

HDDEDATA DdeClientTransaction(*lpvData, cbData, hConv, hszItem, uFmt, uType, uTimeout, lpuResult*)

```
void FAR* lpvData;        /* address of data to pass to server  */
DWORD cbData;             /* length of data                     */
HCONV hConv;              /* handle of conversation             */
HSZ hszItem;              /* handle of item-name string         */
UINT uFmt;                /* clipboard data format              */
UINT uType;               /* transaction type                   */
DWORD uTimeout;           /* timeout duration                   */
DWORD FAR* lpuResult;     /* points to transaction result       */
```

The **DdeClientTransaction** function begins a data transaction between a client and a server. Only a dynamic data exchange (DDE) client application can call this function, and only after establishing a conversation with the server.

Parameters

lpvData

Points to the beginning of the data that the client needs to pass to the server.

Optionally, an application can specify the data handle (HDDEDATA) to pass to the server, in which case the *cbData* parameter should be set to −1. This parameter is required only if the *uType* parameter is XTYP_EXECUTE or XTYP_POKE. Otherwise, this parameter should be NULL.

cbData

Specifies the length, in bytes, of the data pointed to by the *lpvData* parameter. A value of −1 indicates that *lpvData* is a data handle that identifies the data being sent.

hConv

Identifies the conversation in which the transaction is to take place.

hszItem

Identifies the data item for which data is being exchanged during the transaction. This handle must have been created by a previous call to the **DdeCreate-StringHandle** function. This parameter is ignored (and should be set to NULL) if the *uType* parameter is XTYP_EXECUTE.

uFmt

Specifies the standard clipboard format in which the data item is being submitted or requested. For more information about standard clipboard formats, see the *Microsoft Windows Guide to Programming*.

uType

Specifies the transaction type. This parameter can be one of the following values:

Value	Meaning
XTYP_ADVSTART	Begins an advise loop. Any number of distinct advise loops can exist within a conversation. An application can alter the advise loop type by combining the XTYP_ADVSTART transaction type with one or more of the following flags:

Value	Meaning
XTYPF_NODATA	Instructs the server to notify the client of any data changes without actually sending the data. This flag gives the client the option of ignoring the notification or requesting the changed data from the server.

Value	Meaning	
	Value	**Meaning**
	XTYPF_ACKREQ	Instructs the server to wait until the client acknowledges that it received the previous data item before sending the next data item. This flag prevents a fast server from sending data faster than the client can process it.

XTYP_ADVSTOP	Ends an advise loop.
XTYP_EXECUTE	Begins an execute transaction.
XTYP_POKE	Begins a poke transaction.
XTYP_REQUEST	Begins a request transaction.

uTimeout

Specifies the maximum length of time, in milliseconds, that the client will wait for a response from the server application in a synchronous transaction. This parameter should be set to TIMEOUT_ASYNC for asynchronous transactions.

lpuResult

Points to a variable that receives the result of the transaction. An application that does not check the result can set this value to NULL. For synchronous transactions, the low-order word of this variable will contain any applicable DDE_ flags resulting from the transaction. This provides support for applications dependent on DDE_APPSTATUS bits. (It is recommended that applications no longer use these bits because they may not be supported in future versions of the DDE Management Library.) For asynchronous transactions, this variable is filled with a unique transaction identifier for use with the **DdeAbandonTransaction** function and the XTYP_XACT_COMPLETE transaction.

Return Value

The return value is a data handle that identifies the data for successful synchronous transactions in which the client expects data from the server. The return value is TRUE for successful asynchronous transactions and for synchronous transactions in which the client does not expect data. The return value is FALSE for all unsuccessful transactions.

Errors

Use the **DdeGetLastError** function to retrieve the error value, which may be one of the following:

DMLERR_ADVACKTIMEOUT
DMLERR_BUSY
DMLERR_DATAACKTIMEOUT
DMLERR_DLL_NOT_INITIALIZED

DMLERR_EXECACKTIMEOUT
DMLERR_INVALIDPARAMETER
DMLERR_MEMORY_ERROR
DMLERR_NO_CONV_ESTABLISHED
DMLERR_NO_ERROR
DMLERR_NOTPROCESSED
DMLERR_POKEACKTIMEOUT
DMLERR_POSTMSG_FAILED
DMLERR_REENTRANCY
DMLERR_SERVER_DIED
DMLERR_UNADVACKTIMEOUT

Comments   When the application is finished using the data handle returned by the **DdeClient-Transaction** function, the application should free the handle by calling the **Dde-FreeDataHandle** function.

Transactions can be synchronous or asynchronous. During a synchronous transaction, the **DdeClientTransaction** function does not return until the transaction completes successfully or fails. Synchronous transactions cause the client to enter a modal loop while waiting for various asynchronous events. Because of this, the client application can still respond to user input while waiting on a synchronous transaction but cannot begin a second synchronous transaction because of the activity associated with the first. The **DdeClientTransaction** function fails if any instance of the same task has a synchronous transaction already in progress.

During an asynchronous transaction, the **DdeClientTransaction** function returns after the transaction is begun, passing a transaction identifier for reference. When the server's DDE callback function finishes processing an asynchronous transaction, the system sends an XTYP_XACT_COMPLETE transaction to the client. This transaction provides the client with the results of the asynchronous transaction that it initiated by calling the **DdeClientTransaction** function. A client application can choose to abandon an asynchronous transaction by calling the **DdeAbandonTransaction** function.

Example   The following example requests an advise loop with a DDE server application:

```
HCONV hconv;
HSZ hszNow;
HDDEDATA hData;
DWORD dwResult;
```

```
hData = DdeClientTransaction(
    (LPBYTE) NULL, /* pass no data to server */
    0,             /* no data                */
    hconv,         /* conversation handle    */
    hszNow,        /* item name              */
    CF_TEXT,       /* clipboard format       */
    XTYP_ADVSTART, /* start an advise loop    */
    1000,          /* time-out in one second */
    &dwResult);    /* points to result flags */
```

See Also   **DdeAbandonTransaction, DdeAccessData, DdeConnect, DdeConnectList, DdeCreateStringHandle**

DdeCmpStringHandles   3.1

#include <ddeml.h>

int **DdeCmpStringHandles**(*hsz1*, *hsz2*)
HSZ *hsz1*;   /* handle of first string   */
HSZ *hsz2*;   /* handle of second string   */

The **DdeCmpStringHandles** function compares the values of two string handles. The value of a string handle is not related to the case of the associated string.

Parameters   *hsz1*
    Specifies the first string handle.

hsz2
    Specifies the second string handle.

Return Value   The return value can be one of the following:

Value	Meaning
−1	The value of *hsz1* is either 0 or less than the value of *hsz2*.
0	The values of *hsz1* and *hsz2* are equal (both can be 0).
1	The value of *hsz2* is either 0 or less than the value of *hsz1*.

Comments   An application that needs to do a case-sensitive comparison of two string handles should compare the string handles directly. An application should use **DdeComp-StringHandles** for all other comparisons to preserve the case-sensitive nature of dynamic data exchange (DDE).

The **DdeCompStringHandles** function cannot be used to sort string handles alphabetically.

Example

This example compares two service-name string handles and, if the handles are the same, requests a conversation with the server, then issues an XTYP_ADVSTART transaction:

```
HSZ hszClock;    /* service name */
HSZ hszTime;     /* topic name   */
HSZ hsz1;        /* unknown server          */
HCONV hConv;     /* conversation handle     */
DWORD dwResult;  /* result flags            */
DWORD idInst;    /* instance identifier     */

/*
 * Compare unknown service name handle with the string handle
 * for the clock application.
 */

if (!DdeCmpStringHandles(hsz1, hszClock)) {

    /*
     * If this is the clock application, start a conversation
     * with it and request an advise loop.
     */

    hConv = DdeConnect(idInst, hszClock, hszTime, NULL);
    if (hConv != (HCONV) NULL)
        DdeClientTransaction(NULL, 0, hConv, hszNow,
            CF_TEXT, XTYP_ADVSTART, 1000, &dwResult);

}
```

See Also   **DdeAccessData, DdeCreateStringHandle, DdeFreeStringHandle**

DdeConnect   3.1

#include <ddeml.h>

HCONV DdeConnect(*idInst, hszService, hszTopic, pCC*)
DWORD *idInst*;   /* instance identifier   */
HSZ *hszService*;   /* handle of service-name string   */
HSZ *hszTopic*;   /* handle of topic-name string   */
CONVCONTEXT FAR* *pCC*;   /* address of structure with context data */

The **DdeConnect** function establishes a conversation with a server application that supports the specified service name and topic name pair. If more than one such server exists, the system selects only one.

Parameters

idInst
Specifies the application-instance identifier obtained by a previous call to the **DdeInitialize** function.

hszService
Identifies the string that specifies the service name of the server application with which a conversation is to be established. This handle must have been created by a previous call to the **DdeCreateStringHandle** function. If this parameter is NULL, a conversation will be established with any available server.

hszTopic
Identifies the string that specifies the name of the topic on which a conversation is to be established. This handle must have been created by a previous call to the **DdeCreateStringHandle** function. If this parameter is NULL, a conversation on any topic supported by the selected server will be established.

pCC
Points to the **CONVCONTEXT** structure that contains conversation-context information. If this parameter is NULL, the server receives the default **CONVCONTEXT** structure during the XTYP_CONNECT or XTYP_WILDCONNECT transaction.

The **CONVCONTEXT** structure has the following form:

```
#include <ddeml.h>

typedef struct tagCONVCONTEXT { /* cc                    */
    UINT        cb;
    UINT        wFlags;
    UINT        wCountryID;
    int         iCodePage;
    DWORD       dwLangID;
    DWORD       dwSecurity;
} CONVCONTEXT;
```

For a full description of this structure, see the *Microsoft Windows Programmer's Reference, Volume 3*.

Return Value

The return value is the handle of the established conversation if the function is successful. Otherwise, it is NULL.

Errors   Use the **DdeGetLastError** function to retrieve the error value, which may be one
                    of the following:

                    DMLERR_DLL_NOT_INITIALIZED
                    DMLERR_INVALIDPARAMETER
                    DMLERR_NO_CONV_ESTABLISHED
                    DMLERR_NO_ERROR

Comments   The client application should not make assumptions regarding which server will
                    be selected. If an instance-specific name is specified in the *hszService* parameter, a
                    conversation will be established only with the specified instance. Instance-specific
                    service names are passed to an application's dynamic data exchange callback func-
                    tion during the XTYP_REGISTER and XTYP_UNREGISTER transactions.

                    All members of the default **CONVCONTEXT** structure are set to zero except **cb**,
                    which specifies the size of the structure, and **iCodePage**, which specifies
                    CP_WINANSI (the default code page).

Example   The following example creates a service-name string handle and a topic-name
                    string handle, then attempts to establish a conversation with a server that supports
                    the service name and topic name. If the attempt fails, the example retrieves an
                    error value identifying the reason for the failure.

```
DWORD idInst = 0L;
HSZ hszClock;
HSZ hszTime;
HCONV hconv;
UINT uError;

hszClock = DdeCreateStringHandle(idInst, "Clock", CP_WINANSI);
hszTime = DdeCreateStringHandle(idInst, "Time", CP_WINANSI);

if ((hconv = DdeConnect(
    idInst,                     /* instance identifier         */
    hszClock,                   /* server's service name       */
    hszTime,                    /* topic name                  */
    NULL)) == NULL) {           /* use default CONVCONTEXT     */
    uError = DdeGetLastError(idInst);
}
```

See Also   **DdeConnectList**, **DdeCreateStringHandle**, **DdeDisconnect**,
                    DdeDisconnectList, **DdeInitialize**

DdeConnectList

#include <ddeml.h>

HCONVLIST DdeConnectList(*idInst*, *hszService*, *hszTopic*, *hConvList*, *pCC*)
DWORD *idInst*;   /* instance identifier   */
HSZ *hszService*;   /* handle of service-name string   */
HSZ *hszTopic*;   /* handle of topic-name string   */
HCONVLIST *hConvList*;   /* handle of conversation list   */
CONVCONTEXT FAR* *pCC*;   /* address of structure with context data   */

The **DdeConnectList** function establishes a conversation with all server applications that support the specified service/topic name pair. An application can also use this function to enumerate a list of conversation handles by passing the function an existing conversation handle. During enumeration, the Dynamic Data Exchange Management Library (DDEML) removes the handles of any terminated conversations from the conversation list. The resulting conversation list contains the handles of all conversations currently established that support the specified service name and topic name.

Parameters

idInst

Specifies the application-instance identifier obtained by a previous call to the **DdeInitialize** function.

hszService

Identifies the string that specifies the service name of the server application with which a conversation is to be established. If this parameter is NULL, the system will attempt to establish conversations with all available servers that support the specified topic name.

hszTopic

Identifies the string that specifies the name of the topic on which a conversation is to be established. This handle must have been created by a previous call to the **DdeCreateStringHandle** function. If this parameter is NULL, the system will attempt to establish conversations on all topics supported by the selected server (or servers).

hConvList

Identifies the conversation list to be enumerated. This parameter should be set to NULL if a new conversation list is to be established.

pCC

Points to the **CONVCONTEXT** structure that contains conversation-context information. If this parameter is NULL, the server receives the default **CONVCONTEXT** structure during the XTYP_CONNECT or XTYP_WILDCONNECT transaction.

The **CONVCONTEXT** structure has the following form:

```
#include <ddeml.h>

typedef struct tagCONVCONTEXT { /* cc                          */
        UINT        cb;
        UINT        wFlags;
        UINT        wCountryID;
        int         iCodePage;
        DWORD       dwLangID;
        DWORD       dwSecurity;
} CONVCONTEXT;
```

For a full description of this structure, see the *Microsoft Windows Programmer's Reference, Volume 3.*

Return Value   The return value is the handle of a new conversation list if the function is successful. Otherwise, it is NULL. The handle of the old conversation list is no longer valid.

Errors   Use the **DdeGetLastError** function to retrieve the error value, which may be one of the following:

DMLERR_DLL_NOT_INITIALIZED
DMLERR_INVALID_PARAMETER
DMLERR_NO_CONV_ESTABLISHED
DMLERR_NO_ERROR
DMLERR_SYS_ERROR

Comments   An application must free the conversation-list handle returned by this function, regardless of whether any conversation handles within the list are active. To free the handle, an application can call the **DdeDisconnectList** function.

All members of the default **CONVCONTEXT** structure are set to zero except **cb**, which specifies the size of the structure, and **iCodePage**, which specifies CP_WINANSI (the default code page).

Example   The following example uses the **DdeConnectList** function to establish a conversation with all servers that support the System topic, counts the servers, allocates a buffer for storing the server's service-name string handles, and then copies the handles to the buffer:

```
HCONVLIST hconvList; /* conversation list       */
DWORD idInst;          /* instance identifier     */
HSZ hszSystem;         /* System topic            */
HCONV hconv = NULL;    /* conversation handle     */
CONVINFO ci;           /* holds conversation data */
UINT cConv = 0;        /* count of conv. handles  */
HSZ *pHsz, *aHsz;      /* point to string handles */

/* Connect to all servers that support the System topic. */

hconvList = DdeConnectList(idInst, (HSZ) NULL, hszSystem,
    (HCONV) NULL, (LPVOID) NULL);

/* Count the number of handles in the conversation list. */

while ((hconv = DdeQueryNextServer(hconvList, hconv)) != (HCONV) NULL)
    cConv++;

/* Allocate a buffer for the string handles. */

hconv = (HCONV) NULL;
aHsz = (HSZ *) LocalAlloc(LMEM_FIXED, cConv * sizeof(HSZ));

/* Copy the string handles to the buffer. */

pHsz = aHsz;
while ((hconv = DdeQueryNextServer(hconvList, hconv)) != (HCONV) NULL) {
    DdeQueryConvInfo(hconv, QID_SYNC, (PCONVINFO) &ci);
    DdeKeepStringHandle(idInst, ci.hszSvcPartner);
    *pHsz++ = ci.hszSvcPartner;
}

.
. /* Use the handles; converse with servers. */
.

/* Free the memory and terminate conversations. */

LocalFree((HANDLE) aHsz);
DdeDisconnectList(hconvList);
```

See Also

DdeConnect, DdeCreateStringHandle, DdeDisconnect, DdeDisconnectList, DdeInitialize, DdeQueryNextServer

DdeCreateDataHandle

#include <ddeml.h>

HDDEDATA DdeCreateDataHandle(*idInst, lpvSrcBuf, cbInitData, offSrcBuf, hszItem, uFmt, afCmd*)
DWORD *idInst*;	/* instance identifier	*/
void FAR * *lpvSrcBuf*;	/* address of source buffer	*/
DWORD *cbInitData*;	/* length of global memory object	*/
DWORD *offSrcBuf*;	/* offset from beginning of source buffer	*/
HSZ *hszItem*;	/* handle of item-name string	*/
UINT *uFmt*;	/* clipboard data format	*/
UINT *afCmd*;	/* creation flags	*/

The **DdeCreateDataHandle** function creates a global memory object and fills the object with the data pointed to by the *lpvSrcBuf* parameter. A dynamic data exchange (DDE) application uses this function during transactions that involve passing data to the partner application.

Parameters

idInst

Specifies the application-instance identifier obtained by a previous call to the **DdeInitialize** function.

lpvSrcBuf

Points to a buffer that contains data to be copied to the global memory object. If this parameter is NULL, no data is copied to the object.

cbInitData

Specifies the amount, in bytes, of memory to allocate for the global memory object. If this parameter is zero, the *lpvSrcBuf* parameter is ignored.

offSrcBuf

Specifies an offset, in bytes, from the beginning of the buffer pointed to by the *lpvSrcBuf* parameter. The data beginning at this offset is copied from the buffer to the global memory object.

hszItem

Identifies the string that specifies the data item corresponding to the global memory object. This handle must have been created by a previous call to the **DdeCreateStringHandle** function. If the data handle is to be used in an XTYP_EXECUTE transaction, this parameter must be set to NULL.

uFmt

Specifies the standard clipboard format of the data.

afCmd

Specifies the creation flags. This parameter can be HDATA_APPOWNED, which specifies that the server application that calls the **DdeCreate-DataHandle** function will own the data handle that this function creates. This makes it possible for the server to share the data handle with multiple clients instead of creating a separate handle for each request. If this flag is set, the server must eventually free the shared memory object associated with this handle by using the **DdeFreeDataHandle** function. If this flag is not set, after the data handle is returned by the server's DDE callback function or used as a parameter in another DDE Management Library function, the handle becomes invalid in the application that creates the handle.

Return Value   The return value is a data handle if the function is successful. Otherwise, it is NULL.

Errors   Use the **DdeGetLastError** function to retrieve the error value, which may be one of the following:

DMLERR_DLL_NOT_INITIALIZED
DMLERR_INVALIDPARAMETER
DMLERR_MEMORY_ERROR
DMLERR_NO_ERROR

Comments   Any locations in the global memory object that are not filled are undefined.

After a data handle has been used as a parameter in another DDEML function or has been returned by a DDE callback function, the handle may be used only for read access to the global memory object identified by the handle.

If the application will be adding data to the global memory object (using the **DdeAddData** function) so that the object exceeds 64K in length, then the application should specify a total length (*cbInitData* + *offSrcData*) that is equal to the anticipated maximum length of the object. This avoids unnecessary data copying and memory reallocation by the system.

Example   The following example processes the XTYP_WILDCONNECT transaction by returning a data handle to an array of **HSZPAIR** structures—one for each topic name supported:

```
#define CTOPICS 2

UINT type;
UINT fmt;
HSZPAIR ahp[(CTOPICS + 1)];
HSZ ahszTopicList[CTOPICS];
HSZ hszServ, hszTopic;
WORD i, j;

if (type == XTYP_WILDCONNECT) {

    /*
     * Scan the topic list and create array of HSZPAIR data
     * structures.
     */
```

```
            j = 0;
            for (i = 0; i < CTOPICS; i++) {
                if (hszTopic == (HSZ) NULL ||
                        hszTopic == ahszTopicList[i]) {
                    ahp[j].hszSvc = hszServ;
                    ahp[j++].hszTopic = ahszTopicList[i];
                }
            }

            /*
             * End the list with an HSZPAIR structure that contains NULL
             * string handles as its members.
             */

            ahp[j].hszSvc = NULL;
            ahp[j++].hszTopic = NULL;

            /*
             * Return a handle to a global memory object containing the
             * HSZPAIR structures.
             */

            return DdeCreateDataHandle(
                idInst,             /* instance identifier     */
                &ahp,               /* points to HSZPAIR array */
                sizeof(HSZ) * j,    /* length of the array      */
                0,                  /* start at the beginning   */
                NULL,               /* no item-name string      */
                fmt,                /* return the same format   */
                0);                 /* let the system own it    */
        }
```

See Also   **DdeAccessData, DdeFreeDataHandle, DdeGetData, DdeInitialize**

DdeCreateStringHandle   `3.1`

#include <ddeml.h>

HSZ DdeCreateStringHandle(*idInst, lpszString, codepage*)
DWORD *idInst*;   /* instance identifier   */
LPCSTR *lpszString*;   /* address of null-terminated string   */
int *codepage*;   /* code page   */

The **DdeCreateStringHandle** function creates a handle that identifies the string pointed to by the *lpszString* parameter. A dynamic data exchange (DDE) client or server application can pass the string handle as a parameter to other DDE Management Library functions.

Parameters

idInst

Specifies the application-instance identifier obtained by a previous call to the **DdeInitialize** function.

lpszString

Points to a buffer that contains the null-terminated string for which a handle is to be created. This string may be any length.

codepage

Specifies the code page used to render the string. This value should be either CP_WINANSI or the value returned by the **GetKBCodePage** function. A value of zero implies CP_WINANSI.

Return Value

The return value is a string handle if the function is successful. Otherwise, it is NULL.

Errors

Use the **DdeGetLastError** function to retrieve the error value, which may be one of the following:

DMLERR_INVALIDPARAMETER
DMLERR_NO_ERROR
DMLERR_SYS_ERROR

Comments

Two identical strings always correspond to the same string handle. String handles are unique across all tasks that use the DDEML. That is, when an application creates a handle for a string and another application creates a handle for an identical string, the string handles returned to both applications are identical—regardless of case.

The value of a string handle is not related to the case of the string it identifies.

When an application has either created a string handle or received one in the callback function and has used the **DdeKeepStringHandle** function to keep it, the application must free that string handle when it is no longer needed.

An instance-specific string handle is not mappable from string handle to string to string handle again. This is shown in the following example, in which the **DdeQueryString** function creates a string from a string handle and then **DdeCreateStringHandle** creates a string handle from that string, but the two handles are not the same:

```
DWORD idInst;
DWORD cb;
HSZ hszInst, hszNew;
PSZ pszInst;

DdeQueryString(idInst, hszInst, pszInst, cb, CP_WINANSI);
hszNew = DdeCreateStringHandle(idInst, pszInst, CP_WINANSI);
/* hszNew != hszInst ! */
```

Example   The following example creates a service-name string handle and a topic-name string handle and then attempts to establish a conversation with a server that supports the service name and topic name. If the attempt fails, the example obtains an error value identifying the reason for the failure.

```
DWORD idInst = 0L;
HSZ hszClock;
HSZ hszTime;
HCONV hconv;
UINT uError;

hszClock = DdeCreateStringHandle(idInst, "Clock", CP_WINANSI);
hszTime = DdeCreateStringHandle(idInst, "Time", CP_WINANSI);

if ((hconv = DdeConnect(
    idInst,                  /* instance identifier        */
    hszClock,                /* server's service name      */
    hszTime,                 /* topic name                 */
    NULL)) == NULL) {        /* use default CONVCONTEXT    */

    uError = DdeGetLastError(idInst);
}
```

See Also   **DdeAccessData, DdeCmpStringHandles, DdeFreeStringHandle, DdeInitialize, DdeKeepStringHandle, DdeQueryString**

DdeDisconnect   3.1

#include <ddeml.h>

BOOL DdeDisconnect(*hConv*)
HCONV *hConv*;   /* handle of conversation   */

The **DdeDisconnect** function terminates a conversation started by either the **Dde-Connect** or **DdeConnectList** function and invalidates the given conversation handle.

Parameters   *hConv*
    Identifies the active conversation to be terminated.

Return Value   The return value is nonzero if the function is successful. Otherwise, it is zero.

Errors   Use the **DdeGetLastError** function to retrieve the error value, which may be one of the following:

DMLERR_DLL_NOT_INITIALIZED
DMLERR_NO_CONV_ESTABLISHED
DMLERR_NO_ERROR

Comments   Any incomplete transactions started before calling **DdeDisconnect** are immediately abandoned. The XTYP_DISCONNECT transaction type is sent to the dynamic data exchange (DDE) callback function of the partner in the conversation. Generally, only client applications need to terminate conversations.

See Also   **DdeConnect, DdeConnectList, DdeDisconnectList**

DdeDisconnectList   3.1

#include <ddeml.h>

BOOL DdeDisconnectList(*hConvList*)
HCONVLIST *hConvList*;   /* handle of conversation list   */

The **DdeDisconnectList** function destroys the given conversation list and terminates all conversations associated with the list.

Parameters   *hConvList*
Identifies the conversation list. This handle must have been created by a previous call to the **DdeConnectList** function.

Return Value   The return value is nonzero if the function is successful. Otherwise, it is zero.

Errors   Use the **DdeGetLastError** function to retrieve the error value, which may be one of the following:

DMLERR_DLL_NOT_INITIALIZED
DMLERR_INVALIDPARAMETER
DMLERR_NO_ERROR

Comments   An application can use the **DdeDisconnect** function to terminate individual conversations in the list.

See Also   **DdeConnect, DdeConnectList, DdeDisconnect**

DdeEnableCallback

3.1

#include <ddeml.h>

BOOL DdeEnableCallback(*idInst***, *hConv*, *uCmd***)**
DWORD *idInst*;   /* instance identifier   */
HCONV *hConv*;   /* handle of conversation   */
UINT *uCmd*;   /* the enable/disable function code */

The **DdeEnableCallback** function enables or disables transactions for a specific conversation or for all conversations that the calling application currently has established.

After disabling transactions for a conversation, the system places the transactions for that conversation in a transaction queue associated with the application. The application should reenable the conversation as soon as possible to avoid losing queued transactions.

Parameters

idInst
Specifies the application-instance identifier obtained by a previous call to the **DdeInitialize** function.

hConv
Identifies the conversation to enable or disable. If this parameter is NULL, the function affects all conversations.

uCmd
Specifies the function code. This parameter can be one of the following values:

Value	Meaning
EC_ENABLEALL	Enables all transactions for the specified conversation.
EC_ENABLEONE	Enables one transaction for the specified conversation.
EC_DISABLE	Disables all blockable transactions for the specified conversation.
	A server application can disable the following transactions:
	XTYP_ADVSTART
	XTYP_ADVSTOP
	XTYP_EXECUTE
	XTYP_POKE
	XTYP_REQUEST
	A client application can disable the following transactions:
	XTYP_ADVDATA
	XTYP_XACT_COMPLETE

Return Value

The return value is nonzero if the function is successful. Otherwise, it is zero.

Errors   Use the **DdeGetLastError** function to retrieve the error value, which may be one
               of the following:

               DMLERR_DLL_NOT_INITIALIZED
               DMLERR_NO_ERROR
               DMLERR_INVALIDPARAMETER

Comments   An application can disable transactions for a specific conversation by returning
               CBR_BLOCK from its dynamic data exchange (DDE) callback function. When
               the conversation is reenabled by using the **DdeEnableCallback** function, the sys-
               tem generates the same transaction as was in process when the conversation was
               disabled.

See Also   **DdeConnect, DdeConnectList, DdeDisconnect, DdeInitialize**

DdeFreeDataHandle   3.1

#include <ddeml.h>

BOOL DdeFreeDataHandle(*hData*)
HDDEDATA *hData*;   /* handle of global memory object   */

               The **DdeFreeDataHandle** function frees a global memory object and deletes the
               data handle associated with the object.

Parameters   *hData*
               Identifies the global memory object to be freed. This handle must have been
               created by a previous call to the **DdeCreateDataHandle** function or returned
               by the **DdeClientTransaction** function.

Return Value   The return value is nonzero if the function is successful. Otherwise, it is zero.

Errors   Use the **DdeGetLastError** function to retrieve the error value, which may be one
               of the following:

               DMLERR_INVALIDPARAMETER
               DMLERR_NO_ERROR

Comments   An application must call **DdeFreeDataHandle** under the following circumstances:

               ■ To free a global memory object that the application allocated by calling the
                 DdeCreateDataHandle function if the object's data handle was never passed

by the application to another Dynamic Data Exchange Management Library (DDEML) function

- To free a global memory object that the application allocated by specifying the HDATA_APPOWNED flag in a call to the **DdeCreateDataHandle** function

- To free a global memory object whose handle the application received from the **DdeClientTransaction** function

The system automatically frees an unowned object when its handle is returned by a dynamic data exchange (DDE) callback function or used as a parameter in a DDEML function.

Example

The following example creates a global memory object containing help information, then frees the object after passing the object's handle to the client application:

```
DWORD idInst;
HSZ hszItem;
HDDEDATA hDataHelp;

char szDdeHelp[] = "DDEML test server help:\r\n"\
    "\tThe 'Server' (service) and 'Test' (topic) names may change.\r\n"\
    "Items supported under the 'Test' topic are:\r\n"\
    "\tCount:\tThis value increments on each data change.\r\n"\
    "\tRand:\tThis value is changed after each data change. \r\n"\
    "\t\tIn Runaway mode, the above items change after a request.\r\n"\
    "\tHuge:\tThis is randomly generated text data >64k that the\r\n"\
    "\t\ttest client can verify. It is recalculated on each\r\n"\
    "\t\trequest. This also verifies huge data poked or executed\r\n"\
    "\t\tfrom the test client.\r\n"\
    "\tHelp:\tThis help information.  This data is APPOWNED.\r\n";

    /* Create global memory object containing help information. */

    if (!hDataHelp) {
        hDataHelp = DdeCreateDataHandle(idInst, szDdeHelp,
            strlen(szDdeHelp) + 1, 0, hszItem, CF_TEXT, HDATA_APPOWNED);
    }

    .
    . /* Pass help information to client application. */
    .

    /* Free the global memory object. */

    if (hDataHelp)
        DdeFreeDataHandle(hDataHelp);
```

See Also

DdeAccessData, DdeCreateDataHandle

DdeFreeStringHandle

#include <ddeml.h>

BOOL DdeFreeStringHandle(*idInst*, *hsz*)
DWORD *idInst*;   /* instance identifier   */
HSZ *hsz*;   /* handle of string   */

The **DdeFreeStringHandle** function frees a string handle in the calling application.

Parameters

idInst
Specifies the application-instance identifier obtained by a previous call to the **DdeInitialize** function.

hsz
Identifies the string handle to be freed. This handle must have been created by a previous call to the **DdeCreateStringHandle** function.

Return Value

The return value is nonzero if the function is successful. Otherwise, it is zero.

Comments

An application can free string handles that it creates with the **DdeCreateString-Handle** function but should not free those that the system passed to the application's dynamic data exchange (DDE) callback function or those returned in the **CONVINFO** structure by the **DdeQueryConvInfo** function.

Example

The following example frees string handles during the XTYP_DISCONNECT transaction:

```
DWORD idInst = 0L;
HSZ hszClock;
HSZ hszTime;
HSZ hszNow;
UINT type;

if (type == XTYP_DISCONNECT) {

    DdeFreeStringHandle(idInst, hszClock);
    DdeFreeStringHandle(idInst, hszTime);
    DdeFreeStringHandle(idInst, hszNow);

    return (HDDEDATA) NULL;
}
```

See Also

DdeCmpStringHandles, DdeCreateStringHandle, DdeInitialize, DdeKeepStringHandle, DdeQueryString

DdeGetData

#include <ddeml.h>

DWORD DdeGetData(*hData, pDest, cbMax, offSrc*)
HDDEDATA *hData*;   /* handle of global memory object   */
void FAR* *pDest*;   /* address of destination buffer   */
DWORD *cbMax*;   /* amount of data to copy   */
DWORD *offSrc*;   /* offset to beginning of data   */

The **DdeGetData** function copies data from the given global memory object to the specified local buffer.

Parameters

hData
  Identifies the global memory object that contains the data to copy.

pDest
  Points to the buffer that receives the data. If this parameter is NULL, the **DdeGetData** function returns the amount, in bytes, of data that would be copied to the buffer.

cbMax
  Specifies the maximum amount, in bytes, of data to copy to the buffer pointed to by the *pDest* parameter. Typically, this parameter specifies the length of the buffer pointed to by *pDest*.

offSrc
  Specifies an offset within the global memory object. Data is copied from the object beginning at this offset.

Return Value

If the *pDest* parameter points to a buffer, the return value is the size, in bytes, of the memory object associated with the data handle or the size specified in the *cbMax* parameter, whichever is lower.

If the *pDest* parameter is NULL, the return value is the size, in bytes, of the memory object associated with the data handle.

Errors

Use the **DdeGetLastError** function to retrieve the error value, which may be one of the following:

DMLERR_DLL_NOT_INITIALIZED
DMLERR_INVALID_HDDEDATA
DMLERR_INVALIDPARAMETER
DMLERR_NO_ERROR

Example

The following example copies data from a global memory object to a local buffer and then fills the **TIME** structure with data from the buffer:

```
HDDEDATA hData;
char szBuf[32];

typedef struct {
    int hour;
    int minute;
    int second;
} TIME;

DdeGetData(hData, (LPBYTE) szBuf, 32L, 0L);
sscanf(szBuf, "%d:%d:%d", &nTime.hour, &nTime.minute,
    &nTime.second);
```

See Also   **DdeAccessData, DdeCreateDataHandle, DdeFreeDataHandle**

DdeGetLastError   3.1

#include <ddeml.h>

UINT DdeGetLastError(*idInst*)
DWORD *idInst*;   /* instance identifier   */

The **DdeGetLastError** function returns the most recent error value set by the
failure of a Dynamic Data Exchange Management Library (DDEML) function and
resets the error value to DMLERR_NO_ERROR.

Parameters   *idInst*
Specifies the application-instance identifier obtained by a previous call to the
DdeInitialize function.

Return Value   The return value is the last error value. Following are the possible DDEML error
values:

Value	Meaning
DMLERR_ADVACKTIMEOUT	A request for a synchronous advise transaction has timed out.
DMLERR_BUSY	The response to the transaction caused the DDE_FBUSY bit to be set.
DMLERR_DATAACKTIMEOUT	A request for a synchronous data transaction has timed out.

Value	Meaning
DMLERR_DLL_NOT_INITIALIZED	A DDEML function was called without first calling the **DdeInitialize** function, or an invalid instance identifier was passed to a DDEML function.
DMLERR_DLL_USAGE	An application initialized as APPCLASS_MONITOR has attempted to perform a DDE transaction, or an application initialized as APPCMD_CLIENTONLY has attempted to perform server transactions.
DMLERR_EXECACKTIMEOUT	A request for a synchronous execute transaction has timed out.
DMLERR_INVALIDPARAMETER	A parameter failed to be validated by the DDEML. Some of the possible causes are as follows:
	▪ The application used a data handle initialized with a different item-name handle than that required by the transaction.
	▪ The application used a data handle that was initialized with a different clipboard data format than that required by the transaction.
	▪ The application used a client-side conversation handle with a server-side function or vise versa.
	▪ The application used a freed data handle or string handle.
	▪ More than one instance of the application used the same object.
DMLERR_LOW_MEMORY	A DDEML application has created a prolonged race condition (where the server application outruns the client), causing large amounts of memory to be consumed.
DMLERR_MEMORY_ERROR	A memory allocation failed.
DMLERR_NO_CONV_ESTABLISHED	A client's attempt to establish a conversation has failed.
DMLERR_NOTPROCESSED	A transaction failed.
DMLERR_POKEACKTIMEOUT	A request for a synchronous poke transaction has timed out.
DMLERR_POSTMSG_FAILED	An internal call to the **PostMessage** function has failed.

Value	Meaning
DMLERR_REENTRANCY	An application instance with a synchronous transaction already in progress attempted to initiate another synchronous transaction, or the **DdeEnableCallback** function was called from within a DDEML callback function.
DMLERR_SERVER_DIED	A server-side transaction was attempted on a conversation that was terminated by the client, or the server terminated before completing a transaction.
DMLERR_SYS_ERROR	An internal error has occurred in the DDEML.
DMLERR_UNADVACKTIMEOUT	A request to end an advise transaction has timed out.
DMLERR_UNFOUND_QUEUE_ID	An invalid transaction identifier was passed to a DDEML function. Once the application has returned from an XTYP_XACT_COMPLETE callback, the transaction identifier for that callback is no longer valid.

Example

The following example calls the **DdeGetLastError** function if the **DdeCreateDataHandle** function fails:

```
DWORD idInst;
HDDEDATA hddeMyData;
HSZPAIR ahszp[2];
HSZ hszClock, hszTime;

/* Create string handles. */

hszClock = DdeCreateStringHandle(idInst, (LPSTR) "Clock",
    CP_WINANSI);
hszTime = DdeCreateStringHandle(idInst, (LPSTR) "Time",
    CP_WINANSI);

/* Copy handles to an HSZPAIR structure. */

ahszp[0].hszSvc   = hszClock;
ahszp[0].hszTopic = hszTime;
ahszp[1].hszSvc   = (HSZ) NULL;
ahszp[1].hszTopic = (HSZ) NULL;

/* Create a global memory object. */

hddeMyData = DdeCreateDataHandle(idInst, ahszp,
        sizeof(ahszp), 0, NULL, CF_TEXT, 0);
    if (hddeMyData == NULL)
```

```
            /*
             * Pass error value to application-defined error handling
             * function.
             */

            HandleError(DdeGetLastError(idInst));
```

See Also   **DdeInitialize**

DdeInitialize

3.1

#include <ddeml.h>

UINT DdeInitialize(*lpidInst, pfnCallback, afCmd, uRes*)
DWORD FAR* *lpidInst*;   /* address of instance identifier   */
PFNCALLBACK *pfnCallback*;   /* address of callback function   */
DWORD *afCmd*;   /* array of command and filter flags   */
DWORD *uRes*;   /* reserved   */

The **DdeInitialize** function registers an application with the Dynamic Data Exchange Management Library (DDEML). An application must call this function before calling any other DDEML function.

Parameters   *lpidInst*

Points to the application-instance identifier. At initialization, this parameter should point to 0L. If the function is successful, this parameter points to the instance identifier for the application. This value should be passed as the *idInst* parameter in all other DDEML functions that require it. If an application uses multiple instances of the DDEML dynamic link library, the application should provide a different callback function for each instance.

If *lpidInst* points to a nonzero value, this implies a reinitialization of the DDEML. In this case, *lpidInst* must point to a valid application-instance identifier.

pfnCallback

Points to the application-defined DDE callback function. This function processes DDE transactions sent by the system. For more information, see the description of the **DdeCallback** callback function.

afCmd

Specifies an array of APPCMD_ and CBF_ flags. The APPCMD_ flags provide special instructions to the **DdeInitialize** function. The CBF_ flags set filters that prevent specific types of transactions from reaching the callback function. Using these flags enhances the performance of a DDE application by eliminating unnecessary calls to the callback function.

This parameter can be a combination of the following flags:

Flag	Meaning
APPCLASS_MONITOR	Makes it possible for the application to monitor DDE activity in the system. This flag is for use by DDE monitoring applications. The application specifies the types of DDE activity to monitor by combining one or more monitor flags with the APPCLASS_MONITOR flag. For details, see the following Comments section.
APPCLASS_STANDARD	Registers the application as a standard (nonmonitoring) DDEML application.
APPCMD_CLIENTONLY	Prevents the application from becoming a server in a DDE conversation. The application can be only a client. This flag reduces resource consumption by the DDEML. It includes the functionality of the CBF_FAIL_ALLSVRXACTIONS flag.
APPCMD_FILTERINITS	Prevents the DDEML from sending XTYP_CONNECT and XTYP_WILDCONNECT transactions to the application until the application has created its string handles and registered its service names or has turned off filtering by a subsequent call to the **DdeNameService** or **DdeInitialize** function. This flag is always in effect when an application calls **DdeInitialize** for the first time, regardless of whether the application specifies this flag. On subsequent calls to **DdeInitialize**, not specifying this flag turns off the application's service-name filters; specifying this flag turns on the application's service-name filters.
CBF_FAIL_ALLSVRXACTIONS	Prevents the callback function from receiving server transactions. The system will return DDE_FNOTPROCESSED to each client that sends a transaction to this application. This flag is equivalent to combining all CBF_FAIL_ flags.

Flag	Meaning
CBF_FAIL_ADVISES	Prevents the callback function from receiving XTYP_ADVSTART and XTYP_ADVSTOP transactions. The system will return DDE_FNOTPROCESSED to each client that sends an XTYP_ADVSTART or XTYP_ADVSTOP transaction to the server.
CBF_FAIL_CONNECTIONS	Prevents the callback function from receiving XTYP_CONNECT and XTYP_WILDCONNECT transactions.
CBF_FAIL_EXECUTES	Prevents the callback function from receiving XTYP_EXECUTE transactions. The system will return DDE_FNOTPROCESSED to a client that sends an XTYP_EXECUTE transaction to the server.
CBF_FAIL_POKES	Prevents the callback function from receiving XTYP_POKE transactions. The system will return DDE_FNOTPROCESSED to a client that sends an XTYP_POKE transaction to the server.
CBF_FAIL_REQUESTS	Prevents the callback function from receiving XTYP_REQUEST transactions. The system will return DDE_FNOTPROCESSED to a client that sends an XTYP_REQUEST transaction to the server.
CBF_FAIL_SELFCONNECTIONS	Prevents the callback function from receiving XTYP_CONNECT transactions from the application's own instance. This prevents an application from establishing a DDE conversation with its own instance. An application should use this flag if it needs to communicate with other instances of itself but not with itself.
CBF_SKIP_ALLNOTIFICATIONS	Prevents the callback function from receiving any notifications. This flag is equivalent combining all CBF_SKIP_ flags.
CBF_SKIP_CONNECT_CONFIRMS	Prevents the callback function from receiving XTYP_CONNECT_CONFIRM notifications.

Flag	Meaning
CBF_SKIP_DISCONNECTS	Prevents the callback function from receiving XTYP_DISCONNECT notifications.
CBF_SKIP_REGISTRATIONS	Prevents the callback function from receiving XTYP_REGISTER notifications.
CBF_SKIP_UNREGISTRATIONS	Prevents the callback function from receiving XTYP_UNREGISTER notifications.

uRes
　　Reserved; must be set to 0L.

Return Value　　The return value is one of the following:

DMLERR_DLL_USAGE
DMLERR_INVALIDPARAMETER
DMLERR_NO_ERROR
DMLERR_SYS_ERROR

Comments　　An application that uses multiple instances of the DDEML must not pass DDEML objects between instances.

A DDE monitoring application should not attempt to perform DDE (establish conversations, issue transactions, and so on) within the context of the same application instance.

A synchronous transaction will fail with a DMLERR_REENTRANCY error if any instance of the same task has a synchronous transaction already in progress.

A DDE monitoring application can combine one or more of the following monitor flags with the APPCLASS_MONITOR flag to specify the types of DDE activity to monitor:

Flag	Meaning
MF_CALLBACKS	Notifies the callback function whenever a transaction is sent to any DDE callback function in the system.
MF_CONV	Notifies the callback function whenever a conversation is established or terminated.
MF_ERRORS	Notifies the callback function whenever a DDE error occurs.
MF_HSZ_INFO	Notifies the callback function whenever a DDE application creates, frees, or increments the use count of a string handle or whenever a string handle is freed as a result of a call to the **DdeUninitialize** function.

Flag	Meaning
MF_LINKS	Notifies the callback function whenever an advise loop is started or ended.
MF_POSTMSGS	Notifies the callback function whenever the system or an application posts a DDE message.
MF_SENDMSGS	Notifies the callback function whenever the system or an application sends a DDE message.

Example

The following example obtains a procedure-instance address for a DDE callback function, then initializes the application with the DDEML.

```
DWORD idInst = 0L;
FARPROC lpDdeProc;

lpDdeProc = MakeProcInstance((FARPROC) DDECallback, hInst);
if (DdeInitialize((LPDWORD) &idInst, (PFNCALLBACK) lpDdeProc,
        APPCMD_CLIENTONLY, 0L))
    return FALSE;
```

See Also

DdeClientTransaction, DdeConnect, DdeCreateDataHandle, DdeEnable-Callback, DdeNameService, DdePostAdvise, DdeUninitialize

DdeKeepStringHandle

3.1

#include <ddeml.h>

BOOL DdeKeepStringHandle(*idInst***,** *hsz***)**
DWORD *idInst*;   /* instance identifier   */
HSZ *hsz*;   /* handle of string   */

The **DdeKeepStringHandle** function increments the usage count (increases it by one) associated with the given handle. This function makes it possible for an application to save a string handle that was passed to the application's dynamic data exchange (DDE) callback function. Otherwise, a string handle passed to the callback function is deleted when the callback function returns.

Parameters

idInst
Specifies the application-instance identifier obtained by a previous call to the **DdeInitialize** function.

hsz
Identifies the string handle to be saved.

Return Value The return value is nonzero if the function is successful. Otherwise, it is zero.

Example The following example is a portion of a DDE callback function that increases the usage count and saves a local copy of two string handles:

```
HSZ hsz1;
HSZ hsz2;
static HSZ hszServerBase;
static HSZ hszServerInst;
DWORD idInst;

case XTYP_REGISTER:

    /* Keep the handles for later use. */

    DdeKeepStringHandle(idInst, hsz1);
    DdeKeepStringHandle(idInst, hsz2);
    hszServerBase = hsz1;
    hszServerInst = hsz2;

    .
    . /* Finish processing the transaction. */
    .
```

See Also **DdeCreateStringHandle, DdeFreeStringHandle, DdeInitialize, DdeQueryString**

DdeNameService

3.1

#include <ddeml.h>

HDDEDATA DdeNameService(*idInst*, *hsz1*, *hszRes*, *afCmd*)
DWORD *idInst*;	/* instance identifier	*/
HSZ *hsz1*;	/* handle of service-name string	*/
HSZ *hszRes*;	/* reserved	*/
UINT *afCmd*;	/* service-name flags	*/

The **DdeNameService** function registers or unregisters the service names that a dynamic data exchange (DDE) server supports. This function causes the system to send XTYP_REGISTER or XTYP_UNREGISTER transactions to other running DDE Management Library (DDEML) client applications.

A server application should call this function to register each service name that it supports and to unregister names that it previously registered but no longer supports. A server should also call this function to unregister its service names just before terminating.

Parameters   *idInst*

Specifies the application-instance identifier obtained by a previous call to the **DdeInitialize** function.

hsz1

Identifies the string that specifies the service name that the server is registering or unregistering. An application that is unregistering all of its service names should set this parameter to NULL.

hszRes

Reserved; should be set to NULL.

afCmd

Specifies the service-name flags. This parameter can be one of the following values:

Value	Meaning
DNS_REGISTER	Registers the given service name.
DNS_UNREGISTER	Unregisters the given service name. If the *hsz1* parameter is NULL, all service names registered by the server will be unregistered.
DNS_FILTERON	Turns on service-name initiation filtering. This filter prevents a server from receiving XTYP_CONNECT transactions for service names that it has not registered. This is the default setting for this filter.
	If a server application does not register any service names, the application cannot receive XTYP_WILDCONNECT transactions.
DNS_FILTEROFF	Turns off service-name initiation filtering. If this flag is set, the server will receive an XTYP_CONNECT transaction whenever another DDE application calls the **Dde-Connect** function, regardless of the service name.

Return Value   The return value is nonzero if the function is successful. Otherwise, it is zero.

Errors   Use the **DdeGetLastError** function to retrieve the error value, which may be one of the following:

DMLERR_DLL_NOT_INITIALIZED
DMLERR_DLL_USAGE
DMLERR_INVALIDPARAMETER
DMLERR_NO_ERROR

Comments   The service name identified by the *hsz1* parameter should be a base name (that is, the name should contain no instance-specific information). The system generates an instance-specific name and sends it along with the base name during the XTYP_REGISTER and XTYP_UNREGISTER transactions. The receiving applications can then connect to the specific application instance.

Example   The following example initializes an application with the DDEML, creates
frequently used string handles, and registers the application's service name:

```
HSZ hszClock;
HSZ hszTime;
HSZ hszNow;
HINSTANCE hinst;
DWORD idInst = 0L;
FARPROC lpDdeProc;

/* Initialize the application for the DDEML. */

lpDdeProc = MakeProcInstance((FARPROC) DdeCallback, hinst);
if (!DdeInitialize((LPDWORD) &idInst, (PFNCALLBACK) lpDdeProc,
        APPCMD_FILTERINITS | CBF_FAIL_EXECUTES, 0L)) {

    /* Create frequently used string handles. */

    hszTime = DdeCreateStringHandle(idInst, "Time", CP_WINANSI);
    hszNow = DdeCreateStringHandle(idInst, "Now", CP_WINANSI);
    hszClock = DdeCreateStringHandle(idInst, "Clock", CP_WINANSI);

    /* Register the service name. */

    DdeNameService(idInst, hszClock, (HSZ) NULL, DNS_REGISTER);

}
```

See Also   **DdeConnect, DdeConnectList, DdeInitialize**

DdePostAdvise

3.1

#include <ddeml.h>

BOOL DdePostAdvise(*idInst*, *hszTopic*, *hszItem*)
DWORD *idInst*;   /* instance identifier   */
HSZ *hszTopic*;   /* handle of topic-name string   */
HSZ *hszItem*;   /* handle of item-name string   */

The **DdePostAdvise** function causes the system to send an XTYP_ADVREQ
transaction to the calling (server) application's dynamic data exchange (DDE) callback function for each client that has an advise loop active on the specified topic
or item name pair. A server application should call this function whenever the data
associated with the topic or item name pair changes.

Parameters

idInst
Specifies the application-instance identifier obtained by a previous call to the **DdeInitialize** function.

hszTopic
Identifies a string that specifies the topic name. To send notifications for all topics with active advise loops, an application can set this parameter to NULL.

hszItem
Identifies a string that specifies the item name. To send notifications for all items with active advise loops, an application can set this parameter to NULL.

Return Value

The return value is nonzero if the function is successful. Otherwise, it is zero.

Errors

Use the **DdeGetLastError** function to retrieve the error value, which may be one of the following:

DMLERR_DLL_NOT_INITIALIZED
DMLERR_DLL_USAGE
DMLERR_NO_ERROR

Comments

A server that has nonenumerable topics or items should set the *hszTopic* and *hszItem* parameters to NULL so that the system will generate transactions for all active advise loops. The server's DDE callback function returns NULL for any advise loops that do not need to be updated.

If a server calls **DdePostAdvise** with a topic/item/format name set that includes the set currently being handled in a XTYP_ADVREQ callback, a stack overflow may result.

Example

The following example calls the **DdePostAdvise** function whenever the time changes:

```
typedef struct { /* tm */
    int hour;
    int minute;
    int second;
} TIME;

TIME tmTime;
DWORD idInst;
HSZ hszTime;
HSZ hszNow;
TIME tmCurTime;

    .
    . /* Fill tmCurTime with the current time. */
    .
```

```
/* Check for any change in second, minute, or hour. */

if ((tmCurTime.second != tmTime.second) ||
        (tmCurTime.minute != tmTime.minute) ||
        (tmCurTime.hour   != tmTime.hour)) {

    /* Send the current time to the clients. */

    DdePostAdvise(idInst, hszTime, hszNow);
```

See Also   **DdeInitialize**

DdeQueryConvInfo

3.1

#include <ddeml.h>

UINT DdeQueryConvInfo(*hConv*, *idTransaction*, *lpConvInfo*)
HCONV *hConv*;   /* handle of conversation   */
DWORD *idTransaction*;   /* transaction identifier   */
CONVINFO FAR* *lpConvInfo*;   /* address of structure with conversation data   */

The **DdeQueryConvInfo** function retrieves information about a dynamic data exchange (DDE) transaction and about the conversation in which the transaction takes place.

Parameters   *hConv*
Identifies the conversation.

idTransaction
Specifies the transaction. For asynchronous transactions, this parameter should be a transaction identifier returned by the **DdeClientTransaction** function. For synchronous transactions, this parameter should be QID_SYNC.

lpConvInfo
Points to the **CONVINFO** structure that will receive information about the transaction and conversation. The **cb** member of the **CONVINFO** structure must specify the length of the buffer allocated for the structure.

The **CONVINFO** structure has the following form:

```
#include <ddeml.h>

typedef struct tagCONVINFO { /* ci */
    DWORD      cb;
    DWORD      hUser;
    HCONV      hConvPartner;
    HSZ        hszSvcPartner;
    HSZ        hszServiceReq;
    HSZ        hszTopic;
    HSZ        hszItem;
    UINT       wFmt;
    UINT       wType;
    UINT       wStatus;
    UINT       wConvst;
    UINT       wLastError;
    HCONVLIST  hConvList;
    CONVCONTEXT ConvCtxt;
} CONVINFO;
```

For a full description of this structure, see the *Microsoft Windows Programmer's Reference, Volume 3*.

Return Value   The return value is the number of bytes copied into the **CONVINFO** structure, if the function is successful. Otherwise, it is zero.

Errors   Use the **DdeGetLastError** function to retrieve the error value, which may be one of the following:

DMLERR_DLL_NOT_INITIALIZED
DMLERR_NO_CONV_ESTABLISHED
DMLERR_NO_ERROR
DMLERR_UNFOUND_QUEUE_ID

Example   The following example fills a **CONVINFO** structure with information about a synchronous conversation and then obtains the names of the partner application and topic:

```
DWORD idInst;
HCONV hConv;
CONVINFO ci;
WORD wError;
char szSvcPartner[32];
char szTopic[32];
DWORD cchServ, cchTopic;

if (!DdeQueryConvInfo(hConv, QID_SYNC, &ci))
    wError = DdeGetLastError(idInst);
```

```
else {
    cchServ = DdeQueryString(idInst, ci.hszSvcPartner,
        (LPSTR) &szSvcPartner, sizeof(szSvcPartner),
        CP_WINANSI);
    cchTopic =DdeQueryString(idInst, ci.hszTopic,
        (LPSTR) &szTopic, sizeof(szTopic),
        CP_WINANSI);
}
```

See Also   **DdeConnect, DdeConnectList, DdeQueryNextServer**

DdeQueryNextServer   3.1

#include <ddeml.h>

HCONV DdeQueryNextServer(*hConvList*, *hConvPrev*)
HCONVLIST *hConvList*;   /* handle of conversation list   */
HCONV *hConvPrev*;   /* previous conversation handle   */

The **DdeQueryNextServer** function obtains the next conversation handle in the given conversation list.

Parameters   *hConvList*
Identifies the conversation list. This handle must have been created by a previous call to the **DdeConnectList** function.

hConvPrev
Identifies the conversation handle previously returned by this function. If this parameter is NULL, this function returns the first conversation handle in the list.

Return Value   The return value is the next conversation handle in the list if the list contains any more conversation handles. Otherwise, it is NULL.

Example   The following example uses the **DdeQueryNextServer** function to count the number of conversation handles in a conversation list and to copy the service-name string handles of the servers to a local buffer:

```
HCONVLIST hconvList; /* conversation list       */
DWORD idInst;        /* instance identifier     */
HSZ hszSystem;       /* System topic            */
HCONV hconv = NULL;  /* conversation handle     */
CONVINFO ci;         /* holds conversation data */
UINT cConv = 0;      /* count of conv. handles  */
HSZ *pHsz, *aHsz;    /* point to string handles */
```

```
                /* Connect to all servers that support the System topic. */

                hconvList = DdeConnectList(idInst, (HSZ) NULL, hszSystem,
                    (HCONV) NULL, (LPVOID) NULL);

                /* Count the number of handles in the conversation list. */

                while ((hconv = DdeQueryNextServer(hconvList, hconv)) != (HCONV) NULL)
                    cConv++;

                /* Allocate a buffer for the string handles. */

                hconv = (HCONV) NULL;
                aHsz = (HSZ *) LocalAlloc(LMEM_FIXED, cConv * sizeof(HSZ));

                /* Copy the string handles to the buffer. */

                pHsz = aHsz;
                while ((hconv = DdeQueryNextServer(hconvList, hconv)) != (HCONV) NULL) {
                    DdeQueryConvInfo(hconv, QID_SYNC, (PCONVINFO) &ci);
                    DdeKeepStringHandle(idInst, ci.hszSvcPartner);
                    *pHsz++ = ci.hszSvcPartner;
                }

                .
                . /* Use the handles; converse with servers. */
                .

                /* Free the memory and terminate conversations. */

                LocalFree((HANDLE) aHsz);
                DdeDisconnectList(hconvList);
```

See Also   **DdeConnectList, DdeDisconnectList**

DdeQueryString   3.1

#include <ddeml.h>

DWORD DdeQueryString(*idInst, hsz, lpsz, cchMax, codepage*)
DWORD *idInst*;   /* instance identifier   */
HSZ *hsz*;   /* handle of string   */
LPSTR *lpsz*;   /* address of destination buffer */
DWORD *cchMax*;   /* length of buffer   */
int *codepage*;   /* code page   */

The **DdeQueryString** function copies text associated with a string handle into a buffer.

The string returned in the buffer is always null-terminated. If the string is longer than (*cchMax* – 1), only the first (*cchMax* – 1) characters of the string are copied.

If the *lpsz* parameter is NULL, this function obtains the length, in bytes, of the string associated with the string handle. The length does not include the terminating null character.

Parameters

idInst
   Specifies the application-instance identifier obtained by a previous call to the **DdeInitialize** function.

hsz
   Identifies the string to copy. This handle must have been created by a previous call to the **DdeCreateStringHandle** function.

lpsz
   Points to a buffer that receives the string. To obtain the length of the string, this parameter should be set to NULL.

cchMax
   Specifies the length, in bytes, of the buffer pointed to by the *lpsz* parameter. If the string is longer than (*cchMax* – 1), it will be truncated. If the *lpsz* parameter is set to NULL, this parameter is ignored.

codepage
   Specifies the code page used to render the string. This value should be either CP_WINANSI or the value returned by the **GetKBCodePage** function.

Return Value

The return value is the length, in bytes, of the returned text (not including the terminating null character) if the *lpsz* parameter specified a valid pointer. The return value is the length of the text associated with the *hsz* parameter (not including the terminating null character) if the *lpsz* parameter specified a NULL pointer. The return value is NULL if an error occurs.

Example

The following example uses the **DdeQueryString** function to obtain a service name and topic name that a server has registered:

```
UINT type;

HSZ hsz1;
HSZ hsz2;
char szBaseName[16];
char szInstName[16];

if (type == XTYP_REGISTER) {
```

```
/* Copy the base service name to a buffer. */

DdeQueryString(idInst, hsz1, (LPSTR) &szBaseName,
    sizeof(szBaseName), CP_WINANSI);

/* Copy the instance-specific service name to a buffer. */

DdeQueryString(idInst, hsz2, (LPSTR) &szInstName,
    sizeof(szInstName), CP_WINANSI);
return (HDDEDATA) TRUE;
}
```

See Also   **DdeCmpStringHandles**, **DdeCreateStringHandle**, **DdeFreeStringHandle**,
DdeInitialize

DdeReconnect   3.1

#include <ddeml.h>

HCONV DdeReconnect(*hConv*)
HCONV *hConv*;   /* handle of conversation to reestablish   */

The **DdeReconnect** function allows a client Dynamic Data Exchange Management Library (DDEML) application to attempt to reestablish a conversation with a
service that has terminated a conversation with the client. When the conversation
is reestablished, the DDEML attempts to reestablish any preexisting advise loops.

Parameters   *hConv*
      Identifies the conversation to be reestablished. A client must have obtained the
      conversation handle by a previous call to the **DdeConnect** function.

Return Value   The return value is the handle of the reestablished conversation if the function is
      successful. The return value is NULL if the function fails.

Errors   Use the **DdeGetLastError** function to retrieve the error value, which may be one
      of the following:

      DMLERR_DLL_NOT_INITIALIZED
      DMLERR_INVALIDPARAMETER
      DMLERR_NO_CONV_ESTABLISHED
      DMLERR_NO_ERROR

Example   The following example shows the context within which an application should call the **DdeReconnect** function:

```
HDDEDATA EXPENTRY DdeCallback(wType, wFmt, hConv, hsz1,
    hsz2, hData, dwData1, dwData2)
WORD wType;        /* transaction type              */
WORD wFmt;         /* clipboard format              */
HCONV hConv;       /* handle of the conversation    */
HSZ hsz1;          /* handle of a string            */
HSZ hsz2;          /* handle of a string            */
HDDEDATA hData;    /* handle of a global memory object */
DWORD dwData1;     /* transaction-specific data     */
DWORD dwData2;     /* transaction-specific data     */
{
    BOOL fAutoReconnect;

    switch (wType) {
        case XTYP_DISCONNECT:
            if (fAutoReconnect) {
                DdeReconnect(hConv); /* attempt to reconnect */
            }
            return 0;

        .
        . /* Process other transactions. */
        .
    }
}
```

See Also   **DdeConnect, DdeDisconnect**

DdeSetUserHandle   3.1

#include <ddeml.h>

BOOL DdeSetUserHandle(*hConv*, *id*, *hUser*)
HCONV *hConv*;   /* handle of conversation   */
DWORD *id*;   /* transaction identifier   */
DWORD *hUser*;   /* application-defined value   */

The **DdeSetUserHandle** function associates an application-defined 32-bit value with a conversation handle and transaction identifier. This is useful for simplifying the processing of asynchronous transactions. An application can use the **Dde-QueryConvInfo** function to retrieve this value.

Parameters

hConv
Identifies the conversation.

id
Specifies the transaction identifier of an asynchronous transaction. An application should set this parameter to QID_SYNC if no asynchronous transaction is to be associated with the *hUser* parameter.

hUser
Identifies the value to associate with the conversation handle.

Return Value
The return value is nonzero if the function is successful. Otherwise, it is zero.

Errors
Use the **DdeGetLastError** function to retrieve the error value, which may be one of the following:

DMLERR_DLL_NOT_INITIALIZED
DMLERR_INVALIDPARAMETER
DMLERR_NO_ERROR
DMLERR_UNFOUND_QUEUE_ID

See Also
DdeQueryConvInfo

DdeUnaccessData   3.1

#include <ddeml.h>

BOOL DdeUnaccessData(*hData*)
HDDEDATA *hData*;   /* handle of global memory object   */

The **DdeUnaccessData** function frees a global memory object. An application must call this function when it is finished accessing the object.

Parameters

hData
Identifies the global memory object.

Return Value
The return value is nonzero if the function is successful. Otherwise, it is zero.

Errors
Use the **DdeGetLastError** function to retrieve the error value, which may be one of the following:

DMLERR_DLL_NOT_INITIALIZED
DMLERR_INVALIDPARAMETER
DMLERR_NO_ERROR

Example   The following example obtains a pointer to a global memory object, uses the pointer to copy data from the object to a local buffer, and then uses the **Dde-UnaccessData** function to free the object:

```
HDDEDATA hData;
LPBYTE lpszAdviseData;
DWORD cbDataLen;
DWORD i;
char szData[128];

lpszAdviseData = DdeAccessData(hData, &cbDataLen);
for (i = 0; i < cbDataLen; i++)
    szData[i] = *lpszAdviseData++;
DdeUnaccessData(hData);
```

See Also   **DdeAccessData, DdeAddData, DdeCreateDataHandle, DdeFreeDataHandle**

DdeUninitialize
3.1

#include <ddeml.h>

BOOL DdeUninitialize(*idInst*)
DWORD *idInst*;   /* instance identifier   */

The **DdeUninitialize** function frees all Dynamic Data Exchange Management Library (DDEML) resources associated with the calling application.

Parameters   *idInst*
Specifies the application-instance identifier obtained by a previous call to the **DdeInitialize** function.

Return Value   The return value is nonzero if the function is successful. Otherwise, it is zero.

Comments   The **DdeUninitialize** function terminates any conversations currently open for the application. If the partner in a conversation fails to terminate its end of the conversation, the system may enter a modal loop while it waits for the conversation to terminate. A timeout period is associated with this loop. If the timeout period expires before the conversation has terminated, a message box appears that gives the user the choice of waiting for another timeout period (Retry), waiting indefinitely (Ignore), or exiting the modal loop (Abort).

An application should wait until its windows are no longer visible and its message loop has terminated before calling this function.

See Also   **DdeDisconnect, DdeDisconnectList, DdeInitialize**

DebugBreak   3.0

void DebugBreak(void)

The **DebugBreak** function causes a breakpoint exception to occur in the caller. This allows the calling process to signal the debugger, forcing it to take some action. If the process is not being debugged, the system invokes the default breakpoint exception handler. This may cause the calling process to terminate.

Parameters   This function has no parameters.

Return Value   This function does not return a value.

Comments   This function is the only way to break into a **WEP** (Windows exit procedure) in a dynamic-link library.

For more information about using the debugging functions with Microsoft debugging tools, see *Microsoft Windows Programming Tools*.

Example   The following example uses the **DebugBreak** function to signal the debugger immediately before the application handles the WM_DESTROY message:

```
case WM_DESTROY:

    DebugBreak();
    PostQuitMessage(0);
    break;
```

See Also   **WEP**

DebugOutput

void FAR _ cdecl DebugOutput(*flags, lpszFmt, ...*)
UINT *flags*;   /* type of message   */
LPCSTR *lpszFmt*;   /* address of formatting string   */

The **DebugOutput** function sends a message to the debugging terminal. Applications can apply the formatting codes to the message string and use filters and options to control the message category.

Parameters

flags

Specifies the type of message to be sent to the debugging terminal. This parameter can be one of the following values:

Value	Meaning
DBF_TRACE	The message reports that no error has occurred and supplies information that may be useful during debugging. Example: "t Kernel: LoadResource(14AE of GDI)"
DBF_WARNING	The message reports a situation that may or may not be an error, depending on the circumstances. Example: "wn Kernel: GlobalWire(17BE of GDI) (try GlobalLock)"
DBF_ERROR	The message reports an error resulting from a failed call to a Windows function. The application continues to run. Example: "err Kernel: LocalShrink(15EA of GDI) (invalid local heap)"
DBF_FATAL	The message reports an error that will terminate the application. Example: "fatl User: SetDeskWallpaper(16CA of USER)"

lpszFmt

Points to a formatting string identical to the formatting strings used by the Windows function **wsprintf**. This string must be less than 160 characters long. Any additional formatting can be done by supplying additional parameters following *lpszFmt*.

. . .

Specifies zero or more optional arguments. The number and type of arguments depends on the corresponding format-control character sequences specified in the *lpszFmt* parameter.

Return Value

This function does not return a value.

Comments

The messages sent by the **DebugOutput** function are affected by the system debugging options and trace-filter flags that are set and retrieved by using the **GetWinDebugInfo** and **SetWinDebugInfo** functions. These options and flags are stored in a **WINDEBUGINFO** structure.

Unlike most other Windows functions, **DebugOutput** uses the C calling convention (**_cdecl**), rather than the Pascal calling convention. As a result, the caller must pop arguments off the stack. Also, arguments must be pushed on the stack from right to left. In C-language modules, the C compiler performs this task.

See Also

GetWinDebugInfo, OutputDebugString, SetWinDebugInfo, wsprintf

---

DebugProc

3.1

LRESULT CALLBACK DebugProc(*code*, *wParam*, *lParam*)
int *code*;   /* hook code   */
WPARAM *wParam*;   /* type of hook about to be called   */
LPARAM *lParam*;   /* address of structure with debugging information */

The **DebugProc** function is a library-defined callback function that the system calls before calling any other filter installed by the **SetWindowsHookEx** function. The system passes information about the filter about to be called to the **Debug-Proc** callback function. The callback function can examine the information and determine whether to allow the filter to be called.

Parameters

code
Specifies the hook code. Currently, HC_ACTION is the only positive valid value. If this parameter is less than zero, the callback function must call the **CallNextHookEx** function without any further processing.

wParam
Specifies the task handle of the task that installed the filter about to be called.

lParam
Contains a long pointer to a **DEBUGHOOKINFO** structure. The **DEBUGHOOKINFO** structure has the following form:

```
typedef struct tagDEBUGHOOKINFO {
    HMODULE hModuleHook;
    LPARAM  reserved;
    LPARAM  lParam;
    WPARAM  wParam;
    int     code;
} DEBUGHOOKINFO;
```

For a full description of this structure, see the *Microsoft Windows Programmer's Reference, Volume 3*.

Return Value   The callback function should return TRUE to prevent the system from calling another filter. Otherwise, the callback function must pass the filter information to the **CallNextHookEx** function.

Comments   An application must install this callback function by specifying the WH_DEBUG filter type and the procedure-instance address of the callback function in a call to the **SetWindowsHookEx** function.

CallWndProc is a placeholder for the library-defined function name. The actual name must be exported by including it in an **EXPORTS** statement in the library's module-definition file.

See Also   **CallNextHookEx**, **SetWindowsHookEx**

DefDlgProc   3.0

LRESULT DefDlgProc(*hwndDlg*, *uMsg*, *wParam*, *lParam*)
HWND *hwndDlg*;   /* handle of dialog box   */
UINT *uMsg*;   /* message   */
WPARAM *wParam*;   /* first message parameter   */
LPARAM *lParam*;   /* second message parameter   */

The **DefDlgProc** function provides default processing for any Windows messages that a dialog box with a private window class does not process.

Parameters   *hwndDlg*
                      Identifies the dialog box.

                      uMsg
                      Specifies the message to be processed.

                      wParam
                      Specifies 16 bits of additional message-dependent information.

lParam
Specifies 32 bits of additional message-dependent information.

Return Value
The return value specifies the result of the message processing and depends on the message sent.

Comments
The **DefDlgProc** function is the window procedure for the DIALOG window class. An application that creates new window classes that inherit dialog box functionality should use this function. **DefDlgProc** is not intended to be called as the default handler for messages within a dialog box procedure, since doing so will result in recursive execution.

An application creates a dialog box by calling one of the following functions:

Function	Description
CreateDialog	Creates a modeless dialog box.
CreateDialogIndirect	Creates a modeless dialog box.
CreateDialogIndirectParam	Creates a modeless dialog box and passes data to it when it is created.
CreateDialogParam	Creates a modeless dialog box and passes data to it when it is created.
DialogBox	Creates a modal dialog box.
DialogBoxIndirect	Creates a modal dialog box.
DialogBoxIndirectParam	Creates a modal dialog box and passes data to it when it is created.
DialogBoxParam	Creates a modal dialog box and passes data to it when it is created.

See Also
DefWindowProc

DefDriverProc   `3.1`

LRESULT DefDriverProc(*dwDriverIdentifier*, *hdrvr*, *uMsg*, *lParam1*, *lParam2*)
DWORD *dwDriverIdentifier*;   /* installable-driver identifier   */
HDRVR *hdrvr*;   /* handle of installable driver   */
UINT *uMsg*;   /* message number   */
LPARAM *lParam1*;   /* first message parameter   */
LPARAM *lParam2*;   /* second message parameter   */

The **DefDriverProc** function provides default processing for any messages not processed by an installable driver.

Parameters   *dwDriverIdentifier*
                        Identifies an installable driver. This parameter must have been obtained by a
                        previous call to the **OpenDriver** function.

                        hdrvr
                        Identifies the installable driver.

                        uMsg
                        Specifies the message to be processed.

                        lParam1
                        Specifies 32 bits of additional message-dependent information.

                        lParam2
                        Specifies 32 bits of additional message-dependent information.

Return Value   The return value is nonzero if the function is successful. Otherwise, it is zero.

Comments   The **DefDriverProc** function processes messages that are not handled by the
                        DriverProc function.

See Also   **OpenDriver**, **SendDriverMessage**

DeferWindowPos   3.0

HDWP DeferWindowPos(*hdwp*, *hwnd*, *hwndInsertAfter*, *x*, *y*, *cx*, *cy*,*flags***)**
HDWP *hdwp*;   /* handle of internal structure   */
HWND *hwnd*;   /* handle of window to position   */
HWND *hwndInsertAfter*;   /* placement-order handle   */
int *x*;   /* horizontal position   */
int *y*;   /* vertical position   */
int *cx*;   /* width   */
int *cy*;   /* height   */
UINT *flags*;   /* window-positioning flags   */

The **DeferWindowPos** function updates the given internal structure for the given
window. The function then returns the handle of the updated structure. The **End-
DeferWindowPos** function uses the information in this structure to change the
position and size of a number of windows simultaneously.

Parameters   *hdwp*
                        Identifies an internal structure that contains size and position information for
                        one or more windows. This structure is returned by the **BeginDeferWindow-
                        Pos** function or by the most recent call to the **DeferWindowPos** function.

hwnd

Identifies the window for which to store update information in the structure.

hwndInsertAfter

Identifies a window that will precede the positioned window in the Z-order. This parameter must be a window handle, or one of the following values:

Value	Meaning
HWND_BOTTOM	Places the window at the bottom of the Z-order. If *hwnd* identifies a topmost window, the window loses its topmost status.
HWND_TOP	Places the window at the top of the Z-order.
HWND_TOPMOST	Places the window above all non-topmost windows. The window maintains its topmost position even when the window is deactivated.
HWND_NOTOPMOST	Repositions the window to the top of all non-topmost windows (that is, behind all topmost windows).

This parameter is ignored if SWP_NOZORDER is set in the *flags* parameter.

x

Specifies the x-coordinate of the window's upper-left corner.

y

Specifies the y-coordinate of the window's upper-left corner.

cx

Specifies the window's new width.

cy

Specifies the window's new height.

flags

Specifies one of eight possible 16-bit values that affect the size and position of the window. This parameter can be a combination of the following values:

Value	Meaning
SWP_DRAWFRAME	Draws a frame (defined in the window's class description) around the window.
SWP_HIDEWINDOW	Hides the window.
SWP_NOACTIVATE	Does not activate the window.
SWP_NOMOVE	Retains current position (ignores *x* and *y* parameters).
SWP_NOREDRAW	Does not redraw changes. If this flag is set, no repainting occurs. This applies to the client area, the non-client area (including the title and scroll bars), and any part of the parent window uncovered as a result of the moved window. When this flag is set, the application must explicitly invalidate or redraw any parts of the window and parent window that must be redrawn.

Value	Meaning
SWP_NOSIZE	Retains current size (ignores the cx and cy parameters).
SWP_NOZORDER	Retains current ordering (ignores the *hwndInsertAfter* parameter).
SWP_SHOWWINDOW	Displays the window.

Return Value

The return value is a handle of the updated structure if the function is successful. This handle may differ from the one passed to the function as the *hdwp* parameter and should be passed to the next call to **DeferWindowPos** or to the **EndDefer-WindowPos** function.

The return value is NULL if insufficient system resources are available for the function to complete successfully and the repositioning process is terminated.

Comments

If a call to **DeferWindowPos** fails, the application should abandon the window-positioning operation without calling the **EndDeferWindowPos** function.

If SWP_NOZORDER is not specified, Windows places the window identified by *hwnd* in the position following the window identified by *hwndInsertAfter*. If *hwndInsertAfter* is NULL, Windows places the window identified by *hwnd* at the top of the list. If *hwndInsertAfter* is HWND_BOTTOM, Windows places the window identified by *hwnd* at the bottom of the list.

All coordinates for child windows are relative to the upper-left corner of the parent window's client area.

A window can be made a topmost window either by setting *hwndInsertAfter* to HWND_TOPMOST and ensuring that SWP_NOZORDER is not set, or by setting a window's Z-order so that it is above any existing topmost windows. When a non-topmost window is made topmost, its owned windows are also made topmost. Its owners are not changed.

If neither SWP_NOACTIVATE nor SWP_NOZORDER is specified (that is, when the application requests that a window be simultaneously activated and placed in the specified Z-order), the value specified in *hwndInsertAfter* is used only in the following circumstances:

- Neither HWND_TOPMOST nor HWND_NOTOPMOST is specified in the *hwndInsertAfter* parameter.
- The window specified in the *hwnd* parameter is not the active window.

An application cannot activate an inactive window without also bringing it to the top of the Z-order. Applications can change the Z-order of an activated window without restrictions or activate a window and then move it to the top of the topmost or non-topmost windows.

A topmost window is no longer topmost if it is repositioned to the bottom (HWND_BOTTOM) of the Z-order or after any non-topmost window. When a topmost window is made non-topmost, the window and all of its owners, and its owned windows, are also made non-topmost.

A non-topmost window may own a topmost window, but not vice versa. Any window (for example, a dialog box) owned by a topmost window is itself made topmost to ensure that all owned windows stay above their owner.

See Also   **BeginDeferWindowPos, EndDeferWindowPos**

DefFrameProc   3.0

LRESULT DefFrameProc(*hwnd, hwndMDIClient, uMsg, wParam, lParam*)
HWND *hwnd*;   /* handle of frame window   */
HWND *hwndMDIClient*;   /* handle of client window   */
UINT *uMsg*;   /* message   */
WPARAM *wParam*;   /* first message parameter   */
LPARAM *lParam*;   /* second message parameter   */

The **DefFrameProc** function provides default processing for any Windows messages that the window procedure of a multiple document interface (MDI) frame window does not process. All window messages that are not explicitly processed by the window procedure must be passed to the **DefFrameProc** function, not the **DefWindowProc** function.

Parameters   *hwnd*
Identifies the MDI frame window.

hwndMDIClient
Identifies the MDI client window.

uMsg
Specifies the message to be processed.

wParam
Specifies 16 bits of additional message-dependent information.

lParam
Specifies 32 bits of additional message-dependent information.

Return Value   The return value specifies the result of the message processing and depends on the message sent. If the *hwndMDIClient* parameter is NULL, the return value is the same as for the **DefWindowProc** function.

Comments   Typically, when an application's window procedure does not handle a message, it passes the message to the **DefWindowProc** function, which processes the message. MDI applications use the **DefFrameProc** and **DefMDIChildProc** functions instead of **DefWindowProc** to provide default message processing. All messages that an application would usually pass to **DefWindowProc** (such as nonclient messages and WM_SETTEXT) should be passed to **DefFrameProc** instead. In addition to handling these messages, **DefFrameProc** also handles the following messages:

Message	Response
WM_COMMAND	The frame window of an MDI application receives the WM_COMMAND message to activate a particular MDI child window. The window identifier accompanying this message will identify the MDI child window assigned by Windows, starting with the first identifier specified by the application when it created the MDI client window. This value of the first identifier must not conflict with menu-item identifiers.
WM_MENUCHAR	When the user presses the ALT+– key combination, the System menu (often called Control menu) of the active MDI child window will be selected.
WM_SETFOCUS	**DefFrameProc** passes focus on to the MDI client, which in turn passes the focus on to the active MDI child window.
WM_SIZE	If the frame window procedure passes this message to **DefFrameProc**, the MDI client window will be resized to fit in the new client area. If the frame window procedure sizes the MDI client to a different size, it should not pass the message to **DefWindowProc**.

See Also   **DefMDIChildProc, DefWindowProc**

DefHookProc

`2.x`

DWORD DefHookProc(*nCode*, *uParam*, *dwParam*, *lphhook*)
int *nCode*;   /* process code   */
UINT *uParam*;   /* first message parameter   */
DWORD *dwParam*;   /* second message parameter   */
HHOOK FAR* *lphhook*;   /* points to address of next hook function   */

This function is obsolete but has been retained for backward compatibility with Windows versions 3.0 and earlier. Applications written for Windows version 3.1 should use the **CallNextHookEx** function.

The **DefHookProc** function calls the next function in a chain of hook functions. A hook function is a function that processes events before they are sent to an application's message-processing loop in the **WinMain** function. When an application defines more than one hook function by using the **SetWindowsHook** function, Windows forms a linked list or hook chain. Windows places functions of the same type in a chain.

Parameters   *nCode*
Specifies a code used by the Windows hook function (also called the message-filter function) to determine how to process the message.

uParam
Specifies 16 bits of additional message-dependent information.

dwParam
Specifies 32 bits of additional message-dependent information.

lphhook
Points to the variable that contains the procedure-instance address of the previously installed hook function returned by the **SetWindowsHook** function.

Return Value   The return value specifies the result of the event processing and depends on the event.

Comments   Windows changes the value at the location pointed to by the *lphhook* parameter after an application calls the **UnhookWindowsHook** function. For more information, see the description of the **UnhookWindowsHook** function.

See Also   **SetWindowsHook, UnhookWindowsHook**

DefMDIChildProc   `3.0`

LRESULT DefMDIChildProc(*hwnd, uMsg, wParam, lParam*)
HWND *hwnd*;   /* handle of child window   */
UINT *uMsg*;   /* message   */
WPARAM *wParam*;   /* first message parameter   */
LPARAM *lParam*;   /* second message parameter   */

The **DefMDIChildProc** function provides default processing for any Windows messages that the window procedure of a multiple document interface (MDI) child window does not process. All window messages that are not explicitly processed by the window procedure must be passed to the **DefMDIChildProc** function, not the **DefWindowProc** function.

Parameters

hwnd
Identifies the MDI child window.

uMsg
Specifies the message to be processed.

wParam
Specifies 16 bits of additional message-dependent information.

lParam
Specifies 32 bits of additional message-dependent information.

Return Value

The return value specifies the result of the message processing and depends on the message sent.

Comments

This function assumes that the parent of the window identified by the *hwnd* parameter was created with the MDICLIENT class.

Typically, when an application's window procedure does not handle a message, it passes the message to the **DefWindowProc** function, which processes the message. MDI applications use the **DefFrameProc** and **DefMDIChildProc** functions instead of **DefWindowProc** to provide default message processing. All messages that an application would usually pass to **DefWindowProc** (such as nonclient messages and WM_SETTEXT) should be passed to **DefMDIChildProc** instead. In addition to handling these messages, **DefMDIChildProc** also handles the following messages:

Message	Response
WM_CHILDACTIVATE	Performs activation processing when child windows are sized, moved, or shown. This message must be passed.
WM_GETMINMAXINFO	Calculates the size of a maximized MDI child window based on the current size of the MDI client window.
WM_MENUCHAR	Sends the keystrokes to the frame window.
WM_MOVE	Recalculates MDI client scroll bars, if they are present.
WM_SETFOCUS	Activates the child window if it is not the active MDI child window.
WM_SIZE	Performs necessary operations when changing the size of a window, especially when maximizing or restoring an MDI child window. Failing to pass this message to **DefMDIChildProc** will produce highly undesirable results.
WM_SYSCOMMAND	Also handles the next window command.

See Also

DefFrameProc, **DefWindowProc**

DefWindowProc

LRESULT DefWindowProc(*hwnd*, *uMsg*, *wParam*, *lParam*)
HWND *hwnd*;   /* handle of window   */
UINT *uMsg*;   /* type of message   */
WPARAM *wParam*;   /* first message parameter   */
LPARAM *lParam*;   /* second message parameter   */

The **DefWindowProc** function calls the default window procedure. The default window procedure provides default processing for any window messages that an application does not process. This function ensures that every message is processed. It should be called with the same parameters as those received by the window procedure.

Parameters

hwnd
    Identifies the window that received the message.

uMsg
    Specifies the message.

wParam
    Specifies 16 bits of additional message-dependent information.

lParam
    Specifies 32 bits of additional message-dependent information.

Return Value

The return value is the result of the message processing and depends on the message sent.

Comments

The source code for the **DefWindowProc** function is provided on the Microsoft Windows 3.1 Software Development Kit (SDK) disks.

Example

The following example shows a typical window procedure. A switch statement is used to process individual messages. All messages not processed are passed on to the **DefWindowProc** function.

```
LONG FAR PASCAL MainWndProc(hwnd, message, wParam, lParam)
HWND hwnd;       /* handle of window       */
WORD message;    /* type of message        */
WORD wParam;     /* additional information */
LONG lParam;     /* additional information */
{
    switch (message) {
```

```
/*
 * Process whatever messages you want here and send the
 * rest to DefWindowProc.
 */

default:
    return (DefWindowProc(hwnd, message, wParam, lParam));
```

See Also   **DefDlgProc**

DeleteAtom   `2.x`

ATOM DeleteAtom(*atm*)
ATOM *atm*;   /* atom to delete   */

The **DeleteAtom** function decrements (decreases by one) the reference count of a local atom by one. If the atom's reference count is reduced to zero, the string associated with the atom is removed from the local atom table.

An atom's reference count specifies the number of times the atom has been added to the atom table. The **AddAtom** function increments (increases by one) the count on each call. **DeleteAtom** decrements the count on each call and removes the string only if the atom's reference count is reduced to zero.

Parameters   *atm*
    Identifies the atom and character string to be deleted.

Return Value   The return value is zero if the function is successful. Otherwise, it is equal to the *atm* parameter.

Comments   The only way to ensure that an atom has been deleted from the atom table is to call this function repeatedly until it fails. When the count is decremented to zero, the next call to the **FindAtom** or **DeleteAtom** function will fail.

DeleteAtom has no effect on integer atoms (atoms created by using the **MAKE-INTATOM** macro). The function always returns zero for integer atoms.

Example   The following example uses the **DeleteAtom** function to decrement the reference count for the specified atom:

```
ATOM at;

at = DeleteAtom(atTest);
```

```
if (at == NULL)
    MessageBox(hwnd, "atom count decremented",
        "DeleteAtom", MB_OK);
else
    MessageBox(hwnd, "atom count could not be decremented",
        "DeleteAtom", MB_ICONEXCLAMATION);
```

See Also   **AddAtom, FindAtom, GlobalDeleteAtom**

DeleteDC   2.x

BOOL DeleteDC(*hdc*)
HDC *hdc*;   /* handle of device context   */

The **DeleteDC** function deletes the given device context.

Parameters   *hdc*
                     Identifies the device context.

Return Value   The return value is nonzero if the function is successful. Otherwise, it is zero.

Comments   If the *hdc* parameter identifies the last device context for a given device, the
                     device is notified and all storage and system resources used by the device are
                     released.

                     An application must not delete a device context whose handle was retrieved by
                     calling the **GetDC** function. Instead, the application must call the **ReleaseDC**
                     function to free the device context.

                     An application should not call **DeleteDC** if the application has selected objects
                     into the device context. Objects must be selected out of the device context before
                     it is deleted.

Example   The following example uses the **CreateDC** function to create a device context for
                     a printer and then calls the **DeleteDC** function when the device context is no
                     longer needed:

```
/* Retrieves a device context for a printer. */

hdcPrinter = CreateDC(lpDriverName, lpDeviceName, lpOutput,
    lpInitData);

. /* Use the device context. */
.
```

```
/* Delete the device context. */

DeleteDC(hdcPrinter);
```

See Also   **CreateDC**, **GetDC**, **ReleaseDC**

DeleteMenu

BOOL DeleteMenu(*hmenu*, *idItem*, *fuFlags*)
HMENU *hmenu*;   /* handle of menu   */
UINT *idItem*;   /* menu-item identifier   */
UINT *fuFlags*;   /* menu flags   */

The **DeleteMenu** function deletes an item from a menu. If the menu item has an associated pop-up menu, **DeleteMenu** destroys the handle of the pop-up menu and frees the memory used by the pop-up menu.

Parameters   *hmenu*
Identifies the menu to be changed.

idItem
Specifies the menu item to be deleted, as determined by the *fuFlags* parameter.

fuFlags
Specifies how the *idItem* parameter is interpreted. This parameter can be one of the following values:

Value	Meaning
MF_BYCOMMAND	The *idItem* parameter specifies the menu-item identifier.
MF_BYPOSITION	The *idItem* parameter specifies the zero-based relative position of the menu item.

Return Value   The return value is nonzero if the function is successful. Otherwise, it is zero.

Comments   Whenever a menu changes (whether or not the menu is in a window that is displayed), the application should call the **DrawMenuBar** function.

See Also   **AppendMenu**, **CreateMenu**, **DrawMenuBar**, **InsertMenu**, **RemoveMenu**

DeleteMetaFile

2.x

BOOL DeleteMetaFile(*hmf*)
HMETAFILE *hmf*;   /* handle of metafile   */

The **DeleteMetaFile** function invalidates the given metafile handle.

Parameters   *hmf*
                        Identifies the metafile to be deleted.

Return Value   The return value is nonzero if the function is successful. Otherwise, it is zero.

Comments   The **DeleteMetaFile** function does not destroy a metafile that is saved on disk.
                        After calling **DeleteMetaFile**, an application can retrieve a new handle of the
                        metafile by calling the **GetMetaFile** function.

Example   The following example uses the **CreateMetaFile** function to create the handle of a
                        memory metafile device context, draws a line in that device context, retrieves a
                        handle of the metafile by calling the **CloseMetaFile** function, plays the metafile
                        by using the **PlayMetaFile** function, and finally deletes the metafile by using
                        DeleteMetaFile:

```
HDC hdcMeta;
HMETAFILE hmf;

hdcMeta = CreateMetaFile(NULL);
MoveTo(hdcMeta, 10, 10);
LineTo(hdcMeta, 100, 100);
hmf = CloseMetaFile(hdcMeta);
PlayMetaFile(hdc, hmf);
DeleteMetaFile(hmf);
```

See Also   **CreateMetaFile, GetMetaFile**

DeleteObject

2.x

BOOL DeleteObject(*hgdiobj*)
HGDIOBJ *hgdiobj*;   /* handle of object to delete   */

The **DeleteObject** function deletes an object from memory by freeing all system
storage associated with the object. (Objects include pens, brushes, fonts, bitmaps,
regions, and palettes.)

Parameters   *hgdiobj*
                   Identifies a pen, brush, font, bitmap, region, or palette.

Return Value   The return value is nonzero if the function is successful. Otherwise, it is zero.

Comments   After the object is deleted, the handle given in the *hgdiobj* parameter is no longer valid.

                   An application should not delete an object that is currently selected into a device context.

                   When a pattern brush is deleted, the bitmap associated with the brush is not deleted. The bitmap must be deleted independently.

Example   The following example creates a pen, selects it into a device context, and uses the pen to draw a rectangle. To delete the pen, the original pen is selected back into the device context and the **DeleteObject** function is called.

```
HPEN hpen, hpenOld;

hpen = CreatePen(PS_SOLID, 6, RGB(0, 0, 255));
hpenOld = SelectObject(hdc, hpen);

Rectangle(hdc, 10, 10, 100, 100);

SelectObject(hdc, hpenOld);
DeleteObject(hpen);
```

See Also   **SelectObject**

DestroyCaret   2.x

void DestroyCaret(void)

                   The **DestroyCaret** function destroys the current caret shape, frees the caret from the window that currently owns it, and removes the caret from the screen if it is visible. The **DestroyCaret** function checks the ownership of the caret and destroys the caret only if a window in the current task owns it.

                   If the caret shape was previously a bitmap, **DestroyCaret** does not free the bitmap.

Parameters   This function has no parameters.

Return Value   This function does not return a value.

Comments	The caret is a shared resource. If a window has created a caret shape, it should destroy that shape before it loses the input focus or becomes inactive.
See Also	**CreateCaret, HideCaret, ShowCaret**

DestroyCursor   `3.0`

BOOL DestroyCursor(*hcur***)**
HCURSOR *hcur*;   /* handle of cursor to destroy   */

The **DestroyCursor** function destroys a cursor that was previously created by the **CreateCursor** or **LoadCursor** function and frees any memory that the cursor occupied.

Parameters	*hcur* Identifies the cursor to be destroyed. The cursor must not be in current use.
Return Value	The return value is nonzero if the function is successful. Otherwise, it is zero.
See Also	**CreateCursor, CreateIcon, DestroyIcon, LoadCursor**

DestroyIcon   `3.0`

BOOL DestroyIcon(*hicon***)**
HICON *hicon*;   /* handle of icon to destroy   */

The **DestroyIcon** function destroys an icon that was created by the **CreateIcon** or **LoadIcon** function and frees any memory that the icon occupied.

Parameters	*hicon* Identifies the icon to be destroyed.
Return Value	The return value is nonzero if the function is successful. Otherwise, it is zero.
See Also	**CreateCursor, CreateIcon, DestroyCursor, LoadIcon**

DestroyMenu

BOOL DestroyMenu(*hmenu*)
HMENU *hmenu*;   /* handle of menu to destroy   */

The **DestroyMenu** function destroys a menu and frees any memory that the menu occupied.

Parameters   *hmenu*
                        Identifies the menu to be destroyed.

Return Value   The return value is nonzero if the function is successful. Otherwise, it is zero.

See Also   **CreateMenu**

DestroyWindow

BOOL DestroyWindow(*hwnd*)
HWND *hwnd*;   /* handle of window to destroy   */

The **DestroyWindow** function destroys the specified window. The function sends appropriate messages to the window to deactivate it and remove the input focus. It also destroys the window's menu, flushes the application queue, destroys outstanding timers, removes clipboard ownership, and breaks the clipboard-viewer chain (if the window is at the top of the viewer chain). It sends WM_DESTROY and WM_NCDESTROY messages to the window.

If the given window is the parent of any windows, **DestroyWindow** automatically destroys these child windows when it destroys the parent window. The function destroys child windows first, and then the window itself.

The **DestroyWindow** function also destroys modeless dialog boxes created by the **CreateDialog** function.

Parameters   *hwnd*
                        Identifies the window to be destroyed.

Return Value   The return value is nonzero if the function is successful. Otherwise, it is zero.

Comments   If the window being destroyed is a child window and does not have the WS_NOPARENTNOTIFY style set, a WM_PARENTNOTIFY message is sent to the parent.

Example   The following example responds to the application-defined menu command
IDM_EXIT, and then calls **DestroyWindow** to destroy the window:

```
case IDM_EXIT:
    DestroyWindow(hwnd);
    return 0;
```

See Also   **CreateDialog**, **CreateWindow**, **CreateWindowEx**

DeviceCapabilities

3.0

#include <print.h>

DWORD DeviceCapabilities(*lpszDevice, lpszPort, fwCapability, lpszOutput, lpdm***)**
LPSTR *lpszDevice*;   /* address of device-name string   */
LPSTR *lpszPort*;   /* address of port-name string   */
WORD *fwCapability*;   /* device capability to query   */
LPSTR *lpszOutput*;   /* address of the output   */
LPDEVMODE *lpdm*;   /* address of structure with device data */

The **DeviceCapabilities** function retrieves the capabilities of the printer device
driver.

Parameters   *lpszDevice*
Points to a null-terminated string that contains the name of the printer device,
such as PCL/HP LaserJet.

lpszPort
Points to a null-terminated string that contains the name of the port to which the
device is connected, such as LPT1.

fwCapability
Specifies the capabilities to query. This parameter can be one of the following
values:

Value	Meaning
DC_BINNAMES	Copies an array containing a list of the names of the paper bins. This array is in the form **char** *PaperNames[cBinMax][cchBinName]* where *cchBinName* is 24. If the *lpszOutput* parameter is NULL, the return value is the number of bin entries required. Otherwise, the return value is the number of bins copied.

Value	Meaning
DC_BINS	Retrieves a list of available bins. The function copies the list to the *lpszOutput* parameter as a **WORD** array. If *lpszOutput* is NULL, the function returns the number of supported bins to allow the application the opportunity to allocate a buffer with the correct size. For more information about these bins, see the description of the **dmDefaultSource** member of the **DEVMODE** structure.
DC_COPIES	Returns the number of copies the device can print.
DC_DRIVER	Returns the version number of the printer driver.
DC_DUPLEX	Returns the level of duplex support. The function returns 1 if the printer is capable of duplex printing. Otherwise, the return value is zero.
DC_ENUMRESOLUTIONS	Returns a list of available resolutions. If *lpszOutput* is NULL, the function returns the number of available resolution configurations. Resolutions are represented by pairs of **LONG** integers representing the horizontal and vertical resolutions (specified in dots per inch).
DC_EXTRA	Returns the number of bytes required for the device-specific portion of the **DEVMODE** structure for the printer driver.
DC_FIELDS	Returns the **dmFields** member of the printer driver's **DEVMODE** structure. The **dmFields** member indicates which fields in the device-independent portion of the structure are supported by the printer driver.
DC_FILEDEPENDENCIES	Returns a list of files that also need to be loaded when a driver is installed. If the *lpszOutput* parameter is NULL, the function returns the number of files. Otherwise, *lpszOutput* points to an array of filenames in the form **char**[*chFileName*, **64**]. Each filename is a null-terminated string.
DC_MAXEXTENT	Returns a **POINT** structure containing the maximum paper size that the **dmPaperLength** and **dmPaperWidth** members of the printer driver's **DEVMODE** structure can specify.
DC_MINEXTENT	Returns a **POINT** structure containing the minimum paper size that the **dmPaperLength** and **dmPaperWidth** members of the printer driver's **DEVMODE** structure can specify.

Value	Meaning
DC_ORIENTATION	Returns the relationship between portrait and landscape orientations for a device, in terms of the number of degrees that portrait orientation is rotated counterclockwise to produce landscape orientation. The return value can be one of the following:

Value	Meaning
0	No landscape orientation.
90	Portrait is rotated 90 degrees to produce landscape. (For example, Hewlett-Packard PCL printers.)
270	Portrait is rotated 270 degrees to produce landscape. (For example, dot-matrix printers.)

Value	Meaning
DC_PAPERNAMES	Retrieves a list of supported paper names—for example, Letter or Legal. If the *lpszOutput* parameter is NULL, the function returns the number of paper sizes available. Otherwise, *lpszOutput* points to an array for the paper names in the form **char**[*cPaperNames*, **64**]. Each paper name is a null-terminated string.
DC_PAPERS	Retrieves a list of supported paper sizes. The function copies the list to *lpszOutput* as a **WORD** array and returns the number of entries in the array. If *lpszOutput* is NULL, the function returns the number of supported paper sizes to allow the application the opportunity to allocate a buffer with the correct size. For more information on paper sizes, see the description of the **dmPaperSize** member of the **DEVMODE** structure.
DC_PAPERSIZE	Copies the dimensions of all supported paper sizes, in tenths of a millimeter, to an array of **POINT** structures pointed to by the *lpszOutput* parameter. The width (x-dimension) and length (y-dimension) of a paper size are returned as if the paper were in the DMORIENT_PORTRAIT orientation.
DC_SIZE	Returns the **dmSize** member of the printer driver's **DEVMODE** structure.

DC_TRUETYPE | Retrieves the abilities of the driver to use True-Type fonts. The return value can be one or more of the following:

Value	Meaning
DCTT_BITMAP	Device is capable of printing TrueType fonts as graphics. (For example, dot-matrix and PCL printers.)
DCTT_DOWNLOAD	Device is capable of downloading TrueType fonts. (For example, PCL and PostScript printers.)
DCTT_SUBDEV	Device is capable of substituting device fonts for TrueType fonts. (For example, PostScript printers.)

For DC_TRUETYPE, the *lpszOutput* parameter should be NULL.

DC_VERSION | Returns the specification version to which the printer driver conforms.

lpszOutput
Points to an array of bytes. The format of the array depends on the setting of the *fwCapability* parameter. If *lpszOutput* is zero, **DeviceCapabilities** returns the number of bytes required for the output data.

lpdm
Points to a **DEVMODE** structure. If this parameter is NULL, **Device-Capabilities** retrieves the current default initialization values for the specified printer driver. Otherwise, the function retrieves the values contained in the structure to which *lpdm* points.

The **DEVMODE** structure has the following form:

```
#include <print.h>

typedef struct tagDEVMODE {   /* dm */
    char  dmDeviceName[CCHDEVICENAME];
    UINT  dmSpecVersion;
    UINT  dmDriverVersion;
    UINT  dmSize;
    UINT  dmDriverExtra;
    DWORD dmFields;
    int   dmOrientation;
    int   dmPaperSize;
    int   dmPaperLength;
    int   dmPaperWidth;
    int   dmScale;
    int   dmCopies;
    int   dmDefaultSource;
    int   dmPrintQuality;
    int   dmColor;
    int   dmDuplex;
    int   dmYResolution;
    int   dmTTOption;
} DEVMODE;
```

For a full description of this structure, see the *Microsoft Windows Programmer's Reference, Volume 3.*

Return Value

The return value, if the function is successful, depends on the setting of the *fwCapability* parameter. The return value is −1 if the function fails.

Comments

This function is supplied by the printer driver. To use the **DeviceCapabilities** function, an application must retrieve the address of the function by calling the **Load-Library** and **GetProcAddress** functions, and it must include the PRINT.H file.

DeviceCapabilities is not supported by all printer drivers. If the **GetProcAddress** function returns NULL, **DeviceCapabilities** is not supported.

See Also

GetProcAddress, LoadLibrary

DeviceMode

void DeviceMode(*hwnd*, *hModule*, *lpszDevice*, *lpszOutput*)
HWND *hwnd*;   /* handle of window owning dialog box   */
HANDLE *hModule*;   /* handle of printer-driver module   */
LPSTR *lpszDevice*;   /* address of string for device name   */
LPSTR *lpszOutput*;   /* address of string for output name   */

The **DeviceMode** function sets the current printing modes for a specified device by using a dialog box to prompt for those modes. An application calls **Device-Mode** to allow the user to change the printing modes of the corresponding device. **DeviceMode** copies the mode information to the environment block that is associated with the device and maintained by the graphics device interface (GDI).

The **ExtDeviceMode** function provides a superset of the functionality of the **DeviceMode** function; new applications should use **ExtDeviceMode** instead of **DeviceMode** whenever possible. (Applications can use the DM_IN_PROMPT constant with **ExtDeviceMode** to duplicate the functionality of **DeviceMode**.)

Parameters

hwnd
Identifies the window that will own the dialog box.

hModule
Identifies the printer-driver module. The application should retrieve this handle by calling either the **GetModuleHandle** or **LoadLibrary** function.

lpszDevice
Points to a null-terminated string that specifies the name of the specific device to be supported (for example, Epson FX-80). The device name is the same as the name passed to the **CreateDC** function.

lpszOutput
Points to a null-terminated string that specifies the MS-DOS filename or device name for the physical output medium (file or output port). The output name is the same as the name passed to the **CreateDC** function.

Return Value

This function does not return a value.

Comments

The **DeviceMode** function is part of the printer's device driver, not part of GDI. To call this function, an application must load the printer driver by calling the **LoadLibrary** function and retrieve the address of the function by using the **Get-ProcAddress** function. The application can then use the address to set up the printer.

DeviceMode is not supported by all printer drivers. If the **GetProcAddress** function returns NULL, **DeviceMode** is not supported.

See Also

CreateDC, **ExtDeviceMode**, **GetModuleHandle**, **LoadLibrary**

DialogBox

int DialogBox(*hinst, lpszDlgTemp, hwndOwner, dlgprc*)
HINSTANCE *hinst*;   /* handle of application instance   */
LPCSTR *lpszDlgTemp*;   /* address of dialog box template name   */
HWND *hwndOwner*;   /* handle of owner window   */
DLGPROC *dlgprc*;   /* instance address of dialog box procedure */

The **DialogBox** function creates a modal dialog box from a dialog box template resource.

Parameters

hinst
Identifies an instance of the module whose executable file contains the dialog box template.

lpszDlgTemp
Points to a null-terminated string that names the dialog box template.

hwndOwner
Identifies the window that owns the dialog box.

dlgprc
Specifies the procedure-instance address of the dialog box procedure. The address must be created by using the **MakeProcInstance** function. For more information about the dialog box procedure, see the description of the **Dialog-Proc** callback function.

Return Value

The return value specifies the value of the *nResult* parameter specified in the **End-Dialog** function that is used to terminate the dialog box. The system processes values returned by the dialog box procedure and does not return them to the application. The return value is −1 if the function cannot create the dialog box.

Comments

The **CreateWindowEx** function is called to create the dialog box. The dialog box procedure then receives a WM_SETFONT message (if DS_SETFONT style was specified) and a WM_INITDIALOG message, and then the dialog box is displayed.

The **DialogBox** function does not return control until the dialog box procedure terminates the modal dialog box by calling the **EndDialog** function.

A dialog box can contain up to 255 controls.

Example

The following example uses the **DialogBox** function to create a modal dialog box:

```
DLGPROC dlgprc;
HWND hwndParent;
```

```
case IDM_ABOUT:
    dlgprc = (DLGPROC) MakeProcInstance(About, hinst);
    DialogBox(hinst, "AboutBox", hwndParent, dlgprc);
    FreeProcInstance((FARPROC) dlgprc);
    break;
```

See Also   **DialogBoxIndirect, DialogBoxIndirectParam, DialogBoxParam, DialogProc,
                    EndDialog, GetDC, MakeProcInstance**

DialogBoxIndirect

2.x

int **DialogBoxIndirect**(*hinst*, *hglbDlgTemp*, *hwndOwner*, *dlgprc*)
HINSTANCE *hinst*;   /* handle of application instance   */
HGLOBAL *hglbDlgTemp*;   /* handle of memory with dialog box template */
HWND *hwndOwner*;   /* handle of owner window   */
DLGPROC *dlgprc*;   /* instance address of dialog box procedure */

The **DialogBoxIndirect** function creates a modal dialog box from a dialog box template in memory.

Parameters   *hinst*
                   Identifies the instance of the module that will create the dialog box.

                   hglbDlgTemp
                   Identifies the global memory object that contains a dialog box template used to create the dialog box. This template is in the form of a **DialogBoxHeader** structure. For more information about this structure, see Chapter 7, "Resource Formats Within Executable Files," in the *Microsoft Windows Programmer's Reference*, *Volume 4*.

                   hwndOwner
                   Identifies the window that owns the dialog box.

                   dlgprc
                   Specifies the procedure-instance address of the dialog box procedure. The address must be created by using the **MakeProcInstance** function. For more information about the dialog box procedure, see the description of the **Dialog-Proc** callback function.

Return Value   The return value is the value of the *nResult* parameter specified in the **EndDialog** function that is used to terminate the dialog box. The system processes values returned by the dialog box procedure and does not return them to the application. The return value is −1 if the function cannot create the dialog box.

Comments   The **CreateWindowEx** function is called to create the dialog box. The dialog box procedure then receives a WM_SETFONT message (if DS_SETFONT style was specified) and a WM_INITDIALOG message, and then the dialog box is displayed.

The **DialogBoxIndirect** function does not return control until the dialog box procedure terminates the modal dialog box by calling the **EndDialog** function.

A dialog box can contain up to 255 controls.

Example   The following example uses the **DialogBoxIndirect** function to create a dialog box from a dialog box template in memory:

```
#define TEMPLATE_SIZE 100
HGLOBAL hglbDlgTemp;
DLGPROC dlgprc;
int result;
HWND hwndParent;

/* Allocate a global memory object for the dialog box template. */

hglbDlgTemp = GlobalAlloc(GHND, TEMPLATE_SIZE);

.
. /* Build a DLGTEMPLATE structure in the memory object. */
.

dlgprc = (DLGPROC) MakeProcInstance(DialogProc, hinst);
result = DialogBoxIndirect(hinst, hglbDlgTemp, hwndParent, dlgprc);
```

See Also   **DialogBox, DialogBoxIndirectParam, DialogBoxParam, DialogProc, End-Dialog, MakeProcInstance**

DialogBoxIndirectParam   3.0

int DialogBoxIndirectParam(*hinst, hglbDlgTemp, hwndOwner, dlgprc, lParamInit*)
HINSTANCE *hinst*;   /* handle of application instance   */
HGLOBAL *hglbDlgTemp*;   /* handle of memory with dialog box template */
HWND *hwndOwner*;   /* handle of owner window   */
DLGPROC *dlgprc*;   /* instance address of dialog box procedure */
LPARAM *lParamInit*;   /* initialization value   */

The **DialogBoxIndirectParam** function creates a modal dialog box from a dialog box template in memory. Before displaying the dialog box, the function passes an application-defined value to the dialog box procedure as the *lParam* parameter of the WM_INITDIALOG message. An application can use this value to initialize dialog box controls.

Parameters

hinst
Identifies the instance of the module that will create the dialog box.

hglbDlgTemp
Identifies the global memory object that contains a dialog box template used to create the dialog box. This template is in the form of a **DialogBoxHeader** structure. For more information about this structure, see Chapter 7, "Resource Formats Within Executable Files," in the *Microsoft Windows Programmer's Reference, Volume 4.*

hwndOwner
Identifies the window that owns the dialog box.

dlgprc
Specifies the procedure-instance address of the dialog box procedure. The address must be created by using the **MakeProcInstance** function. For more information about the dialog box procedure, see the description of the **Dialog-Proc** callback function.

lParamInit
Specifies a 32-bit value that **DialogBoxIndirectParam** passes to the dialog box when the WM_INITDIALOG message is being processed.

Return Value

The return value is the value of the *nResult* parameter specified in the **EndDialog** function that is used to terminate the dialog box. The system processes values returned by the dialog box procedure and does not return them to the application. The return value is −1 if the function cannot create the dialog box.

Comments

The **CreateWindowEx** function is called to create the dialog box. The dialog box procedure then receives a WM_SETFONT message (if DS_SETFONT style was specified) and a WM_INITDIALOG message, and then the dialog box is displayed.

The **DialogBoxIndirectParam** function does not return control until the dialog box procedure terminates the modal dialog box by calling the **EndDialog** function.

A dialog box can contain up to 255 controls.

Example

The following example uses the **DialogBoxIndirectParam** function to create a modal dialog box from a dialog box template in memory. The example uses the *lParamInit* parameter to send two initialization parameters (wInitParm1 and wInitParm2) to the dialog box procedure when the WM_INITDIALOG message is being processed.

```
#define TEMPLATE_SIZE 100
HGLOBAL hglbDlgTemp;
DLGPROC dlgprc;
int result;
HWND hwndParent;
WORD wInitParm1, wInitParm2;

/* Allocate a global memory object for the dialog box template. */

hglbDlgTemp = GlobalAlloc(GHND, TEMPLATE_SIZE);


.
. /* Build a DLGTEMPLATE structure in the memory object. */
.

dlgprc = (DLGPROC) MakeProcInstance(DialogProc, hinst);
result = DialogBoxIndirectParam(hinst, hglbDlgTemp, hwndParent,
    dlgprc, (LPARAM) MAKELONG(wInitParm1, wInitParm2));
```

See Also   **DialogBox, DialogBoxIndirect, DialogBoxParam, DialogProc, EndDialog,
MakeProcInstance**

DialogBoxParam   3.0

int DialogBoxParam(*hinst, lpszDlgTemp, hwndOwner, dlgprc, lParamInit*)
HINSTANCE *hinst*;   /* handle of application instance   */
LPCSTR *lpszDlgTemp*;   /* address of dialog box template name   */
HWND *hwndOwner*;   /* handle of owner window   */
DLGPROC *dlgprc*;   /* instance address of dialog box procedure */
LPARAM *lParamInit*;   /* initialization value   */

The **DialogBoxParam** function creates a modal dialog box from a dialog box template resource. Before displaying the dialog box, the function passes an application-specified value to the dialog box procedure as the *lParam* parameter of the WM_INITDIALOG message. An application can use this value to initialize dialog box controls.

Parameters   *hinst*
                  Identifies an instance of the module whose executable file contains the dialog box template.

                  lpszDlgTemp
                  Points to a null-terminated string that names the dialog box template.

                  hwndOwner
                  Identifies the window that owns the dialog box.

dlgprc

Specifies the procedure-instance address of the dialog box procedure. The address must be created by using the **MakeProcInstance** function. For more information about the dialog box procedure, see the description of the **Dialog-Proc** callback function.

lParamInit

Specifies a 32-bit value that **DialogBoxParam** passes to the dialog box procedure when creating the dialog box.

Return Value

The return value specifies the value of the *nResult* parameter specified in the **End-Dialog** function that is used to terminate the dialog box. The system processes values returned by the dialog box procedure and does not return them to the application. The return value is −1 if the function cannot create the dialog box.

Comments

The **CreateWindowEx** function is called to create the dialog box. The dialog box procedure then receives a WM_SETFONT message (if DS_SETFONT style was specified) and a WM_INITDIALOG message, and then the dialog box is displayed.

The **DialogBoxParam** function does not return control until the dialog box procedure terminates the modal dialog box by calling the **EndDialog** function.

A dialog box can contain up to 255 controls.

Example

The following example uses the **DialogBoxParam** function to create a modal dialog box. The function passes the dialog box a pointer to a string when the WM_INITDIALOG message is being processed.

```
DLGPROC dlgprc;
HWND hwndParent;
PSTR pszFileName;
int result;

case IDM_OPEN:

    dlgprc = (DLGPROC) MakeProcInstance(FileOpenProc, hinst);
    result = DialogBoxParam(hinst, "FileOpenBox", hwndParent,
        dlgprc, MAKELPARAM(pszFileName, 0));
    FreeProcInstance((FARPROC) dlgprc);
    break;
```

See Also

DialogBox, DialogBoxIndirect, DialogBoxIndirectParam, DialogProc, EndDialog, MakeProcInstance

DialogProc

BOOL CALLBACK DialogProc(*hwndDlg*, *msg*, *wParam*, *lParam*)
HWND *hwndDlg*;   /* handle of dialog box   */
UINT *msg*;   /* message   */
WPARAM *wParam*;   /* first message parameter   */
LPARAM *lParam*;   /* second message parameter   */

The **DialogProc** function is an application-defined callback function that processes messages sent to a modeless dialog box.

Parameters

hwndDlg
Identifies the dialog box.

msg
Specifies the message.

wParam
Specifies 16 bits of additional message-dependent information.

lParam
Specifies 32 bits of additional message-dependent information.

Return Value

Except in response to the WM_INITDIALOG message, the dialog box procedure should return nonzero if it processes the message, and zero if it does not. In response to a WM_INITDIALOG message, the dialog box procedure should return zero if it calls the **SetFocus** function to set the focus to one of the controls in the dialog box. Otherwise, it should return nonzero, in which case the system will set the focus to the first control in the dialog box that can be given the focus.

Comments

The dialog box procedure is used only if the dialog box class is used for the dialog box. This is the default class and is used if no explicit class is given in the dialog box template. Although the dialog box procedure is similar to a window procedure, it must not call the **DefWindowProc** function to process unwanted messages. Unwanted messages are processed internally by the dialog box window procedure.

DialogProc is a placeholder for the application-defined function name. The actual name must be exported by including it in an **EXPORTS** statement in the application's module-definition file.

See Also

CreateDialog, CreateDialogIndirect, CreateDialogIndirectParam, Create-DialogParam, DefWindowProc, SetFocus

DirectedYield

void DirectedYield(*htask*)
HTASK *htask*;

The **DirectedYield** function puts the current task to sleep and awakens the given task.

Parameters

htask
Specifies the task to be executed.

Return Value

This function does not return a value.

Comments

When relinquishing control to other applications (that is, when exiting hard mode), a Windows-based debugger should call **DirectedYield**, identifying the handle of the task being debugged. This ensures that the debugged application runs next and that messages received during debugging are processed by the appropriate windows.

The Windows scheduler executes a task only when there is an event waiting for it, such as a paint message, or a message posted in the message queue.

If an application uses **DirectedYield** for a task with no events scheduled, the task will not be executed. Instead, Windows searches the task queue. In some cases, however, you may want the application to force a specific task to be scheduled. The application can do this by calling the **PostAppMessage** function, specifying a WM_NULL message identifier. Then, when the application calls **DirectedYield**, the scheduler will run the task regardless of the task's event status.

DirectedYield starts the task identified by *htask* at the location where it left off. Typically, debuggers should use **TaskSwitch** instead of **DirectedYield**, because **TaskSwitch** can start a task at any address.

DirectedYield returns when the current task is reawakened. This occurs when the task identified by *htask* waits for messages or uses the **Yield** or **DirectedYield** function. Execution will continue as before the task switch.

DirectedYield is located in KRNL286.EXE and KRNL386.EXE and is available in Windows versions 3.0 and 3.1.

See Also

PostAppMessage, **TaskSwitch**, **TaskGetCSIP**, **TaskSetCSIP**, **Yield**

DispatchMessage

2.x

LONG DispatchMessage(*lpmsg*)
const MSG FAR* *lpmsg*;   /* address of structure with message   */

The **DispatchMessage** function dispatches a message to a window. It is typically used to dispatch a message retrieved by the **GetMessage** function.

Parameters   *lpmsg*
Points to an **MSG** structure that contains the message. The **MSG** structure has the following form:

```
typedef struct tagMSG {      /* msg */
    HWND    hwnd;
    UINT    message;
    WPARAM  wParam;
    LPARAM  lParam;
    DWORD   time;
    POINT   pt;
} MSG;
```

The **MSG** structure must contain valid message values. If the *lpmsg* parameter points to a WM_TIMER message and the *lParam* parameter of the WM_TIMER message is not NULL, then *lParam* points to a function that is called instead of the window procedure.

For a full description of this structure, see the *Microsoft Windows Programmer's Reference, Volume 3*.

Return Value   The return value specifies the value returned by the window procedure. Although its meaning depends on the message being dispatched, generally the return value is ignored.

Example   The following example shows a typical use of the **DispatchMessage** function in an application's main message loop:

```
MSG msg;
HWND hwnd;
HWND hwndDlgModeless;
HANDLE haccl;

while (GetMessage(&msg, NULL, 0, 0)) {
    if ((hwndDlgModeless == NULL ||
            !IsDialogMessage(hwndDlgModeless, &msg)) &&
            !TranslateAccelerator(hwnd, haccl, &msg)) {
        TranslateMessage(&msg);
        DispatchMessage(&msg);
    }
}
```

See Also   GetMessage, PeekMessage, PostAppMessage, PostMessage, TranslateMessage

DlgDirList

2.x

int DlgDirList(*hwndDlg*, *lpszPath*, *idListBox*, *idStaticPath*, *uFileType*)
HWND *hwndDlg*;   /* handle of dialog box with list box   */
LPSTR *lpszPath*;   /* address of path or filename string   */
int *idListBox*;   /* identifier of list box   */
int *idStaticPath*;   /* identifier of static control   */
UINT *uFileType*;   /* file attributes to display   */

The **DlgDirList** function fills a list box with a file or directory listing. It fills the list box with the names of all files matching the specified path or filename.

Parameters   *hwndDlg*
Identifies the dialog box that contains the list box.

lpszPath
Points to a null-terminated string that contains the path or filename. **DlgDirList** modifies this string, which should be long enough to contain the modifications. For more information, see the following Comments section.

idListBox
Specifies the identifier of a list box. If this parameter is zero, **DlgDirList** assumes that no list box exists and does not attempt to fill one.

idStaticPath
Specifies the identifier of the static control used for displaying the current drive and directory. If this parameter is zero, **DlgDirList** assumes that no such control is present.

uFileType
Specifies the attributes of the filenames to be displayed. This parameter can be a combination of the following values:

Value	Meaning
DDL_READWRITE	Read-write data files with no additional attributes.
DDL_READONLY	Read-only files.
DDL_HIDDEN	Hidden files.
DDL_SYSTEM	System files.
DDL_DIRECTORY	Directories.
DDL_ARCHIVE	Archives.

Value	Meaning
DDL_POSTMSGS	LB_DIR flag. If the LB_DIR flag is set, Windows places the messages generated by **DlgDirList** in the application's queue; otherwise, they are sent directly to the dialog box procedure.
DDL_DRIVES	Drives.
DDL_EXCLUSIVE	Exclusive bit. If the exclusive bit is set, only files of the specified type are listed; otherwise, files of the specified type are listed in addition to normal files.

Return Value

The return value is nonzero if the function is successful. Otherwise, it is zero.

Comments

If you specify a zero-length string for the *lpszPath* parameter or if you specify only a directory name but do not include any filename, the string will be changed to *.*.

The **DlgDirList** function shows directories enclosed in brackets ([ ]) and shows drives in the form [-*x*-], where *x* is the drive letter.

The *lpszPath* parameter has the following form:

[*drive*:][[\]*directory*[*directory*]…\][*filename*]

In this example, *drive* is a drive letter, *directory* is a valid MS-DOS directory name, and *filename* is a valid MS-DOS filename that must contain at least one wildcard. The wildcards are a question mark (?), meaning match any character, and an asterisk (*), meaning match any number of characters.

If the *lpszPath* parameter includes a drive or directory name, or both, the current drive and directory are changed to the specified drive and directory before the list box is filled. The static control identified by the *idStaticPath* parameter is also updated with the new drive or directory name, or both.

After the list box is filled, *lpszPath* is updated by removing the drive or directory portion, or both, of the path and filename.

DlgDirList sends LB_RESETCONTENT and LB_DIR messages to the list box.

See Also

DlgDirListComboBox, DlgDirSelect, DlgDirSelectComboBox

DlgDirListComboBox

int **DlgDirListComboBox**(*hwndDlg*, *lpszPath*, *idComboBox*, *idStaticPath*, *uFileType*)
HWND *hwndDlg*;   /* handle of dialog box with combo box   */
LPSTR *lpszPath*;   /* address of path or filename string   */
int *idComboBox*;   /* identifier of combo box   */
int *idStaticPath*;   /* identifier of static control   */
UINT *uFileType*;   /* file attributes to display   */

The **DlgDirListComboBox** function fills the list box of a combo box with a file or directory listing. It fills the list box with the names of all files matching the specified path and filename.

Parameters

hwndDlg
Identifies the dialog box that contains the combo box.

lpszPath
Points to a null-terminated string that contains the path and filename. For more information, see the following Comments section.

idComboBox
Specifies the identifier of a combo box in a dialog box. If this parameter is zero, **DlgDirListComboBox** assumes that no combo box exists and does not attempt to fill one.

idStaticPath
Specifies the identifier of the static control used for displaying the current drive and directory. If this parameter is zero, **DlgDirListComboBox** assumes that no such control is present.

uFileType
Specifies the attributes of the filenames to be displayed. This parameter can be a combination of the following values:

Value	Meaning
DDL_READWRITE	Read-write data files with no additional attributes.
DDL_READONLY	Read-only files.
DDL_HIDDEN	Hidden files.
DDL_SYSTEM	System files.
DDL_DIRECTORY	Directories.
DDL_ARCHIVE	Archives.
DDL_POSTMSGS	CB_DIR flag. If the CB_DIR flag is set, Windows places the messages generated by **DlgDirListComboBox** in the application's queue; otherwise, they are sent directly to the dialog box procedure.
DDL_DRIVES	Drives.

Value	Meaning
DDL_EXCLUSIVE	Exclusive bit. If the exclusive bit is set, only files of the specified type are listed; otherwise, files of the specified type are listed in addition to normal files.

Return Value   The return value is nonzero if the function is successful. Otherwise, it is zero.

Comments   The **DlgDirListComboBox** function shows directories enclosed in brackets ([ ]) and shows drives in the form [-*x*-], where *x* is the drive letter.

The *lpszPath* parameter has the following form:

[*drive*:][[\]*directory*[*directory*]...\][*filename*]

In this example, *drive* is a drive letter, *directory* is a valid MS-DOS directory name, and *filename* is a valid MS-DOS filename that must contain at least one wildcard. The wildcards are a question mark (?), meaning match any character, and an asterisk (*), meaning match any number of characters.

If the *lpszPath* parameter includes a drive or directory name, or both, the current drive and directory are changed to the specified drive and directory before the list box is filled. The static control identified by the *idStaticPath* parameter is also updated with the new drive or directory name, or both.

After the list box of the combo box is filled, *lpszPath* is updated by removing the drive or directory portion, or both, of the path and filename.

DlgDirListComboBox sends CB_RESETCONTENT and CB_DIR messages to the combo box.

See Also   **DlgDirList, DlgDirSelect, DlgDirSelectComboBox**

DlgDirSelect   2.x

BOOL DlgDirSelect(*hwndDlg*, *lpszPath*, *idListBox*)
HWND *hwndDlg*;   /* handle of dialog box with list box   */
LPSTR *lpszPath*;   /* address of buffer for path or filename string   */
int *idListBox*;   /* identifier of list box   */

The **DlgDirSelect** function retrieves the current selection from a list box. It assumes that the list box has been filled by the **DlgDirList** function and that the selection is a drive letter, a file, or a directory name.

Parameters	*hwndDlg* Identifies the dialog box that contains the list box. *lpszPath* Points to a 128-byte buffer for the path or filename. *idListBox* Specifies the integer identifier of a list box in the dialog box.
Return Value	The return value is nonzero if the function is successful. Otherwise, it is zero.
Comments	If the current selection is a directory name or drive letter, **DlgDirSelect** removes the enclosing brackets (and hyphens, for drive letters) so that the name or letter is ready to be inserted into a new path or filename. If there is no selection, the contents of the buffer pointed to by the *lpszPath* parameter do not change. The **DlgDirSelect** function does not allow more than one filename to be returned from a list box. The list box must not be a multiple-selection list box. If it is, this function will not return a zero value and *lpszPath* will remain unchanged. **DlgDirSelect** sends LB_GETCURSEL and LB_GETTEXT messages to the list box.
See Also	**DlgDirList, DlgDirListComboBox, DlgDirSelectComboBox, DlgDirSelectEx**

DlgDirSelectComboBox   3.0

BOOL DlgDirSelectComboBox(*hwndDlg*, *lpszPath*, *idComboBox*)
HWND *hwndDlg*;   /* handle of dialog box with list box   */
LPSTR *lpszPath*;   /* address of buffer for path or filename string   */
int *idComboBox*;   /* identifier of combo box   */

The **DlgDirSelectComboBox** function retrieves the current selection from the list box of a combo box. It assumes that the list box has been filled by the **DlgDirList-ComboBox** function and that the selection is a drive letter, a file, or a directory name.

Parameters	*hwndDlg* Identifies the dialog box that contains the combo box. *lpszPath* Points to a 128-byte buffer for the path or filename.

idComboBox
Specifies the integer identifier of the combo box in the dialog box.

Return Value   The return value is nonzero if the function is successful. Otherwise, it is zero.

Comments   The **DlgDirSelectComboBox** function does not allow more than one selection to be returned from a combo box.

If the current selection is a directory name or drive letter, **DlgDirSelect-ComboBox** removes the enclosing brackets (and hyphens, for drive letters) so that the name or letter is ready to be inserted into a new path or filename. If there is no selection, the contents of buffer pointed to by the *lpszPath* parameter do not change.

DlgDirSelectComboBox sends CB_GETCURSEL and CB_GETLBTEXT messages to the combo box.

See Also   **DlgDirList, DlgDirListComboBox, DlgDirSelect, DlgDirSelectComboBoxEx, DlgDirSelectEx**

DlgDirSelectComboBoxEx   3.0

BOOL DlgDirSelectComboBoxEx(*hwndDlg*, *lpszPath*, *cbPath*, *idComboBox*)
HWND *hwndDlg*;   /* handle of dialog box with list box   */
LPSTR *lpszPath*;   /* address of buffer for path string   */
int *cbPath*;   /* number of bytes in path string   */
int *idComboBox*;   /* identifier of combo box   */

The **DlgDirSelectComboBoxEx** function retrieves the current selection from the list box of a combo box. The list box should have been filled by the **DlgDirList-ComboBox** function, and the selection should be a drive letter, a file, or a directory name.

Parameters   *hwndDlg*
Identifies the dialog box that contains the combo box.

lpszPath
Points to a buffer that receives the selected path or filename.

cbPath
Specifies the length, in bytes, of the path or filename pointed to by the *lpszPath* parameter. This value should not be larger than 128.

idComboBox
Specifies the integer identifier of the combo box in the dialog box.

Return Value   The return value is nonzero if the current combo box selection is a directory name. Otherwise, it is zero.

Comments   The **DlgDirSelectComboBoxEx** function does not allow more than one filename to be returned from a combo box.

If the current selection is a directory name or drive letter, **DlgDirSelect-ComboBoxEx** removes the enclosing square brackets (and hyphens, for drive letters) so that the name or letter is ready to be inserted into a new path or filename. If there is no selection, the contents of buffer pointed to by the *lpszPath* parameter do not change.

DlgDirSelectComboBoxEx sends CB_GETCURSEL and CB_GETLBTEXT messages to the combo box.

See Also   **DlgDirList**, **DlgDirListComboBox**, **DlgDirSelect**, **DlgDirSelectEx**, **DlgDirSelectComboBox**

DlgDirSelectEx   2.x

BOOL DlgDirSelectEx(*hwndDlg*, *lpszPath*, *cbPath*, *idListBox*)
HWND *hwndDlg*;   /* handle of dialog box with list box   */
LPSTR *lpszPath*;   /* address of buffer for path string   */
int *cbPath*;   /* number of bytes in path string   */
int *idListBox*;   /* identifier of list box   */

The **DlgDirSelectEx** function retrieves the current selection from a list box. The specified list box should have been filled by the **DlgDirList** function, and the selection should be a drive letter, a file, or a directory name.

Parameters   *hwndDlg*
                         Identifies the dialog box that contains the list box.

                         lpszPath
                         Points to a buffer that receives the selected path or filename.

                         cbPath
                         Specifies the length, in bytes, of the path or filename pointed to by the *lpszPath* parameter. This value should not be larger than 128.

                         idListBox
                         Specifies the integer identifier of a list box in the dialog box.

Return Value   The return value is nonzero if the current list box selection is a directory name. Otherwise, it is zero.

Comments   If the current selection is a directory name or drive letter, **DlgDirSelectEx** removes the enclosing square brackets (and hyphens, for drive letters) so that the name or letter is ready to be inserted into a new path or filename. If there is no selection, the contents of buffer pointed to by the *lpszPath* parameter do not change.

The **DlgDirSelectEx** function does not allow more than one filename to be returned from a list box.

The list box must not be a multiple-selection list box. If it is, this function will not return a zero value and *lpszPath* will remain unchanged.

DlgDirSelectEx sends LB_GETCURSEL and LB_GETTEXT messages to the list box.

See Also   **DlgDirList, DlgDirListComboBox, DlgDirSelect, DlgDirSelectComboBox**

DOS3Call   3.0

The **DOS3Call** function allows an application to call an MS-DOS Interrupt 21h function. **DOS3Call** can be called only from assembly-language routines. It is exported from KRNL286.EXE and KRNL386.EXE and is not defined in any Windows header or include files.

Parameters   Registers must be set up as required by the desired Interrupt 21h function before the application calls the **DOS3Call** function.

Return Value   The register contents are preserved as they are returned by the Interrupt 21h function.

Comments   Applications should use this function instead of a directly coded MS-DOS Interrupt 21h function. The **DOS3Call** function runs somewhat faster than the equivalent MS-DOS Interrupt 21h function running in Windows.

Example   The following example shows how to prototype the **DOS3Call** function in C:

```
extern void FAR PASCAL DOS3Call(void);
```

To declare the **DOS3Call** function in an assembly-language routine, an application could use the following line:

```
extrn DOS3CALL: far
```

If the application includes CMACROS.INC, the function is declared as follows:

```
extrnFP DOS3Call
```

The following example is a typical use of the **DOS3Call** function:

```
extrn DOS3CALL: far
            .
            .
            .
      ; set registers

      mov     ah, DOSFUNC     ;DOSFUNC = Int 21h function number
      cCall   DOS3Call
```

DPtoLP

BOOL DPtoLP(*hdc*, *lppt*, *cPoints*)
HDC *hdc*;   /* handle of device context   */
POINT FAR* *lppt*;   /* address of array with points */
int *cPoints*;   /* number of points in array   */

The **DPtoLP** function converts device coordinates (points) into logical coordinates.

Parameters

hdc
Identifies the device context.

lppt
Points to an array of **POINT** structures. Each coordinate in each structure is mapped into the logical coordinate system for the current device context. The **POINT** structure has the following form:

```
typedef struct tagPOINT {   /* pt */
    int x;
    int y;
} POINT;
```

For a full description of this structure, see the *Microsoft Windows Programmer's Reference, Volume 3*.

cPoints
Specifies the number of points in the array.

Return Value

The return value is nonzero if the function is successful. Otherwise, it is zero.

Comments   The conversion depends on the current mapping mode and the settings of the
                      origins and extents for the device's window and viewport.

Example   The following example sets the mapping mode to MM_LOENGLISH, and then
                      calls the **DPtoLP** function to convert the coordinates of a rectangle into logical
                      coordinates:

```
RECT rc;

SetMapMode(hdc, MM_LOENGLISH);
SetRect(&rc, 100, 100, 200, 200);
DPtoLP(hdc, (LPPOINT) &rc, 2);
```

See Also   **LPtoDP**

DragAcceptFiles   3.1

#include <shellapi.h>

void DragAcceptFiles(*hwnd, fAccept*)
HWND *hwnd*;   /* handle of the registering window   */
BOOL *fAccept*;   /* flag for whether dropped files are accepted   */

                      The **DragAcceptFiles** function registers whether a given window accepts dropped
                      files.

Parameters   *hwnd*
                      Identifies the window registering whether it accepts dropped files.

                      fAccept
                      Specifies whether the window specified by the *hwnd* parameter accepts
                      dropped files. An application should set this value to TRUE to accept dropped
                      files or FALSE to discontinue accepting dropped files.

Return Value   This function does not return a value.

Comments   When an application calls **DragAcceptFiles** with *fAccept* set to TRUE, Windows
                      File Manager (WINFILE.EXE) sends the specified window a WM_DROPFILES
                      message each time the user drops a file in that window.

DragFinish

#include <shellapi.h>

void DragFinish(*hDrop***)**
HDROP *hDrop*;   /* handle of memory to free   */

> The **DragFinish** function releases memory that Windows allocated for use in transferring filenames to the application.

Parameters   *hDrop*
> Identifies the internal data structure that describes dropped files. This handle is passed to the application in the *wParam* parameter of the WM_DROPFILES message.

Return Value   This function does not return a value.

DragQueryFile

#include <shellapi.h>

UINT DragQueryFile(*hDrop***,** *iFile***,** *lpszFile***,** *cb***)**
HDROP *hDrop*;   /* handle of structure for dropped files   */
UINT *iFile*;   /* index of file to query   */
LPSTR *lpszFile*;   /* address of buffer for returned filename   */
UINT *cb*;   /* size of buffer for filename   */

> The **DragQueryFile** function retrieves the number of dropped files and their filenames.

Parameters   *hDrop*
> Identifies the internal data structure containing filenames for the dropped files. This handle is passed to the application in the *wParam* parameter of the WM_DROPFILES message.

> *iFile*
> Specifies the index of the file to query. The index of the first file is 0. If the value of the *iFile* parameter is −1, **DragQueryFile** returns the number of files dropped. If the value of the *iFile* parameter is between zero and the total number of files dropped, **DragQueryFile** copies the filename corresponding to that value to the buffer pointed to by the *lpszFile* parameter.

lpszFile

Points to a null-terminated string that contains the filename of a dropped file when the function returns. If this parameter is NULL and the *iFile* parameter specifies the index for the name of a dropped file, **DragQueryFile** returns the required size, in bytes, of the buffer for that filename.

cb

Specifies the size, in bytes, of the *lpszFile* buffer.

Return Value

When the function copies a filename to the *lpszFile* buffer, the return value is the number of bytes copied. If the *iFile* parameter is 0xFFFF, the return value is the number of dropped files. If *iFile* is between zero and the total number of dropped files and if *lpszFile* is NULL, the return value is the required size of the *lpszFile* buffer.

See Also

DragQueryPoint

DragQueryPoint

3.1

#include <shellapi.h>

BOOL DragQueryPoint(*hDrop*, *lppt*)
HDROP *hDrop*;   /* handle of structure for dropped file   */
POINT FAR* *lppt*;   /* address of structure for cursor coordinates   */

The **DragQueryPoint** function retrieves the window coordinates of the cursor when a file is dropped.

Parameters

hDrop

Identifies the internal data structure that describes the dropped file. This structure is returned in the *wParam* parameter of the WM_DROPFILES message.

lppt

Points to a **POINT** structure that the function fills with the coordinates of the position at which the cursor was located when the file was dropped. The **POINT** structure has the following form:

```
typedef struct tagPOINT {   /* pt */
    int x;
    int y;
} POINT;
```

For a full description of this structure, see the *Microsoft Windows Programmer's Reference, Volume 3*.

Return Value   The return value is nonzero if the file is dropped in the client area of the window. Otherwise, it is zero.

Comments   The **DragQueryPoint** function fills the **POINT** structure with the coordinates of the position at which the cursor was located when the user released the left mouse button. The window for which coordinates are returned is the window that received the WM_DROPFILES message.

See Also   **DragQueryFile**

DrawFocusRect   `3.0`

void DrawFocusRect(*hdc*, *lprc*)
HDC *hdc*;   /* handle of device context   */
const RECT FAR* *lprc*;   /* address of structure with rectangle   */

The **DrawFocusRect** function draws a rectangle in the style used to indicate that the rectangle has the focus.

Parameters   *hdc*
Identifies the device context.

lprc
Points to a **RECT** structure that contains the logical coordinates of the rectangle. The **RECT** structure has the following form:

```
typedef struct tagRECT {    /* rc */
    int left;
    int top;
    int right;
    int bottom;
} RECT;
```

For a full description of this structure, see the *Microsoft Windows Programmer's Reference, Volume 3*.

Return Value   This function does not return a value.

Comments   Because this is an XOR function, calling it a second time and specifying the same rectangle removes the rectangle from the screen.

The rectangle this function draws cannot be scrolled. To scroll an area containing a rectangle drawn by this function, call **DrawFocusRect** to remove the rectangle from the screen, scroll the area, and then call **DrawFocusRect** to draw the rectangle in the new position.

See Also   **FrameRect**

DrawIcon   2.x

BOOL DrawIcon(*hdc, x, y, hicon*)
HDC *hdc*;	/* handle of device context	*/
int *x*;	/* x-coordinate of upper-left corner	*/
int *y*;	/* y-coordinate of upper-left corner	*/
HICON *hicon*;	/* handle of icon to draw	*/

The **DrawIcon** function draws an icon on the given device. The **DrawIcon** function places the icon's upper-left corner at the specified location.

Parameters   *hdc*
                     Identifies the device context for a window.

                     x
                     Specifies the logical x-coordinate of the upper-left corner of the icon.

                     y
                     Specifies the logical y-coordinate of the upper-left corner of the icon.

                     hicon
                     Identifies the icon to be drawn.

Return Value   The return value is nonzero if the function is successful. Otherwise, it is zero.

Comments   The icon resource must have been loaded by using the **LoadIcon** function. The MM_TEXT mapping mode must be selected before using this function.

See Also   **GetMapMode, LoadIcon, SetMapMode**

DrawMenuBar

void DrawMenuBar(*hwnd*)
HWND *hwnd*;   /* handle of window with menu bar to redraw   */

> The **DrawMenuBar** function redraws the menu bar of the given window. If a menu bar is changed after Windows has created the window, an application should call this function to draw the changed menu bar.

Parameters

hwnd
> Identifies the window whose menu must be redrawn.

Return Value   This function does not return a value.

DrawText

int DrawText(*hdc, lpsz, cb, lprc, fuFormat*)
HDC *hdc*;   /* handle of device context   */
LPCSTR *lpsz*;   /* address of string to draw   */
int *cb*;   /* string length   */
RECT FAR* *lprc*;   /* address of structure with formatting dimensions   */
UINT *fuFormat*;   /* text-drawing flags   */

> The **DrawText** function draws formatted text into a given rectangle. It formats text by expanding tabs into appropriate spaces, aligning text to the left, right, or center of the rectangle, and breaking text into lines that fit within the rectangle.
>
> The **DrawText** function uses the device context's selected font, text color, and background color to draw the text. Unless the DT_NOCLIP format is specified, **DrawText** clips the text so that the text does not appear outside the given rectangle. All formatting is assumed to have multiple lines unless the DT_SINGLELINE format is specified.

Parameters

hdc
> Identifies the device context. This cannot be a metafile device context.

lpsz
> Points to the string to be drawn. If the *cb* parameter is −1, the string must be null-terminated.

cb

Specifies the number of bytes in the string. If this parameter is −1, then the *lpsz* parameter is assumed to be a long pointer to a null-terminated string and **DrawText** computes the character count automatically.

lprc

Points to a **RECT** structure that contains the logical coordinates of the upper-left and lower-right corners of the rectangle in which the text is to be formatted. The **RECT** structure has the following form:

```
typedef struct tagRECT {    /* rc */
    int left;
    int top;
    int right;
    int bottom;
} RECT;
```

For a full description of this structure, see the *Microsoft Windows Programmer's Reference, Volume 3*.

fuFormat

Specifies an array of flags that determine how to draw the text. This parameter can be a combination of the following values:

Value	Meaning
DT_BOTTOM	Specifies bottom-aligned text. This value must be combined with DT_SINGLELINE.
DT_CALCRECT	Determines the width and height of the rectangle. If there are multiple lines of text, **DrawText** will use the width of the rectangle pointed to by the *lprc* parameter and extend the base of the rectangle to bound the last line of text. If there is only one line of text, **DrawText** will modify the right side of the rectangle so that it bounds the last character in the line. In either case, **DrawText** returns the height of the formatted text but does not draw the text.
DT_CENTER	Centers text horizontally.
DT_EXPANDTABS	Expands tab characters. The default number of characters per tab is eight.
DT_EXTERNALLEADING	Includes the font external leading in line height. Normally, external leading is not included in the height of a line of text.
DT_LEFT	Left-aligns text.
DT_NOCLIP	Draws without clipping. **DrawText** is somewhat faster when DT_NOCLIP is used.

Value	Meaning
DT_NOPREFIX	Turns off processing of prefix characters. Normally, **DrawText** interprets the mnemonic & as a directive to underscore the character that follows, and the mnemonic && as a directive to print a single &. By specifying DT_NOPREFIX, this processing is turned off.
DT_RIGHT	Right-aligns text.
DT_SINGLELINE	Specifies single line only. Carriage returns and linefeeds do not break the line.
DT_TABSTOP	Sets tab stops. The high-order byte of the *fuFormat* parameter is the number of characters for each tab. The default number of characters per tab is eight.
DT_TOP	Specifies top-aligned text (single line only).
DT_VCENTER	Specifies vertically centered text (single line only).
DT_WORDBREAK	Specifies word breaking. Lines are automatically broken between words if a word would extend past the edge of the rectangle specified by the *lprc* parameter. A carriage return–linefeed sequence will also break the line.

Note that the DT_CALCRECT, DT_EXTERNALLEADING, DT_INTERNAL, DT_NOCLIP, and DT_NOPREFIX values cannot be used with the DT_TABSTOP value.

Return Value

The return value specifies the height of the text if the function is successful.

Comments

If the selected font is too large for the specified rectangle, the **DrawText** function does not attempt to substitute a smaller font.

If the DT_CALCRECT flag is specified, the **RECT** structure pointed to by the *lprc* parameter will be updated to reflect the width and height needed to draw the text.

If the TA_UPDATECP text-alignment flag has been set (see the **SetTextAlign** function), **DrawText** will display text starting at the current position, rather than at the left of the given rectangle. **DrawText** will not wrap text when the TA_UPDATECP flag has been set (the DT_WORDBREAK flag will have no effect).

The text color must be set by the **SetTextColor** function.

See Also

ExtTextOut, SetTextColor, TabbedTextOut, TextOut

DriverProc

LRESULT CALLBACK DriverProc(*dwDriverIdentifier, hDriver, wMessage, lParam1, lParam2*)
DWORD *dwDriverIdentifier*;   /* identifies installable driver   */
HDRVR *hDriver*;   /* handle of installable driver   */
UINT *wMessage*;   /* message   */
LPARAM *lParam1*;   /* first message parameter   */
LPARAM *lParam2*;   /* second message parameter   */

The **DriverProc** function processes the specified message.

Parameters

dwDriverIdentifier
Specifies an identifier of the installable driver.

hDriver
Identifies the installable driver. This parameter is a unique handle that Windows assigns to the driver.

wMessage
Identifies a message that the driver must process. Following are the messages that Windows or an application can send to an installable driver:

Message	Description
DRV_CLOSE	Notifies the driver that it should decrement (decrease by one) its usage count and unload the driver if the count is zero.
DRV_CONFIGURE	Notifies the driver that it should display a custom-configuration dialog box. (This message should be sent only if the driver returns a nonzero value when the DRV_QUERYCONFIGURE message is processed.)
DRV_DISABLE	Notifies the driver that its allocated memory is about to be freed.
DRV_ENABLE	Notifies the driver that it has been loaded or re-loaded, or that Windows has been enabled.
DRV_FREE	Notifies the driver that it will be discarded.
DRV_INSTALL	Notifies the driver that it has been successfully installed.
DRV_LOAD	Notifies the driver that it has been successfully loaded.
DRV_OPEN	Notifies the driver that it is about to be opened.
DRV_POWER	Notifies the driver that the device's power source is about to be turned off or turned on.
DRV_QUERYCONFIGURE	Determines whether the driver supports the DRV_CONFIGURE message. The message displays a private configuration dialog box.

Message	Description
DRV_REMOVE	Notifies the driver that it is about to be removed from the system.

lParam1
Specifies the first message parameter.

lParam2
Specifies the second message parameter.

Return Value   The return value is nonzero if the function is successful. Otherwise, it is zero.

Comments   The **DriverProc** function is the main function within a Windows installable driver; it is supplied by the driver developer.

When the *wMessage* parameter is DRV_OPEN, *lParam1* is the string following the driver filename from the SYSTEM.INI file and *lParam2* is the value given as the *lParam* parameter in the call to the **OpenDriver** function.

When the *wMessage* parameter is DRV_CLOSE, *lParam1* and *lParam2* are the same values as the *lParam1* and *lParam2* parameters in the call to the **Close-Driver** function.

See Also   **CloseDriver, OpenDriver**

Ellipse

2.x

BOOL Ellipse(*hdc*, *nLeftRect*, *nTopRect*, *nRightRect*, *nBottomRect*)
HDC *hdc*;   /* handle of device context   */
int *nLeftRect*;   /* x-coordinate upper-left corner bounding rectangle   */
int *nTopRect*;   /* y-coordinate upper-left corner bounding rectangle   */
int *nRightRect*;   /* x-coordinate lower-right corner bounding rectangle   */
int *nBottomRect*;   /* y-coordinate lower-right corner bounding rectangle   */

The **Ellipse** function draws an ellipse. The center of the ellipse is the center of the specified bounding rectangle. The ellipse is drawn by using the current pen, and its interior is filled by using the current brush.

If either the width or the height of the bounding rectangle is zero, the function does not draw the ellipse.

Parameters   *hdc*
Identifies the device context.

nLeftRect
Specifies the logical x-coordinate of the upper-left corner of the bounding rectangle.

nTopRect
Specifies the logical y-coordinate of the upper-left corner of the bounding rectangle.

nRightRect
Specifies the logical x-coordinate of the lower-right corner of the bounding rectangle.

nBottomRect
Specifies the logical y-coordinate of the lower-right corner of the bounding rectangle.

Return Value   The return value is nonzero if the function is successful. Otherwise, it is zero.

Comments   The figure drawn by this function extends up to but does not include the right and bottom coordinates. This means that the height of the figure is determined as follows:

nBottomRect – nTopRect

Similarly, the width of the figure is determined as follows:

nRightRect – nLeftRect

Both the width and the height of a rectangle must be greater than 2 units and less than 32,767 units.

See Also   **Arc, Chord**

EmptyClipboard   `2.x`

BOOL EmptyClipboard(void)

The **EmptyClipboard** function empties the clipboard and frees handles to data in the clipboard. It then assigns ownership of the clipboard to the window that currently has the clipboard open.

Parameters   This function has no parameters.

Return Value   The return value is nonzero if the function is successful. Otherwise, it is zero.

Comments   The clipboard must be open when the **EmptyClipboard** function is called.

See Also   **OpenClipboard**

EnableCommNotification   3.1

BOOL EnableCommNotification(*idComDev*, *hwnd*, *cbWriteNotify*, *cbOutQueue*)
int *idComDev*;   /* communications-device identifier   */
HWND *hwnd*;   /* handle of window receiving messages   */
int *cbWriteNotify*;   /* number of bytes written before notification   */
int *cbOutQueue*;   /* minimum number of bytes in output queue   */

The **EnableCommNotification** function enables or disables
WM_COMMNOTIFY message posting to the given window.

Parameters   *idComDev*
Specifies the communications device that is posting notification messages to
the window identified by the *hwnd* parameter. The **OpenComm** function returns the value for the *idComDev* parameter.

hwnd
Identifies the window whose WM_COMMNOTIFY message posting will be
enabled or disabled. If this parameter is NULL, **EnableCommNotification** disables message posting to the current window.

cbWriteNotify
Indicates the number of bytes the COM driver must write to the application's
input queue before sending a notification message. The message signals the application to read information from the input queue.

cbOutQueue
Indicates the minimum number of bytes in the output queue. When the number
of bytes in the output queue falls below this number, the COM driver sends the
application a notification message, signaling it to write information to the output queue.

Return Value   The return value is nonzero if the function is successful. Otherwise, it is zero, indicating an invalid COM port identifier, a port that is not open, or a function not supported by COMM.DRV.

Comments   If an application specifies −1 for the *cbWriteNotify* parameter, the
WM_COMMNOTIFY message is sent to the specified window for CN_EVENT
and CN_TRANSMIT notifications but not for CN_RECEIVE notifications. If −1

is specified for the *cbOutQueue* parameter, CN_EVENT and CN_RECEIVE notifications are sent but CN_TRANSMIT notifications are not.

If a timeout occurs before as many bytes as specified by the *cbWriteNotify* parameter are written to the input queue, a WM_COMMNOTIFY message is sent with the CN_RECEIVE flag set. When this occurs, another message will not be sent until the number of bytes in the input queue falls below the number specified in the *cbWriteNotify* parameter. Similarly, a WM_COMMNOTIFY message in which the CN_RECEIVE flag is set is sent only when the output queue is larger than the number of bytes specified in the *cbOutQueue* parameter.

The Windows 3.0 version of COMM.DRV does not support this function.

EnableHardwareInput

`2.x`

BOOL EnableHardwareInput(*fEnableInput*)
BOOL *fEnableInput*;   /* for enabling or disabling queuing   */

The **EnableHardwareInput** function enables or disables queuing of mouse and keyboard input.

Parameters   *fEnableInput*
Specifies whether to enable or disable queuing of input. If this parameter is TRUE, keyboard and mouse input are queued. If the parameter is FALSE, keyboard and mouse input are disabled.

Return Value   The return value is nonzero if queuing of input was previously enabled. Otherwise, it is zero.

Comments   This function does not disable input from installable drivers, nor does it disable device drivers.

See Also   **GetInputState**

EnableMenuItem

BOOL EnableMenuItem(*hmenu*, *idEnableItem*, *uEnable*)
HMENU *hmenu*;   /* handle of menu   */
UINT *idEnableItem*;   /* menu-item identifier   */
UINT *uEnable*;   /* action flag   */

The **EnableMenuItem** function enables, disables, or grays (dims) a menu item.

Parameters

hmenu
Identifies the menu.

idEnableItem
Specifies the menu item to be enabled, disabled, or grayed. This parameter can specify pop-up menu items as well as standard menu items. The interpretation of this parameter depends on the value of the *uEnable* parameter.

uEnable
Specifies the action to take. This parameter can be MF_DISABLED, MF_ENABLED, or MF_GRAYED, combined with MF_BYCOMMAND or MF_BYPOSITION. These values have the following meanings:

Value	Meaning
MF_BYCOMMAND	Specifies that the *idEnableItem* parameter gives the menu-item identifier.
MF_BYPOSITION	Specifies that the *idEnableItem* parameter gives the position of the menu item (the first item is at position zero).
MF_DISABLED	Specifies that the menu item is disabled.
MF_ENABLED	Specifies that the menu item is enabled.
MF_GRAYED	Specifies that the menu item is grayed.

Return Value

The return value is 0 if the menu item was previously disabled, 1 if the menu item was previously enabled, and −1 if the menu item does not exist.

Comments

To disable or enable input to a menu bar, see the WM_SYSCOMMAND message.

The **CreateMenu**, **InsertMenu**, **ModifyMenu**, and **LoadMenuIndirect** functions can also set the state (enabled, disabled, or grayed) of a menu item.

Using the MF_BYPOSITION value requires an application to specify the correct menu handle. If the menu handle of the menu bar is specified, a top-level menu item (an item in the menu bar) is affected. To set the state of an item in a pop-up or nested pop-up menu by position, an application must specify the handle of the pop-up menu.

When an application specifies the MF_BYCOMMAND flag, Windows checks all pop-up menu items that are subordinate to the menu identified by the specified menu handle; therefore, unless duplicate menu items are present, specifying the menu handle of the menu bar is sufficient.

See Also   **CheckMenuItem, HiliteMenuItem**

EnableScrollBar   3.1

BOOL EnableScrollBar(*hwnd, fnSBFlags, fuArrowFlags*)
HWND *hwnd*;   /* handle of window or scroll bar   */
int *fnSBFlags*;   /* scroll-bar type flag   */
UINT *fuArrowFlags*;   /* scroll-bar arrow flag   */

The **EnableScrollBar** function enables or disables one or both arrows of a scroll bar.

Parameters   *hwnd*
Identifies a window or a scroll bar, depending on the value of the *fnSBFlags* parameter.

fnSBFlags
Specifies the scroll bar type. This parameter can be one of the following values:

Value	Meaning
SB_BOTH	Enables or disables the arrows of the horizontal and vertical scroll bars associated with the given window. The *hwnd* parameter identifies the window.
SB_CTL	Identifies the scroll bar as a scroll bar control. The *hwnd* parameter must identify a scroll bar control.
SB_HORZ	Enables or disables the arrows of the horizontal scroll bar associated with the given window. The *hwnd* parameter identifies the window.
SB_VERT	Enables or disables the arrows of the vertical scroll bar associated with the given window. The *hwnd* parameter identifies the window.

fuArrowFlags
Specifies whether the scroll bar arrows are enabled or disabled, and which arrows are enabled or disabled. This parameter can be one of the following values:

Value	Meaning
ESB_ENABLE_BOTH	Enables both arrows of a scroll bar.
ESB_DISABLE_LTUP	Disables the left arrow of a horizontal scroll bar, or the up arrow of a vertical scroll bar.

Value	Meaning
ESB_DISABLE_RTDN	Disables the right arrow of a horizontal scroll bar, or the down arrow of a vertical scroll bar.
ESB_DISABLE_BOTH	Disables both arrows of a scroll bar.

Return Value

The return value is nonzero if the arrows are enabled or disabled as specified. Otherwise, it is zero, indicating that the arrows are already in the requested state or that an error occurred.

Example

The following example enables an edit control's vertical scroll bar when the control receives the input focus, and disables the scroll bar when the control loses the focus:

```
case EN_SETFOCUS:
    EnableScrollBar(hwndMLEdit, SB_VERT, ESB_ENABLE_BOTH);
    break;

case EN_KILLFOCUS:
    EnableScrollBar(hwndMLEdit, SB_VERT, ESB_DISABLE_BOTH);
    break;
```

See Also

ShowScrollBar

EnableWindow
2.x

BOOL EnableWindow(*hwnd*, *fEnable*)
HWND *hwnd*;   /* handle of window   */
BOOL *fEnable*;   /* flag for enabling or disabling input   */

The **EnableWindow** function enables or disables mouse and keyboard input to the given window or control. When input is disabled, the window ignores input such as mouse clicks and key presses. When input is enabled, the window processes all input.

Parameters

hwnd
Identifies the window to be enabled or disabled.

fEnable
Specifies whether to enable or disable the window. If this parameter is TRUE, the window is enabled. If the parameter is FALSE, the window is disabled.

Return Value

The return value is nonzero if the window was previously disabled. Otherwise, the return value is zero.

Comments   If the enabled state of the window is changing, a WM_ENABLE message is sent before this function returns. If a window is already disabled, all its child windows are implicitly disabled, although they are not sent a WM_ENABLE message.

A window must be enabled before it can be activated. For example, if an application is displaying a modeless dialog box and has disabled its main window, the application must enable the main window before destroying the dialog box. Otherwise, another window will receive the input focus and be activated. If a child window is disabled, it is ignored when Windows tries to determine which window should receive mouse messages.

By default, a window is enabled when it is created. An application can specify the WS_DISABLED style in the **CreateWindow** or **CreateWindowEx** function to create a window that is initially disabled. After a window has been created, an application can use the **EnableWindow** function to enable or disable the window.

An application can use this function to enable or disable a control in a dialog box. A disabled control cannot receive the input focus, nor can a user access it.

Example   The following example enables a Save push button in a dialog box, depending on whether a user-specified filename exists:

```
static char szFileName[128];

case WM_INITDIALOG:

    /* If a filename is specified, enable the Save push button. */

    EnableWindow(GetDlgItem(hdlg, IDOK),
        (szFileName[0] == '\0' ? FALSE : TRUE));
    return TRUE;
```

See Also   **IsWindowEnabled**

EndDeferWindowPos   3.0

BOOL EndDeferWindowPos(*hdwp***)**
HDWP *hdwp*;   /* handle of internal structure   */

The **EndDeferWindowPos** function simultaneously updates the position and size of one or more windows in a single screen-refresh cycle.

Parameters   *hdwp*
                Identifies an internal structure that contains size and position information for
                one or more windows. This structure is returned by the **BeginDeferWindow-**
                Pos function or by the most recent call to the **DeferWindowPos** function.

Return Value   The return value is nonzero if the function is successful. Otherwise, it is zero.

Comments   This function sends the WM_WINDOWPOSCHANGING and
                WM_WINDOWPOSCHANGED messages to each window identified in the inter-
                nal structure.

See Also   **BeginDeferWindowPos, DeferWindowPos**

EndDialog   `2.x`

void EndDialog(*hwndDlg*, *nResult*)
HWND *hwndDlg*;   /* handle of dialog box   */
int *nResult*;   /* value to return   */

                The **EndDialog** function hides a modal dialog box and causes the **DialogBox** func-
                tion to return.

Parameters   *hwndDlg*
                Identifies the dialog box to be destroyed.

                nResult
                Specifies the value that is returned to the caller of **DialogBox**.

Return Value   This function does not return a value.

Comments   The **EndDialog** function is required to complete processing of a modal dialog box
                created by the **DialogBox** function. An application calls **EndDialog** from within
                the dialog box procedure.

                A dialog box procedure can call **EndDialog** at any time, even during the pro-
                cessing of the WM_INITDIALOG message. If the function is called while
                WM_INITDIALOG is being processed, the dialog box is hidden before it is
                shown and before the input focus is set.

EndDialog does not destroy the dialog box immediately. Instead, it sets a flag that directs Windows to destroy the dialog box when the **DialogBox** function returns.

See Also   **DialogBox**

EndDoc   3.1

int **EndDoc**(*hdc*)
HDC *hdc*;   /* handle of device context   */

The **EndDoc** function ends a print job. This function replaces the ENDDOC printer escape for Windows version 3.1.

Parameters   *hdc*
                        Identifies the device context for the print job.

Return Value   The return value is greater than or equal to zero if the function is successful. Otherwise, it is less than zero.

Comments   An application should call the **EndDoc** function immediately after finishing a successful print job. To terminate a print job because of an error or if the user chooses to cancel the job, an application should call the **AbortDoc** function.

Do not use the **EndDoc** function inside metafiles.

See Also   **AbortDoc, Escape, StartDoc**

EndPage   3.1

int **EndPage**(*hdc*)
HDC *hdc*;   /* handle of device context   */

The **EndPage** function signals the device that the application has finished writing to a page. This function is typically used to direct the driver to advance to a new page.

This function replaces the **NEWFRAME** printer escape for Windows 3.1. Unlike **NEWFRAME**, this function is always called after printing a page.

Parameters   *hdc*
                       Identifies the device context for the print job.

Return Value   The return value is greater than or equal to zero if the function is successful. Otherwise, it is an error value.

Errors   If the function fails, it returns one of the following error values:

Value	Meaning
SP_ERROR	General error.
SP_APPABORT	Job was terminated because the application's print-canceling function returned zero.
SP_USERABORT	User terminated the job by using Windows Print Manager (PRINTMAN.EXE).
SP_OUTOFDISK	Not enough disk space is currently available for spooling, and no more space will become available.
SP_OUTOFMEMORY	Not enough memory is available for spooling.

Comments   The **ResetDC** function can be used to change the device mode, if necessary, after calling the **EndPage** function.

See Also   **Escape**, **ResetDC**, **StartPage**

EndPaint   2.x

void EndPaint(*hwnd*, *lpps*)
HWND *hwnd*;   /* handle of window   */
const PAINTSTRUCT FAR* *lpps*;   /* address of structure for paint data   */

The **EndPaint** function marks the end of painting in the given window. This function is required for each call to the **BeginPaint** function, but only after painting is complete.

Parameters   *hwnd*
                       Identifies the window that has been repainted.

                      lpps
                       Points to a **PAINTSTRUCT** structure that contains the painting information retrieved by the **BeginPaint** function. The **PAINTSTRUCT** structure has the following form:

```
typedef struct tagPAINTSTRUCT {      /* ps */
    HDC  hdc;
    BOOL fErase;
    RECT rcPaint;
    BOOL fRestore;
    BOOL fIncUpdate;
    BYTE rgbReserved[16];
} PAINTSTRUCT;
```

For a full description of this structure, see the *Microsoft Windows Programmer's Reference, Volume 3*.

Return Value   This function does not return a value.

Comments   If the caret was hidden by the **BeginPaint** function, the **EndPaint** function restores the caret to the screen.

See Also   **BeginPaint**

EnumChildProc $\boxed{\textbf{2.x}}$

BOOL CALLBACK EnumChildProc(*hwnd*, *lParam***)**
HWND *hwnd*;   /* handle of child window   */
LPARAM *lParam*;   /* application-defined value   */

The **EnumChildProc** function is an application-defined callback function that receives child window handles as a result of a call to the **EnumChildWindows** function.

Parameters   *hwnd*
Identifies a child window of the parent window specified in the **EnumChildWindows** function.

lParam
Specifies the application-defined value specified in the **EnumChildWindows** function.

Return Value   The callback function must return nonzero to continue enumeration; to stop enumeration, it must return zero.

Comments   The callback function can carry out any desired task.

An application must register this callback function by passing its address to the **EnumChildWindows** function. The **EnumChildProc** function is a placeholder for the application-defined function name. The actual name must be exported by including it in an **EXPORTS** statement in the application's module-definition (.DEF) file.

See Also   **EnumChildWindows**

EnumChildWindows   2.x

BOOL EnumChildWindows(*hwndParent, wndenmprc, lParam*)
HWND *hwndParent*;   /* handle of parent window   */
WNDENUMPROC *wndenmprc*;   /* address of callback function */
LPARAM *lParam*;   /* application-defined value   */

The **EnumChildWindows** function enumerates the child windows that belong to the given parent window by passing the handle of each child window, in turn, to an application-defined callback function. **EnumChildWindows** continues until the last child window is enumerated or the callback function returns zero.

Parameters   *hwndParent*
                    Identifies the parent window whose child windows are to be enumerated.

                    wndenmprc
                    Specifies the procedure-instance address of the application-supplied callback function. The address must have been created by using the **MakeProcInstance** function. For more information about the callback function, see the description of the **EnumChildProc** callback function.

                    lParam
                    Specifies a 32-bit application-defined value to pass to the callback function.

Return Value   The return value is nonzero if the function is successful. Otherwise, it is zero.

Comments   This function does not enumerate top-level windows that belong to the parent window.

                    If a child window has created child windows of its own, the function enumerates those windows as well.

                    A child window that is moved or repositioned in the Z-order during the enumeration process will be properly enumerated. The function will not enumerate a child window that is destroyed before it is enumerated or that is created during the enumeration process. These measures ensure that the **EnumChildWindows** function is reliable even when the application causes odd side effects, whereas an application that uses a **GetWindow** loop risks being caught in an infinite loop or referencing a handle to a window that has been destroyed.

See Also   **EnumChildProc, MakeProcInstance**

EnumClipboardFormats   2.x

UINT EnumClipboardFormats(*uFormat*)
UINT *uFormat*;   /* known clipboard format   */

The **EnumClipboardFormats** function enumerates the formats found in a list of available formats that belong to the clipboard. Each call to this function specifies a known available format; the function returns the format that appears next in the list.

Parameters   *uFormat*
Specifies a known format. If this parameter is zero, the function returns the first format in the list.

Return Value   The return value specifies the next known clipboard data format if the function is successful. It is zero if the *uFormat* parameter specifies the last format in the list of available formats, or if the clipboard is not open.

Comments   Before it enumerates the formats by using the **EnumClipboardFormats** function, an application must open the clipboard by using the **OpenClipboard** function.

An application puts (or "donates") alternative formats for the same data into the clipboard in the same order that the enumerator uses when returning them to the pasting application. The pasting application should use the first format enumerated in the list that it can handle. This gives the donor application an opportunity to recommend formats that involve the least loss of data.

See Also   **CountClipboardFormats, GetClipboardFormatName, GetPriorityClipboard-Format, IsClipboardFormatAvailable, OpenClipboard, RegisterClipboard-Format**

EnumFontFamilies

int **EnumFontFamilies**(*hdc*, *lpszFamily*, *fntenmprc*, *lParam*)
HDC *hdc*;   /* handle of device context   */
LPCSTR *lpszFamily*;   /* address of font-family name   */
FONTENUMPROC *fntenmprc*;   /* address of callback function   */
LPARAM *lParam*;   /* application-defined data   */

The **EnumFontFamilies** function enumerates the fonts in a specified font family that are available on a given device. **EnumFontFamilies** continues until there are no more fonts or the callback function returns zero.

Parameters

hdc
Identifies the device context.

lpszFamily
Points to a null-terminated string that specifies the family name of the desired fonts. If this parameter is NULL, the **EnumFontFamilies** function selects and enumerates one font from each available font family.

fntenmprc
Specifies the procedure-instance address of the application-defined callback function. The address must be created by the **MakeProcInstance** function. For more information about the callback function, see the description of the **Enum-FontFamProc** callback function.

lParam
Specifies a 32-bit application-defined value that is passed to the callback function along with the font information.

Return Value

The return value specifies the last value returned by the callback function, if the function is successful. This value depends on which font families are available for the given device.

Comments

The **EnumFontFamilies** function differs from the **EnumFonts** function in that it retrieves the style names associated with a TrueType font. Using **EnumFont-Families**, an application can retrieve information about unusual font styles (for example, Outline) that cannot be enumerated by using the **EnumFonts** function. Applications should use **EnumFontFamilies** instead of **EnumFonts**.

For each font having the font name specified by the *lpszFamily* parameter, the **EnumFontFamilies** function retrieves information about that font and passes it to the function pointed to by the *fntenmprc* parameter. The application-supplied callback function can process the font information, as necessary.

Example

The following example uses the **MakeProcInstance** function to create a pointer to the callback function for the **EnumFontFamilies** function. The **FreeProcInstance** function is called when enumeration is complete. Because the second parameter is NULL, **EnumFontFamilies** enumerates one font from each family that is available in the given device context. The aFontCount variable points to an array that is used inside the callback function.

```
FONTENUMPROC lpEnumFamCallBack;
int aFontCount[] = { 0, 0, 0 };

lpEnumFamCallBack = (FONTENUMPROC) MakeProcInstance(
    (FARPROC) EnumFamCallBack, hAppInstance);
EnumFontFamilies(hdc, NULL, lpEnumFamCallBack, (LPARAM) aFontCount);
FreeProcInstance((FARPROC) lpEnumFamCallBack);
```

See Also   **EnumFonts, EnumFontFamProc**

EnumFontFamProc   `3.1`

int CALLBACK EnumFontFamProc(*lpnlf*, *lpntm*, *FontType*, *lParam*)
LOGFONT FAR* *lpnlf*;   /* address of structure with logical-font data   */
TEXTMETRIC FAR* *lpntm*;   /* address of structure with physical-font data   */
int *FontType*;   /* type of font   */
LPARAM *lParam*;   /* address of application-defined data   */

The **EnumFontFamProc** function is an application-defined callback function that retrieves information about available fonts.

Parameters   *lpnlf*
Points to a NEWLOGFONT structure that contains information about the logical attributes of the font. This structure is locally-defined and is identical to the Windows **LOGFONT** structure except for two new members. The NEWLOGFONT structure has the following form:

```
struct tagNEWLOGFONT {                    /* nlf */
    int   lfHeight;
    int   lfWidth;
    int   lfEscapement;
    int   lfOrientation;
    int   lfWeight;
    BYTE  lfItalic;
    BYTE  lfUnderline;
    BYTE  lfStrikeOut;
```

```
        BYTE    lfCharSet;
        BYTE    lfOutPrecision;
        BYTE    lfClipPrecision;
        BYTE    lfQuality;
        BYTE    lfPitchAndFamily;
        BYTE    lfFaceName[LF_FACESIZE];
        BYTE    lfFullName[2 * LF_FACESIZE]; /* TrueType only */
        BYTE    lfStyle[LF_FACESIZE];        /* TrueType only */
} NEWLOGFONT;
```

The **lfFullName** and **lfStyle** members are appended to a **LOGFONT** structure when a TrueType font is enumerated in the **EnumFontFamProc** function.

The **lfFullName** member is a character array specifying the full name for the font. This name contains the font name and style name.

The **lfStyle** member is a character array specifying the style name for the font.

For example, when bold italic Arial® is enumerated, the last three members of the NEWLOGFONT structure contain the following strings:

lfFaceName = "Arial";
lfFullName = "Arial Bold Italic";
lfStyle = "Bold Italic";

For a full description of the **LOGFONT** structure, see the *Microsoft Windows Programmer's Reference, Volume 3.*

lpntm

Points to a **NEWTEXTMETRIC** structure that contains information about the physical attributes of the font, if the font is a TrueType font. If the font is not a TrueType font, this parameter points to a **TEXTMETRIC** structure.

The **NEWTEXTMETRIC** structure has the following form:

```
typedef struct tagNEWTEXTMETRIC {    /* ntm */
    int    tmHeight;
    int    tmAscent;
    int    tmDescent;
    int    tmInternalLeading;
    int    tmExternalLeading;
    int    tmAveCharWidth;
    int    tmMaxCharWidth;
    int    tmWeight;
    BYTE   tmItalic;
    BYTE   tmUnderlined;
    BYTE   tmStruckOut;
    BYTE   tmFirstChar;
    BYTE   tmLastChar;
    BYTE   tmDefaultChar;
    BYTE   tmBreakChar;
    BYTE   tmPitchAndFamily;
```

```
         BYTE   tmCharSet;
         int    tmOverhang;
         int    tmDigitizedAspectX;
         int    tmDigitizedAspectY;
         DWORD  ntmFlags;
         UINT   ntmSizeEM;
         UINT   ntmCellHeight;
         UINT   ntmAvgWidth;
    } NEWTEXTMETRIC;
```

The **TEXTMETRIC** structure is identical to **NEWTEXTMETRIC** except that it does not include the last four members. For a full description of these structures, see the *Microsoft Windows Programmer's Reference, Volume 3.*

FontType
Specifies the type of the font. This parameter can be a combination of the following masks:

DEVICE_FONTTYPE
RASTER_FONTTYPE
TRUETYPE_FONTTYPE

lParam
Points to the application-defined data passed by **EnumFontFamilies**.

Return Value   This function must return a nonzero value to continue enumeration; to stop enumeration, it must return zero.

Comments   An application must register this callback function by passing its address to the **EnumFontFamilies** function. The **EnumFontFamProc** function is a placeholder for the application-defined function name. The actual name must be exported by including it in an **EXPORTS** statement in the application's module-definition (.DEF) file.

The AND (&) operator can be used with the RASTER_FONTTYPE, DEVICE_FONTTYPE, and TRUETYPE_FONTTYPE constants to determine the font type. If the RASTER_FONTTYPE bit is set, the font is a raster font. If the TRUETYPE_FONTTYPE bit is set, the font is a TrueType font. If neither bit is set, the font is a vector font. A third mask, DEVICE_FONTTYPE, is set when a device (for example, a laser printer) supports downloading TrueType fonts; it is zero if the font is not a device font. (Any device can support device fonts, including display adapters and dot-matrix printers.) An application can also use the DEVICE_FONTTYPE mask to distinguish GDI-supplied raster fonts from device-supplied fonts. GDI can simulate bold, italic, underline, and strikeout attributes for GDI-supplied raster fonts, but not for device-supplied fonts.

See Also   **EnumFontFamilies**, **EnumFonts**

EnumFonts

int **EnumFonts**(*hdc*, *lpszFace*, *fntenmprc*, *lParam*)
HDC *hdc*;   /* handle of device context   */
LPCSTR *lpszFace*;   /* address of font name   */
FONTENUMPROC *fntenmprc*;   /* address of callback function */
LPARAM *lParam*;   /* application-defined data   */

The **EnumFonts** function enumerates the fonts available for a given device. This function is provided for backwards compatibility with earlier versions of Windows; current applications should use the **EnumFontFamilies** function.

EnumFonts continues until there are no more fonts or the callback function returns zero.

Parameters

hdc
Identifies the device context.

lpszFace
Points to a null-terminated string that specifies the names of the requested fonts. If this parameter is NULL, the **EnumFonts** function randomly selects and enumerates one font from each available typeface.

fntenmprc
Specifies the procedure-instance address of the application-defined callback function. The address must be created by the **MakeProcInstance** function. For more information about the callback function, see the description of the **EnumFontsProc** callback function.

lParam
Specifies a 32-bit application-defined value that is passed to the callback function along with the font information.

Return Value

The return value specifies the last value returned by the callback function and is defined by the user.

Comments

The **EnumFonts** function retrieves information about the specified font and passes it to the function pointed to by the *fntenmprc* parameter. The application-supplied callback function can process the font information, as necessary.

If the device is capable of text transformations (scaling, italicizing, and so on), only the base font will be enumerated. The user must know the device's text-transformation abilities to determine which additional fonts are available directly from the device. The graphics device interface (GDI) can simulate the bold, italic, underlined, and strikeout attributes for any GDI-based font.

The **EnumFonts** function enumerates fonts from the GDI internal table only. This does not include fonts that are generated by a device, such as fonts that are transformations of fonts from the internal table. The **GetDeviceCaps** function can be used to determine which transformations a device can perform. This information is available by using the TEXTCAPS index.

GDI can scale GDI-based raster fonts by one to five units horizontally and one to eight units vertically, unless PROOF_QUALITY is being used.

Example

The following example uses the **MakeProcInstance** function to create a pointer to the callback function for the **EnumFonts** function. The **FreeProcInstance** function is called when enumeration is complete. Because the second parameter is "Arial", **EnumFonts** enumerates the Arial fonts available in the given device context. The cArial variable is passed to the callback function.

```
FONTENUMPROC lpEnumFontsCallBack;
int cArial = 0;

lpEnumFontsCallBack = (FONTENUMPROC) MakeProcInstance(
    (FARPROC) EnumFontsCallBack, hAppInstance);
EnumFonts(hdc, "Arial", lpEnumFontsCallBack, (LPARAM) &cArial);
FreeProcInstance((FARPROC) lpEnumFontsCallBack);
```

See Also

EnumFontFamilies, EnumFontsProc

EnumFontsProc

3.1

int CALLBACK EnumFontsProc(lplf**,** lpntm**,** FontType**,** lpData**)**
LOGFONT FAR* lplf;   /* address of logical-font data structure   */
NEWTEXTMETRIC FAR* lpntm;   /* address of physical-font data structure   */
int FontType;   /* type of font   */
LPARAM lpData;   /* address of application-defined data   */

The **EnumFontsProc** function is an application-defined callback function that processes font data from the **EnumFonts** function.

Parameters

lplf
Points to a **LOGFONT** structure that contains information about the logical attributes of the font. The **LOGFONT** structure has the following form:

```
typedef struct tagLOGFONT {     /* lf */
    int   lfHeight;
    int   lfWidth;
    int   lfEscapement;
    int   lfOrientation;
    int   lfWeight;
    BYTE  lfItalic;
```

```
                    BYTE    lfUnderline;
                    BYTE    lfStrikeOut;
                    BYTE    lfCharSet;
                    BYTE    lfOutPrecision;
                    BYTE    lfClipPrecision;
                    BYTE    lfQuality;
                    BYTE    lfPitchAndFamily;
                    BYTE    lfFaceName[LF_FACESIZE];
                } LOGFONT;
```

For a full description of this structure, see the *Microsoft Windows Programmer's Reference, Volume 3.*

lpntm

Points to a **NEWTEXTMETRIC** structure that contains information about the physical attributes of the font, if the font is a TrueType font. If the font is not a TrueType font, this parameter points to a **TEXTMETRIC** structure.

The **NEWTEXTMETRIC** structure has the following form:

```
typedef struct tagNEWTEXTMETRIC {    /* ntm */
    int     tmHeight;
    int     tmAscent;
    int     tmDescent;
    int     tmInternalLeading;
    int     tmExternalLeading;
    int     tmAveCharWidth;
    int     tmMaxCharWidth;
    int     tmWeight;
    BYTE    tmItalic;
    BYTE    tmUnderlined;
    BYTE    tmStruckOut;
    BYTE    tmFirstChar;
    BYTE    tmLastChar;
    BYTE    tmDefaultChar;
    BYTE    tmBreakChar;
    BYTE    tmPitchAndFamily;
    BYTE    tmCharSet;
    int     tmOverhang;
    int     tmDigitizedAspectX;
    int     tmDigitizedAspectY;
    DWORD   ntmFlags;
    UINT    ntmSizeEM;
    UINT    ntmCellHeight;
    UINT    ntmAvgWidth;
} NEWTEXTMETRIC;
```

The **TEXTMETRIC** structure is identical to **NEWTEXTMETRIC** except that it does not include the last four members. For a full description of these structures, see the *Microsoft Windows Programmer's Reference, Volume 3.*

FontType

Specifies the type of the font. This parameter can be a combination of the following masks:

DEVICE_FONTTYPE
RASTER_FONTTYPE
TRUETYPE_FONTTYPE

lpData

Points to the application-defined data passed by the **EnumFonts** function.

Return Value

This function must return a nonzero value to continue enumeration; to stop enumeration, it must return zero.

Comments

An application must register this callback function by passing its address to the **EnumFonts** function. The **EnumFontsProc** function is a placeholder for the application-defined function name. The actual name must be exported by including it in an **EXPORTS** statement in the application's module-definition (.DEF) file.

The AND (&) operator can be used with the RASTER_FONTTYPE, DEVICE_FONTTYPE, and TRUETYPE_FONTTYPE constants to determine the font type. If the RASTER_FONTTYPE bit is set, the font is a raster font. If the TRUETYPE_FONTTYPE bit is set, the font is a TrueType font. If neither bit is set, the font is a vector font. A third mask, DEVICE_FONTTYPE, is set when a device (for example, a laser printer) supports downloading TrueType fonts; it is zero if the device is a display adapter, dot-matrix printer, or other raster device. An application can also use the DEVICE_FONTTYPE mask to distinguish GDI-supplied raster fonts from device-supplied fonts. GDI can simulate bold, italic, underline, and strikeout attributes for GDI-supplied raster fonts, but not for device-supplied fonts.

See Also

EnumFonts, EnumFontFamilies

EnumMetaFile

2.x

BOOL EnumMetaFile(*hdc*, *hmf*, *mfenmprc*, *lParam***)**
HDC *hdc*;   /* handle of device context   */
HLOCAL *hmf*;   /* handle of metafile   */
MFENUMPROC *mfenmprc*;   /* address of callback function   */
LPARAM *lParam*;   /* application-defined data   */

The **EnumMetaFile** function enumerates the metafile records in a given metafile. **EnumMetaFile** continues until there are no more graphics device interface (GDI) calls or the callback function returns zero.

Parameters

hdc
Identifies the device context associated with the metafile.

hmf
Identifies the metafile.

Note The **HLOCAL** type for this parameter is incorrect in the WINDOWS.H file. The type of this parameter is actually **HMETAFILE**. Developers should cast this parameter to an **HLOCAL** type to avoid compiler warnings.

mfenmprc
Specifies the procedure-instance address of the application-supplied callback function. The address must be created by using the **MakeProcInstance** function. For more information about the callback function, see the description of the **EnumMetaFileProc** callback function.

lParam
Specifies a 32-bit application-defined value that is passed to the callback function along with the metafile information.

Return Value

The return value is nonzero if the callback function enumerates all the GDI calls in a metafile. Otherwise, it is zero.

Comments

The **EnumMetaFile** function retrieves metafile records and passes them to a callback function. An application can modify the metafile record inside the callback function. The application can also use the **PlayMetaFileRecord** function inside the callback function; this is useful for very large metafiles, when using the **PlayMetaFile** function might be time-consuming.

Example

The following example creates a dashed green pen and passes it to the callback function for the **EnumMetaFile** function. If the first element in the array of object handles is a handle, that handle is replaced by the handle of the green pen before the **PlayMetaFileRecord** function is called. (For this example, it is assumed that the table of object handles contains only one handle and that it is the handle of a pen.)

```
MFENUMPROC lpEnumMetaProc;
HPEN hpenGreen;

lpEnumMetaProc = (MFENUMPROC) MakeProcInstance(
    (FARPROC) EnumMetaFileProc, hAppInstance);
hpenGreen = CreatePen(PS_DASH, 1, RGB(0, 255, 0));
EnumMetaFile(hdc, hmf, lpEnumMetaProc, (LPARAM) &hpenGreen);
FreeProcInstance((FARPROC) lpEnumMetaProc);
DeleteObject(hpenGreen);
    .
    .
    .
```

```
int FAR PASCAL EnumMetaFileProc(HDC hdc, HANDLETABLE FAR* lpHTable,
    METARECORD FAR* lpMFR, int cObj, BYTE FAR* lpClientData)
{
    if (lpHTable->objectHandle[0] != 0)
        lpHTable->objectHandle[0] = *(HPEN FAR *) lpClientData;
    PlayMetaFileRecord(hdc, lpHTable, lpMFR, cObj);

    return 1;
}
```

See Also   **EnumMetaFileProc, MakeProcInstance, PlayMetaFile, PlayMetaFileRecord**

EnumMetaFileProc   3.1

int CALLBACK EnumMetaFileProc(*hdc, lpht, lpmr, cObj, lParam*)
HDC *hdc*;   /* handle of device context   */
HANDLETABLE FAR* *lpht*;   /* address of table of object handles   */
METARECORD FAR* *lpmr*;   /* address of metafile record   */
int *cObj*;   /* number of objects in handle table   */
LPARAM *lParam*;   /* address of application-defined data   */

The **EnumMetaFileProc** function is an application-defined callback function that processes metafile data from the **EnumMetaFile** function.

Parameters   *hdc*
                     Identifies the special device context that contains the metafile.

                     lpht
                     Points to a table of handles associated with the objects (pens, brushes, and so on) in the metafile.

                     lpmr
                     Points to a metafile record contained in the metafile.

                     cObj
                     Specifies the number of objects with associated handles in the handle table.

                     lParam
                     Points to the application-defined data.

Return Value   The callback function must return a nonzero value to continue enumeration; to stop enumeration, it must return zero.

Comments   An application must register this callback function by passing its address to the **EnumMetaFile** function.

The **EnumMetaFileProc** function is a placeholder for the application-defined function name. The actual name must be exported by including it in an **EXPORTS** statement in the application's module-definition (.DEF) file.

See Also   **EnumMetaFile**

EnumObjects   `2.x`

```
int EnumObjects(hdc, fnObjectType, goenmprc, lParam)
HDC hdc;                        /* handle of device context      */
int fnObjectType;               /* type of object                */
GOBJENUMPROC goenmprc;          /* address of callback function  */
LPARAM lParam;                  /* application-defined data       */
```

The **EnumObjects** function enumerates the pens and brushes available in the given device context. For each object of a given type, the callback function is called with the information for that object. **EnumObjects** continues until there are no more objects or the callback function returns zero.

Parameters

hdc
Identifies the device context.

fnObjectType
Specifies the object type. This parameter can be one of the following values:

Value	Meaning
OBJ_BRUSH	Specifies a brush.
OBJ_PEN	Specifies a pen.

goenmprc
Specifies the procedure-instance address of the application-supplied callback function. The address must be created by the **MakeProcInstance** function. For more information about the callback function, see the description of the **EnumObjectsProc** callback function.

lParam
Specifies a 32-bit application-defined value that is passed to the callback function.

Return Value

The return value specifies the last value returned by the callback function and is defined by the user.

Example   The following example retrieves the number of horizontally hatched brushes and
fills **LOGBRUSH** structures with information about each of them:

```
#define MAXBRUSHES 50

GOBJENUMPROC lpProcCallback;
HGLOBAL hglbl;
LPBYTE lpbCountBrush;

lpProcCallback = (GOBJENUMPROC) MakeProcInstance(
    (FARPROC) Callback, hinst);

hglbl = GlobalAlloc(GMEM_FIXED, sizeof(LOGBRUSH)
    * MAXBRUSHES);
lpbCountBrush = (LPBYTE) GlobalLock(hglbl);
*lpbCountBrush = 0;
EnumObjects(hdc, OBJ_BRUSH, lpProcCallback,
    (LPARAM) lpbCountBrush);

FreeProcInstance((FARPROC) lpProcCallback);

int FAR PASCAL Callback(LPLOGBRUSH lpLogBrush, LPBYTE pbData)
{
    /*
     * The pbData parameter contains the number of horizontally
     * hatched brushes; the lpDest parameter is set to follow the
     * byte reserved for pbData and the LOGBRUSH structures that
     * have been filled with brush information.
     */

    LPLOGBRUSH lpDest =
        (LPLOGBRUSH) (pbData + 1 + (*pbData * sizeof(LOGBRUSH)));

    if (lpLogBrush->lbStyle ==
            BS_HATCHED && /* if horiz hatch */
            lpLogBrush->lbHatch == HS_HORIZONTAL) {
        *lpDest++ = *lpLogBrush; /* fills structure with brush info */
        (*pbData) ++;            /* increments brush count         */
        if (*pbData >= MAXBRUSHES)
            return 0;
    }

    return 1;
}
```

See Also   **EnumObjectsProc, FreeProcInstance, GlobalAlloc, GlobalLock,
MakeProcInstance**

EnumObjectsProc

int CALLBACK EnumObjectsProc(*lpLogObject***,** *lpData***)**
void FAR* *lpLogObject*;   /* address of object   */
LPARAM *lpData*;   /* address of application-defined data   */

The **EnumObjectsProc** function is an application-defined callback function that processes object data from the **EnumObjects** function.

Parameters

lpLogObject
Points to a **LOGPEN** or **LOGBRUSH** structure that contains information about the attributes of the object.

The **LOGPEN** structure has the following form:

```
typedef struct tagLOGPEN {  /* lgpn */
    UINT     lopnStyle;
    POINT    lopnWidth;
    COLORREF lopnColor;
} LOGPEN;
```

The **LOGBRUSH** structure has the following form:

```
typedef struct tagLOGBRUSH {    /* lb */
    UINT     lbStyle;
    COLORREF lbColor;
    int      lbHatch;
} LOGBRUSH;
```

For a full description of these structures, see the *Microsoft Windows Programmer's Reference, Volume 3*.

lpData
Points to the application-defined data passed by the **EnumObjects** function.

Return Value

This function must return a nonzero value to continue enumeration; to stop enumeration, it must return zero.

Comments

An application must register this callback function by passing its address to the **EnumObjects** function. The **EnumObjectsProc** function is a placeholder for the application-supplied function name. The actual name must be exported by including it in an **EXPORTS** statement in the application's module-definition (.DEF) file.

Example   The following example retrieves the number of horizontally hatched brushes and
fills **LOGBRUSH** structures with information about each of them:

```
#define MAXBRUSHES 50

GOBJENUMPROC lpProcCallback;
HGLOBAL hglbl;
LPBYTE lpbCountBrush;

lpProcCallback = (GOBJENUMPROC) MakeProcInstance(
    (FARPROC) Callback, hinst);

hglbl = GlobalAlloc(GMEM_FIXED, sizeof(LOGBRUSH)
    * MAXBRUSHES);
lpbCountBrush = (LPBYTE) GlobalLock(hglbl);
*lpbCountBrush = 0;
EnumObjects(hdc, OBJ_BRUSH, lpProcCallback,
    (LPARAM) lpbCountBrush);

FreeProcInstance((FARPROC) lpProcCallback);

int FAR PASCAL Callback(LPLOGBRUSH lpLogBrush, LPBYTE pbData)
{
    /*
     * The pbData parameter contains the number of horizontally
     * hatched brushes; the lpDest parameter is set to follow the
     * byte reserved for pbData and the LOGBRUSH structures that
     * have been filled with brush information.
     */

    LPLOGBRUSH lpDest =
        (LPLOGBRUSH) (pbData + 1 + (*pbData * sizeof(LOGBRUSH)));

    if (lpLogBrush->lbStyle ==
            BS_HATCHED && /* if horiz hatch */
            lpLogBrush->lbHatch == HS_HORIZONTAL) {
        *lpDest++ = *lpLogBrush; /* fills structure with brush info */
        (*pbData) ++;            /* increments brush count          */
        if (*pbData >= MAXBRUSHES)
            return 0;
    }

    return 1;
}
```

See Also   **EnumObjects, FreeProcInstance, GlobalAlloc, GlobalLock,
MakeProcInstance**

EnumPropFixedProc

2.x

BOOL CALLBACK EnumPropFixedProc(*hwnd*, *lpsz*, *hData*)
HWND *hwnd*;   /* handle of window with property   */
LPCSTR *lpsz*;   /* address of property string or atom */
HANDLE *hData*;   /* handle data of property data   */

The **EnumPropFixedProc** function is an application-defined callback function that receives a window's property data as a result of a call to the **EnumProps** function.

Parameters

hwnd
Identifies the handle of the window that contains the property list.

lpsz
Points to the null-terminated string associated with the property data identified by the *hData* parameter. The application specified the string and data in a previous call to the **SetProp** function. If the application passed an atom instead of a string to **SetProp**, the *lpsz* parameter contains the atom in the low-order word and zero in the high-order word.

hData
Identifies the property data.

Return Value

The callback function must return TRUE to continue enumeration; it must return FALSE to stop enumeration.

Comments

This form of the property-enumeration callback function should be used in applications and dynamic-link libraries with fixed data segments and in dynamic libraries with movable data segments that do not contain a stack.

The following restrictions apply to the callback function:

- The callback function must not yield control or do anything that might yield control to other tasks.

- The callback function can call the **RemoveProp** function. However, **Remove-Prop** can remove only the property passed to the callback function through the callback function's parameters.

- The callback function should not attempt to add properties.

The **EnumPropFixedProc** function is a placeholder for the application-defined function name. The actual name must be exported by including it in an **EXPORTS** statement in the application's module-definition (.DEF) file.

See Also

EnumPropMovableProc, EnumProps, RemoveProp, SetProp

EnumPropMovableProc

BOOL CALLBACK EnumPropMovableProc(*hwnd*, *lpsz*, *hData*)
HWND *hwnd*;   /* handle of window with property   */
LPCSTR *lpsz*;   /* address of property string or atom */
HANDLE *hData*;   /* handle of property data   */

The **EnumPropMovableProc** function is an application-defined callback function that receives a window's property data as a result of a call to the **EnumProps** function.

Parameters

hwnd
Identifies the handle of the window that contains the property list.

lpsz
Points to the null-terminated string associated with the data identified by the *hData* parameter. The application specified the string and data in a previous call to the **SetProp** function. If the application passed an atom instead of a string to **SetProp**, the *lpsz* parameter contains the atom.

hData
Identifies the property data.

Return Value

The callback function must return TRUE to continue enumeration; to stop enumeration, it must return FALSE.

Comments

This form of the property-enumeration callback function should be used in applications with movable data segments and in dynamic libraries whose movable data segments also contain a stack. This form is required since movement of the data will invalidate any long pointer to a variable on the stack, such as the *lpsz* parameter. The data segment typically moves if the callback function allocates more space in the local heap than is currently available.

The following restrictions apply to the callback function:

- The callback function must not yield control or do anything that might yield control to other tasks.

- The callback function can call the **RemoveProp** function. However, **Remove-Prop** can remove only the property passed to the callback function through the callback function's parameters.

- The callback function should not attempt to add properties.

The **EnumPropMovableProc** function is a placeholder for the application-defined function name. The actual name must be exported by including it in an **EXPORTS** statement in the application's module-definition (.DEF) file.

See Also   **EnumPropFixedProc, EnumProps, RemoveProp, SetProp**

EnumProps

2.x

int **EnumProps**(*hwnd*, *prpenmprc*)
HWND *hwnd*;   /* handle of window   */
PROPENUMPROC *prpenmprc*;   /* address of callback function   */

The **EnumProps** function enumerates all entries in the property list of the given window. It enumerates the entries by passing them, one by one, to the specified callback function. **EnumProps** continues until the last entry is enumerated or the callback function returns zero.

Parameters   *hwnd*
Identifies the window whose property list is enumerated.

prpenmprc
Specifies the procedure-instance address of the callback function. For more information, see the descriptions of the **EnumPropFixedProc** and **EnumPropMovableProc** callback functions.

Return Value   The return value specifies the last value returned by the callback function. It is −1 if the function did not find a property to enumerate.

Comments   The form of the callback function depends on whether the application or dynamic-link library (DLL) uses fixed or movable data segments. If the application or library uses fixed data segments (or if the library uses movable data segments that do not contain a stack), see the description of the **EnumPropFixedProc** callback function. If the application uses movable data segments (or if the library uses movable data segments that also contain a stack), see the description of the **EnumPropMovableProc** callback function.

An application's **EnumPropFixedProc** or **EnumPropMovableProc** callback function should not add new properties to a window. If the callback function deletes a window's properties, it should delete only the property currently being enumerated. The callback function should not delete other properties belonging to the window; if it does, the enumeration process terminates early.

The address passed in the *prpenmprc* parameter must be created by using the **MakeProcInstance** function.

See Also   **EnumPropFixedProc, EnumPropMovableProc, GetProp, MakeProcInstance, RemoveProp, SetProp**

EnumTaskWindows

2.x

BOOL EnumTaskWindows(*htask*, *wndenmprc*, *lParam*)
HTASK *htask*;   /* handle of task   */
WNDENUMPROC *wndenmprc*;   /* address of callback function   */
LPARAM *lParam*;   /* application-defined value   */

The **EnumTaskWindows** function enumerates all windows associated with a given task. (A task is any program that executes as an independent unit. All applications are executed as tasks, and each instance of an application is a task.) The function enumerates the windows by passing their handles, one by one, to the specified callback function. **EnumTaskWindows** continues until the last entry is enumerated or the callback function returns zero.

Parameters

htask
Identifies the task. The task handle must be retrieved by a previous call to the **GetCurrentTask** function.

wndenmprc
Specifies the procedure-instance address of the callback function. For more information, see the description of the **EnumTaskWndProc** callback function.

lParam
Specifies a 32-bit application-defined value that is passed to the callback function along with each window handle.

Return Value
The return value is nonzero if the function is successful. Otherwise, it is zero.

Comments
This function enumerates all top-level windows but does not enumerate child windows.

The **EnumTaskWindows** function is reliable even when the application causes odd side effects, whereas an application that uses a **GetWindow** loop risks being caught in an infinite loop or referencing a handle to a window that has been destroyed.

The address passed in the *wndenmprc* parameter must be created by using the **MakeProcInstance** function.

See Also
EnumTaskWndProc, GetCurrentTask

EnumTaskWndProc

BOOL CALLBACK EnumTaskWndProc(*hwnd*, *lParam*)
HWND *hwnd*;   /* handle of a window   */
LPARAM *lParam*;   /* application-defined value   */

The **EnumTaskWndProc** function is an application-defined callback function that receives the window handles associated with a task as a result of a call to the **EnumTaskWindows** function.

Parameters

hwnd
Identifies a window associated with the task specified in the **EnumTask-Windows** function.

lParam
Specifies the application-defined value specified in the **EnumTaskWindows** function.

Return Value

The callback function must return TRUE to continue enumeration; to stop enumeration, it must return FALSE.

Comments

The callback function can carry out any desired task.

The **EnumTaskWndProc** function is a placeholder for the application-defined function name. The actual name must be exported by including it in an **EXPORTS** statement in the application's module-definition (.DEF) file.

See Also

EnumTaskWindows

EnumWindows

BOOL EnumWindows(*wndenmprc*, *lParam*)
WNDENUMPROC *wndenmprc*;   /* address of callback function   */
LPARAM *lParam*;   /* application-defined value   */

The **EnumWindows** function enumerates all parent windows on the screen by passing the handle of each window, in turn, to an application-defined callback function. **EnumWindows** continues until the last parent window is enumerated or the callback function returns zero.

Parameters

wndenmprc
Specifies the procedure-instance address of the callback function. For more information, see the description of the **EnumWindowsProc** callback function.

lParam
Specifies a 32-bit application-defined value that is passed to the callback function.

Return Value   The return value is nonzero if the function is successful. Otherwise, it is zero.

Comments   The **EnumWindows** function does not enumerate child windows.

EnumWindows is reliable even when the application causes odd side effects, whereas an application that uses a **GetWindow** loop risks being caught in an infinite loop or referencing a handle to a window that has been destroyed.

The address passed as the *wndenmprc* parameter must be created by using the **MakeProcInstance** function.

See Also   **EnumWindowsProc, MakeProcInstance**

EnumWindowsProc   `2.x`

BOOL CALLBACK EnumWindowsProc(*hwnd*, *lParam*)
HWND *hwnd*;   /* handle of parent window   */
LPARAM *lParam*;   /* application-defined value   */

The **EnumWindowsProc** function is an application-defined callback function that receives parent window handles as a result of a call to the **EnumWindows** function.

Parameters

hwnd
Identifies a parent window.

lParam
Specifies the application-defined value specified in the **EnumWindows** function.

Return Value   The callback function must return nonzero to continue enumeration; to stop enumeration, it must return zero.

Comments   The callback function can carry out any desired task.

The **EnumWindowsProc** function is a placeholder for the application-defined function name. The actual name must be exported by including it in an **EXPORTS** statement in the application's module-definition (.DEF) file.

See Also   **EnumWindows**

EqualRect

$\boxed{\textbf{2.x}}$

BOOL EqualRect(*lprc1***,** *lprc2***)**
const RECT FAR* *lprc1*;   /* address of structure with first rectangle   */
const RECT FAR* *lprc2*;   /* address of structure with second rectangle   */

The **EqualRect** function determines whether the two given rectangles are equal by comparing the coordinates of their upper-left and lower-right corners.

Parameters   *lprc1*
Points to a **RECT** structure that contains the logical coordinates of the first rectangle. The **RECT** structure has the following form:

```
typedef struct tagRECT {    /* rc */
    int left;
    int top;
    int right;
    int bottom;
} RECT;
```

For a full description of this structure, see the *Microsoft Windows Programmer's Reference, Volume 3*.

lprc2
Points to a **RECT** structure that contains the logical coordinates of the second rectangle.

Return Value   The return value is nonzero if the two rectangles are identical. Otherwise, it is zero.

EqualRgn

BOOL EqualRgn(*hrgnSrc1*, *hrgnSrc2*)
HRGN *hrgnSrc1*;   /* handle of first region to test for equality   */
HRGN *hrgnSrc2*;   /* handle of second region to test for equality   */

The **EqualRgn** function determines whether two given regions are identical.

Parameters   *hrgnSrc1*
                Identifies the first region.

                hrgnSrc2
                Identifies the second region.

Return Value   The return value is nonzero if the two regions are equal. Otherwise, it is zero.

Example   The following example uses the **EqualRgn** function to test the equality of a region
        against two other regions. In this case, hrgn2 is identical to hrgn1, but hrgn3 is not
        identical to hrgn1.

```
BOOL fEqual;
HRGN hrgn1, hrgn2, hrgn3;
LPSTR lpszEqual = "Regions are equal.";
LPSTR lpszNotEqual = "Regions are not equal.";

hrgn1 = CreateRectRgn(10, 10, 110, 110); /* 1 and 2 identical */
hrgn2 = CreateRectRgn(10, 10, 110, 110);
hrgn3 = CreateRectRgn(100, 100, 210, 210); /* same dimensions */

fEqual = EqualRgn(hrgn1, hrgn2);
if (fEqual)
    TextOut(hdc, 10, 10, lpszEqual, lstrlen(lpszEqual));
else
    TextOut(hdc, 10, 10, lpszNotEqual, lstrlen(lpszNotEqual));

fEqual = EqualRgn(hrgn1, hrgn3);
if (fEqual)
    TextOut(hdc, 10, 30, lpszEqual, lstrlen(lpszEqual));
else
    TextOut(hdc, 10, 30, lpszNotEqual, lstrlen(lpszNotEqual));

DeleteObject(hrgn1);
DeleteObject(hrgn2);
DeleteObject(hrgn3);
```

Escape

int Escape(*hdc, nEscape, cbInput, lpszInData, lpvOutData*)
HDC *hdc*;   /* handle of device context   */
int *nEscape*;   /* specifies escape function   */
int *cbInput*;   /* size of structure for input   */
LPCSTR *lpszInData*;   /* address of structure for input */
void FAR* *lpvOutData*;   /* address of structure for output */

The **Escape** function allows applications to access capabilities of a particular device that are not directly available through the graphics device interface (GDI). Escape calls made by an application are translated and sent to the driver.

Parameters

hdc
Identifies the device context.

nEscape
Specifies the escape function to be performed. For a complete list of printer escapes, see the *Microsoft Windows Programmer's Reference, Volume 3*.

cbInput
Specifies the number of bytes of data pointed to by the *lpszInData* parameter.

lpszInData
Points to the input structure required for the specified escape.

lpvOutData
Points to the structure that receives output from this escape. This parameter should be NULL if no data is returned.

Return Value

The return value specifies the outcome of the function. It is greater than zero if the function is successful, except for the QUERYESCSUPPORT printer escape, which checks for implementation only. The return value is zero if the escape is not implemented. A return value less than zero indicates an error.

Errors

If the function fails, the return value is one of the following:

Value	Meaning
SP_ERROR	General error.
SP_OUTOFDISK	Not enough disk space is currently available for spooling, and no more space will become available.
SP_OUTOFMEMORY	Not enough memory is available for spooling.
SP_USERABORT	User terminated the job through Print Manager.

EscapeCommFunction

LONG EscapeCommFunction(*idComDev*, *nFunction*)
int *idComDev*;   /* identifies communications device   */
int *nFunction*;   /* code of extended function   */

The **EscapeCommFunction** function directs the specified communications device to carry out an extended function.

Parameters

idComDev
Specifies the communications device that will carry out the extended function. The **OpenComm** function returns this value.

nFunction
Specifies the function code of the extended function. It can be one of the following values:

Value	Meaning
CLRDTR	Clears the DTR (data-terminal-ready) signal.
CLRRTS	Clears the RTS (request-to-send) signal.
GETMAXCOM	Returns the maximum COM port identifier supported by the system. This value ranges from 0x00 to 0x7F, such that 0x00 corresponds to COM1, 0x01 to COM2, 0x02 to COM3, and so on.
GETMAXLPT	Returns the maximum LPT port identifier supported by the system. This value ranges from 0x80 to 0xFF, such that 0x80 corresponds to LPT1, 0x81 to LPT2, 0x82 to LPT3, and so on.
RESETDEV	Resets the printer device if the *idComDev* parameter specifies an LPT port. No function is performed if *idComDev* specifies a COM port.
SETDTR	Sends the DTR (data-terminal-ready) signal.
SETRTS	Sends the RTS (request-to-send) signal.
SETXOFF	Causes transmission to act as if an XOFF character has been received.
SETXON	Causes transmission to act as if an XON character has been received.

Return Value

The return value is zero if the function is successful. Otherwise, it is less than zero.

ExcludeClipRect

int ExcludeClipRect(*hdc, nLeftRect, nTopRect, nRightRect, nBottomRect*)
HDC *hdc*;   /* handle of device context   */
int *nLeftRect*;   /* x-coordinate top-left corner of rectangle   */
int *nTopRect*;   /* y-coordinate top-left corner of rectangle   */
int *nRightRect*;   /* x-coordinate bottom-right corner of rectangle   */
int *nBottomRect*;   /* y-coordinate bottom-right corner of rectangle   */

The **ExcludeClipRect** function creates a new clipping region that consists of the existing clipping region minus the specified rectangle.

Parameters   *hdc*
Identifies the device context.

nLeftRect
Specifies the logical x-coordinate of the upper-left corner of the rectangle.

nTopRect
Specifies the logical y-coordinate of the upper-left corner of the rectangle.

nRightRect
Specifies the logical x-coordinate of the lower-right corner of the rectangle.

nBottomRect
Specifies the logical y-coordinate of the lower-right corner of the rectangle.

Return Value   The return value is SIMPLEREGION (region has no overlapping borders), COMPLEXREGION (region has overlapping borders), or NULLREGION (region is empty), if the function is successful. Otherwise, the return value is ERROR (no region is created).

Comments   The width of the rectangle, specified by the absolute value of *nRightRect − nLeftRect*, must not exceed 32,767 units. This limit applies to the height of the rectangle as well.

Example   The following example uses the **ExcludeClipRect** function to create a clipping region in the shape of a frame that is 20 units wide. The frame is painted red when the **FillRect** function is used to paint the client area.

```
RECT rc;
HRGN hrgn;
HBRUSH hbrRed;

GetClientRect(hwnd, &rc);
hrgn = CreateRectRgn(10, 10, 110, 110);
SelectClipRgn(hdc, hrgn);

ExcludeClipRect(hdc, 30, 30, 90, 90);
```

```
hbrRed = CreateSolidBrush(RGB(255, 0, 0));
FillRect(hdc, &rc, hbrRed);

DeleteObject(hbrRed);
DeleteObject(hrgn);
```

See Also   **CombineRgn**

ExcludeUpdateRgn
2.x

int ExcludeUpdateRgn(*hdc, hwnd*)
HDC *hdc*;   /* handle of device context   */
HWND *hwnd*;   /* handle of window   */

The **ExcludeUpdateRgn** function prevents drawing within invalid areas of a window by excluding an updated region in the window from a clipping region.

Parameters   *hdc*
Identifies the device context associated with the clipping region.

hwnd
Identifies the window to be updated.

Return Value   The return value is SIMPLEREGION (region has no overlapping borders), COMPLEXREGION (region has overlapping borders), or NULLREGION (region is empty), if the function is successful. Otherwise, the return value is ERROR (no region is created).

See Also   **BeginPaint, GetUpdateRect, GetUpdateRgn, UpdateWindow**

ExitWindows
3.0

BOOL ExitWindows(*dwReturnCode, reserved*)
DWORD *dwReturnCode*;   /* return or restart code   */
UINT *reserved*;   /* reserved; must be zero   */

The **ExitWindows** function can restart Windows, terminate Windows and return control to MS-DOS, or terminate Windows and restart the system. Windows sends the WM_QUERYENDSESSION message to notify all applications that a request has been made to restart or terminate Windows. If all applications "agree" to terminate, Windows sends the WM_ENDSESSION message to all applications before terminating.

Parameters *dwReturnCode*

Specifies whether Windows should restart, terminate and return control to MS-DOS, or terminate and restart the system. The high-order word of this parameter should be zero. The low-order word specifies the return value to be passed to MS-DOS when Windows terminates. The low-order word can be one of the following values:

Value	Meaning
EW_REBOOTSYSTEM	Causes Windows to terminate and the system to restart.
EW_RESTARTWINDOWS	Causes Windows to restart.

reserved

Reserved; must be zero.

Return Value The return value is zero if one or more applications refuse to terminate. The function does not return a value if all applications agree to be terminated.

See Also **ExitWindowsExec**

ExitWindowsExec 3.0

BOOL ExitWindowsExec(*lpszExe*, *lpszParams*)
LPCSTR *lpszExe*;
LPCSTR *lpszParams*;

The **ExitWindowsExec** function terminates Windows, runs a specified MS-DOS application, and then restarts Windows.

Parameters *lpszExe*

Points to a null-terminated string specifying the path and filename of the executable file for the system to run after Windows has been terminated. This string must not be longer than 128 bytes (including the null terminating character).

lpszParams

Points to a null-terminated string specifying any parameters for the executable file specified by the *lpszExe* parameter. This string must not be longer than 127 bytes (including the null terminating character). This value can be NULL.

Return Value   The return value is FALSE if the function fails. (The function could fail because
                          of a memory-allocation error or if one of the applications in the system does not
                          terminate.)

Comments   The **ExitWindowsExec** function is typically used by installation programs to re-
                          place components of Windows which are active when Windows is running.

See Also   **ExitWindows**

ExtDeviceMode   3.0

#include <print.h>

int ExtDeviceMode(*hwnd*, *hDriver*, *lpdmOutput*, *lpszDevice*, *lpszPort*, *lpdmInput*, *lpszProfile*, *fwMode***)**
HWND *hwnd*;   /* handle of window   */
HANDLE *hDriver*;   /* handle of driver   */
LPDEVMODE *lpdmOutput*;   /* address of structure for driver output   */
LPSTR *lpszDevice*;   /* string for name of device   */
LPSTR *lpszPort*;   /* string for name of port   */
LPDEVMODE *lpdmInput*;   /* address of structure for driver input   */
LPSTR *lpszProfile*;   /* string for profile filename   */
WORD *fwMode*;   /* operations mask   */

The **ExtDeviceMode** function retrieves or modifies device initialization information for a given printer driver or displays a driver-supplied dialog box for configur-
ing the printer driver. Printer drivers that support device initialization by
applications export **ExtDeviceMode** so that applications can call it.

Parameters   *hwnd*
                          Identifies a window. If the application calls the **ExtDeviceMode** function to dis-
                          play a dialog box, the specified window is the parent window of the dialog box.

                          hDriver
                          Identifies the device-driver module. The **GetModuleHandle** function or **Load-
                          Library** function returns a module handle.

                          lpdmOutput
                          Points to a **DEVMODE** structure. The driver writes the initialization informa-
                          tion supplied in the *lpdmInput* parameter to this structure. The **DEVMODE**
                          structure has the following form:

```
#include <print.h>

typedef struct tagDEVMODE {    /* dm */
    char dmDeviceName[CCHDEVICENAME];
    UINT dmSpecVersion;
    UINT dmDriverVersion;
    UINT dmSize;
    UINT dmDriverExtra;
    DWORD dmFields;
    int  dmOrientation;
    int  dmPaperSize;
    int  dmPaperLength;
    int  dmPaperWidth;
    int  dmScale;
    int  dmCopies;
    int  dmDefaultSource;
    int  dmPrintQuality;
    int  dmColor;
    int  dmDuplex;
    int  dmYResolution;
    int  dmTTOption;
} DEVMODE;
```

For a full description of this structure, see the *Microsoft Windows Programmer's Reference, Volume 3*.

lpszDevice

Points to a null-terminated string that contains the name of the printer device—for example, PCL/HP LaserJet.

lpszPort

Points to a null-terminated string that contains the name of the port to which the device is connected—for example, LPT1.

lpdmInput

Points to a **DEVMODE** structure that supplies initialization information to the printer driver.

lpszProfile

Points to a null-terminated string that contains the name of the initialization file, where initialization information is recorded and read from. If this parameter is NULL, WIN.INI is the default initialization file.

fwMode

Specifies a mask of values that determines the operations the function performs. If this parameter is zero, the **ExtDeviceMode** function returns the number of bytes required by the printer driver's **DEVMODE** structure. Otherwise, the *fwMode* parameter can be one or more of the following values (to change the print settings, the application must specify at least one input value and one output value):

Value	Meaning
DM_IN_BUFFER	Input value. Before prompting, copying, or updating, this value merges the printer driver's current print settings with the settings in the **DEVMODE** structure identified by the *lpdmInput* parameter. The structure is updated only for those members indicated by the application in the **dmFields** member. This value is also defined as DM_MODIFY.
DM_IN_PROMPT	Input value. This value presents the printer driver's Print Setup dialog box and then changes the settings in the printer's **DEVMODE** structure to values specified by the user. This value is also defined as DM_PROMPT.
DM_OUT_BUFFER	Output value. This value writes the printer driver's current print settings (including private data) to the **DEVMODE** structure identified by the *lpdmOutput* parameter. The calling application must allocate a buffer sufficiently large to contain the information. If this bit is clear, *lpdmOutput* can be NULL. This value is also defined as DM_COPY.
DM_OUT_DEFAULT	Output value. This value updates graphics device interface (GDI)'s current printer environment and the WIN.INI file, using the contents of the printer driver's **DEVMODE** structure. Avoid using this value, because it permanently changes the print settings for all applications. This value is also defined as DM_UPDATE.

Return Value

If the *fwMode* parameter is zero, the return value is the size of the buffer required to contain the printer driver initialization data. (Note that this buffer can be larger than a **DEVMODE** structure, if the printer driver appends private data to the structure.) If the function displays the initialization dialog box, the return value is either IDOK or IDCANCEL, depending on which button the user selects. If the function does not display the dialog box and is successful, the return value is IDOK. The return value is less than zero if the function fails.

Comments

The **ExtDeviceMode** function is part of the printer's device driver and not part of GDI. To use this function, an application must retrieve the address of the function by calling the **LoadLibrary** and **GetProcAddress** functions, and it must include the header file PRINT.H. The application can then use the address to set up the printer.

ExtDeviceMode is not supported by all printer drivers. If the **GetProcAddress** function returns NULL, **ExtDeviceMode** is not supported.

To make changes to print settings that are local to the application, an application should call the **ExtDeviceMode** function, specifying the DM_OUT_BUFFER value; modify the returned **DEVMODE** structure; and then pass the modified **DEVMODE** structure back to **ExtDeviceMode**, specifying DM_IN_BUFFER and DM_OUT_BUFFER (combined by using the OR operator). The **DEVMODE** structure returned by this second call to **ExtDeviceMode** can be used as an argument in a call to the **CreateDC** function.

Any call to **ExtDeviceMode** must set either DM_OUT_BUFFER or DM_OUT_DEFAULT.

An application can set the *fwMode* parameter to DM_OUT_BUFFER to obtain a **DEVMODE** structure filled with the printer driver's initialization data. The application can then pass this structure to the **CreateDC** function to set a private environment for the printer device context.

See Also   **CreateDC, DeviceMode, GetModuleHandle, GetProcAddress, LoadLibrary**

ExtFloodFill   3.0

```
BOOL ExtFloodFill(hdc, nXStart, nYStart, clrref, fuFillType)
HDC hdc;                /* handle of device context        */
int nXStart;            /* x-coordinate where filling begins */
int nYStart;            /* y-coordinate where filling begins */
COLORREF clrref;        /* color of fill                   */
UINT fuFillType;        /* fill type                       */
```

The **ExtFloodFill** function fills an area of the screen surface by using the current brush. The type of flood fill specified determines which part of the screen is filled.

Parameters   *hdc*
Identifies the device context.

nXStart
Specifies the logical x-coordinate at which to begin filling.

nYStart
Specifies the logical y-coordinate at which to begin filling.

clrref
Specifies the color of the boundary or area to be filled. The interpretation of this parameter depends on the value of the *fuFillType* parameter.

fuFillType
Specifies the type of flood fill to be performed. It must be one of the following values:

Value	Meaning
FLOODFILLBORDER	Fill area is bounded by the color specified by the *clrref* parameter. This style is identical to the filling performed by the **FloodFill** function.
FLOODFILLSURFACE	Fill area is defined by the color specified by the *clrref* parameter. Filling continues outward in all directions as long as the color is encountered. This style is useful for filling areas that have multicolored boundaries.

Return Value   The return value is nonzero if the function is successful. It is zero if the filling cannot be completed, if the given point has the boundary color specified by the *clrref* parameter (if FLOODFILLBORDER was requested), if the given point does not have the color specified by *clrref* (if FLOODFILLSURFACE was requested), or if the point is outside the clipping region.

Comments   Only memory device contexts and devices that support raster-display technology support the **ExtFloodFill** function. For more information about raster capabilities, see the description of the **GetDeviceCaps** function.

If the *fuFillType* parameter is the FLOODFILLBORDER value, the area is assumed to be completely bounded by the color specified by the *clrref* parameter. The **ExtFloodFill** function begins at the coordinates specified by the *nXStart* and *nYStart* parameters and fills in all directions to the color boundary.

If *fuFillType* is FLOODFILLSURFACE, **ExtFloodFill** begins at the coordinates specified by *nXStart* and *nYStart* and continues in all directions, filling all adjacent areas containing the color specified by *clrref*.

See Also   **FloodFill**, **GetDeviceCaps**

ExtractIcon   3.1

#include <shellapi.h>

```
HICON ExtractIcon(hinst, lpszExeName, iIcon)
HINSTANCE hinst;        /* instance handle          */
LPCSTR lpszExeName;     /* address of string for file */
UINT iIcon;             /* index of icon to retrieve */
```

The **ExtractIcon** function retrieves the handle of an icon from a specified executable file, dynamic-link library (DLL), or icon file.

Parameters   *hinst*
                        Identifies the instance of the application calling the function.

                     lpszExeName
                        Points to a null-terminated string specifying the name of an executable file,
                        dynamic-link library, or icon file.

                     iIcon
                        Specifies the index of the icon to be retrieved. If this parameter is zero, the
                        function returns the handle of the first icon in the specified file. If the parame-
                        ter is −1, the function returns the total number of icons in the specified file.

Return Value   The return value is the handle of an icon if the function is successful. It is 1 if the
                      file specified in the *lpszExeName* parameter is not an executable file, dynamic-link
                      library, or icon file. Otherwise, it is NULL, indicating that the file contains no
                      icons.

ExtTextOut

2.x

BOOL ExtTextOut(*hdc, nXStart, nYStart, fuOptions, lprc, lpszString, cbString, lpDx*)
HDC *hdc*;   /* handle of device context   */
int *nXStart*;   /* x-coordinate of starting position   */
int *nYStart*;   /* y-coordinate of starting position   */
UINT *fuOptions*;   /* rectangle type   */
const RECT FAR* *lprc*;   /* address of structure with rectangle   */
LPCSTR *lpszString*;   /* address of string   */
UINT *cbString*;   /* number of bytes in string   */
int FAR* *lpDx*;   /* spacing between character cells   */

The **ExtTextOut** function writes a character string within a rectangular region,
using the currently selected font. The rectangular region can be opaque (filled by
using the current background color as set by the **SetBkColor** function), and it can
be a clipping region.

Parameters   *hdc*
                        Identifies the device context.

                     nXStart
                        Specifies the logical x-coordinate at which the string begins.

                     nYStart
                        Specifies the logical y-coordinate at which the string begins.

                     fuOptions
                        Specifies the rectangle type. This parameter can be one, both, or neither of the
                        following values:

Value	Meaning
ETO_CLIPPED	Text is clipped to the rectangle.
ETO_OPAQUE	Current background color fills the rectangle. (An application can set and query the current background color by using the **SetBkColor** and **GetBkColor** functions.)

lprc
Points to a **RECT** structure that determines the dimensions of the rectangle. The **RECT** structure has the following form:

```
typedef struct tagRECT {     /* rc */
    int left;
    int top;
    int right;
    int bottom;
} RECT;
```

For a full description of this structure, see the *Microsoft Windows Programmer's Reference, Volume 3*.

lpszString
Points to the specified character string.

cbString
Specifies the number of bytes in the string.

lpDx
Points to an array of values that indicate the distance, in logical units, between origins of adjacent character cells. The *n*th element in the array specifies the number of logical units that separate the origin of the *n*th item in the string from the origin of item *n* + 1. If this parameter is NULL, **ExtTextOut** uses the default spacing between characters. Otherwise, the array contains the number of elements specified in the *cbString* parameter.

Return Value   The return value is nonzero if the function is successful. Otherwise, it is zero.

Comments   If the *fuOptions* parameter is zero and the *lprc* parameter is NULL, the **Ext-TextOut** function writes text to the device context without using a rectangular region.

By default, the current position is not used or updated by **ExtTextOut**. If an application needs to update the current position when it calls **ExtTextOut**, the application can call the **SetTextAlign** function with the *wFlags* parameter set to TA_UPDATECP. When this flag is set, Windows ignores the *nXStart* and *nYStart* parameters on subsequent calls to **ExtTextOut**, using the current position instead. When an application uses TA_UPDATECP to update the current position, **Ext-TextOut** sets the current position either to the end of the previous line of text or to the position specified by the last element of the array pointed to by the *lpDX* parameter, whichever is greater.

Example

The following example uses the **ExtTextOut** function to clip text to a rectangular region defined by a **RECT** structure:

```
RECT rc;

SetRect(&rc, 90, 190, 250, 220);

ExtTextOut(hdc, 100, 200,    /* x and y coordinates         */
    ETO_CLIPPED,             /* clips text to rectangle      */
    &rc,                     /* address of RECT structure */
    "Test of ExtTextOut function.", /* string to write    */
    28,                      /* characters in string        */
    (LPINT) NULL);           /* default character spacing */
```

See Also

GetBkColor, **SetBkColor**, **SetTextAlign**, **SetTextColor**, **TabbedTextOut**, **TextOut**

FatalAppExit

3.0

void FatalAppExit(*fuAction*, *lpszMessageText*)
UINT *fuAction*;   /* must be zero   */
LPCSTR *lpszMessageText*;   /* string to display in message box   */

The **FatalAppExit** function displays a message box and terminates the application when the message box is closed. If the user is running the debugging version of the Windows operating system, the message box gives the user the opportunity to terminate the application or to cancel the message box and return to the caller.

Parameters

fuAction
Reserved; must be zero.

lpszMessageText
Points to a null-terminated string that is displayed in the message box. The message is displayed on a single line. To accommodate low-resolution screens, the string should contain no more than 35 characters.

Return Value

This function does not return a value.

Comments

An application should call the **FatalAppExit** function only when it is incapable of terminating any other way. **FatalAppExit** may not always free an application's memory or close its files, and it may cause a general failure of Windows. An application that encounters an unexpected error should terminate by freeing all its memory and returning from its main message loop.

See Also

FatalExit, **TerminateApp**

FatalExit

`2.x`

void FatalExit(*nErrCode*)
int *nErrCode*;   /* error value to display   */

The **FatalExit** function sends the current state of Windows to the debugger and prompts for instructions on how to proceed.

An application should call this function for debugging purposes only; it should not call the function in a retail version of the application. Calling this function in the retail version will terminate the application.

Parameters

nErrCode
    Specifies the error value to be displayed.

Return Value

This function does not return a value.

Comments

The displayed information includes an error value followed by a symbolic stack trace, showing the flow of execution up to the point of the call.

The **FatalExit** function prompts the user to respond to an Abort, Break, or Ignore message. Windows processes the response as follows:

Response	Description
A (Abort)	Terminate immediately.
B (Break)	Enter the debugger.
I (Ignore)	Return to the caller.

You can specify any combination of error values for the *nErrCode* parameter, since the meaning of the values is unique to your application. However, the error value −1 must always be reserved for the stack-overflow message. When this value is specified, Windows automatically displays a stack-overflow message.

See Also

FatalAppExit

FillRect

int FillRect(*hdc*, *lprc*, *hbr*)
HDC *hdc*;   /* handle of device context   */
const RECT FAR* *lprc*;   /* address of structure with rectangle   */
HBRUSH *hbr*;   /* handle of brush   */

The **FillRect** function fills a given rectangle by using the specified brush. The **FillRect** function fills the complete rectangle, including the left and top borders, but does not fill the right and bottom borders.

Parameters

hdc
Identifies the device context.

lprc
Points to a **RECT** structure that contains the logical coordinates of the rectangle to be filled. The **RECT** structure has the following form:

```
typedef struct tagRECT {    /* rc */
    int left;
    int top;
    int right;
    int bottom;
} RECT;
```

For a full description of this structure, see the *Microsoft Windows Programmer's Reference, Volume 3*.

hbr
Identifies the brush used to fill the rectangle.

Return Value

The return value is not used and has no meaning.

Comments

The brush must be created by using either the **CreateHatchBrush, CreatePatternBrush**, or **CreateSolidBrush** function, or retrieved by using the **GetStockObject** function.

When filling the specified rectangle, the **FillRect** function does not include the rectangle's right and bottom sides. Graphics device interface (GDI) fills a rectangle up to, but not including, the right column and bottom row, regardless of the current mapping mode.

FillRect compares the values of the **top, bottom, left**, and **right** members of the specified **RECT** structure. If **bottom** is less than or equal to **top**, or if **right** is less than or equal to **left**, the function does not draw the rectangle.

See Also

CreateHatchBrush, CreatePatternBrush, CreateSolidBrush, GetStockObject, InvertRect

FillRgn

BOOL FillRgn(*hdc*, *hrgn*, *hbr*)
HDC *hdc*;   /* handle of device context   */
HRGN *hrgn*;   /* handle of region   */
HBRUSH *hbr*;   /* handle of brush   */

The **FillRgn** function fills the given region by using the specified brush.

Parameters   *hdc*
Identifies the device context.

hrgn
Identifies the region to be filled. The coordinates for the given region are specified in device units.

hbr
Identifies the brush to be used to fill the region.

Return Value   The return value is nonzero if the function is successful. Otherwise, it is zero.

Example   The following example uses a blue brush to fill a rectangular region. Note that it is not necessary to select the brush into the device context before using it to fill the region.

```
HRGN hrgn;
HBRUSH hBrush;

hrgn = CreateRectRgn(10, 10, 110, 110);
SelectObject(hdc, hrgn);

hBrush = CreateSolidBrush(RGB(0, 0, 255));

FillRgn(hdc, hrgn, hBrush);

DeleteObject(hrgn);
```

See Also   **CreateBrushIndirect, CreateDIBPatternBrush, CreateHatchBrush, CreatePatternBrush, CreateSolidBrush, PaintRgn**

FindAtom

2.x

ATOM FindAtom(*lpszString*)
LPCSTR *lpszString*;   /* address of string to find   */

The **FindAtom** function searches the local atom table for the specified character string and retrieves the atom associated with that string.

Parameters   *lpszString*
Points to the null-terminated character string to search for.

Return Value   The return value identifies the atom associated with the given string if the function is successful. Otherwise (if the string is not in the table), the return value is zero.

Example   The following example uses the **FindAtom** function to retrieve the atom for the string "This is an atom":

```
ATOM at;
char szMsg[80];

if ((at = FindAtom("This is an atom")) == 0)
    MessageBox(hwnd, "could not find atom",
        "FindAtom", MB_ICONEXCLAMATION);
else {
    wsprintf(szMsg, "atom = %u", at);
    MessageBox(hwnd, szMsg, "FindAtom", MB_OK);
}
```

See Also   **AddAtom, DeleteAtom**

FindExecutable

3.1

#include <shellapi.h>

HINSTANCE FindExecutable(*lpszFile*, *lpszDir*, *lpszResult*)
LPCSTR *lpszFile*;   /* address of string for filename   */
LPCSTR *lpszDir*;   /* address of string for default directory   */
LPSTR *lpszResult*;   /* address of string for executable file on return */

The **FindExecutable** function finds and retrieves the executable filename that is associated with a specified filename.

Parameters	*lpszFile* Points to a null-terminated string specifying a filename. This can be a document or executable file.

Parameters

lpszFile
Points to a null-terminated string specifying a filename. This can be a document or executable file.

lpszDir
Points to a null-terminated string specifying the drive letter and path for the default directory.

lpszResult
Points to a buffer that receives the name of an executable file when the function returns. This null-terminated string specifies the application that is started when the Open command is chosen from the File menu in File Manager.

Return Value

The return value is greater than 32 if the function is successful. If the return value is less than or equal to 32, it specifies an error code.

Errors

The **FindExecutable** function returns 31 if there is no association for the specified file type. The other possible error values are as follows:

Value	Meaning
0	System was out of memory, executable file was corrupt, or relocations were invalid.
2	File was not found.
3	Path was not found.
5	Attempt was made to dynamically link to a task, or there was a sharing or network-protection error.
6	Library required separate data segments for each task.
8	There was insufficient memory to start the application.
10	Windows version was incorrect.
11	Executable file was invalid. Either it was not a Windows application or there was an error in the .EXE image.
12	Application was designed for a different operating system.
13	Application was designed for MS-DOS 4.0.
14	Type of executable file was unknown.
15	Attempt was made to load a real-mode application (developed for an earlier version of Windows).
16	Attempt was made to load a second instance of an executable file containing multiple data segments that were not marked read-only.
19	Attempt was made to load a compressed executable file. The file must be decompressed before it can be loaded.
20	Dynamic-link library (DLL) file was invalid. One of the DLLs required to run this application was corrupt.
21	Application requires Microsoft Windows 32-bit extensions.

Comments   The filename specified in the *lpszFile* parameter is associated with an executable
                       file when an association has been registered between that file's filename extension
                       and an executable file in the registration database. An application that produces
                       files with a given filename extension typically associates the extension with an ex-
                       ecutable file when the application is installed.

See Also   **RegQueryValue**, **ShellExecute**

FindResource   2.x

HRSRC FindResource(*hinst*, *lpszName*, *lpszType*)
HINSTANCE *hinst*;   /* handle of module containing resource   */
LPCSTR *lpszName*;   /* address of resource name   */
LPCSTR *lpszType*;   /* address of resource type   */

The **FindResource** function determines the location of a resource in the specified
resource file.

Parameters   *hinst*
                       Identifies the instance of the module whose executable file contains the re-
                       source.

                       lpszName
                       Specifies the name of the resource. For details, see the following Comments
                       section.

                       lpszType
                       Specifies the resource type. For details, see the following Comments section.
                       For predefined resource types, this parameter should be one of the following
                       values:

Value	Meaning
RT_ACCELERATOR	Accelerator table
RT_BITMAP	Bitmap resource
RT_CURSOR	Cursor resource
RT_DIALOG	Dialog box
RT_FONT	Font resource
RT_FONTDIR	Font directory resource
RT_ICON	Icon resource
RT_MENU	Menu resource
RT_RCDATA	User-defined resource (raw data)
RT_STRING	String resource

Return Value   The return value is the handle of the named resource if the function is successful. Otherwise, it is NULL.

Comments   If the high-order word of the *lpszName* or *lpszType* parameter is zero, the low-order word specifies the integer identifier of the name or type of the given resource. Otherwise, the parameters are long pointers to null-terminated strings. If the first character of the string is a pound sign (#), the remaining characters represent a decimal number that specifies the integer identifier of the resource's name or type. For example, the string #258 represents the integer ID 258.

To reduce the amount of memory required for the resources used by an application, the application should refer to the resources by integer identifier instead of by name.

An application must not call the **FindResource** and **LoadResource** functions to load cursor, icon, and string resources. Instead, it must load these resources by calling the **LoadCursor**, **LoadIcon**, and **LoadString** functions, respectively.

Although the application can call the **FindResource** and **LoadResource** functions to load other predefined resource types, it should load the corresponding resources by calling the **LoadAccelerators**, **LoadBitmap**, and **LoadMenu** functions.

See Also   **LoadAccelerators, LoadBitmap, LoadCursor, LoadIcon, LoadMenu, LoadResource, LoadString**

FindText

3.1

#include <commdlg.h>

HWND FindText(*lpfr***)**
FINDREPLACE FAR* *lpfr*;   /* address of structure with initialization data   */

The **FindText** function creates a system-defined modeless dialog box that makes it possible for the user to find text within a document. The application must perform the search operation.

Parameters   *lpfr*
Points to a **FINDREPLACE** structure that contains information used to initialize the dialog box. When the user makes a selection in the dialog box, the system fills this structure with information about the user's selection and then sends a message to the application. This message contains a pointer to the **FINDREPLACE** structure.

The **FINDREPLACE** structure has the following form:

```
#include <commdlg.h>

typedef struct tagFINDREPLACE {      /* fr */
    DWORD     lStructSize;
    HWND      hwndOwner;
    HINSTANCE hInstance;
    DWORD     Flags;
    LPSTR     lpstrFindWhat;
    LPSTR     lpstrReplaceWith;
    UINT      wFindWhatLen;
    UINT      wReplaceWithLen;
    LPARAM    lCustData;
    UINT      (CALLBACK* lpfnHook)(HWND, UINT, WPARAM, LPARAM);
    LPCSTR    lpTemplateName;
} FINDREPLACE;
```

For a full description of this structure, see the *Microsoft Windows Programmer's Reference, Volume 3.*

Return Value

The return value is the window handle of the dialog box if the function is successful. Otherwise, it is NULL. An application can use this window handle to communicate with or to close the dialog box.

Errors

Use the **CommDlgExtendedError** function to retrieve the error value, which may be one of the following values:

CDERR_FINDRESFAILURE
CDERR_INITIALIZATION
CDERR_LOCKRESFAILURE
CDERR_LOADRESFAILURE
CDERR_LOADSTRFAILURE
CDERR_MEMALLOCFAILURE
CDERR_MEMLOCKFAILURE
CDERR_NOHINSTANCE
CDERR_NOHOOK
CDERR_NOTEMPLATE
CDERR_STRUCTSIZE
FRERR_BUFFERLENGTHZERO

Comments

The dialog box procedure for the Find dialog box passes user requests to the application through special messages. The *lParam* parameter of each of these messages contains a pointer to a **FINDREPLACE** structure. The procedure sends the messages to the window identified by the **hwndOwner** member of the **FIND-REPLACE** structure. An application can register the identifier for these messages by specifying the "commdlg_FindReplace" string in a call to the **Register-WindowMessage** function.

For the TAB key to function correctly, any application that calls the **FindText** function must also call the **IsDialogMessage** function in its main message loop. (The **IsDialogMessage** function returns a value that indicates whether messages are intended for the Find dialog box.)

If the hook function (to which the **lpfnHook** member of the **FINDREPLACE** structure points) processes the WM_CTLCOLOR message, this function must return a handle of the brush that should be used to paint the control background.

Example   The following example initializes a **FINDREPLACE** structure and calls the **FindText** function to display the Find dialog box:

```
FINDREPLACE fr;

/* Set all structure members to zero. */

memset(&fr, 0, sizeof(FINDREPLACE));

fr.lStructSize = sizeof(FINDREPLACE);
fr.hwndOwner = hwnd;
fr.lpstrFindWhat = szFindWhat;
fr.wFindWhatLen = sizeof(szFindWhat);

hDlg = FindText(&fr);

break;
```

In addition to initializing the members of the **FINDREPLACE** structure and calling the **FindText** function, an application must register the special FINDMSGSTRING message and process messages from the dialog box.

The following example registers the message by using the **RegisterWindowMessage** function:

```
UINT uFindReplaceMsg;

/* Register the FindReplace message. */

uFindReplaceMsg = RegisterWindowMessage(FINDMSGSTRING);
```

After the application registers the FINDMSGSTRING message, it can process messages by using the **RegisterWindowMessage** return value. An application must check the FR_DIALOGTERM bit in the **Flags** member of the **FIND-REPLACE** structure when it processes this message, as in the following example:

```
LRESULT CALLBACK MainWndProc(HWND hwnd, UINT msg, WPARAM wParam,
    LPARAM lParam)
```

```
    {
        static FINDREPLACE FAR* lpfr;

        if (msg == uFindReplaceMsg) {
            lpfr = (FINDREPLACE FAR*) lParam;
            SearchFile((BOOL) (lpfr->Flags & FR_DOWN),
                (BOOL) (lpfr->Flags & FR_MATCHCASE));
            return 0;
        }
        SearchFile((BOOL) (lpfr->Flags & FR_DOWN),
            (BOOL) (lpfr->Flags & FR_MATCHCASE));
        return 0;
    }
```

See Also   **IsDialogMessage, RegisterWindowMessage, ReplaceText**

FindWindow   2.x

HWND FindWindow(*lpszClassName*, *lpszWindow*)
LPCSTR *lpszClassName*;   /* address of class-name string   */
LPCSTR *lpszWindow*;   /* address of window-name string   */

The **FindWindow** function retrieves the handle of the window whose class name and window name match the specified strings. This function does not search child windows.

Parameters   *lpszClassName*
Points to a null-terminated string that contains the window's class name. If this parameter is NULL, all class names match.

lpszWindow
Points to a null-terminated string that specifies the window name (the window's title). If this parameter is NULL, all window names match.

Return Value   The return value is the handle of the window that has the specified class name and window name if the function is successful. Otherwise, it is NULL.

Example   The following example searches for the main window of Windows Control Panel (CONTROL.EXE) and, if it does not find it, starts Control Panel:

```
if (FindWindow("CtlPanelClass", "Control Panel") == NULL)
    WinExec("control.exe", SW_SHOWNA);
```

See Also   **EnumWindows, GetWindow, WindowFromPoint**

FlashWindow

BOOL FlashWindow(*hwnd, fInvert*)
HWND *hwnd*;   /* handle of window to flash   */
BOOL *fInvert*;   /* invert flag   */

The **FlashWindow** function flashes the given window once. Flashing a window means changing the appearance of its title bar as if the window were changing from inactive to active status or vice versa. (An inactive title bar changes to an active title bar or an active title bar changes to an inactive title bar.)

Typically, a window is flashed to inform the user that the window requires attention but that it does not currently have the input focus.

Parameters   *hwnd*
Identifies the window to be flashed. The window can be either open or minimized.

fInvert
Specifies whether to flash the window or return it to its original state. If this parameter is TRUE, the window is flashed from one state to the other. If the parameter is FALSE, the window is returned to its original state (either active or inactive).

Return Value   The return value is nonzero if the window was active before the call to the **FlashWindow** function. Otherwise, it is zero.

Comments   The **FlashWindow** function flashes the window only once; for successive flashing, the application should create a system timer.

The *fInvert* parameter should be FALSE only when the window is receiving the input focus and will no longer be flashing; it should be TRUE on successive calls while waiting to get the input focus.

This function always returns nonzero for minimized windows. If the window is minimized, **FlashWindow** simply flashes the window's icon; *fInvert* is ignored for minimized windows.

See Also   **MessageBeep**

FloodFill

2.x

BOOL FloodFill(*hdc*, *nXStart*, *nYStart*, *clrref*)
HDC *hdc*;   /* handle of device context   */
int *nXStart*;   /* x-coordinate of starting position   */
int *nYStart*;   /* y-coordinate of starting position   */
COLORREF *clrref*;   /* color of fill boundary   */

The **FloodFill** function fills an area of the screen surface by using the current brush. The area is assumed to be bounded as specified by the *clrref* parameter. The **FloodFill** function begins at the point specified by the *nXStart* and *nYStart* parameters and continues in all directions to the color boundary.

Parameters

hdc
Identifies the device context.

nXStart
Specifies the logical x-coordinate at which to begin filling.

nYStart
Specifies the logical y-coordinate at which to begin filling.

clrref
Specifies the color of the boundary.

Return Value

The return value is nonzero if the function is successful. Otherwise, it is zero, indicating that the filling cannot be completed, that the given point has the boundary color specified by *clrref*, or that the point is outside the clipping region.

Comments

Only memory device contexts and devices that support raster-display technology support the **FloodFill** function. For more information about raster capabilities, see the description of the **GetDeviceCaps** function.

See Also

ExtFloodFill, GetDeviceCaps

FlushComm

2.x

int FlushComm(*idComDev*, *fnQueue*)
int *idComDev*;   /* communications-device identifier   */
int *fnQueue*;   /* queue to flush   */

The **FlushComm** function flushes all characters from the transmission or receiving queue of the specified communications device.

Parameters	*idComDev*

Specifies the communication device to be flushed. The **OpenComm** function returns this value.

fnQueue

Specifies the queue to be flushed. If this parameter is zero, the transmission queue is flushed. If the parameter is 1, the receiving queue is flushed.

Return Value   The return value is zero if the function is successful. It is less than zero if *idComDev* is not a valid device or if *fnQueue* is not a valid queue. The return value is positive if there is an error for the specified device. For a list of the possible error values, see the **GetCommError** function.

See Also   **GetCommError, OpenComm**

FMExtensionProc   3.1

#include <wfext.h>

HMENU FAR PASCAL FMExtensionProc(*hwnd*, *wMsg*, *lParam*)
HWND *hwnd*;   /* handle of the extension window   */
WORD *wMsg*;   /* menu-item identifier or message   */
LONG *lParam*;   /* additional message information   */

The **FMExtensionProc** function, an application-defined callback function, processes menu commands and messages sent to a File Manager extension dynamic-link library (DLL).

Parameters   *hwnd*

Identifies the File Manager window. An extension DLL should use this handle to specify the parent for any dialog boxes or message boxes that the DLL may display and to send request messages to File Manager.

wMsg

Specifies the message. This parameter may be one of the following values:

Value	Meaning
1–99	Identifier for the menu item that the user selected.
FMEVENT_INITMENU	User selected the extension's menu.
FMEVENT_LOAD	File Manager is loading the extension DLL.
FMEVENT_SELCHANGE	Selection in File Manager's directory window, or Search Results window, changed.

Value	Meaning
FMEVENT_UNLOAD	File Manager is unloading the extension DLL.
FMEVENT_USER_REFRESH	User chose the Refresh command from the Window menu.

lParam
Specifies 32 bits of additional message-dependent information.

Return Value
The callback function should return the result of the message processing. The actual return value depends on the message that is processed.

Comments
Whenever File Manager calls the **FMExtensionProc** function, it waits to refresh its directory windows (for changes in the file system) until after the function returns. This allows the extension to perform large numbers of file operations without excessive repainting by the File Manager. The extension does not need to send the FM_REFRESH_WINDOWS message to notify File Manager to repaint its windows.

FrameRect

2.x

int FrameRect(*hdc*, *lprc*, *hbr*)
HDC *hdc*;   /* handle of device context   */
const RECT FAR* *lprc*;   /* address of structure with rectangle   */
HBRUSH *hbr*;   /* handle of brush   */

The **FrameRect** function draws a border around a rectangle, using the specified brush. The width and height of the border are always one logical unit.

Parameters
hdc
Identifies the device context in which to draw the border.

lprc
Points to a **RECT** structure that contains the logical coordinates of the upper-left and lower-right corners of the rectangle. The **RECT** structure has the following form:

```
typedef struct tagRECT {    /* rc */
    int left;
    int top;
    int right;
    int bottom;
} RECT;
```

For a full description of this structure, see the *Microsoft Windows Programmer's Reference, Volume 3*.

hbr
Identifies the brush that will be used to draw the border.

Return Value   The return value is not used and has no meaning.

Comments   The border drawn by the **FrameRect** function is in the same position as a border drawn by the **Rectangle** function using the same coordinates (if **Rectangle** uses a pen that is one logical unit wide). The interior of the rectangle is not filled when an application calls **FrameRect**.

FrameRect compares the values of the **top**, **bottom**, **left**, and **right** members of the specified **RECT** structure. If **bottom** is less than or equal to **top**, or if **right** is less than or equal to **left**, **FrameRect** does not draw the rectangle.

See Also   **CreateHatchBrush, CreatePatternBrush, CreateSolidBrush, DrawFocusRect**

FrameRgn   2.x

```
BOOL FrameRgn(hdc, hrgn, hbr, nWidth, nHeight)
HDC hdc;          /* handle of device context   */
HRGN hrgn;        /* handle of region           */
HBRUSH hbr;       /* handle of brush            */
int nWidth;       /* width of region frame      */
int nHeight;      /* height of region frame     */
```

The **FrameRgn** function draws a border around the given region, using the specified brush.

Parameters   *hdc*
Identifies the device context.

hrgn
Identifies the region to be enclosed in a border.

hbr
Identifies the brush to be used to draw the border.

nWidth
Specifies the width, in device units, of vertical brush strokes.

nHeight
Specifies the height, in device units, of horizontal brush strokes.

Return Value   The return value is nonzero if the function is successful. Otherwise, it is zero.

Example   The following example uses a blue brush to frame a rectangular region. Note that it is not necessary to select the brush or the region into the device context.

```
HRGN hrgn;
HBRUSH hBrush;
int Width = 5, Height = 2;

hrgn = CreateRectRgn(10, 10, 110, 110);
hBrush = CreateSolidBrush(RGB(0, 0, 255));

FrameRgn(hdc, hrgn, hBrush, Width, Height);

DeleteObject(hrgn);
DeleteObject(hBrush);
```

See Also   **FillRgn, PaintRgn**

FreeAllGDIMem   3.1

#include <stress.h>

void FreeAllGDIMem(void)

The **FreeAllGDIMem** function frees all memory allocated by the **AllocGDIMem** function.

Parameters   This function has no parameters.

Return Value   This function does not return a value.

See Also   **AllocGDIMem**

FreeAllMem

3.1

#include <stress.h>

void FreeAllMem(void)

> The **FreeAllMem** function frees all memory allocated by the **AllocMem** function.

Parameters   This function has no parameters.

Return Value   This function does not return a value.

See Also   **AllocMem**

FreeAllUserMem

3.1

#include <stress.h>

void FreeAllUserMem(void)

> The **FreeAllUserMem** function frees all memory allocated by the **AllocUserMem** function.

Parameters   This function has no parameters.

Return Value   This function does not return a value.

See Also   **AllocUserMem**

FreeLibrary

2.x

void FreeLibrary(*hinst***)**
HINSTANCE *hinst*;   /* handle of loaded library module   */

> The **FreeLibrary** function decrements (decreases by one) the reference count of the loaded library module. When the reference count reaches zero, the memory occupied by the module is freed.

Parameters	*hinst* Identifies the loaded library module.
Return Value	This function does not return a value.
Comments	A dynamic-link library (DLL) must not call the **FreeLibrary** function within its **WEP** function (Windows exit procedure).
	The reference count for a library module is incremented (increased by one) each time an application calls the **LoadLibrary** function for the library module.
Example	The following example uses the **LoadLibrary** function to load TOOLHELP.DLL and the **FreeLibrary** function to free it:

```
HINSTANCE hinstToolHelp = LoadLibrary("TOOLHELP.DLL");

if ((UINT) hinstToolHelp > 32) {
        .
        . /* use GetProcAddress to use TOOLHELP functions */
        .
}
else {
    ErrorHandler();
}

if ((UINT) hinstToolHelp > 32)
    FreeLibrary(hinstToolHelp); /* free TOOLHELP.DLL        */
```

See Also	**GetProcAddress, LoadLibrary, WEP**

FreeModule

3.0

BOOL FreeModule(*hinst*)
HINSTANCE *hinst*;   /* handle of loaded module   */

The **FreeModule** function decrements (decreases by one) the reference count of the loaded module. When the reference count reaches zero, the memory occupied by the module is freed.

Parameters	*hinst* Identifies the loaded module.
Return Value	The return value is zero if the reference count is decremented to zero and the module's memory is freed. Otherwise, the return value is nonzero.

Comments	The reference count for a module is incremented (increased by one) each time an application calls the **LoadModule** function for the module.
See Also	**LoadModule**

FreeProcInstance

2.x

void FreeProcInstance(*lpProc***)**
FARPROC *lpProc*;   /* instance address of function to free   */

The **FreeProcInstance** function frees the specified function from the data segment bound to it by the **MakeProcInstance** function.

Parameters	*lpProc* Points to the procedure-instance address of the function to be freed. It must be created by using the **MakeProcInstance** function.
Return Value	This function does not return a value.
Comments	After a procedure instance has been freed, attempts to call the function using the freed procedure-instance address will result in an unrecoverable error.
See Also	**MakeProcInstance**

FreeResource

2.x

BOOL FreeResource(*hglbResource***)**
HGLOBAL *hglbResource*;   /* handle of loaded resource   */

The **FreeResource** function decrements (decreases by one) the reference count of a loaded resource. When the reference count reaches zero, the memory occupied by the resource is freed.

Parameters	*hglbResource* Identifies the data associated with the resource. The handle is assumed to have been created by using the **LoadResource** function.

Return Value   The return value is zero if the function is successful. Otherwise, it is nonzero, indicating that the function has failed and the resource has not been freed.

Comments   The reference count for a resource is incremented (increased by one) each time an application calls the **LoadResource** function for the resource.

See Also   **LoadResource**

FreeSelector   `3.0`

UINT FreeSelector(*uSelector*)
UINT *uSelector*;   /* selector to be freed   */

The **FreeSelector** function frees a selector originally allocated by the **AllocSelector** or **AllocDStoCSAlias** function. After the application calls this function, the selector is invalid and must not be used.

An application should not use this function unless it is absolutely necessary, since its use violates preferred Windows programming practices.

Parameters   *uSelector*
    Specifies the selector to be freed.

Return Value   The return value is zero if the function is successful. Otherwise, it is the selector specified by the *uSelector* parameter.

See Also   **AllocDStoCSAlias, AllocSelector**

GetActiveWindow   `2.x`

HWND GetActiveWindow(void)

The **GetActiveWindow** function retrieves the window handle of the active window. The active window is either the top-level window associated with the input focus or the window explicitly made active by the **SetActiveWindow** function.

Parameters   This function has no parameters.

Return Value   The return value is the handle of the active window or NULL if no window was active at the time of the call.

See Also   **GetCapture, GetFocus, GetLastActivePopup, SetActiveWindow**

GetAspectRatioFilter   `2.x`

DWORD GetAspectRatioFilter(*hdc***)**
HDC *hdc*;   /* handle of device context   */

The **GetAspectRatioFilter** function retrieves the setting for the current aspect-ratio filter. The aspect ratio is the ratio formed by a device's pixel width and height. Information about a device's aspect ratio is used in the creation, selection, and display of fonts. Windows provides a special filter, the aspect-ratio filter, to select fonts designed for a particular aspect ratio from all of the available fonts. The filter uses the aspect ratio specified by the **SetMapperFlags** function.

Parameters   *hdc*
Identifies the device context that contains the specified aspect ratio.

Return Value   The low-order word of the return value contains the x-coordinate of the aspect ratio if the function is successful; the high-order word contains the y-coordinate.

See Also   **SetMapperFlags**

GetAspectRatioFilterEx   `3.1`

BOOL GetAspectRatioFilterEx(*hdc, lpAspectRatio***)**
HDC *hdc*;
SIZE FAR* *lpAspectRatio*;

The **GetAspectRatioFilterEx** function retrieves the setting for the current aspect-ratio filter. The aspect ratio is the ratio formed by a device's pixel width and height. Information about a device's aspect ratio is used in the creation, selection, and displaying of fonts. Windows provides a special filter, the aspect-ratio filter, to select fonts designed for a particular aspect ratio from all of the available fonts. The filter uses the aspect ratio specified by the **SetMapperFlags** function.

Parameters   *hDC*
                      Identifies the device context that contains the specified aspect ratio.

                      lpAspectRatio
                      Pointer to a **SIZE** structure where the current aspect ratio filter will be returned.

Return Value   The return value is nonzero if the function is successful. Otherwise, it is zero.

See Also   **SetMapperFlags**

GetAsyncKeyState   2.x

int GetAsyncKeyState(*vkey*)
int *vkey*;   /* virtual-key code   */

                      The **GetAsyncKeyState** function determines whether a key is up or down at the
                      time the function is called and whether the key was pressed after a previous call to
                      the **GetAsyncKeyState** function.

Parameters   *vkey*
                      Specifies one of 256 possible virtual-key codes.

Return Value   The return value specifies whether the key was pressed since the last call to the
                      GetAsyncKeyState function and whether the key is currently up or down. If the
                      most significant bit is set, the key is down, and if the least significant bit is set, the
                      key was pressed after a preceding **GetAsyncKeyState** call.

Comments   If VK_LBUTTON or VK_RBUTTON is specified in the *vkey* parameter, this func-
                      tion returns the state of the physical left or right mouse button regardless of
                      whether the **SwapMouseButton** function has been used to reverse the meaning of
                      the buttons.

See Also   **GetKeyboardState, GetKeyState, SetKeyboardState, SwapMouseButton**

GetAtomHandle

HLOCAL GetAtomHandle(*atm*)
ATOM *atm*;   /* atom to retrieve handle of   */

The **GetAtomHandle** function retrieves a handle of the specified atom.

This function is only provided for compatibility with Windows, versions 1.*x* and 2.*x*. It should not be used with Windows 3.0 and later.

Parameters
atm
Specifies an atom whose handle is to be retrieved.

Return Value
The return value is a handle of the specified atom if the function is successful.

See Also
GetAtomName, GlobalGetAtomName

GetAtomName

UINT GetAtomName(*atm*, *lpszBuffer*, *cbBuffer*)
ATOM *atm*;   /* atom identifying character string   */
LPSTR *lpszBuffer*;   /* address of buffer for atom string   */
int *cbBuffer*;   /* size of buffer   */

The **GetAtomName** function retrieves a copy of the character string associated with the specified local atom.

Parameters
atm
Specifies the local atom that identifies the character string to be retrieved.

lpszBuffer
Points to the buffer for the character string.

cbBuffer
Specifies the maximum size, in bytes, of the buffer.

Return Value
The return value specifies the number of bytes copied to the buffer, if the function is successful.

Comments
The string returned for an integer atom (an atom created by the **MAKEINT-ATOM** macro) will be a null-terminated string, where the first character is a pound sign (#) and the remaining characters make up the **UINT** used in **MAKE-INTATOM**.

Example   The following example uses the **GetAtomName** function to retrieve the character string associated with a local atom:

```
char szBuf[80];

GetAtomName(atTest, szBuf, sizeof(szBuf));

MessageBox(hwnd, szBuf, "GetAtomName", MB_OK);
```

See Also   **AddAtom, DeleteAtom, FindAtom**

GetBitmapBits

2.x

LONG GetBitmapBits(*hbm*, *cbBuffer*, *lpvBits*)
HBITMAP *hbm*;   /* handle of bitmap   */
LONG *cbBuffer*;   /* number of bytes to copy to buffer   */
void FAR* *lpvBits*;   /* address of buffer for bitmap bits   */

The **GetBitmapBits** function copies the bits of the specified bitmap into a buffer.

Parameters   *hbm*
Identifies the bitmap.

cbBuffer
Specifies the number of bytes to be copied.

lpvBits
Points to the buffer that is to receive the bitmap. The bitmap is an array of bytes. This array conforms to a structure in which horizontal scan lines are multiples of 16 bits.

Return Value   The return value specifies the number of bytes in the bitmap if the function is successful. It is zero if there is an error.

Comments   An application can use the **GetObject** function to determine the number of bytes to copy into the buffer pointed to by the *lpvBits* parameter.

See Also   **GetObject, SetBitmapBits**

GetBitmapDimension

2.x

DWORD GetBitmapDimension(*hbm***)**
HBITMAP *hbm*;   /* handle of bitmap   */

The **GetBitmapDimension** function returns the width and height of the specified bitmap. The height and width is assumed to have been set by the **SetBitmap-Dimension** function.

Parameters   *hbm*
            Identifies the bitmap.

Return Value   The low-order word of the return value contains the bitmap width, in tenths of a millimeter, if the function is successful; the high-order word contains the height. If the bitmap width and height have not been set by using the **SetBitmapDimension** function, the return value is zero.

See Also   **SetBitmapDimension**

GetBitmapDimensionEx

2.x

BOOL GetBitmapDimensionEx(*hBitmap***,** *lpDimension***)**
HBITMAP *hBitmap*;   /* handle of bitmap   */
SIZE FAR* *lpDimension*;   /* address of dimension structure   */

The **GetBitmapDimensionEx** function returns the dimensions of the bitmap previously set by the **SetBitmapDimensionEx** function. If no dimensions have been set, a default of 0,0 will be returned.

Parameters   *hBitmap*
            Identifies the bitmap.

            lpDimension
            Points to a **SIZE** structure to which the dimensions are returned. The **SIZE** structure has the following form:

```
typedef struct tagSIZE {
    int cx;
    int cy;
} SIZE;
```

            For a full description of this structure, see the *Microsoft Windows Programmer's Reference, Volume 3.*

Return Value   The return value is nonzero if the function is successful. Otherwise, it is zero.

See Also   **SetBitmapDimensionEx**

GetBkColor

COLORREF GetBkColor(*hdc*)
HDC *hdc*;   /* handle of device context   */

The **GetBkColor** function returns the current background color.

Parameters   *hdc*
                    Identifies the device context.

Return Value   The return value is an RGB (red, green, blue) color value if the function is suc-
                    cessful.

Comments   If the background mode is OPAQUE, the system uses the background color to fill
                    the gaps in styled lines, the gaps between hatched lines in brushes, and the back-
                    ground in character cells. The system also uses the background color when con-
                    verting bitmaps between color and monochrome device contexts.

Example   The following example uses the **GetBkColor** function to determine whether the
                    current background color is white. If it is, the **SetBkColor** function sets it to red.

```
DWORD dwBackColor;

dwBackColor = GetBkColor(hdc);
if (dwBackColor == RGB(255, 255, 255)) { /* if color is white */
    SetBkColor(hdc, RGB(255, 0, 0));      /* sets color to red */
    TextOut(hdc, 100, 200, "SetBkColor test.", 16);
}
```

See Also   **GetBkMode, SetBkColor, SetBkMode**

GetBkMode

int GetBkMode(*hdc*)
HDC *hdc*;   /* handle of device context   */

The **GetBkMode** function returns the background mode. The background mode defines whether the system removes existing background colors on the drawing surface before drawing text, hatched brushes, or any pen style that is not a solid line.

Parameters   *hdc*
                    Identifies the device context.

Return Value   The return value specifies the current background mode if the function is successful. It can be OPAQUE, TRANSPARENT, or TRANSPARENT1.

Example   The following example determines the current background mode by calling the **GetBkMode** function. If the mode is OPAQUE, the **SetBkMode** function sets it to TRANSPARENT.

```
int nBackMode;

nBackMode = GetBkMode(hdc);
if (nBackMode == OPAQUE) {
    TextOut(hdc, 90, 100, "This background mode is OPAQUE.", 31);
    SetBkMode(hdc, TRANSPARENT);
}
```

See Also   **GetBkColor, SetBkColor, SetBkMode**

GetBoundsRect

UINT GetBoundsRect(*hdc*, *lprcBounds*, *flags*)
HDC *hdc*;   /* handle of device context   */
RECT FAR* *lprcBounds*;   /* address of structure for bounding rectangle */
UINT *flags*;   /* specifies information to return   */

The **GetBoundsRect** function returns the current accumulated bounding rectangle for the specified device context.

Parameters   *hdc*
                      Identifies the device context to return the bounding rectangle for.

                      lprcBounds
                      Points to a buffer that will receive the current bounding rectangle. The rectangle
                      is returned in logical coordinates.

                      flags
                      Specifies whether the bounding rectangle is to be cleared after it is returned.
                      This parameter can be DCB_RESET, to clear the rectangle. Otherwise, it
                      should be zero.

Return Value   The return value is DCB_SET if the bounding rectangle is not empty. Otherwise,
                      it is DCB_RESET.

Comments   To ensure that the bounding rectangle is empty, check both the DCB_RESET bit
                      and the DCB_ACCUMULATE bit in the return value. If DCB_RESET is set and
                      DCB_ACCUMULATE is not, the bounding rectangle is empty.

See Also   **SetBoundsRect**

GetBrushOrg   `2.x`

DWORD GetBrushOrg(*hdc***)**
HDC *hdc*;   /* handle of device context   */

                      The **GetBrushOrg** function retrieves the origin, in device coordinates, of the
                      brush currently selected for the given device context.

Parameters   *hdc*
                      Identifies the device context.

Return Value   The low-order word of the return value contains the current x-coordinate of the
                      brush, in device coordinates, if the function is successful; the high-order word con-
                      tains the y-coordinate.

Comments   The initial brush origin is at the coordinates (0,0) in the client area. The return value specifies these coordinates in device units relative to the origin of the desktop window.

Example   The following example uses the **LOWORD** and **HIWORD** macros to extract the x- and y-coordinate of the current brush from the return value of the **GetBrush-Org** function:

```
DWORD dwBrOrg;
WORD wXBrOrg, wYBrOrg;

dwBrOrg = GetBrushOrg(hdc);
wXBrOrg = LOWORD(dwBrOrg);
wYBrOrg = HIWORD(dwBrOrg);
```

See Also   **SelectObject, SetBrushOrg**

GetBrushOrgEx   3.1

BOOL GetBrushOrgEx(*hDC, lpPoint***)**
HDC *hDC*;   /* handle of device context   */
POINT FAR* *lpPoint*;   /* address of structure for brush origin   */

The **GetBrushOrgEx** function retrieves the current brush origin for the given device context.

Parameters   *hDC*
                    Identifies the device context.

                    lpPoint
                    Points to a **POINT** structure to which the device coordinates of the brush origin are to be returned. The **POINT** structure has the following form:

```
typedef struct tagPOINT {   /* pt */
    int x;
    int y;
} POINT;
```

For a full description of this structure, see the *Microsoft Windows Programmer's Reference, Volume 3*.

Return Value   The return value is nonzero if the function is successful. Otherwise, it is zero.

Comments   The initial brush origin is at the coordinate (0,0).

See Also   **SetBrushOrg**

GetCapture   `2.x`

HWND GetCapture(void)

The **GetCapture** function retrieves a handle of the window that has the mouse capture. Only one window has the mouse capture at any given time; this window receives mouse input whether or not the cursor is within its borders.

Parameters   This function has no parameters.

Return Value   The return value is a handle identifying the window that has the mouse capture if the function is successful. It is NULL if no window has the mouse capture.

Comments   A window receives the mouse capture when its handle is passed as the *hwnd* parameter of the **SetCapture** function.

See Also   **SetCapture**

GetCaretBlinkTime   `2.x`

UINT GetCaretBlinkTime(void)

The **GetCaretBlinkTime** function retrieves the caret blink rate. The blink rate is the elapsed time, in milliseconds, between flashes of the caret.

Parameters   This function has no parameters.

Return Value   The return value specifies the blink rate, in milliseconds, if the function is successful.

See Also   **SetCaretBlinkTime**

GetCaretPos   2.x

void GetCaretPos(*lppt*)
POINT FAR* *lppt*;   /* address of structure to receive coordinates   */

The **GetCaretPos** function retrieves the current position of the caret.

Parameters   *lppt*
Points to a **POINT** structure that receives the client coordinates of the caret's current position. The **POINT** structure has the following form:

```
typedef struct tagPOINT {    /* pt */
    int x;
    int y;
} POINT;
```

For a full description of this structure, see the *Microsoft Windows Programmer's Reference, Volume 3*.

Return Value   This function does not return a value.

Comments   The caret position is always given in the client coordinates of the window that contains the caret.

See Also   **SetCaretPos**

GetCharABCWidths   3.1

BOOL GetCharABCWidths(*hdc, uFirstChar, uLastChar, lpabc*)
HDC *hdc*;   /* handle of device context   */
UINT *uFirstChar*;   /* first character in range to query   */
UINT *uLastChar*;   /* last character in range to query   */
LPABC *lpabc*;   /* address of ABC width structures   */

The **GetCharABCWidths** function retrieves the widths of consecutive characters in a specified range from the current TrueType font. The widths are returned in logical units. This function succeeds only with TrueType fonts.

Parameters

hdc
Identifies the device context.

uFirstChar
Specifies the first character in the range of characters from the current font for which character widths are returned.

uLastChar
Specifies the last character in the range of characters from the current font for which character widths are returned.

lpabc
Points to an array of **ABC** structures that receive the character widths when the function returns. This array must contain at least as many **ABC** structures as there are characters in the range specified by the *uFirstChar* and *uLastChar* parameters.

Return Value

The return value is nonzero if the function is successful. Otherwise, it is zero.

Comments

The TrueType rasterizer provides ABC character spacing after a specific point size has been selected. "A" spacing is the distance that is added to the current position before placing the glyph. "B" spacing is the width of the black part of the glyph. "C" spacing is added to the current position to account for the white space to the right of the glyph. The total advanced width is given by A + B + C.

When the **GetCharABCWidths** function retrieves negative "A" or "C" widths for a character, that character includes underhangs or overhangs.

To convert the ABC widths to font design units, an application should create a font whose height (as specified in the **lfHeight** member of the **LOGFONT** structure) is equal to the value stored in the **ntmSizeEM** member of the **NEWTEXT-METRIC** structure. (The value of the **ntmSizeEM** member can be retrieved by calling the **EnumFontFamilies** function.)

The ABC widths of the default character are used for characters that are outside the range of the currently selected font.

To retrieve the widths of characters in non-TrueType fonts, applications should use the **GetCharWidth** function.

See Also

EnumFontFamilies, GetCharWidth

GetCharWidth

BOOL GetCharWidth(*hdc, uFirstChar, uLastChar, lpnWidths*)

HDC *hdc*;	/* handle of device context	*/
UINT *uFirstChar*;	/* first character in range to query	*/
UINT *uLastChar*;	/* last character in range to query	*/
int FAR* *lpnWidths*;	/* address of buffer for widths	*/

The **GetCharWidth** function retrieves the widths of individual characters in a range of consecutive characters in the current font.

Parameters

hdc
Identifies the device context.

uFirstChar
Specifies the first character in a group of consecutive characters in the current font.

uLastChar
Specifies the last character in a group of consecutive characters in the current font.

lpnWidths
Points to a buffer that receives the width values for a group of consecutive characters in the current font.

Return Value

The return value is nonzero if the function is successful. Otherwise, it is zero.

Comments

If a character in the group of consecutive characters does not exist in a particular font, it will be assigned the width value of the default character.

Example

The following example uses the **GetCharWidth** function to retrieve the widths of the characters from "I" through "S" and displays the total number of widths retrieved in a message box:

```
HDC hdc;
WORD wTotalValues;
WORD wFirstChar, wLastChar;
int InfoBuffer[256];
char szMessage[30];

wFirstChar = (WORD) 'I';
wLastChar  = (WORD) 'S';

hdc = GetDC(hwnd);
```

```
if (GetCharWidth(hdc, wFirstChar, wLastChar, (int FAR*) InfoBuffer)) {
    wTotalValues = wLastChar - wFirstChar + 1;
    wsprintf(szMessage, "Total values received: %d", wTotalValues);
    MessageBox(hwnd, szMessage, "GetCharWidth", MB_OK);
}
else
    MessageBox(hwnd, "GetCharWidth was unsuccessful", "ERROR!",
        MB_OK);

ReleaseDC(hwnd, hdc);
```

See Also   **GetCharABCWidths**

GetClassInfo

3.0

BOOL GetClassInfo(*hinst*, *lpszClassName*, *lpwc*)
HINSTANCE *hinst*;   /* handle of application instance   */
LPCSTR *lpszClassName*;   /* address of class-name string   */
WNDCLASS FAR* *lpwc*;   /* address of structure for class data   */

The **GetClassInfo** function retrieves information about a window class. This function is used for creating subclasses of a given class.

Parameters   *hinst*
Identifies the instance of the application that created the class. To retrieve information about classes defined by Windows (such as buttons or list boxes), set this parameter to NULL.

lpszClassName
Points to a null-terminated string containing the class name. The class name is either an application-specified name as defined by the **RegisterClass** function or the name of a preregistered window class. If the high-order word of this parameter is NULL, the low-order word is assumed to be a value returned by the **MAKEINTRESOURCE** macro used when the class was created.

lpwc
Points to a **WNDCLASS** structure that receives the information about the class. The **WNDCLASS** structure has the following form:

```
typedef struct tagWNDCLASS {    /* wc */
    UINT      style;
    WNDPROC   lpfnWndProc;
    int       cbClsExtra;
    int       cbWndExtra;
    HINSTANCE hInstance;
    HICON     hIcon;
```

```
          HCURSOR   hCursor;
          HBRUSH    hbrBackground;
          LPCSTR    lpszMenuName;
          LPCSTR    lpszClassName;
        } WNDCLASS;
```

For a full description of this structure, see the *Microsoft Windows Programmer's Reference, Volume 3*.

Return Value   The return value is nonzero if the function is successful. Otherwise, it is zero, indicating the function did not find a matching class.

Comments   The **GetClassInfo** function does not set the **lpszClassName** and **lpszMenuName** members of the **WNDCLASS** structure. The menu name is not stored internally and cannot be returned. The class name is already known, since it is passed to this function. **GetClassInfo** returns all other members with the values used when the class was registered.

See Also   **GetClassLong**, **GetClassName**, **GetClassWord**, **RegisterClass**

GetClassLong   2.x

LONG GetClassLong(*hwnd*, *offset***)**
HWND *hwnd*;   /* handle of window   */
int *offset*;   /* offset of value to retrieve   */

The **GetClassLong** function retrieves a 32-bit (long) value at the specified offset into the extra class memory for the window class to which the given window belongs. Extra class memory is reserved by specifying a nonzero value in the **cbClsExtra** member of the **WNDCLASS** structure used with the **RegisterClass** function.

Parameters   *hwnd*
               Identifies the window.

               offset
               Specifies the zero-based byte offset of the value to be retrieved. Valid values
               are in the range zero through the number of bytes of class memory minus four
               (for example, if 12 or more bytes of extra class memory was specified, a value
               of 8 would be an index to the third 32-bit integer) or one of the following
               values:

Value	Meaning
GCL_MENUNAME	Retrieves a 32-bit pointer to the menu-name string.
GCL_WNDPROC	Retrieves a 32-bit pointer to the window procedure.

Return Value   The return value is the specified 32-bit value in the extra class memory if the function is successful. Otherwise, it is zero, indicating the *hwnd* or *offset* parameter is invalid.

Comments   To access any extra four-byte values allocated when the window-class structure was created, use a positive byte offset as the index specified by the *offset* parameter, starting at 0 for the first four-byte value in the extra space, 4 for the next four-byte value, and so on.

See Also   **GetClassInfo, GetClassName, GetClassWord, RegisterClass, SetClassLong**

GetClassName

2.x

int GetClassName(*hwnd, lpszClassName, cchClassName*)
HWND *hwnd*;   /* handle of window   */
LPSTR *lpszClassName*;   /* address of buffer for class name   */
int *cchClassName*;   /* size of buffer   */

The **GetClassName** function retrieves the class name of a window.

Parameters   *hwnd*
        Identifies the window.

    lpszClassName
        Points to a buffer that receives the null-terminated class name string.

    cchClassName
        Specifies the length of the buffer pointed to by the *lpszClassName* parameter. The class name string is truncated if it is longer than the buffer.

Return Value   The return value is the length, in bytes, of the returned class name, not including the terminating null character. The return value is zero if the specified window handle is invalid.

GetClassWord

WORD GetClassWord(*hwnd*, *offset*)
HWND *hwnd*;   /* handle of window   */
int *offset*;   /* offset of value to retrieve */

The **GetClassWord** function retrieves a 16-bit (word) value at the specified offset into the extra class memory for the window class to which the given window belongs. Extra class memory is reserved by specifying a nonzero value in the **cbClsExtra** member of the **WNDCLASS** structure used with the **RegisterClass** function.

Parameters

hwnd
Identifies the window.

offset
Specifies the zero-based byte offset of the value to be retrieved. Valid values are in the range zero through the number of bytes of class memory minus two (for example, if 10 or more bytes of extra class memory was specified, a value of 8 would be an index to the fifth 16-bit integer) or one of the following values:

Value	Meaning
GCW_CBCLSEXTRA	Retrieves the number of bytes of additional class information. For information about how to access this memory, see the following Comments section.
GCW_CBWNDEXTRA	Retrieves the number of bytes of additional window information. For information about how to access this memory, see the following Comments section.
GCW_HBRBACKGROUND	Retrieves the handle of the background brush.
GCW_HCURSOR	Retrieves the handle of the cursor.
GCW_HICON	Retrieves the handle of the icon.
GCW_HMODULE	Retrieves the handle of the module.
GCW_STYLE	Retrieves the window-class style bits.

Return Value

The return value is the 16-bit value in the window's reserved memory, if the function is successful. Otherwise, it is zero, indicating the *hwnd* or *offset* parameter is invalid.

Comments

To access any extra two-byte values allocated when the window-class structure was created, use a positive byte offset as the index specified by the *offset* parameter, starting at 0 for the first two-byte value in the extra space, 2 for the next two-byte value, and so on.

See Also

GetClassInfo, GetClassLong, GetClassName, RegisterClass, SetClassWord

GetClientRect

void GetClientRect(*hwnd*, *lprc*)
HWND *hwnd*;   /* handle of window   */
RECT FAR* *lprc*;   /* address of structure for rectangle   */

The **GetClientRect** function retrieves the client coordinates of a window's client area. The client coordinates specify the upper-left and lower-right corners of the client area. Because client coordinates are relative to the upper-left corner of a window's client area, the coordinates of the upper-left corner are (0,0).

Parameters

hwnd
Identifies the window whose client coordinates are to be retrieved.

lprc
Points to a **RECT** structure that receives the client coordinates. The **left** and **top** members will be zero. The **right** and **bottom** members will contain the width and height of the window. The **RECT** structure has the following form:

```
typedef struct tagRECT {    /* rc */
    int left;
    int top;
    int right;
    int bottom;
} RECT;
```

For a full description of this structure, see the *Microsoft Windows Programmer's Reference, Volume 3*.

Return Value

This function does not return a value.

See Also

GetWindowRect

GetClipboardData

HANDLE GetClipboardData(*uFormat*)
UINT *uFormat*;   /* data format   */

The **GetClipboardData** function retrieves a handle of the current clipboard data having a specified format. The clipboard must have been opened previously.

Parameters   *uFormat*

Specifies the format of the data accessed by this function. For a description of the possible data formats, see the description of the **SetClipboardData** function.

Return Value   The return value is a handle of the clipboard data in the specified format, if the function is successful. Otherwise, it is NULL.

Comments   The available formats can be enumerated in advance by using the **EnumClipboardFormats** function.

The data handle returned by the **GetClipboardData** function is controlled by the clipboard, not by the application. The application should copy the data immediately, instead of relying on the data handle for long-term use. The application should not free the data handle or leave it locked.

Windows supports two formats for text: CF_TEXT (the default Windows text clipboard format) and CF_OEMTEXT (the format Windows uses for text in non-Windows applications). If you call **GetClipboardData** to retrieve data in one text format and the other text format is the only available text format, Windows automatically converts the text to the requested format before supplying it to your application.

If the clipboard contains data in the CF_PALETTE (logical color palette) format, the application should assume that any other data in the clipboard is realized against that logical palette.

See Also   **CloseClipboard, EnumClipboardFormats, IsClipboardFormatAvailable, OpenClipboard, SetClipboardData**

GetClipboardFormatName   2.x

int GetClipboardFormatName(*uFormat, lpszFormatName, cbMax***)**
UINT *uFormat*;   /* format to retrieve   */
LPSTR *lpszFormatName*;   /* address of buffer for name */
int *cbMax*;   /* length of name string   */

The **GetClipboardFormatName** function retrieves the name of a registered clipboard format.

Parameters   *uFormat*

Specifies the registered format to retrieve. This parameter must not specify any of the predefined clipboard formats.

lpszFormatName
> Points to a buffer that receives the format name.

cbMax
> Specifies the maximum length, in bytes, of the format-name string. The format-name string is truncated if it is longer.

Return Value   The return value is the length, in bytes, of the returned format name if the function is successful. Otherwise, it is zero, indicating the requested format does not exist or is predefined.

See Also   **CountClipboardFormats, EnumClipboardFormats, GetPriorityClipboard-Format, IsClipboardFormatAvailable, RegisterClipboardFormat**

GetClipboardOwner   `2.x`

HWND GetClipboardOwner(void)

> The **GetClipboardOwner** function retrieves the handle of the window that currently owns the clipboard, if any.

Parameters   This function has no parameters.

Return Value   The return value identifies the window that owns the clipboard if the function is successful. Otherwise, it is NULL.

Comments   The clipboard can still contain data even if the clipboard is not currently owned.

See Also   **CloseClipboard, GetClipboardData, GetClipboardViewer, OpenClipboard**

GetClipboardViewer   `2.x`

HWND GetClipboardViewer(void)

> The **GetClipboardViewer** function retrieves the handle of the first window in the clipboard-viewer chain.

Parameters   This function has no parameters.

Return Value   The return value identifies the window currently responsible for displaying the clipboard, if the function is successful. Otherwise, it is NULL (if there is no viewer, for example).

See Also   **CloseClipboard**, **GetClipboardData**, **GetClipboardOwner**, **OpenClipboard**

GetClipBox   2.x

int GetClipBox(*hdc*, *lprc*)
HDC *hdc*;   /* handle of device context   */
RECT FAR* *lprc*;   /* address of structure with rectangle   */

The **GetClipBox** function retrieves the dimensions of the smallest rectangle that completely contains the current clipping region.

Parameters   *hdc*
                         Identifies the device context.

                         lprc
                         Points to the **RECT** structure that receives the logical coordinates of the rectangle. The **RECT** structure has the following form:

```
typedef struct tagRECT {    /* rc */
    int left;
    int top;
    int right;
    int bottom;
} RECT;
```

                         For a full description of this structure, see the *Microsoft Windows Programmer's Reference, Volume 3*.

Return Value   The return value is SIMPLEREGION (region has no overlapping borders), COMPLEXREGION (region has overlapping borders), or NULLREGION (region is empty), if the function is successful. Otherwise, the return value is ERROR.

See Also   **GetBoundsRect**, **GetRgnBox**, **GetTextExtent**, **SelectClipRgn**

GetClipCursor

void GetClipCursor(*lprc*)
RECT FAR* *lprc*;   /* address of structure for rectangle   */

The **GetClipCursor** function retrieves the screen coordinates of the rectangle to which the cursor has been confined by a previous call to the **ClipCursor** function.

Parameters   *lprc*
Points to a **RECT** structure that receives the screen coordinates of the confining rectangle. The structure receives the dimensions of the screen if the cursor is not confined to a rectangle. The **RECT** structure has the following form:

```
typedef struct tagRECT {    /* rc */
    int left;
    int top;
    int right;
    int bottom;
} RECT;
```

For a full description of this structure, see the *Microsoft Windows Programmer's Reference, Volume 3*.

Return Value   This function does not return a value.

See Also   **ClipCursor, GetCursorPos**

GetCodeHandle

HGLOBAL GetCodeHandle(*lpProc*)
FARPROC *lpProc*;   /* instance address of function   */

The **GetCodeHandle** function determines which code segment contains the specified function.

Parameters   *lpProc*
Points to the procedure-instance address of the function for which to return the code segment. Typically, this address is returned by the **MakeProcInstance** function.

Return Value   The return value identifies the code segment that contains the function if the **Get-CodeHandle** function is successful. Otherwise, it is NULL.

Comments   If the code segment that contains the function is already loaded, the **GetCode-Handle** function marks the segment as recently used. If the code segment is not loaded, **GetCodeHandle** attempts to load it. Thus, an application can use this function to attempt to preload one or more segments necessary to perform a particular task.

See Also   **MakeProcInstance**

GetCodeInfo   3.0

void GetCodeInfo(*lpProc*, *lpSegInfo*)
FARPROC *lpProc*;   /* function address or module handle   */
SEGINFO FAR* *lpSegInfo*;   /* address of structure for segment information   */

The **GetCodeInfo** function retrieves a pointer to a structure containing information about a code segment.

Parameters   *lpProc*
Specifies the procedure-instance address of the function (typically, returned by the **MakeProcInstance** function) in the segment for which information is to be retrieved, or it specifies a module handle (typically, returned by the **Get-ModuleHandle** function) and segment number.

lpSegInfo
Points to a **SEGINFO** structure that will be filled with information about the code segment. The **SEGINFO** structure has the following form:

```
typedef struct tagSEGINFO {
    UINT    offSegment;
    UINT    cbSegment;
    UINT    flags;
    UINT    cbAlloc;
    HGLOBAL h;
    UINT    alignShift;
    UINT    reserved[2];
} SEGINFO;
```

For a full description of this structure, see the *Microsoft Windows Programmer's Reference, Volume 3*.

Return Value   This function does not return a value.

See Also   **GetModuleHandle, MakeProcInstance**

GetCommError

int GetCommError(*idComDev*, *lpStat*)
int *idComDev*;   /* communications device identifier   */
COMSTAT FAR* *lpStat*;   /* address of device-status buffer   */

The **GetCommError** function retrieves the most recent error value and current status for the specified device.

When a communications error occurs, Windows locks the communications port until **GetCommError** clears the error.

Parameters

idComDev

Specifies the communications device to be examined. The **OpenComm** function returns this value.

lpStat

Points to the **COMSTAT** structure that is to receive the device status. If this parameter is NULL, the function returns only the error values. The **COMSTAT** structure has the following form:

```
typedef struct tagCOMSTAT {    /* cmst                               */
    BYTE status;               /* status of transmission             */
    UINT cbInQue;              /* count of characters in Rx Queue */
    UINT cbOutQue;             /* count of characters in Tx Queue */
} COMSTAT;
```

For a full description of this structure, see the *Microsoft Windows Programmer's Reference, Volume 3*.

Return Value

The return value specifies the error value for the most recent communications-function call to the specified device, if **GetCommError** is successful.

Errors

The return value can be a combination of the following values:

Value	Meaning
CE_BREAK	Hardware detected a break condition.
CE_CTSTO	CTS (clear-to-send) timeout. While a character was being transmitted, CTS was low for the duration specified by the **fCtsHold** member of the **COMSTAT** structure.
CE_DNS	Parallel device was not selected.
CE_DSRTO	DSR (data-set-ready) timeout. While a character was being transmitted, DSR was low for the duration specified by the **fDsrHold** member of **COMSTAT**.
CE_FRAME	Hardware detected a framing error.

Value	Meaning
CE_IOE	I/O error occurred during an attempt to communicate with a parallel device.
CE_MODE	Requested mode is not supported, or the *idComDev* parameter is invalid. If set, CE_MODE is the only valid error.
CE_OOP	Parallel device signaled that it is out of paper.
CE_OVERRUN	Character was not read from the hardware before the next character arrived. The character was lost.
CE_PTO	Timeout occurred during an attempt to communicate with a parallel device.
CE_RLSDTO	RLSD (receive-line-signal-detect) timeout. While a character was being transmitted, RLSD was low for the duration specified by the **fRlsdHold** member of **COMSTAT**.
CE_RXOVER	Receiving queue overflowed. There was either no room in the input queue or a character was received after the end-of-file character was received.
CE_RXPARITY	Hardware detected a parity error.
CE_TXFULL	Transmission queue was full when a function attempted to queue a character.

See Also   **OpenComm**

GetCommEventMask   2.x

UINT GetCommEventMask(*idComDev*, *fnEvtClear***)**
int *idComDev*;   /* communications device identifier   */
int *fnEvtClear*;   /* events to clear in the event word   */

The **GetCommEventMask** function retrieves and then clears the event word for a communications device.

Parameters   *idComDev*
Specifies the communication device to be examined. The **OpenComm** function returns this value.

fnEvtClear
Specifies which events are to be cleared in the event word. For a list of the event values, see the description of the **SetCommEventMask** function.

Return Value   The return value specifies the current event-word value for the specified communications device if the function is successful. Each bit in the event word specifies whether a given event has occurred; a bit is set (to 1) if the event has occurred.

Comments   Before the **GetCommEventMask** function can record the occurrence of an event, an application must enable the event by using the **SetCommEventMask** function.

Before the communication device event is a line-status or printer error, the application should call the **GetCommError** function after calling **GetCommEventMask**.

See Also   **GetCommError, OpenComm, SetCommEventMask**

GetCommState   2.x

int GetCommState(*idComDev, lpdcb*)
int *idComDev*;   /* communications device identifier   */
DCB FAR* *lpdcb*;   /* address of structure for device control block   */

The **GetCommState** function retrieves the device control block for the specified device.

Parameters   *idComDev*
Specifies the device to be examined. The **OpenComm** function returns this value.

lpdcb
Points to the **DCB** structure that is to receive the current device control block. The **DCB** structure defines the control settings for the device. It has the following form:

```
typedef struct tagDCB         /* dcb                            */
{
    BYTE Id;                  /* internal device identifier     */
    UINT BaudRate;            /* baud rate                      */
    BYTE ByteSize;            /* number of bits/byte, 4-8        */
    BYTE Parity;              /* 0-4=none,odd,even,mark,space    */
    BYTE StopBits;            /* 0,1,2 = 1, 1.5, 2              */
    UINT RlsTimeout;          /* timeout for RLSD to be set      */
    UINT CtsTimeout;          /* timeout for CTS to be set       */
    UINT DsrTimeout;          /* timeout for DSR to be set       */

    UINT fBinary       :1;    /* binary mode (skip EOF check)    */
    UINT fRtsDisable   :1;    /* don't assert RTS at init time   */
    UINT fParity       :1;    /* enable parity checking          */
    UINT fOutxCtsFlow  :1;    /* CTS handshaking on output       */
    UINT fOutxDsrFlow  :1;    /* DSR handshaking on output       */
    UINT fDummy        :2;    /* reserved                        */
    UINT fDtrDisable   :1;    /* don't assert DTR at init time   */
```

```
UINT fOutX        :1;   /* enable output XON/XOFF           */
UINT fInX         :1;   /* enable input XON/XOFF            */
UINT fPeChar      :1;   /* enable parity err replacement    */
UINT fNull        :1;   /* enable null stripping            */
UINT fChEvt       :1;   /* enable Rx character event        */
UINT fDtrflow     :1;   /* DTR handshake on input           */
UINT fRtsflow     :1;   /* RTS handshake on input           */
UINT fDummy2      :1;

char XonChar;           /* Tx and Rx XON character          */
char XoffChar;          /* Tx and Rx XOFF character         */
UINT XonLim;            /* transmit XON threshold           */
UINT XoffLim;           /* transmit XOFF threshold          */
char PeChar;            /* parity error replacement char    */
char EofChar;           /* end of Input character           */
char EvtChar;           /* received event character         */
UINT TxDelay;           /* amount of time between chars      */
} DCB;
```

For a full description of this structure, see the *Microsoft Windows Programmer's Reference, Volume 3*.

Return Value   The return value is zero if the function is successful. Otherwise, it is less than zcro.

See Also   **OpenComm**, **SetCommState**

GetCurrentPDB   3.0

UINT GetCurrentPDB(void)

The **GetCurrentPDB** function returns the selector address of the current MS-DOS program database (PDB), also known as the program segment prefix (PSP).

Parameters   This function has no parameters.

Return Value   The return value is the selector address of the current PDB if the function is successful.

Example   The following example uses the **GetCurrentPDB** function to list the current command tail:

```
typedef struct {
    WORD pspInt20;              /* Int 20h instruction           */
    WORD pspNextParagraph;      /* segment addr. of next paragraph */
    BYTE res1;                  /* reserved                      */
    BYTE pspDispatcher[5];      /* long call to MS-DOS           */
    DWORD pspTerminateVector;   /* termination address (Int 22h)  */
    DWORD pspControlCVector;    /* addr of CTRL+C (Int 23h)       */
    DWORD pspCritErrorVector;   /* addr of Crit-Error (Int 24h)   */
    WORD res2[11];              /* reserved                      */
    WORD pspEnvironment;        /* segment address of environment */
    WORD res3[23];              /* reserved                      */
    BYTE pspFCB_1[16];          /* default FCB #1                */
    BYTE pspFCB_2[16];          /* default FCB #2                */
    DWORD res4;                 /* reserved                      */
    BYTE pspCommandTail[128];   /* command tail (also default DTA) */
} PSP, FAR* LPSP;

LPSP lpsp = (LPSP) MAKELP(GetCurrentPDB(), 0);

MessageBox(NULL, lpsp->pspCommandTail, "PDB Command Tail", MB_OK);
```

GetCurrentPosition

2.x

DWORD GetCurrentPosition(*hdc*)
HDC *hdc*;   /* handle of device context   */

The **GetCurrentPosition** function retrieves the logical coordinates of the current position. The current position is set by using the **MoveTo** function.

Parameters   *hdc*
Identifies the device context.

Return Value   The low-order word of the return value contains the logical x-coordinate of the current position if the function is successful; the high-order word contains the logical y-coordinate.

See Also   **LineTo, MoveTo**

GetCurrentPositionEx

3.1

BOOL GetCurrentPositionEx(*hdc***,** *lpPoint***)**
HDC *hdc***;**
POINT FAR* *lpPoint***;**

The **GetCurrentPositionEx** function retrieves the current position in logical coordinates.

Parameters   *hdc*
Identifies the device context to get the current position from.

lpPoint
Points to a **POINT** structure that gets filled with the current position.

Return Value   The return value is nonzero if the function is successful. Otherwise, it is zero.

GetCurrentTask

2.x

HTASK GetCurrentTask(void)

The **GetCurrentTask** function retrieves the handle of the current (running) task.

Parameters   This function has no parameters.

Return Value   The return value is a handle of the current task if the function is successful. Otherwise, it is NULL.

GetCurrentTime

2.x

DWORD GetCurrentTime(void)

The **GetCurrentTime** function retrieves the number of milliseconds that have elapsed since Windows was started.

Parameters   This function has no parameters.

Return Value	The return value is the number of milliseconds that have elapsed since Windows was started, if the function was successful.
Comments	The **GetCurrentTime** function is identical to the **GetTickCount** function. Applications should use the **GetTickCount** function, since its name matches more closely with what the function does.
See Also	**GetTickCount**

GetCursor

$\boxed{\text{3.1}}$

HCURSOR GetCursor(void)

The **GetCursor** function retrieves the handle of the current cursor.

Parameters	This function has no parameters.
Return Value	The return value is the handle of the current cursor if a cursor exists. Otherwise, it is NULL.
See Also	**SetCursor**

GetCursorPos

$\boxed{\text{2.x}}$

void GetCursorPos(*lppt***)**
POINT FAR* *lppt*;   /* address of structure for cursor position   */

The **GetCursorPos** function retrieves the screen coordinates of the cursor's current position.

Parameters
lppt
Points to the **POINT** structure that receives the cursor position, in screen coordinates. The **POINT** structure has the following form:

```
typedef struct tagPOINT {   /* pt */
    int x;
    int y;
} POINT;
```

For a full description of this structure, see the *Microsoft Windows Programmer's Reference, Volume 3.*

Return Value   This function does not return a value.

Comments   The cursor position is always given in screen coordinates and is not affected by the mapping mode of the window that contains the cursor.

See Also   **ClipCursor, SetCursorPos**

GetDC   2.x

HDC GetDC(*hwnd*)
HWND *hwnd*;   /* handle of window   */

The **GetDC** function retrieves the handle of a device context for the client area of the given window. The device context can be used in subsequent graphics device interface (GDI) functions to draw in the client area.

The **GetDC** function retrieves a common, class, or private device context, depending on the class style specified for the given window. For common device contexts, **GetDC** assigns default attributes to the context each time it is retrieved. For class and private contexts, **GetDC** leaves the previously assigned attributes unchanged.

Parameters   *hwnd*
    Identifies the window where drawing will occur. If this parameter is NULL, the function returns a device context for the screen.

Return Value   The return value is a handle of the device context for the given window's client area, if the function is successful. Otherwise, it is NULL.

Comments   Unless the device context belongs to a window class, the **ReleaseDC** function must be called to release the context after drawing. Since only five common device contexts are available at any given time, failure to release a device context can prevent other applications from accessing a device context. If the *hwnd* parameter of the **GetDC** function is NULL, the first parameter of **ReleaseDC** should also be NULL.

A device context belonging to the window's class is returned by the **GetDC** function if CS_CLASSDC, CS_OWNDC, or CS_PARENTDC style was specified in the **WNDCLASS** structure when the class was registered.

See Also   **BeginPaint, GetWindowDC, ReleaseDC**

GetDCEx   ▢ 3.1

HDC GetDCEx(*hwnd*, *hrgnClip*, *fdwOptions*)
register HWND *hwnd*;   /* window where drawing will occur   */
HRGN *hrgnClip*;   /* clipping region that may be combined   */
DWORD *fdwOptions*;   /* device-context options   */

The **GetDCEx** function retrieves the handle of a device context for the given window. The device context can be used in subsequent graphics device interface (GDI) functions to draw in the client area.

This function, which is an extension to the **GetDC** function, gives an application more control over how and whether a device context for a window is clipped.

Parameters   *hwnd*
Identifies the window where drawing will occur.

hrgnClip
Identifies a clipping region that may be combined with the visible region of the client window.

fdwOptions
Specifies how the device context is created. This parameter can be a combination of the following values:

Value	Meaning
DCX_CACHE	Returns a device context from the cache, rather than the OWNDC or CLASSDC window. Essentially overrides CS_OWNDC and CS_CLASSDC.
DCX_CLIPCHILDREN	Excludes the visible regions of all child windows below the window identified by the *hwnd* parameter.
DCX_CLIPSIBLINGS	Excludes the visible regions of all sibling windows above the window identified by the *hwnd* parameter.
DCX_EXCLUDERGN	Excludes the clipping region identified by the *hrgnClip* parameter from the visible region of the returned device context.
DCX_INTERSECTRGN	Intersects the clipping region identified by the *hrgnClip* parameter with the visible region of the returned device context.

Value	Meaning
DCX_LOCKWINDOWUPDATE	Allows drawing even if there is a **Lock-WindowUpdate** call in effect that would otherwise exclude this window. This value is used for drawing during tracking.
DCX_PARENTCLIP	Uses the visible region of the parent window, ignoring the parent window's WS_CLIPCHILDREN and WS_PARENTDC style bits. This value sets the device context's origin to the upper-left corner of the window identified by the *hwnd* parameter.
DCX_WINDOW	Returns a device context corresponding to the window rectangle rather than the client rectangle.

Return Value   The return value is a handle of the device context for the specified window, if the function is successful. Otherwise, it is NULL.

Comments   Unless the device context belongs to a window class, the **ReleaseDC** function must be called to release the context after drawing. Since only five common device contexts are available at any given time, failure to release a device context can prevent other applications from accessing a device context.

A device context belonging to the window's class is returned by the **GetDCEx** function if the CS_CLASSDC, CS_OWNDC, or CS_PARENTDC class style was specified in the **WNDCLASS** structure when the class was registered.

In order to obtain a cached device context, an application must specify DCX_CACHE. If DCX_CACHE is not specified and the window is neither CS_OWNDC nor CS_CLASSDC, this function returns NULL.

See Also   **BeginPaint, GetDC, GetWindowDC, ReleaseDC**

GetDCOrg   2.x

DWORD GetDCOrg(*hdc*)
HDC *hdc*;   /* handle of device context   */

The **GetDCOrg** function retrieves the coordinates of the final translation origin for the device context. This origin specifies the offset used by Windows to translate device coordinates into client coordinates for points in an application's window. The final translation origin is relative to the physical origin of the screen.

Parameters   *hdc*
              Identifies the device context whose origin is to be retrieved.

Return Value   The low-order word of the return value contains the x-coordinate of the final trans-
              lation origin, in device coordinates, if the function is successful; the high-order
              word contains the y-coordinate.

Example   The following example uses the **CreateIC** function to create an information con-
              text for the screen and then retrieves the context's origin by using the **GetDCOrg**
              function:

```
HDC   hdcIC;
DWORD dwOrigin;

hdcIC = CreateIC("DISPLAY", NULL, NULL, NULL);
dwOrigin = GetDCOrg(hdcIC);

DeleteDC(hdcIC);
```

See Also   **CreateIC**

GetDesktopWindow   `3.0`

HWND GetDesktopWindow(void)

              The **GetDesktopWindow** function retrieves the handle of the desktop window.
              The desktop window covers the entire screen and is the area on top of which all
              icons and other windows are painted.

Parameters   This function has no parameters.

Return Value   The return value is a handle of the desktop window.

See Also   **GetTopWindow, GetWindow**

GetDeviceCaps

int GetDeviceCaps(*hdc*, *iCapability*)
HDC *hdc*;   /* handle of device context   */
int *iCapability*;   /* index of capability to query   */

The **GetDeviceCaps** function retrieves device-specific information about a given display device.

Parameters

hdc
Identifies the device context.

iCapability
Specifies the type of information to be returned. It can be one of the following indices:

Index	Description
DRIVERVERSION	Version number of the device driver.
TECHNOLOGY	Device technology. It can be one of the following values:

Value	Meaning
DT_PLOTTER	Vector plotter
DT_RASDISPLAY	Raster display
DT_RASPRINTER	Raster printer
DT_RASCAMERA	Raster camera
DT_CHARSTREAM	Character stream
DT_METAFILE	Metafile
DT_DISPFILE	Display file

Index	Description
HORZSIZE	Width of the physical display, in millimeters.
VERTSIZE	Height of the physical display, in millimeters.
HORZRES	Width of the display, in pixels.
VERTRES	Height of the display, in raster lines.
LOGPIXELSX	Number of pixels per logical inch along the display width.
LOGPIXELSY	Number of pixels per logical inch along the display height.
BITSPIXEL	Number of adjacent color bits for each pixel.
PLANES	Number of color planes.
NUMBRUSHES	Number of device-specific brushes.
NUMPENS	Number of device-specific pens.
NUMMARKERS	Number of device-specific markers.
NUMFONTS	Number of device-specific fonts.
NUMCOLORS	Number of entries in the device's color table.

Index	Description
ASPECTX	Relative width of a device pixel used for line drawing.
ASPECTY	Relative height of a device pixel used for line drawing.
ASPECTXY	Diagonal width of a device pixel used for line drawing.
PDEVICESIZE	Size of the **PDEVICE** internal structure, in bytes.
CLIPCAPS	Clipping capabilities the device supports. It can be one of the following values:

Value	Meaning
CP_NONE	Output is not clipped.
CP_RECTANGLE	Output is clipped to rectangles.
CP_REGION	Output is clipped to regions.

Index	Description
SIZEPALETTE	Number of entries in the system palette. This index is valid only if the device driver sets the RC_PALETTE bit in the RASTERCAPS index; it is available only if the driver is written for Windows 3.0 or later.
NUMRESERVED	Number of reserved entries in the system palette. This index is valid only if the device driver sets the RC_PALETTE bit in the RASTERCAPS index; it is available only if the driver is written for Windows 3.0 or later.
COLORRES	Color resolution of the device, in bits per pixel. This index is valid only if the device driver sets the RC_PALETTE bit in the RASTERCAPS index; it is available only if the driver is written for Windows 3.0 or later.
RASTERCAPS	Raster capabilities the device supports. It can be a combination of the following values:

Value	Meaning
RC_BANDING	Supports banding.
RC_BIGFONT	Supports fonts larger than 64K.
RC_BITBLT	Transfers bitmaps.
RC_BITMAP64	Supports bitmaps larger than 64K.
RC_DEVBITS	Supports device bitmaps.
RC_DI_BITMAP	Supports the **SetDIBits** and **GetDIBits** functions.
RC_DIBTODEV	Supports the **SetDIBitsTo-Device** function.
RC_FLOODFILL	Performs flood fills.
RC_GDI20_OUTPUT	Supports Windows version 2.0 features.

Index	Description

Value	Meaning
RC_GDI20_STATE	Includes a state block in the device context.
RC_NONE	Supports no raster operations.
RC_OP_DX_OUTPUT	Supports dev opaque and DX array.
RC_PALETTE	Specifies a palette-based device.
RC_SAVEBITMAP	Saves bitmaps locally.
RC_SCALING	Supports scaling.
RC_STRETCHBLT	Supports the **StretchBlt** function.
RC_STRETCHDIB	Supports the **StretchDIBits** function.

CURVECAPS   Curve capabilities the device supports. It can be a combination of the following values:

Value	Meaning
CC_NONE	Supports curves.
CC_CIRCLES	Supports circles.
CC_PIE	Supports pie wedges.
CC_CHORD	Supports chords.
CC_ELLIPSES	Supports ellipses.
CC_WIDE	Supports wide borders.
CC_STYLED	Supports styled borders.
CC_WIDESTYLED	Supports wide, styled borders.
CC_INTERIORS	Supports interiors.
CC_ROUNDRECT	Supports rectangles with rounded corners.

LINECAPS   Line capabilities the device supports. It can be a combination of the following values:

Value	Meaning
LC_NONE	Supports no lines.
LC_POLYLINE	Supports polylines.
LC_MARKER	Supports markers.
LC_POLYMARKER	Supports polymarkers.

Index	Description

Value	Meaning
LC_WIDE	Supports wide lines.
LC_STYLED	Supports styled lines.
LC_WIDESTYLED	Supports wide, styled lines.
LC_INTERIORS	Supports interiors.

Index	Description
POLYGONALCAPS	Polygonal capabilities the device supports. It can be a combination of the following values:

Value	Meaning
PC_NONE	Supports no polygons.
PC_POLYGON	Supports alternate fill polygons.
PC_RECTANGLE	Supports rectangles.
PC_WINDPOLYGON	Supports winding number fill polygons.
PC_SCANLINE	Supports scan lines.
PC_WIDE	Supports wide borders.
PC_STYLED	Supports styled borders.
PC_WIDESTYLED	Supports wide, styled borders.
PC_INTERIORS	Supports interiors.

Index	Description
TEXTCAPS	Text capabilities the device supports. It can be a combination of the following values:

Value	Meaning
TC_OP_CHARACTER	Supports character output precision, which indicates the device can place device fonts at any pixel location. This is required for any device with device fonts.
TC_OP_STROKE	Supports stroke output precision, which indicates the device can omit any stroke of a device font.
TC_CP_STROKE	Supports stroke clip precision, which indicates the device can clip device fonts to a pixel boundary.

Index	Description	
	Value	**Meaning**
	TC_CR_90	Supports 90-degree character rotation, which indicates the device can rotate characters only 90 degrees at a time.
	TC_CR_ANY	Supports character rotation at any degree, which indicates the device can rotate device fonts through any angle.
	TC_SF_X_YINDEP	Supports scaling independent of x and y directions, which indicates the device can scale device fonts separately in x and y directions.
	TC_SA_DOUBLE	Supports doubled characters for scaling, which indicates the device can double the size of device fonts.
	TC_SA_INTEGER	Supports integer multiples for scaling, which indicates the device can scale the size of device fonts in any integer multiple.
	TC_SA_CONTIN	Supports any multiples for exact scaling, which indicates the device can scale device fonts by any amount but still preserve the x and y ratios.
	TC_EA_DOUBLE	Supports double-weight characters, which indicates the device can make device fonts bold. If this bit is not set for printer drivers, graphics device interface (GDI) attempts to create bold device fonts by printing them twice.
	TC_IA_ABLE	Supports italics, which indicates the device can make device fonts italic. If this bit is not set, GDI assumes italics are not available.

Index	Description	
	Value	**Meaning**
	TC_UA_ABLE	Supports underlining, which indicates the device can underline device fonts. If this bit is not set, GDI creates underlines for device fonts.
	TC_SO_ABLE	Supports strikeouts, which indicates the device can strikeout device fonts. If this bit is not set, GDI creates strikeouts for device fonts.
	TC_RA_ABLE	Supports raster fonts, which indicates that GDI should enumerate any raster or True-Type fonts available for this device in response to a call to the **EnumFonts** or **Enum-FontFamilies** function. If this bit is not set, GDI-supplied raster or TrueType fonts are not enumerated when these functions are called.
	TC_VA_ABLE	Supports vector fonts, which indicates that GDI should enumerate any vector fonts available for this device in response to a call to the **EnumFonts** or **EnumFont-Families** function. This is significant for vector devices only (that is, for plotters). Display drivers (which must be able to use raster fonts) and raster printer drivers always enumerate vector fonts, because GDI rasterizes vector fonts before sending them to the driver.
	TC_RESERVED	Reserved; must be zero.

Return Value   The return value is the value of the requested capability if the function is successful.

Example   The following example uses the **GetDeviceCaps** function to determine whether a device supports raster capabilities and is palette-based. If so, the example calls the **GetSystemPaletteUse** function.

```
WORD nUse;

hdc = GetDC(hwnd);
if ((GetDeviceCaps(hdc, RASTERCAPS) & RC_PALETTE) == 0) {
    ReleaseDC(hwnd, hdc);
    break;
}
nUse = GetSystemPaletteUse(hdc);
ReleaseDC(hwnd, hdc);
```

GetDialogBaseUnits

3.0

DWORD GetDialogBaseUnits(void)

The **GetDialogBaseUnits** function returns the dialog box base units used by Windows when creating dialog boxes. An application should use these values to calculate the average width of characters in the system font.

Parameters   This function has no parameters.

Return Value   The low-order word of the return value contains the width, in pixels, of the current dialog box base-width unit, if the function is successful (this base unit is derived from the system font); the high-order word of the return value contains the height, in pixels.

Comments   The values returned represent dialog box base units before being scaled to dialog box units. The dialog box unit in the x-direction is one-fourth of the width returned by the **GetDialogBaseUnits** function. The dialog box unit in the y-direction is one-eighth of the height returned by the function.

To use **GetDialogBaseUnits** to determine the height and width, in pixels, of a control, given the width (x) and height (y) in dialog box units and the return value (lDlgBaseUnits), use the following formulas:

```
(x * LOWORD(lDlgBaseUnits)) / 4
(y * HIWORD(lDlgBaseUnits)) / 8
```

To avoid rounding problems, perform the multiplication before the division, in case the dialog box base units are not evenly divisible by four.

Example   The following example calculates tab stops based on the dialog box base units:

```
HMENU hmenu;
WORD DlgWidthUnits;
WORD TabStopList[4];

case WM_CREATE:
    hmenu = LoadMenu(hinst, "TabStopsMenu");
    SetMenu(hwnd, hmenu);
    DlgWidthUnits = LOWORD(GetDialogBaseUnits()) / 4;
    TabStopList[0] = (DlgWidthUnits * 16 * 2);
    TabStopList[1] = (DlgWidthUnits * 32 * 2);
    TabStopList[2] = (DlgWidthUnits * 58 * 2);
    TabStopList[3] = (DlgWidthUnits * 84 * 2);
    break;
```

GetDIBits
3.0

int GetDIBits(*hdc, hbmp, nStartScan, cScanLines, lpvBits, lpbmi, fuColorUse*)

HDC *hdc*;	/* handle of device context	*/
HBITMAP *hbmp*;	/* handle of bitmap	*/
UINT *nStartScan*;	/* first scan line to set in destination bitmap	*/
UINT *cScanLines*;	/* number of scan lines to copy	*/
void FAR* *lpvBits*;	/* address of array for bitmap bits	*/
BITMAPINFO FAR* *lpbmi*;	/* address of structure with bitmap data	*/
UINT *fuColorUse*;	/* type of color table	*/

The **GetDIBits** function retrieves the bits of the specified bitmap and copies them, in device-independent format, into the buffer pointed to by the *lpvBits* parameter. The *lpbmi* parameter retrieves the color format for the device-independent bits.

Parameters   *hdc*
Identifies the device context.

hbmp
Identifies the bitmap.

nStartScan
Specifies the first scan line to be set in the bitmap received in the *lpvBits* parameter.

cScanLines
Specifies the number of lines to be copied.

lpvBits

Points to a buffer that will receive the bitmap bits in device-independent format.

lpbmi

Points to a **BITMAPINFO** structure that specifies the color format and dimension for the device-independent bitmap. The **BITMAPINFO** structure has the following form:

```
typedef struct tagBITMAPINFO {  /* bmi */
    BITMAPINFOHEADER    bmiHeader;
    RGBQUAD             bmiColors[1];
} BITMAPINFO;
```

For a full description of this structure, see the *Microsoft Windows Programmer's Reference, Volume 3*.

fuColorUse

Specifies whether the **bmiColors** members of the **BITMAPINFO** structure are to contain explicit RGB values or indices into the currently realized logical palette. The *fuColorUse* parameter must be one of the following values:

Value	Meaning
DIB_PAL_COLORS	Color table is to consist of an array of 16-bit indices into the currently realized logical palette.
DIB_RGB_COLORS	Color table is to contain literal RGB values.

Return Value

The return value specifies the number of scan lines copied from the bitmap if the function is successful. Otherwise, it is zero.

Comments

If the *lpvBits* parameter is NULL, the **GetDIBits** function fills in the **BITMAPINFO** structure to which the *lpbmi* parameter points but does not retrieve bits from the bitmap.

The bitmap identified by the *hbmp* parameter must not be selected into a device context when the application calls this function.

The origin for device-independent bitmaps (DIBs) is the lower-left corner of the bitmap, not the upper-left corner, which is the origin when the mapping mode is MM_TEXT.

See Also

SetDIBits

GetDlgCtrlID

int **GetDlgCtrlID**(*hwnd*)
HWND *hwnd*;   /* handle of child window   */

The **GetDlgCtrlID** function returns a handle of a child window.

Parameters   *hwnd*
                      Identifies the child window.

Return Value   The return value is a handle of the child window if the function is successful.
                      Otherwise, it is NULL.

Comments   This function returns a handle of any child window, not just that of a control in a
                      dialog box.

                      Since top-level windows do not have an identifier, the **GetDlgCtrlID** function's
                      return value is invalid if the *hwnd* parameter identifies a top-level window.

See Also   **GetDlgItem**, **GetDlgItemInt**, **GetDlgItemText**

GetDlgItem

HWND GetDlgItem(*hwndDlg*, *idControl*)
HWND *hwndDlg*;   /* handle of dialog box   */
int *idControl*;   /* identifier of control   */

The **GetDlgItem** function retrieves the handle of a control that is in the given
dialog box.

Parameters   *hwndDlg*
                      Identifies the dialog box that contains the control.

                      idControl
                      Specifies the identifier of the control to be retrieved.

Return Value   The return value is the handle of the given control if the function is successful.
                      Otherwise, it is NULL, indicating either an invalid dialog box handle or a nonex-
                      istent control.

Comments   The **GetDlgItem** function can be used with any parent-child window pair, not just
                      dialog boxes. As long as the *hwndDlg* parameter identifies a parent window and

the child window has a unique identifier (as specified by the *hmenu* parameter in the **CreateWindow** function that created the child window), **GetDlgItem** returns the handle of the child window.

See Also   **CreateWindow, GetDlgCtrlID, GetDlgItemInt, GetDlgItemText, GetWindow**

GetDlgItemInt   2.x

UINT **GetDlgItemInt**(*hwndDlg, idControl, lpfTranslated, fSigned*)
HWND *hwndDlg*;   /* handle of dialog box   */
int *idControl*;   /* identifier of control   */
BOOL FAR* *lpfTranslated*;   /* address of variable for error flag */
BOOL *fSigned*;   /* signed or unsigned indicator   */

The **GetDlgItemInt** function translates the text of a control in the given dialog box into an integer value.

Parameters   *hwndDlg*
                    Identifies the dialog box.

                   idControl
                    Specifies the identifier of the dialog box control to be translated.

                   lpfTranslated
                    Points to the Boolean variable that is to receive the translated flag.

                   fSigned
                    Specifies whether the value to be retrieved is signed.

Return Value   The return value specifies the translated value of the dialog box item text if the
                   function is successful. Since zero is a valid return value, the *lpfTranslated* parame-
                   ter must be used to detect errors. If an application requires a signed return value, it
                   should cast the return value as an **int** type.

Comments   The function retrieves the text of the given control by sending the control a
                   WM_GETTEXT message. The function then translates the text by stripping any
                   extra spaces at the beginning of the text and converting decimal digits. The func-
                   tion stops translating when it reaches the end of the text or encounters a non-
                   numeric character. If the *fSigned* parameter is TRUE, the **GetDlgItemInt** function
                   checks for a minus sign (–) at the beginning of the text and translates the text into
                   a signed number. Otherwise, it creates an unsigned value.

                   GetDlgItemInt returns zero if the translated number is greater than 32,767 (for
                   signed numbers) or 65,535 (for unsigned numbers). When a error occurs, such as

encountering nonnumeric characters and exceeding the given maximum, **Get-DlgItemInt** copies zero to the location pointed to by the *lpfTranslated* parameter. If there are no errors, *lpfTranslated* receives a nonzero value. If *lpfTranslated* is NULL, **GetDlgItemInt** does not warn about errors.

See Also   **GetDlgCtrlID**, **GetDlgItem**, **GetDlgItemText**

GetDlgItemText   `2.x`

int **GetDlgItemText**(*hwndDlg*, *idControl*, *lpsz*, *cbMax*)
HWND *hwndDlg*;   /* handle of dialog box   */
int *idControl*;   /* identifier of control   */
LPSTR *lpsz*;   /* address of buffer for text   */
int *cbMax*;   /* maximum size of string   */

The **GetDlgItemText** function retrieves the title or text associated with a control in a dialog box.

Parameters   *hwndDlg*
        Identifies the dialog box that contains the control.

        idControl
        Specifies the identifier of the control whose title is to be retrieved.

        lpsz
        Points to a buffer that is to receive the control's title or text.

        cbMax
        Specifies the maximum length, in bytes, of the string to be copied to the buffer pointed to by the *lpsz* parameter. The string is truncated if it is longer.

Return Value   The return value specifies the number of bytes copied to the buffer, not including the terminating null character, if the function is successful. Otherwise, it is zero.

Comments   The **GetDlgItemText** function sends a WM_GETTEXT message to the control.

See Also   **GetDlgCtrlID**, **GetDlgItem**, **GetDlgItemInt**

GetDOSEnvironment

3.0

LPSTR GetDOSEnvironment(void)

The **GetDOSEnvironment** function returns a far pointer to the environment string of the current (running) task.

Parameters   This function has no parameters.

Return Value   The return value is a far pointer to the current environment string.

Comments   Unlike an application, a dynamic-link library (DLL) does not have a copy of the environment string. As a result, the library must call this function to retrieve the environment string.

Example   The following example uses the **GetDOSEnvironment** function to return a pointer to the environment, and then lists the environment settings:

```
LPSTR lpszEnv;

lpszEnv = GetDOSEnvironment();
while (*lpszEnv != '\0') {
    .
    . /* process the environment string */
    .

    /* Move to the next environment string */

    lpszEnv += lstrlen(lpszEnv) + 1;
}
```

GetDoubleClickTime

2.x

UINT GetDoubleClickTime(void)

The **GetDoubleClickTime** function retrieves the current double-click time for the mouse. A double-click is a series of two clicks of the mouse button, the second occurring within a specified time after the first. The double-click time is the maximum number of milliseconds that may occur between the first and second click of a double-click.

Parameters   This function has no parameters.

Return Value   The return value specifies the current double-click time, in milliseconds.

See Also   **GetCapture**

GetDriverInfo   3.1

BOOL GetDriverInfo(*hdrvr*, *lpdis*)
HDRVR *hdrvr*;   /* handle of installable driver   */
DRIVERINFOSTRUCT FAR* *lpdis*;   /* address of structure for info   */

The **GetDriverInfo** function retrieves information about an installable driver.

Parameters   *hdrvr*
                        Identifies the installable driver. This handle must be retrieved by the **Open-Driver** function.

                        lpdis
                        Points to a **DRIVERINFOSTRUCT** structure that receives the driver information. The **DRIVERINFOSTRUCT** structure has the following form:

```
typedef struct tagDRIVERINFOSTRUCT {       /* drvinfst */
    UINT      length;
    HDRVR     hDriver;
    HINSTANCE hModule;
    char      szAliasName[128];
} DRIVERINFOSTRUCT;
```

                        For a full description of this structure, see the *Microsoft Windows Programmer's Reference, Volume 3*.

Return Value   The return value is nonzero if the function is successful. Otherwise, it is zero.

GetDriverModuleHandle   3.1

HINSTANCE GetDriverModuleHandle(*hdrvr*)
HDRVR *hdrvr*;   /* handle of installable driver   */

                        The **GetDriverModuleHandle** function retrieves the instance handle of a module that contains an installable driver.

Parameters   *hdrvr*

Identifies the installable driver. This parameter must be retrieved by the **Open-Driver** function.

Return Value   The return value is an instance handle of the driver module if the function is successful. Otherwise, it is NULL.

See Also   **OpenDriver**

GetDriveType   3.0

UINT GetDriveType(*DriveNumber*)
int *DriveNumber*;   /* 0 = A, 1 = B, and so on   */

The **GetDriveType** function determines whether a disk drive is removable, fixed, or remote.

Parameters   *DriveNumber*

Specifies the drive for which the type is to be determined (0 = drive A, 1 = drive B, 2 = drive C, and so on).

Return Value   The return value is DRIVE_REMOVABLE (disk can be removed from the drive), DRIVE_FIXED (disk cannot be removed from the drive), or DRIVE_REMOTE (drive is a remote, or network, drive), if the function is successful. Otherwise, the return value is zero.

Example   The following example uses the **GetDriveType** function to determine the drive type for all possible disk drives (letters A through Z):

```
int  iDrive;
WORD wReturn;
char szMsg[80];

for (iDrive = 0, wReturn = 0;
        (iDrive < 26) && (wReturn != 1); iDrive++) {

    wReturn = GetDriveType(iDrive);

    sprintf(szMsg, "drive %c: ", iDrive + 'A');
```

```
switch (wReturn) {
    case 0:
        strcat(szMsg, "undetermined");
        break;

    case DRIVE_REMOVABLE:
        strcat(szMsg, "removable");
        break;

    case DRIVE_FIXED:
        strcat(szMsg, "fixed");
        break;

    case DRIVE_REMOTE:
        strcat(szMsg, "remote (network)");
        break;
    }
    TextOut(hdc, 10, 15 * iDrive, szMsg, strlen(szMsg));
}
```

GetExpandedName

`3.1`

#include <lzexpand.h>

int GetExpandedName(*lpszSource*, *lpszBuffer*)
LPCSTR *lpszSource*;   /* specifies name of compressed file   */
LPSTR *lpszBuffer*;   /* points to buffer receiving original filename */

The **GetExpandedName** function retrieves the original name of a compressed file if the file was compressed with the COMPRESS.EXE utility and the **/r** option was specified.

Parameters

lpszSource
Points to a string that specifies the name of a compressed file.

lpszBuffer
Points to a buffer that receives the name of the compressed file.

Return Value

The return value is TRUE if the function is successful. Otherwise, it is an error value that is less than zero, and it may be LZERROR_BADINHANDLE, which means that the handle identifying the source file was not valid.

Example   The following example uses the **GetExpandedName** function to retrieve the original filename of a compressed file:

```
char szSrc[] = {"readme.cmp"};
char szFileName[128];
OFSTRUCT ofStrSrc;
OFSTRUCT ofStrDest;
HFILE hfSrcFile, hfDstFile, hfCompFile;
int cbRead;
BYTE abBuf[512];

/* Open the compressed source file. */

hfSrcFile = OpenFile(szSrc, &ofStrSrc, OF_READ);

/*
 * Initialize internal data structures for the decompression
 * operation.
 */

hfCompFile = LZInit(hfSrcFile);

/* Retrieve the original name for the compressed file. */

GetExpandedName(szSrc, szFileName);

/* Create the destination file using the original name. */

hfDstFile = LZOpenFile(szFileName, &ofStrDest, OF_CREATE);

/* Copy the compressed source file to the destination file. */

do {
    if ((cbRead = LZRead(hfCompFile, abBuf, sizeof(abBuf))) > 0)
        _lwrite(hfDstFile, abBuf, cbRead);
    else {
        .
        . /* handle error condition */
        .
    }
} while (cbRead == sizeof(abBuf));

/* Close the files. */

LZClose(hfSrcFile);
LZClose(hfDstFile);
```

Comments

This function retrieves the original filename from the header of the compressed file. If the source file is not compressed, the filename to which *lpszSource* points is copied to the buffer to which *lpszBuffer* points.

If the **/r** option was not set when the file was compressed, the string in the buffer to which *lpszBuffer* points is invalid.

GetFileResource   3.1

#include <ver.h>

BOOL GetFileResource(*lpszFileName*, *lpszResType*, *lpszResID*, *dwFileOffset*, *dwResLen*, *lpvData*)
LPCSTR *lpszFileName*;   /* address of buffer for filename   */
LPCSTR *lpszResType*;   /* address of buffer for resource type   */
LPCSTR *lpszResID*;   /* address of buffer for resource ID   */
DWORD *dwFileOffset*;   /* resource offset in file   */
DWORD *dwResLen*;   /* size of resource buffer   */
void FAR* *lpvData*;   /* address of buffer for resource copy   */

The **GetFileResource** function copies the specified resource from the specified file into the specified buffer. To obtain the appropriate buffer size, the application can call the **GetFileResourceSize** function before calling **GetFileResource**.

Parameters

lpszFileName
  Points to the buffer that contains the name of the file containing the resource.

lpszResType
  Points to a value that is created by using the **MAKEINTRESOURCE** macro with the numbered resource type. This value is typically VS_FILE_INFO.

lpszResID
  Points to a value that is created by using the **MAKEINTRESOURCE** macro with the numbered resource identifier. This value is typically VS_VERSION_INFO.

dwFileOffset
  Specifies the offset of the resource within the file. The **GetFileResourceSize** function returns this value. If this parameter is NULL, the **GetFileResource** function searches the file for the resource.

dwResLen
  Specifies the buffer size, in bytes, identified by the *lpvData* parameter. The **GetFileResourceSize** function returns the buffer size required to hold the resource. If the buffer is not large enough, the resource data is truncated to the size of the buffer.

lpvData
Points to the buffer that will receive a copy of the resource. If the buffer is not large enough, the resource data is truncated.

Return Value   The return value is nonzero if the function is successful. Otherwise, it is zero, indicating the function could not find the file, could not find the resource, or produced an MS-DOS error. The **GetFileResource** function returns no information about the type of error that occurred.

Comments   If the *dwFileOffset* parameter is zero, the **GetFileResource** function determines the location of the resource by using the *lpszResType* and *lpszResID* parameters.

If *dwFileOffset* is not zero, **GetFileResource** assumes that *dwFileOffset* is the return value of **GetFileResourceSize** and, therefore, ignores *lpszResType* and *lpszResID*.

See Also   **GetFileResourceSize**

GetFileResourceSize   3.1

#include <ver.h>

DWORD GetFileResourceSize(*lpszFileName***,** *lpszResType***,** *lpszResID***,** *lpdwFileOffset***)**
LPCSTR *lpszFileName***;**   /* address of buffer for filename   */
LPCSTR *lpszResType***;**   /* address of buffer for resource type */
LPCSTR *lpszResID***;**   /* address of buffer for resource ID   */
DWORD FAR **lpdwFileOffset***;** /* address of resource offset in file   */

The **GetFileResourceSize** function searches the specified file for the resource of the specified type and identifier.

Parameters   *lpszFileName*
Points to the buffer that contains the name of the file in which to search for the resource.

lpszResType
Points to a value that is created by using the **MAKEINTRESOURCE** macro with the numbered resource type. This value is typically VS_FILE_INFO.

lpszResID
Points to a value that is created by using the **MAKEINTRESOURCE** macro with the numbered resource identifier. This value is typically VS_VERSION_INFO.

lpdwFileOffset
  Points to a 16-bit value that the **GetFileResourceSize** function fills with the offset to the resource within the file.

Return Value   The return value is the size of the resource, in bytes. The return value is NULL if the function could not find the file, the file does not have any resources attached, or the function produced an MS-DOS error. The **GetFileResourceSize** function returns no information about the type of error that occurred.

See Also   **GetFileResource**

GetFileTitle   `3.1`

#include <commdlg.h>

int **GetFileTitle**(*lpszFile*, *lpszTitle*, *cbBuf*)
LPCSTR *lpszFile*;   /* pointer to filename (including drive and directory)   */
LPSTR *lpszTitle*;   /* address of buffer that receives filename   */
UINT *cbBuf*;   /* length of buffer   */

The **GetFileTitle** function returns the title of the file identified by the *lpszFile* parameter.

Parameters   *lpszFile*
  Points to the name and location of an MS-DOS file.

lpszTitle
  Points to a buffer into which the function is to copy the name of the file.

cbBuf
  Specifies the length, in bytes, of the buffer to which the *lpszTitle* parameter points.

Return Value   The return value is zero if the function is successful. The return value is a negative number if the filename is invalid. The return value is a positive integer that specifies the required buffer size, in bytes, if the buffer to which the *lpszTitle* parameter points is too small.

Comments   The function returns an error value if the buffer pointed to by the *lpszFile* parameter contains any of the following:

- An empty string
- A string containing a wildcard (*), opening bracket ([), or closing bracket (])

- A string that ends with a colon (:), slash mark (/), or backslash (\)
- A string whose length exceeded the length of the buffer
- An invalid character (for example, a space or unprintable character).

The required buffer size includes the terminating null character.

GetFileVersionInfo

$\boxed{3.1}$

#include <ver.h>

```
BOOL GetFileVersionInfo(lpszFileName, handle, cbBuf, lpvData)
LPCSTR lpszFileName;    /* address of buffer for filename       */
DWORD handle;           /* file-version information              */
DWORD cbBuf;            /* size of buffer                        */
void FAR* lpvData;      /* address of buffer for file-version info */
```

The **GetFileVersionInfo** function returns version information about the specified file. The application must call the **GetFileVersionInfoSize** function before calling **GetFileVersionInfo** to obtain the appropriate handle if the handle is not NULL.

Parameters

lpszFileName
Points to the buffer that contains the name of the file.

handle
Identifies the file-version information. The **GetFileVersionInfoSize** function returns this handle, or it may be NULL. If the *handle* parameter is NULL, the **GetFileVersionInfo** function searches the file for the version information.

cbBuf
Specifies the buffer size, in bytes, identified by the *lpvData* parameter. The **Get-FileVersionInfoSize** function returns the buffer size required to hold the file-version information. If the buffer is not large enough, the file-version information is truncated to the size of the buffer.

lpvData
Points to the buffer that will receive the file-version information. This parameter is used by a subsequent call to the **VerQueryValue** function.

Return Value

The return value is nonzero if the function is successful. Otherwise, it is zero, indicating the file docs not cxist or the *handle* parameter is invalid. The **GetFile-VersionInfo** function returns no information about the type of error that occurred.

Comments

The file version information is organized in a **VERSIONINFO** statement.

Currently, the **GetFileVersionInfo** function recognizes only version-information created by Microsoft Resource Compiler (RC).

See Also   **GetFileVersionInfoSize**, **VerQueryValue**

GetFileVersionInfoSize

[3.1]

#include <ver.h>

DWORD GetFileVersionInfoSize(*lpszFileName*, *lpdwHandle*)
LPCSTR *lpszFileName*;   /* address of buffer for filename   */
DWORD FAR **lpdwHandle*;   /* address of handle for info   */

The **GetFileVersionInfoSize** function determines whether it can obtain version in-formation from the specified file. If version information is available, **GetFile-VersionInfoSize** returns the size of the buffer required to hold the version information. It also returns a handle that can be used in a subsequent call to the **GetFileVersionInfo** function.

Parameters   *lpszFileName*
Points to the buffer that contains the name of the file.

lpdwHandle
Points to a 32-bit value that the **GetFileVersionInfoSize** function fills with the handle to the file-version information. The **GetFileVersionInfo** function can use this handle.

Return Value   The return value is the buffer size, in bytes, required to hold the version informa-tion if the function is successful. The return value is NULL if the function could not find the file, could not find the version information, or produced an MS-DOS error. The **GetFileVersionInfoSize** function returns no information about the type of error that occurred.

Comments   The file version information is organized in a **VERSIONINFO** statement.

See Also   **GetFileVersionInfo**

GetFocus

HWND GetFocus(void)

The **GetFocus** function retrieves the handle of the window that currently has the input focus.

Parameters   This function has no parameters.

Return Value   The return value is the handle of the focus window. If no window has the focus, it is NULL.

See Also   **GetActiveWindow, GetCapture, SetFocus**

GetFontData

```
DWORD GetFontData(hdc, dwTable, dwOffset, lpvBuffer, cbData)
HDC hdc;                /* handle of device context        */
DWORD dwTable;          /* metric table to query           */
DWORD dwOffset;         /* offset into table being queried */
void FAR* lpvBuffer;    /* address of buffer for font data */
DWORD cbData;           /* length of data to query         */
```

The **GetFontData** function retrieves font-metric information from a scalable font file. The information to retrieve is identified by specifying an offset into the font file and the length of the information to return.

Parameters   *hdc*
                      Identifies the device context.

                      dwTable
                      Specifies the name of the metric table to be returned. This parameter can be one of the metric tables documented in the TrueType Font Files specification, published by Microsoft Corporation. If this parameter is zero, the information is retrieved starting at the beginning of the font file.

                      dwOffset
                      Specifies the offset from the beginning of the table at which to begin retrieving information. If this parameter is zero, the information is retrieved starting at the beginning of the table specified by the *dwTable* parameter. If this value is greater than or equal to the size of the table, **GetFontData** returns zero.

lpvBuffer
Points to a buffer that will receive the font information. If this value is NULL, the function returns the size of the buffer required for the font data specified in the *dwTable* parameter.

cbData
Specifies the length, in bytes, of the information to be retrieved. If this parameter is zero, **GetFontData** returns the size of the data specified in the *dwTable* parameter.

Return Value
The return value specifies the number of bytes returned in the buffer pointed to by the *lpvBuffer* parameter, if the function is successful. Otherwise, it is −1.

Comments
An application can sometimes use the **GetFontData** function to save a TrueType font with a document. To do this, the application determines whether the font can be embedded and then retrieves the entire font file, specifying zero for the *dwTable*, *dwOffset*, and *cbData* parameters.

Applications can determine whether a font can be embedded by checking the **otmfsType** member of the **OUTLINETEXTMETRIC** structure. If bit 1 of **otmfsType** is set, embedding is not permitted for the font. If bit 1 is clear, the font can be embedded. If bit 2 is set, the embedding is read-only.

If an application attempts to use this function to retrieve information for a non-TrueType font, the **GetFontData** function returns −1.

Example
The following example retrieves an entire TrueType font file:

```
HGLOBAL hglb;
DWORD dwSize;
void FAR* lpvBuffer;

dwSize = GetFontData(hdc, NULL, 0L, NULL, 0L); /* get file size   */

hglb = GlobalAlloc(GPTR, dwSize);  /* allocate memory */
lpvBuffer = GlobalLock(hglb);
GetFontData(hdc, NULL, 0L, lpvBuffer, dwSize);  /* retrieve data   */
```

The following retrieves an entire TrueType font file 4K at a time:

```
#define SIZE  4096
BYTE Buffer[SIZE];
DWORD dwOffset;
DWORD dwSize;
```

```
dwOffset = 0L;
while(dwSize = GetFontData(hdc, NULL, dwOffset, Buffer, SIZE)) {

   . /* process data in buffer */
   .
   dwOffset += dwSize;
}
```

The following example retrieves a TrueType font table:

```
HGLOBAL hglb;
DWORD dwSize;
void FAR* lpvBuffer;

LPSTR lpszTable;
DWORD dwTable;

lpszTable = "cmap";
dwTable   = *(LPDWORD) lpszTable;              /* construct DWORD type */

dwSize = GetFontData(hdc, dwTable, 0L, NULL, 0L); /* get table size */

hglb = GlobalAlloc(GPTR, dwSize);                 /* allocate memory */
lpvBuffer = GlobalLock(hglb);
GetFontData(hdc, dwTable, 0L, lpvBuffer, dwSize);  /* retrieve data */
```

See Also   **GetOutlineTextMetrics**

GetFreeFileHandles   3.1

#include <stress.h>

int GetFreeFileHandles(void)

The **GetFreeFileHandles** function returns the number of file handles available to the current instance.

Parameters   This function has no parameters.

Return Value   The return value is the number of file handles available to the current instance.

GetFreeSpace

3.0

DWORD GetFreeSpace(*fuFlags*)
UINT *fuFlags*;   /* ignored in Windows 3.1   */

The **GetFreeSpace** function scans the global heap and returns the number of bytes of memory currently available.

Parameters   *fuFlags*
This parameter is ignored in Windows 3.1.

Return Value   The return value is the amount of available memory, in bytes, if the function is successful.

Comments   The amount of memory specified by the return value is not necessarily contiguous; the **GlobalCompact** function returns the number of bytes in the largest block of free global memory.

In standard mode, the value returned represents the number of bytes in the global heap that are not used and that are not reserved for code.

In 386-enhanced mode, the return value is an estimate of the amount of memory available to an application. It does not account for memory held in reserve for non-Windows applications.

See Also   **GlobalCompact**

GetFreeSystemResources

3.1

UINT GetFreeSystemResources(*fuSysResource*)
UINT *fuSysResource*;   /* type of resource to check   */

The **GetFreeSystemResources** function returns the percentage of free space for system resources.

Parameters   *fuSysResource*
Specifies the type of resource to be checked. This parameter can be one of the following values:

Value	Meaning
GFSR_SYSTEMRESOURCES	Returns the percentage of free space for system resources.
GFSR_GDIRESOURCES	Returns the percentage of free space for GDI resources. GDI resources include device-context handles, brushes, pens, regions, fonts, and bitmaps.
GFSR_USERRESOURCES	Returns the percentage of free space for USER resources. These resources include window and menu handles.

Return Value   The return value specifies the percentage of free space for resources, if the function is successful.

Comments   Since the return value from this function does not guarantee that an application will be able to create a new object, applications should not use this function to determine whether it will be possible to create an object.

See Also   **GetFreeSpace**

GetGlyphOutline   3.1

```
DWORD GetGlyphOutline(hdc, uChar, fuFormat, lpgm, cbBuffer, lpBuffer, lpmat2)
HDC hdc;                        /* handle of device context              */
UINT uChar;                     /* character to query                    */
UINT fuFormat;                  /* format of data to return              */
LPGLYPHMETRICS lpgm;            /* address of structure with glyph metrics */
DWORD cbBuffer;                 /* size of buffer for data               */
void FAR* lpBuffer;             /* address of buffer for outline data    */
LPMAT2 lpmat2;                  /* address of structure with transform matrix */
```

The **GetGlyphOutline** function retrieves the outline curve or bitmap for an outline character in the current font.

Parameters   *hdc*
Identifies the device context.

uChar
Specifies the character for which information is to be returned.

fuFormat
Specifies the format in which the function is to return information. It can be one of the following values:

Value	Meaning
GGO_BITMAP	Returns the glyph bitmap. When the function returns, the buffer pointed to by the *lpBuffer* parameter contains a 1-bit-per-pixel bitmap whose rows start on doubleword boundaries.
GGO_NATIVE	Returns the curve data points in the rasterizer's native format, using device units. When this value is specified, any transformation specified in the *lpmat2* parameter is ignored.

When the value of this parameter is zero, the function fills in a **GLYPHMETRICS** structure but does not return glyph-outline data.

lpgm

Points to a **GLYPHMETRICS** structure that describes the placement of the glyph in the character cell. The **GLYPHMETRICS** structure has the following form:

```
typedef struct tagGLYPHMETRICS {   /* gm */
    UINT   gmBlackBoxX;
    UINT   gmBlackBoxY;
    POINT  gmptGlyphOrigin;
    int    gmCellIncX;
    int    gmCellIncY;
} GLYPHMETRICS;
```

For a full description of this structure, see the *Microsoft Windows Programmer's Reference, Volume 3*.

cbBuffer

Specifies the size of the buffer into which the function copies information about the outline character. If this value is zero and the *fuFormat* parameter is either the GGO_BITMAP or GGO_NATIVE values, the function returns the required size of the buffer.

lpBuffer

Points to a buffer into which the function copies information about the outline character. If the *fuFormat* parameter specifies the GGO_NATIVE value, the information is copied in the form of **TTPOLYGONHEADER** and **TTPOLY-CURVE** structures. If this value is NULL and the *fuFormat* parameter is either the GGO_BITMAP or GGO_NATIVE value, the function returns the required size of the buffer.

lpmat2

Points to a **MAT2** structure that contains a transformation matrix for the character. This parameter cannot be NULL, even when the GGO_NATIVE value is specified for the *fuFormat* parameter. The **MAT2** structure has the following form:

```
typedef struct tagMAT2 {   /* mat2 */
    FIXED eM11;
    FIXED eM12;
    FIXED eM21;
    FIXED eM22;
} MAT2;
```

For a full description of this structure, see the *Microsoft Windows Programmer's Reference, Volume 3.*

Return Value   The return value is the size, in bytes, of the buffer required for the retrieved information if the *cbBuffer* parameter is zero or the *lpBuffer* parameter is NULL. Otherwise, it is a positive value if the function is successful, or −1 if there is an error.

Comments   An application can rotate characters retrieved in bitmap format by specifying a 2-by-2 transformation matrix in the structure pointed to by the *lpmat2* parameter.

A glyph outline is returned as a series of contours. Each contour is defined by a **TTPOLYGONHEADER** structure followed by as many **TTPOLYCURVE** structures as are required to describe it. All points are returned as **POINTFX** structures and represent absolute positions, not relative moves. The starting point given by the **pfxStart** member of the **TTPOLYGONHEADER** structure is the point at which the outline for a contour begins. The **TTPOLYCURVE** structures that follow can be either polyline records or spline records. Polyline records are a series of points; lines drawn between the points describe the outline of the character. Spline records represent the quadratic curves used by TrueType (that is, quadratic b-splines).

For example, the **GetGlyphOutline** function retrieves the following information about the lowercase "i" in the Arial TrueType font:

```
dwrc = 88                   /* total size of native buffer    */

TTPOLYGONHEADER #1          /* contour for dot on i           */
  cb    = 44                /* size for contour               */
  dwType = 24               /* TT_POLYGON_TYPE                */
  pfxStart = 1.000, 11.000

  TTPOLYCURVE #1
    wType  = TT_PRIM_LINE
    cpfx   = 3
    pfx[0] = 1.000, 12.000
    pfx[1] = 2.000, 12.000
    pfx[2] = 2.000, 11.000   /* automatically close to pfxStart */

TTPOLYGONHEADER #2          /* contour for body of i          */
  cb    = 44
  dwType = 24               /* TT_POLYGON_TYPE                */
  pfxStart = 1.000, 0.000
```

```
TTPOLYCURVE #1
  wType = TT_PRIM_LINE
  cpfx  = 3
  pfx[0] = 1.000, 9.000
  pfx[1] = 2.000, 9.000
  pfx[2] = 2.000, 0.000      /* automatically close to pfxStart */
```

See Also   **GetOutlineTextMetrics**

GetInputState   `2.x`

BOOL GetInputState(void)

The **GetInputState** function determines whether there are mouse clicks or keyboard events in the system queue that require processing. Keyboard events occur when a user presses one or more keys. The system queue is the location in which Windows stores mouse clicks and keyboard events.

Parameters   This function has no parameters.

Return Value   The return value is nonzero if the function detects a mouse click or keyboard event in the system queue. Otherwise, it is zero.

See Also   **EnableHardwareInput**

GetInstanceData   `2.x`

int GetInstanceData(*hinst, npbData, cbData*)
HINSTANCE *hinst*;   /* handle of previous instance   */
BYTE* *npbData*;   /* address of current instance data buffer   */
int *cbData*;   /* number of bytes to transfer   */

The **GetInstanceData** function copies data from a previous instance of an application into the data area of the current instance.

Parameters   *hinst*
                        Identifies a previous instance of the application.

npbData
Points to a buffer in the current instance.

cbData
Specifies the number of bytes to be copied.

Return Value   The return value specifies the number of bytes copied if the function is successful. Otherwise, it is zero.

GetKBCodePage   3.0

int GetKBCodePage(void)

The **GetKBCodePage** function returns the current Windows code page.

Parameters   This function has no parameters.

Return Value   The return value specifies the code page currently loaded by Windows, if the function is successful. It can be one of the following values:

Value	Meaning
437	Default (United States, used by most countries: indicates that there is no OEMANSI.BIN in the Windows directory)
850	International (OEMANSI.BIN = XLAT850.BIN)
860	Portugal (OEMANSI.BIN = XLAT860.BIN)
861	Iceland (OEMANSI.BIN = XLAT861.BIN)
863	French Canadian (OEMANSI.BIN = XLAT863.BIN)
865	Norway/Denmark (OEMANSI.BIN = XLAT865.BIN)

Comments   The keyboard driver provides the **GetKBCodePage** function. An application using this function must include the following information in its module-definition (.DEF) file:

```
IMPORTS
    KEYBOARD.GETKBCODEPAGE
```

If the OEMANSI.BIN file is in the Windows directory, Windows reads it and overwrites the OEM/ANSI translation tables in the keyboard driver.

When the user selects a language from the Setup program and the language does not use the default code page (437), Setup copies the appropriate file (such as XLAT850.BIN) to OEMANSI.BIN in the Windows system directory. If the language uses the default code page, Setup deletes OEMANSI.BIN, if it exists, from the Windows system directory.

Example

The following example uses the **GetKBCodePage** function to display the current code page:

```
char szBuf[80];
int i, cp, subtype, f_keys, len;

char *apszKeyboards[] = {
    "IBM PX/XT",
    "Olivetti ICO",
    "IBM AT",
    "IBM Enhanced",
    "Nokia 1050",
    "Nokia 9140",
    "Standard Japanese",
    };

cp = GetKBCodePage();

if ((i = GetKeyboardType(0)) == 0 || i > 7) {
    MessageBox(NULL, "invalid keyboard type",
        "GetKeyboardType", MB_ICONSTOP);
    break;
}

subtype = GetKeyboardType(1);
f_keys = GetKeyboardType(2);

len = wsprintf(szBuf, "%s keyboard, subtype %d\n",
    apszKeyboards[i - 1], subtype);
len = wsprintf(szBuf + len, " %d function keys, code page %d",
    f_keys, cp);

MessageBox(NULL, szBuf, "Keyboard Information", MB_OK);
```

See Also   **GetKeyboardType**

GetKerningPairs   3.1

int **GetKerningPairs**(*hdc*, *cPairs*, *lpkrnpair*)
HDC *hdc*;   /* handle of device context   */
int *cPairs*;   /* number of kerning pairs   */
KERNINGPAIR FAR* *lpkrnpair*; /* pointer to structures for kerning pairs */

The **GetKerningPairs** function retrieves the character kerning pairs for the font that is currently selected in the specified device context.

Parameters   *hdc*
Identifies a device context. The **GetKerningPairs** function retrieves kerning pairs for the current font for this device context.

cPairs
Specifies the number of **KERNINGPAIR** structures pointed to by the *lpkrnpair* parameter. The function will not copy more kerning pairs than specified by *cPairs*.

The **KERNINGPAIR** structure has the following form:

```
typedef struct tagKERNINGPAIR {
    WORD wFirst;
    WORD wSecond;
    int  iKernAmount;
} KERNINGPAIR;
```

For a full description of this structure, see the *Microsoft Windows Programmer's Reference, Volume 3.*

lpkrnpair
Points to an array of **KERNINGPAIR** structures that receive the kerning pairs when the function returns. This array must contain at least as many structures as specified by the *cPairs* parameter. If this parameter is NULL, the function returns the total number of kerning pairs for the font.

Return Value   The return value specifies the number of kerning pairs retrieved or the total number of kerning pairs in the font, if the function is successful. It is zero if the function fails or there are no kerning pairs for the font.

GetKeyboardState   2.x

void GetKeyboardState(*lpbKeyState***)**
BYTE FAR* *lpbKeyState*;   /* address of array to receive virtual-key codes   */

The **GetKeyboardState** function copies the status of the 256 virtual-keyboard keys to the specified buffer.

Parameters   *lpbKeyState*
Points to the 256-byte buffer that will receive the virtual-key codes.

Return Value   This function does not return a value.

Comments

An application calls the **GetKeyboardState** function in response to a keyboard-input message. This function retrieves the state of the keyboard at the time the input message was generated.

If the high-order bit is 1, the key is down; otherwise, it is up. If the low-order bit is 1, the key is toggled. A toggle key, such as the CAPSLOCK key, is toggled if it has been pressed an odd number of times since the system was started. The key is un-toggled if the low-order bit is 0.

For a list of virtual-key codes and their corresponding mouse or keyboard equivalents, see the *Microsoft Windows Programmer's Reference, Volume 3*.

Example

The following example simulates a pressed CTRL key:

```
BYTE pbKeyState[256];

GetKeyboardState((LPBYTE) &pbKeyState);
pbKeyState[VK_CONTROL] |= 0x80;
SetKeyboardState((LPBYTE) &pbKeyState);
```

See Also

GetKeyState, SetKeyboardState

GetKeyboardType

3.0

int GetKeyboardType(*fnKeybInfo*)
int *fnKeybInfo*;   /* specifies type of information to retrieve   */

The **GetKeyboardType** function retrieves information about the current keyboard.

Parameters

fnKeybInfo
Determines the type of keyboard information to be retrieved. This parameter can be one of the following values:

Value	Meaning
0	Retrieves the keyboard type.
1	Retrieves the keyboard subtype.
2	Retrieves the number of function keys on the keyboard.

Return Value

The return value specifies the requested information if the function is successful. Otherwise, it is zero.

Comments

The subtype is an OEM-dependent value. The subtype may be one of the following values:

Value	Meaning
1	IBM PC/XT, or compatible (83-key) keyboard
2	Olivetti "ICO" (102-key) keyboard
3	IBM AT (84-key) or similar keyboard
4	IBM Enhanced (101- or 102-key) keyboard
5	Nokia 1050 and similar keyboards
6	Nokia 9140 and similar keyboards
7	Japanese keyboard

The keyboard driver provides the **GetKeyboardType** function. An application using this function must include the following information in its module-definition (.DEF) file:

```
IMPORTS
    KEYBOARD.GETKEYBOARDTYPE
```

The application can also determine the number of function keys on a keyboard from the keyboard type. The number of function keys for each keyboard type follows:

Type	Number of function keys
1	10
2	12 (sometimes 18)
3	10
4	12
5	10
6	24
7	This value is hardware-dependent and must be specified by the OEM.

Example

The following example uses the **GetKeyboardType** function to display information about the current keyboard:

```
char szBuf[80];
int i, cp, subtype, f_keys, len;

char *apszKeyboards[] = {
    "IBM PX/XT",
    "Olivetti ICO",
    "IBM AT",
    "IBM Enhanced",
    "Nokia 1050",
    "Nokia 9140",
    "Standard Japanese",
    };
```

```
cp = GetKBCodePage();

if ((i = GetKeyboardType(0)) == 0 || i > 7) {
    MessageBox(NULL, "invalid keyboard type",
        "GetKeyboardType", MB_ICONSTOP);
    break;
}

subtype = GetKeyboardType(1);
f_keys = GetKeyboardType(2);

len = wsprintf(szBuf, "%s keyboard, subtype %d\n",
    apszKeyboards[i - 1], subtype);
len = wsprintf(szBuf + len, " %d function keys, code page %d",
    f_keys, cp);

MessageBox(NULL, szBuf, "Keyboard Information", MB_OK);
```

GetKeyNameText

3.0

int GetKeyNameText(*lParam, lpszBuffer, cbMaxKey*)
LONG *lParam*;   /* 32-bit parameter of keyboard message   */
LPSTR *lpszBuffer*;   /* address of a buffer for key name   */
int *cbMaxKey*;   /* specifies maximum key string length   */

The **GetKeyNameText** function retrieves a string that represents the name of a key.

Parameters   *lParam*
Specifies the 32-bit parameter of the keyboard message (such as WM_KEYDOWN) to be processed. The **GetKeyNameText** function interprets the following portions of *lParam*:

Bits	Meaning
16–23	Character scan code.
24	Extended bit. Distinguishes some keys on an enhanced keyboard.
25	"Don't care" bit. The application calling this function sets this bit to indicate that the function should not distinguish between left and right CTRL and SHIFT keys, for example.

lpszBuffer
Points to a buffer that will receive the key name.

cbMaxKey

Specifies the maximum length, in bytes, of the key name, not including the terminating null character (this parameter should one less than the size of the buffer pointed to by the *lpszBuffer* parameter).

Return Value

The return value is the length, in bytes, of the string copied to the specified buffer, if the function is successful. Otherwise, it is zero.

Comments

The format of the key-name string depends on the current keyboard driver. This driver maintains a list of names in the form of character strings for keys with names longer than a single character. The key name is translated, according to the layout of the currently installed keyboard, into the principal language supported by the keyboard driver.

GetKeyState

2.x

int GetKeyState(*vkey*)
int *vkey*;   /* virtual key   */

The **GetKeyState** function retrieves the state of the specified virtual key. The state specifies whether the key is up, down, or toggled (on, off—alternating each time the key is pressed).

Parameters

vkey

Specifies a virtual key. If the requested virtual key is a letter or digit (A through Z, a through z, or 0 through 9), *vkey* must be set to the ASCII value of that character. For other keys, it must be a virtual-key code. For a list of virtual-key codes, see the *Microsoft Windows Programmer's Reference, Volume 3*.

Return Value

The return value specifies the state of the given virtual key. If the high-order bit is 1, the key is down; otherwise, it is up. If the low-order bit is 1, the key is toggled. A toggle key, such as the CAPSLOCK key, is toggled if it has been pressed an odd number of times since the system was started. The key is untoggled if the low-order bit is 0.

Comments

An application calls the **GetKeyState** function in response to a keyboard-input message. This function retrieves the state of the key at the time the input message was generated.

See Also

GetAsyncKeyState, GetKeyboardState

GetLastActivePopup

HWND GetLastActivePopup(*hwndOwner*)
HWND *hwndOwner*;   /* handle of owner window   */

The **GetLastActivePopup** function determines which pop-up window owned by the given window was most recently active.

Parameters   *hwndOwner*
Identifies the owner window.

Return Value   The return value is the handle of most-recently active pop-up window if the function is successful.

Comments   The return value handle will be the same as the handle in the *hwndOwner* parameter if any of the following conditions are met:

- The window identified by *hwndOwner* was most recently active.

- The window identified by *hwndOwner* does not own any pop-up windows.

- The window identified by *hwndOwner* is not a top-level window or is owned by another window.

See Also   **AnyPopup, GetActiveWindow, ShowOwnedPopups**

GetMapMode

int GetMapMode(*hdc*)
HDC *hdc*;   /* handle of device context   */

The **GetMapMode** function retrieves the current mapping mode.

Parameters   *hdc*
Identifies the device context.

Return Value   The return value specifies the mapping mode if the function is successful.

Comments   For a complete list of mapping modes, see the description of the **SetMapMode** function.

Example   The following example uses the **GetMapMode** function to determine whether the current mapping mode is MM_TEXT:

```
if (GetMapMode(hdc) != MM_TEXT) {
    TextOut(hdc, 100, -200, "Mapping mode must be MM_TEXT", 28);
    return FALSE;
}
```

See Also   **SetMapMode**

GetMenu

2.x

HMENU GetMenu(*hwnd*)
HWND *hwnd*;   /* handle of window   */

> The **GetMenu** function retrieves the handle of the menu associated with the given window.

Parameters   *hwnd*
> Identifies the window whose menu handle is retrieved.

Return Value   The return value is the handle of the menu if the function is successful. It is NULL if the given window has no menu. It is undefined if the window is a child window.

See Also   **GetSubMenu, SetMenu**

GetMenuCheckMarkDimensions

3.0

DWORD GetMenuCheckMarkDimensions(void)

> The **GetMenuCheckMarkDimensions** function returns the dimensions of the default check mark bitmap. Windows displays this bitmap next to checked menu items. Before calling the **SetMenuItemBitmaps** function to replace the default check mark, an application should determine the correct size for the bitmaps by calling the **GetMenuCheckMarkDimensions** function.

Parameters   This function has no parameters.

Return Value	The low-order word of the return value contains the width, in pixels, of the default check mark bitmap, if the function is successful; the high-order word contains the height.
See Also	**SetMenuItemBitmaps**

GetMenuItemCount

2.x

int GetMenuItemCount(*hmenu*)
HMENU *hmenu*;   /* handle of menu   */

The **GetMenuItemCount** function determines the number of items in a pop-up or top-level menu.

Parameters	*hmenu* Identifies the handle of the menu to be examined.
Return Value	The return value specifies the number of items in the menu if the function is successful. Otherwise, it is −1.
Example	The following example initializes the items in a pop-up menu:

```
WORD wCount;
WORD wItem;
WORD wID;

case WM_INITMENUPOPUP:
    wCount = GetMenuItemCount((HMENU) wParam);
    for (wItem = 0; wItem < wCount; wItem++) {
        wID = GetMenuItemID((HMENU) wParam, wItem);

        .
        . /* Initialize menu items. */
        .
    }
    break;
```

See Also	**GetMenu, GetMenuItemID, GetSubMenu**

GetMenuItemID

UINT GetMenuItemID(*hmenu*, *pos*)
HMENU *hmenu*;   /* handle of menu   */
int *pos*;   /* position of menu item   */

The **GetMenuItemID** function retrieves the identifier for a menu item located at the given position.

Parameters
hmenu
Identifies the pop-up menu that contains the item whose identifier is to be retrieved.

pos
Specifies the zero-based position of the menu item whose identifier is to be retrieved.

Return Value
The return value specifies the identifier of the pop-up menu item if the function is successful. If the *hmenu* parameter is NULL or if the specified item is a pop-up menu (as opposed to an item within the pop-up menu), the return value is −1. If the *pos* parameter corresponds to a SEPARATOR menu item, the return value is zero.

Example
The following example initializes the items in a pop-up menu:

```
WORD wCount;
WORD wItem;
WORD wID;

case WM_INITMENUPOPUP:
    wCount = GetMenuItemCount((HMENU) wParam);
    for (wItem = 0; wItem < wCount; wItem++) {
        wID = GetMenuItemID((HMENU) wParam, wItem);

        .
        . /* Initialize menu items. */
        .

    }
    break;
```

See Also
GetMenu, GetMenuItemCount, GetSubMenu

GetMenuState

2.x

UINT GetMenuState(*hmenu, idItem, fuFlags*)
HMENU *hmenu*;   /* handle of menu   */
UINT *idItem*;   /* menu-item identifier */
UINT *fuFlags*;   /* menu flags   */

The **GetMenuState** function retrieves the status flags associated with the specified menu item. If the menu item is a pop-up menu, this function also returns the number of items in the pop-up menu.

Parameters

hmenu
Identifies the menu.

idItem
Specifies the menu item for which the state is retrieved, as determined by the *fuFlags* parameter.

fuFlags
Specifies the nature of the *idItem* parameter. It can be one of the following values:

Value	Meaning
MF_BYCOMMAND	Specifies the menu-item identifier.
MF_BYPOSITION	Specifies the zero-based position of the menu item.

Return Value

The return value is −1 if the specified item does not exist. If the *idItem* parameter identifies a pop-up menu, the high-order byte of the return value contains the number of items in the pop-up menu, and the low order byte contains the menu flags associated with the pop-up menu. Otherwise, the return value is a mask (Boolean OR) of the values from the following list (this mask describes the status of the menu item that *idItem* identifies):

Value	Meaning
MF_BITMAP	Item is a bitmap.
MF_CHECKED	Check mark is placed next to item (pop-up menus only).
MF_DISABLED	Item is disabled.
MF_ENABLED	Item is enabled. Note that the value of this constant is zero; an application should not test against zero for failure when using this value.
MF_GRAYED	Item is disabled and grayed.
MF_MENUBARBREAK	Same as MF_MENUBREAK, except for pop-up menus where the new column is separated from the old column by a vertical dividing line.

Value	Meaning
MF_MENUBREAK	Item is placed on a new line (static menus) or in a new column (pop-up menus) without separating columns.
MF_SEPARATOR	Horizontal dividing line is drawn (pop-up menus only). This line cannot be enabled, checked, grayed, or highlighted. The *idItem* and *fuFlags* parameters are ignored.
MF_UNCHECKED	Check mark is not placed next to item (default). Note that the value of this constant is zero; an application should not test against zero for failure when using this value.

Example

The following example retrieves the handle of a pop-up menu, retrieves the checked state of a menu item in the menu, and then toggles the checked state of the item:

```
HMENU hmenu;
BOOL fOwnerDraw;

/* Retrieve a handle to the Colors menu. */

hmenu = GetSubMenu(GetMenu(hwnd), ID_COLORS_POS);

/* Retrieve the current state of the item. */

fOwnerDraw = GetMenuState(hmenu, IDM_COLOROWNERDR,
    MF_BYCOMMAND) & MF_CHECKED;

/* Toggle the state of the item. */

CheckMenuItem(hmenu, IDM_COLOROWNERDR,
    MF_BYCOMMAND | (fOwnerDraw ? MF_UNCHECKED : MF_CHECKED));
```

See Also   **GetMenu, GetMenuItemCount, GetSubMenu**

GetMenuString

int GetMenuString(*hmenu, idItem, lpsz, cbMax, fwFlags*)
HMENU *hmenu*;	/* handle of menu	*/
UINT *idItem*;	/* menu-item identifier	*/
LPSTR *lpsz*;	/* address of buffer for label	*/
int *cbMax*;	/* maximum length of label	*/
UINT *fwFlags*;	/* menu flags	*/

The **GetMenuString** function copies the label of a menu item into a buffer.

Parameters

hmenu
Identifies the menu.

idItem
Specifies the menu item whose label is to be copied, as determined by the *fwFlags* parameter.

lpsz
Points to a buffer that will receive the null-terminated label string.

cbMax
Specifies the maximum length, in bytes, of the label string. The label string is truncated if it is longer.

fwFlags
Specifies the nature of the *idItem* parameter. It can be one of the following values:

Value	Meaning
MF_BYCOMMAND	Specifies the menu-item identifier.
MF_BYPOSITION	Specifies the zero-based position of the menu item.

Return Value

The return value is the length, in bytes, of the returned label, if the function is successful. The length does not include the terminating null character.

Comments

The *cbMax* parameter should be one larger than the number of characters in the label to accommodate the null character that terminates the string.

See Also

GetMenu, GetMenuItemID

GetMessage

2.x

BOOL GetMessage(*lpmsg, hwnd, uMsgFilterMin, uMsgFilterMax***)**
MSG FAR* *lpmsg*;   /* address of structure with message   */
HWND *hwnd*;   /* handle of the window   */
UINT *uMsgFilterMin*;   /* first message   */
UINT *uMsgFilterMax*;   /* last message   */

The **GetMessage** function retrieves a message from the application's message queue and places the message in a **MSG** structure. If no message is available, **GetMessage** yields control to other applications until a message becomes available.

GetMessage retrieves messages associated only with the given window and within the given range of message values. The function does not retrieve messages for windows that belong to other applications.

Parameters   *lpmsg*
Points to an **MSG** structure that contains message information from the application's message queue. The **MSG** structure has the following form:

```
typedef struct tagMSG {      /* msg */
    HWND   hwnd;
    UINT   message;
    WPARAM wParam;
    LPARAM lParam;
    DWORD  time;
    POINT  pt;
} MSG;
```

For a full description of this structure, see the *Microsoft Windows Programmer's Reference, Volume 3*.

hwnd
Identifies the window whose messages are to be retrieved. If this parameter is NULL, **GetMessage** retrieves messages for any window that belongs to the application making the call.

uMsgFilterMin
Specifies the integer value of the lowest message value to be retrieved.

uMsgFilterMax
Specifies the integer value of the highest message value to be retrieved.

Return Value   The return value is nonzero if a message other than WM_QUIT is retrieved. It is zero if the WM_QUIT message is retrieved.

Comments

The return value is usually used to decide whether to terminate the application's main loop and exit the program.

The WM_KEYFIRST and WM_KEYLAST constants can be used as filter values to retrieve all messages related to keyboard input; the WM_MOUSEFIRST and WM_MOUSELAST constants can be used to retrieve all mouse-related messages. If the *uMsgFilterMin* and *uMsgFilterMax* parameters are both zero, the **GetMessage** function returns all available messages (without performing any filtering).

In addition to yielding control to other applications when no messages are available, the **GetMessage** and **PeekMessage** functions also yield control when WM_PAINT or WM_TIMER messages for other tasks are available.

The **GetMessage**, **PeekMessage**, and **WaitMessage** functions are the only ways to let other applications run. If your application does not call any of these functions for long periods of time, other applications cannot run.

Example

The following example uses the **GetMessage** function to retrieve messages from a message queue, translates virtual-key messages into character messages, and dispatches messages to the appropriate window procedures:

```
MSG msg;

while (GetMessage(&msg, (HWND) NULL, 0, 0)) {
    TranslateMessage(&msg);
    DispatchMessage(&msg);
}
```

See Also

GetMessageExtraInfo, PeekMessage, PostQuitMessage, SetMessageQueue, WaitMessage

GetMessageExtraInfo

3.1

LONG GetMessageExtraInfo(void)

The **GetMessageExtraInfo** function retrieves the extra information associated with the last message retrieved by the **GetMessage** or **PeekMessage** function. This extra information may be added to a message by the driver for a pointing device or keyboard.

Parameters

This function has no parameters.

Return Value   The return value specifies the extra information if the function is successful. The meaning of the extra information is device-specific.

See Also   **GetMessage**, **hardware_event**, **PeekMessage**

GetMessagePos

DWORD GetMessagePos(void)

The **GetMessagePos** function returns a long value that represents a cursor position, in screen coordinates. This position is the point occupied by the cursor when the last message retrieved by the **GetMessage** function occurred.

Parameters   This function has no parameters.

Return Value   The return value specifies the x- and y-coordinates of the cursor position if the function is successful.

Comments   To retrieve the current position of the cursor instead of the position at the time the last message occurred, use the **GetCursorPos** function.

The x-coordinate is in the low-order word of the return value; the y-coordinate is in the high-order word. If the return value is assigned to a variable, you can use the **MAKEPOINT** macro to obtain a **POINT** structure from the return value. You can also use the **LOWORD** or **HIWORD** macro to extract the x- or the y-coordinate.

See Also   **GetCursorPos**, **GetMessage**, **GetMessageTime**

GetMessageTime

LONG GetMessageTime(void)

The **GetMessageTime** function returns the message time for the last message retrieved by the **GetMessage** function. The time is a long integer that specifies the elapsed time, in milliseconds, from the time the system was started to the time the message was created (placed in the application queue).

Parameters   This function has no parameters.

Return Value   The return value specifies the message time if the function is successful.

Comments   The return value of the **GetMessageTime** function does not necessarily increase between subsequent messages, because the value wraps to zero if the timer count exceeds the maximum value for long integers.

To calculate time delays between messages, verify that the time of the second message is greater than the time of the first message and then subtract the time of the first message from the time of the second message.

See Also   **GetMessage**, **GetMessagePos**

GetMetaFile   2.x

HMETAFILE GetMetaFile(*lpszFile*)
LPCSTR *lpszFile*;   /* address of metafile name   */

The **GetMetaFile** function creates a handle of a specified metafile.

Parameters   *lpszFile*
Points to the null-terminated string that specifies the MS-DOS filename of the metafile. The metafile is assumed to exist.

Return Value   The return value is the handle of a metafile if the function is successful. Otherwise, it is NULL.

Example   The following example uses the **CopyMetaFile** function to copy a metafile to a specified file, plays the copied metafile, uses the **GetMetaFile** function to retrieve a handle to the copied metafile, uses the **SetWindowOrg** function to change the position at which the metafile is played 200 logical units to the right, and then plays the metafile at the new location:

```
HANDLE hmf, hmfSource, hmfOld;
LPSTR lpszFile1 = "MFTest";

hmf = CopyMetaFile(hmfSource, lpszFile1);
PlayMetaFile(hdc, hmf);
DeleteMetaFile(hmf);

hmfOld = GetMetaFile(lpszFile1);
SetWindowOrg(hdc, -200, 0);
PlayMetaFile(hdc, hmfOld);
```

```
DeleteMetaFile(hmfSource);
DeleteMetaFile(hmfOld);
```

See Also   **CopyMetaFile**, **PlayMetaFile**, **SetWindowOrg**

GetMetaFileBits   2.x

HGLOBAL GetMetaFileBits(*hmf*)
HMETAFILE *hmf*;   /* handle of metafile   */

The **GetMetaFileBits** function returns a handle of the global memory object that contains the specified metafile as a collection of bits. The memory object can be used to determine the size of the metafile or to save the metafile as a file. The memory object should not be modified.

Parameters   *hmf*
                        Identifies the memory metafile.

Return Value   The return value is the handle of the global memory object that contains the metafile, if the function is successful. Otherwise, it is NULL.

Comments   The handle contained in the *hmf* parameter becomes invalid when the **GetMeta-FileBits** function returns, so the returned global memory handle must be used to refer to the metafile.

                        When it no longer requires a global memory object that is associated with a metafile, an application should remove the object by using the **GlobalFree** function.

See Also   **GlobalFree**

GetModuleFileName   2.x

int GetModuleFileName(*hinst*, *lpszFilename*, *cbFileName*)
HINSTANCE *hinst*;   /* handle of module   */
LPSTR *lpszFilename*;   /* address of buffer for filename   */
int *cbFileName*;   /* maximum number of bytes to copy   */

The **GetModuleFileName** function retrieves the full path and filename of the executable file from which the specified module was loaded.

Parameters   *hinst*
Identifies the module or the instance of the module.

lpszFilename
Points to the buffer that is to receive the null-terminated filename.

cbFileName
Specifies the maximum number of bytes to copy, including the terminating null character. The filename is truncated if it is longer than *cbFileName*. This parameter should be set to the length of the filename buffer.

Return Value   The return value specifies the length, in bytes, of the string copied to the specified buffer, if the function is successful. Otherwise, it is zero.

Example   The following example retrieves an application's filename by using the instance handle passed to the application in the **WinMain** function:

```
int PASCAL WinMain(HINSTANCE hinst, HINSTANCE hPrevInst,
    LPSTR lpCmdLine, int nCmdShow)
{
    char szModuleName[260];

    GetModuleFileName(hinst, szModuleName, sizeof(szModuleName));
}
```

See Also   **GetModuleHandle**

GetModuleHandle   2.x

HMODULE GetModuleHandle(*lpszModuleName***)**
LPCSTR *lpszModuleName*;   /* address of name of module   */

The **GetModuleHandle** function retrieves the handle of the specified module.

Parameters   *lpszModuleName*
Points to a null-terminated string that specifies the name of the module.

Return Value   The return value is the handle of the module if the function is successful. Otherwise, it is NULL.

See Also   **GetModuleFileName**

GetModuleUsage

`2.x`

int GetModuleUsage(*hinst*)
HINSTANCE *hinst*;   /* handle of module   */

The **GetModuleUsage** function retrieves the reference count of a specified module.

Parameters   *hinst*
Identifies the module or an instance of the module.

Return Value   The return value specifies the reference count of the module if the function is successful.

Comments   Windows increments (increases by one) a module's reference count each time an application calls the **LoadModule** function. The count is decremented (decreased by one) when an application calls the **FreeModule** function.

See Also   **FreeModule, LoadModule**

GetMsgProc

`3.1`

LRESULT CALLBACK GetMsgProc(*code, wParam, lParam*)
int *code*;   /* process-message flag   */
WPARAM *wParam*;   /* undefined   */
LPARAM *lParam*;   /* pointer to MSG structure */

The **GetMsgProc** function is a library-defined callback function that the system calls whenever the **GetMessage** function has retrieved a message from an application queue. The system passes the retrieved message to the callback function before passing the message to the destination window procedure.

Parameters   *code*
Specifies whether the callback function should process the message or call the **CallNextHookEx** function. If this parameter is less than zero, the callback function should pass the message to **CallNextHookEx** without further processing.

wParam
Specifies a NULL value.

lParam
Points to an **MSG** structure that contains information about the message. The **MSG** structure has the following form:

```
typedef struct tagMSG {        /* msg */
    HWND    hwnd;
    UINT    message;
    WPARAM  wParam;
    LPARAM  lParam;
    DWORD   time;
    POINT   pt;
} MSG;
```

For a full description of this structure, see the *Microsoft Windows Programmer's Reference, Volume 3.*

Return Value   The callback function should return zero.

Comments   The **GetMsgProc** callback function can examine or modify the message as desired. Once the callback function returns control to the system, the **GetMessage** function returns the message, with any modifications, to the application that originally called it. The callback function does not require a return value.

This callback function must be in a dynamic-link library (DLL).

An application must install the callback function by specifying the WH_GETMESSAGE filter type and the procedure-instance address of the callback function in a call to the **SetWindowsHookEx** function.

GetMsgProc is a placeholder for the library-defined function name. The actual name must be exported by including it in an **EXPORTS** statement in the library's module-definition (.DEF) file.

See Also   **CallNextHookEx, GetMessage, SetWindowsHookEx**

GetNearestColor

2.x

COLORREF GetNearestColor(*hdc, clrref*)
HDC *hdc*;   /* handle of device context   */
COLORREF *clrref*;   /* color to match   */

The **GetNearestColor** function retrieves the solid color that best matches a specified logical color; the given device must be able to represent this solid color.

Parameters   *hdc*
Identifies the device context.

clrref
Specifies the color to be matched.

Return Value	The return value specifies an RGB (red, green, blue) color value that defines the solid color closest to the *clrref* value that the device can represent.
See Also	**GetNearestPaletteIndex**

GetNearestPaletteIndex

3.0

UINT GetNearestPaletteIndex(*hpal*, *clrref*)
HPALETTE *hpal*;   /* handle of palette   */
COLORREF *clrref*;   /* color to match   */

The **GetNearestPaletteIndex** function retrieves the index of the logical-palette entry that best matches the specified color value.

Parameters	*hpal*
	    Identifies the logical palette.
	
	clrref
	    Specifies the color to be matched.

Return Value	The return value is the index of the logical-palette entry whose corresponding color best matches the specified color.
Example	The following example uses the **GetNearestPaletteIndex** function to retrieve a color index from a palette. It then creates a brush with that retrieved color by using the **PALETTEINDEX** macro in a call to the **CreateSolidBrush** function.

```
WORD nColor;
HPALETTE hpal;
DWORD dwBrushColors[8][8];
HBRUSH hbr;
int x, y;

    .
    . /* Initialize the array of brush colors. */
    .
nColor = GetNearestPaletteIndex(hpal, dwBrushColors[x][y]);
hbr = CreateSolidBrush(PALETTEINDEX(nColor));

    .
    . /* Use the brush handle. */
    .
DeleteObject(hbr);
```

See Also	**CreateSolidBrush, GetNearestColor, GetPaletteEntries, GetSystemPaletteEntries**

GetNextDlgGroupItem

HWND GetNextDlgGroupItem(*hwndDlg*, *hwndCtrl*, *fPrevious*)
HWND *hwndDlg*;   /* handle of dialog box   */
HWND *hwndCtrl*;   /* handle of control   */
BOOL *fPrevious*;   /* direction flag   */

The **GetNextDlgGroupItem** function searches for the previous (or next) control within a group of controls in a dialog box. A group of controls begins with a control with the WS_GROUP style and ends with the last control that does not contain a WS_GROUP style.

Parameters

hwndDlg
Identifies the dialog box to be searched.

hwndCtrl
Identifies the control to be used as the starting point for the search.

fPrevious
Specifies how the function is to search the group of controls in the dialog box. If this parameter is TRUE, the function searches for the previous control in the group. If this parameter is FALSE, the function searches for the next control in the group.

Return Value

The return value is the window handle of the previous (or next) control in the group, if the function is successful.

Comments

If the *hwndCtrl* parameter identifies the last control in the group and the *fPrevious* parameter is FALSE, the **GetNextDlgGroupItem** function returns the window handle of the first control in the group. If *hwndCtrl* identifies the first control in the group and *fPrevious* is TRUE, **GetNextDlgGroupItem** returns the window handle of the last control in the group.

Example

The following example sets the check state of a group of radio buttons. It is assumed that the group contains only radio buttons and no other type of control:

```
HWND hwndStart, hwndCurrent;

case WM_COMMAND:
    switch (HIWORD(lParam)) {
        case BN_CLICKED:

            /*
             * If a radio button was clicked, clear the current
             * selection and select the one that was clicked.
             */

            hwndStart = GetDlgItem(hdlg, wParam);
```

```
                              if (LOWORD(GetWindowLong(hwndStart,
                                      GWL_STYLE) == BS_RADIOBUTTON)) {
                                  hwndCurrent = hwndStart;

                                  do {
                                      hwndCurrent = GetNextDlgGroupItem(hdlg,
                                          hwndCurrent, TRUE);
                                      SendMessage(hwndCurrent, BM_SETCHECK,
                                          hwndCurrent == hwndStart, 0L);
                                  } while (hwndCurrent != hwndStart);
                              }
                                .
                                . /* Process other notification codes. */
                                .
                          }
```

See Also   **GetDlgItem, GetNextDlgTabItem**

GetNextDlgTabItem   <kbd>2.x</kbd>

HWND GetNextDlgTabItem(*hwndDlg*, *hwndCtrl*, *fPrevious*)
HWND *hwndDlg*;   /* handle of dialog box   */
HWND *hwndCtrl*;   /* handle of known control   */
BOOL *fPrevious*;   /* direction flag   */

The **GetNextDlgTabItem** function retrieves the handle of the first control that has the WS_TABSTOP style that precedes (or follows) the specified control.

Parameters   *hwndDlg*
                        Identifies the dialog box to be searched.

                        hwndCtrl
                        Identifies the control to be used as the starting point for the search.

                        fPrevious
                        Specifies how the function is to search the dialog box. If this parameter is TRUE, the function searches for the previous control in the dialog box. If this parameter is FALSE, the function searches for the next control in the dialog box.

Return Value   The return valuc is the window handle of the previous (or next) control that has the WS_TABSTOP style, if the function is successful.

Example   The following example retrieves the handle of the previous control that has the WS_TABSTOP style, relative to the control that has the input focus:

```
HWND hdlg;
HWND hwndControl;

hwndControl = GetNextDlgTabItem(hdlg, GetFocus(), TRUE);
```

See Also   **GetDlgItem**, **GetNextDlgGroupItem**

GetNextDriver

3.1

HDRVR GetNextDriver(*hdrvr, fdwFlag*)
HDRVR *hdrvr*;   /* handle of installable driver   */
DWORD *fdwFlag*;   /* search flag   */

The **GetNextDriver** function enumerates instances of an installable driver.

Parameters   *hdrvr*
Identifies the installable driver for which instances should be enumerated. This parameter must be retrieved by the **OpenDriver** function. If this parameter is NULL, the enumeration begins at either the beginning or end of the list of installable drivers (depending on the setting of the flags in the *fdwFlag* parameter).

fdwFlag
Specifies whether the function should return a handle identifying only the first instance of a driver and whether the function should return handles identifying the instances of the driver in the order in which they were loaded. This parameter can be one or more of the following flags:

Value	Meaning
GND_FIRSTINSTANCEONLY	Returns a handle identifying the first instance of an installable driver. When this flag is set, the function will enumerate only the first instance of an installable driver, no matter how many times the driver has been installed.
GND_FORWARD	Enumerates subsequent instances of the driver. (Using this flag has the same effect as not using the GND_REVERSE flag.)
GND_REVERSE	Enumerates instances of the driver as it was loaded—each subsequent call to the function returns the handle of the next instance.

Return Value   The return value is the instance handle of the installable driver if the function is successful.

GetNextWindow

HWND GetNextWindow(*hwnd*, *uFlag*)
HWND *hwnd*;   /* handle of current window   */
UINT *uFlag*;   /* direction flag   */

The **GetNextWindow** function searches for the handle of the next (or previous) window in the window manager's list. The window manager's list contains entries for all top-level windows, their associated child windows, and the child windows of any child windows. If the given window is a top-level window, the function searches for the next (or previous) handle of a top-level window. If the given window is a child window, the function searches for the handle of the next (or previous) child window.

Parameters

hwnd
Identifies the current window.

uFlag
Specifies whether the function should return a handle to the next window or to the previous window. It can be either of the following values:

Value	Meaning
GW_HWNDNEXT	Returns a handle of the next window.
GW_HWNDPREV	Returns a handle of the previous window.

Return Value

The return value is the handle of the next (or previous) window in the window manager's list if the function is successful.

See Also

GetTopWindow, **GetWindow**

GetNumTasks

UINT GetNumTasks(void)

The **GetNumTasks** function retrieves the number of currently running tasks.

Parameters

This function has no parameters.

Return Value

The return value specifies the number of current tasks if the function is successful. Otherwise, it is zero.

GetObject

int GetObject(*hgdiobj*, *cbBuffer*, *lpvObject*)
HGDIOBJ *hgdiobj*;   /* handle of object   */
int *cbBuffer*;   /* size of buffer for object information   */
void FAR* *lpvObject*;   /* address of buffer for object information   */

The **GetObject** function fills a buffer with information that defines a given object. The function retrieves a **LOGPEN**, **LOGBRUSH**, **LOGFONT**, or **BITMAP** structure, or an integer, depending on the specified object.

Parameters

hgdiobj
   Identifies a logical pen, brush, font, bitmap, or palette.

cbBuffer
   Specifies the number of bytes to be copied to the buffer.

lpvObject
   Points to the buffer that is to receive the information.

Return Value

The return value specifies the number of bytes retrieved if the function is successful. Otherwise, it is zero.

Comments

The buffer pointed to by the *lpvObject* parameter must be sufficiently large to receive the information.

If the *hgdiobj* parameter identifies a bitmap, the **GetObject** function returns only the width, height, and color format information of the bitmap. The bits can be retrieved by using the **GetBitmapBits** function.

If *hgdiobj* identifies a logical palette, **GetObject** retrieves an integer that specifies the number of entries in the palette; the function does not retrieve the **LOG-PALETTE** structure that defines the palette. To retrieve information about palette entries, an application can call the **GetPaletteEntries** function.

Example

The following example uses the **GetObject** function to fill a **LOGBRUSH** structure with the attributes of the current brush and then tests whether the brush style is BS_SOLID:

```
LOGBRUSH lb;

HBRUSH hbr;

GetObject(hbr, sizeof(LOGBRUSH), (LPSTR) &lb);
```

```
                    if (lb.lbStyle == BS_SOLID) {
                          .
                          .
                          .
                    }
```

See Also   **GetBitmapBits, GetPaletteEntries, GetStockObject**

GetOpenClipboardWindow   3.1

HWND GetOpenClipboardWindow(void)

The **GetOpenClipboardWindow** function retrieves the handle of the window that currently has the clipboard open.

Parameters   This function has no parameters.

Return Value   The return value is the handle of the window that has the clipboard open, if the function is successful. Otherwise, it is NULL.

See Also   **GetClipboardOwner, GetClipboardViewer, OpenClipboard**

GetOpenFileName   3.1

#include <commdlg.h>

BOOL GetOpenFileName(*lpofn***)**
OPENFILENAME FAR* *lpofn*;   /* address of structure with initialization data   */

The **GetOpenFileName** function creates a system-defined dialog box that makes it possible for the user to select a file to open.

Parameters   *lpofn*
Points to an **OPENFILENAME** structure that contains information used to initialize the dialog box. When the **GetOpenFileName** function returns, this structure contains information about the user's file selection.

The **OPENFILENAME** structure has the following form:

```
#include <commdlg.h>

typedef struct tagOPENFILENAME { /* ofn */
    DWORD     lStructSize;
    HWND      hwndOwner;
    HINSTANCE hInstance;
    LPCSTR    lpstrFilter;
    LPSTR     lpstrCustomFilter;
    DWORD     nMaxCustFilter;
    DWORD     nFilterIndex;
    LPSTR     lpstrFile;
    DWORD     nMaxFile;
    LPSTR     lpstrFileTitle;
    DWORD     nMaxFileTitle;
    LPCSTR    lpstrInitialDir;
    LPCSTR    lpstrTitle;
    DWORD     Flags;
    UINT      nFileOffset;
    UINT      nFileExtension;
    LPCSTR    lpstrDefExt;
    LPARAM    lCustData;
    UINT      (CALLBACK* lpfnHook) (HWND, UINT, WPARAM, LPARAM);
    LPCSTR    lpTemplateName;
} OPENFILENAME;
```

For a full description of this structure, see the *Microsoft Windows Programmer's Reference, Volume 3.*

Return Value   The return value is nonzero if the user selects a file to open. It is zero if an error occurs, if the user chooses the Cancel button, if the user chooses the Close command on the System menu to close the dialog box, or if the buffer identified by the **lpstrFile** member of the **OPENFILENAME** structure is too small to contain the string that specifies the selected file.

Errors   The **CommDlgExtendedError** function retrieves the error value, which may be one of the following values:

CDERR_FINDRESFAILURE
CDERR_INITIALIZATION
CDERR_LOCKRESFAILURE
CDERR_LOADRESFAILURE
CDERR_LOADSTRFAILURE
CDERR_MEMALLOCFAILURE
CDERR_MEMLOCKFAILURE
CDERR_NOHINSTANCE
CDERR_NOHOOK

CDERR_NOTEMPLATE
CDERR_STRUCTSIZE
FNERR_BUFFERTOOSMALL
FNERR_INVALIDFILENAME
FNERR_SUBCLASSFAILURE

Comments   If the hook function (to which the **lpfnHook** member of the **OPENFILENAME** structure points) processes the WM_CTLCOLOR message, this function must return a handle of the brush that should be used to paint the control background.

Example   The following example copies file-filter strings into a buffer, initializes an **OPEN-FILENAME** structure, and then creates an Open dialog box.

The file-filter strings are stored in the resource file in the following form:

```
STRINGTABLE
BEGIN
  IDS_FILTERSTRING  "Write Files(*.WRI)|*.wri|Word Files(*.DOC)|*.doc|"
END
```

The replaceable character at the end of the string is used to break the entire string into separate strings, while still guaranteeing that all the strings are contiguous in memory.

```
OPENFILENAME ofn;
char szDirName[256];
char szFile[256], szFileTitle[256];
UINT  i, cbString;
char  chReplace;    /* string separator for szFilter */
char  szFilter[256];
HFILE hf;

/* Get the system directory name and store in szDirName */

GetSystemDirectory(szDirName, sizeof(szDirName));
szFile[0] = '\0';

if ((cbString = LoadString(hinst, IDS_FILTERSTRING,
        szFilter, sizeof(szFilter))) == 0) {
    ErrorHandler();
    return 0L;
}
chReplace = szFilter[cbString - 1]; /* retrieve wild character */

for (i = 0; szFilter[i] != '\0'; i++) {
    if (szFilter[i] == chReplace)
        szFilter[i] = '\0';
}
```

```
                    /* Set all structure members to zero. */

                    memset(&ofn, 0, sizeof(OPENFILENAME));

                    ofn.lStructSize = sizeof(OPENFILENAME);
                    ofn.hwndOwner = hwnd;
                    ofn.lpstrFilter = szFilter;
                    ofn.nFilterIndex = 1;
                    ofn.lpstrFile= szFile;
                    ofn.nMaxFile = sizeof(szFile);
                    ofn.lpstrFileTitle = szFileTitle;
                    ofn.nMaxFileTitle = sizeof(szFileTitle);
                    ofn.lpstrInitialDir = szDirName;
                    ofn.Flags = OFN_SHOWHELP | OFN_PATHMUSTEXIST | OFN_FILEMUSTEXIST;

                    if (GetOpenFileName(&ofn)) {
                        hf = _lopen(ofn.lpstrFile, OF_READ);

                            .
                            . /* Perform file operations */
                            .
                    }
                    else
                        ErrorHandler();
```

See Also   **GetSaveFileName**

GetOutlineTextMetrics   3.1

WORD GetOutlineTextMetrics(*hdc*, *cbData*, *lpotm*)
HDC *hdc*;   /* handle of device context   */
UINT *cbData*;   /* size of buffer for information */
OUTLINETEXTMETRIC FAR* *lpotm*;   /* address of structure for metrics */

The **GetOutlineTextMetrics** function retrieves metric information for TrueType fonts.

Parameters   *hdc*
                    Identifies the device context.

                    cbData
                    Specifies the size, in bytes, of the buffer to which information is returned.

                    lpotm
                    Points to an **OUTLINETEXTMETRIC** structure. If this parameter is NULL, the function returns the size of the buffer required for the retrieved metric information. The **OUTLINETEXTMETRIC** structure has the following form:

```
typedef struct tagOUTLINETEXTMETRIC {
    UINT        otmSize;
    TEXTMETRIC  otmTextMetrics;
    BYTE        otmFiller;
    PANOSE      otmPanoseNumber;
    UINT        otmfsSelection;
    UINT        otmfsType;
    UINT        otmsCharSlopeRise;
    UINT        otmsCharSlopeRun;
    UINT        otmItalicAngle;
    UINT        otmEMSquare;
    INT         otmAscent;
    INT         otmDescent;
    UINT        otmLineGap;
    UINT        otmsXHeight;
    UINT        otmsCapEmHeight;
    RECT        otmrcFontBox;
    INT         otmMacAscent;
    INT         otmMacDescent;
    UINT        otmMacLineGap;
    UINT        otmusMinimumPPEM;
    POINT       otmptSubscriptSize;
    POINT       otmptSubscriptOffset;
    POINT       otmptSuperscriptSize;
    POINT       otmptSuperscriptOffset;
    UINT        otmsStrikeoutSize;
    INT         otmsStrikeoutPosition;
    INT         otmsUnderscorePosition;
    UINT        otmsUnderscoreSize;
    PSTR        otmpFamilyName;
    PSTR        otmpFaceName;
    PSTR        otmpStyleName;
    PSTR        otmpFullName;
} OUTLINETEXTMETRIC;
```

For a full description of this structure, see the *Microsoft Windows Programmer's Reference, Volume 3*.

Return Value

The return value is nonzero if the function is successful. Otherwise, it is zero.

Comments

The **OUTLINETEXTMETRIC** structure contains most of the font metric information provided with the TrueType format, including a **TEXTMETRIC** structure. The last four members of the **OUTLINETEXTMETRIC** structure are pointers to strings. Applications should allocate space for these strings in addition to the space required for the other members. Because there is no system-imposed limit to the size of the strings, the simplest method for allocating memory is to retrieve the required size by specifying NULL for the *lpotm* parameter in the first call to the **GetOutlineTextMetrics** function.

See Also   **GetTextMetrics**

GetPaletteEntries

UINT GetPaletteEntries(*hpal*, *iStart*, *cEntries*, *lppe*)
HPALETTE *hpal*;   /* handle of palette   */
UINT *iStart*;   /* first palette entry to retrieve   */
UINT *cEntries*;   /* number of entries to retrieve   */
PALETTEENTRY FAR* *lppe*;   /* address of structure for palette entries   */

The **GetPaletteEntries** function retrieves a range of palette entries in a logical palette.

Parameters

hpal
Identifies the logical palette.

iStart
Specifies the first logical-palette entry to be retrieved.

cEntries
Specifies the number of logical-palette entries to be retrieved.

lppe
Points to an array of **PALETTEENTRY** structures that will receive the palette entries. The array must contain at least as many structures as specified by the *cEntries* parameter. The **PALETTEENTRY** structure has the following form:

```
typedef struct tagPALETTEENTRY {    /* pe */
    BYTE   peRed;
    BYTE   peGreen;
    BYTE   peBlue;
    BYTE   peFlags;
} PALETTEENTRY;
```

For a full description of this structure, see the *Microsoft Windows Programmer's Reference, Volume 3*.

Return Value

The return value is the number of entries retrieved from the logical palette, if the function is successful. Otherwise, it is zero.

See Also

GetSystemPaletteEntries

GetParent

HWND GetParent(*hwnd***)**
HWND *hwnd*;   /* handle of window   */

The **GetParent** function retrieves the handle of the given window's parent window (if any).

Parameters   *hwnd*
    Identifies the window whose parent window handle is to be retrieved.

Return Value   The return value is the handle of the parent window if the function is successful. Otherwise, it is NULL, indicating an error or no parent window.

See Also   **SetParent**

GetPixel

COLORREF GetPixel(*hdc*, *nXPos*, *nYPos***)**
HDC *hdc*;   /* handle of device context   */
int *nXPos*;   /* x-coordinate of pixel to retrieve */
int *nYPos*;   /* y-coordinate of pixel to retrieve */

The **GetPixel** function retrieves the RGB (red, green, blue) color value of the pixel at the specified coordinates. The point must be in the clipping region; if it is not, the function is ignored.

Parameters   *hdc*
    Identifies the device context.

nXPos
    Specifies the logical x-coordinate of the point to be examined.

nYPos
    Specifies the logical y-coordinate of the point to be examined.

Return Value   The return value specifies an RGB color value for the color of the given point, if the function is successful. It is −1 if the coordinates do not specify a point in the clipping region.

Comments   Not all devices support the **GetPixel** function. For more information, see the description of the **GetDeviceCaps** function.

See Also   **GetDeviceCaps, SetPixel**

GetPolyFillMode   2.x

int GetPolyFillMode(*hdc***)**
HDC *hdc*;   /* handle of device context   */

The **GetPolyFillMode** function retrieves the current polygon-filling mode.

Parameters   *hdc*
                    Identifies the device context.

Return Value   The return value specifies the polygon-filling mode, ALTERNATE or WINDING,
                    if the function is successful.

Comments   When the polygon-filling mode is ALTERNATE, the system fills the area be-
                    tween odd-numbered and even-numbered polygon sides on each scan line. That is,
                    the system fills the area between the first and second side, between the third and
                    fourth side, and so on.

                    When the polygon-filling mode is WINDING, the system uses the direction in
                    which a figure was drawn to determine whether to fill an area. Each line segment
                    in a polygon is drawn in either a clockwise or a counterclockwise direction. When-
                    ever an imaginary line drawn from an enclosed area to the outside of a figure
                    passes through a clockwise line segment, a count is incremented. When the line
                    passes through a counterclockwise line segment, the count is decremented. The
                    area is filled if the count is nonzero when the line reaches the outside of the figure.

Example   The following example uses the **GetPolyFillMode** function to determine whether
                    the current polygon-filling mode is ALTERNATE:

```
int nPolyFillMode;

nPolyFillMode = GetPolyFillMode(hdc);
if (nPolyFillMode == ALTERNATE) {
    .
    .
    .
}
```

See Also   **SetPolyFillMode**

GetPriorityClipboardFormat

3.0

int GetPriorityClipboardFormat(*lpuPriorityList, cEntries*)
UINT FAR* *lpuPriorityList*;   /* address of priority list   */
int *cEntries*;   /* count of entries in list   */

The **GetPriorityClipboardFormat** function retrieves the first clipboard format in a list for which data exists in the clipboard.

Parameters   *lpuPriorityList*
Points to an integer array that contains a list of clipboard formats in priority order. For a description of the data formats, see the description of the **Set-ClipboardData** function.

cEntries
Specifies the number of entries in the priority list. This value must not be greater than the number of entries in the list.

Return Value   The return value is the highest priority clipboard format in the list for which data exists. If no data exists in the clipboard, the return value is NULL. If data exists in the clipboard that does not match any format in the list, the return value is −1.

See Also   **CountClipboardFormats, EnumClipboardFormats, GetClipboardFormat-Name, IsClipboardFormatAvailable, RegisterClipboardFormat, SetClipboardData**

GetPrivateProfileInt

3.0

UINT GetPrivateProfileInt(*lpszSection, lpszEntry, default, lpszFilename*)
LPCSTR *lpszSection*;   /* address of section   */
LPCSTR *lpszEntry*;   /* address of entry   */
int *default*;   /* return value if entry not found   */
LPCSTR *lpszFilename*;   /* address of initialization filename   */

The **GetPrivateProfileInt** function retrieves the value of an integer from an entry within a specified section of a specified initialization file.

Parameters   *lpszSection*
Points to a null-terminated string containing the section heading in the initialization file.

lpszEntry

Points to the null-terminated string containing the entry whose value is to be re-trieved.

default

Specifies the default value to return if the entry cannot be found in the initializa-tion file. This value must be a positive integer in the range 0 through 32,767 (0x0000 through 0x7FFF).

lpszFilename

Points to a null-terminated string that names the initialization file. If this pa-rameter does not contain a full path, Windows searches for the file in the Win-dows directory.

Return Value   The return value is the integer value of the specified entry if the function is successful. It is the value of the *default* parameter if the function does not find the entry. The return value is zero if the value that corresponds to the specified entry is not an integer.

Comments   The function searches the file for an entry that matches the name specified by the *lpszEntry* parameter under the section heading specified by the *lpszSection* parame-ter. An integer entry in the initialization file must have the following form:

[*section*]
entry=value

.
.
.

If the value that corresponds to the entry consists of digits followed by non-numeric characters, the function returns the value of the digits. For example, the function would return 102 for the line "Entry=102abc".

The **GetPrivateProfileInt** function is not case-dependent, so the strings in the *lpszSection* and *lpszEntry* parameters may contain a combination of uppercase and lowercase letters.

GetPrivateProfileInt supports hexadecimal notation. When **GetPrivate-ProfileInt** is used to retrieve a negative integer, the value should be cast to an **int**.

An application can use the **GetProfileInt** function to retrieve an integer value from the WIN.INI file.

Example   The following example uses the **GetPrivateProfileInt** function to retrieve the
last line number by reading the LastLine entry from the [MyApp] section of
TESTCODE.INI:

```
WORD wInt;
char szMsg[144];

wInt = GetPrivateProfileInt("MyApp", "LastLine",
    0, "testcode.ini");

sprintf(szMsg, "last line was %d", wInt);
MessageBox(hwnd, szMsg, "GetPrivateProfileInt", MB_OK);
```

See Also   **GetPrivateProfileString, GetProfileInt**

GetPrivateProfileString

`3.0`

int **GetPrivateProfileString**(*lpszSection*, *lpszEntry*, *lpszDefault*, *lpszReturnBuffer*, *cbReturnBuffer*,
  lpszFilename)
LPCSTR *lpszSection*;   /* address of section   */
LPCSTR *lpszEntry*;   /* address of entry   */
LPCSTR *lpszDefault*;   /* address of default string   */
LPSTR *lpszReturnBuffer*;   /* address of destination buffer   */
int *cbReturnBuffer*;   /* size of destination buffer   */
LPCSTR *lpszFilename*;   /* address of initialization filename   */

The **GetPrivateProfileString** function retrieves a character string from the
specified section in the specified initialization file.

Parameters   *lpszSection*
                    Points to a null-terminated string that specifies the section containing the entry.

                    lpszEntry
                    Points to the null-terminated string containing the entry whose associated string
                    is to be retrieved. If this value is NULL, all entries in the section specified by
                    the *lpszSection* parameter are copied to the buffer specified by the *lpszReturn-
                    Buffer* parameter. For more information, see the following Comments section.

                    lpszDefault
                    Points to a null-terminated string that specifies the default value for the given
                    entry if the entry cannot be found in the initialization file. This parameter must
                    never be NULL.

lpszReturnBuffer
> Points to the buffer that receives the character string.

cbReturnBuffer
> Specifies the size, in bytes, of the buffer pointed to by the *lpszReturnBuffer* parameter.

lpszFilename
> Points to a null-terminated string that names the initialization file. If this parameter does not contain a full path, Windows searches for the file in the Windows directory.

Return Value   The return value specifies the number of bytes copied to the specified buffer, not including the terminating null character.

Comments   The function searches the file for an entry that matches the name specified by the *lpszEntry* parameter under the section heading specified by the *lpszSection* parameter. If the entry is found, its corresponding string is copied to the buffer. If the entry does not exist, the default character string specified by the *lpszDefault* parameter is copied. A string entry in the initialization file must have the following form:

[*section*]
entry=string
> .
> .
> .

If *lpszEntry* is NULL, the **GetPrivateProfileString** function copies all entries in the specified section to the supplied buffer. Each string will be null-terminated, with the final string ending with two zero-termination characters. If the supplied destination buffer is too small to hold all the strings, the last string will be truncated and followed with two zero-termination characters.

If the string associated with *lpszEntry* is enclosed in single or double quotation marks, the marks are discarded when **GetPrivateProfileString** returns the string.

GetPrivateProfileString is not case-dependent, so the strings in *lpszSection* and *lpszEntry* may contain a combination of uppercase and lowercase letters.

An application can use the **GetProfileString** function to retrieve a string from the WIN.INI file.

The *lpszDefault* parameter must point to a valid string, even if the string is empty (its first character is zero).

Example	The following example uses the **GetPrivateProfileString** function to determine the last file saved by the [MyApp] application by reading the LastFile entry in TESTCODE.INI:

```
char szMsg[144], szBuf[80];

GetPrivateProfileString("MyApp", "LastFile",
    "", szBuf, sizeof(szBuf), "testcode.ini");

sprintf(szMsg, "last file was %s", szBuf);
MessageBox(hwnd, szMsg, "GetPrivateProfileString", MB_OK);
```

See Also	**GetProfileString, WritePrivateProfileString**

GetProcAddress   2.x

FARPROC GetProcAddress(*hinst, lpszProcName*)
HINSTANCE *hinst*;   /* handle of module   */
LPCSTR *lpszProcName*;   /* address of function   */

The **GetProcAddress** function retrieves the address of the given module function.

Parameters	*hinst* Identifies the module that contains the function. *lpszProcName* Points to a null-terminated string containing the function name, or specifies the ordinal value of the function. If it is an ordinal value, the value must be in the low-order word and the high-order word must be zero.
Return Value	The return value is the address of the module function's entry point if the **GetProcAddress** function is successful. Otherwise, it is NULL. If the *lpszProcName* parameter is an ordinal value and a function with the specified ordinal does not exist in the module, **GetProcAddress** can still return a non-NULL value. In cases where the function may not exist, specify the function by name rather than ordinal value.
Comments	Use the **GetProcAddress** function to retrieve addresses of exported functions in dynamic-link libraries (DLLs). The **MakeProcInstance** function can be used to access functions within different instances of the current module.

The spelling of the function name (pointed to by the *lpszProcName* parameter) must be identical to the spelling as it appears in the **EXPORTS** section of the source DLL's module-definition (.DEF) file.

Example

The following example uses the **GetProcAddress** function to retrieve the address of the **TimerCount** function in TOOLHELP.DLL:

```
char szBuf[80];
TIMERINFO timerinfo;
HINSTANCE hinstToolHelp;
BOOL (FAR *lpfnTimerCount) (TIMERINFO FAR*);

/* Turn off the "File not found" error box. */

SetErrorMode(SEM_NOOPENFILEERRORBOX);

/* Load the TOOLHELP.DLL library module. */

hinstToolHelp = LoadLibrary("TOOLHELP.DLL");

if (hinstToolHelp > HINSTANCE_ERROR) {      /* loaded successfully */

    /* Retrieve the address of the TimerCount function. */

    (FARPROC) lpfnTimerCount =
        GetProcAddress(hinstToolHelp, "TimerCount");

    if (lpfnTimerCount != NULL) {

        /* Call the TimerCount function. */

        timerinfo.dwSize = sizeof(TIMERINFO);

        if ((*lpfnTimerCount) ((TIMERINFO FAR *) &timerinfo)) {
            sprintf(szBuf, "task: %lu seconds\nVM: %lu seconds",
                timerinfo.dwmsSinceStart / 1000,
                timerinfo.dwmsThisVM / 1000);
        }
        else {
            strcpy(szBuf, "TimerCount failed");
        }
    }
    else {
        strcpy(szBuf, "GetProcAddress failed");
    }

    /* Free the TOOLHELP.DLL library module. */

    FreeLibrary(hinstToolHelp);
}
```

```
else {
    strcpy(szBuf, "LoadLibrary failed");
}

MessageBox(NULL, szBuf, "Library Functions", MB_ICONHAND);
```

See Also   **MakeProcInstance**

GetProfileInt   2.x

UINT GetProfileInt(*lpszSection*, *lpszEntry*, *default*)
LPCSTR *lpszSection*;   /* address of section   */
LPCSTR *lpszEntry*;   /* address of entry   */
int *default*;   /* return value if entry is not found */

The **GetProfileInt** function retrieves the value of an integer from an entry within a specified section of the WIN.INI initialization file.

Parameters   *lpszSection*
                        Points to a null-terminated string that specifies the section containing the entry.

                        lpszEntry
                        Points to the null-terminated string containing the entry whose value is to be retrieved.

                        default
                        Specifies the default value to return if the entry cannot be found. This value can be an unsigned value in the range 0 through 65,536 or a signed value in the range −32,768 through 32,768. Hexadecimal notation is accepted for both positive and negative values.

Return Value   The return value is the integer value of the string following the specified entry, if the function is successful. The return value is the value of the *default* parameter if the function does not find the entry. The return value is zero if the value that corresponds to the specified entry is not an integer.

Comments   The **GetProfileInt** function is not case-dependent, so the strings in the *lpszSection* and *lpszEntry* parameters may contain a combination of uppercase and lowercase letters.

                        GetProfileInt supports hexadecimal notation. When the function is used to retrieve a negative integer, the value should be cast to an **int**.

                        An integer entry in the WIN.INI file must have the following form:

[section]
entry=value

.
.
.

If the value that corresponds to the entry consists of digits followed by non-numeric characters, the function returns the value of the digits. For example, the function would return 102 for the line "Entry=102abc".

An application can use the **GetPrivateProfileInt** function to retrieve an integer from a specified file.

Example

The following example uses the **GetProfileInt** function to retrieve the screen-save timeout time from the WIN.INI file:

```
WORD wTimeOut;
char szMsg[80];

wTimeOut = GetProfileInt("windows",
    "ScreenSaveTimeOut", 0);

sprintf(szMsg, "timeout time is %d", wTimeOut);
MessageBox(hwnd, szMsg, "GetProfileInt", MB_OK);
```

See Also

GetPrivateProfileInt, GetProfileString

GetProfileString

2.x

int GetProfileString(*lpszSection*, *lpszEntry*, *lpszDefault*, *lpszReturnBuffer*, *cbReturnBuffer*)
LPCSTR *lpszSection*;   /* address of section   */
LPCSTR *lpszEntry*;   /* address of entry   */
LPCSTR *lpszDefault*;   /* address of default string   */
LPSTR *lpszReturnBuffer*;   /* address of destination buffer   */
int *cbReturnBuffer*;   /* size of destination buffer   */

The **GetProfileString** function retrieves the string associated with an entry within the specified section in the WIN.INI initialization file.

Parameters

lpszSection
Points to a null-terminated string that specifies the section containing the entry.

lpszEntry
Points to the null-terminated string containing the entry whose associated string is to be retrieved. If this value is NULL, all entries in the section specified by

the *lpszSection* parameter are copied to the buffer specified by the *lpszReturn-Buffer* parameter. For more information, see the following Comments section.

lpszDefault
   Points to the default value for the given entry if the entry cannot be found in the initialization file. This parameter must never be NULL.

lpszReturnBuffer
   Points to the buffer that will receive the character string.

cbReturnBuffer
   Specifies the size, in bytes, of the buffer pointed to by the *lpszReturnBuffer* parameter.

Return Value   The return value is the number of bytes copied to the buffer, not including the terminating zero, if the function is successful.

Comments   If the *lpszEntry* parameter is NULL, the **GetProfileString** function copies all entries in the specified section to the supplied buffer. Each string will be null-terminated, with the final string terminating with two null characters. If the supplied destination buffer is too small to hold all the strings, the last string will be truncated and followed by two terminating null characters.

If the string associated with *lpszEntry* is enclosed in single or double quotation marks, the marks are discarded when **GetProfileString** returns the string.

GetProfileString is not case-dependent, so the strings in the *lpszSection* and *lpszEntry* parameters may contain a combination of uppercase and lowercase letters.

A string entry in the WIN.INI file must have the following form:

[*section*]
entry=string
.
.
.

An application can use the **GetPrivateProfileString** function to retrieve a string from a specified file.

The *lpszDefault* parameter must point to a valid string, even if the string is empty (its first character is zero).

Example   The following example uses the **GetProfileString** function to list all the entries and strings in the [windows] section of the WIN.INI file:

```
                    int c, cc;
                    PSTR pszBuf, pszKey;
                    char szMsg[80], szVal[80];

                    /* Allocate a buffer for the entries. */

                    pszBuf = (PSTR) LocalAlloc(LMEM_FIXED, 1024);

                    /* Retrieve all the entries in the [windows] section. */

                    GetProfileString("windows", NULL, "", pszBuf, 1024);

                     /*
                      *  Retrieve the string for each entry, until
                      *  reaching the double null character.
                      */

                    for (pszKey = pszBuf, c = 0;
                          *pszKey != '\0'; pszKey += strlen(pszKey) + 1) {

                       /* Retrieve the value for each entry in the buffer. */

                       GetProfileString("windows", pszKey, "not found",
                          szVal, sizeof(szVal));

                       cc = sprintf(szMsg, "%s = %s", pszKey, szVal);
                       TextOut(hdc, 10, 15 * c++, szMsg, cc);
                    }

                    LocalFree((HANDLE) pszBuf);
```

See Also   **GetPrivateProfileString, WriteProfileString**

GetProp

HANDLE GetProp(*hwnd, lpsz*)
HWND *hwnd*;   /* handle of window   */
LPCSTR *lpsz*;   /* atom or address of string   */

The **GetProp** function retrieves a data handle from the property list of a window. The character string pointed to by the *lpsz* parameter identifies the handle to be retrieved. The string and handle must be added to the property list by a previous call to the **SetProp** function.

Parameters   *hwnd*
                    Identifies the window whose property list is to be searched.

lpsz

Points to a null-terminated string or an atom that identifies a string. If an atom is given, it must be a global atom created by a previous call to the **GlobalAdd-Atom** function. The atom, a 16-bit value, must be placed in the low-order word of the *lpsz* parameter; the high-order word must be zero.

Return Value

The return value is the associated data handle if the property list contains the given string. Otherwise, it is NULL.

Comments

The value retrieved by the **GetProp** function can be any 16-bit value useful to the application.

See Also

GlobalAddAtom, RemoveProp, SetProp

GetQueueStatus   3.1

DWORD GetQueueStatus(*fuFlags*)
UINT *fuFlags*;   /* queue-status flags   */

The **GetQueueStatus** function returns a value that indicates the type of messages in the queue.

This function is very fast and is typically used inside speed-critical loops to determine whether the **GetMessage** or **PeekMessage** function should be called to process input.

GetQueueStatus returns two sets of information: whether any new messages have been added to the queue since **GetQueueStatus**, **GetMessage**, or **PeekMessage** was last called, and what kinds of events are currently in the queue.

Parameters

fuFlags

Specifies the queue-status flags to be retrieved. This parameter can be a combination of the following values:

Value	Meaning
QS_KEY	WM_CHAR message is in the queue.
QS_MOUSE	WM_MOUSEMOVE or WM_*BUTTON* message is in the queue.
QS_MOUSEMOVE	WM_MOUSEMOVE message is in the queue.
QS_MOUSEBUTTON	WM_*BUTTON* message is in the queue.
QS_PAINT	WM_PAINT message is in the queue.

Value	Meaning
QS_POSTMESSAGE	Posted message other than those listed above is in the queue.
QS_SENDMESSAGE	Message sent by another application is in the queue.
QS_TIMER	WM_TIMER message is in the queue.

Return Value

The high-order word of the return value indicates the types of messages currently in the queue. The low-order word shows the types of messages added to the queue and are still in the queue since the last call to the **GetQueueStatus**, **GetMessage**, or **PeekMessage** function.

Comments

The existence of a QS_ flag in the return value does not guarantee that a subsequent call to the **PeekMessage** or **GetMessage** function will return a message. **GetMessage** and **PeekMessage** perform some internal filtering computation that may cause the message to be processed internally. For this reason, the return value from **GetQueueStatus** should be considered only a hint as to whether **GetMessage** or **PeekMessage** should be called.

See Also

GetInputState, GetMessage, PeekMessage

GetRasterizerCaps

3.1

BOOL GetRasterizerCaps(lpraststat**,** cb**)**
RASTERIZER_STATUS FAR* lpraststat; /* address of structure for status */
int cb; /* number of bytes in structure */

The **GetRasterizerCaps** function returns flags indicating whether TrueType fonts are installed in the system.

Parameters

lpraststat

Points to a **RASTERIZER_STATUS** structure that receives information about the rasterizer. The **RASTERIZER_STATUS** structure has the following form:

```
typedef struct  tagRASTERIZER_STATUS {    /* rs */
    int    nSize;
    int    wFlags;
    int    nLanguageID;
} RASTERIZER_STATUS;
```

For a full description of this structure, see the *Microsoft Windows Programmer's Reference, Volume 3.*

cb

Specifies the number of bytes that will be copied into the structure pointed to by the *lpraststat* parameter.

Return Value   The return value is nonzero if the function is successful. Otherwise, it is zero.

Comments   The **GetRasterizerCaps** function enables applications and printer drivers to determine whether TrueType is installed.

If the TT_AVAILABLE flag is set in the **wFlags** member of the **RASTERIZER_STATUS** structure, at least one TrueType font is installed. If the TT_ENABLED flag is set, TrueType is enabled for the system.

See Also   **GetOutlineTextMetrics**

GetRgnBox   3.0

int GetRgnBox(*hrgn***,** *lprc***)**
HRGN *hrgn*;   /* handle of region   */
RECT FAR* *lprc*;   /* address of structure with rectangle   */

The **GetRgnBox** function retrieves the coordinates of the bounding rectangle of the given region.

Parameters   *hrgn*

Identifies the region.

lprc

Points to a **RECT** structure that receives the coordinates of the bounding rectangle. The **RECT** structure has the following form:

```
typedef struct tagRECT {    /* rc */
    int left;
    int top;
    int right;
    int bottom;
} RECT;
```

For a full description of this structure, see the *Microsoft Windows Programmer's Reference, Volume 3*.

Return Value   The return value is SIMPLEREGION (region has no overlapping borders), COMPLEXREGION (region has overlapping borders), or NULLREGION (region is empty), if the function is successful. Otherwise, the return value is ERROR.

Example

The following example uses the **GetRgnBox** function to determine the type of a region:

```
RECT rc;
HRGN hrgn;
int RgnType;

RgnType = GetRgnBox(hrgn, &rc);

if (RgnType == COMPLEXREGION)
    TextOut(hdc, 10, 10, "COMPLEXREGION", 13);
else if (RgnType == SIMPLEREGION)
    TextOut(hdc, 10, 10, "SIMPLEREGION", 12);
else
    TextOut(hdc, 10, 10, "NULLREGION", 10);
```

GetROP2

`2.x`

int GetROP2(*hdc***)**
HDC *hdc*;   /* handle of device context   */

The **GetROP2** function retrieves the current drawing mode. The drawing mode specifies how the colors of the pen and the interior of filled objects are combined with the color already on the screen surface.

Parameters

hdc
    Identifies the device context.

Return Value

The return value specifies the drawing mode if the function is successful.

Comments

The drawing mode is for raster devices only and does not apply to vector devices. It can be any of the following values:

Value	Meaning
R2_BLACK	Pixel is always black.
R2_WHITE	Pixel is always white.
R2_NOP	Pixel remains unchanged.
R2_NOT	Pixel is the inverse of the screen color.
R2_COPYPEN	Pixel is the pen color.
R2_NOTCOPYPEN	Pixel is the inverse of the pen color.
R2_MERGEPENNOT	Pixel is a combination of the pen color and the inverse of the screen color (final pixel = (~screen pixel)	pen).

Value	Meaning
R2_MASKPENNOT	Pixel is a combination of the colors common to both the pen and the inverse of the screen (final pixel = (~screen pixel) & pen).
R2_MERGENOTPEN	Pixel is a combination of the screen color and the inverse of the pen color (final pixel = (~pen)	screen pixel).
R2_MASKNOTPEN	Pixel is a combination of the colors common to both the screen and the inverse of the pen (final pixel = (~pen) & screen pixel).
R2_MERGEPEN	Pixel is a combination of the pen color and the screen color (final pixel = pen | screen pixel).
R2_NOTMERGEPEN	Pixel is the inverse of the R2_MERGEPEN color (final pixel = ~(pen | screen pixel)).
R2_MASKPEN	Pixel is a combination of the colors common to both the pen and the screen (final pixel = pen & screen pixel).
R2_NOTMASKPEN	Pixel is the inverse of the R2_MASKPEN color (final pixel = ~(pen & screen pixel)).
R2_XORPEN	Pixel is a combination of the colors that are in the pen and in the screen, but not in both (final pixel = pen ^ screen pixel).
R2_NOTXORPEN	Pixel is the inverse of the R2_XORPEN color (final pixel = ~(pen ^ screen pixel)).

Example

The following example uses the **GetROP2** function to test whether the current drawing mode is R2_COPYPEN:

```
int nROP;

nROP = GetROP2(hdc);
if (nROP == R2_COPYPEN)
    TextOut(hdc, 100, 100, "ROP is R2_COPYPEN.", 18);
```

See Also

GetDeviceCaps, SetROP2

GetSaveFileName

#include <commdlg.h>

BOOL GetSaveFileName(*lpofn***)**
OPENFILENAME FAR* *lpofn*;   /* address of structure with initialization data   */

The **GetSaveFileName** function creates a system-defined dialog box that makes it possible for the user to select a file to save.

Parameters   *lpofn*

Points to an **OPENFILENAME** structure that contains information used to initialize the dialog box. When the **GetSaveFileName** function returns, this structure contains information about the user's file selection.

The **OPENFILENAME** structure has the following form:

```
#include <commdlg.h>

typedef struct tagOPENFILENAME { /* ofn */
    DWORD      lStructSize;
    HWND       hwndOwner;
    HINSTANCE  hInstance;
    LPCSTR     lpstrFilter;
    LPSTR      lpstrCustomFilter;
    DWORD      nMaxCustFilter;
    DWORD      nFilterIndex;
    LPSTR      lpstrFile;
    DWORD      nMaxFile;
    LPSTR      lpstrFileTitle;
    DWORD      nMaxFileTitle;
    LPCSTR     lpstrInitialDir;
    LPCSTR     lpstrTitle;
    DWORD      Flags;
    UINT       nFileOffset;
    UINT       nFileExtension;
    LPCSTR     lpstrDefExt;
    LPARAM     lCustData;
    UINT       (CALLBACK* lpfnHook) (HWND, UINT, WPARAM, LPARAM);
    LPCSTR     lpTemplateName;
} OPENFILENAME;
```

For a full description of this structure, see the *Microsoft Windows Programmer's Reference, Volume 3*.

Return Value   The return value is nonzero if the user selects a file to save. It is zero if an error occurs, if the user clicks the Cancel button, if the user chooses the Close command on the System menu to close the dialog box, or if the buffer identified by the **lpstrFile** member of the **OPENFILENAME** structure is too small to contain the string that specifies the selected file.

Errors

The **CommDlgExtendedError** retrieves the error value, which may be one of the following values:

CDERR_FINDRESFAILURE
CDERR_INITIALIZATION
CDERR_LOCKRESFAILURE
CDERR_LOADRESFAILURE
CDERR_LOADSTRFAILURE
CDERR_MEMALLOCFAILURE
CDERR_MEMLOCKFAILURE
CDERR_NOHINSTANCE
CDERR_NOHOOK
CDERR_NOTEMPLATE
CDERR_STRUCTSIZE
FNERR_BUFFERTOOSMALL
FNERR_INVALIDFILENAME
FNERR_SUBCLASSFAILURE

Comments

If the hook function (to which the **lpfnHook** member of the **OPENFILENAME** structure points) processes the WM_CTLCOLOR message, this function must return a handle for the brush that should be used to paint the control background.

Example

The following example copies file-filter strings (filename extensions) into a buffer, initializes an **OPENFILENAME** structure, and then creates a Save As dialog box.

The file-filter strings are stored in the resource file in the following form:

```
STRINGTABLE
BEGIN
  IDS_FILTERSTRING  "Write Files(*.WRI)|*.wri|Word Files(*.DOC)|*.doc|"
END
```

The replaceable character at the end of the string is used to break the entire string into separate strings, while still guaranteeing that all the strings are contiguous in memory.

```
OPENFILENAME ofn;
char szDirName[256];
char szFile[256], szFileTitle[256];
UINT  i, cbString;
char  chReplace;    /* string separator for szFilter */
char  szFilter[256];
HFILE hf;

/*
 * Retrieve the system directory name and store it in
 * szDirName.
```

```
    */
    GetSystemDirectory(szDirName, sizeof(szDirName));

    if ((cbString = LoadString(hinst, IDS_FILTERSTRING,
            szFilter, sizeof(szFilter))) == 0) {
        ErrorHandler();
        return 0;
    }

    chReplace = szFilter[cbString - 1]; /* retrieve wild character */

    for (i = 0; szFilter[i] != '\0'; i++) {
        if (szFilter[i] == chReplace)
            szFilter[i] = '\0';
    }

    /* Set all structure members to zero. */

    memset(&ofn, 0, sizeof(OPENFILENAME));

    /* Initialize the OPENFILENAME members. */

    szFile[0] = '\0';

    ofn.lStructSize = sizeof(OPENFILENAME);
    ofn.hwndOwner = hwnd;
    ofn.lpstrFilter = szFilter;
    ofn.lpstrFile= szFile;
    ofn.nMaxFile = sizeof(szFile);
    ofn.lpstrFileTitle = szFileTitle;
    ofn.nMaxFileTitle = sizeof(szFileTitle);
    ofn.lpstrInitialDir = szDirName;
    ofn.Flags = OFN_SHOWHELP | OFN_OVERWRITEPROMPT;

    if (GetSaveFileName(&ofn)) {

        .
        . /* Perform file operations. */
        .
    }
    else
        ErrorHandler();
```

See Also   **GetOpenFileName**

GetScrollPos

`2.x`

int GetScrollPos(*hwnd*, *fnBar*)
HWND *hwnd*;   /* handle of window with scroll bar   */
int *fnBar*;   /* scroll bar flags   */

The **GetScrollPos** function retrieves the current position of the scroll box (thumb) of a scroll bar. The current position is a relative value that depends on the current scrolling range. For example, if the scrolling range is 0 through 100 and the scroll box is in the middle of the bar, the current position is 50.

Parameters

hwnd
Identifies a window that has standard scroll bars or a scroll bar control, depending on the value of the *fnBar* parameter.

fnBar
Specifies the scroll bar to examine. It can be one of the following values:

Value	Meaning
SB_CTL	Retrieves the position of a scroll bar control. In this case, the *hwnd* parameter must be the window handle of a scroll bar control.
SB_HORZ	Retrieves the position of a window's horizontal scroll bar.
SB_VERT	Retrieves the position of a window's vertical scroll bar.

Return Value

The return value specifies the current position of the scroll box in the scroll bar, if the function is successful. Otherwise, it is zero, indicating that the *hwnd* parameter is invalid or that the window does not have a scroll bar.

See Also

GetScrollRange, SetScrollPos, SetScrollRange

GetScrollRange

`2.x`

void GetScrollRange(*hwnd*, *fnBar*, *lpnMinPos*, *lpnMaxPos*)
HWND *hwnd*;   /* handle of window with scroll bar   */
int *fnBar*;   /* scroll bar flags   */
int FAR* *lpnMinPos*;   /* receives minimum position   */
int FAR* *lpnMaxPos*;   /* receives maximum position   */

The **GetScrollRange** function retrieves the current minimum and maximum scroll bar positions for the given scroll bar.

Parameters   *hwnd*
Identifies a window that has standard scroll bars or a scroll bar control, depending on the value of the *fnBar* parameter.

fnBar
Specifies which scroll bar to retrieve. This parameter can be one of the following values:

Value	Meaning
SB_CTL	Retrieves the position of a scroll bar control; in this case, the *hwnd* parameter must be the handle of a scroll bar control.
SB_HORZ	Retrieves the position of a window's horizontal scroll bar.
SB_VERT	Retrieves the position of a window's vertical scroll bar.

lpnMinPos
Points to the integer variable that receives the minimum position.

lpnMaxPos
Points to the integer variable that receives the maximum position.

Return Value   This function does not return a value.

Comments   If the given window does not have standard scroll bars or is not a scroll bar control, the **GetScrollRange** function copies zero to the *lpnMinPos* and *lpnMaxPos* parameters.

The default range for a standard scroll bar is 0 through 100. The default range for a scroll bar control is empty (both values are zero).

See Also   **GetScrollPos, SetScrollPos, SetScrollRange**

GetSelectorBase   3.1

DWORD GetSelectorBase(*uSelector*)
UINT *uSelector*;

The **GetSelectorBase** function retrieves the base address of a selector.

Parameters   *uSelector*
Specifies the selector whose base address is retrieved.

Return Value   This function returns the base address of the specified selector.

See Also   **GetSelectorLimit, SetSelectorBase, SetSelectorLimit**

GetSelectorLimit   3.1

DWORD GetSelectorLimit(*uSelector*)
UINT *uSelector*;

The **GetSelectorLimit** function retrieves the limit of a selector.

Parameters   *uSelector*
     Specifies the selector whose limit is being retrieved.

Return Value   This function returns the limit of the specified selector.

See Also   **GetSelectorBase, SetSelectorBase, SetSelectorLimit**

GetStockObject   2.x

HGDIOBJ GetStockObject(*fnObject*)
int *fnObject*;   /* type of stock object   */

The **GetStockObject** function retrieves a handle of one of the predefined stock pens, brushes, or fonts.

Parameters   *fnObject*
     Specifies the type of stock object for which to retrieve a handle. This parameter can be one of the following values:

Value	Meaning
BLACK_BRUSH	Black brush.
DKGRAY_BRUSH	Dark-gray brush.
GRAY_BRUSH	Gray brush.
HOLLOW_BRUSH	Hollow brush.
LTGRAY_BRUSH	Light-gray brush.
NULL_BRUSH	Null brush.

Value	Meaning
WHITE_BRUSH	White brush.
BLACK_PEN	Black pen.
NULL_PEN	Null pen.
WHITE_PEN	White pen.
ANSI_FIXED_FONT	Windows fixed-pitch system font.
ANSI_VAR_FONT	Windows variable-pitch system font.
DEVICE_DEFAULT_FONT	Device-dependent font.
OEM_FIXED_FONT	OEM-dependent fixed font.
SYSTEM_FONT	System font. By default, Windows uses the system font to draw menus, dialog box controls, and other text. In Windows versions 3.0 and later, the system font is a variable-pitch font width; earlier versions of Windows use a fixed-pitch system font.
SYSTEM_FIXED_FONT	Fixed-pitch system font used in Windows versions earlier than 3.0. This object is available for compatibility with earlier versions of Windows.
DEFAULT_PALETTE	Default color palette. This palette consists of the static colors in the system palette.

Return Value

The return value is the handle of the specified object if the function is successful. Otherwise, it is NULL.

Comments

The DKGRAY_BRUSH, GRAY_BRUSH, and LTGRAY_BRUSH objects should be used only in windows with the CS_HREDRAW and CS_VREDRAW class styles. Using a gray stock brush in any other style of window can lead to misalignment of brush patterns after a window is moved or sized. The origins of stock brushes cannot be adjusted.

Example

The following example retrieves the handle of a black brush by calling the **GetStockObject** function, selects the brush into the device context, and fills a rectangle by using the black brush:

```
HBRUSH hbr, hbrOld;

hbr = GetStockObject(BLACK_BRUSH);
hbrOld = SelectObject(hdc, hbr);
Rectangle(hdc, 10, 10, 100, 100);
```

See Also

GetObject, SetBrushOrg

GetStretchBltMode

2.x

int GetStretchBltMode(*hdc*)
HDC *hdc*;   /* handle of device context   */

The **GetStretchBltMode** function retrieves the current bitmap-stretching mode. The bitmap-stretching mode defines how information is removed from bitmaps that were compressed by using the **StretchBlt** function.

Parameters   *hdc*
                Identifies the device context.

Return Value   The return value specifies the current bitmap-stretching mode—
                STRETCH_ANDSCANS, STRETCH_DELETESCANS, or
                STRETCH_ORSCANS—if the function is successful.

Comments   The STRETCH_ANDSCANS and STRETCH_ORSCANS modes are
                typically used to preserve foreground pixels in monochrome bitmaps. The
                STRETCH_DELETESCANS mode is typically used to preserve color in color bit-
                maps. For more information, see the **SetStretchBltMode** function.

Example   The following example uses the **GetStretchBltMode** function to determine
                whether the current bitmap-stretching mode is STRETCH_DELETESCANS; if
                so, it uses the **StretchBlt** function to display a compressed bitmap.

```
HDC hdcMem;

int nStretchMode;

nStretchMode = GetStretchBltMode(hdc);
if (nStretchMode == STRETCH_DELETESCANS) {
    StretchBlt(hdc, 50, 175, 32, 32, hdcMem, 0, 0, 64, 64,
        SRCCOPY);
        .
        .
        .
}
```

See Also   **SetStretchBltMode, StretchBlt**

GetSubMenu

2.x

HMENU GetSubMenu(*hmenu, nPos*)
HMENU *hmenu*;   /* handle of menu with pop-up menu   */
int *nPos*;   /* position of pop-up menu   */

The **GetSubMenu** function retrieves the handle of a pop-up menu.

Parameters   *hmenu*
Identifies the menu with the pop-up menu whose handle is to be retrieved.

nPos
Specifies the position in the given menu of the pop-up menu. Position values start at zero (zero-based) for the first menu item. The pop-up menu's identifier cannot be used in this function.

Return Value   The return value is the handle of the given pop-up menu if the function is successful. Otherwise, it is NULL, indicating that no pop-up menu exists at the given position.

See Also   **CreatePopupMenu, GetMenu**

GetSysColor

2.x

COLORREF GetSysColor(*nDspElement*)
int *nDspElement*;   /* display element   */

The **GetSysColor** function retrieves the current color of the specified display element. Display elements are the various parts of a window and the Windows display that appear on the system screen.

Parameters   *nDspElement*
Specifies the display element whose color is to be retrieved. This parameter can be one of the following values:

Value	Meaning
COLOR_ACTIVEBORDER	Active window border.
COLOR_ACTIVECAPTION	Active window title.
COLOR_APPWORKSPACE	Background color of multiple document interface (MDI) applications.
COLOR_BACKGROUND	Desktop.

Value	Meaning
COLOR_BTNFACE	Face shading on push buttons.
COLOR_BTNHIGHLIGHT	Selected button in a control.
COLOR_BTNSHADOW	Edge shading on push buttons.
COLOR_BTNTEXT	Text on push buttons.
COLOR_CAPTIONTEXT	Text in title bar, size button, scroll-bar arrow button.
COLOR_GRAYTEXT	Grayed (dimmed) text. This color is zero if the current display driver does not support a solid gray color.
COLOR_HIGHLIGHT	Background of selected item in a control.
COLOR_HIGHLIGHTTEXT	Text of selected item in a control.
COLOR_INACTIVEBORDER	Inactive window border.
COLOR_INACTIVECAPTION	Inactive window title.
COLOR_INACTIVECAPTIONTEXT	Color of text in an inactive title.
COLOR_MENU	Menu background.
COLOR_MENUTEXT	Text in menus.
COLOR_SCROLLBAR	Scroll-bar gray area.
COLOR_WINDOW	Window background.
COLOR_WINDOWFRAME	Window frame.
COLOR_WINDOWTEXT	Text in windows.

Return Value   The return value is a red, green, blue (RGB) color value for the specified display element, if the function is successful.

Comments   An application can use the **GetRValue**, **GetGValue**, and **GetBValue** macros to extract the various colors from the return value.

See Also   **GetSystemMetrics, SetSysColors**

GetSysModalWindow

2.x

HWND GetSysModalWindow(void)

The **GetSysModalWindow** function retrieves the handle of the system-modal window, if one is present.

Parameters   This function has no parameters.

Return Value   The return value is the handle of the system-modal window, if one is present. Otherwise, it is NULL.

See Also   **SetSysModalWindow**

GetSystemDebugState

3.1

LONG GetSystemDebugState(void)

The **GetSystemDebugState** function retrieves information about the state of the system. A Windows-based debugger can use this information to determine whether to enter hard mode or soft mode upon encountering a breakpoint.

Parameters   This function has no parameters.

Return Value   The return value can be one or more of the following values:

Value	Meaning
SDS_MENU	Menu is displayed.
SDS_SYSMODAL	System-modal dialog box is displayed.
SDS_NOTASKQUEUE	Application queue does not exist yet and, therefore, the application cannot accept posted messages.
SDS_DIALOG	Dialog box is displayed.
SDS_TASKLOCKED	Current task is locked and, therefore, no other task is permitted to run.

GetSystemDir

3.1

#include <ver.h>

UINT GetSystemDir(*lpszWinDir*, *lpszBuf*, *cbBuf*)
LPCSTR *lpszWinDir*;   /* address of Windows directory   */
LPSTR *lpszBuf*;   /* address of buffer for path   */
int *cbBuf*;   /* size of buffer   */

The **GetSystemDir** function retrieves the path of the Windows system directory. This directory contains such files as Windows libraries, drivers, and fonts.

GetSystemDir is used by MS-DOS applications that set up Windows applications; it exists only in the static-link version of the File Installation library. Windows applications should use the **GetSystemDirectory** function to determine the Windows directory.

Parameters
lpszWinDir
Points to the Windows directory retrieved by a previous call to the **Get-WindowsDir** function.

lpszBuf
Points to the buffer that is to receive the null-terminated string containing the path.

cbBuf
Specifies the size, in bytes, of the buffer pointed to by the *lpszBuf* parameter.

Return Value
The return value is the length of the string copied to the buffer, in bytes, including the terminating null character, if the function is sucessful. If the return value is greater than the *cbBuf* parameter, the return value is the size of the buffer required to hold the path. The return value is zero if the function fails.

Comments
An application must call the **GetWindowsDir** function before calling the **Get-SystemDir** function to obtain the correct *lpszWinDir* value.

The path that this function retrieves does not end with a backslash unless the Windows system directory is the root directory. For example, if the system directory is named WINDOWS\SYSTEM on drive C, the path of the system directory retrieved by this function is C:\WINDOWS\SYSTEM.

See Also
GetSystemDirectory, **GetWindowsDir**

GetSystemDirectory

UINT **GetSystemDirectory**(*lpszSysPath*, *cbSysPath*)
LPSTR *lpszSysPath*;   /* address of buffer for system directory   */
UINT *cbSysPath*;   /* size of directory buffer   */

The **GetSystemDirectory** function retrieves the path of the Windows system directory. The system directory contains such files as Windows libraries, drivers, and font files.

Parameters

lpszSysPath
Points to the buffer that is to receive the null-terminated string containing the path of the system directory.

cbSysPath
Specifies the maximum size, in bytes, of the buffer. This value should be set to at least 144 to allow sufficient room in the buffer for the path.

Return Value

The return value is the length, in bytes, of the string copied to the *lpszSysPath* parameter, not including the terminating null character. If the return value is greater than the size specified in the *cbSysPath* parameter, the return value is the size of the buffer required to hold the path. The return value is zero if the function fails.

Comments

Applications should *not* create files in the system directory. If the user is running a shared version of Windows, the application will not have write access to the system directory. Applications should create files only in the directory returned by the **GetWindowsDirectory** function.

The path that this function retrieves does not end with a backslash unless the system directory is the root directory. For example, if the system directory is named WINDOWS\SYSTEM on drive C, the path of the system directory retrieved by this function is C:\WINDOWS\SYSTEM.

A similar function, **GetSystemDir**, is intended for use by MS-DOS applications that set up Windows applications. Windows applications should use **GetSystemDirectory**, not **GetSystemDir**.

Example

The following example uses the **GetSystemDirectory** function to determine the path of the Windows system directory:

```
WORD wReturn;
char szBuf[144];

wReturn = GetSystemDirectory((LPSTR) szBuf, sizeof(szBuf));
```

```
            if (wReturn == 0)
                MessageBox(hwnd, "function failed",
                    "GetSystemDirectory", MB_ICONEXCLAMATION);

            else if (wReturn > sizeof(szBuf))
                MessageBox(hwnd, "buffer is too small",
                    "GetSystemDirectory", MB_ICONEXCLAMATION);

            else
                MessageBox(hwnd, szBuf, "GetSystemDirectory", MB_OK);
```

See Also   **GetWindowsDirectory**

GetSystemMenu   2.x

HMENU GetSystemMenu(*hwnd, fRevert*)
HWND *hwnd*;   /* handle of window to own the System menu   */
BOOL *fRevert*;   /* reset flag   */

The **GetSystemMenu** function allows the application to access the System menu for copying and modification.

Parameters   *hwnd*
Identifies the window that will own a copy of the System menu.

fRevert
Specifies the action to be taken. If this parameter is FALSE, the **GetSystem-Menu** function returns a handle of a copy of the System menu currently in use. This copy is initially identical to the System menu, but can be modified.

If the parameter is TRUE, **GetSystemMenu** resets the System menu back to the Windows default state. The previous System menu, if any, is destroyed. The return value is undefined in this case.

Return Value   The return value is the handle of a copy of the System menu, if the *fRevert* parameter is FALSE. If *fRevert* is TRUE, the return value is undefined.

Comments   Any window that does not use the **GetSystemMenu** function to make its own copy of the System menu receives the standard System menu.

The handle that **GetSystemMenu** returns can be used with the **AppendMenu**, **InsertMenu**, or **ModifyMenu** function to change the System menu. The System menu initially contains items identified by various identifier values such as SC_CLOSE, SC_MOVE, and SC_SIZE. Menu items on the System menu send WM_SYSCOMMAND messages. All predefined System-menu items have identifier numbers greater than 0xF000. If an application adds commands to the System menu, it should use identifier numbers less than 0xF000.

Windows automatically grays (dims) items on the standard System menu, depending on the situation. The application can carry out its own checking or graying by responding to the WM_INITMENU message, which is sent before any menu is displayed.

Example

The following example appends the About item to the System menu:

```
HMENU hmenu;

hmenu = GetSystemMenu(hwnd, FALSE);
AppendMenu(hmenu, MF_SEPARATOR, 0, (LPSTR) NULL);
AppendMenu(hmenu, MF_STRING, IDM_ABOUT, "About...");
```

See Also

AppendMenu, InsertMenu, ModifyMenu

GetSystemMetrics

2.x

int GetSystemMetrics(*nIndex*)
int *nIndex*;   /* system measurement to retrieve   */

The **GetSystemMetrics** function retrieves the system metrics. The system metrics are the widths and heights of the various elements displayed by Windows. **GetSystemMetrics** can also return flags that indicate whether the current version of the Windows operating system is a debugging version, whether a mouse is present, or whether the meanings of the left and right mouse buttons have been exchanged.

Parameters

nIndex
Specifies the system measurement to be retrieved. All measurements are given in pixels. The system measurement must be one of the following values:

Value	Meaning
SM_CXBORDER	Width of window frame that cannot be sized.
SM_CYBORDER	Height of window frame that cannot be sized.
SM_CYCAPTION	Height of window title. This is the title height plus the height of the window frame that cannot be sized (SM_CYBORDER).
SM_CXCURSOR	Width of cursor.
SM_CYCURSOR	Height of cursor.

Value	Meaning
SM_CXDOUBLECLK	Width of the rectangle around the location of the first click in a double-click sequence. The second click must occur within this rectangle for the system to consider the two clicks a double-click.
SM_CYDOUBLECLK	Height of the rectangle around the location of the first click in a double-click sequence. The second click must occur within this rectangle for the system to consider the two clicks a double-click.
SM_CXDLGFRAME	Width of frame when window has the WS_DLGFRAME style.
SM_CYDLGFRAME	Height of frame when window has the WS_DLGFRAME style.
SM_CXFRAME	Width of window frame that can be sized.
SM_CYFRAME	Height of window frame that can be sized.
SM_CXFULLSCREEN	Width of window client area for a full-screen window.
SM_CYFULLSCREEN	Height of window client area for a full-screen window (equivalent to the height of the screen minus the height of the window title).
SM_CXICON	Width of icon.
SM_CYICON	Height of icon.
SM_CXICONSPACING	Width of rectangles the system uses to position tiled icons.
SM_CYICONSPACING	Height of rectangles the system uses to position tiled icons.
SM_CYKANJIWINDOW	Height of Kanji window.
SM_CYMENU	Height of single-line menu bar. This is the menu height minus the height of the window frame that cannot be sized (SM_CYBORDER).
SM_CXMIN	Minimum width of window.
SM_CYMIN	Minimum height of window.
SM_CXMINTRACK	Minimum tracking width of window.
SM_CYMINTRACK	Minimum tracking height of window.
SM_CXSCREEN	Width of screen.
SM_CYSCREEN	Height of screen.
SM_CXHSCROLL	Width of arrow bitmap on a horizontal scroll bar.
SM_CYHSCROLL	Height of arrow bitmap on a horizontal scroll bar.

Value	Meaning
SM_CXVSCROLL	Width of arrow bitmap on a vertical scroll bar.
SM_CYVSCROLL	Height of arrow bitmap on a vertical scroll bar.
SM_CXSIZE	Width of bitmaps contained in the title bar.
SM_CYSIZE	Height of bitmaps contained in the title bar.
SM_CXHTHUMB	Width of scroll box (thumb) on horizontal scroll bar.
SM_CYVTHUMB	Height of scroll box on vertical scroll bar.
SM_DBCSENABLED	Nonzero if current version of Windows uses double-byte characters; otherwise, this value returns zero.
SM_DEBUG	Nonzero if the Windows version is a debugging version.
SM_MENUDROPALIGNMENT	Alignment of pop-up menus. If this value is zero, the left side of a pop-up menu is aligned with the left side of the corresponding menu-bar item. If this value is nonzero, the left side of a pop-up menu is aligned with the right side of the corresponding menu-bar item.
SM_MOUSEPRESENT	Nonzero if the mouse hardware is installed.
SM_PENWINDOWS	Handle of the Pen Windows dynamic-link library (DLL) if Pen Windows is installed.
SM_SWAPBUTTON	Nonzero if the left and right mouse buttons are swapped.

Return Value The return value specifies the requested system metric if the function is successful.

Comments System metrics depend on the type of screen and may vary from screen to screen.

See Also **GetSysColor, SystemParametersInfo**

GetSystemPaletteEntries 3.0

UINT GetSystemPaletteEntries(*hdc***,** *iStart***,** *cEntries***,** *lppe***)**
HDC *hdc***;**   /* handle of device context   */
UINT *iStart***;**   /* first palette entry to retrieve   */
UINT *cEntries***;**   /* number of entries to retrieve   */
PALETTEENTRY FAR* *lppe***;**   /* address of structure for palette entries */

The **GetSystemPaletteEntries** function retrieves a range of palette entries from the system palette.

Parameters

hdc
Identifies the device context.

iStart
Specifies the first system-palette entry to be retrieved.

cEntries
Specifies the number of system-palette entries to be retrieved.

lppe
Points to an array of **PALETTEENTRY** structures that receives the palette entries. The array must contain at least as many structures as specified by the *cEntries* parameter. The **PALETTEENTRY** structure has the following form:

```
typedef struct tagPALETTEENTRY {    /* pe */
    BYTE   peRed;
    BYTE   peGreen;
    BYTE   peBlue;
    BYTE   peFlags;
} PALETTEENTRY;
```

For a full description of this structure, see the *Microsoft Windows Programmer's Reference, Volume 3*.

Return Value

The return value is the number of entries retrieved from the system palette, if the function is successful. Otherwise, it is zero.

Example

The following example uses the **GetDeviceCaps** function to determine whether the specified device is palette-based. If the device supports palettes, the **GetSystemPaletteEntries** function is called, using **GetDeviceCaps** again, this time to determine the number of entries in the system palette.

```
PALETTEENTRY pe[MAXNUMBER];

hdc = GetDC(hwnd);
if (!(GetDeviceCaps(hdc, RASTERCAPS) & RC_PALETTE)) {
    ReleaseDC(hwnd, hdc);
    break;
}
GetSystemPaletteEntries(hdc, 0, GetDeviceCaps(hdc, SIZEPALETTE),
    pe);
ReleaseDC(hwnd, hdc);
```

See Also

GetDeviceCaps, GetPaletteEntries

GetSystemPaletteUse

UINT GetSystemPaletteUse(*hdc*)
HDC *hdc*;   /* handle of device context   */

The **GetSystemPaletteUse** function determines whether an application has access to the entire system palette.

Parameters

hdc
Identifies the device context. This device context must support color palettes.

Return Value

The return value specifies the current use of the system palette, if the function is successful. This parameter can be one of the following values:

Value	Meaning
SYSPAL_NOSTATIC	System palette contains no static colors except black and white.
SYSPAL_STATIC	System palette contains static colors that do not change when an application realizes its logical palette.

Comments

The system palette contains 20 default static colors that are not changed when an application realizes its logical palette. An application can gain access to most of these colors by calling the **SetSystemPaletteUse** function.

Example

The following example uses the **GetDeviceCaps** function to determine whether the specified device is palette-based. If the device supports palettes, the **Get-SystemPaletteUse** function is called.

```
WORD nUse;

hdc = GetDC(hwnd);
if ((GetDeviceCaps(hdc, RASTERCAPS) & RC_PALETTE) == 0) {
    ReleaseDC(hwnd, hdc);
    break;
}
nUse = GetSystemPaletteUse(hdc);
ReleaseDC(hwnd, hdc);
```

See Also

GetDeviceCaps, SetSystemPaletteUse

GetTabbedTextExtent

DWORD GetTabbedTextExtent(*hdc*, *lpszString*, *cChars*, *cTabs*, *lpnTabs*)
HDC *hdc*;   /* handle of device context   */
LPCSTR *lpszString*;   /* address of string   */
int *cChars*;   /* number of characters in string   */
int *cTabs*;   /* number of tab positions   */
int FAR* *lpnTabs*;   /* address of array of tab positions */

The **GetTabbedTextExtent** function computes the width and height of a character string. If the string contains one or more tab characters, the width of the string is based upon the specified tab stops. **GetTabbedTextExtent** uses the currently selected font to compute the dimensions of the string.

Parameters

hdc
Identifies the device context.

lpszString
Points to a character string.

cChars
Specifies the number of characters in the text string.

cTabs
Specifies the number of tab-stop positions in the array pointed to by the *lpnTabs* parameter.

lpnTabs
Points to an array containing the tab-stop positions, in device units. The tab stops must be sorted in increasing order; the smallest x-value should be the first item in the array.

Return Value

The low-order word of the return value contains the string width, in logical units, if the function is successful; the high-order word contains the string height.

Comments

The current clipping region does not affect the width and height returned by the **GetTabbedTextExtent** function.

Since some devices do not place characters in regular cell arrays (that is, they kern the characters), the sum of the extents of the characters in a string may not be equal to the extent of the string.

If the *cTabs* parameter is zero and the *lpnTabs* parameter is NULL, tabs are expanded to eight times the average character width. If *cTabs* is 1, the tab stops are separated by the distance specified by the first value in the array to which *lpnTabs* points.

Example

The following example uses the **LOWORD** and **HIWORD** macros to retrieve the width and height of the string from the value returned by the **GetTabbedTextExtent** function:

```
LPSTR lpszTabbedText = "Column 1\tColumn 2\tTest of TabbedTextOut";
int aTabs[2] = { 150, 300 };
DWORD dwTabExtent;
WORD wStringWidth, wStringHeight;

dwTabExtent = GetTabbedTextExtent(hdc, /* handle of device context */
    lpszTabbedText,                     /* address of text          */
    lstrlen(lpszTabbedText),            /* number of characters     */
    sizeof(aTabs) / sizeof(int),        /* number of tabs in array  */
    aTabs);                             /* array for tab positions  */

wStringWidth = LOWORD(dwTabExtent);  /* gets width of string  */
wStringHeight = HIWORD(dwTabExtent); /* gets height of string */
```

See Also   **GetTextExtent, TabbedTextOut**

GetTempDrive
`2.x`

BYTE GetTempDrive(*chDriveLetter*)
char *chDriveLetter*;   /* ignored   */

The **GetTempDrive** function returns a letter that specifies a disk drive the application can use for temporary files.

Parameters   *chDriveLetter*
This parameter is ignored.

Return Value   The return value specifies a disk drive for temporary files if the function is successful. If at least one hard disk drive is available, the function returns the letter of the first hard disk drive (usually C). If no hard disk drives are available, the function returns the letter of the current drive.

Example

The following example uses the **GetTempDrive** function to determine a suitable disk drive for temporary files:

```
char szMsg[80];
BYTE bTempDrive;

bTempDrive = GetTempDrive(0);

sprintf(szMsg, "temporary drive: %c", bTempDrive);

MessageBox(hwnd, szMsg, "GetTempDrive", MB_OK);
```

See Also   **GetTempFileName**

GetTempFileName   2.x

int **GetTempFileName**(*bDriveLetter*, *lpszPrefixString*, *uUnique*, *lpszTempFileName*)
BYTE *bDriveLetter*;   /* suggested drive   */
LPCSTR *lpszPrefixString*;   /* address of filename prefix   */
UINT *uUnique*;   /* number to use as prefix   */
LPSTR *lpszTempFileName*;   /* address of buffer for created filename */

The **GetTempFileName** function creates a temporary filename of the following form:

*drive:\path\prefixuuuu.***TMP**

The following list describes the filename syntax:

Element	Description
drive	Drive letter specified by the *bDriveLetter* parameter
path	Path of the temporary file (either the Windows directory or the directory specified in the TEMP environment variable)
prefix	All the letters (up to the first three) of the string pointed to by the *lpszPrefixString* parameter
uuuu	Hexadecimal value of the number specified by the *uUnique* parameter

Parameters

bDriveLetter
Specifies the suggested drive for the temporary filename. If this parameter is zero, Windows uses the current default drive.

lpszPrefixString
Points to a null-terminated string to be used as the temporary filename prefix. This string must consist of characters in the OEM-defined character set.

uUnique
Specifies an unsigned short integer. If this parameter is nonzero, it will be appended to the temporary filename. If the parameter is zero, Windows uses the current system time to create a number to append to the filename.

lpszTempFileName
Points to the buffer that will receive the temporary filename. This string consists of characters in the OEM-defined character set. This buffer should be at least 144 bytes in length to allow sufficient room for the path.

Return Value
The return value specifies a unique numeric value used in the temporary filename. If the *uUnique* parameter is nonzero, the return value specifies this same number.

Comments
Temporary files created with this function are *not* automatically deleted when Windows shuts down.

To avoid problems resulting from converting an OEM character string to a Windows string, an application should call the **_lopen** function to create the temporary file.

The **GetTempFileName** function uses the suggested drive letter for creating the temporary filename, except in the following cases:

- If a hard disk is present, **GetTempFileName** always uses the drive letter of the first hard disk.

- If, however, a TEMP environment variable is defined and its value begins with a drive letter, that drive letter is used.

If the TF_FORCEDRIVE bit of the *bDriveLetter* parameter is set, the preceding exceptions do not apply. The temporary filename will always be created in the current directory of the drive specified by *bDriveLetter*, regardless of the presence of a hard disk or the TEMP environment variable.

If the *uUnique* parameter is zero, **GetTempFileName** attempts to form a unique number based on the current system time. If a file with the resulting filename exists, the number is increased by one and the test for existence is repeated. This continues until a unique filename is found; **GetTempFileName** then creates a file by that name and closes it. No attempt is made to create and open the file when *uUnique* is nonzero.

Example
The following example uses the **GetTempFileName** function to create a unique temporary filename on the first available hard disk:

```
HFILE hfTempFile;
char szBuf[144];
```

```
                 /* Create a temporary file. */

                 GetTempFileName(0, "tst", 0, szBuf);

                 hfTempFile = _lcreat(szBuf, 0);

                 if (hfTempFile == HFILE_ERROR) {
                     ErrorHandler();
                 }
```

See Also   **GetTempDrive, _lopen**

GetTextAlign   2.x

UINT GetTextAlign(*hdc*)
HDC *hdc*;   /* handle of device context   */

The **GetTextAlign** function retrieves the status of the text-alignment flags for the given device context.

Parameters   *hdc*
                    Identifies the device context.

Return Value   The return value specifies the status of the text-alignment flags. This parameter can be one or more of the following values:

Value	Meaning
TA_BASELINE	Specifies alignment of the x-axis and the base line of the chosen font within the bounding rectangle.
TA_BOTTOM	Specifies alignment of the x-axis and the bottom of the bounding rectangle.
TA_CENTER	Specifies alignment of the y-axis and the center of the bounding rectangle.
TA_LEFT	Specifies alignment of the y-axis and the left side of the bounding rectangle.
TA_NOUPDATECP	Specifies that the current position is not updated.
TA_RIGHT	Specifies alignment of the y-axis and the right side of the bounding rectangle.
TA_TOP	Specifies alignment of the x-axis and the top of the bounding rectangle.
TA_UPDATECP	Specifies that the current position is updated.

Comments

The text-alignment flags retrieved by the **GetTextAlign** function are used by the **TextOut** and **ExtTextOut** functions. These flags determine how **TextOut** and **ExtTextOut** align a string of text in relation to the string's starting point.

The text-alignment flags are not necessarily single-bit flags and may be equal to zero. To test whether a flag is set, an application should follow three steps:

1. Apply the bitwise OR operator to the flag and its related flags.

   Following are the groups of related flags:

   - TA_LEFT, TA_CENTER, and TA_RIGHT
   - TA_BASELINE, TA_BOTTOM, and TA_TOP
   - TA_NOUPDATECP and TA_UPDATECP

2. Apply the bitwise AND operator to the result and the return value of the **GetTextAlign** function.

3. Test for the equality of this result and the flag.

Example

The following example uses the method described in the preceding Comments section to determine whether text is aligned at the right, left, or center of the bounding rectangle. If the TA_RIGHT flag is set, the **SetTextAlign** function is used to set the text alignment to the left side of the rectangle.

```
switch ((TA_LEFT | TA_CENTER | TA_RIGHT) & GetTextAlign(hdc)) {
    case TA_RIGHT:
        TextOut(hdc, 200, 100, "This is TA_RIGHT.", 17);
        SetTextAlign(hdc, TA_LEFT);
        TextOut(hdc, 200, 120, "This is TA_LEFT.", 16);
        break;
    case TA_LEFT:
        .
        .
        .
    case TA_CENTER:
        .
        .
        .
}
```

See Also

ExtTextOut, SetTextAlign, TextOut

GetTextCharacterExtra

int GetTextCharacterExtra(*hdc*)
HDC *hdc*;   /* handle of device context   */

The **GetTextCharacterExtra** function retrieves the current setting for the amount of intercharacter spacing. Graphics device interface (GDI) adds this spacing to each character, including break characters, when it writes a line of text to the device context.

Parameters   *hdc*
                              Identifies the device context.

Return Value   The return value specifies the amount of intercharacter spacing if the function is successful.

Comments   The default value for the amount of intercharacter spacing is zero.

See Also   **SetTextCharacterExtra**

GetTextColor

COLORREF GetTextColor(*hdc*)
HDC *hdc*;   /* handle of device context   */

The **GetTextColor** function retrieves the current text color. The text color is the foreground color of characters drawn by using the graphics device interface (GDI) text-output functions.

Parameters   *hdc*
                              Identifies the device context.

Return Value   The return value specifies the current text color as a red, green, blue (RGB) color value, if the function is successful.

Example   The following example sets the text color to red if the **GetTextColor** function determines that the current text color is black:

```
DWORD dwColor;

dwColor = GetTextColor(hdc);
if (dwColor == RGB(0, 0, 0))     /* if current color is black */
    SetTextColor(hdc, RGB(255, 0, 0)); /* sets color to red  */
```

See Also   **GetBkColor, GetBkMode, SetBkMode, SetTextColor**

GetTextExtent   `2.x`

DWORD GetTextExtent(*hdc, lpszString, cbString***)**
HDC *hdc*;   /* handle of device context   */
LPCSTR *lpszString*;   /* address of string   */
int *cbString*;   /* number of bytes in string   */

The **GetTextExtent** function computes the width and height of a line of text, using the current font to compute the dimensions.

Parameters   *hdc*
                         Identifies the device context.

                         lpszString
                         Points to a character string.

                         cbString
                         Specifies the number of bytes in the string.

Return Value   The low-order word of the return value contains the string width, in logical units, if the function is successful; the high-order word contains the string height.

Comments   The current clipping region does not affect the width and height returned by the **GetTextExtent** function.

                         Since some devices do not place characters in regular cell arrays (that is, they kern characters), the sum of the extents of the characters in a string may not be equal to the extent of the string.

Example   The following example retrieves the number of characters in a string by using the **lstrlen** function, calls the **GetTextExtent** function to retrieve the dimensions of the string, and then uses the **LOWORD** macro to determine the string width, in logical units:

```
DWORD dwExtent;
WORD wTextWidth;
LPSTR lpszJustified = "Text to be justified in this test.";

dwExtent = GetTextExtent(hdc, lpszJustified, lstrlen(lpszJustified));
wTextWidth = LOWORD(dwExtent);
```

See Also   **GetTabbedTextExtent, SetTextJustification**

GetTextExtentPoint

3.1

BOOL GetTextExtentPoint(*hdc*, *lpszString*, *cbString*, *lpSize*)
HDC *hdc*;   /* handle of device context   */
LPCSTR *lpszString*;   /* address of text string   */
int *cbString*;   /* number of bytes in string   */
SIZE FAR* *lpSize*;   /* address if structure for string size */

The **GetTextExtentPoint** function computes the width and height of the specified text string. The **GetTextExtentPoint** function uses the currently selected font to compute the dimensions of the string. The width and height, in logical units, are computed without considering any clipping.

The **GetTextExtentPoint** function may be used as either a wide-character function (where text arguments must use Unicode) or an ANSI function (where text arguments must use characters from the Windows 3.*x* character set).

Parameters   *hdc*
                      Identifies the device context.

                      lpszString
                      Points to a text string.

                      cbString
                      Specifies the number of bytes in the text string.

                      lpSize
                      Points to a **SIZE** structure that will receive the dimensions of the string The **SIZE** structure has the following form:

```
typedef struct tagSIZE {
    int cx;
    int cy;
} SIZE;
```

For a full description of this structure, see the *Microsoft Windows Programmer's Reference, Volume 3*.

Return Value   The return value is nonzero if the function is successful. Otherwise, it is zero.

Comments   Because some devices do not place characters in regular cell arrays—that is, because they carry out kerning—the sum of the extents of the characters in a string may not be equal to the extent of the string.

The calculated width takes into account the intercharacter spacing set by the **SetTextCharacterExtra** function.

See Also   **SetTextCharacterExtra**

GetTextFace   `2.x`

```
int GetTextFace(hdc, cbBuffer, lpszFace)
HDC hdc;              /* handle of device context        */
int cbBuffer;         /* size of buffer for face name    */
LPSTR lpszFace;       /* pointer to buffer for face name  */
```

The **GetTextFace** function copies the typeface name of the current font into a buffer. The typeface name is copied as a null-terminated string.

Parameters   *hdc*
Identifies the device context.

cbBuffer
Specifies the buffer size, in bytes. If the typeface name is longer than the number of bytes specified by this parameter, the name is truncated.

lpszFace
Points to the buffer for the typeface name.

Return Value   The return value specifies the number of bytes copied to the buffer, not including the terminating null character, if the function is successful. Otherwise, it is zero.

Example   The following example uses the **GetTextFace** function to retrieve the name of the current typeface, calls the **SetTextAlign** function so that the current position is updated when the **TextOut** function is called, and then writes some introductory text and the name of the typeface by calling **TextOut**:

```
int nFaceNameLen;
char aFaceName[80];
```

```
nFaceNameLen = GetTextFace(hdc, /* returns length of string */
    sizeof(aFaceName),          /* size of face-name buffer   */
    (LPSTR) aFaceName);         /* address of face-name buffer */

SetTextAlign(hdc,
    TA_UPDATECP);               /* updates current position      */
MoveTo(hdc, 100, 100);          /* sets current position         */
TextOut(hdc, 0, 0,              /* uses current position for text */
    "This is the current face name: ", 31);
TextOut(hdc, 0, 0, aFaceName, nFaceNameLen);
```

See Also   **GetTextMetrics, SetTextAlign, TextOut**

GetTextMetrics   2.x

BOOL GetTextMetrics(*hdc*, *lptm*)
HDC *hdc*;   /* handle of device context   */
TEXTMETRIC FAR* *lptm*;   /* pointer to structure for font metrics */

The **GetTextMetrics** function retrieves the metrics for the current font.

Parameters   *hdc*
                        Identifies the device context.

                        lptm
                        Points to the **TEXTMETRIC** structure that receives the metrics. The **TEXT-METRIC** structure has the following form:

```
typedef struct tagTEXTMETRIC {  /* tm */
    int  tmHeight;
    int  tmAscent;
    int  tmDescent;
    int  tmInternalLeading;
    int  tmExternalLeading;
    int  tmAveCharWidth;
    int  tmMaxCharWidth;
    int  tmWeight;
    BYTE tmItalic;
    BYTE tmUnderlined;
    BYTE tmStruckOut;
    BYTE tmFirstChar;
    BYTE tmLastChar;
    BYTE tmDefaultChar;
    BYTE tmBreakChar;
    BYTE tmPitchAndFamily;
    BYTE tmCharSet;
```

```
        int  tmOverhang;
        int  tmDigitizedAspectX;
        int  tmDigitizedAspectY;
    } TEXTMETRIC;
```

For a full description of this structure, see the *Microsoft Windows Programmer's Reference, Volume 3*.

Return Value   The return value is nonzero if the function is successful. Otherwise, it is zero.

Example   The following example calls the **GetTextMetrics** function and then uses information in a **TEXTMETRIC** structure to determine how many break characters are in a string of text:

```
TEXTMETRIC tm;
int j, cBreakChars, cchString;
LPSTR lpszJustified = "Text to be justified in this test.";

GetTextMetrics(hdc, &tm);

cchString = lstrlen(lpszJustified);

for (cBreakChars = 0, j = 0; j < cchString; j++)
    if(*(lpszJustified + j) == (char) tm.tmBreakChar)
        cBreakChars++;
```

See Also   **GetTextAlign, GetTextExtent, GetTextFace, SetTextJustification**

GetThresholdEvent   `2.x`

int FAR* GetThresholdEvent(void)

This function is obsolete. Use the Windows multimedia audio functions instead. For information about these functions, see the *Microsoft Windows Multimedia Programmer's Reference*.

GetThresholdStatus

int GetThresholdStatus(void)

> This function is obsolete. Use the Windows multimedia audio functions instead. For information about these functions, see the *Microsoft Windows Multimedia Programmer's Reference*.

GetTickCount

DWORD GetTickCount(void)

> The **GetTickCount** function retrieves the number of milliseconds that have elapsed since Windows was started.

Parameters   This function has no parameters.

Return Value   The return value specifies the number of milliseconds that have elapsed since Windows was started.

Comments   The internal timer will wrap around to zero if Windows is run continuously for approximately 49 days.

The **GetTickCount** function is identical to the **GetCurrentTime** function. Applications should use **GetTickCount**, because its name matches more closely with what the function does.

Example   The following example calls **GetTickCount** to determine the number of milliseconds that Windows has been running, converts the value into seconds, and displays the value in a message box:

```
char szBuf[255];

sprintf(szBuf, "Windows has been running for %lu seconds\n",
    GetTickCount() / 1000L);
MessageBox(hwnd, szBuf, "", MB_OK);
```

GetTimerResolution $\boxed{3.1}$

DWORD GetTimerResolution(void)

The **GetTimerResolution** function retrieves the number of microseconds per timer tick.

Parameters   This function has no parameters.

Return Value   The return value is the number of microseconds per timer tick.

See Also   **GetTickCount, SetTimer**

GetTopWindow $\boxed{2.x}$

HWND GetTopWindow(*hwnd*)
HWND *hwnd*;   /* handle of parent window   */

The **GetTopWindow** function retrieves the handle of the top-level child window that belongs to the given parent window. If the parent window has no child windows, this function returns NULL.

Parameters   *hwnd*
Identifies the parent window. If this parameter is NULL, the function returns the first child window of the desktop window.

Return Value   The return value is the handle of the top-level child window in a parent window's linked list of child windows. The return value is NULL if no child windows exist.

See Also   **EnumWindows, GetParent, IsChild**

GetUpdateRect $\boxed{2.x}$

BOOL GetUpdateRect(*hwnd, lprc, fErase*)
HWND *hwnd*;   /* handle of window   */
RECT FAR* *lprc*;   /* address of structure for update rectangle   */
BOOL *fErase*;   /* erase flag   */

The **GetUpdateRect** function retrieves the coordinates of the smallest rectangle that completely encloses the update region of the given window. If the window was created with the CS_OWNDC style and the mapping mode is not MM_TEXT, **GetUpdateRect** gives the rectangle in logical coordinates; otherwise, **GetUpdateRect** gives the rectangle in client coordinates. If there is no update region, **GetUpdateRect** makes the rectangle empty (sets all coordinates to zero).

Parameters

hwnd
Identifies the window whose update region is to be retrieved.

lprc
Points to the **RECT** structure that receives the client coordinates of the enclosing rectangle. The **RECT** structure has the following form:

```
typedef struct tagRECT {    /* rc */
    int left;
    int top;
    int right;
    int bottom;
} RECT;
```

For a full description of this structure, see the *Microsoft Windows Programmer's Reference, Volume 3*.

An application can set this parameter to NULL to determine whether an update region exists for the window. If this parameter is NULL, the **GetUpdateRect** function returns nonzero if an update region exists, and zero if one does not. This provides a simple and efficient means of determining whether a WM_PAINT message resulted from an invalid area.

fErase
Specifies whether to erase the background in the update region. If this parameter is TRUE and the update region is not empty, the background is erased. To erase the background, the **GetUpdateRect** function sends a WM_ERASEBKGND message to the given window.

Return Value

The return value is nonzero if the update region is not empty. Otherwise, it is zero.

Comments

The update rectangle retrieved by the **BeginPaint** function is identical to that retrieved by the **GetUpdateRect** function.

BeginPaint automatically validates the update region, so any call to **GetUpdateRect** made immediately after the call to **BeginPaint** retrieves an empty update region.

See Also

BeginPaint, GetUpdateRgn, InvalidateRect, UpdateWindow, ValidateRect

GetUpdateRgn

int GetUpdateRgn(*hwnd, hrgn, fErase*)
HWND *hwnd*;   /* handle of window   */
HRGN *hrgn*;   /* handle of region   */
BOOL *fErase*;   /* erase flag   */

The **GetUpdateRgn** function retrieves the update region of a window. The coordinates of the update region are relative to the upper-left corner of the window (that is, they are client coordinates).

Parameters

hwnd
Identifies the window whose update region is to be retrieved.

hrgn
Identifies the update region.

fErase
Specifies whether the window background should be erased and whether non-client areas of child windows should be drawn. If this parameter is FALSE, no drawing is done.

Return Value

The return value is SIMPLEREGION (region has no overlapping borders), COMPLEXREGION (region has overlapping borders), or NULLREGION (region is empty), if the function is successful. Otherwise, the return value is ERROR.

Comments

The **BeginPaint** function automatically validates the update region, so any call to the **GetUpdateRgn** function made immediately after the call to **BeginPaint** retrieves an empty update region.

See Also

BeginPaint, GetUpdateRect, InvalidateRgn, UpdateWindow, ValidateRgn

---

GetVersion

DWORD GetVersion(void)

The **GetVersion** function retrieves the current version numbers of the Windows and MS-DOS operation systems.

Parameters

This function has no parameters.

Return Value

The return value specifies the major and minor version numbers of Windows and of MS-DOS, if the function is successful.

Comments   The low-order word of the return value contains the version of Windows, if the
function is successful. The high-order byte contains the minor version (revision)
number as a two-digit decimal number. For example, in Windows 3.1, the minor
version number is 10. The low-order byte contains the major version number.

The high-order word contains the version of MS-DOS, if the function is successful. The high-order byte contains the major version; the low-order byte contains
the minor version (revision) number.

Example   The following example uses the **GetVersion** function to display the Windows and
MS-DOS version numbers:

```
int len;
char szBuf[80];
DWORD dwVersion;

dwVersion = GetVersion();

len = sprintf(szBuf, "Windows version %d.%d\n",
    LOBYTE(LOWORD(dwVersion)),
    HIBYTE(LOWORD(dwVersion)));

sprintf(szBuf + len, "MS-DOS version %d.%d",
    HIBYTE(HIWORD(dwVersion)),
    LOBYTE(HIWORD(dwVersion)));

MessageBox(NULL, szBuf, "GetVersion", MB_ICONINFORMATION);
```

Note that the major and minor version information is reversed between the Windows version and MS-DOS version.

GetViewportExt   2.x

DWORD GetViewportExt(*hdc***)**
HDC *hdc*;   /* handle of device context   */

The **GetViewportExt** function retrieves the x- and y-extents of the device context's viewport.

Parameters   *hdc*
                Identifies the device context.

Return Value   The low-order word of the return value contains the x-extent, in device units, if the
function is successful; the high-order word contains the y-extent.

Example   The following example uses the **GetViewportExt** function and the **LOWORD** and **HIWORD** macros to retrieve the x- and y-extents for a device context:

```
HDC  hdc;
DWORD dw;
int xViewExt, yViewExt;

hdc = GetDC(hwnd);
dw  = GetViewportExt(hdc);
ReleaseDC(hwnd, hdc);
xViewExt = LOWORD(dw);
yViewExt = HIWORD(dw);
```

See Also   **SetViewportExt**

GetViewportExtEx

3.1

BOOL GetViewportExtEx(*hdc*, *lpSize***)**
HDC *hdc*;
SIZE FAR* *lpSize*;

The **GetViewportExtEx** function retrieves the x- and y-extents of the device context's viewport,

Parameters   *hdc*
    Identifies the device context.

lpSize
    Points to a **SIZE** structure. The x- and y-extents (in device units) are placed in this structure.

Return Value   The return value is nonzero if the function is successful. Otherwise, it is zero.

GetViewportOrg

2.x

DWORD GetViewportOrg(*hdc***)**
HDC *hdc*;   /* handle of device context   */

The **GetViewportOrg** function retrieves the x- and y-coordinates of the origin of the viewport associated with the given device context.

Parameters	*hdc*
	Identifies the device context.

Return Value   The low-order word of the return value contains the viewport origin's x-coordinate, in device coordinates, if the function is successful; the high-order word contains the y-coordinate of the viewport origin.

Example   The following example uses the **GetViewportOrg** function and the **LOWORD** and **HIWORD** macros to retrieve the x- and y-coordinates of the viewport origin:

```
HDC  hdc;
DWORD dw;
int xViewOrg, yViewOrg;

hdc = GetDC(hwnd);
dw  = GetViewportOrg(hdc);
ReleaseDC(hwnd, hdc);
xViewOrg = LOWORD(dw);
yViewOrg = HIWORD(dw);
```

See Also   **GetWindowOrg, SetViewportOrg**

GetViewportOrgEx   3.1

BOOL GetViewportOrgEx(*hdc*, *lpPoint*)
HDC *hdc*;
POINT FAR* *lpPoint*;

The **GetViewportOrgEx** function retrieves the x- and y-coordinates of the origin of the viewport associated with the specified device context.

Parameters   *hdc*
    Identifies the device context.

lpPoint
    Points to a **POINT** structure. The origin of the viewport (in device coordinates) is placed in this structure.

Return Value   The return value is nonzero if the function is successful. Otherwise, it is zero.

GetWinDebugInfo

BOOL GetWinDebugInfo(*lpwdi*, *flags*)
WINDEBUGINFO FAR* *lpwdi*;   /* address of WINDEBUGINFO structure   */
UINT *flags*;   /* flags for returned information   */

The **GetWinDebugInfo** function retrieves current system-debugging information for the debugging version of the Windows 3.1 operating system.

Parameters

lpwdi
Points to a **WINDEBUGINFO** structure that is filled with debugging information. The **WINDEBUGINFO** structure has the following form:

```
typedef struct tagWINDEBUGINFO {
    UINT    flags;
    DWORD   dwOptions;
    DWORD   dwFilter;
    char    achAllocModule[8];
    DWORD   dwAllocBreak;
    DWORD   dwAllocCount;
} WINDEBUGINFO;
```

For a full description of this structure, see the *Microsoft Windows Programmer's Reference, Volume 3*.

flags
Specifies which members of the **WINDEBUGINFO** structure should be filled in. This parameter can be one or more of the following values:

Value	Meaning
WDI_OPTIONS	Fill in the **dwOptions** member of **WINDEBUGINFO**.
WDI_FILTER	Fill in the **dwFilter** member of **WINDEBUGINFO**.
WDI_ALLOCBREAK	Fill in the **achAllocModule**, **dwAllocBreak**, and **dwAllocCount** members of **WINDEBUGINFO**.

Return Value

The return value is nonzero if the function is successful. It is zero if the pointer specified in the *lpwdi* parameter is invalid or if the function is not called in the debugging version of Windows 3.1.

Comments

The **flags** member of the returned **WINDEBUGINFO** structure is set to the values supplied in the *flags* parameter of this function.

See Also

SetWinDebugInfo

GetWindow

HWND GetWindow(*hwnd, fuRel*)
HWND *hwnd*;   /* handle of original window   */
UINT *fuRel*;   /* relationship flag   */

The **GetWindow** function retrieves the handle of a window that has the specified relationship to the given window. The function searches the system's list of top-level windows, their associated child windows, the child windows of any child windows, and any siblings of the owner of a window.

Parameters

hwnd
Identifies the original window.

fuRel
Specifies the relationship between the original window and the returned window. This parameter can be one of the following values:

Value	Meaning
GW_CHILD	Identifies the window's first child window.
GW_HWNDFIRST	Returns the first sibling window for a child window; otherwise, it returns the first top-level window in the list.
GW_HWNDLAST	Returns the last sibling window for a child window; otherwise, it returns the last top-level window in the list.
GW_HWNDNEXT	Returns the sibling window that follows the given window in the list.
GW_HWNDPREV	Returns the previous sibling window in the list.
GW_OWNER	Identifies the window's owner.

Return Value

The return value is the handle of the window if the function is successful. Otherwise, it is NULL, indicating either the end of the system's list or an invalid *fuRel* parameter.

See Also

EnumWindows, FindWindow

GetWindowDC

HDC GetWindowDC(*hwnd*)
HWND *hwnd*;   /* handle of window   */

The **GetWindowDC** function retrieves a device context for the entire window, including title bar, menus, and scroll bars. A window device context permits painting anywhere in the window, because the origin of the context is the upper-left corner of the window instead of the client area.

GetWindowDC assigns default attributes to the device context each time it retrieves the context. Previous attributes are lost.

Parameters

hwnd
Identifies the window whose device context is to be retrieved.

Return Value

The return value is the handle of the device context for the given window, if the function is successful. Otherwise, it is NULL, indicating an error or an invalid *hwnd* parameter.

Comments

The **GetWindowDC** function is intended to be used for special painting effects within a window's nonclient area. Painting in nonclient areas of any window is not recommended.

The **GetSystemMetrics** function can be used to retrieve the dimensions of various parts of the nonclient area, such as the title bar, menu, and scroll bars.

After painting is complete, the **ReleaseDC** function must be called to release the device context. Failure to release a window device context will have serious effects on painting requested by applications.

See Also

BeginPaint, GetDC, GetSystemMetrics, ReleaseDC

GetWindowExt
2.x

DWORD GetWindowExt(*hdc*)
HDC *hdc*;   /* handle of device context   */

The **GetWindowExt** function retrieves the x- and y-extents of the window associated with the given device context.

Parameters

hdc
Identifies the device context.

Return Value

The return value specifies the x- and y-extents, in logical units, if the function is successful. The x-extent is in the low-order word; the y-extent is in the high-order word.

Example   The following example uses the **GetWindowExt** function and the **LOWORD** and
HIWORD macros to retrieve the x- and y-extents of a window:

```
HDC  hdc;
DWORD dw;
int xWindExt, yWindExt;

hdc = GetDC(hwnd);
dw  = GetWindowExt(hdc);
ReleaseDC(hwnd, hdc);
xWindExt = LOWORD(dw);
yWindExt = HIWORD(dw);
```

See Also   **SetWindowExt**

GetWindowExtEx   3.1

BOOL GetWindowExtEx(*hdc*, *lpSize*)
HDC *hdc*;
SIZE FAR* *lpSize*;

The **GetWindowExtEx** function retrieves the x- and y-extents of the window
associated with the specified device context.

Parameters   *hdc*
                          Identifies the device context.

                     lpSize
                          Points to a **SIZE** structure. The x- and y-extents (in logical units) are placed in
                          this structure.

Return Value   The return value is nonzero if the function is successful. Otherwise, it is zero.

GetWindowLong   2.x

LONG GetWindowLong(*hwnd*, *nOffset*)
HWND *hwnd*;   /* handle of window   */
int *nOffset*;   /* offset of value to retrieve   */

The **GetWindowLong** function retrieves a long value at the specified offset into
the extra window memory of the given window. Extra window memory is re-

served by specifying a nonzero value in the **cbWndExtra** member of the
WNDCLASS structure used with the **RegisterClass** function.

Parameters

hwnd
Identifies the window.

nOffset
Specifies the zero-based byte offset of the value to be retrieved. Valid values
are in the range zero through the number of bytes of extra window memory,
minus four (for example, if 12 or more bytes of extra memory was specified, a
value of 8 would be an index to the third long integer), or one of the following
values:

Value	Meaning
GWL_EXSTYLE	Extended window style
GWL_STYLE	Window style
GWL_WNDPROC	Long pointer to the window procedure

The following values are also available when the *hwnd* parameter identifies a
dialog box:

Value	Meaning
DWL_DLGPROC	Specifies the address of the dialog box procedure.
DWL_MSGRESULT	Specifies the return value of a message processed in the dialog box procedure.
DWL_USER	Specifies extra information that is private to the application, such as handles or pointers.

Return Value

The return value specifies information about the given window if the function is
successful.

Comments

To access any extra 4-byte values allocated when the window-class structure was
created, use a positive byte offset as the index specified by the *nOffset* parameter,
starting at 0 for the first 4-byte value in the extra space, 4 for the next 4-byte
value, and so on.

See Also

GetWindowWord, SetWindowLong, SetWindowWord

GetWindowOrg

2.x

DWORD GetWindowOrg(*hdc*)
HDC *hdc*;   /* handle of device context   */

The **GetWindowOrg** function retrieves the x- and y-coordinates of the origin of the window associated with the given device context.

Parameters   *hdc*
                    Identifies the device context.

Return Value   The low-order word of the return value contains the logical x-coordinate of the window's origin, if the function is successful; the high-order word contains the y-coordinate.

Example   The following example uses the **GetWindowOrg** function and the **LOWORD** and **HIWORD** macros to retrieve the x- and y-coordinates for the window origin:

```
HDC  hdc;
DWORD dw;
int xWindOrg, yWindOrg;

hdc = GetDC(hwnd);
dw  = GetWindowOrg(hdc);
ReleaseDC(hwnd, hdc);
xWindOrg = LOWORD(dw);
yWindOrg = HIWORD(dw);
```

See Also   **GetViewportOrg, SetWindowOrg**

GetWindowOrgEx

3.1

BOOL GetWindowOrgEx(*hdc*, *lpPoint*)
HDC *hdc*;
POINT FAR* *lpPoint*;

This function retrieves the x- and y-coordinates of the origin of the window associated with the specified device context.

Parameters   *hdc*
                    Identifies the device context.

lpPoint
Points to a **POINT** structure. The origin of the window (in logical coordinates) is placed in this structure.

Return Value   The return value is nonzero if the function is successful. Otherwise, it is zero.

GetWindowPlacement

3.1

BOOL GetWindowPlacement(*hwnd*, *lpwndpl*)
HWND *hwnd*;   /* handle of window   */
WINDOWPLACEMENT FAR* *lpwndpl*;   /* address of structure for position data   */

The **GetWindowPlacement** function retrieves the show state and the normal (restored), minimized, and maximized positions of a window.

Parameters   *hwnd*
Identifies the window.

lpwndpl
Points to the **WINDOWPLACEMENT** structure that receives the show state and position information. The **WINDOWPLACEMENT** structure has the following form:

```
typedef struct tagWINDOWPLACEMENT {     /* wndpl */
    UINT  length;
    UINT  flags;
    UINT  showCmd;
    POINT ptMinPosition;
    POINT ptMaxPosition;
    RECT  rcNormalPosition;
} WINDOWPLACEMENT;
```

For a full description of this structure, see the *Microsoft Windows Programmer's Reference, Volume 3*.

Return Value   The return value is nonzero if the function is successful. Otherwise, it is zero.

See Also   **SetWindowPlacement**

GetWindowRect

void GetWindowRect(*hwnd***,** *lprc***)**
HWND *hwnd*;   /* handle of window   */
RECT FAR* *lprc*;   /* address of structure for window coordinates   */

The **GetWindowRect** function retrieves the dimensions of the bounding rectangle of a given window. The dimensions are given in screen coordinates, relative to the upper-left corner of the display screen, and include the title bar, border, and scroll bars, if present.

Parameters   *hwnd*
          Identifies the window.

          lprc
          Points to a **RECT** structure that receives the screen coordinates of the upper-left and lower-right corners of the window. The **RECT** structure has the following form:

```
typedef struct tagRECT {    /* rc */
    int left;
    int top;
    int right;
    int bottom;
} RECT;
```

          For a full description of this structure, see the *Microsoft Windows Programmer's Reference*, *Volume 3*.

Return Value   This function does not return a value.

Example   The following example calls the **GetWindowRect** function to retrieve the dimensions of the desktop window, and uses the dimensions to create a window that fills the right third of the desktop window:

```
RECT rc;
WORD wWidth;

GetWindowRect(GetDesktopWindow(), &rc);

/* Set the width to be 1/3 of the desktop window's width. */

wWidth = (rc.right - rc.left) / 3;
```

```
/* Create a main window for this application instance. */

hwndFrame = CreateWindow("MyClass", "My Title", WS_OVERLAPPEDWINDOW,
    rc.right - wWidth,      /* horizontal position */
    0,                      /* vertical position   */
    wWidth,                 /* width               */
    rc.bottom,              /* height              */
    (HWND) NULL, (HMENU) NULL, hinst, (LPSTR) NULL);
```

See Also   **GetClientRect, MoveWindow, SetWindowPos**

GetWindowsDir   3.1

#include <ver.h>

UINT GetWindowsDir(*lpszAppDir*, *lpszPath*, *cbPath*)
LPCSTR *lpszAppDir*;   /* address of Windows directory   */
LPSTR *lpszPath*;   /* address of buffer for path   */
int *cbPath*;   /* size of buffer for path   */

The **GetWindowsDir** function retrieves the path of the Windows directory. This directory contains such files as Windows applications, initialization files, and help files.

GetWindowsDir is used by MS-DOS applications that set up Windows applications; it exists only in the static-link version of the File Installation library. Windows applications should use the **GetWindowsDirectory** function to determine the Windows directory.

Parameters   *lpszAppDir*
Specifies the current directory in a search for Windows files. If the Windows directory is not on the path, the application must prompt the user for its location and pass that string to the **GetWindowsDir** function in the *lpszAppDir* parameter.

lpszPath
Points to the buffer that will receive the null-terminated string containing the path.

cbPath
Specifies the size, in bytes, of the buffer pointed to by the *lpszPath* parameter.

Return Value   The return value is the length of the string copied to the *lpszPath* parameter, including the terminating null character, if the function is successful. If the return value is greater than the *cbPath* parameter, it is the size of the buffer required to hold the path. The return value is zero if the function fails.

Comments   The path that this function retrieves does not end with a backslash unless the Windows directory is the root directory. For example, if the Windows directory is named WINDOWS on drive C, the path retrieved by this function is C:\WINDOWS. If Windows is installed in the root directory of drive C, the path retrieved is C:\.

After the **GetWindowsDir** function locates the Windows directory, it caches the location for use by subsequent calls to the function.

See Also   **GetSystemDir**, **GetWindowsDirectory**

GetWindowsDirectory $\boxed{3.0}$

UINT **GetWindowsDirectory**(*lpszSysPath*, *cbSysPath*)
LPSTR *lpszSysPath*;   /* address of buffer for Windows directory   */
UINT *cbSysPath*;   /* size of directory buffer   */

The **GetWindowsDirectory** function retrieves the path of the Windows directory. The Windows directory contains such files as Windows applications, initialization files, and help files.

Parameters   *lpszSysPath*
    Points to the buffer that will receive the null-terminated string containing the path.

cbSysPath
    Specifies the maximum size, in bytes, of the buffer. This value should be set to at least 144 to allow sufficient room in the buffer for the path.

Return Value   The return value is the length, in bytes, of the string copied to the *lpszSysPath* parameter, not including the terminating null character. If the return value is greater than the number specified in the *cbSysPath* parameter, it is the size of the buffer required to hold the path. The return value is zero if the function fails.

Comments   The Windows directory is the *only* directory where an application should create files. If the user is running a shared version of Windows, the Windows directory is the only directory guaranteed private to the user.

The path this function retrieves does not end with a backslash unless the Windows directory is the root directory. For example, if the Windows directory is named

WINDOWS on drive C, the path retrieved by this function is C:\WINDOWS. If Windows is installed in the root directory of drive C, the path retrieved is C:\.

A similar function, **GetWindowsDir**, is intended for use by MS-DOS applications that set up Windows applications. Windows applications should use **Get-WindowsDirectory**, not **GetWindowsDir**.

Example

The following example uses the **GetWindowsDirectory** function to determine the path of the Windows directory:

```
WORD wReturn;
char szBuf[144];

wReturn = GetWindowsDirectory((LPSTR)szBuf, sizeof(szBuf));

if (wReturn == 0)
    MessageBox(hwnd, "function failed",
        "GetWindowsDirectory", MB_ICONEXCLAMATION);

else if (wReturn > sizeof(szBuf))
    MessageBox(hwnd, "buffer is too small",
        "GetWindowsDirectory", MB_ICONEXCLAMATION);

else
    MessageBox(hwnd, szBuf, "GetWindowsDirectory", MB_OK);
```

See Also

GetSystemDirectory

GetWindowTask

2.x

HTASK GetWindowTask(*hwnd*)
HWND *hwnd*;   /* handle of window   */

The **GetWindowTask** function searches for the handle of a task associated with a window. A task is any program that executes as an independent unit. All applications are executed as tasks. Each instance of an application is a task.

Parameters

hwnd
Identifies the window for which to retrieve a task handle.

Return Value

The return value is the handle of the task associated with a particular window, if the function is successful. Otherwise, it is NULL.

See Also

EnumTaskWindows, GetCurrentTask

GetWindowText

int **GetWindowText**(*hwnd*, *lpsz*, *cbMax*)
HWND *hwnd*;   /* handle of window   */
LPSTR *lpsz*;   /* address of buffer for text   */
int *cbMax*;   /* maximum number of bytes to copy   */

The **GetWindowText** function copies text of the given window's title bar (if it has one) into a buffer. If the given window is a control, the text within the control is copied.

Parameters   *hwnd*
Identifies the window or control containing the title bar or text.

lpsz
Points to a buffer that will receive the title bar or text.

cbMax
Specifies the maximum number of characters to copy to the buffer. The title bar or text is truncated if it is longer than the number of characters specified in *cbMax*.

Return Value   The return value specifies the length, in bytes, of the copied string, not including the terminating null character. It is zero if the window has no title bar, the title bar is empty, or the *hwnd* parameter is invalid.

Comments   This function causes a WM_GETTEXT message to be sent to the given window or control.

See Also   **GetWindowTextLength**

GetWindowTextLength

int **GetWindowTextLength**(*hwnd*)
HWND *hwnd*;   /* handle of window with text   */

The **GetWindowTextLength** function retrieves the length, in bytes, of the text in the given window's title bar. If the window is a control, the length of the text within the control is retrieved.

Parameters   *hwnd*
Identifies the window or control.

Return Value	The return value specifies the text length, in bytes, not including any null terminating character, if the function is successful. Otherwise, it is zero.
Comments	This function causes the WM_GETTEXTLENGTH message to be sent to the given window or control.
See Also	**GetWindowText**

GetWindowWord   `2.x`

WORD GetWindowWord(*hwnd*, *nOffset*)
HWND *hwnd*;   /* handle of window   */
int *nOffset*;   /* offset of value to retrieve   */

The **GetWindowWord** function retrieves a word value at the specified offset into the extra window memory of the given window. Extra window memory is reserved by specifying a nonzero value in the **cbWndExtra** member of the **WNDCLASS** structure used with the **RegisterClass** function.

Parameters   *hwnd*
                       Identifies the window.

                       nOffset
                       Specifies the zero-based byte offset of the value to be retrieved. Valid values are in the range zero through the number of bytes of extra window memory, minus two (for example, if 10 or more bytes of extra memory was specified, a value of 8 would be an index to the fifth integer), or one of the following values:

Value	Meaning
GWW_HINSTANCE	Specifies the instance handle of the module that owns the window.
GWW_HWNDPARENT	Specifies the handle of the parent window, if any. The **SetParent** function changes the parent window of a child window. An application should not call the **SetWindowWord** function to change the parent of a child window.
GWW_ID	Specifies the identifier of the child window.

Return Value   The return value specifies information about the given window if the function is successful.

Comments   To access any extra two-byte values allocated when the window-class structure was created, use a positive byte offset as the index specified by the *nOffset* parameter, starting at 0 for the first two-byte value in the extra space, 2 for the next two-byte value, and so on.

See Also   **GetWindowLong, SetParent, SetWindowLong, SetWindowWord**

GetWinFlags

3.0

DWORD GetWinFlags(void)

The **GetWinFlags** function retrieves the current Windows system and memory configuration.

Parameters   This function has no parameters.

Return Value   The return value specifies the current system and memory configuration if the function is successful.

Comments   The configuration returned by **GetWinFlags** can be a combination of the following values:

Value	Meaning
WF_80x87	System contains an Intel math coprocessor.
WF_CPU086	System CPU is an 8086. Windows 3.1 will not return this flag.
WF_CPU186	System CPU is an 80186. Windows 3.1 will not return this flag.
WF_CPU286	System CPU is an 80286.
WF_CPU386	System CPU is an 80386.
WF_CPU486	System CPU is an i486.
WF_ENHANCED	Windows is running in 386-enhanced mode. The WF_PMODE flag is always set when WF_ENHANCED is set.
WF_PAGING	Windows is running on a system with paged memory.
WF_PMODE	Windows is running in protected mode. In Windows 3.1, this flag is always set.
WF_STANDARD	Windows is running in standard mode. The WF_PMODE flag is always set when WF_STANDARD is set.
WF_WIN286	Same as WF_STANDARD.
WF_WIN386	Same as WF_ENHANCED.
WF_WLO	Identifies an application running Windows-emulation libraries in a non-Windows operating system.

Example   The following example uses the **GetWinFlags** function to display information about the current Windows system configuration:

```
int len;
char szBuf[80];
DWORD dwFlags;

dwFlags = GetWinFlags();

len = sprintf(szBuf, "system %s a coprocessor",
    (dwFlags & WF_80x87) ? "contains" : "does not contain");
TextOut(hdc, 10, 15, szBuf, len);

len = sprintf(szBuf, "processor is an %s",
    (dwFlags & WF_CPU286) ? "80286" :
    (dwFlags & WF_CPU386) ? "80386" :
    (dwFlags & WF_CPU486) ? "i486" : "unknown");
TextOut(hdc, 10, 30, szBuf, len);

len = sprintf(szBuf, "running in %s mode",
    (dwFlags & WF_ENHANCED) ? "enhanced" : "standard");
TextOut(hdc, 10, 45, szBuf, len);

len = sprintf(szBuf, "%s WLO",
    (dwFlags & WF_WLO) ? "using" : "not using");
TextOut(hdc, 10, 60, szBuf, len);
```

GetWinMem32Version

3.0

#include <winmem32.h>

WORD GetWinMem32Version(void)

The **GetWinMem32Version** function retrieves the application programming interface (API) version implemented by the WINMEM32.DLL dynamic-link library. This is not the version number of the library itself.

Parameters   This function has no parameters.

Return Value   The return value specifies the version of the 32-bit memory API implemented by WINMEM32.DLL. The high-order 8 bits contain the major version number, and the low-order 8 bits contain the minor version number.

Global16PointerAlloc

#include <winmem32.h>

WORD Global16PointerAlloc(*wSelector*, *dwOffset*, *lpBuffer*, *dwSize*, *wFlags*)
WORD *wSelector*;   /* selector of object   */
DWORD *dwOffset*;   /* offset of first byte for alias   */
LPDWORD *lpBuffer*;   /* address of location for alias   */
DWORD *dwSize*;   /* size of region   */
WORD *wFlags*;   /* reserved, must be zero   */

The **Global16PointerAlloc** function converts a 16:32 pointer into a 16:16 pointer alias that the application can pass to a Windows function or to other 16:16 functions.

Parameters

wSelector
Specifies the selector of the object for which an alias is to be created. This must be the selector returned by a previous call to the **Global32Alloc** function.

dwOffset
Specifies the offset of the first byte for which an alias is to be created. The offset is from the first byte of the object specified by the *wSelector* parameter. Note that *wSelector.dwOffset* forms a 16:32 address of the first byte of the region for which an alias is to be created.

lpBuffer
Points to a four-byte location in memory that receives the 16:16 pointer alias for the specified region.

dwSize
Specifies the addressable size, in bytes, of the region for which an alias is to be created. This value must be no larger than 64K.

wFlags
Reserved; must be zero.

Return Value

The return value is zero if the function is successful. Otherwise, it is an error value, which can be one of the following:

WM32_Insufficient_Mem
WM32_Insufficient_Sels
WM32_Invalid_Arg
WM32_Invalid_Flags
WM32_Invalid_Func

Comments

When this function returns successfully, the location pointed to by the *lpBuffer* parameter contains a 16:16 pointer to the first byte of the region. This is the same byte to which *wSelector.dwOffset* points.

The returned selector identifies a descriptor for a data segment that has the following attributes: read-write, expand up, and small (B bit clear). The descriptor privilege level (DPL) and the granularity (the G bit) are set at the system's discretion, so you should make no assumptions regarding their settings. The DPL and requestor privilege level (RPL) are appropriate for a Windows application.

Note An application must not change the setting of any bits in the DPL or the RPL selector. Doing so can result in a system crash and will prevent the application from running on compatible platforms.

Because of tiling schemes implemented by some systems, the offset portion of the returned 16:16 pointer is not necessarily zero.

When writing your application, you should not assume the size limit of the returned selector. Instead, assume that at least *dwSize* bytes can be addressed starting at the 16:16 pointer created by this function.

See Also   **Global16PointerFree**

Global16PointerFree   3.0

#include <winmem32.h>

WORD Global16PointerFree(*wSelector*, *dwAlias*, *wFlags*)
WORD *wSelector*;   /* selector of object   */
DWORD *dwAlias*;   /* pointer alias to free   */
WORD *wFlags*;   /* reserved, must be zero   */

The **Global16PointerFree** function frees the 16:16 pointer alias previously created by a call to the **Global16PointerAlloc** function.

Parameters   *wSelector*
              Specifies the selector of the object for which the alias is to be freed. This must be the selector returned by a previous call to the **Global32Alloc** function.

              dwAlias
              Specifies the 16:16 pointer alias to be freed. This must be the alias (including the original offset) returned by a previous call to the **Global16PointerAlloc** function.

              wFlags
              Reserved; must be zero.

Return Value   The return value is zero if the function is successful. Otherwise, it is an error value, which can be one of the following:

WM32_Insufficient_Mem
WM32_Insufficient_Sels
WM32_Invalid_Arg
WM32_Invalid_Flags
WM32_Invalid_Func

Comments   An application should free a 16:16 pointer alias as soon as it is no longer needed. Freeing the alias releases space in the descriptor table, a limited system resource.

See Also   **Global16PointerAlloc**

Global32Alloc   `3.0`

#include <winmem32.h>

WORD Global32Alloc(*dwSize*, *lpSelector*, *dwMaxSize*, *wFlags*)
DWORD *dwSize*;   /* size of block to allocate   */
LPWORD *lpSelector*;   /* address of location for selector   */
DWORD *dwMaxSize*;   /* maximum size of object   */
WORD *wFlags*;   /* sharing flag   */

The **Global32Alloc** function allocates a memory object to be used as a 16:32 (USE32) code or data segment and retrieves the selector portion of the 16:32 address of the memory object. The first byte of the object is at offset 0 from this selector.

Parameters   *dwSize*
Specifies the initial size, in bytes, of the object to be allocated. This value must be in the range 1 through (16 megabytes – 64K).

lpSelector
Points to a 2-byte location in memory that receives the selector portion of the 16:32 address of the allocated object.

dwMaxSize
Specifies the maximum size, in bytes, that the object will reach when it is reallocated by the **Global32Realloc** function. This value must be in the range 1 through (16 megabytes – 64 K). If the application will never reallocate this memory object, the *dwMaxSize* parameter should be set to the same value as the *dwSize* parameter.

wFlags
Depends on the return value of the **GetWinMem32Version** function. If the return value is less than 0x0101, this parameter must be zero. If the return value is greater than or equal to 0x0101, this parameter can be set to GMEM_DDESHARE (to make the object shareable). Otherwise, this parameter should be zero. For more information about GMEM_DDESHARE, see the description of the **GlobalAlloc** function.

Return Value   The return value is zero if the function is successful. Otherwise, it is an error value, which can be one of the following:

WM32_Insufficient_Mem
WM32_Insufficient_Sels
WM32_Invalid_Arg
WM32_Invalid_Flags
WM32_Invalid_Func

Comments   If the **Global32Alloc** function fails, the value to which the *lpSelector* parameter points is zero. If the function succeeds, *lpSelector* points to the selector of the object. The valid range of offsets for the object referenced by this selector is 0 through (but not including) *dwSize*.

In Windows 3.0 and later, the largest object that can be allocated is 0x00FF0000 (16 megabytes – 64K). This is the limitation placed on WINMEM32.DLL by the current Windows kernel.

The returned selector identifies a descriptor for a data segment that has the following attributes: read-write, expand-up, and big (B bit set). The descriptor privilege level (DPL) and the granularity (the G bit) are set at the system's discretion, so you should make no assumptions regarding these settings. Because the system sets the granularity, the size of the object (and the selector size limit) may be greater than the requested size by up to 4095 bytes (4K minus 1). The DPL and requestor privilege level (RPL) will be appropriate for a Windows application.

Note   An application must not change the setting of any bits in the DPL or the RPL selector. Doing so can result in a system crash and will prevent the application from running on compatible platforms.

The allocated object is neither movable nor discardable but can be paged. An application should not page-lock a 32-bit memory object. Page-locking an object is useful only if the object contains code or data that is used at interrupt time, and 32-bit memory cannot be used at interrupt time.

See Also   **Global32Free, Global32Realloc**

Global32CodeAlias

3.0

#include <winmem32.h>

WORD Global32CodeAlias(*wSelector*, *lpAlias*, *wFlags*)
WORD *wSelector*;   /* selector of object for alias   */
LPWORD *lpAlias*;   /* address of location for alias selector */
WORD *wFlags*;   /* reserved, must be zero   */

The **Global32CodeAlias** function creates a 16:32 (USE32) code-segment alias selector for a 32-bit memory object previously created by the **Global32Alloc** function. This allows the application to execute code contained in the memory object.

Parameters   *wSelector*
Specifies the selector of the object for which an alias is to be created. This must be the selector returned by a previous call to the **Global32Alloc** function.

lpAlias
Points to a 2-byte location in memory that receives the selector portion of the 16:32 code-segment alias for the specified object.

wFlags
Reserved; must be zero.

Return Value   The return value is zero if the function is successful. Otherwise, it is an error value, which can be one of the following:

WM32_Insufficient_Mem
WM32_Insufficient_Sels
WM32_Invalid_Arg
WM32_Invalid_Flags
WM32_Invalid_Func

Comments   If the function fails, the value pointed to by the *lpAlias* parameter is zero. If the function is successful, *lpAlias* points to a USE32 code-segment alias for the object specified by the *wSelector* parameter. The first byte of the object is at offset 0 from the selector returned in *lpAlias*. Valid offsets are determined by the size of the object as set by the most recent call to the **Global32Alloc** or **Global32Realloc** function.

The returned selector identifies a descriptor for a code segment that has the following attributes: read-execute, nonconforming, and USE32 (D bit set). The descriptor privilege level (DPL) and the granularity (the G bit) are set at the system's discretion, so you should make no assumptions regarding their settings. The granularity will be consistent with the current data selector for the object. The DPL and requestor privilege level (RPL) are appropriate for a Windows application.

Note An application must not change the setting of any bits in the DPL or the RPL selector. Doing so can result in a system crash and will prevent the application from running on compatible platforms.

An application should not call this function more than once for an object. Depending on the system, the function might fail if an application calls it a second time for a given object without first calling the **Global32CodeAliasFree** function for the object.

See Also   **Global32Alloc**, **Global32CodeAliasFree**

Global32CodeAliasFree   3.0

#include <winmem32.h>

WORD **Global32CodeAliasFree**(*wSelector*, *wAlias*, *wFlags*)
WORD *wSelector*;   /* selector of object   */
WORD *wAlias*;   /* code-segment alias selector to free */
WORD *wFlags*;   /* reserved, must be zero   */

The **Global32CodeAliasFree** function frees the 16:32 (USE32) code-segment alias selector previously created by a call to the **Global32CodeAlias** function.

Parameters   *wSelector*
                        Specifies the selector of the object for which the alias is to be freed. This must be the selector returned by a previous call to the **Global32Alloc** function.

                        wAlias
                        Specifies the USE32 code-segment alias selector to be freed. This must be the alias returned by a previous call to the **Global32CodeAlias** function.

                        wFlags
                        Reserved; must be zero.

Return Value   The return value is zero if the function is successful. Otherwise, it is an error value, which can be one of the following:

                        WM32_Insufficient_Mem
                        WM32_Insufficient_Sels
                        WM32_Invalid_Arg
                        WM32_Invalid_Flags
                        WM32_Invalid_Func

See Also   **Global32CodeAlias**

Global32Free

3.0

#include <winmem32.h>

WORD Global32Free(*wSelector*, *wFlags*)
WORD *wSelector*;   /* selector of object to free   */
WORD *wFlags*;   /* reserved, must be zero   */

The **Global32Free** function frees an object previously allocated by the **Global32Alloc** function.

Parameters

wSelector
Specifies the selector of the object to be freed. This must be the selector returned by a previous call to the **Global32Alloc** function.

wFlags
Reserved; must be zero.

Return Value

The return value is zero if the function is successful. Otherwise, it is an error value, which can be one of the following:

WM32_Insufficient_Mem
WM32_Insufficient_Sels
WM32_Invalid_Arg
WM32_Invalid_Flags
WM32_Invalid_Func

Comments

The **Global32Alloc** function frees the object itself; it also frees all aliases created for the object by the 32-bit memory application programming interface (API).

Note Before terminating, an application must call this function to free each object allocated by the **Global32Alloc** function to ensure that all aliases created for the object are freed.

See Also

Global32Alloc, Global32Realloc

Global32Realloc

#include <winmem32.h>

WORD Global32Realloc(*wSelector*, *dwNewSize*, *wFlags*)
WORD *wSelector*;   /* selector of object to reallocate   */
DWORD *dwNewSize*;   /* new size of object   */
WORD *wFlags*;   /* reserved, must be zero   */

The **Global32Realloc** function changes the size of a 32-bit memory object previously allocated by the **Global32Alloc** function.

Parameters

wSelector
Specifies the selector of the object to be changed. This must be the selector returned by a previous call to the **Global32Alloc** function.

dwNewSize
Specifies the new size, in bytes, of the object. This value must be greater than zero and less than or equal to the size specified by the *dwMaxSize* parameter of the **Global32Alloc** function call that created the object.

wFlags
Reserved; must be zero.

Return Value

The return value is zero if the function is successful. Otherwise, it is an error value, which can be one of the following:

WM32_Insufficient_Mem
WM32_Insufficient_Sels
WM32_Invalid_Arg
WM32_Invalid_Flags
WM32_Invalid_Func

Comments

If this function fails, the previous state of the object is unchanged. If the function succeeds, it updates the state of the object and the state of all aliases to the object created by the 32-bit memory application programming interface (API) functions. For this reason, an application must call the the **Global32Realloc** function to change the size of the object. Using other Windows functions to manipulate the object results in corrupted aliases.

This function does not change the selector specified by the *wSelector* parameter. If this function succeeds, the new valid range of offsets for the selector is zero through (but not including) *dwNewSize*.

The system determines the appropriate granularity of the object. As a result, the size of the object (and the selector size limit) may be greater than the requested size by up to 4095 bytes (4K minus 1).

See Also   **Global32Alloc, Global32Free**

GlobalAddAtom   2.x

ATOM GlobalAddAtom(*lpszString*)
LPCSTR *lpszString*;   /* address of string to add   */

The **GlobalAddAtom** function adds a string to the system atom table and returns a unique value identifying the string.

Parameters   *lpszString*
Points to the null-terminated string to be added. The case of the first string added is preserved and returned by the **GlobalGetAtomName** function. Strings that differ only in case are considered identical.

Return Value   The return value identifies the string if the function is successful. Otherwise, it is zero.

Comments   If the string exists already in the system atom table, the atom for the existing string will be returned and the atom's reference count will be incremented (increased by one). The string associated with the atom will not be deleted from memory until its reference count is zero. For more information, see the description of the **Global-DeleteAtom** function.

Global atoms are not deleted automatically when the application terminates. For every call to the **GlobalAddAtom** function, there must be a corresponding call to the **GlobalDeleteAtom** function.

Example   The following example adds the string "This is a global atom" to the system atom table:

```
ATOM atom;
char szMsg[80];

atom = GlobalAddAtom("This is a global atom");

if (atom == 0)
    MessageBox(hwnd, "GlobalAddAtom failed", "",
        MB_ICONSTOP);
```

```
else {
    wsprintf(szMsg, "GlobalAddAtom returned %u", atom);
    MessageBox(hwnd, szMsg, "", MB_OK);
}
```

See Also   **AddAtom, GlobalDeleteAtom, GlobalGetAtomName**

GlobalAlloc   2.x

HGLOBAL GlobalAlloc(*fuAlloc, cbAlloc*)
UINT *fuAlloc*;   /* how to allocate object   */
DWORD *cbAlloc*;   /* size of object   */

The **GlobalAlloc** function allocates the specified number of bytes from the global heap.

Parameters   *fuAlloc*
Specifies how to allocate memory. This parameter can be a combination of the following values:

Value	Meaning
GHND	Combines the GMEM_MOVEABLE and GMEM_ZEROINIT flags.
GMEM_DDESHARE	Allocates sharable memory. This flag is used for dynamic data exchange (DDE) only. This flag is equivalent to GMEM_SHARE.
GMEM_DISCARDABLE	Allocates discardable memory. This flag can only be used with the GMEM_MOVEABLE flag.
GMEM_FIXED	Allocates fixed memory. The GMEM_FIXED and GMEM_MOVEABLE flags cannot be combined.
GMEM_LOWER	Same as GMEM_NOT_BANKED. This flag is ignored in Windows 3.1.
GMEM_MOVEABLE	Allocates movable memory. The GMEM_FIXED and GMEM_MOVEABLE flags cannot be combined.
GMEM_NOCOMPACT	Does not compact or discard memory to satisfy the allocation request.
GMEM_NODISCARD	Does not discard memory to satisfy the allocation request.
GMEM_NOT_BANKED	Allocates non-banked memory (memory is not within the memory provided by expanded memory). This flag cannot be used with the GMEM_NOTIFY flag. This flag is ignored in Windows 3.1.

Value	Meaning
GMEM_NOTIFY	Calls the notification routine if the memory object is discarded.
GMEM_SHARE	Allocates memory that can be shared with other applications. This flag is equivalent to GMEM_DDESHARE.
GMEM_ZEROINIT	Initializes memory contents to zero.
GPTR	Combines the GMEM_FIXED and GMEM_ZEROINIT flags.

cbAlloc
Specifies the number of bytes to be allocated.

Return Value   The return value is the handle of the newly allocated global memory object, if the function is successful. Otherwise, it is NULL.

Comments   To convert the handle returned by the **GlobalAlloc** function into a pointer, an application should use the **GlobalLock** function.

If this function is successful, it allocates at least the amount requested. If the amount allocated is greater than the amount requested, the application can use the entire amount. To determine the size of a global memory object, an application can use the **GlobalSize** function.

To free a global memory object, an application should use the **GlobalFree** function. To change the size or attributes of an allocated memory object, an application can use the **GlobalReAlloc** function.

The largest memory object that an application can allocate on an 80286 processor is 1 megabyte less 80 bytes. The largest block on an 80386 processor is 16 megabytes less 64K.

If the *cbAlloc* parameter is zero, the **GlobalAlloc** function returns a handle of a memory object that is marked as discarded.

Example   The following example uses the **GlobalAlloc** and **GlobalLock** functions to allocate memory, and then calls the **GlobalUnlock** and **GlobalFree** functions to free it.

```
HGLOBAL hglb;
void FAR* lpvBuffer;

hglb = GlobalAlloc(GPTR, 1024);
lpvBuffer = GlobalLock(hglb);
        .
        .
        .
GlobalUnlock(hglb);
GlobalFree(hglb);
```

See Also   **GlobalFree, GlobalLock, GlobalNotify, GlobalReAlloc, GlobalSize, LocalAlloc**

GlobalCompact   2.x

DWORD GlobalCompact(*dwMinFree*)
DWORD *dwMinFree*;   /* amount of memory requested   */

The **GlobalCompact** function rearranges memory currently allocated to the global heap so that the specified amount of memory is free. If the function cannot free the requested amount of memory, it frees as much as possible.

Parameters   *dwMinFree*
Specifies the number of contiguous free bytes desired. If this parameter is zero, the function does not discard memory, but the return value is valid.

Return Value   The return value specifies the number of bytes in the largest free global memory object in the global heap. If the *dwMinFree* parameter is zero, the return value specifies the number of bytes in the largest free object that Windows can generate if it removes all discardable objects.

Comments   If an application passes the return value to the **GlobalAlloc** function, the GMEM_NOCOMPACT or GMEM_NODISCARD flag should not be used.

This function always rearranges movable memory objects before checking for free memory. Then it checks the memory currently allocated to the global heap for the number of contiguous free bytes specified by the *dwMinFree* parameter. If the specified amount of memory is not available, the function discards unlocked discardable objects, until the requested space is generated (if possible).

See Also   **GlobalAlloc**

GlobalDeleteAtom

2.x

ATOM GlobalDeleteAtom(*atm*)
ATOM *atm*;   /* atom to delete   */

The **GlobalDeleteAtom** function decrements (decreases by one) the reference count of a global atom. If the atom's reference count reaches zero, the string associated with the atom is removed from the system atom table.

Parameters   *atm*
                    Identifies the atom to be deleted.

Return Value   The return value is zero if the function is successful. The return value is equal to the *atm* parameter if the function failed to decrement the reference count for the specified atom.

Comments   An atom's reference count specifies the number of times the string has been added to the atom table. The **GlobalAddAtom** function increments (increases by one) the reference count each time it is called with a string that already exists in the system atom table.

                    The only way to ensure that an atom has been deleted from the atom table is to call this function repeatedly until it fails. When the count is decremented to zero, the next **GlobalFindAtom** or **GlobalDeleteAtom** function call will fail.

Example   The following example repeatedly calls the **GlobalDeleteAtom** function to decrement the reference count for the atom until the atom is deleted and the **Global-DeleteAtom** function does not return zero:

```
int cRef;
ATOM atom;
char szMsg[80];

for (cRef = 0; ((atom = GlobalFindAtom("This is a global atom")) != 0);
        cRef++)
    GlobalDeleteAtom(atom);

wsprintf(szMsg, "reference count was %d", cRef);
MessageBox(hwnd, szMsg, "GlobalDeleteAtom", MB_OK);
```

See Also   **DeleteAtom, GlobalAddAtom, GlobalFindAtom**

GlobalDosAlloc

DWORD GlobalDosAlloc(*cbAlloc*)
DWORD *cbAlloc*;   /* number of bytes to allocate   */

The **GlobalDosAlloc** function allocates global memory that can be accessed by MS-DOS running in real mode. The memory is guaranteed to exist in the first megabyte of linear address space.

An application should not use this function unless it is absolutely necessary, because the memory pool from which the object is allocated is a scarce system resource.

Parameters   *cbAlloc*
Specifies the number of bytes to be allocated.

Return Value   The return value contains a paragraph-segment value in its high-order word and a selector in its low-order word. An application can use the paragraph-segment value to access memory in real mode and the selector to access memory in protected mode. If Windows cannot allocate a block of memory of the requested size, the return value is zero.

Comments   Memory allocated by using the **GlobalDosAlloc** function does not need to be locked by using the **GlobalLock** function.

See Also   **GlobalDosFree**

GlobalDosFree

UINT GlobalDosFree(*uSelector*)
UINT *uSelector*;   /* memory to free   */

The **GlobalDosFree** function frees a global memory object previously allocated by the **GlobalDosAlloc** function.

Parameters   *uSelector*
Identifies the memory object to be freed.

Return Value   The return value is zero if the function is successful. Otherwise, it is equal to the *uSelector* parameter.

See Also   **GlobalDosAlloc**

GlobalEntryHandle   3.1

#include <toolhelp.h>

BOOL GlobalEntryHandle(*lpge*, *hglb***)**
GLOBALENTRY FAR* *lpge*;   /* address of structure for object   */
HGLOBAL *hglb*;   /* handle of item   */

The **GlobalEntryHandle** function fills the specified structure with information that describes the given global memory object.

Parameters   *lpge*
Points to a **GLOBALENTRY** structure that receives information about the global memory object. The **GLOBALENTRY** structure has the following form:

```
#include <toolhelp.h>

typedef struct tagGLOBALENTRY {  /* ge */
    DWORD   dwSize;
    DWORD   dwAddress;
    DWORD   dwBlockSize;
    HGLOBAL hBlock;
    WORD    wcLock;
    WORD    wcPageLock;
    WORD    wFlags;
    BOOL    wHeapPresent;
    HGLOBAL hOwner;
    WORD    wType;
    WORD    wData;
    DWORD   dwNext;
    DWORD   dwNextAlt;
} GLOBALENTRY;
```

For a full description of this structure, see the *Microsoft Windows Programmer's Reference, Volume 3*.

hglb
Identifies the global memory object to be described.

Return Value   The return value is nonzero if the function is successful. Otherwise, it is zero. The function fails if the *hglb* value is an invalid handle or selector.

Comments   This function retrieves information about a global memory handle or selector. Debuggers use this function to obtain the segment number of a segment loaded from an executable file.

Before calling the **GlobalEntryHandle** function, an application must initialize the **GLOBALENTRY** structure and specify its size, in bytes, in the **dwSize** member.

See Also   **GlobalEntryModule, GlobalFirst, GlobalInfo, GlobalNext**

GlobalEntryModule   3.1

#include <toolhelp.h>

BOOL GlobalEntryModule(*lpge*, *hmod*, *wSeg*)
GLOBALENTRY FAR* *lpge*;   /* address of structure for segment   */
HMODULE *hmod*;   /* handle of module   */
WORD *wSeg*;   /* segment to describe   */

The **GlobalEntryModule** function fills the specified structure by *lpge* with information about the specified module segment.

Parameters   *lpge*
Points to a **GLOBALENTRY** structure that receives information about the segment specified in the *wSeg* parameter. The **GLOBALENTRY** structure has the following form:

```
#include <toolhelp.h>

typedef struct tagGLOBALENTRY {   /* ge */
    DWORD   dwSize;
    DWORD   dwAddress;
    DWORD   dwBlockSize;
    HGLOBAL hBlock;
    WORD    wcLock;
    WORD    wcPageLock;
    WORD    wFlags;
    BOOL    wHeapPresent;
    HGLOBAL hOwner;
```

```
        WORD    wType;
        WORD    wData;
        DWORD   dwNext;
        DWORD   dwNextAlt;
} GLOBALENTRY;
```

For a full description of this structure, see the *Microsoft Windows Programmer's Reference, Volume 3.*

hmod
Identifies the module that owns the segment.

wSeg
Specifies the segment to be described in the **GLOBALENTRY** structure. The number of the first segment in the module is 1. Segment numbers are always contiguous, so if the last valid segment number is 10, all segment numbers 1 through 10 are also valid.

Return Value   The return value is nonzero if the function is successful. Otherwise, it is zero. This function fails if the segment in the *wSeg* parameter does not exist in the module specified in the *hmod* parameter.

Comments   Debuggers can use the **GlobalEntryModule** function to retrieve global heap information about a specific segment loaded from an executable file. Typically, the debugger will have symbols that refer to segment numbers; this function translates the segment numbers to heap information.

Before calling **GlobalEntryModule**, an application must initialize the **GLOBALENTRY** structure and specify its size, in bytes, in the **dwSize** member.

See Also   **GlobalEntryHandle, GlobalFirst, GlobalInfo, GlobalNext**

GlobalFindAtom   2.x

ATOM GlobalFindAtom(*lpszString*)
LPCSTR *lpszString*;   /* address of string to find   */

The **GlobalFindAtom** function searches the system atom table for the specified character string and retrieves the global atom associated with that string. (A global atom is an atom that is available to all Windows applications.)

Parameters   *lpszString*
Points to the null-terminated character string to search for.

Return Value	The return value identifies the global atom associated with the given string, if the function is successful. Otherwise, if the string is not in the table, the return value is zero.

Example	The following example repeatedly calls the **GlobalFindAtom** function to retrieve the atom associated with the string "This is a global atom". The example uses the **GlobalDeleteAtom** function to decrement (decrease by one) the reference count for the atom until the atom is deleted and **GlobalFindAtom** returns zero.

```
int cRef;
ATOM atom;
char szMsg[80];

for (cRef = 0; ((atom = GlobalFindAtom("This is a global atom")) != 0);
        cRef++)
    GlobalDeleteAtom(atom);

wsprintf(szMsg, "reference count was %d", cRef);
MessageBox(hwnd, szMsg, "GlobalDeleteAtom", MB_OK);
```

See Also	**FindAtom, GlobalAddAtom, GlobalDeleteAtom**

# GlobalFirst	3.1

#include <toolhelp.h>

BOOL GlobalFirst(*lpge*, *wFlags***)**
GLOBALENTRY FAR* *lpge*;	/* address of structure for object	*/
WORD *wFlags*;	/* specifies the heap to use	*/

The **GlobalFirst** function fills the specified structure with information that describes the first object on the global heap.

Parameters	*lpge*
Points to a **GLOBALENTRY** structure that receives information about the global memory object. The **GLOBALENTRY** structure has the following form:

```
#include <toolhelp.h>

typedef struct tagGLOBALENTRY {  /* ge */
    DWORD   dwSize;
    DWORD   dwAddress;
    DWORD   dwBlockSize;
    HGLOBAL hBlock;
```

```
        WORD     wcLock;
        WORD     wcPageLock;
        WORD     wFlags;
        BOOL     wHeapPresent;
        HGLOBAL hOwner;
        WORD     wType;
        WORD     wData;
        DWORD    dwNext;
        DWORD    dwNextAlt;
} GLOBALENTRY;
```

For a full description of this structure, see the *Microsoft Windows Programmer's Reference, Volume 3.*

wFlags
Specifies the heap to use. This parameter can be one of the following values:

Value	Meaning
GLOBAL_ALL	Structure pointed to by *lpge* will receive information about the first object on the complete global heap.
GLOBAL_FREE	Structure will receive information about the first object on the free list.
GLOBAL_LRU	Structure will receive information about the first object on the least-recently-used (LRU) list.

Return Value

The return value is nonzero if the function is successful. Otherwise, it is zero.

Comments

The **GlobalFirst** function can be used to begin a global heap walk. An application can examine subsequent objects on the global heap by using the **GlobalNext** function. Calls to **GlobalNext** must have the same *wFlags* value as that specified in **GlobalFirst**.

Before calling **GlobalFirst**, an application must initialize the **GLOBALENTRY** structure and specify its size, in bytes, in the **dwSize** member.

See Also

GlobalEntryHandle, GlobalEntryModule, GlobalInfo, GlobalNext

GlobalFix
3.0

void GlobalFix(*hglb*)
HGLOBAL *hglb*;   /* handle of object to fix   */

The **GlobalFix** function prevents the given global memory object from moving in linear memory.

This function interferes with effective Windows memory management and can result in linear-address fragmentation. Few applications need to fix memory in linear address space.

Parameters   *hglb*
Identifies the global memory object to be fixed in linear memory.

Return Value   This function does not return a value.

Comments   The object is locked into linear memory at its current address, and its lock count is incremented (increased by one). Locked memory is not subject to moving or discarding except when the memory object is being reallocated by the **Global-ReAlloc** function. The object remains locked in memory until its lock count is decreased to zero.

Each time an application calls the **GlobalFix** function for a memory object, it must eventually call the **GlobalUnfix** function, which decrements (decreases by one) the lock count for the object. Other functions also can affect the lock count of a memory object. For a list of these functions, see the description of the **Global-Flags** function.

See Also   **GlobalFlags, GlobalReAlloc, GlobalUnfix**

GlobalFlags   2.x

UINT GlobalFlags(*hglb***)**
HGLOBAL *hglb*;   /* handle of global memory object   */

The **GlobalFlags** function returns information about the given global memory object.

Parameters   *hglb*
Identifies the global memory object.

Return Value   The return value specifies the memory-allocation flag and the lock count for the memory object, if the function is successful.

Comments   When an application masks out the lock count in the low-order byte of the return value, the return value contains one of the following allocation flags:

Value	Meaning
GMEM_DISCARDABLE	Object can be discarded.
GMEM_DISCARDED	Object has been discarded.

The low-order byte of the return value contains the lock count of the object. Use the GMEM_LOCKCOUNT mask to retrieve the lock count from the return value.

The following functions can affect the lock count of a global memory object:

Increments lock count	Decrements lock count
GlobalFix	**GlobalUnfix**
GlobalLock	**GlobalUnlock**

See Also   **GlobalFix, GlobalLock, GlobalUnfix, GlobalUnlock**

GlobalFree

2.x

HGLOBAL GlobalFree(*hglb***)**
HGLOBAL *hglb*;   /* handle of object to free   */

The **GlobalFree** function frees the given global memory object (if the object is not locked) and invalidates its handle.

Parameters   *hglb*
    Identifies the global memory object to be freed.

Return Value   The return value is NULL if the function is successful. Otherwise, it is equal to the *hglb* parameter.

Comments   The **GlobalFree** function cannot be used to free a locked memory object—that is, a memory object with a lock count greater than zero. For a list of the functions that affect the lock count, see the description of the **GlobalFlags** function.

Once freed, the handle of the memory object must not be used again. Attempting to free the same memory object more than once can cause Windows to terminate abnormally.

See Also   **GlobalDiscard, GlobalFlags, GlobalLock**

GlobalGetAtomName

UINT GlobalGetAtomName(*atom*, *lpszBuffer*, *cbBuffer*)
ATOM *atom*;   /* atom identifier   */
LPSTR *lpszBuffer*;   /* address of buffer for atom string   */
int *cbBuffer*;   /* size of buffer   */

The **GlobalGetAtomName** function retrieves a copy of the character string associated with the given global atom. (A global atom is an atom that is available to all Windows applications.)

Parameters
atom
Identifies the global atom associated with the character string to be retrieved.

lpszBuffer
Points to the buffer for the character string.

cbBuffer
Specifies the size, in bytes, of the buffer.

Return Value
The return value specifies the number of bytes copied to the buffer, not including the terminating null character, if the function is successful.

Example
The following example uses the **GlobalGetAtomName** function to retrieve the character string associated with a global atom:

```
char szBuf[80];

GlobalGetAtomName(atGlobal, szBuf, sizeof(szBuf));

MessageBox(hwnd, szBuf, "GlobalGetAtomName", MB_OK);
```

GlobalHandle

DWORD GlobalHandle(*uGlobalSel*)
UINT *uGlobalSel*;   /* selector of global memory object   */

The **GlobalHandle** function retrieves the handle of the specified global memory object.

Parameters
uGlobalSel
Specifies the selector of a global memory object.

Return Value   The low-order word of the return value contains the handle of the global memory object, and the high-order word contains the selector of the memory object, if the function is successful. The return value is NULL if no handle exists for the memory object.

GlobalHandleToSel   3.1

#include <toolhelp.h>

WORD GlobalHandleToSel(*hglb*)
HGLOBAL *hglb*;

The **GlobalHandleToSel** function converts the given handle to a selector.

Parameters   *hglb*
                   Identifies the global memory object to be converted.

Return Value   The return value is the selector of the given object if the function is successful. Otherwise, it is zero.

Comments   The **GlobalHandleToSel** function converts a global handle to a selector appropriate for Windows, version 3.0 or 3.1, depending on which version is running. A debugging application might use this selector to access a global memory object if the object is not discardable or if the object's attributes are irrelevant.

See Also   **GlobalAlloc**

GlobalInfo   3.1

#include <toolhelp.h>

BOOL GlobalInfo(*lpgi*)
GLOBALINFO FAR* *lpgi*;   /* address of global-heap structure   */

The **GlobalInfo** function fills the specified structure with information that describes the global heap.

Parameters   *lpgi*
Points to a **GLOBALINFO** structure that receives information about the global heap. The **GLOBALINFO** structure has the following form:

```
#include <toolhelp.h>

typedef struct tagGLOBALINFO {  /* gi */
    DWORD dwSize;
    WORD  wcItems;
    WORD  wcItemsFree;
    WORD  wcItemsLRU;
} GLOBALINFO;
```

For a full description of this structure, see the *Microsoft Windows Programmer's Reference, Volume 3*.

Return Value   The return value is nonzero if the function successful. Otherwise, it is zero.

Comments   The information in the structure can be used to determine how much memory to allocate for a global heap walk.

Before calling the **GlobalInfo** function, an application must initialize the **GLOBALINFO** structure and specify its size, in bytes, in the **dwSize** member.

See Also   **GlobalEntryHandle, GlobalEntryModule, GlobalFirst, GlobalNext**

GlobalLock

2.x

void FAR* GlobalLock(*hglb***)**
HGLOBAL *hglb*;   /* handle of memory object to lock   */

The **GlobalLock** function returns a pointer to the given global memory object. **GlobalLock** increments (increases by one) the lock count of movable objects and locks the memory. Locked memory will not be moved or discarded unless the memory object is reallocated by the **GlobalReAlloc** function. The object remains locked in memory until its lock count is decreased to zero.

Parameters   *hglb*
Identifies the global memory object to be locked.

Return Value   The return value points to the first byte of memory in the global object, if the function is successful. It is NULL if the object has been discarded or an error occurs.

Comments   Each time an application calls the **GlobalLock** function for an object, it must eventually call the **GlobalUnlock** function for the object.

This function will return NULL if an application attempts to lock a memory object with a zero-byte size.

If **GlobalLock** incremented the lock count for the object, **GlobalUnlock** decrements the lock count for the object. Other functions can also affect the lock count of a memory object. For a list of these functions, see the description of the **GetGlobalFlags** function.

Discarded objects always have a lock count of zero.

See Also   **GlobalFlags, GlobalReAlloc, GlobalUnlock**

GlobalLRUNewest   2.x

HGLOBAL GlobalLRUNewest(*hglb***)**
HGLOBAL *hglb*;   /* handle of memory object to move   */

The **GlobalLRUNewest** function moves a global memory object to the newest least-recently-used (LRU) position in memory. This greatly reduces the likelihood that the object will be discarded soon, but does not prevent the object from eventually being discarded.

Parameters   *hglb*
                   Identifies the global memory object to be moved.

Return Value   The return value is NULL if the *hglb* parameter is not a valid handle.

Comments   The **GlobalLRUNewest** function is useful only if the given object is discardable.

See Also   **GlobalLRUOldest**

GlobalLRUOldest

HGLOBAL GlobalLRUOldest(*hglb*)
HGLOBAL *hglb*;   /* handle of memory object to move   */

The **GlobalLRUOldest** function moves a global memory object to the oldest least-recently-used (LRU) position in memory. This makes the memory object the next candidate for discarding.

Parameters   *hglb*
Identifies the global memory object to be moved.

Return Value   The return value is NULL if the *hglb* parameter does not identify a valid handle.

Comments   The **GlobalLRUOldest** function is useful only if the *hglb* object is discardable.

See Also   **GlobalLRUNewest**

GlobalNext

#include <toolhelp.h>

BOOL GlobalNext(*lpge*, *flags*)
GLOBALENTRY FAR* *lpge*;   /* address of structure for object   */
WORD *flags*;   /* heap to use   */

The **GlobalNext** function fills the specified structure with information that describes the next object on the global heap.

Parameters   *lpge*
Points to a **GLOBALENTRY** structure that receives information about the global memory object. The **GLOBALENTRY** structure has the following form:

```
#include <toolhelp.h>

typedef struct tagGLOBALENTRY {  /* ge */
    DWORD   dwSize;
    DWORD   dwAddress;
    DWORD   dwBlockSize;
    HGLOBAL hBlock;
    WORD    wcLock;
    WORD    wcPageLock;
```

```
         WORD     wFlags;
         BOOL     wHeapPresent;
         HGLOBAL  hOwner;
         WORD     wType;
         WORD     wData;
         DWORD    dwNext;
         DWORD    dwNextAlt;
     } GLOBALENTRY;
```

For a full description of this structure, see the *Microsoft Windows Programmer's Reference, Volume 3*.

flags

Specifies heap to use. This parameter can be one of the following values:

Value	Meaning
GLOBAL_ALL	Structure pointed by the *lpge* parameter will receive information about the first object on the complete global heap.
GLOBAL_FREE	Structure will receive information about the first object on the free list.
GLOBAL_LRU	Structure will receive information about the first object on the least-recently-used (LRU) list.

Return Value

The return value is nonzero if the function is successful. Otherwise, it is zero.

Comments

The **GlobalNext** function can be used to continue a global heap walk started by the **GlobalFirst**, **GlobalEntryHandle**, or **GlobalEntryModule** functions.

If **GlobalFirst** starts a heap walk, the *flags* value used in **GlobalNext** must be the same as the value used in **GlobalFirst**.

See Also

GlobalEntryHandle, GlobalEntryModule, GlobalFirst, GlobalInfo

---

GlobalNotify

2.x

void GlobalNotify(*lpNotifyProc***)**
GNOTIFYPROC *lpNotifyProc*;   /* instance address of callback function   */

The **GlobalNotify** function installs a notification procedure for the current task. A notification procedure is a library-defined callback function that the system calls whenever a global memory object allocated with the GMEM_NOTIFY flag is about to be discarded.

Parameters   *lpNotifyProc*
Specifies the address of the current task's notification procedure. For more information, see the description of the **NotifyProc** callback function.

Return Value   This function does not return a value.

Comments   An application must not call the **GlobalNotify** function more than once per instance.

The system does not call the notification procedure when discarding memory that belongs to a dynamic-link library (DLL).

If the object is discarded, the application must use the GMEM_NOTIFY flag when it calls the **GlobalRealloc** function to recreate the object. Otherwise, the application will not be notified when the object is discarded again.

If the notification procedure returns a nonzero value, Windows discards the global memory object. If the procedure returns zero, the block is not discarded.

The address of the **NotifyProc** callback function (specified in the *lpNotifyProc* parameter) must be in a fixed code segment of a dynamic-link library.

See Also   **GlobalReAlloc**, **NotifyProc**

GlobalPageLock

3.0

UINT GlobalPageLock(*hglb*)
HGLOBAL *hglb*;   /* selector of global memory to lock   */

The **GlobalPageLock** function increments (increases by one) the page-lock count for the memory associated with the given global selector. As long as its page-lock count is nonzero, the data that the selector references is guaranteed to remain in memory at the same physical address.

Parameters   *hglb*
Specifies the selector of the memory to be page-locked.

Return Value   The return value specifies the page-lock count after the function has incremented it. If the function fails, the return value is zero.

Comments   Because using this function violates preferred Windows programming practices, an application should not use it unless absolutely necessary. The function is intended to be used for dynamically allocated data that must be accessed at interrupt time. For this reason, it must be called only from a dynamic-link library (DLL).

The **GlobalPageLock** function increments the page-lock count for the block of memory, and the **GlobalPageUnlock** function decrements (decreases by one) the page-lock count. Page-locking operations can be nested, but each page-locking must be balanced by a corresponding unlocking.

See Also   **GlobalPageUnlock**

GlobalPageUnlock   3.0

UINT GlobalPageUnlock(*hglb***)**
HGLOBAL *hglb*;   /* selector of global memory to unlock   */

The **GlobalPageLock** function decrements (decreases by one) the page-lock count for the memory associated with the specified global selector. When the page-lock count reaches zero, the data that the selector references is no longer guaranteed to remain in memory at the same physical address.

Parameters   *hglb*
                         Specifies the selector of the memory to be page-unlocked.

Return Value   The return value specifies the page-lock count after the function has decremented it. If the function fails, the return value is zero.

Comments   Because using this function violates preferred Windows programming practices, an application should not use it unless absolutely necessary. The function is intended to be used for dynamically allocated data that must be accessed at interrupt time. For this reason, it must only be called from a dynamic-link library (DLL).

The **GlobalPageLock** function increments the page-lock count for the block of memory, and the **GlobalPageUnlock** function decrements the page-lock count. Page-locking operations can be nested, but each page-locking must be balanced by a corresponding unlocking.

See Also   **GlobalPageLock**

GlobalReAlloc

HGLOBAL GlobalReAlloc(*hglb*, *cbNewSize*, *fuAlloc*)
HGLOBAL *hglb*;   /* handle of memory object to reallocate   */
DWORD *cbNewSize*;   /* new size of object   */
UINT *fuAlloc*;   /* how object is reallocated   */

The **GlobalReAlloc** function changes the size or attributes of the given global memory object.

Parameters

hglb
Identifies the global memory object to be reallocated.

cbNewSize
Specifies the new size of the memory object.

fuAlloc
Specifies how to reallocate the global object. If this parameter includes GMEM_MODIFY, the **GlobalReAlloc** function ignores the *cbNewSize* parameter.

Value	Meaning
GMEM_DISCARDABLE	Causes a previously movable object to become discardable. This flag can be used only with GMEM_MODIFY.
GMEM_MODIFY	Modifies the object's memory flags. This flag can be used with GMEM_DISCARDABLE and GMEM_MOVEABLE.
GMEM_MOVEABLE	Causes a previously movable and discardable object to be discarded, if the *cbNewSize* parameter is zero and the object's lock count is zero. If *cbNewSize* is zero and the object is not movable and discardable, this flag causes the **GlobalReAlloc** function to fail.
	If *cbNewSize* is nonzero and the object identified by the *hglb* parameter is fixed, this flag allows the reallocated object to be moved to a new fixed location.
	If a movable object is locked, this flag allows the object to be moved to a new locked location without invalidating the handle. This may occur even if the object is currently locked by a previous call to the **GlobalLock** function.
	If this flag is used with GMEM_MODIFY, the **GlobalReAlloc** function changes a fixed memory object to a movable memory object.
GMEM_NODISCARD	Prevents memory from being discarded to satisfy the allocation request. This flag cannot be used with GMEM_MODIFY.

Value	Meaning
GMEM_ZEROINIT	Causes the additional memory to be initialized to zero if the object is growing. This flag cannot be used with GMEM_MODIFY.

Return Value

The return value is the handle of the reallocated global memory if the function is successful. It is NULL if the object cannot be reallocated as specified.

Comments

If **GlobalReAlloc** reallocates a movable object, the return value is a handle to the memory. To access the memory, an application must use the **GlobalLock** function to convert the handle to a pointer.

To free a global memory object, an application should use the **GlobalFree** function.

The GMEM_ZEROINIT flag will cause applications to fail if it is used as shown in the following sequence:

```
hMem = GlobalAlloc(GMEM_ZEROINIT | (other flags), dwSize1);
        .
        .
        .
hMem = GlobalReAlloc(hMem, dwSize2, GMEM_ZEROINIT | (other flags));

/* where dwSize2 > dwSize1. */
        .
        .
        .
hMem = GlobalReAlloc(hMem, dwSize3, GMEM_ZEROINIT | (other flags));

/* where dwSize3 < dwSize2. */
        .
        .
        .
hMem = GlobalReAlloc(hMem, dwSize4, GMEM_ZEROINIT | (other flags));

/* GMEM_ZEROINIT fails when dwSize4 > dwSize3. */
```

In the last step of the preceding example, the memory between dwSize3 and the internal allocation boundary is not set to zero. After the last step, the contents of the buffer equal its contents prior to the call to **GlobalReAlloc** that specified dwSize3.

See Also

GlobalAlloc, GlobalDiscard, GlobalFree, GlobalLock

GlobalSize

DWORD **GlobalSize**(*hglb*)
HGLOBAL *hglb*;   /* handle of memory object to return size of   */

The **GlobalSize** function retrieves the current size, in bytes, of the given global memory object.

Parameters   *hglb*
Identifies the global memory object.

Return Value   The return value specifies the size, in bytes, of the memory object. It is zero if the specified handle is not valid or if the object has been discarded.

Comments   The size of a memory object is sometimes larger than the size requested at the time the memory was allocated.

An application should call the **GlobalFlags** function prior to calling the **GlobalSize** function, to verify that the specified memory object was not discarded. If the memory object has been discarded, the return value for **GlobalSize** is meaningless.

See Also   **GlobalAlloc**, **GlobalFlags**

GlobalUnfix

void **GlobalUnfix**(*hglb*)
HGLOBAL *hglb*;   /* handle of global memory to unlock   */

The **GlobalUnfix** function cancels the effects of the **GlobalFix** function and allows a global memory object to be moved in linear memory.

Parameters   *hglb*
Identifies the global memory object to be unlocked.

Return Value   This function does not return a value.

Comments   This function interferes with effective Windows memory management and can result in linear-address fragmentation. Few applications need to fix memory in linear address space.

Each time an application calls the **GlobalFix** function for an object, it must eventually call the **GlobalUnfix** function for the object.

GlobalUnfix decrements (decreases by one) the object's lock count and returns the new lock count in the CX register. The object is completely unlocked and subject to moving or discarding if the lock count is decremented to zero. Other functions also can affect the lock count of a memory object. For a list of these functions, see the description of the **GlobalFlags** function.

See Also   **GlobalFix, GlobalFlags**

GlobalUnlock   2.x

BOOL GlobalUnlock(*hglb*)
HGLOBAL *hglb*;   /* handle of global memory to unlock   */

The **GlobalUnlock** function unlocks the given global memory object. This function has no effect on fixed memory.

Parameters   *hglb*
                Identifies the global memory object to be unlocked.

Return Value   The return value is zero if the object's lock count was decremented (decreased by one) to zero. Otherwise, the return value is nonzero.

Comments   With movable or discardable memory, this function decrements the object's lock count. The object is completely unlocked and subject to moving or discarding if the lock count is decreased to zero.

                This function returns nonzero if the given memory object is not movable. An application should not rely on the return value to determine the number of times it must subsequently call the **GlobalUnlock** function for the memory object.

                Other functions can also affect the lock count of a memory object. For a list of the functions that affect the lock count, see the description of the **GlobalFlags** function.

                Each time an application calls **GlobalLock** for an object, it must eventually call the **GlobalUnlock** function for the object.

See Also   **GlobalFlags, GlobalLock, UnlockResource**

GlobalUnWire

2.x

BOOL GlobalUnWire(*hglb*)
HGLOBAL *hglb*;

This function should not be used in Windows 3.1.

See Also   **GlobalUnlock**

GlobalWire

2.x

void FAR* GlobalWire(*hglb*)
HGLOBAL *hglb*;

This function should not be used in Windows 3.1.

See Also   **GlobalLock**

GrayString

2.x

```
BOOL GrayString(hdc, hbr, gsprc, lParam, cch, x, y, cx, cy)
HDC hdc;                    /* handle of device context              */
HBRUSH hbr;                 /* handle of brush for graying           */
GRAYSTRINGPROC gsprc;       /* address of callback function          */
LPARAM lParam;              /* address of application-defined data    */
int cch;                    /* number of characters to output         */
int x;                      /* horizontal position                   */
int y;                      /* vertical position                      */
int cx;                     /* width                                 */
int cy;                     /* height                                */
```

The **GrayString** function draws gray (dim) text at the given location by writing the text in a memory bitmap, graying the bitmap, and then copying the bitmap to the display. The function grays the text regardless of the selected brush and background. **GrayString** uses the font currently selected for the given device context.

Parameters   *hdc*
Identifies the device context.

hbr

Identifies the brush to be used for graying.

gsprc

Specifies the procedure-instance address of the application-supplied callback function that will draw the string. The address must be created by the **Make-ProcInstance** function. For more information about the callback function, see the description of the **GrayStringProc** callback function.

If this parameter is NULL, the system uses the **TextOut** function to draw the string, and the *lParam* parameter is assumed to be a long pointer to the character string to be output.

lParam

Points to data to be passed to the output function. If the *gsprc* parameter is NULL, the *lParam* parameter must point to the string to be output.

cch

Specifies the number of characters to be output. If this parameter is zero, the **GrayString** function calculates the length of the string (assuming that the *lParam* parameter is a pointer to the string). If *cch* is −1 and the function pointed to by the *gsprc* parameter returns zero, the image is shown but not grayed.

x

Specifies the logical x-coordinate of the starting position of the rectangle that encloses the string.

y

Specifies the logical y-coordinate of the starting position of the rectangle that encloses the string.

cx

Specifies the width, in logical units, of the rectangle that encloses the string. If this parameter is zero, the **GrayString** function calculates the width of the area, assuming the *lParam* parameter is a pointer to the string.

cy

Specifies the height, in logical units, of the rectangle that encloses the string. If this parameter is zero, the **GrayString** function calculates the height of the area, assuming the *lParam* parameter is a pointer to the string.

Return Value   The return value is nonzero if the function is successful. It is zero if either the **TextOut** function or the application-supplied output function returns zero, or if there is insufficient memory to create a memory bitmap for graying.

Comments   An application must select the MM_TEXT mapping mode before using this function.

If **TextOut** cannot handle the string to be output (for example, if the string is stored as a bitmap), the *gsprc* parameter must point to a callback function that will draw the string.

An application can draw grayed strings on devices that support a solid gray color without calling the **GrayString** function. The system color COLOR_GRAYTEXT is the solid-gray system color used to draw disabled text. The application can call the **GetSysColor** function to retrieve the color value of COLOR_GRAYTEXT. If the color is other than zero (black), the application can call the **SetTextColor** function to set the text color to the color value and then draw the string directly. If the retrieved color is black, the application must call **GrayString** to gray the text.

See Also   **GetSysColor, MakeProcInstance, SetTextColor, TextOut**

GrayStringProc   2.x

BOOL CALLBACK GrayStringProc(*hdc*, *lpData*, *cch*)
HDC *hdc*;   /* handle of device context   */
LPARAM *lpData*;   /* address of string to be drawn   */
int *cch*;   /* length of string to be drawn   */

The **GrayStringProc** function is an application-defined callback function that draws a string as a result of a call to the **GrayString** function.

Parameters   *hdc*
Identifies a device context with a bitmap of at least the width and height specified by the *cx* and *cy* parameters passed to the **GrayString** function.

lpData
Points to the string to be drawn.

cch
Specifies the length, in characters, of the string.

Return Value   The callback function should return TRUE to indicate success. Otherwise it should return FALSE.

Comments   The callback function must draw an image relative to the coordinates (0,0).

GrayStringProc is a placeholder for the application-defined function name. The actual name must be exported by including it in an **EXPORTS** statement in the application's module-definition (.DEF) file.

See Also   **GrayString**

HardwareProc

LRESULT CALLBACK HardwareProc(*code*, *wParam*, *lParam*)
int *code*;   /* hook code   */
WPARAM *wParam*;   /* undefined   */
LPARAM *lParam*;   /* address of structure with event information */

The **HardwareProc** function is an application-defined callback function that the system calls whenever the application calls the **GetMessage** or **PeekMessage** function and there is a hardware event to process. Mouse events and keyboard events are not processed by this hook.

Parameters   *code*
Specifies whether the callback function should process the message or call the **CallNextHookEx** function. If this value is less than zero, the callback function should pass the message to **CallNextHookEx** without further processing. If this value is HC_NOREMOVE, the application is using the **PeekMessage** function with the PM_NOREMOVE option, and the message will not be removed from the system queue.

wParam
Specifies a NULL value.

lParam
Points to a **HARDWAREHOOKSTRUCT** structure. The **HARDWARE-HOOKSTRUCT** structure has the following form:

```
typedef struct tagHARDWAREHOOKSTRUCT {   /* hhs */
    HWND    hWnd;
    UINT    wMessage;
    WPARAM  wParam;
    LPARAM  lParam;
} HARDWAREHOOKSTRUCT;
```

For a full description of this structure, see the *Microsoft Windows Programmer's Reference, Volume 3*.

Return Value   The callback function should return zero to allow the system to process the message; it should be 1 if the message is to be discarded.

Comments   This callback function should not install a playback hook because the function cannot use the **GetMessageExtraInfo** function to get the extra information associated with the message.

The callback function must use the Pascal calling convention and must be declared **FAR**. An application must install the callback function by specifying the WH_HARDWARE filter type and the procedure-instance address of the callback function in a call to the **SetWindowsHookEx** function.

HardwareProc is a placeholder for the library-defined function name. The actual name must be exported by including it in an **EXPORTS** statement in the library's module-definition (.DEF) file.

See Also   **CallNextHookEx, GetMessageExtraInfo, SetWindowsHookEx**

hardware_event

3.1

```
extrn hardware_event :far

mov    ax, Msg        ; message
mov    cx, ParamL     ; low-order word of lParam of the message
mov    dx, ParamH     ; high-order word of lParam of the message
mov    si, hwnd       ; handle of the destination window
mov    di, wParam     ; wParam of the message
cCall hardware_event
```

The **hardware_event** function places a hardware-related message into the system message queue. This function allows a driver for a non-standard hardware device to place a message into the queue.

Parameters   *Msg*
Specifies the message to place in the system message queue.

ParamL
Specifies the low-order word of the *lParam* parameter of the message.

lParamH
Specifies the high-order word of the *lParam* parameter of the message.

hwnd
Identifies the window to which the message is directed. This parameter also becomes the low-order word of the *dwExtraInfo* parameter associated with the message. An application can determine the value of this parameter by calling the **GetMessageExtraInfo** function.

wParam
Specifies the *wParam* parameter of the message.

Return Value   The return value is nonzero if the function is successful. Otherwise, it is zero.

Comments   An application should not use this function to place keyboard or mouse messages into the system message queue.

An application may only call the **hardware_ event** function from an assembly language routine. The application must declare the function as follows:

```
extrn hardware_event :far
```

If the application includes CMACROS.INC, the application can declare the function as follows:

```
extrnFP hardware_event.
```

See Also   **GetMessageExtraInfo**

HideCaret   2.x

void HideCaret(*hwnd*)
HWND *hwnd*;   /* handle of window with caret   */

The **HideCaret** function hides the caret by removing it from the screen. Although the caret is no longer visible, it can be displayed again by using the **ShowCaret** function. Hiding the caret does not destroy its current shape.

Parameters   *hwnd*
Identifies the window that owns the caret. This parameter can be set to NULL to specify indirectly the window in the current task that owns the caret.

Return Value   This function does not return a value.

Comments   The **HideCaret** function hides the caret only if the given window owns the caret. If the *hwnd* parameter is NULL, the function hides the caret only if a window in the current task owns the caret.

Hiding is cumulative. If **HideCaret** has been called five times in a row, **Show-Caret** must be called five times before the caret will be shown.

See Also   **CreateCaret, ShowCaret**

HiliteMenuItem

2.x

BOOL HiliteMenuItem(*hwnd*, *hmenu*, *idHiliteItem*, *fuHilite*)
HWND *hwnd*;   /* handle of window with menu   */
HMENU *hmenu*;   /* handle of menu   */
UINT *idHiliteItem*;   /* menu-item identifier   */
UINT *fuHilite*;   /* highlight flags   */

The **HiliteMenuItem** function highlights or removes the highlighting from a top-level (menu-bar) menu item.

Parameters

hwnd
Identifies the window that contains the menu.

hmenu
Identifies the top-level menu that contains the item to be highlighted.

idHiliteItem
Specifies the menu item to be highlighted, as determined by the *fuHilite* parameter.

fuHilite
Specifies whether the menu item is highlighted or the highlight is removed. It can be a combination of the MF_HILITE or MF_UNHILITE value with the MF_BYCOMMAND or MF_BYPOSITION value. These values have the following meanings:

Value	Meaning
MF_BYCOMMAND	Menu-item identifier is specified by the *idHiliteItem* parameter (the default interpretation).
MF_BYPOSITION	Zero-based position of the menu item is specified by the *idHiliteItem* parameter.
MF_HILITE	Menu item is highlighted. If this value is not given, highlighting is removed from the menu item.
MF_UNHILITE	Highlighting is removed from the menu item.

Return Value

The return value is nonzero if the function is successful. Otherwise, it is zero.

Comments

The MF_HILITE and MF_UNHILITE flags can be used only with the **Hilite-MenuItem** function; they cannot be used with the **ModifyMenu** function.

See Also

CheckMenuItem, **EnableMenuItem**, **ModifyMenu**

hmemcpy

void hmemcpy(*hpvDest*, *hpvSource*, *cbCopy*)
void _huge* *hpvDest*;   /* address of destination buffer   */
const void _huge* *hpvSource*;   /* address of source buffer   */
long *cbCopy*;   /* number of bytes to copy   */

The **hmemcpy** function copies bytes from a source buffer to a destination buffer. This function supports huge memory objects (that is, objects larger than 64K, allocated using the **GlobalAlloc** function).

Parameters   *hpvDest*
                     Points to a buffer that receives the copied bytes.

                     hpvSource
                     Points to a buffer that contains the bytes to be copied.

                     cbCopy
                     Specifies the number of bytes to be copied.

Return Value   This function does not return a value.

See Also   **_hread**, **_hwrite**, **lstrcpy**

_hread

long _hread(*hf*, *hpvBuffer*, *cbBuffer*)
HFILE *hf*;   /* file handle   */
void _huge* *hpvBuffer*;   /* address of buffer for read data   */
long *cbBuffer*;   /* length of data buffer   */

The **_hread** function reads data from the specified file. This function supports huge memory objects (that is, objects larger than 64K, allocated using the **GlobalAlloc** function).

Parameters   *hf*
                     Identifies the file to be read.

                     hpvBuffer
                     Points to a buffer that is to receive the data read from the file.

                     cbBuffer
                     Specifies the number of bytes to be read from the file.

Return Value   The return value indicates the number of bytes that the function read from the file, if the function is successful. If the number of bytes read is less than the number specified in *cbBuffer*, the function reached the end of the file (EOF) before reading the specified number of bytes. The return value is –1L if the function fails.

See Also   **_lread, hmemcpy, _hwrite**

_hwrite

3.1

long _hwrite(*hf*, *hpvBuffer*, *cbBuffer*)
HFILE *hf*;   /* file handle   */
const void _huge* *hpvBuffer*;   /* address of buffer for write data   */
long *cbBuffer*;   /* size of data   */

The **_hwrite** function writes data to the specified file. This function supports huge memory objects (that is, objects larger than 64K, allocated using the **GlobalAlloc** function).

Parameters   *hf*
        Identifies the file to be written to.

        hpvBuffer
        Points to a buffer that contains the data to be written to the file.

        cbBuffer
        Specifies the number of bytes to be written to the file.

Return Value   The return value indicates the number of bytes written to the file, if the function is successful. Otherwise, the return value is –1L.

Comments   MS-DOS error values are not available when an application calls this function.

See Also   **hmemcpy, _hread, _lwrite**

InflateRect

void InflateRect(*lprc***,** *xAmt***,** *yAmt***)**
RECT FAR* *lprc*;   /* address of rectangle   */
int *xAmt*;   /* amount to increase or decrease width   */
int *yAmt*;   /* amount to increase or decrease height   */

The **InflateRect** function increases or decreases the width and height of a rectangle. The **InflateRect** function adds *xAmt* units to the left and right ends of the rectangle and adds *yAmt* units to the top and bottom. The *xAmt* and *yAmt* parameters are signed values; positive values increase the width and height, and negative values decrease them.

Parameters
lprc
Points to the **RECT** structure that increases or decreases in size. The **RECT** structure has the following form:

```
typedef struct tagRECT {    /* rc */
    int left;
    int top;
    int right;
    int bottom;
} RECT;
```

For a full description of this structure, see the *Microsoft Windows Programmer's Reference, Volume 3.*

xAmt
Specifies the amount to increase or decrease the rectangle width. It must be negative to decrease the width.

yAmt
Specifies the amount to increase or decrease the rectangle height. It must be negative to decrease the height.

Return Value
This function does not return a value.

Comments
The width and height of a rectangle must not be greater than 32,767 units or less than −32,768 units.

See Also
IntersectRect, OffsetRect, UnionRect

InitAtomTable

BOOL InitAtomTable(*cTableEntries*)
int *cTableEntries*;   /* size of atom table   */

The **InitAtomTable** function initializes the local atom hash table and sets it to the specified size.

An application need not use this function to use a local atom table. The default size of the local and global atom hash tables is 37 table entries. If an application uses **InitAtomTable**, however, it should call the function before any other atom-management function.

Parameters   *cTableEntries*
        Specifies the size, in table entries, of the atom hash table. This value should be a prime number.

Return Value   The return value is nonzero if the function is successful. Otherwise, it is zero.

Comments   If an application uses a large number of local atoms, it can increase the size of the local atom table, reducing the time required to add an atom to the local atom table or to find an atom in the table. However, this increases the amount of memory required to maintain the table.

        The size of the global atom table cannot be changed from its default size of 37 entries.

Example   The following example uses the **InitAtomTable** function to change the size of the local atom table to 73:

```
BOOL fSuccess;

fSuccess = InitAtomTable(73);

if (fSuccess)
    MessageBox(hwnd, "table initialization succeeded",
        "InitAtomTable", MB_OK);
else
    MessageBox(hwnd, "table initialization failed",
        "InitAtomTable", MB_ICONEXCLAMATION);
```

InSendMessage

2.x

BOOL InSendMessage(void)

The **InSendMessage** function specifies whether the current window procedure is processing a message that was sent from another task by a call to the **Send-Message** function.

Parameters   This function has no parameters.

Return Value   The return value is nonzero if the window procedure is processing a message sent to it from another task by the **SendMessage** function. Otherwise, the return value is zero.

Comments   Applications use the **InSendMessage** function to determine how to handle errors that occur when an inactive window processes messages. For example, if the active window uses the **SendMessage** function to send a request for information to another window, the other window cannot become active until it returns control from the **SendMessage** call. The only method an inactive window has to inform the user of an error is to create a message box.

See Also   **PostAppMessage**, **SendMessage**

InsertMenu

3.0

BOOL InsertMenu(_hmenu, idItem, fuFlags, idNewItem, lpNewItem_**)**
HMENU _hmenu_;   /* handle of menu   */
UINT _idItem_;   /* menu item that new menu item is to precede   */
UINT _fuFlags_;   /* menu flags   */
UINT _idNewItem_;   /* item identifier or pop-up menu handle   */
LPCSTR _lpNewItem_;   /* item content   */

The **InsertMenu** function inserts a new menu item into a menu, moving other items down the menu. The function also sets the state of the menu item.

Parameters   _hmenu_
                   Identifies the menu to be changed.

                 idItem
                   Specifies the menu item before which the new menu item is to be inserted, as determined by the _fuFlags_ parameter.

fuFlags

Specifies how the *idItem* parameter is interpreted and information about the state of the new menu item when it is added to the menu. This parameter consists of a combination of one of the following values and the values listed in the Comments section.

Value	Meaning
MF_BYCOMMAND	The *idItem* parameter specifies the menu-item identifier.
MF_BYPOSITION	The *idItem* parameter specifies the zero-based position of the menu item. If *idItem* is −1, the new menu item is appended to the end of the menu.

idNewItem

Specifies either the identifier of the new menu item or, if *fuFlags* is set to MF_POPUP, the menu handle of the pop-up menu.

lpNewItem

Specifies the contents of the new menu item. If *fuFlags* is set to MF_STRING (the default value), this parameter points to a null-terminated string. If *fuFlags* is set to MF_BITMAP instead, *lpNewItem* contains a bitmap handle in its low-order word. If *fuFlags* is set to MF_OWNERDRAW, *lpNewItem* specifies an application-defined 32-bit value, which the application can use to maintain additional data associated with the menu item. This 32-bit value is available to the application in the **itemData** member of the structure pointed to by the *lParam* parameter of the WM_MEASUREITEM and WM_DRAWITEM messages. These messages are sent when the menu item is initially displayed or is changed.

Return Value

The return value is nonzero if the function is successful. Otherwise, it is zero.

Comments

If the active multiple document interface (MDI) child window is maximized and an application inserts a pop-up menu into the MDI application's menu by calling this function and specifying the MF_BYPOSITION flag, the menu is inserted one position farther left than expected. This occurs because the System menu of the active MDI child window is inserted into the first position of the MDI frame window's menu bar. To avoid this behavior, the application must add 1 to the position value that would otherwise be used. An application can use the WM_MDIGETACTIVE message to determine whether the currently active child window is maximized.

Whenever a menu changes (whether or not the menu is in a window that is displayed), the application should call the **DrawMenuBar** function.

Each of the following groups lists flags that should not be used together:

- MF_BYCOMMAND and MF_BYPOSITION
- MF_DISABLED, MF_ENABLED, and MF_GRAYED

- MF_BITMAP, MF_STRING, MF_OWNERDRAW, and MF_SEPARATOR
- MF_MENUBARBREAK and MF_MENUBREAK
- MF_CHECKED and MF_UNCHECKED

The following list describes the flags that may be set in the *fuFlags* parameter:

Value	Meaning
MF_BITMAP	Uses a bitmap as the item. The low-order word of the *lpNewItem* parameter contains the handle of the bitmap.
MF_BYCOMMAND	Specifies that the *idItem* parameter gives the menu-item identifier (default).
MF_BYPOSITION	Specifies that the *idItem* parameter gives the position of the menu item rather than the menu-item identifier.
MF_CHECKED	Places a check mark next to (selects) the menu item. If the application has supplied check-mark bitmaps (see the **SetMenuItemBitmaps** function), setting this flag displays the check-mark bitmap next to the menu item.
MF_DISABLED	Disables the menu item so that it cannot be selected, but does not gray (dim) it.
MF_ENABLED	Enables the menu item so that it can be selected, and restores it from its grayed state.
MF_GRAYED	Disables the menu item so that it cannot be selected, and grays it.
MF_MENUBARBREAK	Same as MF_MENUBREAK except, for pop-up menus, separates the new column from the old column by using a vertical line.
MF_MENUBREAK	Places the menu item on a new line for static menu-bar items. For pop-up menus, places the menu item in a new column, with no dividing line between the columns.
MF_OWNERDRAW	Specifies that the item is an owner-drawn item. The window that owns the menu receives a WM_MEASUREITEM message (when the menu is displayed for the first time) to retrieve the height and width of the menu item. The WM_DRAWITEM message is then sent to the owner whenever the owner must update the visual appearance of the menu item. This option is not valid for a top-level menu item.
MF_POPUP	Specifies that the menu item has a pop-up menu associated with it. The *idNewItem* parameter specifies a handle of a pop-up menu to be associated with the item. Use the MF_OWNERDRAW flag to add either a top-level pop-up menu or a hierarchical pop-up menu to a pop-up menu item.

Value	Meaning
MF_SEPARATOR	Draws a horizontal dividing line. You can use this flag in a pop-up menu. This line cannot be grayed, disabled, or highlighted. Windows ignores the *lpNewItem* and *idNewItem* parameters.
MF_STRING	Specifies that the menu item is a character string; the *lpNewItem* parameter points to the string for the item.
MF_UNCHECKED	Does not place a check mark next to the item (default value). If the application has supplied check-mark bitmaps (see **SetMenuItemBitmaps**), setting this flag displays the check-mark-off bitmap next to the menu item.

See Also   **AppendMenu, CreateMenu, DrawMenuBar, RemoveMenu, SetMenuItemBitmaps**

InterruptRegister   3.1

#include <toolhelp.h>

BOOL InterruptRegister(*htask*, *lpfnIntCallback*)
HTASK *htask*;   /* handle of task   */
FARPROC *lpfnIntCallback*;   /* address of callback function   */

The **InterruptRegister** function installs a callback function to handle all system interrupts.

Parameters   *htask*
Identifies the task that is registering the callback function. The *htask* value is for registration purposes, not for filtering interrupts. Typically, this value is NULL, indicating the current task. The only time this value is not NULL is when an application requires more than one interrupt handler.

lpfnIntCallback
Points to the interrupt callback function that will handle interrupts. The Tool Helper library calls this function whenever a task receives an interrupt.

The *lpfnIntCallback* value is normally the return value of a call to the **MakeProcInstance** function. This causes the interrupt callback function to be entered with the AX register set to the selector of the application's data segment. Usually, an exported function prolog contains the following code:

```
mov   ds,ax
```

Return Value   The return value is nonzero if the function is successful. Otherwise, it is zero.

Comments   The syntax of the function pointed to by *lpfnIntCallback* is as follows:

void InterruptRegisterCallback(void)

InterruptRegisterCallback is a placeholder for the application-defined function name. The actual name must be exported by including it an **EXPORTS** in the application's module-definition file.

An interrupt callback function must be reentrant, must be page-locked, and must explicitly preserve all register values. When the Tool Helper library calls the function, the stack will be organized as shown in the following illustration.

⋮	
SS (fault)	*SP + 12h*
SP (fault)	*SP + 10h*
Flags (fault)	*SP + 0Eh*
CS (fault)	*SP + 0Ch*
IP (fault)	*SP + 0Ah*
Handle (internal)	*SP + 08h*
Interrupt number	*SP + 06h*
AX	*SP + 04h*
CS (TOOLHELP.DLL)	*SP + 02h*
IP (TOOLHELP.DLL)	*SP + 00h*

The SS and SP values will not be on the stack unless a low-stack fault occurred. This fault is indicated by the high bit of the interrupt number being set.

When Windows calls a callback function, the AX register contains the DS value for the instance of the application that contains the callback function. For more information about this process, see the **MakeProcInstance** function.

Typically, an interrupt callback function is exported. If it is not exported, the developer should verify that the appropriate stack frame is generated, including the correct DS value.

An interrupt callback function must save and restore all register values. The function must also do one of the following:

- Execute an **retf** instruction if it does not handle the interrupt. The Tool Helper library will pass the interrupt to the next appropriate handler in the interrupt handler list.

- Terminate the application by using the **TerminateApp** function.

- Correct the problem that caused the interrupt, clear the first 10 bytes of the stack, and execute an **iret** instruction. This action will restart execution at the specified address. An application may change this address, if necessary.

- Execute a nonlocal goto to a known position in the application by using the **Catch** and **Throw** functions. This type of interrupt handling can be hazardous; the system may be in an unstable state and another fault may occur. Applications that handle interrupts in this way must verify that the fault was a result of the application's code.

The Tool Helper library supports the following interrupts:

Name	Number	Meaning
INT_DIV0	0	Divide-error exception
INT_1	1	Debugger interrupt
INT_3	3	Breakpoint interrupt
INT_UDINSTR	6	Invalid-opcode exception
INT_STKFAULT	12	Stack exception
INT_GPFAULT	13	General protection violation
INT_BADPAGEFAULT	14	Page fault not caused by normal virtual-memory operation
INT_CTLALTSYS RQ	256	User pressed CTRL+ALT+SYS RQ

The Tool Helper library returns interrupt numbers as word values. Normal software interrupts and processor faults are represented by numbers in the range 0 through 255. Interrupts specific to Tool Helper are represented by numbers greater than 255.

Some developers may wish to use CTRL+ALT+SYS RQ (Interrupt 256) to break into the debugger. Be cautious about implementing this interrupt, because the point at which execution stops will probably be in a sensitive part of the Windows kernel. All **InterruptRegisterCallback** functions must be page-locked to prevent problems when this interrupt is used. In addition, the debugger probably will not be able to perform user-interface functions. However, the debugger can use Tool Helper functions to set breakpoints and gather information. The debugger may also be able to use a debugging terminal or secondary screen to display information.

Low-stack Faults

A low-stack fault occurs when inadequate stack space is available on the faulting application's stack. For example, if any fault occurs when there is less than 128 bytes of stack space available or if runaway recursion depletes the stack, a low-stack fault occurs. The Tool Helper library processes a low-stack fault differently than it processes other faults.

A low-stack fault is indicated by the high-order bit of the interrupt number being set. For example, if a stack fault occurs and the SP value becomes invalid, the Tool Helper library will return the fault number as 0x800C rather than 0x000C.

Interrupt handlers designed to process low-stack faults must be aware that the Tool Helper library has passed a fault frame on a stack other that the faulting application's stack. The SS:SP value is on the stack because it was pushed before the rest of the information in the stack frame. The SS:SP value is available only for advisory purposes.

An interrupt handler should never restart the faulting instruction, because this will cause the system to crash. The handler may terminate the application with **TerminateApp** or pass the fault to the next handler in the interrupt-handler list.

Interrupt handlers should not assume that all stack faults are low-stack faults. For example, if an application accesses a stack-relative variable that is out of range, a stack fault will occur. This type of fault can be processed in the same manner as any general protection (GP) fault. If the high-order bit of the interrupt number is not set, the instruction can be restarted.

Interrupt handlers also should not assume that all low-stack faults are stack faults. Any fault that occurs when there is less than 128 bytes of stack available will cause a low-stack fault.

Interrupt callback functions that are not designed to process low-stack faults should execute an **retf** instruction so that the Tool Helper library will pass the fault to the next appropriate handler in the interrupt-handler list.

See Also   **Catch, InterruptUnRegister, NotifyRegister, NotifyUnRegister, TerminateApp, Throw**

InterruptUnRegister   3.1

#include <toolhelp.h>

BOOL InterruptUnRegister(*htask*)
HTASK *htask*;   /* handle of task   */

The **InterruptUnRegister** function restores the default interrupt handle for system interrupts.

Parameters

htask
  Identifies the task. If this value is NULL, it identifies the current task.

Return Value

The return value is nonzero if the function is successful. Otherwise, it is zero.

Comments

After this function is executed, the Tool Helper library will pass all interrupts it receives to the system's default interrupt handler.

See Also

InterruptRegister, NotifyRegister, NotifyUnRegister, TerminateApp

---

IntersectClipRect   `2.x`

```
int IntersectClipRect(hdc, nLeftRect, nTopRect, nRightRect, nBottomRect)
HDC hdc;                /* handle of device context                    */
int nLeftRect;          /* x-coordinate top-left corner of rectangle   */
int nTopRect;           /* y-coordinate top-left corner of rectangle   */
int nRightRect;         /* x-coordinate bottom-right corner of rectangle */
int nBottomRect;        /* y-coordinate bottom-right corner of rectangle */
```

The **IntersectClipRect** function creates a new clipping region from the intersection of the current region and a specified rectangle.

Parameters

hdc
  Identifies the device context.

nLeftRect
  Specifies the logical x-coordinate of the upper-left corner of the rectangle.

nTopRect
  Specifies the logical y-coordinate of the upper-left corner of the rectangle.

nRightRect
  Specifies the logical x-coordinate of the lower-right corner of the rectangle.

nBottomRect
  Specifies the logical y-coordinate of the lower-right corner of the rectangle.

Return Value

The return value specifies that the resulting region has overlapping borders (COMPLEXREGION), is empty (NULLREGION), or has no overlapping borders (SIMPLEREGION). Otherwise, the return value is ERROR.

Comments

An application uses the **IntersectClipRect** function to create a clipping region from the intersection of the current region and a specified rectangle. An application can also create a clipping region that is the intersection of two regions, by specifying RGN_AND in a call to the **CombineRgn** function and then making this combined region the clipping region by calling the **SelectClipRgn** function.

The width of the rectangle, specified by the absolute value of *nRightRect* − *nLeftRect*, must not exceed 32,767 units. This limit applies to the height of the rectangle as well.

Example

The following example creates a square clipping region and colors it red by using a red brush to fill the client area. The **IntersectClipRect** function is called with coordinates that overlap the region, and the client area is filled with a yellow brush. The only region colored yellow is the overlap between the region and the coordinates specified in the call to **IntersectClipRect.**

```
RECT rc;
HRGN hrgn;
HBRUSH hbrRed, hbrYellow;

GetClientRect(hwnd, &rc);
hrgn = CreateRectRgn(10, 10, 110, 110);
SelectClipRgn(hdc, hrgn);
hbrRed = CreateSolidBrush(RGB(255, 0, 0));
FillRect(hdc, &rc, hbrRed);

IntersectClipRect(hdc, 100, 100, 200, 200);

hbrYellow = CreateSolidBrush(RGB(255, 255, 0));
FillRect(hdc, &rc, hbrYellow);

DeleteObject(hbrRed);
DeleteObject(hbrYellow);
DeleteObject(hrgn);
```

See Also

CombineRgn, SelectClipRgn

IntersectRect

BOOL IntersectRect(*lprcDst, lprcSrc1, lprcSrc2***)**
RECT FAR* *lprcDst*;   /* address of structure for intersection   */
const RECT FAR* *lprcSrc1*;   /* address of structure with 1st rectangle   */
const RECT FAR* *lprcSrc2*;   /* address of structure with 2nd rectangle   */

The **IntersectRect** function calculates the intersection of two source rectangles and places the coordinates of the intersection rectangle into the destination rectangle. If the rectangles do not intersect, an empty rectangle (0, 0, 0, 0) is placed into the destination rectangle.

Parameters   *lprcDst*

Points to a **RECT** structure that receives the intersection of the rectangles pointed to by the *lprcSrc1* and *lprcSrc2* parameters. The **RECT** structure has the following form:

```
typedef struct tagRECT {    /* rc */
    int left;
    int top;
    int right;
    int bottom;
} RECT;
```

For a full description of this structure, see the *Microsoft Windows Programmer's Reference, Volume 3*.

lprcSrc1

Points to the **RECT** structure that contains the first source rectangle.

lprcSrc2

Points to the **RECT** structure that contains the second source rectangle.

Return Value   The return value is nonzero if the rectangles intersect. Otherwise, it is zero.

See Also   **InflateRect, SubtractRect, UnionRect**

InvalidateRect   2.x

void InvalidateRect(*hwnd, lprc, fErase***)**
HWND *hwnd*;   /* handle of window with changed update region   */
const RECT FAR* *lprc*;   /* address of structure with rectangle   */
BOOL *fErase*;   /* erase-background flag   */

The **InvalidateRect** function adds a rectangle to a window's update region. The update region represents the client area of the window that must be redrawn.

Parameters   *hwnd*

Identifies the window whose update region has changed.

lprc
> Points to a **RECT** structure that contains the client coordinates of the rectangle to be added to the update region. If the *lprc* parameter is NULL, the entire client area is added to the update region.
>
> The **RECT** structure has the following form:
>
> ```
> typedef struct tagRECT {    /* rc */
>     int left;
>     int top;
>     int right;
>     int bottom;
> } RECT;
> ```
>
> For a full description of this structure, see the *Microsoft Windows Programmer's Reference, Volume 3*.

fErase
> Specifies whether the background within the update region is to be erased when the update region is processed. It this parameter is TRUE, the background is erased when the **BeginPaint** function is called. If this parameter is FALSE, the background remains unchanged.

Return Value   This function does not return a value.

Comments   The invalidated areas accumulate in the update region until the region is processed when the next WM_PAINT message occurs, or until the region is validated by using the **ValidateRect** or **ValidateRgn** function.

Windows sends a WM_PAINT message to a window whenever its update region is not empty and there are no other messages in the application queue for that window.

If the *fErase* parameter is TRUE for any part of the update region, the background is erased in the entire region, not just in the given part.

See Also   **BeginPaint, InvalidateRgn, ValidateRect, ValidateRgn**

InvalidateRgn   2.x

void InvalidateRgn(*hwnd*, *hrgn*, *fErase*)
HWND *hwnd*;	/* handle of window with changed update region	*/
HRGN *hrgn*;	/* handle of region to add	*/
BOOL *fErase*;	/* erase-background flag	*/

The **InvalidateRgn** function adds a region to a window's update region. The update region represents the client area of the window that must be redrawn.

Parameters

hwnd
Identifies the window whose update region has changed.

hrgn
Identifies the region to be added to the update region. The region is assumed to have client coordinates. If this parameter is NULL, the entire client area is added to the update region.

fErase
Specifies whether the background within the update region is to be erased when the update region is processed. If this parameter is TRUE, the background is erased when the **BeginPaint** function is called. If the parameter is FALSE, the background remains unchanged.

Return Value
This function does not return a value.

Comments
The invalidated regions accumulate in the update region until the region is processed when the next WM_PAINT message occurs, or until the region is validated by using the **ValidateRect** or **ValidateRgn** function.

Windows sends a WM_PAINT message to a window whenever its update region is not empty and there are no other messages in the application queue for that window.

If the *fErase* parameter is TRUE for any part of the update region, the background is erased in the entire region, not just in the given part.

See Also
BeginPaint, InvalidateRect, ValidateRect, ValidateRgn

InvertRect

2.x

```
void InvertRect(hdc, lprc)
HDC hdc;                    /* handle of device context          */
const RECT FAR* lprc;       /* address of structure with rectangle  */
```

The **InvertRect** function inverts a rectangular area. Inversion is a logical NOT operation and flips the bits of each pixel.

Parameters

hdc
Identifies the device context.

lprc
Points to a **RECT** structure that contains the logical coordinates of the rectangle to be inverted. The **RECT** structure has the following form:

```
typedef struct tagRECT {    /* rc */
    int left;
    int top;
    int right;
    int bottom;
} RECT;
```

For a full description of this structure, see the *Microsoft Windows Programmer's Reference, Volume 3.*

Return Value   This function does not return a value.

Comments   On monochrome screens, the **InvertRect** function makes white pixels black and black pixels white. On color screens, the inversion depends on how colors are generated for the screen. Calling **InvertRect** twice, specifying the same rectangle, restores the display to its previous colors.

The **InvertRect** function compares the values of the **top**, **bottom**, **left**, and **right** members of the specified rectangle. If **bottom** is less than or equal to **top**, or if **right** is less than or equal to **left**, the function does not draw the rectangle.

See Also   **FillRect**

InvertRgn   2.x

BOOL InvertRgn(*hdc***, ***hrgn***)**
HDC *hdc*;   /* handle of device context   */
HRGN *hrgn*;   /* handle of region   */

The **InvertRgn** function inverts the colors in a given region.

Parameters   *hdc*
Identifies the device context.
hrgn
Identifies the region for which colors are to be inverted.

Return Value   The return value is nonzero if the function is successful. Otherwise, it is zero.

Comments   On monochrome screens, the **InvertRgn** function makes white pixels black and black pixels white. On color screens, the inversion depends on how the colors are generated for the screen.

Example   The following example sets the device coordinates of and creates a rectangular region, selects the region into a device context, and then calls the **InvertRgn** function to display the region in inverted colors:

```
HRGN hrgn;

hrgn = CreateRectRgn(10, 10, 110, 110);
SelectObject(hdc, hrgn);
InvertRgn(hdc, hrgn);

DeleteObject(hrgn);
```

See Also   **FillRgn, PaintRgn**

IsBadCodePtr

3.1

BOOL IsBadCodePtr(*lpfn***)**
FARPROC *lpfn*;   /* pointer to test   */

The **IsBadCodePtr** function determines whether a pointer to executable code is valid.

Parameters   *lpfn*
          Points to a function.

Return Value   The return value is nonzero if the pointer is bad (that is, if it does not point to executable code). The return value is zero if the pointer is good.

See Also   **IsBadHugeReadPtr, IsBadHugeWritePtr, IsBadReadPtr, IsBadStringPtr, IsBadWritePtr**

IsBadHugeReadPtr

3.1

BOOL IsBadHugeReadPtr(*lp***, ***cb***)**
const void _huge* *lp*;   /* pointer to test   */
DWORD *cb*;   /* number of allocated bytes   */

The **IsBadHugeReadPtr** function determines whether a huge pointer to readable memory is valid.

Parameters   *lp*
Points to the beginning of a block of allocated memory. The data object may reside anywhere in memory and may exceed 64K in size.

cb
Specifies the number of bytes of memory that were allocated.

Return Value   The return value is nonzero if the pointer is bad (that is, if it does not point to readable memory of the specified size). The return value is zero if the pointer is good.

See Also   **IsBadCodePtr**, **IsBadHugeWritePtr**, **IsBadReadPtr**, **IsBadStringPtr**, **IsBadWritePtr**

IsBadHugeWritePtr

3.1

BOOL IsBadHugeWritePtr(*lp***, ***cb***)**
void _huge* *lp*;   /* pointer to test   */
DWORD *cb*;   /* number of allocated bytes   */

The **IsBadHugeWritePtr** function determines whether a huge pointer to writable memory is valid.

Parameters   *lp*
Points to the beginning of a block of allocated memory. The data object may reside anywhere in memory and may exceed 64K in size.

cb
Specifies the number of bytes of memory that were allocated.

Return Value   The return value is nonzero if the pointer is bad (that is, if it does not point to writable memory of the specified size). The return value is zero if the pointer is good.

See Also   **IsBadCodePtr**, **IsBadHugeReadPtr**, **IsBadReadPtr**, **IsBadStringPtr**, **IsBadWritePtr**

IsBadReadPtr   3.1

BOOL IsBadReadPtr(*lp***,** *cb***)**
const void FAR* *lp***;**   /* pointer to test   */
UINT *cb***;**   /* number of allocated bytes   */

The **IsBadReadPtr** function determines whether a pointer to readable memory is valid.

Parameters   *lp*
      Points to the beginning of a block of allocated memory.

      cb
      Specifies the number of bytes of memory that were allocated.

Return Value   The return value is nonzero if the pointer is bad (that is, if it does not point to readable memory of the specified size). The return value is zero if the pointer is good.

See Also   **IsBadCodePtr**, **IsBadHugeReadPtr**, **IsBadHugeWritePtr**, **IsBadStringPtr**, **IsBadWritePtr**

IsBadStringPtr   3.1

BOOL IsBadStringPtr(*lpsz***,** *cchMax***)**
const void FAR* *lpsz***;**   /* pointer to test   */
UINT *cchMax***;**   /* maximum size of string   */

The **IsBadStringPtr** function determines whether a pointer to a string is valid.

Parameters   *lpsz*
      Points to a null-terminated string.

cchMax
   Specifies the maximum size of the string, in bytes.

Return Value   The return value is nonzero if the pointer is bad (that is, if it does not point to a string of the specified size). The return value is zero if the pointer is good.

See Also   **IsBadCodePtr, IsBadHugeReadPtr, IsBadHugeWritePtr, IsBadReadPtr, IsBadWritePtr**

IsBadWritePtr   3.1

BOOL IsBadWritePtr(*lp***,** *cb***)**
void FAR* *lp*;   /* pointer to test   */
UINT *cb*;   /* number of allocated bytes   */

The **IsBadWritePtr** function determines whether a pointer to writable memory is valid.

Parameters   *lp*
   Points to the beginning of a block of allocated memory.
   cb
   Specifies the number of bytes of memory that were allocated.

Return Value   The return value is nonzero if the pointer is bad (that is, if it does not point to writable memory of the specified size). The return value is zero if the pointer is good.

See Also   **IsBadCodePtr, IsBadHugeReadPtr, IsBadHugeWritePtr, IsBadReadPtr, IsBadStringPtr**

IsCharAlpha   3.0

BOOL IsCharAlpha(*chTest***)**
char *chTest*;   /* character to test   */

The **IsCharAlpha** function determines whether a character is in the set of language-defined alphabetic characters.

Parameters   *chTest*
                      Specifies the character to be tested.

Return Value   The return value is nonzero if the character is in the set of alphabetic characters. Otherwise, it is zero.

Comments   The language driver for the current language (the language the user selected at setup or by using Control Panel) determines whether the character is in the set. If no language has been set, Windows uses an internal function.

Example   The following example uses the **IsCharAlpha** function to find the first nonalphabetic character in a string:

```
for (lpszNon = lpsz; IsCharAlpha(*lpszNon);
    lpszNon = AnsiNext(lpszNon));
```

See Also   **IsCharAlphaNumeric**

IsCharAlphaNumeric

`3.0`

BOOL IsCharAlphaNumeric(*chTest*)
char *chTest*;   /* character to test   */

The **IsCharAlphaNumeric** function determines whether a character is in the set of language-defined alphabetic or numeric characters.

Parameters   *chTest*
                      Specifies the character to be tested.

Return Value   The return value is nonzero if the character is in either the set of alphabetic characters or the set of numeric characters. Otherwise, it is zero.

Comments   The language driver for the current language (the language the user selected at setup or by using Control Panel) determines whether the character is in the set. If no language driver is selected, Windows uses an internal function.

Example   The following example uses the **IsCharAlphaNumeric** function to find the first nonalphanumeric character in a string:

```
for (lpszNon = lpsz; IsCharAlphaNumeric(*lpszNon);
        lpszNon = AnsiNext(lpszNon));
```

See Also   **IsCharAlpha**

IsCharLower

BOOL IsCharLower(*chTest***)**
char *chTest*;   /* character to test   */

The **IsCharLower** function determines whether a character is in the set of language-defined lowercase characters.

Parameters   *chTest*
                Specifies the character to be tested.

Return Value   The return value is nonzero if the character is lowercase. Otherwise, it is zero.

Comments   The language driver for the current language (the language selected at setup or by using Control Panel) determines whether the character is in the set. If no language driver is selected, Windows uses an internal function.

Example   The following example uses the **IsCharLower** function to find the first lowercase character in a string:

```
/* Look through string for a lowercase character. */

for (lpszLower = lpsz;
        !IsCharLower(*lpszLower) && lpszLower != '\0';
        lpszLower = AnsiNext(lpszLower));

/* Return NULL if no lowercase character is found. */

if (lpszLower == '\0')
    lpszLower = NULL;
```

See Also   **IsCharUpper**

IsCharUpper

`3.0`

BOOL IsCharUpper(*chTest*)
char *chTest*;   /* character to test   */

The **IsCharUpper** function determines whether a character is in the set of language-defined uppercase characters.

Parameters

chTest
   Specifies the character to be tested.

Return Value

The return value is nonzero if the character is uppercase. Otherwise, it is zero.

Comments

The language driver for the current language (the language the user selected at setup or by using Control Panel) determines whether the character is in the set. If no language driver is selected, Windows uses an internal function.

Example

The following example uses the **IsCharUpper** function to find the first uppercase character in a string:

```
/* Look through the string for an uppercase character. */

for (lpszUpper = lpsz;
        !IsCharUpper(*lpszUpper) && lpszUpper != '\0';
        lpszUpper = AnsiNext(lpszUpper));

/* Return NULL if no uppercase character is found. */

if (lpszUpper == '\0')
    lpszUpper = NULL;
```

See Also

IsCharLower

IsChild

`2.x`

BOOL IsChild(*hwndParent*, *hwndChild*)
HWND *hwndParent*;   /* handle of parent window   */
HWND *hwndChild*;   /* handle of child window   */

The **IsChild** function tests whether a given window is a child or other direct descendant of a given parent window. A child window is the direct descendant of a given parent window if that parent window is in the chain of parent windows leading from the original pop-up window to the child window.

Parameters	*hwndParent*
	Identifies the parent window.
	hwndChild
	Identifies the child window to be tested.
Return Value	The return value is nonzero if the child window is a descendant of the parent window. Otherwise, it is zero.
See Also	**SetParent**

IsClipboardFormatAvailable   `2.x`

BOOL IsClipboardFormatAvailable(*uFormat*)
UINT *uFormat*;   /* registered clipboard format   */

The **IsClipboardFormatAvailable** function specifies whether data of a certain format exists on the clipboard.

Parameters	*uFormat*
	Specifies a registered clipboard format. For information about clipboard formats, see the description of the **SetClipboardData function**.
Return Value	The return value is nonzero if data of the specified format is on the clipboard. Otherwise, the return value is zero.
Comments	This function is typically called during processing of the WM_INITMENU or WM_INITMENUPOPUP message to determine whether the clipboard contains data that the application can paste. If such data is present, the application typically enables the Paste command (in its Edit menu).
See Also	**CountClipboardFormats, EnumClipboardFormats, GetClipboardFormatName, GetPriorityClipboardFormat, RegisterClipboardFormat, SetClipboardData**

IsDBCSLeadByte   `3.1`

BOOL IsDBCSLeadByte(*bTestChar*)
BYTE *bTestChar*;   /* character to test   */

IsDialogMessage   553

The **IsDBCSLeadByte** function determines whether a character is a lead byte, the first byte of a character in a double-byte character set (DBCS).

Parameters

bTestChar
Specifies the character to be tested.

Return Value

The return value is nonzero if the character is a DBCS lead byte. Otherwise, it is zero.

Comments

The language driver for the current language (the language the user selected at setup or by using Control Panel) determines whether the character is in the set. If no language driver is selected, Windows uses an internal function.

Each double-byte character set has a unique set of lead-byte values. By itself, a lead byte has no character value; together, the lead byte and the following byte represent a single character. The second, or following, byte is called a trailing byte.

See Also

GetKeyboardType

IsDialogMessage

2.x

BOOL IsDialogMessage(*hwndDlg*, *lpmsg*)
HWND *hwndDlg*;   /* handle of dialog box   */
MSG FAR* *lpmsg*;   /* address of structure with message   */

The **IsDialogMessage** function determines whether the specified message is intended for the given modeless dialog box and, if it is, processes the message.

Parameters

hwndDlg
Identifies the dialog box.

lpmsg
Points to an **MSG** structure that contains the message to be checked. The **MSG** structure has the following form:

```
typedef struct tagMSG {     /* msg */
    HWND    hwnd;
    UINT    message;
    WPARAM  wParam;
    LPARAM  lParam;
    DWORD   time;
    POINT   pt;
} MSG;
```

For a full description of this structure, see the *Microsoft Windows Programmer's Reference, Volume 3*.

Return Value   The return value is nonzero if the message has been processed. Otherwise, it is zero.

Comments   Although **IsDialogMessage** is intended for modeless dialog boxes, it can be used with any window that contains controls, enabling such windows to provide the same keyboard selection as in a dialog box.

When **IsDialogMessage** processes a message, it checks for keyboard messages and converts them into selection commands for the corresponding dialog box. For example, the TAB key, when pressed, selects the next control or group of controls, and the DOWN ARROW key, when pressed, selects the next control in a group.

If a message is processed by **IsDialogMessage**, it must not be passed to the **TranslateMessage** or **DispatchMessage** function. This is because **IsDialog-Message** performs all necessary translating and dispatching of messages.

IsDialogMessage sends WM_GETDLGCODE messages to the dialog box procedure to determine which keys should be processed.

IsDialogMessage can send DM_GETDEFID and DM_SETDEFID messages to the window. These messages are defined in the WINDOWS.H header file as WM_USER and WM_USER+1, so conflicts are possible with application-defined messages having the same values.

See Also   **DispatchMessage, SendDlgItemMessage, TranslateMessage**

IsDlgButtonChecked   2.x

UINT IsDlgButtonChecked(*hwndDlg*, *idButton*)
HWND *hwndDlg*;   /* handle of dialog box   */
int *idButton*;   /* button identifier   */

The **IsDlgButtonChecked** function determines whether a button has a check mark next to it and whether a three-state button is grayed, checked, or neither.

Parameters   *hwndDlg*
Identifies the dialog box that contains the button.

idButton
Specifies the identifier of the button.

Return Value   The return value is nonzero if the specified button is checked, 0 if it is not, or −1 if the *hwndDlg* parameter is invalid. For three-state buttons, the return value is 2 if the button is grayed, 1 if the button is checked, 0 if it is unchecked, or −1 if *hwndDlg* is invalid.

Comments   The **IsDlgButtonChecked** function sends a BM_GETCHECK message to the button.

See Also   **CheckDlgButton, CheckRadioButton**

IsGDIObject   3.1

BOOL IsGDIObject(*hobj*)
HGDIOBJ *hobj*;   /* handle of a menu   */

The **IsGDIObject** function determines whether the specified handle is not the handle of a graphics device interface (GDI) object.

Parameters   *hobj*
     Specifies a handle to test.

Return Value   The return value is nonzero if the handle may be the handle of a GDI object. It is zero if the handle is not the handle of a GDI object.

Comments   An application cannot use **IsGDIObject** to guarantee that a given handle is to a GDI object. However, this function can be used to guarantee that a given handle is not to a GDI object.

See Also   **GetObject**

IsIconic   2.x

BOOL IsIconic(*hwnd*)
HWND *hwnd*;   /* handle of window   */

The **IsIconic** function determines whether the given window is minimized (iconic).

Parameters	*hwnd*
	Identifies the window.

Return Value	The return value is nonzero if the window is minimized. Otherwise, it is zero.

See Also	**CloseWindow, IsZoomed**

IsMenu

3.1

BOOL IsMenu(*hmenu*)
HMENU *hmenu*;   /* handle of menu   */

The **IsMenu** function determines whether the given handle is a menu handle.

Parameters	*hmenu*
	Identifies the handle to be tested.

Return Value	The return value is zero if the handle is definitely *not* a menu handle. A nonzero return value does not guarantee that the handle is a menu handle, however; for nonzero return values, the application should conduct further tests to verify the handle.

Comments	An application should use this function only to ensure that a given handle is *not* a menu handle.

See Also	**CreateMenu, CreatePopupMenu, DestroyMenu, GetMenu**

IsRectEmpty

2.x

BOOL IsRectEmpty(*lprc*)
const RECT FAR* *lprc*;   /* address of structure with rectangle   */

The **IsRectEmpty** function determines whether the specified rectangle is empty. A rectangle is empty if its width or height is zero, or if both are zero.

Parameters	*lprc*
	Points to a **RECT** structure that contains the coordinates of the rectangle. The **RECT** structure has the following form:

```
typedef struct tagRECT {      /* rc */
    int left;
    int top;
    int right;
    int bottom;
} RECT;
```

For a full description of this structure, see the *Microsoft Windows Programmer's Reference, Volume 3*.

Return Value   The return value is nonzero if the rectangle is empty. Otherwise, it is zero.

Example   The following example uses the **IsRectEmpty** function to determine whether a rectangle is empty and then displays a message box giving the status of the rectangle:

```
RECT rc;

if (IsRectEmpty((LPRECT) &rc))
    MessageBox(hwnd, "Rectangle is empty.",
        "Rectangle Status", MB_OK);
else
    MessageBox(hwnd, "Rectangle is not empty.",
        "Rectangle Status", MB_OK);
```

IsTask   3.1

BOOL IsTask(*htask*)
HTASK *htask*;   /* handle of task   */

The **IsTask** function determines whether the given task handle is valid.

Parameters   *htask*
    Identifies a task.

Return Value   The return value is nonzero if the task handle is valid. Otherwise, it is zero.

IsWindow

BOOL IsWindow(*hwnd*)
HWND *hwnd*;   /* handle of window   */

The **IsWindow** function determines whether the given window handle is valid.

Parameters   *hwnd*
                        Identifies a window.

Return Value   The return value is nonzero if the window handle is valid. Otherwise, it is zero.

See Also   **IsWindowEnabled, IsWindowVisible**

IsWindowEnabled

BOOL IsWindowEnabled(*hwnd*)
HWND *hwnd*;   /* handle of window to test   */

The **IsWindowEnabled** function determines whether the given window is enabled for mouse and keyboard input.

Parameters   *hwnd*
                        Identifies the window.

Return Value   The return value is nonzero if the window is enabled. Otherwise, it is zero.

Comments   A child window receives input only if it is both enabled and visible.

See Also   **IsWindow, IsWindowVisible**

IsWindowVisible

BOOL IsWindowVisible(*hwnd*)
HWND *hwnd*;   /* handle of window to test   */

The **IsWindowVisible** function determines the visibility state of the given window.

Parameters	*hwnd* Identifies the window.
Return Value	The return value is nonzero if the specified window is visible on the screen (has the WS_VISIBLE style bit set). The return value is zero if the window is not visible. Because the return value reflects the value of the window's WS_VISIBLE flag, it may be nonzero even if the window is totally obscured by other windows.
Comments	A window possesses a visibility state indicated by the WS_VISIBLE style bit. When this style bit is set, the window is displayed and subsequent drawing into the window is displayed as long as the window has the style bit set. Any drawing to a window that has the WS_VISIBLE style will not be displayed if the window is covered by other windows or is clipped by its parent window.
See Also	**ShowWindow**

IsZoomed
2.x

BOOL IsZoomed(*hwnd*)
HWND *hwnd*;   /* handle of window   */

The **IsZoomed** function determines whether the given window is maximized.

Parameters	*hwnd* Identifies the window.
Return Value	The return value is nonzero if the window is maximized. Otherwise, it is zero.
See Also	**IsIconic**

JournalPlaybackProc
3.1

LRESULT CALLBACK JournalPlaybackProc(*code*, *wParam*, *lParam*)
int *code*;   /* process-message flag   */
WPARAM *wParam*;   /* undefined   */
LPARAM *lParam*;   /* address of structure for message   */

The **JournalPlaybackProc** function is a library-defined callback function that a library can use to insert mouse and keyboard messages into the system message queue. Typically, a library uses this function to play back a series of mouse and keyboard messages that were recorded earlier by using the **JournalRecordProc** function. Regular mouse and keyboard input is disabled as long as a **Journal-PlaybackProc** function is installed.

Parameters

code
Specifies whether the callback function should process the message or call the **CallNextHookEx** function. If this parameter is less than zero, the callback function should pass the message to **CallNextHookEx** without further processing.

wParam
Specifies a NULL value.

lParam
Points to an **EVENTMSG** structure that represents the message being processed by the callback function. The **EVENTMSG** structure has the following form:

```
typedef struct tagEVENTMSG {     /* em */
    UINT  message;
    UINT  paramL;
    UINT  paramH;
    DWORD time;
} EVENTMSG;
```

For a full description of this structure, see the *Microsoft Windows Programmer's Reference, Volume 3.*

Return Value

The callback function should return a value that represents the amount of time, in clock ticks, that the system should wait before processing the message. This value can be computed by calculating the difference between the **time** members of the current and previous input messages. If the function returns zero, the message is processed immediately.

Comments

The **JournalPlaybackProc** function should copy an input message to the *lParam* parameter. The message must have been recorded by using a **JournalRecordProc** callback function, which should not modify the message.

Once the function returns control to the system, the message continues to be processed. If the *code* parameter is HC_SKIP, the filter function should prepare to return the next recorded event message on its next call.

This callback function should reside in a dynamic-link library.

An application must install the callback function by specifying the WH_JOURNALPLAYBACK filter type and the procedure-instance address of the callback function in a call to the **SetWindowsHookEx** function.

JournalPlaybackProc is a placeholder for the library-defined function name. The actual name must be exported by including it in an **EXPORTS** statement in the library's module-definition file.

See Also   **CallNextHookEx**, **JournalRecordProc**, **SetWindowsHookEx**

JournalRecordProc   3.1

LRESULT CALLBACK JournalRecordProc(*code*, *wParam*, *lParam*)
int *code*;   /* process-message flag   */
WPARAM *wParam*;   /* undefined   */
LPARAM *lParam*;   /* address of structure for message */

The **JournalRecordProc** function is a library-defined callback function that records messages that the system removes from the system message queue. Later, a library can use a **JournalPlaybackProc** function to play back the messages.

Parameters   *code*
Specifies whether the callback function should process the message or call the **CallNextHookEx** function. If this parameter is less than zero, the callback function should pass the message to **CallNextHookEx** without further processing.

wParam
Specifies a NULL value.

lParam
Points to an **MSG** structure. The **MSG** structure has the following form:

```
typedef struct tagMSG {     /* msg */
    HWND    hwnd;
    UINT    message;
    WPARAM  wParam;
    LPARAM  lParam;
    DWORD   time;
    POINT   pt;
} MSG;
```

For a full description of this structure, see the *Microsoft Windows Programmer's Reference, Volume 3*.

Return Value   The callback function should return zero.

Comments   A **JournalRecordProc** callback function should copy but not modify the messages. After control returns to the system, the message continues to be processed. The callback function does not require a return value.

This callback function must be in a dynamic-link library.

An application must install the callback function by specifying the WH_JOURNALRECORD filter type and the procedure-instance address of the callback function in a call to the **SetWindowsHookEx** function.

JournalRecordProc is a placeholder for the library-defined function name. The actual name must be exported by including it in an **EXPORTS** statement in the library's module-definition file.

See Also   **CallNextHookEx, JournalPlaybackProc, SetWindowsHookEx**

KeyboardProc   3.1

LRESULT CALLBACK KeyboardProc(*code*, *wParam*, *lParam*)
int *code*;   /* process-message flag   */
WPARAM *wParam*;   /* virtual-key code   */
LPARAM *lParam*;   /* keyboard-message information */

The **KeyboardProc** function is a library-defined callback function that the system calls whenever the application calls the **GetMessage** or **PeekMessage** function and there is a WM_KEYUP or WM_KEYDOWN keyboard message to process.

Parameters   *code*

Specifies whether the callback function should process the message or call the **CallNextHookEx** function. If this value is HC_NOREMOVE, the application is using the **PeekMessage** function with the PM_NOREMOVE option, and the message will not be removed from the system queue. If this value is less than zero, the callback function should pass the message to **CallNextHookEx** without further processing.

wParam
Specifies the virtual-key code of the given key.

lParam
Specifies the repeat count, scan code, extended key, previous key state, context code, and key-transition state, as shown in the following table. (Bit 0 is the low-order bit):

Bit	Description
0–15	Specifies the repeat count. The value is the number of times the keystroke is repeated as a result of the user holding down the key.
16–23	Specifies the scan code. The value depends on the original equipment manufacturer (OEM).

Bit	Description
24	Specifies whether the key is an extended key, such as a function key or a key on the numeric keypad. The value is 1 if it is an extended key; otherwise, it is 0.
25–26	Not used.
27–28	Used internally by Windows.
29	Specifies the context code. The value is 1 if the ALT key is held down while the key is pressed; otherwise, the value is 0.
30	Specifies the previous key state. The value is 1 if the key is down before the message is sent, or it is 0 if the key is up.
31	Specifies the key-transition state. The value is 1 if the key is being released, or it is 0 if the key is being pressed.

Return Value   The callback function should return 0 if the message should be processed by the system; it should return 1 if the message should be discarded.

Comments   This callback function must be in a dynamic-link library.

An application must install the callback function by specifying the WH_KEYBOARD filter type and the procedure-instance address of the callback function in a call to the **SetWindowsHookEx** function.

KeyboardProc is a placeholder for the library-defined function name. The actual name must be exported by including it in an **EXPORTS** statement in the library's module-definition file.

See Also   **CallNextHookEx, GetMessage, PeekMessage, SetWindowsHookEx**

KillTimer   `2.x`

BOOL KillTimer(*hwnd*, *idTimer*)
HWND *hwnd*;   /* handle of window that installed timer   */
UINT *idTimer*;   /* timer identifier   */

The **KillTimer** function removes the specified timer. Any pending WM_TIMER messages associated with the timer are removed from the message queue.

Parameters   *hwnd*
    Identifies the window associated with the timer to be removed. This must be the same value passed as the *hwnd* parameter of the **SetTimer** function that created the timer.

idTimer
: Identifies the timer to be removed. If the application called **SetTimer** with the *hwnd* parameter set to NULL, this parameter must be the timer identifier returned by **SetTimer**. If the *hwnd* parameter of **SetTimer** was a valid window handle, this parameter must be the value of the *idTimer* parameter passed to **SetTimer**.

Return Value
The return value is nonzero if the function is successful. It is zero if the **KillTimer** function could not find the specified timer.

See Also
SetTimer

_lclose

2.x

HFILE _lclose(*hf*)
HFILE *hf*;   /* handle of file to close   */

The **_lclose** function closes the given file. As a result, the file is no longer available for reading or writing.

Parameters
hf
: Identifies the file to be closed. This handle is returned by the function that created or last opened the file.

Return Value
The return value is zero if the function is successful. Otherwise, it is HFILE_ERROR.

Example
The following example copies a file to a temporary file, then closes both files:

```
int cbRead;
PBYTE pbBuf;

/* Allocate a buffer for file I/O. */

pbBuf = (PBYTE) LocalAlloc(LMEM_FIXED, 2048);

/* Copy the input file to the temporary file. */

do {
    cbRead = _lread(hfReadFile, pbBuf, 2048);
    _lwrite(hfTempFile, pbBuf, cbRead);
} while (cbRead != 0);

/* Free the buffer and close the files. */
```

```
LocalFree((HLOCAL) pbBuf);

_lclose(hfReadFile);
_lclose(hfTempFile);
```

See Also   **_lopen**, **OpenFile**

_lcreat

2.x

HFILE _lcreat(*lpszFilename*, *fnAttribute*)
LPCSTR *lpszFilename*;   /* address of file to open   */
int *fnAttribute*;   /* file attributes   */

The **_lcreat** function creates or opens a specified file. If the file does not exist, the function creates a new file and opens it for writing. If the file does exist, the function truncates the file size to zero and opens it for reading and writing. When the function opens the file, the pointer is set to the beginning of the file.

Parameters   *lpszFilename*
Points to a null-terminated string that names the file to be opened. The string must consist of characters from the Windows character set.

fnAttribute
Specifies the file attributes. This parameter must be one of the following values:

Value	Meaning
0	Normal; can be read or written without restriction.
1	Read-only; cannot be opened for writing.
2	Hidden; not found by directory search.
3	System; not found by directory search.

Return Value   The return value is a file handle if the function is successful. Otherwise, it is HFILE_ERROR.

Comments   Use this function carefully. It is possible to open any file, even one that has already been opened by another function.

Example   The following example uses the **_lcreat** function to open a temporary file:

```
HFILE hfTempFile;
char szBuf[144];
```

```
/* Create a temporary file. */

GetTempFileName(0, "tst", 0, szBuf);

hfTempFile = _lcreat(szBuf, 0);

if (hfTempFile == HFILE_ERROR) {
    ErrorHandler();
}
```

LibMain

2.x

int CALLBACK LibMain(*hinst, wDataSeg, cbHeapSize, lpszCmdLine*)
HINSTANCE *hinst*;   /* handle of library instance   */
WORD *wDataSeg*;   /* library data segment   */
WORD *cbHeapSize*;   /* default heap size   */
LPSTR *lpszCmdLine*;   /* command-line arguments   */

The **LibMain** function is called by the system to initialize a dynamic-link library (DLL). A DLL must contain the **LibMain** function if the library is linked with the file LIBENTRY.OBJ.

Parameters   *hinst*
                   Identifies the instance of the DLL.

                   wDataSeg
                   Specifies the value of the data segment (DS) register.

                   cbHeapSize
                   Specifies the size of the heap defined in the module-definition file. (The LibEntry routine in LIBENTRY.OBJ uses this value to initialize the local heap.)

                   lpszCmdLine
                   Points to a null-terminated string specifying command-line information. This parameter is rarely used by DLLs.

Return Value   The function should return 1 if it is successful. Otherwise, it should return 0.

Comments   The **LibMain** function is called by LibEntry, which is called by Windows when the DLL is loaded. The LibEntry routine is provided in the LIBENTRY.OBJ module. LibEntry initializes the DLL's heap (if a **HEAPSIZE** value is specified in the DLL's module-definition file) before calling the **LibMain** function.

Example   The following example shows a typical **LibMain** function:

```
int CALLBACK LibMain(HINSTANCE hinst, WORD wDataSeg, WORD cbHeap,
    LPSTR lpszCmdLine )
{
    HGLOBAL    hgblClassStruct;
    LPWNDCLASS lpClassStruct;
    static HINSTANCE hinstLib;

    /* Has the library been initialized yet? */

    if (hinstLib == NULL) {
        hgblClassStruct = GlobalAlloc(GHND, sizeof(WNDCLASS));
        if (hgblClassStruct != NULL) {
            lpClassStruct = (LPWNDCLASS) GlobalLock(hgblClassStruct);
            if (lpClassStruct != NULL) {

                /* Define the class attributes. */

                lpClassStruct->style = CS_HREDRAW | CS_VREDRAW |
                    CS_DBLCLKS | CS_GLOBALCLASS;
                lpClassStruct->lpfnWndProc = DllWndProc;
                lpClassStruct->cbWndExtra = 0;
                lpClassStruct->hInstance = hinst;
                lpClassStruct->hIcon = NULL;
                lpClassStruct->hCursor = LoadCursor(NULL, IDC_ARROW);
                lpClassStruct->hbrBackground =
                    (HBRUSH) (COLOR_WINDOW + 1);
                lpClassStruct->lpszMenuName = NULL;
                lpClassStruct->lpszClassName = "MyClassName";

                hinstLib = (RegisterClass(lpClassStruct)) ?
                    hinst : NULL;

                GlobalUnlock(hgblClassStruct);
            }

            GlobalFree(hgblClassStruct);
        }
    }
    return (hinstLib ? 1 : 0);  /* return 1 = success; 0 = fail */
}
```

See Also   **GlobalAlloc, GlobalFree, GlobalLock, GlobalUnlock, WEP**

LimitEmsPages

void LimitEmsPages(*cAppKB*)
DWORD *cAppKB*;   /* amount of expanded memory available to application   */

In Windows version 3.1, this function is obsolete and does nothing.

LineDDA

void LineDDA(*nXStart,* *nYStart,* *nXEnd,* *nYEnd,* *lnddaprc,* *lParam*)
int *nXStart*;   /* x-coordinate of line beginning   */
int *nYStart*;   /* y-coordinate of line beginning   */
int *nXEnd*;   /* x-coordinate of line end   */
int *nYEnd*;   /* y-coordinate of line end   */
LINEDDAPROC *lnddaprc*;   /* address of callback function   */
LPARAM *lParam*;   /* address of application-defined data   */

The **LineDDA** function computes all successive points in a line specified by
starting and ending coordinates. For each point on the line, the system calls an
application-defined callback function, specifying the coordinates of that point.

Parameters   *nXStart*
            Specifies the logical x-coordinate of the first point.

            nYStart
            Specifies the logical y-coordinate of the first point.

            nXEnd
            Specifies the logical x-coordinate of the endpoint. This endpoint is not part of
            the line.

            nYEnd
            Specifies the logical y-coordinate of the endpoint. This endpoint is not part of
            the line.

            lnddaprc
            Specifies the procedure-instance address of the application-defined callback
            function. The address must have been created by using the **MakeProcInstance**
            function. For more information about the callback function, see the description
            of the **LineDDAProc** callback function.

            lParam
            Points to 32 bits of application-defined data that is passed to the callback
            function.

Return Value   This function does not return a value.

Example   The following example uses the **LineDDA** function to draw a dot every two spaces between the beginning and ending points of a line:

```
/* Callback function */

void CALLBACK DrawDots(int xPos, int yPos, LPSTR lphdc)
{
    static short cSpaces = 1;

    if (cSpaces == 3) {

        /* Draw a black dot. */

        SetPixel(*(HDC FAR*) lphdc, xPos, yPos, 0);

        /* Initialize the space count. */

        cSpaces = 1;
    }
    else
        cSpaces++;
}
```

See Also   **LineDDAProc, MakeProcInstance**

LineDDAProc

3.1

void CALLBACK LineDDAProc(*xPos*, *yPos*, *lpData*)
int *xPos*;   /* x-coordinate of current position   */
int *yPos*;   /* y-coordinate of current position   */
LPARAM *lpData*;   /* address of application-defined data   */

The **LineDDAProc** function is an application-defined callback function that processes coordinates from the **LineDDA** function.

Parameters   *xPos*
      Specifies the x-coordinate of the current point.

yPos
      Specifies the y-coordinate of the current point.

lpData
      Points to the application-defined data.

Return Value   This function does not return a value.

Comments   An application must register this function by passing its address to the **LineDDA** function.

LineDDAProc is a placeholder for the application-defined function name. The actual name must be exported by including it in an **EXPORTS** statement in the application's module-definition file.

See Also   **LineDDA**

LineTo   2.x

BOOL LineTo(*hdc*, *nXEnd*, *nYEnd*)
HDC *hdc*;   /* handle of device context   */
int *nXEnd*;   /* x-coordinate of line endpoint   */
int *nYEnd*;   /* y-coordinate of line endpoint   */

The **LineTo** function draws a line from the current position up to, but not including, the specified endpoint. The function uses the selected pen to draw the line and sets the current position to the coordinates (*nXEnd,nYEnd*).

Parameters   *hdc*
                     Identifies the device context.

                     nXEnd
                     Specifies the logical x-coordinate of the line's endpoint.

                     nYEnd
                     Specifies the logical y-coordinate of the line's endpoint.

Return Value   The return value is nonzero if the function is successful. Otherwise, it is zero.

Example   The following example sets the current position by using the **MoveTo** function before calling the **LineTo** function. The example uses **POINT** structures to store the coordinates.

```
HDC hdc;

POINT ptStart = {  12,  12 };
POINT ptEnd = { 128, 135 };

MoveTo(hdc, ptStart.x, ptStart.y);
LineTo(hdc, ptEnd.x, ptEnd.y);
```

See Also   **MoveTo**

_llseek

[2.x]

LONG _llseek(*hf*, *lOffset*, *nOrigin*)
HFILE *hf*;   /* file handle   */
LONG *lOffset*;   /* number of bytes to move   */
int *nOrigin*;   /* position to move from   */

The **_llseek** function repositions the pointer in a previously opened file.

Parameters   *hf*
                    Identifies the file.

                    lOffset
                    Specifies the number of bytes the pointer is to be moved.

                    nOrigin
                    Specifies the starting position and direction of the pointer. This parameter must
                    be one of the following values:

Value	Meaning
0	Move the file pointer *lOffset* bytes from the beginning of the file.
1	Move the file pointer *lOffset* bytes from its current position.
2	Move the file pointer *lOffset* bytes from the end of the file.

Return Value   The return value specifies the new offset, in bytes, of the pointer from the begin-
                    ning of the file, if the function is successful. Otherwise, the return value is
                    HFILE_ERROR.

Comments   When a file is initially opened, the file pointer is positioned at the beginning of the
                    file. The **_llseek** function permits random access to a file's contents by moving
                    the pointer an arbitrary amount without reading data.

Example   The following example uses the **_llseek** function to move the file pointer to the
                    end of an existing file:

```
HFILE hfAppendFile;

/* Open the write file. */

hfAppendFile = _lopen("append.txt", WRITE);
```

```
                  /* Move to the end of the file. */

                  if (_llseek(hfAppendFile, 0L, 2) == -1) {
                      ErrorHandler();
                  }
```

See Also   **_lopen**

LoadAccelerators   2.x

HACCEL LoadAccelerators(*hinst*, *lpszTableName*)
HINSTANCE *hinst*;   /* handle of module to load from   */
LPCSTR *lpszTableName*;   /* address of table name   */

The **LoadAccelerators** function loads the specified accelerator table.

Parameters   *hinst*
                    Identifies an instance of the module whose executable file contains the accelera-
                    tor table to be loaded.

                    lpszTableName
                    Points to a null-terminated string that names the accelerator table to be loaded.

Return Value   The return value is the handle of the loaded accelerator table if the function is
                    successful. Otherwise, it is NULL.

Comments   If the accelerator table has not yet been loaded, the function loads it from the given
                    executable file.

                    Accelerator tables loaded from resources are freed automatically when the applica-
                    tion terminates.

LoadBitmap

2.x

HBITMAP LoadBitmap(*hinst*, *lpszBitmap*)
HINSTANCE *hinst*;   /* handle of application instance   */
LPCSTR *lpszBitmap*;   /* address of bitmap name   */

The **LoadBitmap** function loads the specified bitmap resource from the given module's executable file.

Parameters   *hinst*
Identifies the instance of the module whose executable file contains the bitmap to be loaded.

lpszBitmap
Points to a null-terminated string that contains the name of the bitmap resource to be loaded. Alternatively, this parameter can consist of the resource identifier in the low-order word and zero in the high-order word. The **MAKEINT-RESOURCE** macro can be used to create this value.

Return Value   The return value is the handle of the specified bitmap if the function is successful. Otherwise, it is NULL.

Comments   If the bitmap pointed to by *lpszBitmap* does not exist or if there is insufficient memory to load the bitmap, the function fails.

The application must call the **DeleteObject** function to delete each bitmap handle returned by the **LoadBitmap** function. This also applies to the following prede-fined bitmaps.

An application can use the **LoadBitmap** function to access the predefined bitmaps used by Windows. To do so, the application must set the *hinst* parameter to NULL and the *lpszBitmap* parameter to one of the following values:

OBM_BTNCORNERS
OBM_BTSIZE
OBM_CHECK
OBM_CHECKBOXES
OBM_CLOSE
OBM_COMBO
OBM_DNARROW
OBM_DNARROWD
OBM_DNARROWI
OBM_LFARROW
OBM_LFARROWD
OBM_LFARROWI
OBM_MNARROW
OBM_OLD_CLOSE

OBM_OLD_DNARROW
OBM_OLD_LFARROW
OBM_OLD_REDUCE
OBM_OLD_RESTORE
OBM_OLD_RGARROW
OBM_OLD_UPARROW
OBM_OLD_ZOOM
OBM_REDUCE
OBM_REDUCED
OBM_RESTORE
OBM_RESTORED
OBM_RGARROW
OBM_RGARROWD
OBM_RGARROWI
OBM_SIZE
OBM_UPARROW
OBM_UPARROWD
OBM_UPARROWI
OBM_ZOOM
OBM_ZOOMD

Bitmap names that begin with OBM_OLD represent bitmaps used by Windows versions earlier than 3.0.

The bitmaps identified by OBM_DNARROWI, OBM_LFARROWI, OBM_RGARROWI, and OBM_UPARROWI are new for Windows 3.1. These bitmaps are not found in device drivers for previous versions of Windows.

Note that for an application to use any of the OBM_ constants, the constant OEMRESOURCE must be defined before the WINDOWS.H header file is included.

The following shows the appearance of each of the OBM_ bitmaps.

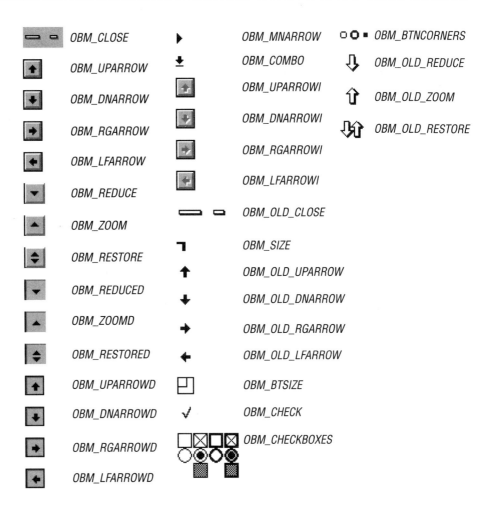

See Also   **DeleteObject**

LoadCursor

2.x

HCURSOR LoadCursor(*hinst, pszCursor*)
HINSTANCE *hinst*;   /* handle of application instance   */
LPCSTR *pszCursor*;   /* cursor-name string or cursor resource identifier   */

The **LoadCursor** function loads the specified cursor resource from the executable file associated with the given application instance.

Parameters

hinst

Identifies an instance of the module whose executable file contains the cursor to be loaded.

pszCursor

Points to a null-terminated string that contains the name of the cursor resource to be loaded. Alternatively, this parameter can consist of the resource identifier in the low-order word and zero in the high-order word. The **MAKEINT-RESOURCE** macro can be used to create this value.

Return Value

The return value is the handle of the newly loaded cursor if the function is successful. Otherwise, it is NULL.

Comments

The function loads the cursor resource only if it has not been loaded; otherwise, it retrieves a handle of the existing resource. The **LoadCursor** function returns a valid cursor handle only if the *pszCursor* parameter points to a cursor resource. If *pszCursor* points to any type of resource other than a cursor (such as an icon), the return value will not be NULL, even though it is not a valid cursor handle.

An application can use the **LoadCursor** function to access the predefined cursors used by Windows. To do this, the application must set the *hinst* parameter to NULL and the *pszCursor* parameter to one the following values:

Value	Meaning
IDC_ARROW	Standard arrow cursor.
IDC_CROSS	Crosshair cursor.
IDC_IBEAM	Text I-beam cursor.
IDC_ICON	Empty icon.
IDC_SIZE	A square with a smaller square inside its lower-right corner.
IDC_SIZENESW	Double-pointed cursor with arrows pointing northeast and southwest.
IDC_SIZENS	Double-pointed cursor with arrows pointing north and south.
IDC_SIZENWSE	Double-pointed cursor with arrows pointing northwest and southeast.
IDC_SIZEWE	Double-pointed cursor with arrows pointing west and east.
IDC_UPARROW	Vertical arrow cursor.
IDC_WAIT	Hourglass cursor.

It is not necessary to destroy these system cursors. An application should use the **DestroyCursor** function to destroy any private cursors it loads.

See Also

DestroyCursor, **SetCursor**, **ShowCursor**

LoadIcon

2.x

HICON LoadIcon(*hinst, pszIcon*)
HINSTANCE *hinst*;   /* handle of application instance   */
LPCSTR *pszIcon*;   /* icon-name string or icon resource identifier   */

The **LoadIcon** function loads the specified icon resource from the executable file associated with the given application instance.

Parameters

hinst
Identifies an instance of the module whose executable file contains the icon to be loaded. This parameter must be NULL when a system icon is being loaded.

pszIcon
Points to a null-terminated string that contains the name of the icon resource to be loaded. Alternatively, this parameter can consist of the resource identifier in the low-order word and zero in the high-order word. The **MAKEINT-RESOURCE** macro can be used to create this value.

Return Value

The return value is the handle of the newly loaded icon if the function is successful. Otherwise, it is NULL.

Comments

This function loads the icon resource only if it has not been loaded; otherwise, it retrieves a handle of the existing resource.

An application can use the **LoadIcon** function to access the predefined icons used by Windows. To do this, the application must set the *hinst* parameter to NULL and the *pszIcon* parameter to one of the following values:

Value	Meaning
IDI_APPLICATION	Default application icon.
IDI_ASTERISK	Asterisk (used in informative messages).
IDI_EXCLAMATION	Exclamation point (used in warning messages).
IDI_HAND	Hand-shaped icon (used in serious warning messages).
IDI_QUESTION	Question mark (used in prompting messages).

It is not necessary to destroy these system icons. An application should use the **DestroyIcon** function to destroy any private icons it loads.

The following shows all of the system icons.

 IDI_APPLICATION

 IDI_HAND

 IDI_QUESTION

 IDI_EXCLAMATION

 IDI_ASTERISK

See Also   **DestroyIcon, DrawIcon**

LoadLibrary   2.x

HINSTANCE LoadLibrary(*lpszLibFileName*)
LPCSTR *lpszLibFileName*;   /* address of name of library file   */

The **LoadLibrary** function loads the specified library module.

Parameters   *lpszLibFileName*
Points to a null-terminated string that names the library file to be loaded. If the string does not contain a path, Windows searches for the library in this order:

1. The current directory.

2. The Windows directory (the directory containing WIN.COM); the **Get-WindowsDirectory** function retrieves the path of this directory.

3. The Windows system directory (the directory containing such system files as GDI.EXE); the **GetSystemDirectory** function retrieves the path of this directory.

4. The directory containing the executable file for the current task; the **Get-ModuleFileName** function retrieves the path of this directory.

5. The directories listed in the PATH environment variable.

6. The list of directories mapped in a network.

Return Value   The return value is the instance handle of the loaded library module if the function is successful. Otherwise, it is an error value less than HINSTANCE_ERROR.

Errors

If the function fails, it returns one of the following error values:

Value	Meaning
0	System was out of memory, executable file was corrupt, or relocations were invalid.
2	File was not found.
3	Path was not found.
5	Attempt was made to dynamically link to a task, or there was a sharing or network-protection error.
6	Library required separate data segments for each task.
8	There was insufficient memory to start the application.
10	Windows version was incorrect.
11	Executable file was invalid. Either it was not a Windows application or there was an error in the .EXE image.
12	Application was designed for a different operating system.
13	Application was designed for MS-DOS 4.0.
14	Type of executable file was unknown.
15	Attempt was made to load a real-mode application (developed for an earlier version of Windows).
16	Attempt was made to load a second instance of an executable file containing multiple data segments that were not marked read-only.
19	Attempt was made to load a compressed executable file. The file must be decompressed before it can be loaded.
20	Dynamic-link library (DLL) file was invalid. One of the DLLs required to run this application was corrupt.
21	Application requires Microsoft Windows 32-bit extensions.

Comments

If the module has been loaded, **LoadLibrary** increments (increases by one) the module's reference count. If the module has not been loaded, the function loads it from the specified file.

LoadLibrary increments the reference count for a library module each time an application calls the function. When it has finished using the module, the application should use the **FreeLibrary** function to decrement (decrease by one) the reference count.

An application can use the **GetProcAddress** function to access functions in a library that was loaded using **LoadLibrary**.

Example

The following example uses the **LoadLibrary** function to load the Tool Helper Library TOOLHELP.DLL and the **FreeLibrary** function to free it:

```
HINSTANCE hinstToolHelp = LoadLibrary("TOOLHELP.DLL");
```

```
if ((UINT) hinstToolHelp > 32) {
        .
        . /* use GetProcAddress to use TOOLHELP functions */
        .
}
else {
    ErrorHandler();
}

if ((UINT) hinstToolHelp > 32)
    FreeLibrary(hinstToolHelp); /* free TOOLHELP.DLL     */
```

See Also   **FreeLibrary, GetProcAddress**

LoadMenu   2.x

HMENU LoadMenu(*hinst*, *lpszMenuName*)
HINSTANCE *hinst*;   /* handle of application instance   */
LPCSTR *lpszMenuName*;   /* menu-name string or menu resource identifier   */

The **LoadMenu** function loads the specified menu resource from the executable file associated with the given application instance.

Parameters   *hinst*
Identifies an instance of the module whose executable file contains the menu to be loaded.

lpszMenuName
Points to a null-terminated string that contains the name of the menu resource to be loaded. Alternatively, this parameter can consist of the resource identifier in the low-order word and zero in the high-order word. The **MAKEINT-RESOURCE** macro can be used to create this value.

Return Value   The return value is the handle of the menu resource if the function is successful. Otherwise, it is NULL.

Comments   Before exiting, an application must free system resources associated with a menu if the menu is not assigned to a window. An application frees a menu by calling the **DestroyMenu** function.

Example   The following example loads a menu resource, and then assigns the menu to a window:

```
HMENU hmenu;

hmenu = LoadMenu(hinst, "ColorMenu");
SetMenu(hwnd, hmenu);
```

See Also   **DestroyMenu, LoadMenuIndirect, SetMenu**

LoadMenuIndirect   2.x

HMENU LoadMenuIndirect(*lpmith*)
const void FAR* *lpmith*;   /* address of menu template   */

The **LoadMenuIndirect** function loads the specified menu template in memory.
A menu template is a header followed by a collection of one or more **MENU-
ITEMTEMPLATE** structures, each of which may contain one or more menu
items and pop-up menus.

Parameters   *lpmith*
          Points to a menu template, which consists of a menu-template header and one
          or more menu item templates. The menu template header consists of a **MENU-
          ITEMTEMPLATEHEADER** structure, which has the following form:

```
typedef struct {      /* mith */
    UINT    versionNumber;
    UINT    offset;
} MENUITEMTEMPLATEHEADER;
```

          Each menu item template consists of a **MENUITEMTEMPLATE** structure.
          The **MENUITEMTEMPLATE** structure has the following form:

```
typedef  struct {    /* mit */
    UINT mtOption;
    UINT mtID;
    char mtString[1];
} MENUITEMTEMPLATE;
```

          For a full description of these two structures, see the *Microsoft Windows Pro-
          grammer's Reference, Volume 3.*

Return Value   The return value is the handle of a menu if the function is successful. Otherwise, it
          is NULL.

Comments   Before exiting, an application must free system resources associated with a menu if the menu is not assigned to a window. An application frees a menu by calling the **DestroyMenu** function.

Example   The following example retrieves a menu handle for a menu template resource that has been loaded into memory, gives the menu handle to a window, and then unlocks and frees the resource:

```
HRSRC hrsrcResInfo;
HGLOBAL hglbResMenu;
char FAR* lpResMenu;
HMENU hmenu;

case IDM_NEWMENU:
    hrsrcResInfo = FindResource(hinst, "DynaMenu", RT_MENU);
    hglbResMenu = LoadResource(hinst, hrsrcResInfo);
    lpResMenu = LockResource(hglbResMenu);
    hmenu = LoadMenuIndirect(lpResMenu);

    DestroyMenu(GetMenu(hwnd));
    SetMenu(hwnd, hmenu);

    UnlockResource(hglbResMenu);
    FreeResource(hglbResMenu);

    break;
```

See Also   **DestroyMenu, LoadMenu, SetMenu**

LoadModule   `3.0`

HINSTANCE LoadModule(*lpszModuleName, lpvParameterBlock*)
LPCSTR *lpszModuleName*;   /* address of filename to load   */
LPVOID *lpvParameterBlock*;   /* address of parameter block for new module   */

The **LoadModule** function loads and executes a Windows application or creates a new instance of an existing Windows application.

Parameters   *lpszModuleName*
              Points to a null-terminated string that contains the complete filename (including the file extension) of the application to be run. If the string does not contain a path, Windows searches for the executable file in this order:
              1. The current directory.

2. The Windows directory (the directory containing WIN.COM), whose path the **GetWindowsDirectory** function retrieves.

3. The Windows system directory (the directory containing such system files as GDI.EXE), whose path the **GetSystemDirectory** function retrieves.

4. The directory containing the executable file for the current task; the **GetModuleFileName** function obtains the path of this directory.

5. The directories listed in the PATH environment variable.

6. The list of directories mapped in a network.

lpvParameterBlock
Points to an application-defined LOADPARMS structure that defines the new application's parameter block. The LOADPARMS structure has the following form:

```
struct _LOADPARMS {
    WORD      segEnv;        /* child environment  */
    LPSTR     lpszCmdLine;   /* child command tail */
    UINT FAR* lpShow;        /* how to show child  */
    UINT FAR* lpReserved;    /* must be NULL        */
} LOADPARMS;
```

Member	Description
segEnv	Specifies whether the child application receives a copy of the parent application's environment or a new environment created by the parent application. If this member is zero, the child application receives an exact duplicate of the parent application's environment block. If the member is nonzero, the value entered must be the segment address of a memory object containing a copy of the new environment for the child application.
lpszCommandLine	Points to a null-terminated string that specifies the command line (excluding the child application name). This string must not exceed 120 characters. If there is no command line, this member must point to a zero-length string (it cannot be set to NULL).
lpShow	Points to an array containing two 16-bit values. The first value must always be set to two. The second value specifies how the application window is to be shown. For a list of the acceptable values, see the description of the *nCmdShow* parameter of the **ShowWindow** function.
lpReserved	Reserved; must be NULL.

Return Value

The return value is the instance handle of the loaded module if the function is successful. If the function fails, it returns an error value less than HINSTANCE_ERROR.

Errors

If the function fails, it returns one of the following error values:

Value	Meaning
0	System was out of memory, executable file was corrupt, or relocations were invalid.
2	File was not found.
3	Path was not found.
5	Attempt was made to dynamically link to a task, or there was a sharing or network-protection error.
6	Library required separate data segments for each task.
8	There was insufficient memory to start the application.
10	Windows version was incorrect.
11	Executable file was invalid. Either it was not a Windows application or there was an error in the .EXE image.
12	Application was designed for a different operating system.
13	Application was designed for MS-DOS 4.0.
14	Type of executable file was unknown.
15	Attempt was made to load a real-mode application (developed for an earlier version of Windows).
16	Attempt was made to load a second instance of an executable file containing multiple data segments that were not marked read-only.
19	Attempt was made to load a compressed executable file. The file must be decompressed before it can be loaded.
20	Dynamic-link library (DLL) file was invalid. One of the DLLs required to run this application was corrupt.
21	Application requires Microsoft Windows 32-bit extensions.

Comments

The **WinExec** function provides an alternative method for executing an application.

Example

The following example uses the **LoadModule** function to run an executable file named DRAW.EXE:

```
struct LOADPARMS {
    WORD   segEnv;              /* child environment  */
    LPSTR  lpszCmdLine;        /* child command tail */
    LPWORD lpwShow;            /* how to show child  */
    LPWORD lpwReserved;        /* must be NULL       */
};

char szMsg[80];
HINSTANCE hinstMod;
struct LOADPARMS parms;
WORD awShow[2] = { 2, SW_SHOWMINIMIZED };
```

```
        parms.segEnv = 0;                    /* child inherits environment */
        parms.lpszCmdLine = (LPSTR) "";      /* no command line           */
        parms.lpwShow = (LPWORD) awShow;     /* shows child as an icon */
        parms.lpwReserved = (LPWORD) NULL;   /* must be NULL              */

        hinstMod = LoadModule("draw.exe", &parms);

        if ((UINT) hinstMod < 32) {
            sprintf(szMsg, "LoadModule failed; error code = %d",
                hinstMod);
            MessageBox(hwnd, szMsg, "Error", MB_ICONSTOP);
        }
        else {
            sprintf(szMsg, "LoadModule returned %d", hinstMod);
            MessageBox(hwnd, szMsg, "", MB_OK);
        }
```

See Also   **FreeModule, GetModuleFileName, GetSystemDirectory, GetWindowsDirectory, ShowWindow, WinExec**

LoadProc   2.x

HGLOBAL CALLBACK LoadProc(*hglbMem, hinst, hrsrcResInfo***)**
HGLOBAL *hglbMem*;   /* handle of object containing resource   */
HINSTANCE *hinst*;   /* handle of application instance   */
HRSRC *hrsrcResInfo*;   /* handle of a resource   */

The **LoadProc** function is an application-defined callback function that receives information about a resource to be locked and can process that information as needed.

Parameters   *hglbMem*
Identifies a memory object that contains a resource. This parameter is NULL if the resource has not yet been loaded.

hinst
Identifies the instance of the module whose executable file contains the resource.

hrsrcResInfo
Identifies the resource. The resource must have been created by using the **FindResource** function.

Return Value   The return value is a global memory handle for memory that was allocated using the GMEM_DDESHARE flag in the **GlobalAlloc** function.

Comments If an attempt to lock the memory object identified by the *hglbMem* parameter fails, this means the resource has been discarded and must be reloaded.

LoadProc is a placeholder for the application-defined function name. The actual name must be exported by including it in an **EXPORTS** statement in the application's module-definition file.

See Also **FindResource, GlobalAlloc, SetResourceHandler**

LoadResource

2.x

```
HGLOBAL LoadResource(hinst, hrsrc)
HINSTANCE hinst;        /* handle of file containing resource    */
HRSRC hrsrc;            /* handle of resource                    */
```

The **LoadResource** function loads the specified resource in global memory.

Parameters *hinst*
Identifies an instance of the module whose executable file contains the resource to be loaded.

hrsrc
Identifies the resource to be loaded. This handle must have been created by using the **FindResource** function.

Return Value The return value is the instance handle of the global memory object containing the data associated with the resource. It is NULL if no such resource exists.

Comments When finished with a resource, an application should free the global memory associated with it by using the **FreeResource** function.

If the specified resource has been loaded, this function simply increments the reference count for the resource.

The resource is not loaded until the **LockResource** function is called to translate the handle returned by **LoadResource** into a far pointer to the resource data.

See Also **FindResource, FreeResource, LockResource**

LoadString

int **LoadString**(*hinst*, *idResource*, *lpszBuffer*, *cbBuffer*)
HINSTANCE *hinst*;   /* handle of module containing string resource   */
UINT *idResource*;   /* resource identifier   */
LPSTR *lpszBuffer*;   /* address of buffer for resource   */
int *cbBuffer*;   /* size of buffer   */

The **LoadString** function loads the specified string resource.

Parameters   *hinst*
Identifies an instance of the module whose executable file contains the string resource to be loaded.

idResource
Specifies the integer identifier of the string to be loaded.

lpszBuffer
Points to the buffer that will receive the null-terminated string.

cbBuffer
Specifies the buffer size, in bytes. The buffer should be large enough for the string and its terminating null character. The string is truncated if it is longer than the number of bytes specified.

Return Value   The return value specifies the number of bytes copied into the buffer, if the function is successful. It is zero if the string resource does not exist.

LocalAlloc

HLOCAL LocalAlloc(*fuAllocFlags*, *fuAlloc*)
UINT *fuAllocFlags*;   /* allocation attributes   */
UINT *fuAlloc*;   /* number of bytes to allocate   */

The **LocalAlloc** function allocates the specified number of bytes from the local heap.

Parameters   *fuAllocFlags*
Specifies how to allocate memory. This parameter can be a combination of the following values:

Value	Meaning
LHND	Combines the LMEM_MOVEABLE and LMEM_ZEROINIT flags.
LMEM_DISCARDABLE	Allocates discardable memory.
LMEM_FIXED	Allocates fixed memory. The LMEM_FIXED and LMEM_MOVEABLE flags cannot be combined.
LMEM_MOVEABLE	Allocates movable memory. The LMEM_FIXED and LMEM_MOVEABLE flags cannot be combined.
LMEM_NOCOMPACT	Does not compact or discard memory to satisfy the allocation request.
LMEM_NODISCARD	Does not discard memory to satisfy the allocation request.
LMEM_ZEROINIT	Initializes memory contents to zero.
LPTR	Combines the LMEM_FIXED and LMEM_ZEROINIT flags.
NONZEROLHND	Same as the LMEM_MOVEABLE flag.
NONZEROLPTR	Same as the LMEM_FIXED flag.

fuAlloc
Specifies the number of bytes to be allocated.

Return Value   The return value is the instance handle of the newly allocated local memory object, if the function is successful. Otherwise, it is NULL.

Comments   If **LocalAlloc** allocates movable memory, the return value is a local handle of the memory. To access the memory, an application must use the **LocalLock** function to convert the handle to a pointer.

If **LocalAlloc** allocates fixed memory, the return value is a pointer to the memory. To access the memory, an application can simply cast the return value to a pointer.

Fixed memory will be slightly faster than movable memory. If memory will be allocated and freed without an intervening local allocation or reallocation, then the memory should be allocated as fixed.

If this function is successful, it allocates at least the amount requested. If the amount allocated is greater than the amount requested, the application can use the entire amount. To determine the size of a local memory object, an application can use the **LocalSize** function.

To free a local memory object, an application should use the **LocalFree** function. To change the size or attributes of an allocated memory object, an application can use the **LocalReAlloc** function.

See Also   **LocalFree, LocalLock, LocalReAlloc, LocalSize, LocalUnlock**

LocalCompact

2.x

UINT **LocalCompact**(*uMinFree*)
UINT *uMinFree*;   /* amount of memory requested   */

The **LocalCompact** function rearranges the local heap so that the specified amount of memory is free.

Parameters   *uMinFree*
Specifies the number of contiguous free bytes requested. If this parameter is zero, the function does not compact memory, but the return value is valid.

Return Value   The return value specifies the number of bytes in the largest free local memory object. If the *uMinFree* parameter is zero, the return value specifies the number of bytes in the largest free object that Windows can generate if it removes all discardable objects.

Comments   The function first checks the local heap for the specified number of contiguous free bytes. If the bytes do not exist, the function compacts local memory by moving all unlocked, movable objects into high memory. If this does not generate the requested amount of space, the function discards movable and discardable objects that are not locked, until the requested amount of space is generated (if possible).

See Also   **LocalAlloc, LocalLock**

LocalFirst

3.1

#include <toolhelp.h>

BOOL **LocalFirst**(*lple, hglbHeap*)
LOCALENTRY FAR* *lple*;   /* address of LOCALENTRY structure   */
HGLOBAL *hglbHeap*;   /* handle of local heap   */

The **LocalFirst** function fills the specified structure with information that describes the first object on the local heap.

Parameters   *lple*
Points to a **LOCALENTRY** structure that will receive information about the local memory object. The **LOCALENTRY** structure has the following form:

```
#include <toolhelp.h>

typedef struct tagLOCALENTRY {   /* le */
    DWORD   dwSize;
    HLOCAL  hHandle;
    WORD    wAddress;
    WORD    wSize;
    WORD    wFlags;
    WORD    wcLock;
    WORD    wType;
    WORD    hHeap;
    WORD    wHeapType;
    WORD    wNext;
} LOCALENTRY;
```

For a full description of this structure, see the *Microsoft Windows Programmer's Reference, Volume 3.*

hglbHeap
Identifies the local heap.

Return Value   The return value is nonzero if the function is successful. Otherwise, it is zero.

Comments   The **LocalFirst** function can be used to begin a local heap walk. An application can examine subsequent objects on the local heap by using the **LocalNext** function.

Before calling **LocalFirst**, an application must initialize the **LOCALENTRY** structure and specify its size, in bytes, in the **dwSize** member.

See Also   **LocalInfo, LocalNext**

LocalFlags
2.x

UINT LocalFlags(*hloc*)
HLOCAL *hloc*;   /* handle of local memory object   */

The **LocalFlags** function retrieves information about the given local memory object.

Parameters   *hloc*
Identifies the local memory object.

Return Value	The low-order byte of the return value contains the lock count of the object; the high-order byte contains either LMEM_DISCARDABLE (object has been marked as discardable) or LMEM_DISCARDED (object has been discarded).
Comments	To retrieve the lock count from the return value, use the LMEM_LOCKCOUNT mask.
See Also	**LocalAlloc, LocalLock, LocalReAlloc, LocalUnlock**

LocalFree 2.x

HLOCAL LocalFree(*hloc*)
HLOCAL *hloc*;   /* handle of local memory object   */

The **LocalFree** function frees the given local memory object (if the object is not locked) and invalidates its handle.

Parameters	*hloc* Identifies the local memory object to be freed.
Return Value	The return value is NULL if the function is successful. Otherwise, it is equal to the *hloc* parameter.
Comments	An application cannot use the **LocalFree** function to free a locked memory object—that is, a memory object with a lock count greater than zero. After freeing the handle of the memory object, an application cannot use the handle again. An attempt to free the same memory object more than once can cause Windows to terminate abnormally.
See Also	**LocalFlags, LocalLock**

LocalHandle 2.x

HLOCAL LocalHandle(*pvMem*)
void NEAR* *pvMem*;   /* address of local memory object   */

The **LocalHandle** function retrieves the handle of the specified local memory object.

Parameters	*pvMem*
	Specifies the address of the local memory object.

Return Value   The return value is the handle of the specified local memory object if the function is successful. It is NULL if the specified address has no handle.

See Also   **LocalAlloc**

LocalInfo

3.1

#include <toolhelp.h>

BOOL LocalInfo(*lpli*, *hglbHeap***)**
LOCALINFO FAR* *lpli*;   /* address of LOCALINFO structure   */
HGLOBAL *hglbHeap*;   /* handle of local heap   */

The **LocalInfo** function fills the specified structure with information that describes the local heap.

Parameters   *lpli*
Points to a **LOCALINFO** structure that will receive information about the local heap. The **LOCALINFO** structure has the following form:

```
#include <toolhelp.h>

typedef struct tagLOCALINFO {  /* li */
    DWORD  dwSize;
    WORD   wcItems;
} LOCALINFO;
```

For a full description of this structure, see the *Microsoft Windows Programmer's Reference, Volume 3.*

hglbHeap
Identifies the local heap to be described.

Return Value   The return value is nonzero if the function is successful. Otherwise, it is zero.

Comments   The information in the **LOCALINFO** structure can be used to determine how much memory to allocate for a local heap walk.

Before calling **LocalInfo**, an application must initialize the **LOCALINFO** structure and specify its size, in bytes, in the **dwSize** member.

See Also   **LocalFirst, LocalNext**

LocalInit

BOOL LocalInit(*uSegment*, *uStartAddr*, *uEndAddr*)
UINT *uSegment*;   /* segment to contain local heap   */
UINT *uStartAddr*;   /* starting address for heap   */
UINT *uEndAddr*;   /* ending address for heap   */

The **LocalInit** function initializes a local heap in the specified segment.

Parameters   *uSegment*
    Identifies the segment that is to contain the local heap.

    uStartAddr
    Specifies the starting address of the local heap within the segment.

    uEndAddr
    Specifies the ending address of the local heap within the segment.

Return Value   The return value is nonzero if the function is successful. Otherwise, it is zero.

Comments   The first 16 bytes of the segment containing a local heap must be reserved for use by the system.

See Also   **GlobalLock, LocalAlloc, LocalReAlloc**

LocalLock

void NEAR* LocalLock(*hloc*)
HLOCAL *hloc*;   /* handle of local memory object   */

The **LocalLock** function retrieves a pointer to the given local memory object. **LocalLock** increments (increases by one) the lock count of movable objects and locks the memory.

Parameters   *hloc*
    Identifies the local memory object to be locked.

Return Value   The return value points to the first byte of memory in the local object, if the function is successful. It is NULL if the object has been discarded or an error occurs.

Comments   Each time an application calls **LocalLock** for an object, it must eventually call **LocalUnlock** for the object.

This function will return NULL if an application attempts to lock a memory object with a size of 0 bytes.

The **LocalUnlock** function decrements (decreases by one) the lock count for the object if **LocalLock** incremented the count. Other functions can also affect the lock count of a memory object.

Locked memory will not be moved or discarded unless the memory object is reallocated by the **LocalReAlloc** function. The object remains locked in memory until its lock count is decreased to zero.

Discarded objects always have a lock count of zero.

See Also   **LocalFlags, LocalReAlloc, LocalUnlock**

LocalNext   3.1

#include <toolhelp.h>

BOOL LocalNext(*lple***)**
LOCALENTRY FAR* *lple*;   /* address of LOCALENTRY structure   */

The **LocalNext** function fills the specified structure with information that describes the next object on the local heap.

Parameters   *lple*
Points to a **LOCALENTRY** structure that will receive information about the local memory object. The **LOCALENTRY** structure has the following form:

```
#include <toolhelp.h>

typedef struct tagLOCALENTRY {  /* le */
    DWORD   dwSize;
    HLOCAL  hHandle;
    WORD    wAddress;
    WORD    wSize;
    WORD    wFlags;
    WORD    wcLock;
    WORD    wType;
```

```
            WORD    hHeap;
            WORD    wHeapType;
            WORD    wNext;
        } LOCALENTRY;
```

For a full description of this structure, see the *Microsoft Windows Programmer's Reference, Volume 3*.

Return Value   The return value is nonzero if the function is successful. Otherwise, it is zero.

Comments   The **LocalNext** function can be used to continue a local heap walk started by the **LocalFirst** function.

See Also   **LocalFirst**, **LocalInfo**

LocalReAlloc   `2.x`

HLOCAL LocalReAlloc(*hloc*, *fuNewSize*, *fuFlags*)
HLOCAL *hloc*;   /* handle of local memory object   */
UINT *fuNewSize*;   /* new size of object   */
UINT *fuFlags*;   /* new allocation attributes   */

The **LocalReAlloc** function changes the size or attributes of the given local memory object.

Parameters   *hloc*
Identifies the local memory object to be reallocated.

fuNewSize
Specifies the new size of the local memory object.

fuFlags
Specifies how to reallocate the local memory object. If this parameter includes the LMEM_MODIFY and LMEM_DISCARDABLE flags, **LocalReAlloc** ignores the *fuNewSize* parameter. The *fuFlags* parameter can be a combination of the following values.

Value	Meaning
LMEM_DISCARDABLE	Causes a previously movable object to become discardable. This flag can be used only with LMEM_MODIFY.
LMEM_MODIFY	Modifies the object's memory flags. This flag can be used only with LMEM_DISCARDABLE.

Value	Meaning
LMEM_MOVEABLE	If *fuNewSize* is zero, this flag causes a previously fixed object to be freed or a previously movable object to be discarded (if the object's lock count is zero). This flag cannot be used with LMEM_MODIFY.
	If *fuNewSize* is nonzero and the object identified by the *hloc* parameter is fixed, this flag allows the reallocated object to be moved to a new fixed location.
LMEM_NOCOMPACT	Prevents memory from being compacted or discarded to satisfy the allocation request. This flag cannot be used with LMEM_MODIFY.
LMEM_ZEROINIT	If the object is growing, this flag causes the additional memory contents to be initialized to zero. This flag cannot be used with LMEM_MODIFY.

Return Value

The return value is the handle of the reallocated local memory object, if the function is successful. Otherwise, it is NULL.

Comments

If **LocalReAlloc** reallocates a movable object, the return value is a local handle of the memory. To access the memory, an application must use the **LocalLock** function to convert the handle to a pointer.

If **LocalReAlloc** reallocates a fixed object, the return value is a pointer to the memory. To access the memory, an application can simply cast the return value to a pointer.

To free a local memory object, an application should use the **LocalFree** function.

See Also

LocalAlloc, LocalDiscard, LocalFree, LocalLock

LocalShrink

2.x

UINT LocalShrink(*hloc*, *cbNewSize***)**
HLOCAL *hloc*;   /* segment containing local heap   */
UINT *cbNewSize*;   /* new size of local heap   */

The **LocalShrink** function shrinks the local heap in the given segment.

Parameters

hloc
Identifies the segment that contains the local heap. If this parameter is zero, the function shrinks the heap in the current data segment.

cbNewSize
  Specifies the new size, in bytes, of the local heap.

Return Value   The return value specifies the new size of the local heap if the function is successful.

Comments   Windows will not shrink the portion of the data segment that contains the stack and the static variables.

Use the **GlobalSize** function to determine the new size of the data segment.

See Also   **GlobalSize**

LocalSize   2.x

UINT LocalSize(*hloc*)
HLOCAL *hloc*;   /* handle of local memory object   */

The **LocalSize** function returns the current size, in bytes, of the given local memory object.

Parameters   *hloc*
  Identifies the local memory object.

Return Value   The return value specifies the size, in bytes, of the memory object, if the function is successful. It is zero if the specified handle is invalid or if the object has been discarded.

Comments   The size of a memory object sometimes is larger than the size requested when the memory was allocated.

To verify that the memory object has not been discarded, an application should call the **LocalFlags** function prior to calling the **LocalSize** function. If the memory object has been discarded, the return value for **LocalSize** is meaningless.

See Also   **LocalAlloc, LocalFlags**

LocalUnlock

BOOL LocalUnlock(*hloc*)
HLOCAL *hloc*;   /* handle of local memory object   */

The **LocalUnlock** function unlocks the given local memory object. This function has no effect on fixed memory.

Parameters   *hloc*
     Identifies the local memory object to be unlocked.

Return Value   The return value is zero if the function is successful. Otherwise, it is nonzero.

Comments   With discardable memory, this function decrements (decreases by one) the object's lock count. The object is completely unlocked, and subject to discarding, if the lock count is decreased to zero.

See Also   **LocalLock**

LockInput

BOOL LockInput(*hReserved*, *hwndInput*, *fLock*)
HANDLE *hReserved*;   /* reserved, must be NULL   */
HWND *hwndInput*;   /* handle of window to receive all input   */
BOOL *fLock*;   /* the lock/unlock flag   */

The **LockInput** function locks input to all tasks except the current one, if the *fLock* parameter is TRUE. The given window is made system modal; that is, it will receive all input. If *fLock* is FALSE, **LockInput** unlocks input and restores the system to its unlocked state.

Parameters   *hReserved*
     This parameter is reserved and must be NULL.

     hwndInput
     Identifies the window that is to receive all input. This window must be in the current task. If *fLock* is FALSE, this parameter should be NULL.

     fLock
     Indicates whether to lock or unlock input. A value of TRUE locks input; a value of FALSE unlocks input.

Return Value   The return value is nonzero if the function is successful. Otherwise, it is zero.

Comments   Before entering hard mode, a Windows-based debugger calls **LockInput**, specifying TRUE for the *fLock* parameter. This action saves the current global state. To exit hard mode, the debugger calls **LockInput**, specifying FALSE for *fLock*. This restores the global state to the conditions that existed when the debugger entered hard mode. A debugger must restore the global state before exiting. Calls to **LockInput** cannot be nested.

See Also   **DirectedYield**

LockResource   `2.x`

void FAR* LockResource(*hglb***)**
HGLOBAL *hglb*;   /* handle of resource   */

The **LockResource** function locks the given resource. The resource is locked in memory and its reference count is incremented (increased by one). The locked resource is not subject to discarding.

Parameters   *hglb*
Identifies the resource to be locked. This handle must have been created by using the **LoadResource** function.

Return Value   The return value points to the first byte of the loaded resource if the function is successful. Otherwise, it is NULL.

Comments   The resource remains locked in memory until its reference count is decreased to zero by calls to the **FreeResource** function.

If the resource identified by the *hglb* parameter has been discarded, the resource-handler function (if any) associated with the resource is called before the **LockResource** function returns. The resource-handler function can recalculate and reload the resource if necessary. After the resource-handler function returns, **LockResource** makes another attempt to lock the resource and returns with the result.

Using the handle returned by the **FindResource** function for the *hglb* parameter causes an error.

Use the **UnlockResource** macro to unlock a resource that was locked by **LockResource**.

See Also   **FindResource, FreeResource, SetResourceHandler**

LockSegment

2.x

HGLOBAL LockSegment(*uSegment*)
UINT *uSegment*;   /* segment to lock   */

The **LockSegment** function locks the specified discardable segment. The segment
is locked into memory at the given address and its lock count is incremented
(increased by one).

Parameters   *uSegment*
Specifies the segment address of the segment to be locked. If this parameter
is −1, the **LockSegment** function locks the current data segment.

Return Value   The return value specifies the data segment if the function is successful. It is
NULL if the segment has been discarded or an error occurs.

Comments   Locked memory is not subject to discarding except when a portion of the segment
is being reallocated by the **GlobalReAlloc** function. The segment remains locked
in memory until its lock count is decreased to zero by the **UnlockSegment** function.

Each time an application calls **LockSegment** for a segment, it must eventually call
UnlockSegment for the segment. The **UnlockSegment** function decrements the
lock count for the segment. Other functions also can affect the lock count of a
memory object. For a list of these functions, see the description of the **Global-
Flags** function.

See Also   **GlobalFlags, GlobalReAlloc, LockData, UnlockSegment**

LockWindowUpdate

3.1

BOOL LockWindowUpdate(*hwndLock*)
HWND *hwndLock*;   /* handle of window   */

The **LockWindowUpdate** function disables or reenables drawing in the given
window. A locked window cannot be moved. Only one window can be locked at a
time.

Parameters   *hwndLock*
Identifies the window in which drawing will be disabled. If this parameter is
NULL, drawing in the locked window is enabled.

Return Value The return value is nonzero if the function is successful. It is zero if a failure occurs or if the **LockWindowUpdate** function has been used to lock another window.

Comments If an application with a locked window (or any locked child windows) calls the **GetDC**, **GetDCEx**, or **BeginPaint** function, the called function returns a device context whose visible region is empty. This will occur until the application unlocks the window by calling **LockWindowUpdate**, specifying a value of NULL for *hwndLock*.

While window updates are locked, the system keeps track of the bounding rectangle of any drawing operations to device contexts associated with a locked window. When drawing is reenabled, this bounding rectangle is invalidated in the locked window and its child windows to force an eventual WM_PAINT message to update the screen. If no drawing has occurred while the window updates were locked, no area is invalidated.

The **LockWindowUpdate** function does not make the given window invisible and does not clear the WS_VISIBLE style bit.

LogError   `3.1`

void LogError(*uErr*, *lpvInfo*)
UINT *uErr*;   /* error type   */
void FAR* *lpvInfo*;   /* address of error information   */

The **LogError** function identifies the most recent system error. An application's interrupt callback function typically calls **LogError** to return error information to the user.

Parameters *uErr*
Specifies the type of error that occurred. The *lpvInfo* parameter may point to more information about the error, depending on the value of *uErr*. This parameter may be one or more of the following values:

Value	Meaning
ERR_ALLOCRES	**AllocResource** failed.
ERR_BADINDEX	Bad index to **GetClassLong**, **GetClassWord**, **GetWindowLong**, **GetWindowWord**, **SetClassLong**, **SetClassWord**, **SetWindowLong**, or **SetWindowWord**.
ERR_BYTE	Invalid 8-bit parameter.

Value	Meaning
ERR_CREATEDC	**CreateCompatibleDC**, **CreateDC**, or **CreateIC** failed.
ERR_CREATEDLG	Could not create dialog box because **LoadMenu** failed.
ERR_CREATEDLG2	Could not create dialog box because **CreateWindow** failed.
ERR_CREATEMENU	Could not create menu.
ERR_CREATEMETA	**CreateMetaFile** failed.
ERR_CREATEWND	Could not create window because the class was not found.
ERR_DCBUSY	Device context (DC) cache is full.
ERR_DELOBJSELECTED	Program is trying to delete a bitmap that is selected into the DC.
ERR_DWORD	Invalid 32-bit parameter.
ERR_GALLOC	**GlobalAlloc** failed.
ERR_GLOCK	**GlobalLock** failed.
ERR_GREALLOC	**GlobalReAlloc** failed.
ERR_LALLOC	**LocalAlloc** failed.
ERR_LLOCK	**LocalLock** failed.
ERR_LOADMENU	**LoadMenu** failed.
ERR_LOADMODULE	**LoadModule** failed.
ERR_LOADSTR	**LoadString** failed.
ERR_LOCKRES	**LockResource** failed.
ERR_LREALLOC	**LocalReAlloc** failed.
ERR_NESTEDBEGINPAINT	Program contains nested **BeginPaint** calls.
ERR_REGISTERCLASS	**RegisterClass** failed because the class is already registered.
ERR_SELBITMAP	Program is trying to select a bitmap that is already selected.
ERR_SIZE_MASK	Identifies which 2 bits of *uErr* specify the size of the invalid parameter.
ERR_STRUCEXTRA	Program is using unallocated space.
ERR_WARNING	A non-fatal error occurred.
ERR_WORD	Invalid 16-bit parameter.

lpvInfo

Points to more information about the error. The value of *lpvInfo* depends on the value of *uErr*. If the value of (*uErr* & ERR_SIZE_MASK) is 0, *lpvInfo* is undefined. Currently, no *uErr* code has defined meanings for *lpvInfo*.

Return Value   This function does not return a value.

Comments   The errors identified by **LogError** may be trapped by the callback function that **NotifyRegister** installs.

Error values whose low 12 bits are less than 0x07FF are reserved for use by Windows.

See Also   **LogParamError, NotifyRegister**

LogParamError   3.1

void LogParamError(*uErr, lpfn, lpvParam*)
UINT *uErr*;   /* error type   */
FARPROC *lpfn*;   /* address where error occurred   */
void FAR* *lpvParam*; /* address of more error information   */

The **LogParamError** function identifies the most recent parameter validation error. An application's interrupt callback function typically calls **LogParamError** to return information about an invalid parameter to the user.

Parameters   *uErr*
Specifies the type of parameter validation error that occurred. The *lpvParam* parameter may point to more information about the error, depending on the value of *uErr*. This parameter may be one or more of the following values:

Value	Meaning
ERR_BAD_ATOM	Invalid atom.
ERR_BAD_CID	Invalid communications identifier (CID).
ERR_BAD_COORDS	Invalid x,y coordinates.
ERR_BAD_DFLAGS	Invalid 32-bit flags.
ERR_BAD_DINDEX	Invalid 32-bit index or index out-of-range.
ERR_BAD_DVALUE	Invalid 32-bit signed or unsigned value.
ERR_BAD_FLAGS	Invalid bit flags.
ERR_BAD_FUNC_PTR	Invalid function pointer.
ERR_BAD_GDI_OBJECT	Invalid graphics device interface (GDI) object.
ERR_BAD_GLOBAL_HANDLE	Invalid global handle.
ERR_BAD_HANDLE	Invalid generic handle.
ERR_BAD_HBITMAP	Invalid bitmap handle.
ERR_BAD_HBRUSH	Invalid brush handle.
ERR_BAD_HCURSOR	Invalid cursor handle.

Value	Meaning
ERR_BAD_HDC	Invalid device context (DC) handle.
ERR_BAD_HDRVR	Invalid driver handle.
ERR_BAD_HDWP	Invalid handle of a window-position structure.
ERR_BAD_HFILE	Invalid file handle.
ERR_BAD_HFONT	Invalid font handle.
ERR_BAD_HICON	Invalid icon handle.
ERR_BAD_HINSTANCE	Invalid instance handle.
ERR_BAD_HMENU	Invalid menu handle.
ERR_BAD_HMETAFILE	Invalid metafile handle.
ERR_BAD_HMODULE	Invalid module handle.
ERR_BAD_HPALETTE	Invalid palette handle.
ERR_BAD_HPEN	Invalid pen handle.
ERR_BAD_HRGN	Invalid region handle.
ERR_BAD_HWND	Invalid window handle.
ERR_BAD_INDEX	Invalid index or index out-of-range.
ERR_BAD_LOCAL_HANDLE	Invalid local handle.
ERR_BAD_PTR	Invalid pointer.
ERR_BAD_SELECTOR	Invalid selector.
ERR_BAD_STRING_PTR	Invalid zero-terminated string pointer.
ERR_BAD_VALUE	Invalid 16-bit signed or unsigned value.
ERR_BYTE	Invalid 8-bit parameter.
ERR_DWORD	Invalid 32-bit parameter.
ERR_PARAM	A parameter validation error occurred. This flag is always set.
ERR_SIZE_MASK	Identifies which 2 bits of *uErr* specify the size of the invalid parameter.
ERR_WARNING	An invalid parameter was detected, but the error is not serious enough to cause the function to fail. The invalid parameter is reported, but the call runs as usual.
ERR_WORD	Invalid 16-bit parameter.

lpfn
Specifies the address at which the parameter error occurred. This value is NULL if the address is unknown.

lpvParam
Points to more information about the error. The value of *lpvParam* depends on the value of *uErr*. If the value of (*uErr* & ERR_SIZE_MASK) is 0, *lpvParam* is undefined. Currently, no *uErr* code has defined meanings for *lpvParam*.

Return Value   This function does not return a value.

Comments   The errors identified by **LogParamError** may be trapped by the callback function that **NotifyRegister** installs.

Error values whose low 12 bits are less than 0x07FF are reserved for use by Windows.

The size of the value passed in *lpvParam* is determined by the values of the bits selected by ERR_SIZE_MASK, as follows:

```
switch (err & ERR_SIZE_MASK)
{
case ERR_BYTE:              /* 8-bit invalid parameter */
    b = LOBYTE(param);
    break;

case ERR_WORD:              /* 16-bit invalid parameter */
    w = LOWORD(param);
    break;

case ERR_DWORD:             /* 32-bit invalid parameter */
    l = (DWORD)param;
    break:

default:                    /* invalid parameter value is unknown */
    break;
}
```

See Also   **LogError**, **NotifyRegister**

_lopen

HFILE _lopen(*lpszFilename, fnOpenMode*)
LPCSTR *lpszFilename*;   /* address of file to open   */
int *fnOpenMode*;   /* file access   */

The **_lopen** function opens an existing file and sets the file pointer to the beginning of the file.

Parameters   *lpszFilename*
      Points to a null-terminated string that names the file to be opened. The string must consist of characters from the Windows character set.

fnOpenMode

Specifies the modes in which to open the file. This parameter consists of one access mode and an optional share mode.

Value	Access mode
READ	Opens the file for reading only.
READ_WRITE	Opens the file for reading and writing.
WRITE	Opens the file for writing only.

Value	Share mode (optional)
OF_SHARE_COMPAT	Opens the file in compatibility mode, allowing any process on a given machine to open the file any number of times. If the file has been opened by using any of the other sharing modes, **_lopen** fails.
OF_SHARE_DENY_NONE	Opens the file without denying other programs read or write access to the file. If the file has been opened in compatibility mode by any other program, **_lopen** fails.
OF_SHARE_DENY_READ	Opens the file and denies other programs read access to the file. If the file has been opened in compatibility mode or for read access by any other program, **_lopen** fails.
OF_SHARE_DENY_WRITE	Opens the file and denies other programs write access to the file. If the file has been opened in compatibility mode or for write access by any other program, **_lopen** fails.
OF_SHARE_EXCLUSIVE	Opens the file in exclusive mode, denying other programs both read and write access to the file. If the file has been opened in any other mode for read or write access, even by the current program, **_lopen** fails.

Return Value

The return value is a file handle if the function is successful. Otherwise, it is HFILE_ERROR.

Example

The following example uses the **_lopen** function to open an input file:

```
HFILE hfReadFile;
/* Open the input file (read only). */

hfReadFile = _lopen("testfile", READ);

if (hfReadFile == HFILE_ERROR) {
    ErrorHandler();
}
```

See Also   OpenFile

LPtoDP   2.x

BOOL LPtoDP(*hdc*, *lppt*, *cPoints*)
HDC *hdc*;   /* handle of device context   */
POINT FAR* *lppt*;   /* address of array with points   */
int *cPoints*;   /* number of points in array   */

The **LPtoDP** function converts logical coordinates (points) into device coordinates.

Parameters   *hdc*
                    Identifies the device context.

                    lppt
                    Points to an array of **POINT** structures. The coordinates in each structure are
                    mapped to the device coordinates of the current device context. The **POINT**
                    structure has the following form:

```
typedef struct tagPOINT {   /* pt */
    int x;
    int y;
} POINT;
```

                    For a full description of this structure, see the *Microsoft Windows Program-
                    mer's Reference, Volume 3*.

                    cPoints
                    Specifies the number of points in the array.

Return Value   The return value is nonzero if the function is successful. Otherwise, it is zero.

Comments   The conversion depends on the current mapping mode and the settings of the
                    origins and extents of the device's window and viewport.

                    The x- and y-coordinates of points are 2-byte signed integers in the range −32,768
                    through 32,767. In cases where the mapping mode would result in values larger
                    than these limits, the system sets the values to −32,768 and 32,767, respectively.

Example   The following example sets the mapping mode to MM_LOENGLISH and then
                    calls the **LPtoDP** function to convert the coordinates of a rectangle into device
                    coordinates:

```
                RECT rc;

                SetMapMode(hdc, MM_LOENGLISH);
                SetRect(&rc, 100, -100, 200, -200);
                LPtoDP(hdc, (LPPOINT) &rc, 2);
```

See Also   **DPtoLP**

_lread

2.x

UINT _lread(*hf, hpvBuffer, cbBuffer*)
HFILE *hf*;   /* file handle   */
void _huge* *hpvBuffer*;   /* address of buffer for read data */
UINT *cbBuffer*;   /* length of data buffer   */

The **_lread** function reads data from the specified file.

Parameters   *hf*
                     Identifies the file to be read.

                     hpvBuffer
                     Points to a buffer that is to receive the data read from the file.

                     cbBuffer
                     Specifies the number of bytes to be read from the file. This value cannot be
                     greater than 0xFFFE (65,534).

Return Value   The return value indicates the number of bytes that the function read from the file,
                     if the function is successful. If the number of bytes read is less than the number
                     specified in *cbBuffer*, the function reached the end of the file (EOF) before reading
                     the specified number of bytes. The return value is HFILE_ERROR if the function
                     fails.

Example   The following example uses the **_lread** and **_lwrite** functions to copy data from
                     one file to another:

```
HFILE hfReadFile;
int cbRead;
PBYTE pbBuf;

/* Allocate a buffer for file I/O. */

pbBuf = (PBYTE) LocalAlloc(LMEM_FIXED, 2048);

/* Copy the input file to the temporary file. */
```

```
do {
    cbRead = _lread(hfReadFile, pbBuf, 2048);
    _lwrite(hfTempFile, pbBuf, cbRead);
} while (cbRead != 0);

/* Free the buffer and close the files. */

LocalFree((HLOCAL) pbBuf);

_lclose(hfReadFile);
_lclose(hfTempFile);
```

See Also   **_hread, _lwrite**

lstrcat   `2.x`

LPSTR lstrcat(*lpszString1*, *lpszString2*)
LPSTR *lpszString1*;   /* address of buffer for concatenated strings   */
LPCSTR *lpszString2*;   /* address of string to add to string1   */

The **lstrcat** function appends one string to another.

Parameters   *lpszString1*
Points to a byte array containing a null-terminated string. The byte array containing the string must be large enough to contain both strings.

lpszString2
Points to the null-terminated string to be appended to the string specified in the *lpszString1* parameter.

Return Value   The return value points to *lpszString1* if the function is successful.

Comments   Both strings must be less than 64K in size.

Example   The following example uses the **lstrcat** function to append a test string to a buffer:

```
char szBuf[80] = { "the test string is " };

lstrcat(szBuf, lpsz);
MessageBox(hwnd, szBuf, "lstrcat", MB_OK);
```

lstrcmp

int lstrcmp(*lpszString1*, *lpszString2*)
LPCSTR *lpszString1*;   /* address of first string   */
LPCSTR *lpszString2*;   /* address of second string   */

The **lstrcmp** function compares two character strings. The comparison is case-sensitive.

Parameters

lpszString1
Points to the first null-terminated string to be compared.

lpszString2
Points to the second null-terminated string to be compared.

Return Value

The return value is less than zero if the string specified in *lpszString1* is less than the string specified in *lpszString2*, is greater than zero if *lpszString1* is greater than *lpszString2*, and is zero if the two strings are equal.

Comments

The **lstrcmp** function compares two strings by checking the first characters against each other, the second characters against each other, and so on, until it finds an inequality or reaches the ends of the strings. The function returns the difference of the values of the first unequal characters it encounters. For example, **lstrcmp** determines that "abcz" is greater than "abcdefg" and returns the difference of "z" and "d".

The language driver for the language selected by the user determines which string is greater (or whether the strings are the same). If no language driver is selected, Windows uses an internal function. With the Windows United States language functions, uppercase characters have lower values than lowercase characters.

With a double-byte character set (DBCS) version of Windows, this function can compare two DBCS strings.

Both strings must be less than 64K in size.

See Also   **lstrcmpi**

lstrcmpi

int lstrcmpi(*lpszString1*, *lpszString2*)
LPCSTR *lpszString1*;   /* address of first string   */
LPCSTR *lpszString2*;   /* address of second string   */

The **lstrcmpi** function compares the two strings. The comparison is not case-sensitive.

Parameters

lpszString1
  Points to the first null-terminated string to be compared.

lpszString2
  Points to the second null-terminated string to be compared.

Return Value

The return value is less than zero if the string specified in *lpszString1* is less than the string specified in *lpszString2*, is greater than zero if *lpszString1* is greater than *lpszString2*, and is zero if the two strings are equal.

Comments

The **lstrcmpi** function compares two strings by checking the first characters against each other, the second characters against each other, and so on, until it finds an inequality or reaches the ends of the strings. The function returns the difference of the values of the first unequal characters it encounters. For example, **lstrcmpi** determines that "abcz" is greater than "abcdefg" and returns the difference of "z" and "d".

The language driver for the language selected by the user determines which string is greater (or whether the strings are the same). If no language driver is selected, Windows uses an internal function.

With a double-byte character set (DBCS) version of Windows, this function can compare two DBCS strings.

Both strings must be less than 64K in size.

See Also

lstrcmp

lstrcpy

2.x

LPSTR lstrcpy(*lpszString1***, ***lpszString2***)**
LPSTR *lpszString1*;   /* address of buffer   */
LPCSTR *lpszString2*;   /* address of string to copy */

The **lstrcpy** function copies a string to a buffer.

Parameters

lpszString1
  Points to a buffer that will receive the contents of the string pointed to by the *lpszString2* parameter. The buffer must be large enough to contain the string, including the terminating null character.

lpszString2
>   Points to the null-terminated string to be copied.

Return Value   The return value is a pointer to *lpszString1* if the function is successful. Otherwise, it is NULL.

Comments   This function can be used to copy a double-byte character set (DBCS) string.

>   Both strings must be less than 64K in size.

See Also   **lstrlen**

---

lstrlen

2.x

int lstrlen(*lpszString*)
LPCSTR *lpszString*;   /* address of string to count   */

>   The **lstrlen** function returns the length, in bytes, of the specified string (not including the terminating null character).

Parameters   *lpszString*
>   Points to a null-terminated string. This string must be less than 64K in size.

Return Value   The return value specifies the length, in bytes, of the string pointed to by the *lpszString* parameter. There is no error return.

See Also   **lstrcpy**

_lwrite

2.x

UINT _lwrite(*hf, hpvBuffer, cbBuffer*)
HFILE *hf*;   /* file handle   */
const void _huge* *hpvBuffer*;   /* address of buffer for write data   */
UINT *cbBuffer*;   /* size of data   */

>   The **_lwrite** function writes data to the specified file.

Parameters

hf
    Identifies the file to be written to.

hpvBuffer
    Points to a buffer that contains the data to be written to the file.

cbBuffer
    Specifies the number of bytes to be written to the file. If this parameter is zero, the file is expanded or truncated to the current file-pointer position.

Return Value

The return value indicates the number of bytes written to the file, if the function is successful. Otherwise, the return value is HFILE_ERROR.

Comments

The buffer specified by *hpvBuffer* cannot extend past the end of a segment.

Example

The following example uses the **_lread** and **_lwrite** functions to copy data from one file to another:

```
int cbRead;
PBYTE pbBuf;

/* Allocate a buffer for file I/O. */

pbBuf = (PBYTE) LocalAlloc(LMEM_FIXED, 2048);

/* Copy the input file to the temporary file. */

do {
    cbRead = _lread(hfReadFile, pbBuf, 2048);
    _lwrite(hfTempFile, pbBuf, cbRead);
} while (cbRead != 0);

/* Free the buffer and close the files. */

LocalFree((HLOCAL) pbBuf);

_lclose(hfReadFile);
_lclose(hfTempFile);
```

See Also

_hwrite, _lread

LZClose

#include <lzexpand.h>

void LZClose(*hf***)**
HFILE *hf*;   /* handle of file to be closed   */

The **LZClose** function closes a file that was opened by the **LZOpenFile** or **Open-File** function.

Parameters   *hf*
                    Identifies the source file.

Return Value   This function does not return a value.

Comments   If the file was compressed by Microsoft File Compression Utility
                    (COMPRESS.EXE) and opened by the **LZOpenFile** function, **LZClose**
                    frees any global heap space that was required to expand the file.

Example   The following example uses **LZClose** to close a file opened by **LZOpenFile**:

```
char szSrc[] = {"readme.txt"};
char szDst[] = {"readme.bak"};
OFSTRUCT ofStrSrc;
OFSTRUCT ofStrDest;
HFILE hfSrcFile, hfDstFile;

/* Open the source file. */

hfSrcFile = LZOpenFile(szSrc, &ofStrSrc, OF_READ);

/* Create the destination file. */

hfDstFile = LZOpenFile(szDst, &ofStrDest, OF_CREATE);

/* Copy the source file to the destination file. */

LZCopy(hfSrcFile, hfDstFile);

/* Close the files. */

LZClose(hfSrcFile);
LZClose(hfDstFile);
```

See Also   **OpenFile, LZOpenFile**

LZCopy

#include <lzexpand.h>

LONG LZCopy(*hfSource*, *hfDest*)
HFILE *hfSource*;   /* handle of source file   */
HFILE *hfDest*;   /* handle of destination file   */

The **LZCopy** function copies a source file to a destination file. If the source file was compressed by Microsoft File Compression Utility (COMPRESS.EXE), this function creates a decompressed destination file. If the source file was not compressed, this function duplicates the original file.

Parameters

hfSource
Identifies the source file. (This handle is returned by the **LZOpenFile** function when a compressed file is opened.)

hfDest
Identifies the destination file.

Return Value

The return value is the size, in bytes, of the destination file if the function is successful. Otherwise, it is an error value that is less than zero and may be one of the following:

Value	Meaning
LZERROR_BADINHANDLE	The handle identifying the source file was not valid.
LZERROR_BADOUTHANDLE	The handle identifying the destination file was not valid.
LZERROR_GLOBALLOC	There is insufficient memory for the required buffers.
LZERROR_GLOBLOCK	The handle identifying the internal data structures is invalid.
LZERROR_READ	The source file format was not valid.
LZERROR_UNKNOWNALG	The source file was compressed with an unrecognized compression algorithm.
LZERROR_WRITE	There is insufficient space for the output file.

Comments

This function is designed for single-file copy operations. (Use the **CopyLZFile** function for multiple-file copy operations.)

If the function is successful, the file identified by *hfDest* is uncompressed.

If the source or destination file is opened by a C run-time function (rather than the **_lopen** or **OpenFile** function), it must be opened in binary mode.

Example   The following example uses the **LZCopy** function to copy a file:

```
char szSrc[] = {"readme.txt"};
char szDst[] = {"readme.bak"};
OFSTRUCT ofStrSrc;
OFSTRUCT ofStrDest;
HFILE hfSrcFile, hfDstFile;

/* Open the source file. */

hfSrcFile = LZOpenFile(szSrc, &ofStrSrc, OF_READ);

/* Create the destination file. */

hfDstFile = LZOpenFile(szDst, &ofStrDest, OF_CREATE);

/* Copy the source file to the destination file. */

LZCopy(hfSrcFile, hfDstFile);

/* Close the files. */

LZClose(hfSrcFile);
LZClose(hfDstFile);
```

See Also   **CopyLZFile, _lopen, LZOpenFile, OpenFile**

LZDone

3.1

#include <lzexpand.h>

void LZDone(void)

The **LZDone** function frees buffers that the **LZStart** function allocated for multiple-file copy operations.

Parameters   This function has no parameters.

Return Value   This function does not return a value.

Comments   Applications that copy multiple files should call **LZStart** before copying the files with the **CopyLZFile** function. **LZStart** allocates buffers for the file copy operations.

Example   The following example uses **LZDone** to free buffers allocated by **LZStart**:

```
#define NUM_FILES    4

char *szSrc[NUM_FILES] =
    {"readme.txt", "data.txt", "update.txt", "list.txt"};
char *szDest[NUM_FILES] =
    {"readme.bak", "data.bak", "update.bak", "list.bak"};
OFSTRUCT ofStrSrc;
OFSTRUCT ofStrDest;
HFILE hfSrcFile, hfDstFile;
int i;

/* Allocate internal buffers for the CopyLZFile function. */

LZStart();

/* Open, copy, and then close the files. */

for (i = 0; i < NUM_FILES; i++) {
    hfSrcFile = LZOpenFile(szSrc[i], &ofStrSrc, OF_READ);
    hfDstFile = LZOpenFile(szDest[i], &ofStrDest, OF_CREATE);
    CopyLZFile(hfSrcFile, hfDstFile);
    LZClose(hfSrcFile);
    LZClose(hfDstFile);
}

LZDone(); /* free the internal buffers */
```

See Also   **CopyLZFile, LZCopy, LZStart**

LZInit   3.1

#include <lzexpand.h>

HFILE LZInit(*hfSrc*)
HFILE *hfSrc*;   /* handle of source file   */

The **LZInit** function allocates memory for, creates, and initializes the internal data structures that are required to decompress files.

Parameters   *hfSrc*
                Identifies the source file.

Return Value   The return value is the original file handle if the function is successful and the file is not compressed. If the function is successful and the file is compressed, the return value is a new file handle. If the function fails, the return value is an error value that is less than zero and may be one of the following:

Value	Meaning
LZERROR_BADINHANDLE	The handle identifying the source file is invalid.
LZERROR_GLOBALLOC	There is insufficient memory for the required internal data structures. This value is returned when an application attempts to open more than 16 files.
LZERROR_GLOBLOCK	The handle identifying global memory is invalid. (The internal call to the **GlobalLock** function failed.)
LZERROR_READ	The source file format is invalid.
LZERROR_UNKNOWNALG	The file was compressed with an unrecognized compression algorithm.

Comments   A maximum of 16 compressed files can be open at any given time.

Example   The following example uses **LZInit** to initialize the internal structures that are required to decompress a file:

```
char szSrc[] = {"readme.cmp"};
char szFileName[128];
OFSTRUCT ofStrSrc;
OFSTRUCT ofStrDest;
HFILE hfSrcFile, hfDstFile, hfCompFile;
int cbRead;
BYTE abBuf[512];

/* Open the compressed source file. */

hfSrcFile = OpenFile(szSrc, &ofStrSrc, OF_READ);

/*
 * Initialize internal data structures for the decompression
 * operation.
 */

hfCompFile = LZInit(hfSrcFile);

/* Retrieve the original name for the compressed file. */

GetExpandedName(szSrc, szFileName);

/* Create the destination file using the original name. */

hfDstFile = LZOpenFile(szFileName, &ofStrDest, OF_CREATE);

/* Copy the compressed source file to the destination file. */

do {
    if ((cbRead = LZRead(hfCompFile, abBuf, sizeof(abBuf))) > 0)
        _lwrite(hfDstFile, abBuf, cbRead);
```

```
        else {
             .
             . /* handle error condition */
             .
        }
    } while (cbRead == sizeof(abBuf));

    /* Close the files. */

    LZClose(hfSrcFile);
    LZClose(hfDstFile);
```

LZOpenFile

3.1

#include <lzexpand.h>

HFILE LZOpenFile(*lpszFile*, *lpof*, *style*)
LPCSTR *lpszFile*;   /* address of filename   */
OFSTRUCT FAR* *lpof*;   /* address of structure for file info */
UINT *style*;   /* action to be taken   */

The **LZOpenFile** function creates, opens, reopens, or deletes the file specified by the string to which *lpszFile* points.

Parameters   *lpszFile*
Points to a string that specifies the name of a file.

lpof
Points to the **OFSTRUCT** structure that is to receive information about the file when the file is opened. The structure can be used in subsequent calls to **LZOpenFile** to refer to the open file.

The **szPathName** member of this structure contains characters from the OEM character set. For more information about the OEM character set, see the *Microsoft Windows Guide to Programming*.

style
Specifies the action to be taken. These styles can be combined by using the bitwise OR operator:

Value	Meaning
OF_CANCEL	Adds a Cancel button to the OF_PROMPT dialog box. Choosing the Cancel button directs **LZOpenFile** to return a file-not-found error message.
OF_CREATE	Directs **LZOpenFile** to create a new file. If the file already exists, it is truncated to zero length.

Value	Meaning
OF_DELETE	Deletes the file.
OF_EXIST	Opens the file, and then closes it. This action is used to test for file existence.
OF_PARSE	Fills the **OFSTRUCT** structure, but carries out no other action.
OF_PROMPT	Displays a dialog box if the requested file does not exist. The dialog box informs the user that Windows cannot find the file and prompts the user to insert the disk containing the file in drive A.
OF_READ	Opens the file for reading only.
OF_READWRITE	Opens the file for reading and writing.
OF_REOPEN	Opens the file using information in the reopen buffer.
OF_SHARE_DENY_NONE	Opens the file without denying other programs read access or write access to the file. **LZOpen-File** fails if the file has been opened in compatibility mode by any other program.
OF_SHARE_DENY_READ	Opens the file and denies other programs read access to the file. **LZOpenFile** fails if the file has been opened in compatibility mode or for read access by any other program.
OF_SHARE_DENY_WRITE	Opens the file and denies other programs write access to the file. **LZOpenFile** fails if the file has been opened in compatibility mode or for write access by any other program.
OF_SHARE_EXCLUSIVE	Opens the file in exclusive mode, denying other programs both read access and write access to the file. **LZOpenFile** fails if the file has been opened in any other mode for read access or write access, even by the current program.
OF_WRITE	Opens the file for writing only.

Return Value   The return value is a handle identifying the file if the function is successful and the value specified by *style* is not OF_READ. If the file is compressed and opened with *style* set to the OF_READ value, the return value is a special file handle. If the function fails, the return value is −1.

Comments   If *style* is OF_READ (or OF_READ and any of the OF_SHARE_ flags) and the file is compressed, **LZOpenFile** calls the **LZInit** function, which performs the required initialization for the decompression operations.

Example   The following example uses **LZOpenFile** to open a source file and create a destination file into which the source file can be copied:

```
char szSrc[] = {"readme.txt"};
char szDst[] = {"readme.bak"};
OFSTRUCT ofStrSrc;
OFSTRUCT ofStrDest;
HFILE hfSrcFile, hfDstFile;

/* Open the source file. */

hfSrcFile = LZOpenFile(szSrc, &ofStrSrc, OF_READ);

/* Create the destination file. */

hfDstFile = LZOpenFile(szDst, &ofStrDest, OF_CREATE);

/* Copy the source file to the destination file. */

LZCopy(hfSrcFile, hfDstFile);

/* Close the files. */

LZClose(hfSrcFile);
LZClose(hfDstFile);
```

See Also   **LZInit**

LZRead

$\boxed{3.1}$

#include <lzexpand.h>

int **LZRead**(*hf*, *lpvBuf*, *cb*)
HFILE *hf*;   /* handle of the file   */
void FAR* *lpvBuf*;   /* address of buffer for file data */
int *cb*;   /* number of bytes to read   */

The **LZRead** function reads into a buffer bytes from a file.

Parameters   *hf*
                      Identifies the source file.

                      lpvBuf
                      Points to a buffer that is to receive the bytes read from the file.

                      cb
                      Specifies the maximum number of bytes to be read.

Return Value   The return value is the actual number of bytes read if the function is successful. Otherwise, it is an error value that is less than zero and may be any of the following:

Value	Meaning
LZERROR_BADINHANDLE	The handle identifying the source file was invalid.
LZERROR_BADVALUE	The *cb* parameter specified a negative value.
LZERROR_GLOBLOCK	The handle identifying required initialization data is invalid.
LZERROR_READ	The format of the source file was invalid.
LZERROR_UNKNOWNALG	The file was compressed with an unrecognized compression algorithm.

Comments   If the file is not compressed, **LZRead** calls the **_lread** function, which performs the read operation.

If the file is compressed, **LZRead** emulates **_lread** on an expanded image of the file and copies the bytes of data into the buffer to which *lpvBuf* points.

If the source file was compressed by Microsoft File Compression Utility (COMPRESS.EXE), the **LZOpenFile**, **LZSeek**, and **LZRead** functions can be called instead of the **OpenFile**, **_llseek**, and **_lread** functions.

Example   The following example uses **LZRead** to copy and decompress a compressed file:

```
char szSrc[] = {"readme.cmp"};
char szFileName[128];
OFSTRUCT ofStrSrc;
OFSTRUCT ofStrDest;
HFILE hfSrcFile, hfDstFile, hfCompFile;
int cbRead;
BYTE abBuf[512];

/* Open the compressed source file. */

hfSrcFile = OpenFile(szSrc, &ofStrSrc, OF_READ);

/*
 * Initialize internal data structures for the decompression
 * operation.
 */

hfCompFile = LZInit(hfSrcFile);

/* Retrieve the original name for the compressed file. */

GetExpandedName(szSrc, szFileName);
```

```
                    /* Create the destination file using the original name. */

                    hfDstFile = LZOpenFile(szFileName, &ofStrDest, OF_CREATE);

                    /* Copy the compressed source file to the destination file. */

                    do {
                        if ((cbRead = LZRead(hfCompFile, abBuf, sizeof(abBuf))) > 0)
                            _lwrite(hfDstFile, abBuf, cbRead);
                        else {
                            .
                            . /* handle error condition */
                            .
                        }
                    } while (cbRead == sizeof(abBuf));

                    /* Close the files. */

                    LZClose(hfSrcFile);
                    LZClose(hfDstFile);
```

See Also   **_llseek, _lread, LZOpenFile, LZRead, LZSeek**

LZSeek   3.1

#include <lzexpand.h>

LONG LZSeek(*hf, lOffset, nOrigin*)
HFILE *hf*;   /* handle of file   */
long *lOffset*;   /* number of bytes to move   */
int *nOrigin*;   /* original position   */

The **LZSeek** function moves a file pointer from its original position to a new position.

Parameters   *hf*
                    Identifies the source file.

                    lOffset
                    Specifies the number of bytes by which the file pointer should be moved.

                    nOrigin
                    Specifies the starting position of the pointer. This parameter must be one of the following values:

Value	Meaning
0	Move the file pointer *lOffset* bytes from the beginning of the file.
1	Move the file pointer *lOffset* bytes from the current position.
2	Move the file pointer *lOffset* bytes from the end of the file.

Return Value   The return value is the offset from the beginning of the file to the new pointer position, if the function is successful. Otherwise, it is an error value that is less than zero and may be one of the following:

Value	Meaning
LZERROR_BADINHANDLE	The handle identifying the source file was invalid.
LZERROR_BADVALUE	One of the parameters exceeds the range of valid values.
LZERROR_GLOBLOCK	The handle identifying the initialization data is invalid.

Comments   If the file is not compressed, **LZSeek** calls the **_llseek** function and moves the file pointer by the specified offset.

If the file is compressed, **LZSeek** emulates **_llseek** on an expanded image of the file.

See Also   **_llseek**

LZStart   3.1

#include <lzexpand.h>

int LZStart(void)

The **LZStart** function allocates the buffers that the **CopyLZFile** function uses to copy a source file to a destination file.

Parameters   This function has no parameters.

Return Value   The return value is nonzero if the function is successful. Otherwise, it is LZERROR_GLOBALLOC.

Comments   Applications that copy (or copy and decompress) multiple consecutive files should call the **LZStart**, **CopyLZFile**, and **LZDone** functions. Applications that copy a single file should call the **LZCopy** function.

Example

The following example uses **LZStart** to allocate buffers used by **CopyLZFile**:

```
#define NUM_FILES    4

char *szSrc[NUM_FILES] =
    {"readme.txt", "data.txt", "update.txt", "list.txt"};
char *szDest[NUM_FILES] =
    {"readme.bak", "data.bak", "update.bak", "list.bak"};
OFSTRUCT ofStrSrc;
OFSTRUCT ofStrDest;
HFILE hfSrcFile, hfDstFile;
int i;

/* Allocate internal buffers for the CopyLZFile function. */

LZStart();

/* Open, copy, and then close the files. */

for (i = 0; i < NUM_FILES; i++) {
    hfSrcFile = LZOpenFile(szSrc[i], &ofStrSrc, OF_READ);
    hfDstFile = LZOpenFile(szDest[i], &ofStrDest, OF_CREATE);
    CopyLZFile(hfSrcFile, hfDstFile);
    LZClose(hfSrcFile);
    LZClose(hfDstFile);
}

LZDone(); /* free the internal buffers */
```

See Also

CopyLZFile, LZCopy, LZDone

MakeProcInstance

2.x

FARPROC MakeProcInstance(*lpProc, hinst***)**
FARPROC *lpProc*;   /* address of function   */
HINSTANCE *hinst*;   /* instance to bind to function */

The **MakeProcInstance** function returns the address of the prolog code for an exported function. The prolog code binds an instance data segment to an exported function. When the function is called, it has access to variables and data in that instance data segment.

Parameters

lpProc
Specifies the address of an exported function.

hinst
> Identifies the instance associated with the desired data segment.

Return Value   The return value points to the prolog code for the specified exported function, if **MakeProcInstance** is successful. Otherwise, it is NULL.

Comments   The **MakeProcInstance** function is used to retrieve a calling address for a function that must be called by Windows, such as an About procedure. This function must be used only to access functions from instances of the current module. If the address specified in the *lpProc* parameter identifies a procedure in a dynamic-link library, **MakeProcInstance** returns the same address specified in *lpProc*.

After **MakeProcInstance** has been called for a particular function, all calls to that function should be made through the retrieved address.

The **FreeProcInstance** function frees the function from the data segment bound to it by the **MakeProcInstance** function.

MakeProcInstance will create more than one procedure instance. To avoid wasting memory, an application should not call **MakeProcInstance** more than once using the same function and instance handle.

See Also   **FreeProcInstance, GetProcAddress**

MapDialogRect

2.x

void MapDialogRect(*hwndDlg*, *lprc*)
HWND *hwndDlg*;   /* handle of dialog box   */
RECT FAR* *lprc*;   /* address of structure with rectangle   */

The **MapDialogRect** function converts (maps) the specified dialog box units to screen units (pixels).

Parameters   *hwndDlg*
> Identifies a dialog box. This dialog box must have been created by using the **CreateDialog** or **DialogBox** function.

lprc
> Points to a **RECT** structure that contains the dialog box coordinates to be converted. The **RECT** structure has the following form:

```
typedef struct tagRECT {      /* rc */
    int left;
    int top;
    int right;
    int bottom;
} RECT;
```

For a full description of this structure, see the *Microsoft Windows Programmer's Reference, Volume 3*.

Return Value   This function does not return a value.

Comments   The **MapDialogRect** function converts the dialog box units of a rectangle to screen units. Dialog box units are defined in terms of the current dialog base unit, which is derived from the average width and height of characters in the font used for dialog box text. Typically, dialog boxes use the System font, but an application can specify a different font by using the DS_SETFONT style in the resource-definition file.

One horizontal unit is one-fourth of the dialog box base width unit, and one vertical unit is one-eighth of the dialog box base height unit. The **GetDialogBaseUnits** function retrieves the dialog box base units in pixels.

See Also   **CreateDialog**, **DialogBox**, **GetDialogBaseUnits**

MapVirtualKey   3.0

UINT MapVirtualKey(*uKeyCode, fuMapType*)
UINT *uKeyCode*;   /* virtual-key code or scan code   */
UINT *fuMapType*;   /* translation to perform   */

The **MapVirtualKey** function translates (maps) a virtual-key code into a scan code or ASCII value, or it translates a scan code into a virtual-key code.

Parameters   *uKeyCode*
     Specifies the virtual-key code or scan code for a key. How this parameter is interpreted depends on the value of the *fuMapType* parameter.

fuMapType
     Specifies the translation to perform. If this parameter is 0, the *uKeyCode* parameter is a virtual-key code and is translated into its corresponding scan code. If *fuMapType* is 1, *uKeyCode* is a scan code and is translated to a virtual-key code. If *fuMapType* is 2, *uKeyCode* is a virtual-key code and is translated to an unshifted ASCII value. Other values are reserved.

Return Value   The return value depends on the value of the *uKeyCode* and *fuMapType* parameters. For more information, see the description of the *fuMapType* parameter.

See Also   **OemKeyScan**, **VkKeyScan**

MapWindowPoints

3.1

void MapWindowPoints(*hwndFrom*, *hwndTo*, *lppt*, *cPoints*)
HWND *hwndFrom*;   /* handle of window to be mapped from   */
HWND *hwndTo*;   /* handle of window to be mapped to   */
POINT FAR* *lppt*;   /* address of structure array with points to map   */
UINT *cPoints*;   /* number of structures in array   */

The **MapWindowPoints** function converts (maps) a set of points from a coordinate space relative to one window to a coordinate space relative to another window.

Parameters   *hwndFrom*
             Identifies the window from which points are converted. If this parameter is
             NULL or HWND_DESKTOP, the points are assumed to be in screen coordi-
             nates.

             hwndTo
             Identifies the window to which points are converted. If this parameter is NULL
             or HWND_DESKTOP, the points are converted to screen coordinates.

             lppt
             Points to an array of **POINT** structures that contain the set of points to be con-
             verted. This parameter can also point to a **RECT** structure, in which case the
             cPoints parameter should be set to 2. The **POINT** structure has the following
             form:

```
typedef struct tagPOINT {   /* pt */
    int x;
    int y;
} POINT;
```

             The **RECT** structure has the following form:

```
typedef struct tagRECT {    /* rc */
    int left;
    int top;
    int right;
    int bottom;
} RECT;
```

For a full description of these structures, see the *Microsoft Windows Programmer's Reference, Volume 3.*

cPoints
Specifies the number of **POINT** structures in the array pointed to by the *lppt* parameter.

Return Value   This function does not return a value.

See Also   **ClientToScreen, ScreenToClient**

MemManInfo   3.1

#include <toolhelp.h>

BOOL MemManInfo(*lpmmi*)
MEMMANINFO FAR* *lpmmi*;   /* address of MEMMANINFO structure   */

The **MemManInfo** function fills the specified structure with status and performance information about the memory manager. This function is most useful in 386 enhanced mode but can also be used in standard mode.

Parameters   *lpmmi*
Points to a **MEMMANINFO** structure that will receive information about the memory manager. The **MEMMANINFO** structure has the following form:

```
#include <toolhelp.h>

typedef struct tagMEMMANINFO {  /* mmi */
    DWORD dwSize;
    DWORD dwLargestFreeBlock;
    DWORD dwMaxPagesAvailable;
    DWORD dwMaxPagesLockable;
    DWORD dwTotalLinearSpace;
    DWORD dwTotalUnlockedPages;
    DWORD dwFreePages;
    DWORD dwTotalPages;
    DWORD dwFreeLinearSpace;
    DWORD dwSwapFilePages;
    WORD  wPageSize;
} MEMMANINFO;
```

For a full description of this structure, see the *Microsoft Windows Programmer's Reference, Volume 3.*

Return Value   The return value is nonzero if the function is successful. Otherwise, it is zero.

Comments   This function is included for advisory purposes.

Before calling **MemManInfo**, an application must initialize the **MEM-MANINFO** structure and specify its size, in bytes, in the **dwSize** member.

MemoryRead

3.1

#include <toolhelp.h>

DWORD MemoryRead(*wSel, dwOffset, lpvBuf, dwcb*)
WORD *wSel*; /* selector of global heap object */
DWORD *dwOffset*; /* offset to object   */
void FAR* *lpvBuf*; /* address of buffer to read to */
DWORD *dwcb*; /* number of bytes to read */

The **MemoryRead** function copies memory from the specified global heap object to the specified buffer.

Parameters   *wSel*
Specifies the global heap object from which to read. This value must be a selector on the global heap; if the value is an alias selector or a selector in a tiled selector array, **MemoryRead** will fail.

dwOffset
Specifies the offset in the object specified in the *wSel* parameter at which to begin reading. The *dwOffset* value may point anywhere within the object; it may be greater than 64K if the object is larger than 64K.

lpvBuf
Points to the buffer to which **MemoryRead** will copy the memory from the object. This buffer must be large enough to contain the entire amount of memory copied to it. If the application is running under low memory conditions, *lpvBuf* should be in a fixed object while **MemoryRead** copies data to it.

dwcb
Specifies the number of bytes to copy from the object to the buffer pointed to by *lpvBuf*.

Return Value   The return value is the number of bytes copied from *wSel* to *lpvBuf*. If *wSel* is invalid or if *dwOffset* is out of the selector's range, the return value is zero.

Comments   The **MemoryRead** function enables developers to examine memory without consideration for selector tiling and aliasing. **MemoryRead** reads memory in read-write or read-only objects. This function can be used in any size object owned by any task. It is not necessary to compute selector array offsets.

The **MemoryRead** and **MemoryWrite** functions are designed to read and write objects loaded by the **LoadModule** function or allocated by the **GlobalAlloc** function. Developers should *not* split off the selector portion of a far pointer and use this as the value for *wSel*, unless the selector is known to be on the global heap.

See Also   **MemoryWrite**

MemoryWrite   3.1

#include <toolhelp.h>

DWORD MemoryWrite(*wSel, dwOffset, lpvBuf, dwcb*)
WORD *wSel*;   /* selector of global heap object   */
DWORD *dwOffset*;   /* offset to object   */
void FAR* *lpvBuf*; /* address of buffer to write from   */
DWORD *dwcb*;   /* number of bytes to write   */

The **MemoryWrite** function copies memory from the specified buffer to the specified global heap object.

Parameters   *wSel*
Specifies the global heap object to which **MemoryWrite** will write. This value must be a selector on the global heap; if the value is an alias selector or a selector in a tiled selector array, **MemoryWrite** will fail.

dwOffset
Specifies the offset in the object at which to begin writing. The *dwOffset* value may point anywhere within the object; it may be greater than 64K if the object is larger than 64K.

lpvBuf
Points to the buffer from which **MemoryWrite** will copy the memory to the object. If the application is running under low memory conditions, *lpvBuf* should be in a fixed object while **MemoryWrite** copies data from it.

dwcb
Specifies the number of bytes to copy to the object from the buffer pointed to by *lpvBuf*.

Return Value   The return value is the number of bytes copied from *lpvBuf* to *wSel*. If the selector is invalid or if *dwOffset* is out of the selector's range, the return value is zero.

Comments	The **MemoryWrite** function enables developers to modify memory without consideration for selector tiling and aliasing. **MemoryWrite** writes memory in read-write or read-only objects. This function can be used in any size object owned by any task. It is not necessary to make alias objects writable or to compute selector array offsets.

The **MemoryRead** and **MemoryWrite** functions are designed to read and write objects loaded by the **LoadModule** function or allocated by the **GlobalAlloc** function. Developers should *not* split off the selector portion of a far pointer and use this as the value for *wSel*, unless the selector is known to be on the global heap.

See Also   **MemoryRead**

MessageBeep   2.x

void MessageBeep(*uAlert*)
UINT *uAlert*;   /* alert level   */

The **MessageBeep** function plays a waveform sound corresponding to a given system alert level. The sound for each alert level is identified by an entry in the [sounds] section of the WIN.INI initialization file.

Parameters   *uAlert*
Specifies the alert level. This parameter can be one of the following values:

Value	Meaning
−1	Produces a standard beep sound by using the computer speaker.
MB_ICONASTERISK	Plays the sound identified by the SystemAsterisk entry in the [sounds] section of WIN.INI.
MB_ICONEXCLAMATION	Plays the sound identified by the System-Exclamation entry in the [sounds] section of WIN.INI.
MB_ICONHAND	Plays the sound identified by the SystemHand entry in the [sounds] section of WIN.INI.
MB_ICONQUESTION	Plays the sound identified by the SystemQuestion entry in the [sounds] section of WIN.INI.
MB_OK	Plays the sound identified by the SystemDefault entry in the [sounds] section of WIN.INI.

Return Value   This function does not return a value.

Comments   **MessageBeep** returns control to the caller after queuing the sound and plays the
                    sound asynchronously.

                    If it cannot play the specified alert sound, **MessageBeep** attempts to play the sys-
                    tem default sound. If it cannot play the system default sound, the function pro-
                    duces a standard beep sound by using the computer speaker.

                    The user can disable the warning beep by using the Windows Control Panel appli-
                    cation Sounds.

See Also   **FlashWindow**, **MessageBox**

MessageBox   2.x

int **MessageBox**(*hwndParent*, *lpszText*, *lpszTitle*, *fuStyle*)
HWND *hwndParent*;   /* handle of parent window   */
LPCSTR *lpszText*;   /* address of text in message box   */
LPCSTR *lpszTitle*;   /* address of title of message box   */
UINT *fuStyle*;   /* style of message box   */

The **MessageBox** function creates, displays, and operates a message-box window.
The message box contains an application-defined message and title, plus any combination of the predefined icons and push buttons described in the *fuStyle* parameter.

Parameters   *hwndParent*
                    Identifies the parent window of the message box to be created. If this parameter
                    is NULL, the message box will have no parent window.

                    lpszText
                    Points to a null-terminated string containing the message to be displayed.

                    lpszTitle
                    Points to a null-terminated string to be used for the dialog box title. If this pa-
                    rameter is NULL, the default title Error is used.

                    fuStyle
                    Specifies the contents and behavior of the dialog box. This parameter can be a
                    combination of the following values:

Value	Meaning
MB_ABORTRETRYIGNORE	The message box contains three push buttons: Abort, Retry, and Ignore.

Value	Meaning
MB_APPLMODAL	The user must respond to the message box before continuing work in the window identified by the *hwndParent* parameter. However, the user can move to the windows of other applications and work in those windows. MB_APPLMODAL is the default if neither MB_SYSTEMMODAL nor MB_TASKMODAL is specified.
MB_DEFBUTTON1	The first button is the default. Note that the first button is always the default unless MB_DEFBUTTON2 or MB_DEFBUTTON3 is specified.
MB_DEFBUTTON2	The second button is the default.
MB_DEFBUTTON3	The third button is the default.
MB_ICONASTERISK	Same as MB_ICONINFORMATION.
MB_ICONEXCLAMATION	An exclamation-point icon appears in the message box.
MB_ICONHAND	Same as MB_ICONSTOP.
MB_ICONINFORMATION	An icon consisting of a lowercase letter "I" in a circle appears in the message box.
MB_ICONQUESTION	A question-mark icon appears in the message box.
MB_ICONSTOP	A stop-sign icon appears in the message box.
MB_OK	The message box contains one push button: OK.
MB_OKCANCEL	The message box contains two push buttons: OK and Cancel.
MB_RETRYCANCEL	The message box contains two push buttons: Retry and Cancel.
MB_SYSTEMMODAL	All applications are suspended until the user responds to the message box. Unless the application specifies MB_ICONHAND, the message box does not become modal until after it is created; consequently, the parent window and other windows continue to receive messages resulting from its activation. System-modal message boxes are used to notify the user of serious, potentially damaging errors that require immediate attention (for example, running out of memory).

Value	Meaning
MB_TASKMODAL	Same as MB_APPLMODAL except that all the top-level windows belonging to the current task are disabled if the *hwndParent* parameter is NULL. This flag should be used when the calling application or library does not have a window handle available but still needs to prevent input to other windows in the current application without suspending other applications.
MB_YESNO	The message box contains two push buttons: Yes and No.
MB_YESNOCANCEL	The message box contains three push buttons: Yes, No, and Cancel.

Return Value

The return value is zero if there is not enough memory to create the message box. Otherwise, it is one of the following menu-item values returned by the dialog box:

Value	Meaning
IDABORT	Abort button was selected.
IDCANCEL	Cancel button was selected.
IDIGNORE	Ignore button was selected.
IDNO	No button was selected.
IDOK	OK button was selected.
IDRETRY	Retry button was selected.
IDYES	Yes button was selected.

If a message box has a Cancel button, the IDCANCEL value will be returned if either the ESC key is pressed or the Cancel button is selected. If the message box has no Cancel button, pressing ESC has no effect.

Comments

When a system-modal message box is created to indicate that the system is low on memory, the strings pointed to by the *lpszText* and *lpszTitle* parameters should not be taken from a resource file, because an attempt to load the resource may fail.

When an application calls the **MessageBox** function and specifies the MB_ICONHAND and MB_SYSTEMMODAL flags for the *fuStyle* parameter, Windows displays the resulting message box regardless of available memory. When these flags are specified, Windows limits the length of the message-box text to three lines. Windows does *not* automatically break the lines to fit in the message box, however, so the message string must contain carriage returns to break the lines at the appropriate places.

If a message box is created while a dialog box is present, use the handle of the dialog box as the *hwndParent* parameter. The *hwndParent* parameter should not identify a child window, such as a control in a dialog box.

Following are the various system icons that can be used in a message box:

 MB_ICONHAND and MB_ICONSTOP

 MB_ICONQUESTION

 MB_ICONEXCLAMATION

 MB_ICONASTERISK and MB_ICONINFORMATION

See Also   **FlashWindow**, **MessageBeep**

MessageProc   `3.1`

LRESULT CALLBACK MessageProc(*code*, *wParam*, *lParam*)
int *code*;   /* message type   */
WPARAM *wParam*;   /* undefined   */
LPARAM *lParam*;   /* address of structure with message data   */

The **MessageProc** function is an application- or library-defined callback function that the system calls after a dialog box, message box, or menu has retrieved a message, but before the message is processed. The callback function can process or modify the messages.

Parameters   *code*
Specifies the type of message being processed. This parameter can be one of the following values:

Value	Meaning
MSGF_DIALOGBOX	Messages inside a dialog box or message box procedure are being processed.
MSGF_MENU	Keyboard and mouse messages in a menu are being processed.

If the *code* parameter is less than zero, the callback function must pass the message to **CallNextHookEx** without further processing and return the value returned by **CallNextHookEx**.

wParam
Specifies a NULL value.

lParam

Points to an **MSG** structure. The **MSG** structure has the following form:

```
typedef struct tagMSG {      /* msg */
    HWND    hwnd;
    UINT    message;
    WPARAM  wParam;
    LPARAM  lParam;
    DWORD   time;
    POINT   pt;
} MSG;
```

For a full description of this structure, see the *Microsoft Windows Programmer's Reference, Volume 3.*

Return Value   The callback function should return a nonzero value if it processes the message; it should return zero if it does not process the message.

Comments   The WH_MSGFILTER filter type is the only task-specific filter. A task may install this filter.

An application must install the callback function by specifying the WH_MSGFILTER filter type and the procedure-instance address of the callback function in a call to the **SetWindowsHookEx** function.

MessageProc is a placeholder for the library-defined function name. The actual name must be exported by including it in an **EXPORTS** statement in the library's module-definition file.

See Also   **CallNextHookEx, SetWindowsHookEx**

ModifyMenu   3.0

BOOL ModifyMenu(*hmenu, idItem, fuFlags, idNewItem, lpNewItem*)
HMENU *hmenu*;   /* handle of menu   */
UINT *idItem*;   /* menu-item identifier   */
UINT *fuFlags*;   /* menu-item flags   */
UINT *idNewItem*;   /* new menu-item identifier   */
LPCSTR *lpNewItem*;   /* menu-item content   */

The **ModifyMenu** function changes an existing menu item.

Parameters   *hmenu*

Identifies the menu to change.

idItem

Specifies the menu item to change, as determined by the *fuFlags* parameter. When the *fuFlags* parameter is MF_BYCOMMAND, the *idItem* parameter specifies the menu-item identifier. When the *fuFlags* parameter is MF_BY-POSITION, the *idItem* parameter specifies the zero-based position of the menu item.

fuFlags

Specifies how the *idItem* parameter is interpreted and information about the changes to be made to the menu item. It consists of one or more values listed in the following Comments section.

idNewItem

Specifies either the identifier of the modified menu item or, if *fuFlags* is set to MF_POPUP, the menu handle of the pop-up menu.

lpNewItem

Specifies the content of the changed menu item. If *fuFlags* is set to MF_STRING (the default), *lpNewItem* is a long pointer to a null-terminated string. If *fuFlags* is set to MF_BITMAP instead, *lpNewItem* contains a bitmap handle in its low-order word. If *fuFlags* is set to MF_OWNERDRAW, *lpNewItem* specifies an application-defined 32-bit value that the application can use to maintain additional data associated with the menu item. This 32-bit value is available to the application in the **itemData** member of the **MEASUREITEMSTRUCT** or **DRAWITEMSTRUCT** structure pointed to by the *lParam* parameter of the WM_MEASUREITEM or WM_DRAWITEM message. These messages are sent when the menu item is initially displayed or is changed.

Return Value

The return value is nonzero if the function is successful. Otherwise, it is zero.

Comments

If the **ModifyMenu** function replaces a pop-up menu associated with the menu item, it destroys the old pop-up menu and frees the memory used by the pop-up menu.

Whenever a menu changes (whether or not it is in a window that is displayed), the application should call **DrawMenuBar**. To change the attributes of existing menu items, it is much faster to use the **CheckMenuItem** and **EnableMenuItem** functions.

Each of the following groups lists flags that should not be used together:

- MF_BYCOMMAND and MF_BYPOSITION

- MF_DISABLED, MF_ENABLED, and MF_GRAYED

- MF_BITMAP, MF_STRING, MF_OWNERDRAW, and MF_SEPARATOR

- MF_MENUBARBREAK and MF_MENUBREAK
- MF_CHECKED and MF_UNCHECKED

The following list describes the flags that may be set in the *fuFlags* parameter:

Value	Meaning
MF_BITMAP	Uses a bitmap as the menu item. The low-order word of the *lpNewItem* parameter contains the handle of the bitmap.
MF_BYCOMMAND	Specifies that the *idItem* parameter gives the menu-item identifier. This is the default if neither MF_BYCOMMAND nor MF_POSITION is set.
MF_BYPOSITION	Specifies that the *idItem* parameter gives the position of the menu item to be changed rather than the menu-item identifier.
MF_CHECKED	Places a check mark next to the menu item. If the application has supplied check-mark bitmaps (see **SetMenuItemBitmaps**), setting this flag displays the check-mark bitmap next to the menu item.
MF_DISABLED	Disables the menu item so that it cannot be selected, but does not gray (dim) it.
MF_ENABLED	Enables the menu item so that it can be selected and restores it from its grayed state.
MF_GRAYED	Disables the menu item so that it cannot be selected and grays it.
MF_MENUBARBREAK	Same as MF_MENUBREAK except, for pop-up menus, separates the new column from the old column with a vertical line.
MF_MENUBREAK	Places the menu item on a new line for static menu-bar items. For pop-up menus, this flag places the item in a new column, with no dividing line between the columns.
MF_OWNERDRAW	Specifies that the menu item is an owner-drawn item. The window that owns the menu receives a WM_MEASUREITEM message when the menu is displayed for the first time to retrieve the height and width of the menu item. The WM_DRAWITEM message is then sent whenever the owner must update the visual appearance of the menu item. This option is not valid for a top-level menu item.
MF_POPUP	Specifies that the item has a pop-up menu associated with it. The *idNewItem* parameter specifies a handle of a pop-up menu to be associated with the menu item. Use this flag for adding either a top-level pop-up menu or a hierarchical pop-up menu to a pop-up menu item.

Value	Meaning
MF_SEPARATOR	Draws a horizontal dividing line. This line cannot be grayed, disabled, or highlighted. You can use this flag only in a pop-up menu. The *lpNewItem* and *idNewItem* parameters are ignored.
MF_STRING	Specifies that the menu item is a character string; the *lpNewItem* parameter points to the string for the menu item.
MF_UNCHECKED	Does not select (place a check mark next to) the menu item. No check mark is the default condition if neither MF_CHECKED nor MF_UNCHECKED is set. If the application has supplied check-mark bitmaps (see the **Set-MenuItemBitmaps** function), setting this flag displays the "check mark off" bitmap next to the menu item.

See Also   **CheckMenuItem, DrawMenuBar, EnableMenuItem, SetMenuItemBitmaps**

ModuleFindHandle   3.1

#include <toolhelp.h>

HMODULE ModuleFindHandle(*lpme***,** *hmod***)**
MODULEENTRY FAR* *lpme***;**   /* address of MODULEENTRY structure   */
HMODULE *hmod***;**   /* handle of module   */

The **ModuleFindHandle** function fills the specified structure with information that describes the given module.

Parameters   *lpme*
Points to a **MODULEENTRY** structure that will receive information about the module. The **MODULEENTRY** structure has the following form:

```
#include <toolhelp.h>

typedef struct tagMODULEENTRY {  /* me */
    DWORD   dwSize;
    char    szModule[MAX_MODULE_NAME + 1];
    HMODULE hModule;
    WORD    wcUsage;
    char    szExePath[MAX_PATH + 1];
    WORD    wNext;
} MODULEENTRY;
```

For a full description of this structure, see the *Microsoft Windows Programmer's Reference, Volume 3*.

hmod
Identifies the module to be described.

Return Value

The return value is the handle of the given module if the function is successful. Otherwise, it is NULL.

Comments

The **ModuleFindHandle** function returns information about a currently loaded module whose module handle is known.

This function can be used to begin a walk through the list of all currently loaded modules. An application can examine subsequent items in the module list by using the **ModuleNext** function.

Before calling **ModuleFindHandle**, an application must initialize the **MODULEENTRY** structure and specify its size, in bytes, in the **dwSize** member.

See Also

ModuleFindName, **ModuleFirst**, **ModuleNext**

ModuleFindName

3.1

#include <toolhelp.h>

HMODULE ModuleFindName(*lpme*, *lpszName*)
MODULEENTRY FAR* *lpme*;   /* address of MODULEENTRY structure   */
LPCSTR *lpszName*;   /* address of module name   */

The **ModuleFindName** function fills the specified structure with information that describes the module with the specified name.

Parameters

lpme
Points to a **MODULEENTRY** structure that will receive information about the module. The **MODULEENTRY** structure has the following form:

```
#include <toolhelp.h>

typedef struct tagMODULEENTRY {   /* me */
    DWORD   dwSize;
    char    szModule[MAX_MODULE_NAME + 1];
    HMODULE hModule;
    WORD    wcUsage;
    char    szExePath[MAX_PATH + 1];
    WORD    wNext;
} MODULEENTRY;
```

For a full description of this structure, see the *Microsoft Windows Programmer's Reference, Volume 3*.

lpszName
Specifies the name of the module to be described.

Return Value   The return value is the handle named in the **lpszName** parameter, if the function is successful. Otherwise, it is NULL.

Comments   The **ModuleFindName** function returns information about a currently loaded module by looking up the module's name in the module list.

This function can be used to begin a walk through the list of all currently loaded modules. An application can examine subsequent items in the module list by using the **ModuleNext** function.

Before calling **ModuleFindName**, an application must initialize the **MODULEENTRY** structure and specify its size, in bytes, in the **dwSize** member.

See Also   **ModuleFindHandle, ModuleFirst, ModuleNext**

ModuleFirst   3.1

#include <toolhelp.h>

BOOL ModuleFirst(*lpme***)**
MODULEENTRY FAR* *lpme*;   /* address of MODULEENTRY structure   */

The **ModuleFirst** function fills the specified structure with information that describes the first module in the list of all currently loaded modules.

Parameters

lpme

Points to a **MODULEENTRY** structure that will receive information about the first module. The **MODULEENTRY** structure has the following form:

```
#include <toolhelp.h>

typedef struct tagMODULEENTRY {   /* me */
    DWORD   dwSize;
    char    szModule[MAX_MODULE_NAME + 1];
    HMODULE hModule;
    WORD    wcUsage;
    char    szExePath[MAX_PATH + 1];
    WORD    wNext;
} MODULEENTRY;
```

For a full description of this structure, see the *Microsoft Windows Programmer's Reference, Volume 3*.

Return Value

The return value is nonzero if the function is successful. Otherwise, it is zero.

Comments

The **ModuleFirst** function can be used to begin a walk through the list of all currently loaded modules. An application can examine subsequent items in the module list by using the **ModuleNext** function.

Before calling **ModuleFirst**, an application must initialize the **MODULEENTRY** structure and specify its size, in bytes, in the **dwSize** member.

See Also

ModuleFindHandle, ModuleFindName, ModuleNext

ModuleNext

$\boxed{3.1}$

#include <toolhelp.h>

BOOL ModuleNext(*lpme***)**
MODULEENTRY FAR* *lpme*;   /* address of MODULEENTRY structure   */

The **ModuleNext** function fills the specified structure with information that describes the next module in the list of all currently loaded modules.

Parameters

lpme

Points to a **MODULEENTRY** structure that will receive information about the next module. The **MODULEENTRY** structure has the following form:

```
#include <toolhelp.h>

typedef struct tagMODULEENTRY {   /* me */
    DWORD    dwSize;
    char     szModule[MAX_MODULE_NAME + 1];
    HMODULE  hModule;
    WORD     wcUsage;
    char     szExePath[MAX_PATH + 1];
    WORD     wNext;
} MODULEENTRY;
```

For a full description of this structure, see the *Microsoft Windows Programmer's Reference, Volume 3.*

Return Value   The return value is nonzero if the function is successful. Otherwise, it is zero.

Comments   The **ModuleNext** function can be used to continue a walk through the list of all currently loaded modules. The walk must have been started by the **ModuleFirst**, **ModuleFindName**, or **ModuleFindHandle** function.

See Also   **ModuleFindHandle, ModuleFindName, ModuleFirst**

MouseProc   3.1

LRESULT CALLBACK MouseProc(*code, wParam, lParam*)
int *code*;   /* process-message flag   */
WPARAM *wParam*;   /* message identifier   */
LPARAM *lParam*;   /* address of MOUSEHOOKSTRUCT structure   */

The **MouseProc** function is a library-defined callback function that the system calls whenever an application calls the **GetMessage** or **PeekMessage** function and there is a mouse message to be processed.

Parameters   *code*
Specifies whether the callback function should process the message or call the **CallNextHookEx** function. If this value is less than zero, the callback function should pass the message to **CallNextHookEx** without further processing. If this value is HC_NOREMOVE, the application is using a **PeekMessage** function with the PM_NOREMOVE option, and the message will not be removed from the system queue.

wParam
Specifies the identifier of the mouse message.

lParam

Points to a **MOUSEHOOKSTRUCT** structure containing information about the mouse. The **MOUSEHOOKSTRUCT** structure has the following form:

```
typedef struct tagMOUSEHOOKSTRUCT { /* ms */
    POINT   pt;
    HWND    hwnd;
    UINT    wHitTestCode;
    DWORD   dwExtraInfo;
} MOUSEHOOKSTRUCT;
```

For a full description of this structure, see the *Microsoft Windows Programmer's Reference*, *Volume 3*.

The callback function should return 0 to allow the system to process the message; it should return 1 to discard the message.

Comments

This callback function should not install a **JournalPlaybackProc** callback function.

An application must install the callback function by specifying the WH_MOUSE filter type and the procedure-instance address of the callback function in a call to the **SetWindowsHookEx** function.

MouseProc is a placeholder for the library-defined function name. The actual name must be exported by including it in an **EXPORTS** statement in the library's module-definition file.

See Also

CallNextHookEx, **GetMessage**, **PeekMessage**, **SetWindowsHookEx**

MoveTo

2.x

DWORD MoveTo(*hdc*, *nXPos*, *nYPos*)
HDC *hdc*;   /* handle of device context   */
int *nXPos*;   /* x-coordinate of new position   */
int *nYPos*;   /* y-coordinate of new position   */

The **MoveTo** function moves the current position to the specified coordinates.

Parameters

hdc

Identifies the device context.

nXPos

Specifies the logical x-coordinate of the new position.

nYPos

Specifies the logical y-coordinate of the new position.

Return Value   The low-order word of the return value contains the logical x-coordinate of the previous position, if the function is successful; the high-order word contains the logical y-coordinate.

Example   The following example uses the **MoveTo** function to set the current position and then calls the **LineTo** function. The example uses **POINT** structures to store the coordinates.

```
HDC hdc;

POINT ptStart = {  12,  12 };
POINT ptEnd = { 128, 135 };

MoveTo(hdc, ptStart.x, ptStart.y);
LineTo(hdc, ptEnd.x, ptEnd.y);
```

See Also   **GetCurrentPosition, LineTo**

MoveToEx   3.1

BOOL MoveToEx(*hdc*, *nX*, *nY*, *lpPoint***)**
HDC *hdc*;	/* handle of device context	*/
int *nX*;	/* x-coordinate of new position	*/
int *nY*;	/* y-coordinate of new position	*/
POINT FAR* *lpPoint*;	/* pointer to structure for previous position	*/

The **MoveToEx** function moves the current position to the point specified by the *nX* and *nY* parameters, optionally returning the previous position.

Parameters   *hdc*

Identifies the device context.

nX

Specifies the logical x-coordinate of the new position.

nY

Specifies the logical y-coordinate of the new position.

lpPoint

Points to a **POINT** structure in which the previous current position will be stored. If this parameter is NULL, no previous position is returned. The **POINT** structure has the following form:

```
typedef struct tagPOINT {    /* pt */
    int x;
    int y;
} POINT;
```

For a full description of this structure, see the *Microsoft Windows Programmer's Reference, Volume 3*.

Return Value   The return value is nonzero if the call is successful. Otherwise, it is zero.

See Also   **MoveTo**

MoveWindow   2.x

BOOL MoveWindow(*hwnd, nLeft, nTop, nWidth, nHeight, fRepaint***)**
HWND *hwnd*;   /* handle of window   */
int *nLeft*;   /* left coordinate   */
int *nTop*;   /* top coordinate   */
int *nWidth*;   /* width   */
int *nHeight*;   /* height   */
BOOL *fRepaint*;   /* repaint flag   */

The **MoveWindow** function changes the position and dimensions of a window. For top-level windows, the position and dimensions are relative to the upper-left corner of the screen. For child windows, they are relative to the upper-left corner of the parent window's client area.

Parameters   *hwnd*
Identifies the window to be changed.

nLeft
Specifies the new position of the left side of the window.

nTop
Specifies the new position of the top of the window.

nWidth
Specifies the new width of the window.

nHeight
Specifies the new height of the window.

fRepaint
Specifies whether the window is to be repainted. If this parameter is TRUE, the window receives a WM_PAINT message. If this parameter is FALSE, no repainting of any kind occurs. This applies to the client area, the nonclient area

(including the title and scroll bars), and any part of the parent window un-covered as a result of the moved window. When this parameter is FALSE, the application must explicitly invalidate or redraw any parts of the window and parent window that must be redrawn.

Return Value   The return value is nonzero if the function is successful. Otherwise, it is zero.

Comments   The **MoveWindow** function sends a WM_GETMINMAXINFO message to the window being moved, giving it an opportunity to modify the default values for the largest and smallest possible windows. If the **MoveWindow** parameters exceed these values, they will be replaced by the minimum or maximum values specified in the WM_GETMINMAXINFO message.

Example   The following example changes the dimensions of a child window in response to a WM_SIZE message. In this example, the child window would always fill the client area of the parent window.

```
case WM_SIZE:
    MoveWindow(hwndChild, 0, 0, LOWORD(lParam), HIWORD(lParam),
        TRUE);
    break;
```

See Also   **ClientToScreen, GetWindowRect, ScreenToClient, SetWindowPos**

MulDiv   3.0

int MulDiv(*nMultiplicand*, *nMultiplier*, *nDivisor*)
int *nMultiplicand*;   /* 16-bit signed multiplicand   */
int *nMultiplier*;   /* 16-bit signed multiplier   */
int *nDivisor*;   /* 16-bit signed divisor   */

The **MulDiv** function multiplies two 16-bit values and then divides the 32-bit re-sult by a third 16-bit value. The return value is the 16-bit result of the division, rounded up or down to the nearest integer.

Parameters   *nMultiplicand*
Specifies the multiplicand.

nMultiplier
Specifies the multiplier.

nDivisor
Specifies the number by which the result of the multiplication (*nMultiplicand* * *nMultiplier*) is to be divided.

Return Value   The return value is the result of the multiplication and division if the function is successful. The return value is −32,768 if either an overflow occurs or the *nDivisor* parameter is 0.

See Also   **CreateFontIndirect, GetDeviceCaps**

NetBIOSCall

3.0

The **NetBIOSCall** function allows an application to issue the NETBIOS Interrupt 5Ch. This function can be called only from assembly-language routines. It is exported from KRNL286.EXE and KRNL386.EXE and is not defined in any Windows header files.

Parameters   Registers must be set up as required by Interrupt 5Ch before the application calls the **NetBIOSCall** function.

Return Value   The register contents are preserved as they are returned by Interrupt 5Ch.

Comments   Applications should use this function instead of directly issuing a NETBIOS Interrupt 5Ch.

Example   To use this function, an application should declare it in an assembly-language routine, as follows:

```
extrn NETBIOSCALL: far
```

If the application includes CMACROS.INC, the function is declared as follows:

```
externFP NetBIOSCall
```

Following is an example of how to use the **NetBIOSCall** function:

```
extrn NETBIOSCALL: far
        .
        .
        ;set registers

        cCall NetBIOSCall
```

NotifyProc

2.x

BOOL CALLBACK NotifyProc(*hglbl*)
HGLOBAL *hglbl*;   /* handle of global memory object   */

The **NotifyProc** function is a library-defined callback function that the system calls whenever it is about to discard a global memory object allocated with the GMEM_NOTIFY flag.

Parameters   *hglbl*
Identifies the global memory object being discarded.

Return Value   The callback function should return nonzero if the system is to discard the memory object, or zero if it should not.

Comments   The callback function is not necessarily called in the context of the application that owns the routine. For this reason, the callback function should not assume it is using the stack segment of the application. The callback function should not call any routine that might move memory.

The callback function must be in a fixed code segment of a dynamic-link library.

NotifyProc is a placeholder for the application-defined function name. The actual name must be exported by including it in an **EXPORTS** statement in the library's module-definition statement.

See Also   **GlobalNotify**

NotifyRegister

3.1

#include <toolhelp.h>

BOOL NotifyRegister(*htask*, *lpfnCallback*, *wFlags*)
HTASK *htask*;   /* handle of task   */
LPFNNOTIFYCALLBACK *lpfnCallback*;   /* address of callback function   */
WORD *wFlags*;   /* notification flags   */

The **NotifyRegister** function installs a notification callback function for the given task.

Parameters

htask

Identifies the task associated with the callback function. If this parameter is NULL, it identifies the current task.

lpfnCallback

Points to the notification callback function that is installed for the task. The kernel calls this function whenever it sends a notification to the task.

The callback-function address is normally the return value of a call to **Make-ProcInstance**. This causes the callback function to be entered with the AX register set to the selector of the application's data segment. Usually, an exported function prolog contains the following code:

```
mov  ds,ax
```

wFlags

Specifies the optional notifications that the application will receive, in addition to the default notifications. This parameter can be NF_NORMAL or any combination of the following values:

Value	Meaning
NF_NORMAL	The application will receive the default notifications but none of the notifications of task switching, system debugging errors, or debug strings.
NF_TASKSWITCH	The application will receive task-switching notifications. To avoid poor performance, an application should not receive these notifications unless absolutely necessary.
NF_RIP	The application will receive notifications of system debugging errors.

Return Value

The return value is nonzero if the function was successful. Otherwise, it is zero.

Callback Function

The syntax of the function pointed to by *lpfnCallback* is as follows:

BOOL NotifyRegisterCallback(*wID*, *dwData*)
WORD *wID*;
DWORD *dwData*;

Parameters

wID

Indicates the type of notification and the value of the *dwData* parameter. The *wID* parameter may be one of the following values in Windows versions 3.0 and later:

Value	Meaning
NFY_DELMODULE	The low-order word of *dwData* is the handle of the module to be freed.

Value	Meaning
NFY_EXITTASK	The low-order byte of *dwData* contains the program exit code.
NFY_FREESEG	The low-order word of *dwData* is the selector of the segment to be freed.
NFY_INCHAR	The *dwData* parameter is not used. The notification callback function should return either the ASCII value for the keystroke or NULL.
NFY_LOADSEG	The *dwData* parameter points to an **NFYLOADSEG** structure.
NFY_OUTSTR	The *dwData* parameter points to the string to be displayed.
NFY_RIP	The *dwData* parameter points to an **NFYRIP** structure.
NFY_STARTDLL	The *dwData* parameter points to an **NFYSTARTDLL** structure.
NFY_STARTTASK	The *dwData* parameter is the CS:IP of the starting address of the task.
NFY_UNKNOWN	The kernel returned an unknown notification.

In Windows version 3.1, *wID* may be one of the following values:

Value	Meaning
NFY_LOGERROR	The *dwData* parameter points to an **NFYLOG-ERROR** structure.
NFY_LOGPARAMERROR	The *dwData* parameter points to an **NFYLOG-PARAMERROR** structure.
NFY_TASKIN	The *dwData* parameter is undefined. The callback function should call the **GetCurrentTask** function.
NFY_TASKOUT	The *dwData* parameter is undefined. The callback function should call **GetCurrentTask**.

dwData
    Specifies data, or specifies a pointer to data, or is undefined, depending on the value of *wID*.

Return Value
    The return value of the callback function is nonzero if the callback function handled the notification. Otherwise, it is zero and the notification is passed to other callback functions.

Comments
    A notification callback function must be able to ignore any unknown notification value. Typically, the notification callback function cannot use any Windows function, with the exception of the Tool Helper functions and **PostMessage**.

    NotifyRegisterCallback is a placeholder for the application-defined function name. The actual name must be exported by including it in an **EXPORTS** statement in the application's module-definition file.

See Also   InterruptRegister, InterruptUnRegister, MakeProcInstance,
                               NotifyUnRegister, TerminateApp

NotifyUnRegister   3.1

#include <toolhelp.h>

BOOL NotifyUnRegister(*htask*)
HTASK *htask*;   /* handle of task   */

                               The **NotifyUnRegister** function restores the default notification handler.

Parameters   *htask*
                               Identifies the task. If *htask* is NULL, it identifies the current task.

Return Value   The return value is nonzero if the function is successful. Otherwise, it is zero.

Comments   After this function is executed, the given task no longer receives notifications from
                               the kernel.

See Also   **InterruptRegister, InterruptUnRegister, NotifyRegister, TerminateApp**

OemKeyScan   3.0

DWORD OemKeyScan(*uOemChar*)
UINT *uOemChar*;   /* OEM ASCII character   */

                               The **OemKeyScan** function translates (maps) OEM ASCII codes 0 through 0xFF
                               to their corresponding OEM scan codes and shift states.

Parameters   *uOemChar*
                               Specifies the ASCII value of the OEM character.

Return Value   The low-order word of the return value contains the scan code of the specified
                               OEM character; the high-order word contains flags that indicate the shift state: If
                               bit 1 is set, a SHIFT key is pressed; if bit 2 is set, a CTRL key is pressed. Both the
                               low-order and high-order words of the return value contain −1 if the character is
                               not defined in the OEM character tables.

Comments   The **OemKeyScan** function does not translate characters that require CTRL+ALT or dead keys. Characters not translated by this function must be copied by simulating input, using the ALT+ keypad mechanism. For this to work, the NUM LOCK key must be off.

This function calls the **VkKeyScan** function in recent versions of the keyboard device drivers.

OemKeyScan allows an application to send OEM text to another application by simulating keyboard input. It is used specifically for this purpose by Windows in 386 enhanced mode.

See Also   **VkKeyScan**

OemToAnsi $\boxed{\text{2.x}}$

void OemToAnsi(*hpszOemStr*, *hpszWindowsStr*)
const char _huge* *hpszOemStr*;   /* address of string to translate   */
char _huge* *hpszWindowsStr*;   /* address of translated string buffer   */

The **OemToAnsi** function translates a string from the OEM-defined character set into the Windows character set.

Parameters   *hpszOemStr*
　　Points to a null-terminated string of characters from the OEM-defined character set.

hpszWindowsStr
　　Points to the location where the translated string is to be copied. To translate the string in place, the *hpszWindowsStr* parameter can be the same as the *hpszOemStr* parameter.

Return Value   This function does not return a value.

See Also   **AnsiToOem, OemToAnsiBuff**

OemToAnsiBuff

void OemToAnsiBuff(*lpszOemStr*, *lpszWindowsStr*, *cbOemStr*)
LPCSTR *lpszOemStr*;   /* address of OEM character string   */
LPSTR *lpszWindowsStr*;   /* address of buffer for Windows string   */
UINT *cbOemStr*;   /* length of OEM string   */

The **OemToAnsiBuff** function translates a string from the OEM-defined character set into the Windows character set.

Parameters

lpszOemStr
Points to a buffer containing one or more characters from the OEM-defined character set.

lpszWindowsStr
Points to the location where the translated string is to be copied. To translate the string in place, the *lpszWindowsStr* parameter can be the same as the *lpszOemStr* parameter.

cbOemStr
Specifies the length, in bytes, of the buffer pointed to by *lpszOemStr*. If *cbOemStr* is 0, the length is 64K.

Return Value

This function does not return a value.

See Also

AnsiToOem, OemToAnsi

OffsetClipRgn

int OffsetClipRgn(*hdc*, *nXOffset*, *nYOffset*)
HDC *hdc*;   /* device-context handle   */
int *nXOffset*;   /* offset along x-axis   */
int *nYOffset*;   /* offset along y-axis   */

The **OffsetClipRgn** function moves the clipping region of the given device by the specified offsets.

Parameters

hdc
Identifies the device context.

nXOffset
Specifies the number of logical units to move left or right.

nYOffset
Specifies the number of logical units to move up or down.

Return Value   The return value is SIMPLEREGION (region has no overlapping borders), COMPLEXREGION (region has overlapping borders), or NULLREGION (region is empty), if the function is successful. Otherwise, the return value is ERROR.

Example   The following example creates an elliptical region and selects it as the clipping region for a device context. The **OffsetClipRgn** function is called repeatedly to move the clipping region from left to right across the screen. Because only the new clipping region is redrawn each time the **Rectangle** function is called, the left side of each ellipse remains on the screen when the clipping region moves. When the loop has finished, a wide blue line with rounded ends stretches from one side of the client area to the other.

```
RECT rc;
HRGN hrgn;
HBRUSH hbr, hbrPrevious;
int i;

GetClientRect(hwnd, &rc);
hrgn = CreateEllipticRgn(0, 100, 100, 200);
SelectClipRgn(hdc, hrgn);
hbr = CreateSolidBrush(RGB(0, 0, 255));
hbrPrevious = SelectObject(hdc, hbr);

for (i = 0; i < rc.right - 100; i++) {
    OffsetClipRgn(hdc, 1, 0);
    Rectangle(hdc, rc.left, rc.top, rc.right, rc.bottom);
}

SelectObject(hdc, hbrPrevious);
DeleteObject(hbr);
DeleteObject(hrgn);
```

See Also   **CreateEllipticRgn, SelectClipRgn**

OffsetRect   2.x

void OffsetRect(*lprc, x, y*)
RECT FAR* *lprc*;   /* address of structure with rectangle   */
int *x*;   /* horizontal offset   */
int *y*;   /* vertical offset   */

The **OffsetRect** function moves the given rectangle by the specified offsets.

Parameters   *lprc*

Points to a **RECT** structure that contains the coordinates of the rectangle to be moved. The **RECT** structure has the following form:

```
typedef struct tagRECT {    /* rc */
    int left;
    int top;
    int right;
    int bottom;
} RECT;
```

For a full description of this structure, see the *Microsoft Windows Programmer's Reference, Volume 3*.

x

Specifies the amount to move left or right. It must be negative to move left.

y

Specifies the amount to move up or down. It must be negative to move up.

Return Value   This function does not return a value.

Comments   The coordinate values of a rectangle must not be greater than 32,767 or less than −32,768. The *x* and *y* parameters must be chosen carefully to prevent invalid rectangles.

See Also   **InflateRect, IntersectRect, UnionRect**

OffsetRgn

2.x

int OffsetRgn(*hrgn, nXOffset, nYOffset*)
HRGN *hrgn*;   /* handle of region   */
int *nXOffset*;   /* offset along x-axis   */
int *nYOffset*;   /* offset along y-axis   */

The **OffsetRgn** function moves the given region by the specified offsets.

Parameters   *hrgn*

Identifies the region to be moved.

nXOffset

Specifies the number of logical units to move left or right.

nYOffset

Specifies the number of logical units to move up or down.

Return Value   The return value is SIMPLEREGION (region has no overlapping borders), COMPLEXREGION (region has overlapping borders), or NULLREGION (region is empty), if the function is successful. Otherwise, the return value is ERROR.

Comments   The coordinate values of a region must not be greater than 32,767 or less than −32,768. The *nXOffset* and *nYOffset* parameters must be carefully chosen to prevent invalid regions.

Example   The following example creates a rectangular region, uses the **OffsetRgn** function to move the region 50 positive units in the x- and y-directions, selects the offset region into the device context, and then fills it by using a blue brush:

```
HDC hdcLocal;
HRGN hrgn;
HBRUSH hbrBlue;
int RgnType;

hdcLocal = GetDC(hwnd);
hrgn = CreateRectRgn(100, 10, 210, 110);
SelectObject(hdc, hrgn);
PaintRgn(hdc, hrgn);

RgnType = OffsetRgn(hrgn, 50, 50);
SelectObject(hdc, hrgn);

if (RgnType == ERROR)
    TextOut(hdcLocal, 10, 135, "ERROR", 5);
else if (RgnType == SIMPLEREGION)
    TextOut(hdcLocal, 10, 135, "SIMPLEREGION", 12);
else if (RgnType == NULLREGION)
    TextOut(hdcLocal, 10, 135, "NULLREGION", 10);
else
    TextOut(hdcLocal, 10, 135, "Unrecognized value.", 19);

hbrBlue = CreateSolidBrush(RGB(0, 0, 255));
FillRgn(hdc, hrgn, hbrBlue);

DeleteObject(hrgn);
DeleteObject(hbrBlue);
ReleaseDC(hwnd, hdcLocal);
```

OffsetViewportOrg

2.x

DWORD OffsetViewportOrg(*hdc*, *nXOffset*, *nYOffset*)
HDC *hdc*;   /* handle of device context   */
int *nXOffset*;   /* offset along x-axis   */
int *nYOffset*;   /* offset along y-axis   */

The **OffsetViewportOrg** function modifies the coordinates of the viewport origin relative to the coordinates of the current viewport origin.

Parameters

hdc
Identifies the device context.

nXOffset
Specifies the value, in device units, to add to the x-coordinate of the current origin.

nYOffset
Specifies the value, in device units, to add to the y-coordinate of the current origin.

Return Value

The low-order word of the return value contains the x-coordinate, in device units, of the previous viewport origin, if the function is successful; the high-order word contains the y-coordinate.

Comments

The viewport origin is the origin of the device coordinate system for a window. By changing the viewport origin, an application can change the way the graphics device interface (GDI) maps points from the logical coordinate system. GDI maps all points in the logical coordinate system to the viewport in the same way as it maps the origin.

To map points to the right, specify a negative value for the *nXOffset* parameter. Similarly, to map points down (in the MM_TEXT mapping mode), specify a negative value for the *nYOffset* parameter.

Example

The following example uses the **OffsetWindowOrg** and **OffsetViewportOrg** functions to reposition the output of the **PlayMetaFile** function on the screen:

```
HDC hdcMeta;
HANDLE hmf;

hdcMeta = CreateMetaFile((LPSTR) NULL);
    .
    . /* Record the metafile. */
    .

PlayMetaFile(hdc, hmf);
```

```
OffsetWindowOrg(hdc, -200, -200);
PlayMetaFile(hdc, hmf);    /* MM_TEXT screen output +200 x, +200 y */

OffsetViewportOrg(hdc, 0, -200);
PlayMetaFile(hdc, hmf);    /* outputs -200 y from last PlayMetaFile */

DeleteMetaFile(hmf);
```

See Also   **GetViewportOrg, OffsetWindowOrg, SetViewportOrg**

OffsetViewportOrgEx   3.1

BOOL OffsetViewportOrgEx(*hdc, nX, nY, lpPoint*)
HDC *hdc*;   /* handle of device context   */
int *nX*;   /* device units to add to x-coordinate */
int *nY*;   /* device units to add to y-coordinate */
POINT FAR* *lpPoint*;   /* address of POINT structure   */

The **OffsetViewportOrgEx** function modifies the viewport origin relative to the current values. The formulas are written as follows:

```
xNewVO = xOldVO + X
yNewVO = yOldVO + Y
```

The new origin is the sum of the current origin and the *nX* and *nY* values.

Parameters   *hdc*
                   Identifies the device context.

                   nX
                   Specifies the number of device units to add to the current origin's x-coordinate.

                   nY
                   Specifies the number of device units to add to the current origin's y-coordinate.

                   lpPoint
                   Points to a **POINT** structure. The previous viewport origin (in device coordinates) is placed in this structure. If *lpPoint* is NULL, the previous viewport origin in not returned.

Return Value   The return value is nonzero if the function is successful. Otherwise, it is zero.

OffsetWindowOrg

DWORD OffsetWindowOrg(*hdc*, *nXOffset*, *nYOffset*)
HDC *hdc*;   /* handle of device context   */
int *nXOffset*;   /* offset along x-axis   */
int *nYOffset*;   /* offset along y-axis   */

The **OffsetWindowOrg** function modifies the window origin relative to the coordinates of the current window origin.

Parameters

hdc
Identifies the device context.

nXOffset
Specifies the value, in logical units, to add to the x-coordinate of the current origin.

nYOffset
Specifies the value, in logical units, to add to y-coordinate of the current origin.

Return Value

The low-order word of the return value contains the logical x-coordinate of the previous window origin, if the function is successful; the high-order word contains the logical y-coordinate.

Comments

The window origin is the origin of the logical coordinate system for a window. By changing the window origin, an application can change the way the graphics device interface (GDI) maps logical points to the physical coordinate system (the viewport). GDI maps all points in the logical coordinate system to the viewport in the same way as it maps the origin.

To map points to the right, specify a negative value for the *nXOffset* parameter. Similarly, to map points down (in the MM_TEXT mapping mode), specify a negative value for the *nYOffset* parameter.

Example

The following example uses the **OffsetWindowOrg** and **OffsetViewportOrg** functions to reposition the output of the **PlayMetaFile** function on the screen:

```
HDC hdcMeta;
HANDLE hmf;

hdcMeta = CreateMetaFile((LPSTR) NULL);
    .
    . /* Record the metafile. */
    .

PlayMetaFile(hdc, hmf);
```

```
OffsetWindowOrg(hdc, -200, -200);
PlayMetaFile(hdc, hmf);   /* MM_TEXT screen output +200 x, +200 y */

OffsetViewportOrg(hdc, 0, -200);
PlayMetaFile(hdc, hmf);   /* outputs -200 y from last PlayMetaFile */

DeleteMetaFile(hmf);
```

See Also **GetWindowOrg**, **OffsetViewportOrg**, **SetWindowOrg**

OffsetWindowOrgEx   3.1

BOOL OffsetWindowOrgEx(*hdc, nX, nY, lpPoint***)**
HDC *hdc*;   /* handle of device context   */
int *nX*;   /* logical units to add to x-coordinate */
int *nY*;   /* logical units to add to y-coordinate */
POINT FAR* *lpPoint*;   /* address of POINT structure   */

The **OffsetWindowOrgEx** function modifies the viewport origin relative to the current values. The formulas are written as follows:

```
xNewWO = xOldWO + X
yNewWO = yOldWO + Y
```

The new origin is the sum of the current origin and the *nX* and *nY* values.

Parameters   *hdc*
                      Identifies the device context.

                      nX
                      Specifies the number of logical units to add to the current origin's x-coordinate.

                      nY
                      Specifies the number of logical units to add to the current origin's y-coordinate.

                      lpPoint
                      Points to a **POINT** structure. The previous window origin (in logical coordinates) is placed in this structure. If *lpPoint* is NULL, the previous origin is not returned.

Return Value   The return value is nonzero if the function is successful. Otherwise, it is zero.

OleActivate

#include <ole.h>

OLESTATUS OleActivate(*lpObject*, *verb*, *fShow*, *fTakeFocus*, *hwnd*, *lprcBound*)
LPOLEOBJECT *lpObject*;	/* address of object to activate	*/
UINT *verb*;	/* operation to perform	*/
BOOL *fShow*;	/* whether to show window	*/
BOOL *fTakeFocus*;	/* whether server gets focus	*/
HWND *hwnd*;	/* window handle of destination document	*/
const RECT FAR* *lprcBound*;	/* bounding rectangle for object display	*/

The **OleActivate** function opens an object for an operation. Typically, the object is edited or played.

Parameters

lpObject
Points to the object to activate.

verb
Specifies which operation to perform (0 = the primary verb, 1 = the secondary verb, and so on).

fShow
Specifies whether the window is to be shown. If the window is to be shown, this value is TRUE; otherwise, it is FALSE.

fTakeFocus
Specifies whether the server should get the focus. If the server should get the focus, this value is TRUE; otherwise, it is FALSE. This parameter is relevant only if the *fShow* parameter is TRUE.

hwnd
Identifies the window of the document containing the object.

lprcBound
Points to a **RECT** structure containing the coordinates of the bounding rectangle in which the destination document displays the object. The mapping mode of the device context determines the units for these coordinates.

Return Value

The return value is OLE_OK if the function is successful. Otherwise, it is an error value, which may be one of the following:

OLE_BUSY
OLE_ERROR_OBJECT
OLE_WAIT_FOR_RELEASE

Comments   Typically, a server is launched in a separate window; editing then occurs asyn-
                     chronously. The client is notified of changes to the object through the callback
                     function.

                     A client application might set the *fShow* parameter to FALSE if a server needed to
                     remain active without being visible on the display. (In this case, the application
                     would also use the **OleSetData** function.)

                     Client applications typically specify the primary verb when the user double-clicks
                     an object. The server can take any action in response to the specified verb. If the
                     server supports only one action, it takes that action no matter which value is
                     passed in the *verb* parameter.

                     In future releases of the object linking and embedding (OLE) protocol, the *hwnd*
                     and *lprcBound* parameters will be used to help determine the placement of the
                     server's editing window.

See Also   **OleQueryOpen**, **OleSetData**

OleBlockServer   3.1

#include <ole.h>

OLESTATUS OleBlockServer(*lhSrvr***)**
LHSERVER *lhSrvr*;   /* handle of server   */

                     The **OleBlockServer** function causes requests to the server to be queued until the
                     server calls the **OleUnblockServer** function.

Parameters   *lhSrvr*
                        Identifies the server for which requests are to be queued.

Return Value   The return value is OLE_OK if the function is successful. Otherwise, it is an error
                     value, which may be OLE_ERROR_HANDLE.

Comments   The server must call the **OleUnblockServer** function after calling the **OleBlock-**
                     Server function.

                     A server application can use the **OleBlockServer** and **OleUnblockServer** func-
                     tions to control when the server library processes requests from client applications.
                     Because only messages from the client to the server are blocked, a blocked server
                     can continue to send messages to client applications.

A server application receives a handle when it calls the **OleRegisterServer** function.

See Also   **OleRegisterServer, OleUnblockServer**

OleClone

#include <ole.h>

OLESTATUS OleClone(*lpObject*, *lpClient*, *lhClientDoc*, *lpszObjname*, *lplpObject*)
LPOLEOBJECT *lpObject*;   /* address of object to copy   */
LPOLECLIENT *lpClient*;   /* address of OLECLIENT for new object   */
LHCLIENTDOC *lhClientDoc*;   /* long handle of client document   */
LPCSTR *lpszObjname*;   /* address of string for object name   */
LPOLEOBJECT FAR* *lplpObject*;   /* address of pointer to new object   */

The **OleClone** function makes a copy of an object. The copy is identical to the source object, but it is not connected to the server.

Parameters   *lpObject*
                   Points to the object to copy.

                   lpClient
                   Points to an **OLECLIENT** structure for the new object.

                   lhClientDoc
                   Identifies the client document in which the object is to be created.

                   lpszObjname
                   Points to a null-terminated string specifying the client's name for the object. This name must be unique with respect to the names of any other objects in the document and cannot contain a slash mark (/).

                   lplpObject
                   Points to a variable where the library will store the long pointer to the new object.

Return Value   The return value is OLE_OK if the function is successful. Otherwise, it is an error value, which may be one of the following:

                   OLE_BUSY
                   OLE_ERROR_HANDLE
                   OLE_ERROR_OBJECT
                   OLE_WAIT_FOR_RELEASE

Comments	Client applications often use the **OleClone** function to support the Undo command.
	A client application can supply a new **OLECLIENT** structure for the cloned object, if required.
See Also	**OleEqual**

OleClose

#include <ole.h>

OLESTATUS OleClose(*lpObject***)**
LPOLEOBJECT *lpObject*;   /* address of object to close   */

The **OleClose** function closes the specified open object. Closing an object terminates the connection with the server application.

Parameters	*lpObject*
	Points to the object to close.
Return Value	The return value is OLE_OK if the function is successful. Otherwise, it is an error value, which may be one of the following:
	OLE_BUSY
	OLE_ERROR_OBJECT
	OLE_WAIT_FOR_RELEASE
See Also	**OleActivate**, **OleDelete**, **OleReconnect**

OleCopyFromLink

#include <ole.h>

OLESTATUS OleCopyFromLink(*lpObject, lpszProtocol, lpClient, lhClientDoc, lpszObjname,*
   *lplpObject***)**

LPOLEOBJECT *lpObject*;	/* address of object to embed	*/
LPCSTR *lpszProtocol*;	/* address of protocol name	*/
LPOLECLIENT *lpClient*;	/* address of client structure	*/
LHCLIENTDOC *lhClientDoc*;	/* long handle of client document	*/
LPCSTR *lpszObjname*;	/* address of string for object name	*/
LPOLEOBJECT FAR* *lplpObject*;	/* address of pointer to new object	*/

The **OleCopyFromLink** function makes an embedded copy of a linked object.

Parameters

lpObject
   Points to the linked object that is to be embedded.

lpszProtocol
   Points to a null-terminated string specifying the name of the protocol required
   for the new embedded object. Currently, this value can be StdFileEditing (the
   name of the object linking and embedding protocol).

lpClient
   Points to an **OLECLIENT** structure for the new object.

lhClientDoc
   Identifies the client document in which the object is to be created.

lpszObjname
   Points to a null-terminated string specifying the client's name for the object.

lplpObject
   Points to a variable where the long pointer to the new object will be stored.

Return Value

The return value is OLE_OK if the function is successful. Otherwise, it is an error
value, which may be one of the following:

OLE_BUSY
OLE_ERROR_HANDLE
OLE_ERROR_NAME
OLE_ERROR_OBJECT
OLE_ERROR_PROTOCOL
OLE_WAIT_FOR_RELEASE

Comments

Making an embedded copy of a linked object may involve starting the server application.

See Also

OleObjectConvert

OleCopyToClipboard

#include <ole.h>

OLESTATUS OleCopyToClipboard(*lpObject*)
LPOLEOBJECT *lpObject*;   /* address of object   */

The **OleCopyToClipboard** function puts the specified object on the clipboard.

Parameters   *lpObject*
                          Points to the object to copy to the clipboard.

Return Value   The return value is OLE_OK if the function is successful. Otherwise, it is an error
                        value, which may be OLE_ERROR_OBJECT.

Comments   A client application typically calls the **OleCopyToClipboard** function when a
                        user chooses the Copy or Cut command from the Edit menu.

                        The client application should open and empty the clipboard, call the **OleCopyTo-
                        Clipboard** function, and close the clipboard.

OleCreate

#include <ole.h>

OLESTATUS OleCreate(*lpszProtocol, lpClient, lpszClass, lhClientDoc, lpszObjname, lplpObject,*
    renderopt, cfFormat)
LPCSTR *lpszProtocol*;   /* address of string for protocol name   */
LPOLECLIENT *lpClient*;   /* address of client structure   */
LPCSTR *lpszClass*;   /* address of string for classname   */
LHCLIENTDOC *lhClientDoc*;   /* long handle of client document   */
LPCSTR *lpszObjname*;   /* address of string for object name   */
LPOLEOBJECT FAR* *lplpObject*;   /* address of pointer to object   */
OLEOPT_RENDER *renderopt*;   /* rendering options   */
OLECLIPFORMAT *cfFormat*;   /* clipboard format   */

The **OleCreate** function creates an embedded object of a specified class. The server is opened to perform the initial editing.

Parameters   *lpszProtocol*
                          Points to a null-terminated string specifying the name of the protocol required
                          for the new embedded object. Currently, this value can be StdFileEditing (the
                          name of the object linking and embedding protocol).

lpClient
Points to an **OLECLIENT** structure for the new object.

lpszClass
Points to a null-terminated string specifying the registered name of the class of the object to be created.

lhClientDoc
Identifies the client document in which the object is to be created.

lpszObjname
Points to a null-terminated string specifying the client's name for the object. This name must be unique with respect to the names of any other objects in the document and cannot contain a slash mark (/).

lplpObject
Points to a variable where the library will store the long pointer to the new object.

renderopt
Specifies the client's preference for presentation data for the object. This parameter can be one of the following values:

Value	Meaning
olerender_draw	The client calls the **OleDraw** function, and the library obtains and manages presentation data.
olerender_format	The client calls the **OleGetData** function to retrieve data in a specific format. The library obtains and manages the data in the requested format, as specified by the *cfFormat* parameter.
olerender_none	The client library does not obtain any presentation data and does not draw the object.

cfFormat
Specifies the clipboard format when the *renderopt* parameter is **olerender_format**. This clipboard format is used in a subsequent call to **OleGetData**. If this clipboard format is CF_METAFILEPICT, CF_DIB, or CF_BITMAP, the library manages the data and draws the object. The library does not support drawing for any other formats.

Return Value

The return value is OLE_OK if the function is successful. Otherwise, it is an error value, which may be one of the following:

OLE_ERROR_HANDLE
OLE_ERROR_NAME
OLE_ERROR_PROTOCOL
OLE_WAIT_FOR_RELEASE

Comments

The **olerender_none** rendering option is typically used to support hyperlinks. With this option, the client does not call **OleDraw** and calls **OleGetData** only for ObjectLink, OwnerLink, and Native formats.

The **olerender_ format** rendering option allows a client to compute data (instead of painting it), use an unusual data format, or modify a standard data format. With this option, the client does not call **OleDraw**. The client calls **OleGetData** to retrieve data in the specified format.

The **olerender_ draw** rendering option is the most typical option. It is the easiest rendering option for the client to implement (the client simply calls **OleDraw**), and it allows the most flexibility. An object handler can exploit this flexibility to store no presentation data, a private presentation data format, or several different formats that it can choose among dynamically. Future implementations of object linking and embedding (OLE) may also exploit the flexibility that is inherent in this option.

See Also   **OleCreateFromClip, OleCreateFromTemplate, OleDraw, OleGetData**

OleCreateFromClip   3.1

#include <ole.h>

OLESTATUS OleCreateFromClip(*lpszProtocol, lpClient, lhClientDoc, lpszObjname, lplpObject,*
   *renderopt, cfFormat***)**
LPCSTR *lpszProtocol*;   /* address of string for protocol name   */
LPOLECLIENT *lpClient*;   /* address of client structure   */
LHCLIENTDOC *lhClientDoc*;   /* long handle of client document   */
LPCSTR *lpszObjname*;   /* address of string for object name   */
LPOLEOBJECT FAR* *lplpObject*;   /* address of pointer to object   */
OLEOPT_ RENDER *renderopt*;   /* rendering options   */
OLECLIPFORMAT *cfFormat*;   /* clipboard format   */

The **OleCreateFromClip** function creates an object from the clipboard.

Parameters   *lpszProtocol*
          Points to a null-terminated string specifying the name of the protocol required for the new embedded object. Currently, this value can be StdFileEditing (the name of the object linking and embedding protocol) or Static (for uneditable pictures only).

lpClient
          Points to an **OLECLIENT** structure allocated and initialized by the client application. This pointer is used to locate the callback function and is passed in callback notifications.

lhClientDoc
          Identifies the client document in which the object is being created.

lpszObjname
  Points to a null-terminated string specifying the client's name for the object. This name must be unique with respect to the names of any other objects in the document and cannot contain a slash mark (/).

lplpObject
  Points to a variable where the library will store the long pointer to the new object.

renderopt
  Specifies the client's preference for presentation data for the object. This parameter can be one of the following values:

Value	Meaning
olerender_draw	The client calls the **OleDraw** function, and the library obtains and manages presentation data.
olerender_format	The client calls the **OleGetData** function to retrieve data in a specific format. The library obtains and manages the data in the requested format, as specified by the *cfFormat* parameter.
olerender_none	The client library does not obtain any presentation data and does not draw the object.

cfFormat
  Specifies the clipboard format when the *renderopt* parameter is **olerender_format**. This clipboard format is used in a subsequent call to **OleGetData**. If this clipboard format is CF_METAFILEPICT, CF_DIB, or CF_BITMAP, the library manages the data and draws the object. The library does not support drawing for any other formats.

Return Value
  The return value is OLE_OK if the function is successful. Otherwise, it is an error value, which may be one of the following:

  OLE_ERROR_CLIP
  OLE_ERROR_FORMAT
  OLE_ERROR_HANDLE
  OLE_ERROR_NAME
  OLE_ERROR_OPTION
  OLE_ERROR_PROTOCOL
  OLE_WAIT_FOR_RELEASE

Comments
  The client application should open and empty the clipboard, call the **OleCreateFromClip** function, and close the clipboard.

  The **olerender_none** rendering option is typically used to support hyperlinks. With this option, the client does not call **OleDraw** and calls **OleGetData** only for ObjectLink, OwnerLink, and Native formats.

The **olerender_ format** rendering option allows a client to compute data (instead of painting it), use an unusual data format, or modify a standard data format. With this option, the client does not call **OleDraw**. The client calls **OleGetData** to retrieve data in the specified format.

The **olerender_ draw** rendering option is the most typical option. It is the easiest rendering option for the client to implement (the client simply calls **OleDraw**), and it allows the most flexibility. An object handler can exploit this flexibility to store no presentation data, a private presentation data format, or several different formats that it can choose among dynamically. Future implementations of object linking and embedding (OLE) may also exploit the flexibility that is inherent in this option.

See Also   **OleCreate, OleCreateFromTemplate, OleDraw, OleGetData, OleQueryCreateFromClip**

OleCreateFromFile   3.1

#include <ole.h>

OLESTATUS OleCreateFromFile(*lpszProtocol, lpClient, lpszClass, lpszFile, lhClientDoc,*
  lpszObjname, lplpObject, renderopt, cfFormat)
LPCSTR *lpszProtocol*;	/* address of string for protocol name */
LPOLECLIENT *lpClient*;	/* address of client structure */
LPCSTR *lpszClass*;	/* address of string for class name */
LPCSTR *lpszFile*;	/* address of string for filename */
LHCLIENTDOC *lhClientDoc*;	/* long handle of client document */
LPCSTR *lpszObjname*;	/* address of string for object name */
LPOLEOBJECT FAR* *lplpObject*;	/* address of pointer to object */
OLEOPT_ RENDER *renderopt*;	/* rendering options */
OLECLIPFORMAT *cfFormat*;	/* clipboard format */

The **OleCreateFromFile** function creates an embedded object from the contents of a named file.

Parameters   *lpszProtocol*
      Points to a null-terminated string specifying the name of the protocol required for the new embedded object. Currently, this value can be StdFileEditing (the name of the object linking and embedding protocol).

lpClient
      Points to an **OLECLIENT** structure allocated and initialized by the client application. This pointer is used to locate the callback function and is passed in callback notifications.

lpszClass
Points to a null-terminated string specifying the name of the class for the new object. If this value is NULL, the library uses the extension of the filename pointed to by the *lpszFile* parameter to find the class name for the object.

lpszFile
Points to a null-terminated string specifying the name of the file containing the object.

lhClientDoc
Identifies the client document in which the object is being created.

lpszObjname
Points to a null-terminated string specifying the client's name for the object. This name must be unique with respect to the names of any other objects in the document and cannot contain a slash mark (/).

lplpObject
Points to a variable where the library will store the long pointer to the new object.

renderopt
Specifies the client's preference for presentation data for the object. This parameter can be one of the following values:

Value	Meaning
olerender_draw	The client calls the **OleDraw** function, and the library obtains and manages presentation data.
olerender_format	The client calls the **OleGetData** function to retrieve data in a specific format. The library obtains and manages the data in the requested format, as specified by the *cfFormat* parameter.
olerender_none	The client library does not obtain any presentation data and does not draw the object.

cfFormat
Specifies the clipboard format when the *renderopt* parameter is **olerender_format**. This clipboard format is used in a subsequent call to **OleGetData**. If this clipboard format is CF_METAFILEPICT, CF_DIB, or CF_BITMAP, the library manages the data and draws the object. The library does not support drawing for any other formats.

Return Value

The return value is OLE_OK if the function is successful. Otherwise, it is an error value, which may be one of the following:

OLE_ERROR_CLASS
OLE_ERROR_HANDLE
OLE_ERROR_MEMORY
OLE_ERROR_NAME
OLE_ERROR_PROTOCOL
OLE_WAIT_FOR_RELEASE

Comments   When a client application calls the **OleCreateFromFile** function, the server is
started to render the Native and presentation data and then is closed. (If the server
and document are already open, this function simply retrieves the information,
without closing the server.) The server does not show the object to the user for
editing.

The **olerender_none** rendering option is typically used to support hyperlinks.
With this option, the client does not call **OleDraw** and calls **OleGetData** only for
ObjectLink, OwnerLink, and Native formats.

The **olerender_format** rendering option allows a client to compute data (instead
of painting it), use an unusual data format, or modify a standard data format. With
this option, the client does not call **OleDraw**. The client calls **OleGetData** to retrieve data in the specified format.

The **olerender_draw** rendering option is the most typical option. It is the easiest
rendering option for the client to implement (the client simply calls **OleDraw**),
and it allows the most flexibility. An object handler can exploit this flexibility to
store no presentation data, a private presentation data format, or several different
formats that it can choose among dynamically. Future implementations of object
linking and embedding (OLE) may also exploit the flexibility that is inherent in
this option.

If a client application accepts files dropped from File Manager, it should respond
to the **WM_DROPFILES** message by calling **OleCreateFromFile** and specifying Packager for the *lpszClass* parameter to indicate Microsoft Windows Object
Packager.

See Also   **OleCreate, OleCreateFromTemplate, OleDraw, OleGetData**

OleCreateFromTemplate   3.1

#include <ole.h>

OLESTATUS OleCreateFromTemplate(*lpszProtocol***,** *lpClient***,** *lpszTemplate***,** *lhClientDoc***,**
    *lpszObjname***,** *lplpObject***,** *renderopt***,** *cfFormat***)**

LPCSTR *lpszProtocol*;	/* address of string for protocol name	*/
LPOLECLIENT *lpClient*;	/* address of client structure	*/
LPCSTR *lpszTemplate*;	/* address of string for path of file	*/
LHCLIENTDOC *lhClientDoc*;	/* long handle of client document	*/
LPCSTR *lpszObjname*;	/* address of string for object name	*/
LPOLEOBJECT FAR* *lplpObject*;	/* address of pointer to object	*/
OLEOPT_RENDER *renderopt*;	/* rendering options	*/
OLECLIPFORMAT *cfFormat*;	/* clipboard format	*/

The **OleCreateFromTemplate** function creates an object by using another object as a template. The server is opened to perform the initial editing.

Parameters

lpszProtocol
Points to a null-terminated string specifying the name of the protocol required for the new embedded object. Currently, this value can be StdFileEditing (the name of the object linking and embedding protocol).

lpClient
Points to an **OLECLIENT** structure for the new object.

lpszTemplate
Points to a null-terminated string specifying the path of the file to be used as a template for the new object. The server is opened for editing and loads the initial state of the new object from the named template file.

lhClientDoc
Identifies the client document in which the object is being created.

lpszObjname
Points to a null-terminated string specifying the client's name for the object. This name must be unique with respect to the names of any other objects in the document and cannot contain a slash mark (/).

lplpObject
Points to a variable where the library will store the long pointer to the new object.

renderopt
Specifies the client's preference for presentation data for the object. This parameter can be one of the following values:

Value	Meaning
olerender_draw	The client calls the **OleDraw** function, and the library obtains and manages presentation data.
olerender_format	The client calls the **OleGetData** function to retrieve data in a specific format. The library obtains and manages the data in the requested format, as specified by the *cfFormat* parameter.
olerender_none	The client library does not obtain any presentation data and does not draw the object.

cfFormat
Specifies the clipboard format when the *renderopt* parameter is **olerender_format**. This clipboard format is used in a subsequent call to the **OleGetData** function. If this clipboard format is CF_METAFILEPICT, CF_DIB, or CF_BITMAP, the library manages the data and draws the object. The library does not support drawing for any other formats.

Return Value   The return value is OLE_OK if the function is successful. Otherwise, it is an error value, which may be one of the following:

OLE_ERROR_CLASS
OLE_ERROR_HANDLE
OLE_ERROR_MEMORY
OLE_ERROR_NAME
OLE_ERROR_PROTOCOL
OLE_WAIT_FOR_RELEASE

Comments   The client library uses the filename extension of the file specified in the *lpszTemplate* parameter to identify the server for the object. The association between the extension and the server is stored in the registration database.

The **olerender_none** rendering option is typically used to support hyperlinks. With this option, the client does not call **OleDraw** and calls **OleGetData** only for ObjectLink, OwnerLink, and Native formats.

The **olerender_format** rendering option allows a client to compute data (instead of painting it), use an unusual data format, or modify a standard data format. With this option, the client does not call **OleDraw**. The client calls **OleGetData** to retrieve data in the specified format.

The **olerender_draw** rendering option is the most typical option. It is the easiest rendering option for the client to implement (the client simply calls **OleDraw**), and it allows the most flexibility. An object handler can exploit this flexibility to store no presentation data, a private presentation data format, or several different formats that it can choose among dynamically. Future implementations of object linking and embedding (OLE) may also exploit the flexibility that is inherent in this option.

See Also   **OleCreate, OleCreateFromClip, OleDraw, OleGetData, OleObjectConvert**

OleCreateInvisible

#include <ole.h>

OLESTATUS OleCreateInvisible(*lpszProtocol*, *lpClient*, *lpszClass*, *lhClientDoc*, *lpszObjname*,
    lplpObject, *renderopt*, *cfFormat*, *fActivate*)

LPCSTR *lpszProtocol*;	/* address of string for protocol name	*/
LPOLECLIENT *lpClient*;	/* address of client structure	*/
LPCSTR *lpszClass*;	/* address of string for classname	*/
LHCLIENTDOC *lhClientDoc*;	/* long handle of client document	*/
LPCSTR *lpszObjname*;	/* address of string for object name	*/
LPOLEOBJECT FAR* *lplpObject*;	/* address of pointer to object	*/
OLEOPT_RENDER *renderopt*;	/* rendering options	*/
OLECLIPFORMAT *cfFormat*;	/* clipboard format	*/
BOOL *fActivate*;	/* server activation flag	*/

The **OleCreateInvisible** function creates an object without displaying the server application to the user. The function either starts the server to create the object or creates a blank object of the specified class and format without starting the server.

Parameters

lpszProtocol
Points to a null-terminated string specifying the name of the protocol required for the new embedded object. Currently, this value can be StdFileEditing (the name of the object linking and embedding protocol) or Static (for uneditable pictures only).

lpClient
Points to an **OLECLIENT** structure allocated and initialized by the client application. This pointer is used to locate the callback function and is passed in callback notifications.

lpszClass
Points to a null-terminated string specifying the registered name of the class of the object to be created.

lhClientDoc
Identifies the client document in which the object is being created.

lpszObjname
Points to a null-terminated string specifying the client's name for the object. This name must be unique with respect to the names of any other objects in the document and cannot contain a slash mark (/).

lplpObject
Points to a variable where the library will store the long pointer to the new object.

renderopt
Specifies the client's preference for presentation data for the object. This parameter can be one of the following values:

Value	Meaning
olerender_draw	The client calls the **OleDraw** function, and the library obtains and manages presentation data.
olerender_format	The client calls the **OleGetData** function to retrieve data in a specific format. The library obtains and manages the data in the requested format, as specified by the *cfFormat* parameter.
olerender_none	The client library does not obtain any presentation data and does not draw the object.

cfFormat
Specifies the clipboard format when the *renderopt* parameter is **olerender_format**. This clipboard format is used in a subsequent call to **OleGetData**. If this clipboard format is CF_METAFILEPICT, CF_DIB, or CF_BITMAP, the library manages the data and draws the object. The library does not support drawing for any other formats.

fActivate
Specifies whether to start the server for the object. If this parameter is TRUE the server is started (but not shown). If this parameter is FALSE, the server is not started and the function creates a blank object of the specified class and format.

Return Value

The return value is OLE_OK if the function is successful. Otherwise, it is an error value, which may be one of the following:

OLE_ERROR_HANDLE
OLE_ERROR_NAME
OLE_ERROR_PROTOCOL

Comments

An application can avoid redrawing an object repeatedly by calling the **OleCreateInvisible** function before using such functions as **OleSetBounds**, **OleSetColorScheme**, and **OleSetTargetDevice** to set up the object. After setting up the object, the application can either call the **OleActivate** function to display the object or call the **OleUpdate** and **OleClose** functions to update the object without displaying it.

See Also

OleActivate, OleClose, OleSetBounds, OleSetColorScheme, OleSetTargetDevice, OleUpdate

OleCreateLinkFromClip

#include <ole.h>

OLESTATUS OleCreateLinkFromClip(*lpszProtocol, lpClient, lhClientDoc, lpszObjname, lplpObject,*
   renderopt, cfFormat)
LPCSTR *lpszProtocol*;   /* address of string for protocol name   */
LPOLECLIENT *lpClient*;   /* address of client structure   */
LHCLIENTDOC *lhClientDoc*;   /* long handle of client document   */
LPCSTR *lpszObjname*;   /* address of string for object name   */
LPOLEOBJECT FAR* *lplpObject*;   /* address of pointer to object   */
OLEOPT_RENDER *renderopt*;   /* rendering options   */
OLECLIPFORMAT *cfFormat*;   /* clipboard format   */

The **OleCreateLinkFromClip** function typically creates a link to an object from
the clipboard.

Parameters   *lpszProtocol*
        Points to a null-terminated string specifying the name of the required protocol.
        Currently, this value can be StdFileEditing (the name of the object linking and
        embedding protocol).

      lpClient
        Points to an **OLECLIENT** structure allocated and initialized by the client appli-
        cation. This pointer is used to locate the callback function and is passed in call-
        back notifications.

      lhClientDoc
        Identifies the client document in which the object is being created.

      lpszObjname
        Points to a null-terminated string specifying the client's name for the object.
        This name must be unique with respect to the names of any other objects in the
        document and cannot contain a slash mark (/).

      lplpObject
        Points to a variable where the library will store the long pointer to the new ob-
        ject.

      renderopt
        Specifies the client's preference for presentation data for the object. This pa-
        rameter can be one of the following values:

Value	Meaning
olerender_draw	The client calls the **OleDraw** function, and the library ob-tains and manages presentation data.
olerender_format	The client calls the **OleGetData** function to retrieve data in a specific format. The library obtains and manages the data in the requested format, as specified by the *cfFormat* parameter.

Value	Meaning
olerender_none	The client library does not obtain any presentation data and does not draw the object.

cfFormat
   Specifies the clipboard format when the *renderopt* parameter is
   olerender_format. This clipboard format is used in a subsequent call to
   OleGetData. If this clipboard format is CF_METAFILEPICT, CF_DIB, or
   CF_BITMAP, the library manages the data and draws the object. The library
   does not support drawing for any other formats.

Return Value   The return value is OLE_OK if the function is successful. Otherwise, it is an error
value, which may be one of the following:

OLE_ERROR_CLIP
OLE_ERROR_FORMAT
OLE_ERROR_HANDLE
OLE_ERROR_NAME
OLE_ERROR_PROTOCOL
OLE_WAIT_FOR_RELEASE

Comments   The **olerender_none** rendering option is typically used to support hyperlinks.
With this option, the client does not call the **OleDraw** function and calls **OleGet-Data** only for ObjectLink, OwnerLink, and Native formats.

The **olerender_format** rendering option allows a client to compute data (instead
of painting it), use an unusual data format, or modify a standard data format. With
this option, the client does not call **OleDraw**. The client calls **OleGetData** to re-trieve data in the specified format.

The **olerender_draw** rendering option is the most typical option. It is the easiest
rendering option for the client to implement (the client simply calls **OleDraw**),
and it allows the most flexibility. An object handler can exploit this flexibility to
store no presentation data, a private presentation data format, or several different
formats that it can choose among dynamically. Future implementations of object
linking and embedding (OLE) may also exploit the flexibility that is inherent in
this option.

See Also   **OleCreate, OleCreateFromTemplate, OleDraw, OleGetData,
OleQueryLinkFromClip**

OleCreateLinkFromFile

#include <ole.h>

OLESTATUS OleCreateLinkFromFile(*lpszProtocol, lpClient, lpszClass, lpszFile, lpszItem,*
   lhClientDoc, lpszObjname, lplpObject, renderopt, cfFormat)

LPCSTR *lpszProtocol*;	/* address of string for protocol name */
LPOLECLIENT *lpClient*;	/* address of client structure */
LPCSTR *lpszClass*;	/* string for class name */
LPCSTR *lpszFile*;	/* address of string for filename */
LPCSTR *lpszItem*;	/* address of string for document part to link */
LHCLIENTDOC *lhClientDoc*;	/* long handle of client document */
LPCSTR *lpszObjname*;	/* address of string for object name */
LPOLEOBJECT FAR* *lplpObject*;	/* address of pointer to new object */
OLEOPT_RENDER *renderopt*;	/* rendering options */
OLECLIPFORMAT *cfFormat*;	/* clipboard format */

The **OleCreateLinkFromFile** function creates a linked object from a file that contains an object. If necessary, the library starts the server to render the presentation data, but the object is not shown in the server for editing.

Parameters

lpszProtocol
Points to a null-terminated string specifying the name of the required protocol. Currently, this value can be StdFileEditing (the name of the object linking and embedding protocol).

lpClient
Points to an **OLECLIENT** structure allocated and initialized by the client application. This pointer is used to locate the callback function and is passed in callback notifications.

lpszClass
Points to a null-terminated string specifying the name of the class for the new object. If this value is NULL, the library uses the extension of the filename pointed to by the *lpszFile* parameter to find the class name for the object.

lpszFile
Points to a null-terminated string specifying the name of the file containing the object.

lpszItem
Points to a null-terminated string identifying the part of the document to link to. If this value is NULL, the link is to the entire document.

lhClientDoc
Identifies the client document in which the object is being created.

lpszObjname
> Points to a null-terminated string specifying the client's name for the object. This name must be unique with respect to the names of any other objects in the document and cannot contain a slash mark (/).

lplpObject
> Points to a variable where the library will store the long pointer to the new object.

renderopt
> Specifies the client's preference for presentation data for the object. This parameter can be one of the following values:

Value	Meaning
olerender_draw	The client calls the **OleDraw** function, and the library obtains and manages presentation data.
olerender_format	The client calls the **OleGetData** function to retrieve data in a specific format. The library obtains and manages the data in the requested format, as specified by the *cfFormat* parameter.
olerender_none	The client library does not obtain any presentation data and does not draw the object.

cfFormat
> Specifies the clipboard format when the *renderopt* parameter is **olerender_format**. This clipboard format is used in a subsequent call to **OleGetData**. If this clipboard format is CF_METAFILEPICT, CF_DIB, or CF_BITMAP, the library manages the data and draws the object. The library does not support drawing for any other formats.

Return Value

The return value is OLE_OK if the function is successful. Otherwise, it is an error value, which may be one of the following:

OLE_ERROR_CLASS
OLE_ERROR_HANDLE
OLE_ERROR_MEMORY
OLE_ERROR_NAME
OLE_ERROR_PROTOCOL
OLE_WAIT_FOR_RELEASE

Comments

The **olerender_none** rendering option is typically used to support hyperlinks. With this option, the client does not call **OleDraw** and calls **OleGetData** only for ObjectLink, OwnerLink, and Native formats.

The **olerender_format** rendering option allows a client to compute data (instead of painting it), use an unusual data format, or modify a standard data format. With this option, the client does not call **OleDraw**. The client calls **OleGetData** to retrieve data in the specified format.

The **olerender_draw** rendering option is the most typical option. It is the easiest rendering option for the client to implement (the client simply calls **OleDraw**), and it allows the most flexibility. An object handler can exploit this flexibility to store no presentation data, a private presentation data format, or several different formats that it can choose among dynamically. Future implementations of object linking and embedding (OLE) may also exploit the flexibility that is inherent in this option.

See Also

OleCreate, **OleCreateFromFile**, **OleCreateFromTemplate**, **OleDraw**, **OleGetData**

OleDelete

#include <ole.h>

OLESTATUS OleDelete(*lpObject*)
LPOLEOBJECT *lpObject*;   /* address of object to delete   */

The **OleDelete** function deletes an object and frees memory that was associated with that object. If the object was open, it is closed.

Parameters

lpObject
Points to the object to delete.

Return Value

The return value is OLE_OK if the function is successful. Otherwise, it is an error value, which may be one of the following:

OLE_BUSY
OLE_ERROR_OBJECT
OLE_WAIT_FOR_RELEASE

Comments

An application uses the **OleDelete** function when the object is no longer part of the client document.

The **OleDelete** function, unlike **OleRelease**, indicates that the object has been permanently removed.

See Also

OleClose, **OleRelease**

OleDraw

#include <ole.h>

OLESTATUS OleDraw(*lpObject, hdc, lprcBounds, lprcWBounds, hdcFormat*)
LPOLEOBJECT *lpObject*;   /* address of object to draw   */
HDC *hdc*;   /* handle of DC for drawing object   */
const RECT FAR* *lprcBounds*;   /* bounding rectangle for drawing object */
const RECT FAR* *lprcWBounds*; /* bounding rectangle for metafile DC   */
HDC *hdcFormat*;   /* handle of DC for formatting object   */

The **OleDraw** function draws a specified object into a bounding rectangle in a device context.

Parameters

lpObject
Points to the object to draw.

hdc
Identifies the device context in which to draw the object.

lprcBounds
Points to a **RECT** structure defining the bounding rectangle, in logical units for the device context specified by the *hdc* parameter, in which to draw the object.

lprcWBounds
Points to a **RECT** structure defining the bounding rectangle if the *hdc* parameter specifies a metafile. The **left** and **top** members of the **RECT** structure should specify the window origin, and the **right** and **bottom** members should specify the window extents.

hdcFormat
Identifies a device context describing the target device for which to format the object.

Return Value

The return value is OLE_OK if the function is successful. Otherwise, it is an error value, which may be one of the following:

OLE_ERROR_ABORT
OLE_ERROR_BLANK
OLE_ERROR_DRAW
OLE_ERROR_MEMORY
OLE_ERROR_OBJECT

Comments

This function returns OLE_ERROR_ABORT if the callback function returns FALSE during drawing.

When the *hdc* parameter specifies a metafile device context, the rectangle specified by the *lprcWBounds* parameter contains the rectangle specified by the *lprcBounds* parameter. If *hdc* does not specify a metafile device context, the *lprcWBounds* parameter is ignored.

The library may use an object handler to render the object, and this object handler may need information about the target device. Therefore, the device-context handle specified by the *hdcFormat* parameter is required. The *lprcBounds* parameter identifies the rectangle on the device context (relative to its current mapping mode) that the object should be mapped onto. This may involve scaling the picture and can be used by client applications to impose a view scaling between the displayed view and the final printed image.

An object handler should format an object as if it were to be drawn at the size specified by a call to the **OleSetBounds** function for the device context specified by the *hdcFormat* parameter. Often this formatting will already have been done by the server application; in this case, the library simply renders the presentation data with suitable scaling for the required bounding rectangle. If cropping or banding is required, the device context in which the object is drawn may include a clipping region smaller than the specified bounding rectangle.

See Also   **OleSetBounds**

OleEnumFormats   3.1

#include <ole.h>

OLECLIPFORMAT OleEnumFormats(*lpObject*, *cfFormat*)
LPOLEOBJECT *lpObject*;   /* address of object to query   */
OLECLIPFORMAT *cfFormat*;   /* format from previous function call   */

The **OleEnumFormats** function enumerates the data formats that describe a specified object.

Parameters   *lpObject*
                   Points to the object to be queried.

                   cfFormat
                   Specifies the format returned by the last call to the **OleEnumFormats** function. For the first call to this function, this parameter is zero.

Return Value   The return value is the next available format if any further formats are available. Otherwise, the return value is NULL.

Comments   When an application specifies NULL for the *cfFormat* parameter, the **OleEnum-Formats** function returns the first available format. Whenever an application specifies a format that was returned by a previous call to **OleEnumFormats**, the function returns the next available format, in sequence. When no more formats are available, the function returns NULL.

See Also   **OleGetData**

OleEnumObjects   3.1

#include <ole.h>

OLESTATUS OleEnumObjects(_lhDoc_, _lplpObject_**)**
LHCLIENTDOC _lhDoc_;   /* document handle   */
LPOLEOBJECT FAR* _lplpObject_;   /* address of pointer to object   */

The **OleEnumObjects** function enumerates the objects in a specified document.

Parameters   _lhDoc_
                      Identifies the document for which the objects are enumerated.

                      lplpObject
                      Points to an object in the document when the function returns. For the first call
                      to this function, this parameter should point to a NULL object.

Return Value   The return value is OLE_OK if the function is successful. Otherwise, it is an error
                      value, which may be one of the following:

                      OLE_ERROR_HANDLE
                      OLE_ERROR_OBJECT

Comments   When an application specifies a NULL object for the _lplpObject_ parameter, the
                      OleEnumObjects function returns the first object in the document. Whenever
                      an application specifies an object that was returned by a previous call to
                      OleEnumObjects, the function returns the next object, in sequence. When there
                      are no more objects in the document, the _lplpObject_ parameter points to a NULL
                      object.

                      Only objects that have been loaded and not released are enumerated by this func-
                      tion.

See Also   **OleDelete, OleRelease**

OleEqual

#include <ole.h>

OLESTATUS OleEqual(*lpObject1*, *lpObject2*)
LPOLEOBJECT *lpObject1*;   /* address of first object to compare   */
LPOLEOBJECT *lpObject2*;   /* address of second object to compare   */

The **OleEqual** function compares two objects for equality.

Parameters

lpObject1
Points to the first object to test for equality.

lpObject2
Points to the second object to test for equality.

Return Value

The return value is OLE_OK if the specified objects are equal. Otherwise, it is an error value, which may be one of the following:

OLE_ERROR_OBJECT
OLE_ERROR_NOT_EQUAL

Comments

Embedded objects are equal if their class, item, and native data are identical. Linked objects are equal if their class, document, and item are identical.

See Also

OleClone, OleQueryOutOfDate

OleExecute

#include <ole.h>

OLESTATUS OleExecute(*lpObject*, *hglbCmds*, *reserved*)
LPOLEOBJECT *lpObject*;   /* address of object receiving DDE commands   */
HGLOBAL *hglbCmds*;   /* handle of memory with commands   */
UINT *reserved*;   /* reserved   */

The **OleExecute** function sends dynamic data exchange (DDE) execute commands to the server for the specified object.

Parameters

lpObject
Points to an object identifying the server to which DDE execute commands are sent.

hglbCmds
　Identifies the memory containing one or more DDE execute commands.

reserved
　Reserved; must be zero.

Return Value　　The return value is OLE_OK if the function is successful. Otherwise, it is an error value, which may be one of the following:

OLE_BUSY
OLE_ERROR_COMMAND
OLE_ERROR_MEMORY
OLE_ERROR_NOT_OPEN
OLE_ERROR_OBJECT
OLE_ERROR_PROTOCOL
OLE_ERROR_STATIC
OLE_WAIT_FOR_RELEASE

Comments　　The client application should call the **OleQueryProtocol** function, specifying StdExecute, before calling the **OleExecute** function. The **OleQueryProtocol** function succeeds if the server for an object supports the **OleExecute** function.

See Also　　**OleQueryProtocol**

OleGetData

3.1

#include <ole.h>

OLESTATUS OleGetData(*lpObject, cfFormat, lphData*)
LPOLEOBJECT *lpObject*;　　　/* address of object to query　　　*/
OLECLIPFORMAT *cfFormat*;　　/* format for retrieved data　　　*/
HANDLE FAR* *lphData*;　　　　/* address of memory to contain data　*/

The **OleGetData** function retrieves data in the requested format from the specified object and supplies the handle of a memory or graphics device interface (GDI) object containing the data.

Parameters　　*lpObject*
　Points to the object from which data is retrieved.

cfFormat
　Specifies the format in which data is returned. This parameter can be one of the predefined clipboard formats or the value returned by the **RegisterClipboard-Format** function.

lphData
> Points to the handle of a memory object that contains the data when the function returns.

Return Value
The return value is OLE_OK if the function is successful. Otherwise, it is an error value, which may be one of the following:

OLE_ERROR_BLANK
OLE_ERROR_FORMAT
OLE_ERROR_OBJECT
OLE_WARN_DELETE_DATA

Comments
If the **OleGetData** function returns OLE_WARN_DELETE_DATA, the client application owns the data and should free the memory associated with the data when the client has finished using it. For other return values, the client should not free the memory or modify the data, because the data is controlled by the client library. If the application needs the data for long-term use, it should copy the data.

The **OleGetData** function typically returns OLE_WARN_DELETE_DATA if an object handler generates data for an object that the client library cannot interpret. In this case, the client application is responsible for controlling that data.

When the **OleGetData** function specifies CF_METAFILE or CF_BITMAP, the *lphData* parameter points to a GDI object, not a memory object, when the function returns. **OleGetData** supplies the handle of a memory object for all other formats.

See Also
OleEnumFormats, **OleSetData**, **RegisterClipboardFormat**

OleGetLinkUpdateOptions
3.1

#include <ole.h>

OLESTATUS OleGetLinkUpdateOptions(*lpObject***, ***lpUpdateOpt***)**
LPOLEOBJECT *lpObject*;   /* address of object to query   */
OLEOPT_UPDATE FAR* *lpUpdateOpt*;   /* address of update options   */

> The **OleGetLinkUpdateOptions** function retrieves the link-update options for the presentation of a specified object.

Parameters
lpObject
> Points to the object to query.

lpUpdateOpt
Points to a variable in which the function stores the current value of the link-update option for the specified object. The link-update option setting may be one of the following values:

Value	Meaning
oleupdate_always	Update the linked object whenever possible. This option supports the Automatic link-update radio button in the Links dialog box.
oleupdate_oncall	Update the linked object only on request from the client application. This option supports the Manual link-update radio button in the Links dialog box.
oleupdate_onsave	Update the linked object when the source document is saved by the server.

Return Value   The return value is OLE_OK if the function is successful. Otherwise, it is an error value, which may be one of the following:

OLE_ERROR_OBJECT
OLE_ERROR_STATIC

See Also   **OleSetLinkUpdateOptions**

OleIsDcMeta   3.1

#include <ole.h>

BOOL OleIsDcMeta(*hdc***)**
HDC *hdc*;   /* device-context handle   */

The **OleIsDcMeta** function determines whether the specified device context is a metafile device context.

Parameters   *hdc*
Identifies the device context to query.

Return Value   The return value is a positive value if the device context is a metafile device context. Otherwise, it is NULL.

OleLoadFromStream

3.1

#include <ole.h>

OLESTATUS OleLoadFromStream(*lpStream*, *lpszProtocol*, *lpClient*, *lhClientDoc*, *lpszObjname*,
    lplpObject)
LPOLESTREAM *lpStream*;   /* address of stream for object   */
LPCSTR *lpszProtocol*;   /* address of string for protocol name   */
LPOLECLIENT *lpClient*;   /* address of client structure   */
LHCLIENTDOC *lhClientDoc*;   /* long handle of client document   */
LPCSTR *lpszObjname*;   /* address of string for object name   */
LPOLEOBJECT FAR* *lplpObject*;   /* address of pointer to object   */

The **OleLoadFromStream** function loads an object from the containing document.

Parameters   *lpStream*
    Points to an **OLESTREAM** structure that was allocated and initialized by the
    client application. The library calls the **Get** function in the
    OLESTREAMVTBL structure to obtain the data for the object.

lpszProtocol
    Points to a null-terminated string specifying the name of the required protocol.
    Currently, this value can be StdFileEditing (the name of the object linking and
    embedding protocol) or Static (for uneditable pictures only).

lpClient
    Points to an **OLECLIENT** structure allocated and initialized by the client appli-
    cation. This pointer is used to locate the callback function and is passed in call-
    back notifications.

lhClientDoc
    Identifies the client document in which the object is being created.

lpszObjname
    Points to a null-terminated string specifying the client's name for the object.

lplpObject
    Points to a variable in which the library stores a pointer to the loaded object.

Return Value   The return value is OLE_OK if the function is successful. Otherwise, it is an error
    value, which may be one of the following:

    OLE_ERROR_HANDLE
    OLE_ERROR_NAME
    OLE_ERROR_PROTOCOL
    OLE_ERROR_STREAM
    OLE_WAIT_FOR_RELEASE

Comments

To load an object, the client application needs only the location of that object in a file. A client typically loads an object only when the object is needed (for example, when it must be displayed).

If an object cannot be loaded when the *lpszProtocol* parameter specifies StdFileEditing, the application can call the **OleLoadFromStream** function again, specifying Static.

If the object is linked and the server and document are open, the library automatically makes the link between the client and server applications when an application calls **OleLoadFromStream**.

See Also

OleQuerySize, **OleSaveToStream**

OleLockServer

3.1

#include <ole.h>

OLESTATUS OleLockServer(*lpObject*, *lphServer*)
LPOLEOBJECT *lpObject*;   /* address of object   */
LHSERVER FAR* *lphServer*;   /* address of handle of server   */

The **OleLockServer** function is called by a client application to keep an open server application in memory. Keeping the server application in memory allows the client library to use the server application to open objects quickly.

Parameters

lpObject
Points to an object the client library uses to identify the open server application to keep in memory. When the server has been locked, this object can be deleted.

lphServer
Points to the handle of the server application when the function returns.

Return Value

The return value is OLE_OK if the function is successful. Otherwise, it is an error value, which may be one of the following:

OLE_ERROR_COMM
OLE_ERROR_LAUNCH
OLE_ERROR_OBJECT

Comments

A client calls **OleLockServer** to speed the opening of objects when the same server is used for a number of different objects. Before the client terminates, it must call the **OleUnlockServer** function to release the server from memory.

When **OleLockServer** is called more than once for a given server, even by different client applications, the server's lock count is increased. Each call to **Ole-UnlockServer** decrements the lock count. The server remains locked until the lock count is zero. If the object identified by the *lpObject* parameter is deleted before calling the **OleUnlockServer** function, **OleUnlockServer** must still be called to decrement the lock count.

If necessary, a server can terminate even though a client has called the **OleLock-Server** function.

See Also   **OleUnlockServer**

OleObjectConvert

3.1

#include <ole.h>

OLESTATUS OleObjectConvert(*lpObject, lpszProtocol, lpClient, lhClientDoc, lpszObjname, lplpObject*)

LPOLEOBJECT *lpObject*;	/* address of object to convert	*/
LPCSTR *lpszProtocol*;	/* address of string for protocol name	*/
LPOLECLIENT *lpClient*;	/* address of client for new object	*/
LHCLIENTDOC *lhClientDoc*;	/* long handle of client document	*/
LPCSTR *lpszObjname*;	/* address of string for object name	*/
LPOLEOBJECT FAR* *lplpObject*;	/* address of pointer to new object	*/

The **OleObjectConvert** function creates a new object that supports a specified protocol by converting an existing object. This function neither deletes nor replaces the original object.

Parameters   *lpObject*
Points to the object to convert.

lpszProtocol
Points to a null-terminated string specifying the name of the required protocol. Currently this value can be Static (for uneditable pictures only).

lpClient
Points to an **OLECLIENT** structure for the new object.

lhClientDoc
Identifies the client document in which the object is being created.

lpszObjname
Points to a null-terminated string specifying the client's name for the object. This name must be unique with respect to the names of any other objects in the document and cannot contain a slash mark (/).

lplpObject
   Points to a variable in which the library stores a pointer to the new object.

Return Value   The return value is OLE_OK if the function is successful. Otherwise, it is an error value, which may be one of the following:

OLE_BUSY
OLE_ERROR_HANDLE
OLE_ERROR_NAME
OLE_ERROR_OBJECT
OLE_ERROR_STATIC

Comments   The only conversion currently supported is that of changing a linked or embedded object to a static object.

See Also   **OleClone**

OleQueryBounds   3.1

#include <ole.h>

OLESTATUS OleQueryBounds(*lpObject, lpBounds*)
LPOLEOBJECT *lpObject*;   /* address of object to query   */
RECT FAR* *lpBounds*;   /* address of structure for bounding rectangle   */

The **OleQueryBounds** function retrieves the extents of the bounding rectangle on the target device for the specified object. The coordinates are in MM_HIMETRIC units.

Parameters   *lpObject*
   Points to the object to query.

lpBounds
   Points to a **RECT** structure for the extents of the bounding rectangle. The members of the **RECT** structure have the following meanings:

Member	Meaning
rect.left	0
rect.top	0
rect.right	x-extent
rect.bottom	y-extent

Return Value   The return value is OLE_OK if the function is successful. Otherwise, it is an error value, which may be one of the following:

OLE_ERROR_BLANK
OLE_ERROR_MEMORY
OLE_ERROR_OBJECT

See Also   **OleSetBounds**, **SetMapMode**

OleQueryClientVersion   `3.1`

#include <ole.h>

DWORD OleQueryClientVersion(void)

The **OleQueryClientVersion** function retrieves the version number of the client library.

Parameters   This function has no parameters.

Return Value   The return value is a doubleword value. The major version number is in the low-order byte of the low-order word, and the minor version number is in the high-order byte of the low-order word. The high-order word is reserved.

See Also   **OleQueryServerVersion**

OleQueryCreateFromClip   `3.1`

#include <ole.h>

OLESTATUS OleQueryCreateFromClip(_lpszProtocol_, _renderopt_, _cfFormat_**)**
LPCSTR _lpszProtocol_;   /* address of string for protocol name   */
OLEOPT_RENDER _renderopt_;   /* rendering options   */
OLECLIPFORMAT _cfFormat_;   /* format for clipboard data   */

The **OleQueryCreateFromClip** function checks whether the object on the clipboard supports the specified protocol and rendering options.

Parameters

lpszProtocol

Points to a null-terminated string specifying the name of the protocol needed by the client. Currently, this value can be StdFileEditing (the name of the object linking and embedding protocol) or Static (for uneditable pictures only).

renderopt

Specifies the client's preference for presentation data for the object. This parameter can be one of the following values:

Value	Meaning
olerender_draw	The client calls the **OleDraw** function, and the library obtains and manages presentation data.
olerender_format	The library obtains and manages the data in the requested format, as specified by the *cfFormat* parameter.
olerender_none	The client library does not obtain any presentation data and does not draw the object.

cfFormat

Specifies the clipboard format. This parameter is used only when the *renderopt* parameter is **olerender_format**. If the clipboard format is CF_METAFILEPICT, CF_DIB, or CF_BITMAP, the library manages the data and draws the object. The library does not support drawing for any other formats.

Return Value

The return value is OLE_OK if the function is successful. Otherwise, it is an error value, which may be one of the following:

OLE_ERROR_FORMAT
OLE_ERROR_PROTOCOL

Comments

The **OleQueryCreateFromClip** function is typically used to check whether to enable a Paste command.

The **olerender_none** rendering option is typically used to support hyperlinks. With this option, the client does not call **OleDraw** and calls the **OleGetData** function only for ObjectLink, OwnerLink, and Native formats.

The **olerender_format** rendering option allows a client to compute data (instead of painting it), use an unusual data format, or modify a standard data format. With this option the client does not call **OleDraw**. The client calls **OleGetData** to retrieve data in the specified format.

The **olerender_draw** rendering option is the most typical option. It is the easiest rendering option for the client to implement (the client simply calls **OleDraw**), and it allows the most flexibility. An object handler can exploit this flexibility to store no presentation data, a private presentation data format, or several different formats that it can choose among dynamically. Future implementations of object linking and embedding (OLE) may also exploit the flexibility that is inherent in this option.

See Also   **OleCreateFromClip**, **OleDraw**, **OleGetData**

OleQueryLinkFromClip   `3.1`

#include <ole.h>

OLESTATUS OleQueryLinkFromClip(*lpszProtocol*, *renderopt*, *cfFormat*)
LPCSTR *lpszProtocol*;   /* address of string for protocol name   */
OLEOPT_RENDER *renderopt*;   /* rendering options   */
OLECLIPFORMAT *cfFormat*;   /* format for clipboard data   */

The **OleQueryLinkFromClip** function checks whether a client application can use the data on the clipboard to produce a linked object that supports the specified protocol and rendering options.

Parameters   *lpszProtocol*
Points to a null-terminated string specifying the name of the protocol needed by the client. Currently this value can be StdFileEditing (the name of the object linking and embedding protocol).

renderopt
Specifies the client's preference for presentation data for the object. This parameter can be one of the following values:

Value	Meaning
olerender_draw	The client calls the **OleDraw** function, and the library obtains and manages presentation data.
olerender_format	The library obtains and manages the data in the requested format, as specified by the *cfFormat* parameter.
olerender_none	The client library does not obtain any presentation data and does not draw the object.

cfFormat
Specifies the clipboard format. This parameter is used only when the *renderopt* parameter is **olerender_format**. If this clipboard format is CF_METAFILEPICT, CF_DIB, or CF_BITMAP, the library manages the data and draws the object. The library does not support drawing for any other formats.

Return Value   The return value is OLE_OK if the function is successful. Otherwise, it is an error value, which may be one of the following:

OLE_ERROR_FORMAT
OLE_ERROR_PROTOCOL

Comments   The **OleQueryLinkFromClip** function is typically used to check whether to enable a Paste Link command.

The **olerender_none** rendering option is typically used to support hyperlinks. With this option, the client does not call **OleDraw** and calls the **OleGetData** function only for ObjectLink, OwnerLink, and Native formats.

The **olerender_format** rendering option allows a client to compute data (instead of painting it), use an unusual data format, or modify a standard data format. With this option, the client does not call **OleDraw**. The client calls **OleGetData** to retrieve data in the specified format.

The **olerender_draw** rendering option is the most typical option. It is the easiest rendering option for the client to implement (the client simply calls **OleDraw**), and it allows the most flexibility. An object handler can exploit this flexibility to store no presentation data, a private presentation data format, or several different formats that it can choose among dynamically. Future implementations of object linking and embedding (OLE) may also exploit the flexibility that is inherent in this option.

See Also   **OleCreateLinkFromClip, OleDraw, OleGetData**

OleQueryName   3.1

#include <ole.h>

OLESTATUS OleQueryName(*lpObject*, *lpszObject*, *lpwBuffSize*)
LPOLEOBJECT *lpObject*;   /* address of object   */
LPSTR *lpszObject*;   /* address of string for object name   */
UINT FAR* *lpwBuffSize*;   /* address of word for size of buffer   */

The **OleQueryName** function retrieves the name of a specified object.

Parameters   *lpObject*
Points to the object whose name is being queried.

lpszObject
> Points to a character array that contains a null-terminated string. When the function returns, this string specifies the name of the object.

lpwBuffSize
> Points to a variable containing the size, in bytes, of the buffer pointed to by the *lpszObject* parameter. When the function returns, this value is the number of bytes copied to the buffer.

Return Value
The return value is OLE_OK if the function is successful. Otherwise, it is an error value, which may be OLE_ERROR_OBJECT.

See Also
OleRename

OleQueryOpen

3.1

#include <ole.h>

OLESTATUS OleQueryOpen(*lpObject*)
LPOLEOBJECT *lpObject*;   /* address of object to query   */

The **OleQueryOpen** function checks whether the specified object is open.

Parameters
lpObject
> Points to the object to query.

Return Value
The return value is OLE_OK if the object is open. Otherwise, it is an error value, which may be one of the following:

OLE_ERROR_COMM
OLE_ERROR_OBJECT
OLE_ERROR_STATIC

See Also
OleActivate

OleQueryOutOfDate

3.1

#include <ole.h>

OLESTATUS OleQueryOutOfDate(*lpObject*)
LPOLEOBJECT *lpObject*;   /* address of object to query   */

The **OleQueryOutOfDate** function checks whether an object is out-of-date.

Parameters	*lpObject* Points to the object to query.
Return Value	The return value is OLE_OK if the object is up-to-date. Otherwise, it is an error value, which may be one of the following: OLE_ERROR_OBJECT OLE_ERROR_OUTOFDATE
Comments	The **OleQueryOutOfDate** function has not been implemented for the current version of object linking and embedding (OLE). For linked objects, **OleQueryOutOf-Date** always returns OLE_OK. A linked object might be out-of-date if the document that is the source for the link has been updated. An embedded object that contains links to other objects might also be out-of-date.
See Also	**OleEqual, OleUpdate**

OleQueryProtocol

3.1

#include <ole.h>

void FAR* OleQueryProtocol(*lpobj,* *lpszProtocol*)
LPOLEOBJECT *lpobj*;   /* address of object to query   */
LPCSTR *lpszProtocol*;   /* address of string for protocol to query   */

The **OleQueryProtocol** function checks whether an object supports a specified protocol.

Parameters	*lpobj* Points to the object to query.

lpszProtocol

Points to a null-terminated string specifying the name of the requested protocol. This value can be StdFileEditing or StdExecute.

Return Value

The return value is a void pointer to an **OLEOBJECT** structure if the function is successful, or it is NULL if the object does not support the requested protocol. The library can return OLE_WAIT_FOR_RELEASE when an application calls this function.

Comments

The **OleQueryProtocol** function queries whether the specified protocol is supported and returns a modified object pointer that allows access to the function table for the protocol. This modified object pointer points to a structure that has the same form as the **OLEOBJECT** structure; the new structure also points to a table of functions and may contain additional state information. The new pointer does not point to a different object—if the object is deleted, secondary pointers become invalid. If a protocol includes delete functions, calling a delete function invalidates all pointers to that object.

A client application typically calls **OleQueryProtocol**, specifying StdExecute for the *lpszProtocol* parameter, before calling the **OleExecute** function. This allows the client application to check whether the server for an object supports dynamic data exchange (DDE) execute commands.

See Also

OleExecute

OleQueryReleaseError

3.1

#include <ole.h>

OLESTATUS OleQueryReleaseError(*lpobj*)
LPOLEOBJECT *lpobj*;   /* address of object to query   */

The **OleQueryReleaseError** function checks the error value for an asynchronous operation on an object.

Parameters

lpobj

Points to an object for which the error value is to be queried.

Return Value

The return value, if the function is successful, is either OLE_OK if the asynchronous operation completed successfully or the error value for that operation. If the pointer passed in the *lpobj* parameter is invalid, the function returns OLE_ERROR_OBJECT.

Comments   A client application receives the OLE_RELEASE notification when an asynchronous operation has terminated. The client should then call **OleQueryRelease-Error** to check whether the operation has terminated successfully or with an error value.

See Also   **OleQueryReleaseMethod, OleQueryReleaseStatus**

OleQueryReleaseMethod

3.1

#include <ole.h>

OLE_RELEASE_METHOD OleQueryReleaseMethod(*lpobj***)**
LPOLEOBJECT *lpobj*;   /* address of object to query   */

The **OleQueryReleaseMethod** function finds out the operation that finished for the specified object.

Parameters   *lpobj*
    Points to an object for which the operation is to be queried.

Return Value   The return value indicates the server operation (method) that finished. It can be one of the following values:

Value	Server operation
OLE_ACTIVATE	Activate
OLE_CLOSE	Close
OLE_COPYFROMLNK	CopyFromLink (autoreconnect)
OLE_CREATE	Create
OLE_CREATEFROMFILE	CreateFromFile
OLE_CREATEFROMTEMPLATE	CreateFromTemplate
OLE_CREATEINVISIBLE	CreateInvisible
OLE_CREATELINKFROMFILE	CreateLinkFromFile
OLE_DELETE	Object Delete
OLE_EMBPASTE	Paste and Update
OLE_LNKPASTE	PasteLink (autoreconnect)
OLE_LOADFROMSTREAM	LoadFromStream (autoreconnect)
OLE_NONE	No operation active
OLE_OTHER	Other miscellaneous asynchronous operations
OLE_RECONNECT	Reconnect

Value	Server operation
OLE_REQUESTDATA	OleRequestData
OLE_RUN	Run
OLE_SERVERUNLAUNCH	Server is stopping
OLE_SETDATA	OleSetData
OLE_SETUPDATEOPTIONS	Setting update options
OLE_SHOW	Show
OLE_UPDATE	Update

If the pointer passed in the *lpobj* parameter is invalid, the function returns OLE_ERROR_OBJECT.

Comments   A client application receives the OLE_RELEASE notification when an asynchronous operation has ended. The client can then call **OleQueryReleaseMethod** to check which operation caused the library to send the OLE_RELEASE notification. The client calls **OleQueryReleaseError** to determine whether the operation terminated successfully or with an error value.

See Also   **OleQueryReleaseError**, **OleQueryReleaseStatus**

OleQueryReleaseStatus $\boxed{3.1}$

#include <ole.h>

OLESTATUS OleQueryReleaseStatus(*lpobj***)**
LPOLEOBJECT *lpobj*;   /* address of object to query   */

The **OleQueryReleaseStatus** function determines whether an operation has finished for the specified object.

Parameters   *lpobj*
    Points to an object for which the operation is queried.

Return Value   The return value, if the function is successful, is either OLE_BUSY if an operation is in progress or OLE_OK. If the pointer passed in the *lpobj* parameter is invalid, the function returns OLE_ERROR_OBJECT.

See Also   **OleQueryReleaseError**, **OleQueryReleaseMethod**

OleQueryServerVersion

#include <ole.h>

DWORD OleQueryServerVersion(void)

The **OleQueryServerVersion** function retrieves the version number of the server library.

Parameters   This function has no parameters.

Return Value   The return value is a doubleword value. The major version number is in the low-order byte of the low-order word, and the minor version number is in the high-order byte of the low-order word. The high-order word is reserved.

See Also   **OleQueryClientVersion**

OleQuerySize

#include <ole.h>

OLESTATUS OleQuerySize(*lpObject, pdwSize***)**
LPOLEOBJECT *lpObject*;   /* address of object to query   */
DWORD FAR* *pdwSize*;   /* address of size of object   */

The **OleQuerySize** function retrieves the size of the specified object.

Parameters   *lpObject*
Points to the object to query.

pdwSize
Points to a variable for the size of the object. This variable contains the size of the object when the function returns.

Return Value   The return value is OLE_OK if the function is successful. Otherwise, it is an error value, which may be one of the following:

OLE_ERROR_BLANK
OLE_ERROR_MEMORY
OLE_ERROR_OBJECT

See Also   **OleLoadFromStream**

OleQueryType

#include <ole.h>

OLESTATUS OleQueryType(*lpObject*, *lpType*)
LPOLEOBJECT *lpObject*;   /* address of object to query   */
LONG FAR* *lpType*;   /* address of type of object   */

The **OleQueryType** function checks whether a specified object is embedded, linked, or static.

Parameters

lpObject
Points to the object for which the type is to be queried.

lpType
Points to a long variable that contains the type of the object when the function returns. This parameter can be one of the following values:

Value	Meaning
OT_EMBEDDED	Object is embedded.
OT_LINK	Object is a link.
OT_STATIC	Object is a static picture.

Return Value

The return value is OLE_OK if the function is successful. Otherwise, it is an error value, which may be one of the following:

OLE_ERROR_GENERIC
OLE_ERROR_OBJECT

See Also

OleEnumFormats

OleReconnect

#include <ole.h>

OLESTATUS OleReconnect(*lpObject*)
LPOLEOBJECT *lpObject*;   /* address of object to reconnect to   */

The **OleReconnect** function reestablishes a link to an open linked object. If the specified object is not open, this function does not open it.

Parameters	*lpObject*
	Points to the object to reconnect to.

Return Value   The return value is OLE_OK if the function is successful. Otherwise, it is an error value, which may be one of the following:

OLE_BUSY
OLE_ERROR_NOT_LINK
OLE_ERROR_OBJECT
OLE_ERROR_STATIC
OLE_WAIT_FOR_RELEASE

Comments   A client application can use **OleReconnect** to keep the presentation for a linked object up-to-date.

See Also   **OleActivate, OleClose, OleUpdate**

OleRegisterClientDoc   3.1

#include <ole.h>

OLESTATUS OleRegisterClientDoc(*lpszClass*, *lpszDoc*, *reserved*, *lplhDoc*)
LPCSTR *lpszClass*;   /* address of string for class name   */
LPCSTR *lpszDoc*;   /* address of string for document name   */
LONG *reserved*;   /* reserved   */
LHCLIENTDOC FAR* *lplhDoc*;   /* address of handle of document   */

The **OleRegisterClientDoc** function registers an open client document with the library and returns the handle of that document.

Parameters   *lpszClass*
          Points to a null-terminated string specifying the class of the client document.

     lpszDoc
          Points to a null-terminated string specifying the location of the client document. (This value should be a fully qualified path.)

     reserved
          Reserved. Must be zero.

     lplhDoc
          Points to the handle of the client document when the function returns. This handle is used to identify the document in other document-management functions.

Return Value
The return value is OLE_OK if the function is successful. Otherwise, it is an error value, which may be one of the following:

OLE_ERROR_ALREADY_REGISTERED
OLE_ERROR_MEMORY
OLE_ERROR_NAME

Comments
When a document being copied onto the clipboard exists only because the client application is copying Native data that contains objects, the name specified in the *lpszDoc* parameter must be Clipboard.

Client applications should register open documents with the library and notify the library when a document is renamed, closed, saved, or restored to a changed state.

See Also
OleRenameClientDoc, OleRevertClientDoc, OleRevokeClientDoc, OleSavedClientDoc

---

OleRegisterServer

3.1

#include <ole.h>

OLESTATUS OleRegisterServer(*lpszClass*, *lpsrvr*, *lplhserver*, *hinst*, *srvruse*)
LPCSTR *lpszClass*;   /* address of string for class name   */
LPOLESERVER *lpsrvr*;   /* address of OLESERVER structure   */
LHSERVER FAR* *lplhserver*;   /* address of server handle   */
HINSTANCE *hinst*;   /* instance handle   */
OLE_SERVER_USE *srvruse*;   /* single or multiple instances   */

The **OleRegisterServer** function registers the specified server, class name, and instance with the server library.

Parameters
lpszClass
　　Points to a null-terminated string specifying the class name being registered.

lpsrvr
　　Points to an **OLESERVER** structure allocated and initialized by the server application.

lplhserver
　　Points to a variable of type **LHSERVER** in which the library stores the handle of the server. This handle is used in such functions as **OleRegisterServerDoc** and **OleRevokeServer**.

hinst
> Identifies the instance of the server application. This handle is used to ensure that clients connect to the correct instance of a server application.

srvruse
> Specifies whether the server uses a single instance or multiple instances to support multiple objects. This value must be either OLE_SERVER_SINGLE or OLE_SERVER_MULTI.

Return Value   The return value is OLE_OK if the function is successful. Otherwise, it is an error value, which may be one of the following:

OLE_ERROR_CLASS
OLE_ERROR_MEMORY
OLE_ERROR_PROTECT_ONLY

Comments   When the server application starts, it creates an **OLESERVER** structure and calls the **OleRegisterServer** function. Servers that support several class names can allocate a structure for each or reuse the same structure. The class name is passed to server-application functions that are called through the library, so that servers supporting more than one class can check which class is being requested.

The *srvruse* parameter is used when the libraries open an object. When OLE_SERVER_MULTI is specified for this parameter and all current instances are already editing an object, a new instance of the server is started. Servers that support the multiple document interface (MDI) typically specify OLE_SERVER_SINGLE.

See Also   **OleRegisterServerDoc, OleRevokeServer**

OleRegisterServerDoc   3.1

#include <ole.h>

OLESTATUS OleRegisterServerDoc(*lhsrvr, lpszDocName, lpdoc, lplhdoc***)**
LHSERVER *lhsrvr*;   /* server handle   */
LPCSTR *lpszDocName*;   /* address of string for document name   */
LPOLESERVERDOC *lpdoc*;   /* address of OLESERVERDOC structure   */
LHSERVERDOC FAR* *lplhdoc*;   /* handle of registered document   */

> The **OleRegisterServerDoc** function registers a document with the server library in case other client applications have links to it. A server application uses this function when the server is started with the **/Embedding** *filename* option or when it creates or opens a document that is not requested by the library.

Parameters   *lhsrvr*

Identifies the server. Server applications obtain this handle by calling the **OleRegisterServer** function.

lpszDocName

Points to a null-terminated string specifying the permanent name for the document. This parameter should be a fully qualified path.

lpdoc

Points to an **OLESERVERDOC** structure allocated and initialized by the server application.

lplhdoc

Points to a handle that will identify the document. This parameter points to the handle when the function returns.

Return Value   If the function is successful, the return value is OLE_OK. Otherwise, it is an error value, which may be one of the following:

OLE_ERROR_ADDRESS
OLE_ERROR_HANDLE
OLE_ERROR_MEMORY

Comments   If the document was created or opened in response to a request from the server library, the server should not register the document by using **OleRegisterServer-Doc**. Instead, the server should return a pointer to the **OLESERVERDOC** structure through the parameter to the relevant function.

See Also   **OleRegisterServer, OleRevokeServerDoc**

OleRelease

3.1

#include <ole.h>

OLESTATUS OleRelease(*lpObject***)**
LPOLEOBJECT *lpObject*;   /* address of object to release   */

The **OleRelease** function releases an object from memory and closes it if it was open. This function does not indicate that the object has been deleted from the client document.

Parameters   *lpObject*

Points to the object to release.

Return Value	If the function is successful, the return value is OLE_OK. Otherwise, it is an error value, which may be one of the following: OLE_BUSY OLE_ERROR_OBJECT OLE_WAIT_FOR_RELEASE
Comments	The **OleRelease** function should be called for all objects when closing the client document.
See Also	**OleDelete**

OleRename ⬚3.1

#include <ole.h>

OLESTATUS OleRename(*lpObject*, *lpszNewname*)
LPOLEOBJECT *lpObject*;   /* address of object being renamed   */
LPCSTR *lpszNewname*;   /* address of string for new object name   */

The **OleRename** function renames an object.

Parameters	*lpObject*
	    Points to the object that is being renamed.
	
	lpszNewname
	    Points to a null-terminated string specifying the new name of the object.

Return Value	The return value is OLE_OK if the function is successful. Otherwise, it is an error value, which may be OLE_ERROR_OBJECT.
Comments	Object names need not be seen by the user. They must be unique within the containing document and must be preserved when the document is saved.
See Also	**OleQueryName**

OleRenameClientDoc

#include <ole.h>

OLESTATUS OleRenameClientDoc(*lhClientDoc*, *lpszNewDocname*)
LHCLIENTDOC *lhClientDoc*;   /* handle of client document   */
LPCSTR *lpszNewDocname*;   /* address of string for new document name   */

The **OleRenameClientDoc** function informs the client library that a document has been renamed. A client application calls this function when a document name has changed—for example, when the user chooses the Save or Save As command from the File menu.

Parameters

lhClientDoc
Identifies the document that has been renamed.

lpszNewDocname
Points to a null-terminated string specifying the new name of the document.

Return Value

The return value is OLE_OK if the function is successful. Otherwise, it is an error value, which may be OLE_ERROR_HANDLE.

Comments

Client applications should register open documents with the library and notify the library when a document is renamed, closed, saved, or restored to a changed state.

See Also

OleRegisterClientDoc, **OleRevertClientDoc**, **OleRevokeClientDoc**, **OleSavedClientDoc**

OleRenameServerDoc

#include <ole.h>

OLESTATUS OleRenameServerDoc(*lhDoc*, *lpszDocName*)
LHSERVERDOC *lhDoc*;   /* handle of document   */
LPCSTR *lpszDocName*;   /* address of string for path and filename   */

The **OleRenameServerDoc** function informs the server library that a document has been renamed.

Parameters

lhDoc
Identifies the document that has been renamed.

lpszDocName
> Points to a null-terminated string specifying the new name of the document.
> This parameter is typically a fully qualified path.

Return Value   The return value is OLE_OK if the function is successful. Otherwise, it is an error value, which may be one of the following:

OLE_ERROR_HANDLE
OLE_ERROR_MEMORY

Comments   The **OleRenameServerDoc** function has the same effect as sending the OLE_RENAMED notification to the client application's callback function. The server application calls this function when it renames a document to which the active links need to be reconnected or when the user chooses the Save As command from the File menu while working with an embedded object.

Server applications should register open documents with the server library and notify the library when a document is renamed, closed, saved, or restored to a changed state.

See Also   **OleRegisterServerDoc, OleRevertServerDoc, OleRevokeServerDoc, OleSavedServerDoc**

OleRequestData   [3.1]

#include <ole.h>

OLESTATUS OleRequestData(*lpObject, cfFormat*)
LPOLEOBJECT *lpObject*;   /* address of object to query   */
OLECLIPFORMAT *cfFormat*;   /* format for retrieved data   */

The **OleRequestData** function requests the library to retrieve data in a specified format from a server.

Parameters   *lpObject*
> Points to the object that is associated with the server from which data is to be retrieved.

cfFormat
> Specifies the format in which data is to be returned. This parameter can be one of the predefined clipboard formats or the value returned by the **Register-ClipboardFormat** function.

Return Value   The return value is OLE_OK if the function is successful. Otherwise, it is an error value, which may be one of the following:

OLE_BUSY
OLE_ERROR_NOT_OPEN
OLE_ERROR_OBJECT
OLE_ERROR_STATIC
OLE_WAIT_FOR_RELEASE

Comments   The client application should be connected to the server application when the client calls the **OleRequestData** function. When the client receives the OLE_RELEASE notification, it can retrieve the data from the object by using the **OleGetData** function or query the data by using such functions as **OleQueryBounds**.

If the requested data format is the same as the presentation data for the object, the library manages the data and updates the presentation.

The **OleRequestData** function returns OLE_WAIT_FOR_RELEASE if the server is busy. In this case, the application should continue to dispatch messages until it receives a callback notification with the OLE_RELEASE argument.

See Also   **OleEnumFormats, OleGetData, OleSetData, RegisterClipboardFormat**

OleRevertClientDoc   3.1

#include <ole.h>

OLESTATUS OleRevertClientDoc(*lhClientDoc*)
LHCLIENTDOC *lhClientDoc*;   /* handle of client document   */

The **OleRevertClientDoc** function informs the library that a document has been restored to a previously saved condition.

Parameters   *lhClientDoc*
     Identifies the document that has been restored to its saved state.

Return Value   The return value is OLE_OK if the function is successful. Otherwise, it is an error value, which may be OLE_ERROR_HANDLE.

Comments   A client application should call the **OleRevertClientDoc** function when it reloads a document without saving changes to the document.

Client applications should register open documents with the library and notify the library when a document is renamed, closed, saved, or restored to a saved state.

See Also   **OleRegisterClientDoc**, **OleRenameClientDoc**, **OleRevokeClientDoc**, **OleSavedClientDoc**

OleRevertServerDoc   3.1

#include <ole.h>

OLESTATUS OleRevertServerDoc(*lhDoc*)
LHSERVERDOC *lhDoc*;   /* handle of document   */

The **OleRevertServerDoc** function informs the server library that the server has restored a document to its saved state without closing it.

Parameters   *lhDoc*
Identifies the document that has been restored to its saved state.

Return Value   The return value is OLE_OK if the function is successful. Otherwise, it is an error value, which may be OLE_ERROR_HANDLE.

Comments   Server applications should register open documents with the server library and notify the library when a document is renamed, closed, saved, or restored to a saved state.

See Also   **OleRegisterServerDoc**, **OleRenameServerDoc**, **OleRevokeServerDoc**, **OleSavedServerDoc**

OleRevokeClientDoc   3.1

#include <ole.h>

OLESTATUS OleRevokeClientDoc(*lhClientDoc*)
LHCLIENTDOC *lhClientDoc*;   /* handle of client document   */

The **OleRevokeClientDoc** function informs the client library that a document is no longer open.

Parameters   *lhClientDoc*
                        Identifies the document that is no longer open. This handle is invalid following
                        the call to **OleRevokeClientDoc**.

Return Value   The return value is OLE_OK if the function is successful. Otherwise, it is an error
                        value, which may be one of the following:

                        OLE_ERROR_HANDLE
                        OLE_ERROR_NOT_EMPTY

Comments   The client application should delete all the objects in a document before calling
                        OleRevokeClientDoc.

                        Client applications should register open documents with the library and notify the
                        library when a document is renamed, closed, saved, or restored to a changed state.

See Also   **OleRegisterClientDoc, OleRenameClientDoc, OleRevertClientDoc,
                        OleSavedClientDoc**

OleRevokeObject   3.1

#include <ole.h>

OLESTATUS OleRevokeObject(*lpClient*)
LPOLECLIENT *lpClient*;   /* address of OLECLIENT structure   */

                        The **OleRevokeObject** function revokes access to an object. A server application
                        typically calls this function when the user destroys an object.

Parameters   *lpClient*
                        Points to the **OLECLIENT** structure associated with the object being revoked.

Return Value   The return value is OLE_OK if the function is successful. Otherwise, it is an error
                        value.

See Also   **OleRevokeServer, OleRevokeServerDoc**

OleRevokeServer

3.1

#include <ole.h>

OLESTATUS OleRevokeServer(*lhServer*)
LHSERVER *lhServer*;   /* server handle   */

> The **OleRevokeServer** function is called by a server application to close any registered documents.

Parameters   *lhServer*
> Identifies the server to revoke. A server application obtains this handle in a call to the **OleRegisterServer** function.

Return Value   The return value is OLE_OK if the function is successful. Otherwise, it is an error value, which may be one of the following:

> OLE_ERROR_HANDLE
> OLE_WAIT_FOR_RELEASE

Comments   The **OleRevokeServer** function returns OLE_WAIT_FOR_RELEASE if communications between clients and the server are in the process of terminating. In this case, the server application should continue to send and dispatch messages until the library calls the server's **Release** function.

See Also   **OleRegisterServer, OleRevokeObject, OleRevokeServerDoc**

OleRevokeServerDoc

3.1

#include <ole.h>

OLESTATUS OleRevokeServerDoc(*lhdoc*)
LHSERVERDOC *lhdoc*;   /* document handle   */

> The **OleRevokeServerDoc** function revokes the specified document. A server application calls this function when a registered document is being closed or otherwise made unavailable to client applications.

Parameters   *lhdoc*
> Identifies the document to revoke. This handle was returned by a call to the **OleRegisterServerDoc** function or was associated with a document by using one of the server-supplied functions that create documents.

Return Value   The return value is OLE_OK if the function is successful. Otherwise, it is an error value, which may be one of the following:

OLE_ERROR_HANDLE
OLE_WAIT_FOR_RELEASE

Comments   If this function returns OLE_WAIT_FOR_RELEASE, the server application should not free the **OLESERVERDOC** structure or exit until the library calls the server's **Release** function.

See Also   **OleRegisterServerDoc, OleRevokeObject, OleRevokeServer**

OleSavedClientDoc

3.1

#include <ole.h>

OLESTATUS OleSavedClientDoc(*lhClientDoc*)
LHCLIENTDOC *lhClientDoc*;   /* handle of client document   */

The **OleSavedClientDoc** function informs the client library that a document has been saved.

Parameters   *lhClientDoc*
Identifies the document that has been saved.

Return Value   The return value is OLE_OK if the function is successful. Otherwise, it is an error value, which may be OLE_ERROR_HANDLE.

Comments   Client applications should register open documents with the client library and notify the library when a document is renamed, closed, saved, or restored to a saved state.

See Also   **OleRegisterClientDoc, OleRenameClientDoc, OleRevertClientDoc, OleRevokeClientDoc**

OleSavedServerDoc

3.1

#include <ole.h>

OLESTATUS OleSavedServerDoc(*lhDoc***)**
LHSERVERDOC *lhDoc***;**   /* handle of document   */

> The **OleSavedServerDoc** function informs the server library that a document has been saved.

Parameters   *lhDoc*
> Identifies the document that has been saved.

Return Value   The return value is OLE_OK if the function is successful. Otherwise, it is an error value, which may be one of the following:

> OLE_ERROR_CANT_UPDATE_CLIENT
> OLE_ERROR_HANDLE

Comments   The **OleSavedServerDoc** function has the same effect as sending the OLE_SAVED notification to the client application's callback function. The server application calls this function when saving a document or when updating an embedded object without closing the document.

> When a server application receives OLE_ERROR_CANT_UPDATE_CLIENT as an error value, it should display a message box indicating that the user cannot update the document until the server terminates.

> Server applications should register open documents with the server library and notify the library when a document is renamed, closed, saved, or restored to a saved state.

See Also   **OleRegisterServerDoc**, **OleRenameServerDoc**, **OleRevertServerDoc**, **OleRevokeServerDoc**

OleSaveToStream

#include <ole.h>

OLESTATUS OleSaveToStream(*lpObject*, *lpStream*)
LPOLEOBJECT *lpObject*;   /* address of object to save   */
LPOLESTREAM *lpStream*;   /* address of OLESTREAM structure   */

The **OleSaveToStream** function saves an object to the stream.

Parameters

lpObject
  Points to the object to be saved to the stream.

lpStream
  Points to an **OLESTREAM** structure allocated and initialized by the client application. The library calls the **Put** function in the **OLESTREAM** structure to store the data from the object.

Return Value

The return value is OLE_OK if the function is successful. Otherwise, it is an error value, which may be one of the following:

OLE_ERROR_BLANK
OLE_ERROR_MEMORY
OLE_ERROR_OBJECT
OLE_ERROR_STREAM

Comments

An application can use the **OleQuerySize** function to find the number of bytes to allocate for the object.

See Also

OleLoadFromStream, OleQuerySize

OleSetBounds

#include <ole.h>

OLESTATUS OleSetBounds(*lpObject*, *lprcBound*)
LPOLEOBJECT *lpObject*;   /* address of object   */
RECT FAR* *lprcBound*;   /* address of structure for bounding rectangle */

The **OleSetBounds** function sets the coordinates of the bounding rectangle for the specified object on the target device.

Parameters   *lpObject*
                          Points to the object for which the bounding rectangle is set.

                       lprcBound
                          Points to a **RECT** structure containing the coordinates of the bounding
                          rectangle. The coordinates are specified in MM_HIMETRIC units. Neither the
                          width nor height of an object should exceed 32,767 MM_HIMETRIC units.

Return Value   The return value is OLE_OK if the function is successful. Otherwise, it is an error
                       value, which may be one of the following:

                       OLE_BUSY
                       OLE_ERROR_MEMORY
                       OLE_ERROR_OBJECT
                       OLE_WAIT_FOR_RELEASE

                       The **OleSetBounds** function returns OLE_ERROR_OBJECT when it is called for
                       a linked object.

Comments   The **OleSetBounds** function is ignored for linked objects, because the size of a
                       linked object is determined by the source document for the link.

                       A client application uses **OleSetBounds** to change the bounding rectangle. The
                       client does not need to call **OleSetBounds** every time a server is opened.

                       The bounding rectangle specified in the **OleSetBounds** function does not neces-
                       sarily have the same dimensions as the rectangle specified in the call to the **Ole-
                       Draw** function. These dimensions may be different because of the view scaling
                       used by the container application. An application can use **OleSetBounds** to cause
                       the server to reformat the picture to fit the rectangle more closely.

                       In the MM_HIMETRIC mapping mode, the positive y-direction is up.

See Also   **OleDraw**, **OleQueryBounds**, **SetMapMode**

OleSetColorScheme   3.1

#include <ole.h>

OLESTATUS OleSetColorScheme(*lpObject*, *lpPalette*)
LPOLEOBJECT *lpObject*;   /* address of object   */
const LOGPALETTE FAR* *lpPalette*;   /* address of preferred palette   */

The **OleSetColorScheme** function specifies the palette a client application recommends be used when the server application edits the specified object. The server application can ignore the recommended palette.

Parameters

lpObject
Points to an **OLEOBJECT** structure describing the object for which a palette is recommended.

lpPalette
Points to a **LOGPALETTE** structure specifying the recommended palette.

Return Value

The return value is OLE_OK if the function is successful. Otherwise, it is an error value, which may be one of the following:

OLE_BUSY
OLE_ERROR_COMM
OLE_ERROR_MEMORY
OLE_ERROR_OBJECT
OLE_ERROR_PALETTE
OLE_ERROR_STATIC
OLE_WAIT_FOR_RELEASE

The **OleSetColorScheme** function returns OLE_ERROR_OBJECT when it is called for a linked object.

Comments

A client application uses **OleSetColorScheme** to change the color scheme. The client does not need to call **OleSetColorScheme** every time a server is opened.

The first palette entry in the **LOGPALETTE** structure specifies the foreground color recommended by the client application. The second palette entry specifies the background color. The first half of the remaining palette entries are fill colors, and the second half are colors for lines and text.

Client applications should specify an even number of palette entries. When there is an uneven number of entries, the server interprets the odd entry as a fill color; that is, if there are five entries, three are interpreted as fill colors and two as line and text colors.

When server applications render metafiles, they should use the suggested palette.

OleSetData

3.1

#include <ole.h>

OLESTATUS OleSetData(*lpObject*, *cfFormat*, *hData*)
LPOLEOBJECT *lpObject*;   /* address of object   */
OLECLIPFORMAT *cfFormat*;   /* format of data to send   */
HANDLE *hData*;   /* memory containing data   */

The **OleSetData** function sends data in the specified format to the server associated with a specified object.

Parameters

lpObject
Points to an object specifying the server to which data is to be sent.

cfFormat
Specifies the format of the data.

hData
Identifies a memory object containing the data in the specified format.

Return Value

The return value is OLE_OK if the function is successful. Otherwise, it is an error value, which may be one of the following:

OLE_BUSY
OLE_ERROR_BLANK
OLE_ERROR_MEMORY
OLE_ERROR_NOT_OPEN
OLE_ERROR_OBJECT
OLE_WAIT_FOR_RELEASE

If the specified object cannot accept the data, the function returns an error value. If the server is not open and the requested data format is different from the format of the presentation data, the return value is OLE_ERROR_NOT_OPEN.

See Also

OleGetData, **OleRequestData**

OleSetHostNames

3.1

#include <ole.h>

OLESTATUS OleSetHostNames(*lpObject*, *lpszClient*, *lpszClientObj*)
LPOLEOBJECT *lpObject*;　　　/* address of object　　　　　　　　　　*/
LPCSTR *lpszClient*;　　　　　/* address of string with name of client app　*/
LPCSTR *lpszClientObj*;　　　/* address of string with client's name for object　*/

The **OleSetHostNames** function specifies the name of the client application and the client's name for the specified object. This information is used in window titles when the object is being edited in the server application.

Parameters

lpObject
　　Points to the object for which a name is to be set.

lpszClient
　　Points to a null-terminated string specifying the name of the client application.

lpszClientObj
　　Points to a null-terminated string specifying the client's name for the object.

Return Value

The return value is OLE_OK if the function is successful. Otherwise, it is an error value, which may be one of the following:

OLE_BUSY
OLE_ERROR_MEMORY
OLE_ERROR_OBJECT
OLE_WAIT_FOR_RELEASE

The **OleSetHostNames** function returns OLE_ERROR_OBJECT when it is called for a linked object.

Comments

When a server application is started for editing of an embedded object, it displays in its title bar the string specified in the *lpszClientObj* parameter. The object name specified in this string should be the name of the client document containing the object.

A client application uses **OleSetHostNames** to set the name of an object the first time that object is activated or to change the name of an object. The client does not need to call **OleSetHostNames** every time a server is opened.

OleSetLinkUpdateOptions

3.1

#include <ole.h>

OLESTATUS OleSetLinkUpdateOptions(*lpObject*, *UpdateOpt*)
LPOLEOBJECT *lpObject*;   /* address of object   */
OLEOPT_ UPDATE *UpdateOpt*;   /* link-update options   */

The **OleSetLinkUpdateOptions** function sets the link-update options for the presentation of the specified object.

Parameters

lpObject
Points to the object for which the link-update option is set.

UpdateOpt
Specifies the link-update option for the specified object. This parameter can be one of the following values:

Option	Description
oleupdate_always	Update the linked object whenever possible. This option supports the Automatic link-update radio button in the Links dialog box.
oleupdate_oncall	Update the linked object only on request from the client application. This option supports the Manual link-update radio button in the Links dialog box.
oleupdate_onsave	Update the linked object when the source document is saved by the server.

Return Value

The return value is OLE_OK if the function is successful. Otherwise, it is an error value, which may be one of the following:

OLE_BUSY
OLE_ERROR_OBJECT
OLE_ERROR_OPTION
OLE_ERROR_STATIC
OLE_WAIT_FOR_RELEASE

See Also

OleGetLinkUpdateOptions

OleSetTargetDevice

#include <ole.h>

OLESTATUS OleSetTargetDevice(*lpObject*, *hotd*)
LPOLEOBJECT *lpObject*;   /* address of object   */
HGLOBAL *hotd*;   /* handle of OLETARGETDEVICE structure   */

The **OleSetTargetDevice** function specifies the target output device for an object.

Parameters

lpObject
Points to the object for which a target device is specified.

hotd
Identifies an **OLETARGETDEVICE** structure that describes the target device for the object.

Return Value

The return value is OLE_OK if the function is successful. Otherwise, it is an error value, which may be one of the following:

OLE_BUSY
OLE_ERROR_MEMORY
OLE_ERROR_OBJECT
OLE_ERROR_STATIC
OLE_WAIT_FOR_RELEASE

Comments

The **OleSetTargetDevice** function allows a linked or embedded object to be formatted correctly for a target device, even when the object is rendered on a different device. A client application should call this function whenever the target device changes, so that servers can be notified to change the rendering of the object, if necessary. The client application should call the **OleUpdate** function to ensure that the information is sent to the server, so that the server can make the necessary changes to the object's presentation. The client application should call the library to redraw the object if it receives a notification from the server that the object has changed.

A client application uses the **OleSetTargetDevice** function to change the target device. The client does not need to call **OleSetTargetDevice** every time a server is opened.

OleUnblockServer   3.1

#include <ole.h>

OLESTATUS OleUnblockServer(*lhSrvr*, *lpfRequest*)
LHSERVER *lhSrvr*;   /* handle of server   */
BOOL FAR* *lpfRequest*;   /* address of flag for more requests   */

The **OleUnblockServer** function processes a request from a queue created by
calling the **OleBlockServer** function.

Parameters   *lhSrvr*
                   Identifies the server for which requests were queued.

                   lpfRequest
                   Points to a flag indicating whether there are further requests in the queue. If
                   there are further requests in the queue, this flag is TRUE when the function re-
                   turns. Otherwise, it is FALSE when the function returns.

Return Value   The return value is OLE_OK if the function is successful. Otherwise, it is an error
                   value, which may be one of the following:

                   OLE_ERROR_HANDLE
                   OLE_ERROR_MEMORY

Comments   A server application can use the **OleBlockServer** and **OleUnblockServer** func-
                   tions to control when the server library processes requests from client applications.
                   It is best to use **OleUnblockServer** outside the **GetMessage** function in a message
                   loop, unblocking all blocked messages before getting the next message. Unblock-
                   ing message loops should not be run inside server-defined functions that are called
                   by the library.

See Also   **OleBlockServer**

OleUnlockServer   3.1

#include <ole.h>

OLESTATUS OleUnlockServer(*hServer*)
LHSERVER *hServer*;   /* handle of server to unlock   */

The **OleUnlockServer** function unlocks a server that was locked by the **OleLock-
Server** function.

Parameters   *hServer*

Identifies the server to release from memory. This handle was retrieved by a call to the **OleLockServer** function.

Return Value   The return value is OLE_OK if the function is successful. Otherwise, it is an error value, which may be one of the following:

OLE_ERROR_HANDLE
OLE_WAIT_FOR_RELEASE

Comments   When the **OleLockServer** function is called more than once for a given server, the server's lock count is incremented. Each call to **OleUnlockServer** decrements the lock count. The server remains locked until the lock count is zero.

If the **OleUnlockServer** function returns OLE_WAIT_FOR_RELEASE, the application should call the **OleQueryReleaseStatus** function to determine whether the unlocking process has finished. In the call to **OleQueryReleaseStatus**, the application can cast the server handle to a long pointer to an object linking and embedding (OLE) object (**LPOLEOBJECT**):

```
OleQueryReleaseStatus((LPOLEOBJECT) lhserver);
```

When **OleQueryReleaseStatus** no longer returns OLE_BUSY, the server has been unlocked.

See Also   **OleLockServer, OleQueryReleaseStatus**

OleUpdate   3.1

#include <ole.h>

OLESTATUS OleUpdate(*lpObject***)**
LPOLEOBJECT *lpObject*;   /* address of object   */

The **OleUpdate** function updates the specified object. This function updates the presentation of the object and ensures that the object is up-to-date with respect to any linked objects it contains.

Parameters   *lpObject*

Points to the object to be updated.

Return Value   The return value is OLE_OK if the function is successful. Otherwise, it is an error value, which may be one of the following:

OLE_BUSY
OLE_ERROR_OBJECT
OLE_ERROR_STATIC
OLE_WAIT_FOR_RELEASE

See Also   **OleQueryOutOfDate**

OpenClipboard   `2.x`

BOOL OpenClipboard(*hwnd***)**
HWND *hwnd*;   /* handle of window to associate ownership with   */

The **OpenClipboard** function opens the clipboard. Other applications will not be able to modify the clipboard until the **CloseClipboard** function is called.

Parameters   *hwnd*
Identifies the window to be associated with the open clipboard.

Return Value   The return value is nonzero if the function is successful. It is zero if another application or window has the clipboard opened.

Comments   The window identified by the *hwnd* parameter will not become the owner of the clipboard until the **EmptyClipboard** function is called.

See Also   **CloseClipboard**, **EmptyClipboard**

OpenComm   `2.x`

int OpenComm(*lpszDevControl***,** *cbInQueue***,** *cbOutQueue***)**
LPCSTR *lpszDevControl*;   /* address of device-control information   */
UINT *cbInQueue*;   /* size of receiving queue   */
UINT *cbOutQueue*;   /* size of transmission queue   */

The **OpenComm** function opens a communications device.

Parameters   *lpszDevControl*

Points to a null-terminated string that specifies the device in the form COM*n* or LPT*n*, where *n* is the device number.

cbInQueue

Specifies the size, in bytes, of the receiving queue. This parameter is ignored for LPT devices.

cbOutQueue

Specifies the size, in bytes, of the transmission queue. This parameter is ignored for LPT devices.

Return Value   The return value identifies the open device if the function is successful. Otherwise, it is less than zero.

Errors   If the function fails, it may return one of the following error values:

Value	Meaning
IE_BADID	The device identifier is invalid or unsupported.
IE_BAUDRATE	The device's baud rate is unsupported.
IE_BYTESIZE	The specified byte size is invalid.
IE_DEFAULT	The default parameters are in error.
IE_HARDWARE	The hardware is not available (is locked by another device).
IE_MEMORY	The function cannot allocate the queues.
IE_NOPEN	The device is not open.
IE_OPEN	The device is already open.

If this function is called with both queue sizes set to zero, the return value is IE_OPEN if the device is already open or IE_MEMORY if the device is not open.

Comments   Windows allows COM ports 1 through 9 and LPT ports 1 through 3. If the device driver does not support a communications port number, the **OpenComm** function will fail.

The communications device is initialized to a default configuration. The **Set-CommState** function should be used to initialize the device to alternate values.

The receiving and transmission queues are used by interrupt-driven device drivers. LPT ports are not interrupt driven—for these ports, the *cbInQueue* and *cbOutQueue* parameters are ignored and the queue size is set to zero.

Example   The following example uses the **OpenComm** function to open communications port 1:

```
idComDev = OpenComm("COM1", 1024, 128);
if (idComDev < 0) {
    ShowError(idComDev, "OpenComm");
    return 0;
}

err = BuildCommDCB("COM1:9600,n,8,1", &dcb);
if (err < 0) {
    ShowError(err, "BuildCommDCB");
    return 0;
}

err = SetCommState(&dcb);
if (err < 0) {
    ShowError(err, "SetCommState");
    return 0;
}
```

See Also   **CloseComm, SetCommState**

OpenDriver   3.1

HDRVR OpenDriver(*lpDriverName*, *lpSectionName*, *lParam*)
LPCSTR *lpDriverName*;   /* address of driver name   */
LPCSTR *lpSectionName*;   /* address of .INI file section name   */
LPARAM *lParam*;   /* address of driver-specific information   */

The **OpenDriver** function performs necessary initialization operations such as set-ting members in installable-driver structures to their default values.

Parameters   *lpDriverName*
                     Points to a null-terminated string that specifies the name of an installable driver.

                     lpSectionName
                     Points to a null-terminated string that specifies the name of a section in the
                     SYSTEM.INI file.

                     lParam
                     Specifies driver-specific information.

Return Value   The return value is a handle of the installable driver, if the function is successful.
                     Otherwise it is NULL.

Comments   The string to which *lpDriverName* points must be identical to the name of the in-stallable driver as it appears in the SYSTEM.INI file.

If the name of the installable driver appears in the [driver] section of the SYSTEM.INI file, the string pointed to by *lpSectionName* should be NULL. Otherwise this string should specify the name of the section in SYSTEM.INI that contains the driver name.

When an application opens a driver for the first time, Windows calls the **Driver-Proc** function with the DRV_LOAD, DRV_ENABLE, and DRV_OPEN messages. When subsequent instances of the driver are opened, only DRV_OPEN is sent.

The value specified in the *lParam* parameter is passed to the *lParam2* parameter of the **DriverProc** function.

See Also   **CloseDriver**, **DriverProc**

OpenFile

2.x

HFILE OpenFile(*lpszFileName***, ***lpOpenBuff***, ***fuMode***)**
LPCSTR *lpszFileName*;	/* address of filename */
OFSTRUCT FAR* *lpOpenBuff*;	/* address of buffer for file information */
UINT *fuMode*;	/* action and attributes */

The **OpenFile** function creates, opens, reopens, or deletes a file.

Parameters   *lpszFileName*
Points to a null-terminated string that names the file to be opened. The string must consist of characters from the Windows character set and cannot contain wildcards.

lpOpenBuff
Points to the **OFSTRUCT** structure that will receive information about the file when the file is first opened. The structure can be used in subsequent calls to the **OpenFile** function to refer to the open file. The **OFSTRUCT** structure has the following form:

```
typedef struct tagOFSTRUCT {    /* of */
    BYTE  cBytes;
    BYTE  fFixedDisk;
    UINT  nErrCode;
    BYTE  reserved[4];
    BYTE  szPathName[128];
} OFSTRUCT;
```

The **szPathName** member of **OFSTRUCT** contains characters from the OEM character set.

For a full description of this structure, see the *Microsoft Windows Programmer's Reference, Volume 3*.

fuMode
Specifies the action to take and the attributes for the file. This parameter can be a combination of the following values:

Value	Meaning
OF_CANCEL	Adds a Cancel button to the OF_PROMPT dialog box. Pressing the Cancel button directs **OpenFile** to return a file-not-found error message.
OF_CREATE	Creates a new file. If the file already exists, it is truncated to zero length.
OF_DELETE	Deletes the file.
OF_EXIST	Opens the file, and then closes it. This value is used to test for file existence. Using this value does not change the file date.
OF_PARSE	Fills the **OFSTRUCT** structure but carries out no other action.
OF_PROMPT	Displays a dialog box if the requested file does not exist. The dialog box informs the user that Windows cannot find the file and prompts the user to insert the file in drive A.
OF_READ	Opens the file for reading only.
OF_READWRITE	Opens the file for reading and writing.
OF_REOPEN	Opens the file using information in the reopen buffer.
OF_SEARCH	Windows searches in directories even when the file name includes a full path.
OF_SHARE_COMPAT	Opens the file with compatibility mode, allowing any program on a given machine to open the file any number of times. **OpenFile** fails if the file has been opened with any of the other sharing modes.
OF_SHARE_DENY_NONE	Opens the file without denying other programs read or write access to the file. **OpenFile** fails if the file has been opened in compatibility mode by any other program.
OF_SHARE_DENY_READ	Opens the file and denies other programs read access to the file. **OpenFile** fails if the file has been opened in compatibility mode or for read access by any other program.
OF_SHARE_DENY_WRITE	Opens the file and denies other programs write access to the file. **OpenFile** fails if the file has been opened in compatibility or for write access by any other program.

Value	Meaning
OF_SHARE_EXCLUSIVE	Opens the file with exclusive mode, denying other programs both read and write access to the file. **OpenFile** fails if the file has been opened in any other mode for read or write access, even by the current program.
OF_VERIFY	Compares the time and date in the OF_STRUCT with the time and date of the specified file. The function returns HFILE_ERROR if the dates and times do not agree.
OF_WRITE	Opens the file for writing only.

Return Value

The return value is an MS-DOS file handle if the function is successful. (This handle is not necessarily valid; for example, if the *fuMode* parameter is OF_EXIST, the handle does not identify an open file, and if the *fuMode* parameter is OF_DELETE, the handle is invalid.) The return value is HFILE_ERROR if an error occurs.

Comments

If the *lpszFileName* parameter specifies a filename and extension only (or if the OF_SEARCH flag is specified), the **OpenFile** function searches for a matching file in the following directories (in this order):

1. The current directory.
2. The Windows directory (the directory containing WIN.COM), whose path the **GetWindowsDirectory** function retrieves.
3. The Windows system directory (the directory containing such system files as GDI.EXE), whose path the **GetSystemDirectory** function retrieves.
4. The directory containing the executable file for the current task; the **Get-ModuleFileName** function obtains the path of this directory.
5. The directories listed in the PATH environment variable.
6. The list of directories mapped in a network.

To close the file after use, the application should call the **_lclose** function.

See Also

GetSystemDirectory, **GetWindowsDirectory**

OpenIcon

2.x

BOOL OpenIcon(*hwnd*)
HWND *hwnd*;   /* handle of window   */

The **OpenIcon** function activates and displays a minimized window. Windows restores the window to its original size and position.

Parameters   *hwnd*
                     Identifies the window.

Return Value   The return value is nonzero if the function is successful. Otherwise, it is zero.

Comments   Using **OpenIcon** is the same as specifying the SW_SHOWNORMAL flag in a call to the **ShowWindow** function.

See Also   **CloseWindow**, **IsIconic**, **ShowWindow**

OpenSound

2.x

int OpenSound(void)

This function is obsolete. Use the Windows multimedia audio functions instead. For information about these functions, see the *Microsoft Windows Multimedia Programmer's Reference*.

OutputDebugString

3.0

void OutputDebugString(*lpszOutputString*)
LPCSTR *lpszOutputString*;   /* address of string to display   */

The **OutputDebugString** function displays the specified character string on the debugging terminal if a debugger is running.

Parameters   *lpszOutputString*
Points to a null-terminated string to be displayed.

Return Value   This function does not return a value.

Comments   This function preserves all registers.

Example   The following example uses the **OutputDebugString** function to display information on the debugging terminal:

```
OutputDebugString("\n\rcalling ValidateCodeSegments");

ValidateCodeSegments();

OutputDebugString("\n\rdone");
```

See Also   **DebugOutput**

PaintRgn   2.x

BOOL PaintRgn(*hdc*, *hrgn*)
HDC *hdc*;   /* handle of device context   */
HRGN *hrgn*;   /* handle of region   */

The **PaintRgn** function fills a region by using the current brush for the given device context.

Parameters   *hdc*
Identifies the device context that contains the region to be filled.

hrgn
Identifies the region to be filled. The coordinates for the given region are specified in device units.

Return Value   The return value is nonzero if the function is successful. Otherwise, it is zero.

Example   The following example uses the current brush for a device context to fill an elliptical region:

```
HDC hdc;
HRGN hrgn;

hrgn = CreateEllipticRgn(10, 10, 110, 110);
SelectObject(hdc, hrgn);
PaintRgn(hdc, hrgn);

DeleteObject(hrgn);
```

See Also   **CreateBrushIndirect, CreateDIBPatternBrush, CreateHatchBrush, CreatePatternBrush, CreateSolidBrush, FillRgn**

PatBlt

2.x

BOOL PatBlt(*hdc, nLeftRect, nTopRect, nwidth, nheight, fdwRop***)**
HDC *hdc*;	/* handle of device context	*/
int *nLeftRect*;	/* x-coordinate top-left corner destination rectangle	*/
int *nTopRect*;	/* y-coordinate top-left corner destination rectangle	*/
int *nwidth*;	/* width of destination rectangle	*/
int *nheight*;	/* height of destination rectangle	*/
DWORD *fdwRop*;	/* raster operation	*/

The **PatBlt** function creates a bit pattern on the specified device. The pattern is a combination of the selected brush and the pattern already on the device. The specified raster-operation code defines how the patterns are combined.

Parameters   *hdc*
Identifies the device context.

nLeftRect
Specifies the logical x-coordinate of the upper-left corner of the rectangle that receives the pattern.

nTopRect
Specifies the logical y-coordinate of the upper-left corner of the rectangle that receives the pattern.

nwidth
Specifies the width, in logical units, of the rectangle that will receive the pattern.

nheight
Specifies the height, in logical units, of the rectangle that will receive the pattern.

fdwRop

Specifies the raster-operation code that determines how the graphics device interface (GDI) combines the colors in the output operation. This parameter can be one of the following values:

Value	Meaning
PATCOPY	Copies the pattern to the destination bitmap.
PATINVERT	Combines the destination bitmap with the pattern by using the Boolean XOR operator.
PATPAINT	Paints the destination bitmap.
DSTINVERT	Inverts the destination bitmap.
BLACKNESS	Turns all output black.
WHITENESS	Turns all output white.

Return Value

The return value is nonzero if the function is successful. Otherwise, it is zero.

Comments

The raster operations listed for this function are a limited subset of the full 256 ternary raster-operation codes; in particular, a raster-operation code that refers to a source cannot be used.

Not all devices support the **PatBlt** function. To determine whether a device supports **PatBlt**, an application can call the **GetDeviceCaps** function with the RASTERCAPS index.

Example

The following example uses the **CreateBitmap** function to create a bitmap with a zig-zag pattern, and then uses the **PatBlt** function to fill the client area with that pattern:

```
HDC hdc;
HBITMAP hbmp;
HBRUSH hbr, hbrPrevious;
RECT rc;

int aZigzag[] = { 0xFF, 0xF7, 0xEB, 0xDD, 0xBE, 0x7F, 0xFF, 0xFF };

hbmp = CreateBitmap(8, 8, 1, 1, aZigzag);
hbr = CreatePatternBrush(hbmp);

hdc = GetDC(hwnd);
UnrealizeObject(hbr);
hbrPrevious = SelectObject(hdc, hbr);
GetClientRect(hwnd, &rc);
```

```
PatBlt(hdc, rc.left, rc.top,
    rc.right - rc.left, rc.bottom - rc.top, PATCOPY);
SelectObject(hdc, hbrPrevious);
ReleaseDC(hwnd, hdc);

DeleteObject(hbr);
DeleteObject(hbmp);
```

See Also   **GetDeviceCaps**

PeekMessage   2.x

BOOL PeekMessage(*lpmsg, hwnd, uFilterFirst, uFilterLast, fuRemove***)**
MSG FAR* *lpmsg*;   /* address of structure for message   */
HWND *hwnd*;   /* handle of filter window   */
UINT *uFilterFirst*;   /* first message   */
UINT *uFilterLast*;   /* last message   */
UINT *fuRemove*;   /* removal flags   */

The **PeekMessage** function checks the application's message queue for a message and places the message (if any) in the specified **MSG** structure.

Parameters   *lpmsg*
Points to an **MSG** structure that will receive message information from the application's message queue. The **MSG** structure has the following form:

```
typedef struct tagMSG {     /* msg */
    HWND    hwnd;
    UINT    message;
    WPARAM  wParam;
    LPARAM  lParam;
    DWORD   time;
    POINT   pt;
} MSG;
```

For a full description of this structure, see the *Microsoft Windows Programmer's Reference, Volume 3.*

hwnd
Identifies the window whose messages are to be examined.

uFilterFirst
Specifies the value of the first message in the range of messages to be examined.

uFilterLast
Specifies the value of the last message in the range of messages to be examined.

fuRemove

Specifies how messages are handled. This parameter can be a combination of the following values (PM_NOYIELD can be combined with either PM_NOREMOVE or PM_REMOVE):

Value	Meaning
PM_NOREMOVE	Messages are not removed from the queue after processing by **PeekMessage**.
PM_NOYIELD	Prevents the current task from halting and yielding system resources to another task.
PM_REMOVE	Messages are removed from the queue after processing by **PeekMessage**.

Return Value

The return value is nonzero if a message is available. Otherwise, it is zero.

Comments

Unlike the **GetMessage** function, the **PeekMessage** function does not wait for a message to be placed in the queue before returning. It does, however, yield control to other tasks (if the PM_NOYIELD flag is not set).

PeekMessage retrieves only messages associated with the window identified by the *hwnd* parameter, or any of its children as specified by the **IsChild** function, and within the range of message values given by the *uFilterFirst* and *uFilterLast* parameters. If *hwnd* is NULL, **PeekMessage** retrieves messages for any window that belongs to the application making the call. (**PeekMessage** does not retrieve messages for windows that belong to other applications.) If *uFilterFirst* and *uFilterLast* are both zero, **PeekMessage** returns all available messages (no range filtering is performed).

The WM_KEYFIRST and WM_KEYLAST flags can be used as filter values to retrieve all key messages; the WM_MOUSEFIRST and WM_MOUSELAST flags can be used to retrieve all mouse messages.

PeekMessage does not remove WM_PAINT messages from the queue. The messages remain in the queue until processed. The **GetMessage**, **PeekMessage**, and **WaitMessage** functions yield control to other applications. These calls provide the only way to let other applications run. If your application does not call any of these functions for long periods of time, other applications cannot run.

As long as an application is in a **PeekMessage** loop, Windows cannot become idle. Therefore, an application should not remain in a **PeekMessage** loop after the application's background processing has completed.

When an application uses the **PeekMessage** function without removing the message and then calls the **WaitMessage** function, **WaitMessage** does not return until the message is received. Applications that use the **PeekMessage** function should remove any retrieved messages from the queue before calling **WaitMessage**.

Example   The following example checks the message queue for keystrokes that have special meaning to the application. Note that the CheckSpecialKeys function is application-defined.

```
MSG msg;
BOOL fRetVal = TRUE;

while (PeekMessage(&msg, NULL, 0, 0, PM_REMOVE)) {

    if (msg.message == WM_QUIT)
        fRetVal = FALSE;

    if (CheckSpecialKeys(&msg)) /* application defined */
        continue;

    TranslateMessage(&msg);
    DispatchMessage(&msg);
}
return fRetVal;
```

See Also   **GetMessage, IsChild, PostAppMessage, SetMessageQueue, WaitMessage**

Pie

2.x

BOOL Pie(*hdc, nLeftRect, nTopRect, nRightRect, nBottomRect, nxStartArc, nyStartArc, nxEndArc, nyEndArc*)

HDC *hdc*;	/* handle of device context	*/
int *nLeftRect*;	/* x-coordinate upper-left corner bounding rectangle	*/
int *nTopRect*;	/* y-coordinate upper-left corner bounding rectangle	*/
int *nRightRect*;	/* x-coordinate lower-right corner bounding rectangle	*/
int *nBottomRect*;	/* y-coordinate lower-right corner bounding rectangle	*/
int *nxStartArc*;	/* x-coordinate arc starting point	*/
int *nyStartArc*;	/* y-coordinate arc starting point	*/
int *nxEndArc*;	/* x-coordinate arc ending point	*/
int *nyEndArc*;	/* y-coordinate arc ending point	*/

The **Pie** function draws a pie-shaped wedge by drawing an elliptical arc whose center and two endpoints are joined by lines.

Parameters   *hdc*
    Identifies the device context.

nLeftRect
    Specifies the logical x-coordinate of the upper-left corner of the bounding rectangle.

nTopRect
> Specifies the logical y-coordinate of the upper-left corner of the bounding rectangle.

nRightRect
> Specifies the logical x-coordinate of the lower-right corner of the bounding rectangle.

nBottomRect
> Specifies the logical y-coordinate of the lower-right corner of the bounding rectangle.

nxStartArc
> Specifies the logical x-coordinate of the arc's starting point. This point does not have to lie exactly on the arc.

nyStartArc
> Specifies the logical y-coordinate of the arc's starting point. This point does not have to lie exactly on the arc.

nxEndArc
> Specifies the logical x-coordinate of the arc's endpoint. This point does not have to lie exactly on the arc.

nyEndArc
> Specifies the logical y-coordinate of the arc's endpoint. This point does not have to lie exactly on the arc.

Return Value   The return value is nonzero if the function is successful. Otherwise, it is zero.

Comments   The center of the arc drawn by the **Pie** function is the center of the bounding rectangle specified by the *nLeftRect*, *nTopRect*, *nRightRect*, and *nBottomRect* parameters. The starting and ending points of the arc are specified by the *nxStartArc*, *nyStartArc*, *nxEndArc*, and *nyEndArc* parameters. The function draws the arc by using the selected pen, moving in a counterclockwise direction. It then draws two additional lines from each endpoint to the arc's center. Finally, it fills the pie-shaped area by using the current brush.

If *nxStartArc* equals *nxEndArc* and *nyStartArc* equals *nyEndArc*, the result is an ellipse with a single line from the center of the ellipse to the point (*nxStartArc*, *nyStartArc*) or (*nxEndArc*,*nyEndArc*).

The figure drawn by this function extends up to but does not include the right and bottom coordinates. This means that the height of the figure is *nBottomRect* – *nTopRect* and the width of the figure is *nRightRect* – *nLeftRect*.

Both the width and the height of a rectangle must be greater than 2 units and less than 32,767 units.

Example

The following example uses a **RECT** structure to store the points that define the bounding rectangle and uses **POINT** structures to store the coordinates that specify the beginning and end of the wedge:

```
HDC hdc;

RECT rc = { 10, 10, 180, 140 };
POINT ptStart = {  12,  12 };
POINT ptEnd = { 128, 135 };

Pie(hdc, rc.left, rc.top, rc.right, rc.bottom,
    ptStart.x, ptStart.y, ptEnd.x, ptEnd.y);
```

See Also   **Chord**

PlayMetaFile   2.x

BOOL PlayMetaFile(*hdc*, *hmf*)
HDC *hdc*;   /* handle of device context   */
HMETAFILE *hmf*;   /* handle of metafile   */

The **PlayMetaFile** function plays the contents of the specified metafile on the given device. The metafile can be played any number of times.

Parameters

hdc
   Identifies the device context of the output device.

hmf
   Identifies the metafile to be played.

Return Value   The return value is nonzero if the function is successful. Otherwise, it is zero.

Example   The following example uses the **CreateMetaFile** function to create a device-context handle of a memory metafile, draws a line in the device context, retrieves a metafile handle by calling the **CloseMetaFile** function, plays the metafile by using the **PlayMetaFile** function, and finally deletes the metafile by using the **DeleteMetaFile** function:

```
HDC hdcMeta;
HMETAFILE hmf;
```

```
hdcMeta = CreateMetaFile(NULL);
MoveTo(hdcMeta, 10, 10);
LineTo(hdcMeta, 100, 100);
hmf = CloseMetaFile(hdcMeta);
PlayMetaFile(hdc, hmf);
DeleteMetaFile(hmf);
```

See Also   **PlayMetaFileRecord**

PlayMetaFileRecord   2.x

void PlayMetaFileRecord(*hdc, lpht, lpmr, cHandles*)
HDC *hdc*;   /* handle of device context   */
HANDLETABLE FAR* *lpht*;   /* address of table of object handles */
METARECORD FAR* *lpmr*;   /* address of metafile record   */
UINT *cHandles*;   /* number of handles in table   */

The **PlayMetaFileRecord** function plays a metafile record by executing the graphics device interface (GDI) function contained in the record.

Parameters   *hdc*
Identifies the device context of the output device.

lpht
Points to a table of handles associated with the objects (pens, brushes, and so on) in the metafile.

lpmr
Points to the metafile record to be played.

cHandles
Specifies the number of handles in the handle table.

Return Value   This function does not return a value.

Comments   An application typically uses this function in conjunction with the **EnumMetafile** function to modify and then play a metafile.

Example   The following example creates a dashed green pen and passes it to the callback function for the **EnumMetaFile** function. If the first element in the array of object handles contains a handle, that handle is replaced by the handle of the green pen before the **PlayMetaFileRecord** function is called. (For this example, it is assumed that the table of object handles contains only one handle and that it is a pen handle.)

```
              MFENUMPROC lpEnumMetaProc;
              HPEN hpenGreen;

              lpEnumMetaProc = (MFENUMPROC) MakeProcInstance(
                  (FARPROC) EnumMetaFileProc, hAppInstance);
              hpenGreen = CreatePen(PS_DASH, 1, RGB(0, 255, 0));
              EnumMetaFile(hdc, hmf, lpEnumMetaProc, (LPARAM) &hpenGreen);
              FreeProcInstance((FARPROC) lpEnumMetaProc);
              DeleteObject(hpenGreen);
                   .
                   .
                   .

              int FAR PASCAL EnumMetaFileProc(HDC hdc, HANDLETABLE FAR* lpHTable,
                  METARECORD FAR* lpMFR, int cObj, BYTE FAR* lpClientData)
              {
                  if (lpHTable->objectHandle[0] != 0)
                      lpHTable->objectHandle[0] = *(HPEN FAR *) lpClientData;
                  PlayMetaFileRecord(hdc, lpHTable, lpMFR, cObj);

                  return 1;
              }
```

See Also   **EnumMetafile, PlayMetaFile**

Polygon   2.x

BOOL Polygon(*hdc, lppt, cPoints*)
HDC *hdc*;   /* handle of device context   */
const POINT FAR* *lppt*;   /* address of array with points for vertices */
int *cPoints*;   /* number of points in array   */

The **Polygon** function draws a polygon consisting of two or more points (vertices)
connected by lines. The system closes the polygon automatically, if necessary, by
drawing a line from the last vertex to the first. Polygons are surrounded by a frame
drawn by using the current pen and filled by using the current brush.

Parameters   *hdc*
                        Identifies the device context.

                        lppt
                        Points to an array of **POINT** structures that specify the vertices of the polygon.
                        Each structure in the array specifies a vertex. The **POINT** structure has the fol-
                        lowing form:

```
typedef struct tagPOINT {    /* pt */
    int x;
    int y;
} POINT;
```

For a full description of this structure, see the *Microsoft Windows Programmer's Reference, Volume 3.*

cPoints
Specifies the number of vertices in the array.

Return Value   The return value is nonzero if the function is successful. Otherwise, it is zero.

Comments   The current polygon-filling mode can be retrieved or set by using the **GetPolyFillMode** and **SetPolyFillMode** functions.

Example   The following example assigns values to an array of points and then calls the **Polygon** function:

```
HDC hdc;

POINT aPoints[3];

aPoints[0].x = 50;
aPoints[0].y = 10;
aPoints[1].x = 250;
aPoints[1].y = 50;
aPoints[2].x = 125;
aPoints[2].y = 130;

Polygon(hdc, aPoints, sizeof(aPoints) / sizeof(POINT));
```

See Also   **GetPolyFillMode, Polyline, PolyPolygon, SetPolyFillMode**

Polyline   2.x

BOOL Polyline(*hdc, lppt, cPoints***)**
HDC *hdc*;   /* handle of device context   */
const POINT FAR* *lppt*;   /* address of array with points to connect */
int *cPoints*;   /* number of points in array   */

The **Polyline** function draws a set of line segments, connecting the specified points. The lines are drawn from the first point through subsequent points, using the current pen. Unlike the **LineTo** function, the **Polyline** function neither uses nor updates the current position.

Parameters	*hdc* Identifies the device context.

lppt
Points to an array of **POINT** structures. Each structure in the array specifies a point. The **POINT** structure has the following form:

```
typedef struct tagPOINT {   /* pt */
    int x;
    int y;
} POINT;
```

For a full description of this structure, see the *Microsoft Windows Programmer's Reference, Volume 3*.

cPoints
Specifies the number of points in the array. This value must be at least 2.

Return Value   The return value is nonzero if the function is successful. Otherwise, it is zero.

Example   The following example assigns values to an array of points and then calls the **Polyline** function:

```
HDC hdc;

POINT aPoints[3];

aPoints[0].x = 50;
aPoints[0].y = 10;
aPoints[1].x = 250;
aPoints[1].y = 50;
aPoints[2].x = 125;
aPoints[2].y = 130;

Polyline(hdc, aPoints, sizeof(aPoints) / sizeof(POINT));
```

See Also   **LineTo**, **Polygon**

PolyPolygon   `3.0`

BOOL PolyPolygon(*hdc, lppt, lpnPolyCounts, cPolygons***)**
HDC *hdc*;   /* handle of device context   */
const POINT FAR* *lppt*;   /* address of array with vertices   */
int FAR* *lpnPolyCounts*;   /* address of array with point counts   */
int *cPolygons*;   /* number of polygons to draw   */

The **PolyPolygon** function creates two or more polygons that are filled by using the current polygon-filling mode. The polygons may be disjoint or overlapping.

Parameters

hdc
Identifies the device context.

lppt
Points to an array of **POINT** structures. Each structure in the array specifies a vertext of a polygon. The **POINT** structure has the following form:

```
typedef struct tagPOINT {   /* pt */
    int x;
    int y;
} POINT;
```

For a full description of this structure, see the *Microsoft Windows Programmer's Reference, Volume 3.*

lpnPolyCounts
Points to an array of integers, each of which specifies the number of points in one of the polygons in the array pointed to by the *lppt* parameter.

cPolygons
Specifies the number of polygons to be drawn. This value must be at least 2.

Return Value

The return value is nonzero if the function is successful. Otherwise, it is zero.

Comments

Each polygon specified in a call to the **PolyPolygon** function must be closed. Unlike polygons created by the **Polygon** function, the polygons created by **PolyPolygon** are not closed automatically.

The **PolyPolygon** function creates two or more polygons. To create a single polygon, an application should use the **Polygon** function.

The current polygon-filling mode can be retrieved or set by using the **GetPolyFillMode** and **SetPolyFillMode** functions.

Example

The following example draws two overlapping polygons by assigning values to an array of points and then calling the **PolyPolygon** function:

```
HDC hdc;

POINT aPolyPoints[8];
int aVertices[] = { 4, 4 };

aPolyPoints[0].x = 50;
aPolyPoints[0].y = 10;
aPolyPoints[1].x = 250;
aPolyPoints[1].y = 50;
aPolyPoints[2].x = 125;
```

```
            aPolyPoints[2].y = 130;
            aPolyPoints[3].x = 50;
            aPolyPoints[3].y = 10;

            aPolyPoints[4].x = 100;
            aPolyPoints[4].y = 25;
            aPolyPoints[5].x = 300;
            aPolyPoints[5].y = 125;
            aPolyPoints[6].x = 70;
            aPolyPoints[6].y = 150;
            aPolyPoints[7].x = 100;
            aPolyPoints[7].y = 25;

            PolyPolygon(hdc, aPolyPoints, aVertices,
                sizeof(aVertices) / sizeof(int));
```

See Also   **GetPolyFillMode, Polygon, Polyline, SetPolyFillMode**

PostAppMessage   2.x

BOOL PostAppMessage(*htask***,** *uMsg***,** *wParam***,** *lParam***)**
HTASK *htask***;**   /* handle of task to receive message   */
UINT *uMsg***;**   /* message to post   */
WPARAM *wParam***;**   /* first message parameter   */
LPARAM *lParam***;**   /* second message parameter   */

The **PostAppMessage** function posts (places) a message in the message queue of the given application (task) and then returns without waiting for the application to process the message. The application to which the message is posted retrieves the message by calling the **GetMessage** or **PeekMessage** function. The **hwnd** member of the returned **MSG** structure is NULL.

Parameters   *htask*
                        Identifies the task to which the message is posted. The **GetCurrentTask** function returns this handle.

                        uMsg
                        Specifies the type of message to be posted.

                        wParam
                        Specifies 16 bits of additional message-dependent information.

                        lParam
                        Specifies 32 bits of additional message-dependent information.

Return Value   The return value is nonzero if the function is successful. Otherwise, it is zero.

See Also   GetCurrentTask, GetMessage, PeekMessage

PostMessage

BOOL PostMessage(*hwnd*, *uMsg*, *wParam*, *lParam*)
HWND *hwnd*;   /* handle of the destination window   */
UINT *uMsg*;   /* message to post   */
WPARAM *wParam*;   /* first message parameter   */
LPARAM *lParam*;   /* second message parameter   */

The **PostMessage** function posts (places) a message in a window's message queue and then returns without waiting for the corresponding window to process the message. Messages in a message queue are retrieved by calls to the **GetMessage** or **PeekMessage** function.

hwnd
Identifies the window to which the message will be posted. If this parameter is HWND_BROADCAST, the message will be posted to all top-level windows, including disabled or invisible unowned windows.

uMsg
Specifies the message to be posted.

wParam
Specifies 16 bits of additional message-dependent information.

lParam
Specifies 32 bits of additional message-dependent information.

Return Value   The return value is nonzero if the function is successful. Otherwise, it is zero.

Comments   An application should never use the **PostMessage** function to post a message to a control.

If the message is being posted to another application and the *wParam* or *lParam* parameter is used to pass a handle or pointer to a global memory object, the memory should be allocated by the **GlobalAlloc** function, using the GMEM_SHARE flag.

See Also   GetMessage, PeekMessage, PostAppMessage, SendDlgItemMessage, SendMessage

PostQuitMessage

void PostQuitMessage(*nExitCode*)
int *nExitCode*;   /* exit code   */

The **PostQuitMessage** function posts a message to Windows indicating that an application is requesting to terminate execution (quit). This function is typically used in response to a WM_DESTROY message.

Parameters   *nExitCode*
Specifies an application-defined exit code. It must be the *wParam* parameter of the WM_QUIT message.

Return Value   This function does not return a value.

Comments   The **PostQuitMessage** function posts a WM_QUIT message to the application and returns immediately; the function simply indicates to the system that the application will request to quit some time in the future.

When the application receives the WM_QUIT message, it should exit the message loop in the main function and return control to Windows.

See Also   **GetMessage**

PrestoChangoSelector

UINT PrestoChangoSelector(*uSourceSelector*, *uDestSelector*)
UINT *uSourceSelector*;   /* selector to convert   */
UINT *uDestSelector*;   /* converted selector (allocated by AllocSelector)   */

The **PrestoChangoSelector** function generates a code selector that corresponds to a given data selector, or it generates a data selector that corresponds to a given code selector.

An application should not use this function unless it is absolutely necessary, because its use violates preferred Windows programming practices.

Parameters   *uSourceSelector*
Specifies the selector to be converted.

uDestSelector
Specifies a selector previously allocated by the **AllocSelector** function. This previously allocated selector receives the converted selector.

Return Value   The return value is the copied and converted selector if the function is successful. Otherwise, it is zero.

Comments   Windows does not track changes to the source selector. Consequently, before any memory can be moved, the application should use the converted destination selector immediately after it is returned by this function.

The **PrestoChangoSelector** function modifies the destination selector to have the same properties as the source selector, but with the opposite code or data attribute. This function changes only the attributes of the selector, not the value of the selector.

This function was named **ChangeSelector** in the Windows 3.0 documentation.

See Also   **AllocDStoCSAlias**, **AllocSelector**

PrintDlg

3.1

#include <commdlg.h>

BOOL PrintDlg(*lppd***)**
PRINTDLG FAR* *lppd*;   /* address of structure with initialization data   */

The **PrintDlg** function displays a Print dialog box or a Print Setup dialog box. The Print dialog box makes it possible for the user to specify the properties of a particular print job. The Print Setup dialog box makes it possible for the user to select additional job properties and configure the printer.

Parameters   *lppd*
Points to a **PRINTDLG** structure that contains information used to initialize the dialog box. When the **PrintDlg** function returns, this structure contains information about the user's selections.

The **PRINTDLG** structure has the following form:

```
#include <commdlg.h>

typedef struct tagPD {  /* pd */
    DWORD    lStructSize;
    HWND     hwndOwner;
    HGLOBAL  hDevMode;
    HGLOBAL  hDevNames;
    HDC      hDC;
    DWORD    Flags;
    UINT     nFromPage;
```

```
        UINT       nToPage;
        UINT       nMinPage;
        UINT       nMaxPage;
        UINT       nCopies;
        HINSTANCE  hInstance;
        LPARAM     lCustData;
        UINT       (CALLBACK* lpfnPrintHook)(HWND, UINT, WPARAM, LPARAM);
        UINT       (CALLBACK* lpfnSetupHook)(HWND, UINT, WPARAM, LPARAM);
        LPCSTR     lpPrintTemplateName;
        LPCSTR     lpSetupTemplateName;
        HGLOBAL    hPrintTemplate;
        HGLOBAL    hSetupTemplate;
    } PRINTDLG;
```

For a full description of this structure, see the *Microsoft Windows Programmer's Reference, Volume 3*.

Return Value   The return value is nonzero if the function successfully configures the printer. The return value is zero if an error occurs, if the user chooses the Cancel button, or if the user chooses the Close command on the System menu to close the dialog box. (The return value is also zero if the user chooses the Setup button to display the Print Setup dialog box, chooses the OK button in the Print Setup dialog box, and then chooses the Cancel button in the Print dialog box.)

Errors   Use the **CommDlgExtendedError** function to retrieve the error value, which may be one of the following:

CDERR_FINDRESFAILURE	PDERR_CREATEICFAILURE
CDERR_INITIALIZATION	PDERR_DEFAULTDIFFERENT
CDERR_LOADRESFAILURE	PDERR_DNDMMISMATCH
CDERR_LOADSTRFAILURE	PDERR_GETDEVMODEFAIL
CDERR_LOCKRESFAILURE	PDERR_INITFAILURE
CDERR_MEMALLOCFAILURE	PDERR_LOADDRVFAILURE
CDERR_MEMLOCKFAILURE	PDERR_NODEFAULTPRN
CDERR_NOHINSTANCE	PDERR_NODEVICES
CDERR_NOHOOK	PDERR_PARSEFAILURE
CDERR_NOTEMPLATE	PDERR_PRINTERNOTFOUND
CDERR_STRUCTSIZE	PDERR_RETDEFFAILURE
	PDERR_SETUPFAILURE

Example   The following example initializes the **PRINTDLG** structure, calls the **PrintDlg** function to display the Print dialog box, and prints a sample page of text if the return value is nonzero:

```
PRINTDLG pd;

/* Set all structure fields to zero. */

memset(&pd, 0, sizeof(PRINTDLG));

/* Initialize the necessary PRINTDLG structure fields. */

pd.lStructSize = sizeof(PRINTDLG);
pd.hwndOwner = hwnd;
pd.Flags = PD_RETURNDC;

/* Print a test page if successful */

if (PrintDlg(&pd) != 0) {
    Escape(pd.hDC, STARTDOC, 8, "Test-Doc", NULL);

    /* Print text and rectangle */

    TextOut(pd.hDC, 50, 50, "Common Dialog Test Page", 23);
    Rectangle(pd.hDC, 50, 90, 625, 105);
    Escape(pd.hDC, NEWFRAME, 0, NULL, NULL);
    Escape(pd.hDC, ENDDOC, 0, NULL, NULL);
    DeleteDC(pd.hDC);
    if (pd.hDevMode != NULL)
        GlobalFree(pd.hDevMode);
    if (pd.hDevNames != NULL)
        GlobalFree(pd.hDevNames);
}
else
    ErrorHandler();
```

ProfClear

3.0

void ProfClear(void)

The **ProfClear** function discards all Microsoft Windows Profiler samples currently in the sampling buffer.

Parameters	This function has no parameters.

Return Value	This function does not return a value.

Comments	For more information about using Profiler, see *Microsoft Windows Programming Tools.*

Example   The following example uses the **ProfClear** function to clear the Profiler sampling buffer before changing the sampling rate:

```
ProfClear();              /* clears existing buffer */
ProfSampRate(5, 1);       /* changes sampling rate  */
```

ProfFinish   3.0

void ProfFinish(void)

The **ProfFinish** function stops Microsoft Windows Profiler sampling and flushes the output buffer to disk.

Parameters   This function has no parameters.

Return Value   This function does not return a value.

Comments   If Profiler is running in 386 enhanced mode, the **ProfFinish** function also frees the buffer for system use.

For more information about using Profiler, see *Microsoft Windows Programming Tools*.

Example   The following example uses the **ProfFinish** function to stop sampling and flush the output buffer during WM_DESTROY message processing:

```
case WM_DESTROY:
    ProfFinish();
    PostQuitMessage(0);
    break;
```

ProfFlush   3.0

void ProfFlush(void)

The **ProfFlush** function flushes the Microsoft Windows Profiler sampling buffer to disk.

Parameters   This function has no parameters.

Return Value   This function does not return a value.

Comments   Excessive use of the **ProfFlush** function can seriously impair application performance. An application should not use **ProfFlush** when MS-DOS may be unstable
(inside an interrupt handler, for example).

For more information about using Profiler, see *Microsoft Windows Programming
Tools*.

Example   The following example uses the **ProfFlush** function to flush the Profiler buffer
before changing the buffer size:

```
ProfFlush();              /* flushes existing buffer */
ProfSetup(1024, 0);       /* uses a 1024K buffer     */
```

ProfInsChk   3.0

int ProfInsChk(void)

The **ProfInsChk** function determines whether Microsoft Windows Profiler is installed.

Parameters   This function has no parameters.

Return Value   The return value is 1 if Profiler is installed for a mode other than 386 enhanced
mode, or it is 2 if Profiler is installed for 386 enhanced mode. Otherwise, the return value is 0, indicating that Profiler is not installed.

Comments   For more information about using Profiler, see *Microsoft Windows Programming
Tools*.

Example   The following example uses the **ProfInsChk** function to determine whether the
Profiler is installed:

```
int ick;
char szMsg[80];

if ((ick = ProfInsChk()) == 0)
    MessageBox(hwnd, "Profiler is not installed!",
        "ProfInsChk", MB_ICONSTOP);
```

```
else {
    strcpy(szMsg, "Profiler is installed");
    if (ick == 2) {
        strcat(szMsg, " in 386 enhanced mode");
        ProfSetup(128, 0);        /* uses a 128K buffer */
    }
    MessageBox(hwnd, szMsg, "ProfInsChk", MB_OK);
}
```

ProfSampRate   3.0

void ProfSampRate(*nRate286*, *nRate386*)
int *nRate286*;   /* sample rate for non–386 enhanced mode   */
int *nRate386*;   /* sample rate for 386 enhanced mode   */

The **ProfSampRate** function sets the Microsoft Windows Profiler code-sampling rate.

Parameters   *nRate286*
Specifies the sampling rate if the application is not running in 386 enhanced mode. The *nRate286* parameter can be one of the following values:

Value	Sampling rate
1	122.070 microseconds
2	244.141 microseconds
3	488.281 microseconds
4	976.562 microseconds
5	1.953125 milliseconds
6	3.90625 milliseconds
7	7.8125 milliseconds
8	15.625 milliseconds
9	31.25 milliseconds
10	62.5 milliseconds
11	125 milliseconds
12	250 milliseconds
13	500 milliseconds

nRate386
Specifies the sampling rate, in milliseconds if the application is running in 386 enhanced mode. This value is in the range 1 through 1000.

Return Value   This function does not return a value.

Comments   Only the rate parameter appropriate to the current mode is used; the other parameter is ignored.

The default rate is 2 milliseconds in 386 enhanced mode; in any other mode, the value is 5, which specifies a rate of 1.953125 milliseconds.

For more information about using Profiler, see *Microsoft Windows Programming Tools.*

Example   The following example uses the **ProfSampRate** function to change the Profiler sampling rate to 1 millisecond in 386 enhanced mode:

```
ProfClear();                    /* clears existing buffer */
ProfSampRate(5, 1);             /* changes sampling rate  */
```

ProfSetup

$\boxed{3.0}$

void ProfSetup(*nBufferKB*, *nSamplesKB*)
int *nBufferKB*;   /* size of output buffer   */
int *nSamplesKB*;   /* amount of sample data written to disk   */

The **ProfSetup** function specifies the size of the Microsoft Windows Profiler output buffer and how much sampling data Profiler is to write to the disk.

Profiler ignores the **ProfSetup** function when running with Windows in any mode other than 386 enhanced mode.

Parameters   *nBufferKB*
Specifies the size, in kilobytes, of the output buffer. This value is in the range 1 through 1064. The default value is 64.

nSamplesKB
Specifies the amount, in kilobytes, of sampling data Profiler writes to the disk. A value of zero (the default value) specifies unlimited sampling data.

Return Value   This function does not return a value.

Comments   Do not call the **ProfSetup** function after calling **ProfStart**. To resize memory after **ProfStart** has been called, first call the **ProfStop** function.

For more information about using Profiler, see *Microsoft Windows Programming Tools.*

Example   The following example uses the **ProfSetup** function to set the output buffer size to 128K if Profiler is installed in 386 enhanced mode:

```
int ick;
char szMsg[80];

if ((ick = ProfInsChk()) == 0)
    MessageBox(hwnd, "Profiler is not installed!",
        "ProfInsChk", MB_ICONSTOP);
else {
    strcpy(szMsg, "Profiler is installed");
    if (ick == 2) {
        strcat(szMsg, " in 386 enhanced mode");
        ProfSetup(128, 0);      /* uses a 128K buffer */
    }
    MessageBox(hwnd, szMsg, "ProfInsChk", MB_OK);
}
```

See Also   **ProfStart**, **ProfStop**

ProfStart   `3.0`

void ProfStart(void)

The **ProfStart** function starts Microsoft Windows Profiler sampling.

Parameters   This function has no parameters.

Return Value   This function does not return a value.

Comments   For more information about using Profiler, see *Microsoft Windows Programming Tools*.

Example   The following example uses the **ProfStart** and **ProfStop** functions to sample during the message-queue dispatch process:

```
/* Acquire and dispatch messages until WM_QUIT is received. */

while (GetMessage(&msg, /* message structure                 */
        (HWND) NULL,      /* handle of window receiving message */
        0,                /* lowest message to examine          */
        0))               /* highest message to examine         */
```

```
    {
        ProfStart();

        TranslateMessage(&msg); /* translates virtual-key codes   */
        DispatchMessage(&msg);  /* dispatches message to window    */

        ProfStop();
    }
```

See Also   **ProfStop**

ProfStop $\boxed{3.0}$

void ProfStop(void)

The **ProfStop** function stops Microsoft Windows Profiler sampling.

Parameters   This function has no parameters.

Return Value   This function does not return a value.

Comments   For more information about using Profiler, see *Microsoft Windows Programming Tools*.

Example   The following example uses the **ProfStart** and **ProfStop** functions to sample during the message-queue dispatch process:

```
/* Acquire and dispatch messages until WM_QUIT is received. */

while (GetMessage(&msg, /* message structure                    */
        (HWND) NULL,     /* handle of window receiving message   */
        0,               /* lowest message to examine            */
        0))              /* highest message to examine           */
    {
    ProfStart();

    TranslateMessage(&msg); /* translates virtual-key codes   */
    DispatchMessage(&msg);  /* dispatches message to window    */

    ProfStop();
    }
```

See Also   **ProfStart**

PtInRect

BOOL PtInRect(*lprc*, *pt*)
const RECT FAR* *lprc*;   /* address of structure with rectangle   */
POINT *pt*;   /* structure with point   */

The **PtInRect** function determines whether the specified point lies within a given rectangle. A point is within a rectangle if it lies on the left or top side or is within all four sides. A point on the right or bottom side is considered outside the rectangle.

Parameters   *lprc*
Points to a **RECT** structure that contains the specified rectangle. The **RECT** structure has the following form:

```
typedef struct tagRECT {    /* rc */
    int left;
    int top;
    int right;
    int bottom;
} RECT;
```

For a full description of this structure, see the *Microsoft Windows Programmer's Reference*, *Volume 3*.

pt
Specifies a **POINT** structure that contains the specified point. The **POINT** structure has the following form:

```
typedef struct tagPOINT {    /* pt */
    int x;
    int y;
} POINT;
```

For a full description of this structure, see the *Microsoft Windows Programmer's Reference*, *Volume 3*.

Return Value   The return value is nonzero if the point lies within the given rectangle. Otherwise, it is zero.

See Also   **EqualRect, IsRectEmpty**

PtInRegion

BOOL PtInRegion(*hrgn*, *nXPos*, *nYPos*)
HRGN *hrgn*;   /* handle of region   */
int *nXPos*;   /* x-coordinate of point   */
int *nYPos*;   /* y-coordinate of point   */

The **PtInRegion** function determines whether a specified point is in the given region.

Parameters

hrgn
Identifies the region to be examined.

nXPos
Specifies the logical x-coordinate of the point.

nYPos
Specifies the logical y-coordinate of the point.

Return Value

The return value is nonzero if the point is in the region. Otherwise, it is zero.

Example

The following example uses the **PtInRegion** function to determine whether the point (50, 50) is in the specified region and prints the result:

```
HRGN hrgn;
BOOL fPtIn;
LPSTR lpszInRegion = "Specified point is in region.";
LPSTR lpszNotInRegion = "Specified point is not in region.";

fPtIn = PtInRegion(hrgn, 50, 50);
if (!fPtIn)
    TextOut(hdc, 10, 10, lpszNotInRegion,
        lstrlen(lpszNotInRegion));
else
    TextOut(hdc, 10, 10, lpszInRegion, lstrlen(lpszInRegion));
```

See Also   **RectInRegion**

PtVisible

BOOL PtVisible(*hdc*, *nXPos*, *nYPos*)
HDC *hdc*;   /* handle of device context   */
int *nXPos*;   /* x-coordinate of point to query */
int *nYPos*;   /* y-coordinate of point to query */

The **PtVisible** function determines whether the specified point is within the clipping region of the given device context.

Parameters

hdc
Identifies the device context.

nXPos
Specifies the logical x-coordinate of the point.

nYPos
Specifies the logical y-coordinate of the point.

Return Value

The return is nonzero if the point is within the clipping region. Otherwise, it is zero.

Example

The following example creates a rectangular region, displays a message inside it, and selects the region as the clipping region. The **PtVisible** function is used to determine whether coordinates generated by a double-click are inside the region. If so, the message changes to "Thank you." If not, the **CombineRgn** function is used to create a clipping region that combines the first region with a new region that surrounds the specified coordinates, and the word "Missed!" is displayed at the coordinates.

```
HDC hdcLocal;
HRGN hrgnClick, hrgnMiss, hrgnCombine;
HBRUSH hbr;

hdcLocal = GetDC(hwnd);
hbr = GetStockObject(BLACK_BRUSH);

hrgnClick = CreateRectRgn(90, 95, 225, 120);
FrameRgn(hdcLocal, hrgnClick, hbr, 1, 1);
TextOut(hdcLocal, 100, 100, "Double-click here.", 18);
SelectClipRgn(hdcLocal, hrgnClick);

if (PtVisible(hdcLocal, XClick, YClick)) {
    PaintRgn(hdcLocal, hrgnClick);
    FrameRgn(hdcLocal, hrgnClick, hbr, 1, 1);
    TextOut(hdcLocal, 100, 100, "Thank you.", 10);
}
else if (XClick > 0) {
    hrgnMiss = CreateRectRgn(XClick - 5, YClick - 5, XClick + 60,
        YClick + 20);
    hrgnCombine = CreateRectRgn(0, 0, 0, 0);
    CombineRgn(hrgnCombine, hrgnClick, hrgnMiss, RGN_OR);
    SelectClipRgn(hdcLocal, hrgnCombine);
    FrameRgn(hdcLocal, hrgnCombine, hbr, 1, 1);
    TextOut(hdcLocal, XClick, YClick, "Missed!", 7);
}

InvalidateRect(hwnd, NULL, FALSE);
```

```
DeleteObject(hrgnClick);
DeleteObject(hrgnMiss);
DeleteObject(hrgnCombine);
ReleaseDC(hwnd, hdcLocal);
```

See Also   **CombineRgn, RectVisible**

QueryAbort   3.1

BOOL QueryAbort(*hdc*, *reserved*)
HDC *hdc*;   /* device-context handle   */
int *reserved*;   /* reserved; should be zero   */

The **QueryAbort** function calls the **AbortProc** callback function for a printing application and queries whether the printing should be terminated.

Parameters   *hdc*
Identifies the device context.

reserved
Specifies a reserved value. It should be zero.

Return Value   The return value is TRUE if printing should continue or if there is no abort procedure. It is FALSE if the print job should be terminated. The return value is supplied by the **AbortProc** callback function.

See Also   **AbortDoc, AbortProc, SetAbortProc**

QuerySendMessage   3.1

BOOL QuerySendMessage(*hreserved1*, *hreserved2*, *hreserved3*, *lpMessage*)
HANDLE *hreserved1*;
HANDLE *hreserved2*;
HANDLE *hreserved3*;
LPMSG *lpMessage*;   /* address of structure for message   */

The **QuerySendMessage** function determines whether a message sent by **SendMessage** originated from within the current task. If the message is an intertask message, **QuerySendMessage** puts it into the specified **MSG** structure.

Parameters   *hreserved1*
                            Reserved; must be NULL.

                        hreserved2
                            Reserved; must be NULL.

                        hreserved3
                            Reserved; must be NULL.

                        lpMessage
                            Specifies the **MSG** structure in which to place an intertask message. The **MSG**
                            structure has the following form:

```
typedef struct tagMSG {      /* msg */
    HWND    hwnd;
    UINT    message;
    WPARAM  wParam;
    LPARAM  lParam;
    DWORD   time;
    POINT   pt;
} MSG;
```

                            For a full description of this structure, see the *Microsoft Windows Program-
                            mer's Reference, Volume 3.*

Return Value   The return value is zero if the message originated within the current task. Other-
                        wise, it is nonzero.

Comments   If the Windows debugger is entering soft mode, the application being debugged
                        should reply to intertask messages by using the **ReplyMessage** function.

                        The NULL parameters are reserved for future use.

See Also   **SendMessage**, **ReplyMessage**

ReadComm   `2.x`

int ReadComm(*idComDev, lpvBuf, cbRead***)**
int *idComDev*;   /* identifier of device to read from   */
void FAR* *lpvBuf*;   /* address of buffer for read bytes   */
int *cbRead*;   /* number of bytes to read   */

                        The **ReadComm** function reads up to a specified number of bytes from the given
                        communications device.

Parameters	*idComDev*

Parameters

idComDev
Specifies the communications device to be read from. The **OpenComm** function returns this value.

lpvBuf
Points to the buffer for the read bytes.

cbRead
Specifies the number of bytes to be read.

Return Value

The return value is the number of bytes read, if the function is successful. Otherwise, it is less than zero and its absolute value is the number of bytes read.

For parallel I/O ports, the return value is always zero.

Comments

When an error occurs, the cause of the error can be determined by using the **GetCommError** function to retrieve the error value and status. Since errors can occur when no bytes are present, if the return value is zero, the **GetCommError** function should be used to ensure that no error occurred.

The return value is less than the number specified by the *cbRead* parameter only if the number of bytes in the receiving queue is less than that specified by *cbRead*. If the return value is equal to *cbRead*, additional bytes may be queued for the device. If the return value is zero, no bytes are present.

See Also

GetCommError, OpenComm

RealizePalette

3.0

UINT RealizePalette(*hdc*)
HDC *hdc*;   /* handle of device context   */

The **RealizePalette** function maps palette entries from the current logical palette to the system palette.

Parameters

hdc
Identifies the device context containing a logical palette.

Return Value

The return value indicates how many entries in the logical palette were mapped to different entries in the system palette. This represents the number of entries that this function remapped to accommodate changes in the system palette since the logical palette was last realized.

Comments

A logical color palette acts as a buffer between color-intensive applications and the system, allowing an application to use as many colors as necessary without interfering with either its own displayed color or with colors displayed by other windows. When a window has the input focus and calls the **RealizePalette** function, Windows ensures that the window will display all the requested colors (up to the maximum number simultaneously available on the screen) and Windows displays additional colors by matching them to available colors. In addition, Windows matches the colors requested by inactive windows that call **RealizePalette** as closely as possible to the available colors. This significantly reduces undesirable changes in the colors displayed in inactive windows.

Example

The following example uses the **SelectPalette** function to select a palette into a device context and then calls the **RealizePalette** function to map the colors to the system palette:

```
HPALETTE hpal, hPalPrevious;

hdc = GetDC(hwnd);

hPalPrevious = SelectPalette(hdc, hpal, FALSE);
if (RealizePalette(hdc) == NULL)
    MessageBox(hwnd, "Can't realize palette", "Error", MB_OK);

ReleaseDC(hwnd, hdc);
```

See Also   **SelectPalette**

Rectangle

`2.x`

BOOL Rectangle(*hdc, nLeftRect, nTopRect, nRightRect, nBottomRect***)**
HDC *hdc*;   /* handle of device context   */
int *nLeftRect*;   /* x-coordinate upper-left corner   */
int *nTopRect*;   /* y-coordinate upper-left corner   */
int *nRightRect*;   /* x-coordinate lower-right corner   */
int *nBottomRect*; /* y-coordinate lower-right corner   */

The **Rectangle** function draws a rectangle, using the current pen. The interior of the rectangle is filled by using the current brush.

Parameters

hdc
  Identifies the device context.

nLeftRect
  Specifies the logical x-coordinate of the upper-left corner of the rectangle.

nTopRect
Specifies the logical y-coordinate of the upper-left corner of the rectangle.

nRightRect
Specifies the logical x-coordinate of the lower-right corner of the rectangle.

nBottomRect
Specifies the logical y-coordinate of the lower-right corner of the rectangle.

Return Value   The return value is nonzero if the function is successful. Otherwise, it is zero.

Comments   The figure this function draws extends up to, but does not include, the right and bottom coordinates. This means that the height of the figure is *nBottomRect – nTopRect* and the width of the figure is *nRightRect – nLeftRect*.

Both the width and the height of a rectangle must be greater than 2 units and less than 32,767 units.

Example   The following example uses a **RECT** structure to store the coordinates used by the **Rectangle** function:

```
HDC hdc;

RECT rc = { 10, 10, 180, 140 };
Rectangle(hdc, rc.left, rc.top,
    rc.right, rc.bottom);
```

See Also   **PolyLine**, **RoundRect**

RectInRegion   3.0

BOOL RectInRegion(*hrgn*, *lprc*)
HRGN *hrgn*;   /* handle of region   */
const RECT FAR* *lprc*;   /* address of structure with rectangle   */

The **RectInRegion** function determines whether any part of the specified rectangle is within the boundaries of the given region.

Parameters   *hrgn*
Identifies the region.

lprc
Points to a **RECT** structure containing the coordinates of the rectangle. The **RECT** structure has the following form:

```
typedef struct tagRECT {    /* rc */
    int left;
    int top;
    int right;
    int bottom;
} RECT;
```

For a full description of this structure, see the *Microsoft Windows Programmer's Reference, Volume 3.*

Return Value   The return value is nonzero if any part of the specified rectangle lies within the boundaries of the region. Otherwise, it is zero.

Example   The following example uses the **RectInRegion** function to determine whether a specified rectangle is in a region and prints the result:

```
HRGN hrgn;
RECT rc = { 100, 10, 130, 50 };
BOOL fRectIn;
LPSTR lpszOverlap = "Some overlap between rc and region.";
LPSTR lpszNoOverlap = "No common points in rc and region.";

fRectIn = RectInRegion(hrgn, &rc);
if (!fRectIn)
    TextOut(hdc, 10, 10, lpszNoOverlap, lstrlen(lpszNoOverlap));
else
    TextOut(hdc, 10, 10, lpszOverlap, lstrlen(lpszOverlap));
```

See Also   **PtInRegion**

RectVisible   2.x

BOOL RectVisible(*hdc, lprc***)**
HDC *hdc*;   /* handle of device context   */
const RECT FAR* *lprc*;   /* address of structure with rectangle   */

The **RectVisible** function determines whether any part of the specified rectangle lies within the clipping region of the given device context.

Parameters   *hdc*
    Identifies the device context.

lprc
    Points to a **RECT** structure that contains the logical coordinates of the specified rectangle. The **RECT** structure has the following form:

```
typedef struct tagRECT {    /* rc */
    int left;
    int top;
    int right;
    int bottom;
} RECT;
```

For a full description of this structure, see the *Microsoft Windows Programmer's Reference, Volume 3.*

Return Value

The return value is nonzero if some portion of the rectangle is within the clipping region. Otherwise, it is zero.

Example

The following example paints a clipping region yellow by painting the client area. The **RectVisible** function is called to determine whether a specified rectangle overlaps the clipping region. If there is some overlap, the rectangle is filled by using a red brush. If there is no overlap, text is displayed inside the clipping region. In this case, the rectangle and the region do not overlap, even though they both specify 110 as a boundary on the y-axis, because regions are defined as including the pixels up to but not including the specified right and bottom coordinates.

```
RECT rc, rcVis;
HRGN hrgn;
HBRUSH hbrRed, hbrYellow;

GetClientRect(hwnd, &rc);
hrgn = CreateRectRgn(10, 10, 310, 110);
SelectClipRgn(hdc, hrgn);

hbrYellow = CreateSolidBrush(RGB(255, 255, 0));
FillRect(hdc, &rc, hbrYellow);

SetRect(&rcVis, 10, 110, 310, 300);
if (RectVisible(hdc, &rcVis)) {
    hbrRed = CreateSolidBrush(RGB(255, 0, 0));
    FillRect(hdc, &rcVis, hbrRed);
    DeleteObject(hbrRed);
}
else {
    SetBkColor(hdc, RGB(255, 255, 0));
    TextOut(hdc, 20, 50, "Rectangle outside clipping region.", 34);
}

DeleteObject(hbrYellow);
DeleteObject(hrgn);
```

See Also

CreateRectRgn, PtVisible, SelectClipRgn

RedrawWindow

BOOL RedrawWindow(*hwnd*, *lprcUpdate*, *hrgnUpdate*, *fuRedraw*)
HWND *hwnd*;   /* handle of window   */
const RECT FAR* *lprcUpdate*;   /* address of structure with update rect.   */
HRGN *hrgnUpdate*;   /* handle of update region   */
UINT *fuRedraw*;   /* redraw flags   */

The **RedrawWindow** function updates the specified rectangle or region in the given window's client area.

Parameters

hwnd
Identifies the window to be redrawn. If this parameter is NULL, the desktop window is updated.

lprcUpdate
Points to a **RECT** structure containing the coordinates of the update rectangle. This parameter is ignored if the *hrgnUpdate* parameter contains a valid region handle. The **RECT** structure has the following form:

```
typedef struct tagRECT {    /* rc */
    int left;
    int top;
    int right;
    int bottom;
} RECT;
```

For a full description of this structure, see the *Microsoft Windows Programmer's Reference, Volume 3*.

hrgnUpdate
Identifies the update region. If both the *hrgnUpdate* and *lprcUpdate* parameters are NULL, the entire client area is added to the update region.

fuRedraw
Specifies one or more redraw flags. This parameter can be a combination of flags:

The following flags are used to invalidate the window:

Value	Meaning
RDW_ERASE	Causes the window to receive a WM_ERASEBKGND message when the window is repainted. The RDW_INVALIDATE flag must also be specified; otherwise, RDW_ERASE has no effect.

Value	Meaning
RDW_FRAME	Causes any part of the non-client area of the window that intersects the update region to receive a WM_NCPAINT message. The RDW_INVALIDATE flag must also be specified; otherwise, RDW_FRAME has no effect. The WM_NCPAINT message is typically not sent during the execution of the **RedrawWindow** function unless either RDW_UPDATENOW or RDW_ERASENOW is specified.
RDW_INTERNALPAINT	Causes a WM_PAINT message to be posted to the window regardless of whether the window contains an invalid region.
RDW_INVALIDATE	Invalidate *lprcUpdate* or *hrgnUpdate* (only one may be non-NULL). If both are NULL, the entire window is invalidated.

The following flags are used to validate the window:

Value	Meaning
RDW_NOERASE	Suppresses any pending WM_ERASEBKGND messages.
RDW_NOFRAME	Suppresses any pending WM_NCPAINT messages. This flag must be used with RDW_VALIDATE and is typically used with RDW_NOCHILDREN. This option should be used with care, as it could cause parts of a window from painting properly.
RDW_NOINTERNALPAINT	Suppresses any pending internal WM_PAINT messages. This flag does not affect WM_PAINT messages resulting from invalid areas.
RDW_VALIDATE	Validates *lprcUpdate* or *hrgnUpdate* (only one may be non-NULL). If both are NULL, the entire window is validated. This flag does not affect internal WM_PAINT messages.

The following flags control when repainting occurs. No painting is performed by the **RedrawWindow** function unless one of these bits is specified.

Value	Meaning
RDW_ERASENOW	Causes the affected windows (as specified by the RDW_ALLCHILDREN and RDW_NOCHILDREN flags) to receive WM_NCPAINT and WM_ERASEBKGND messages, if necessary, before the function returns. WM_PAINT messages are deferred.

Value	Meaning
RDW_UPDATENOW	Causes the affected windows (as specified by the RDW_ALLCHILDREN and RDW_NOCHILDREN flags) to receive WM_NCPAINT, WM_ERASEBKGND, and WM_PAINT messages, if necessary, before the function returns.

By default, the windows affected by the **RedrawWindow** function depend on whether the specified window has the WS_CLIPCHILDREN style. The child windows of WS_CLIPCHILDREN windows are not affected; however, non-WS_CLIPCHILDREN windows are recursively validated or invalidated until a WS_CLIPCHILDREN window is encountered. The following flags control which windows are affected by the **RedrawWindow** function:

Value	Meaning
RDW_ALLCHILDREN	Includes child windows, if any, in the repainting operation.
RDW_NOCHILDREN	Excludes child windows, if any, from the repainting operation.

Return Value   The return value is nonzero if the function is successful. Otherwise, it is zero.

Comments   When the **RedrawWindow** function is used to invalidate part of the desktop window, the desktop window does not receive a WM_PAINT message. To repaint the desktop, an application should use the RDW_ERASE flag to generate a WM_ERASEBKGND message.

See Also   **GetUpdateRect, GetUpdateRgn, InvalidateRect, InvalidateRgn, UpdateWindow**

RegCloseKey   3.1

#include <shellapi.h>

LONG RegCloseKey(*hkey*)
HKEY *hkey*;   /* handle of key to close   */

The **RegCloseKey** function closes a key. Closing a key releases the key's handle. When all keys are closed, the registration database is updated.

Parameters   *hkey*
Identifies the open key to close.

Return Value   The return value is ERROR_SUCCESS if the function is successful. Otherwise, it
                            is an error value.

Comments   The **RegCloseKey** function should be called only if a key has been opened by
                            either the **RegOpenKey** function or the **RegCreateKey** function. The handle for a
                            given key should not be used after it has been closed, because it may no longer be
                            valid. Key handles should not be left open any longer than necessary.

Example   The following example uses the **RegCreateKey** function to create the handle of a
                            protocol, uses the **RegSetValue** function to set up the subkeys of the protocol, and
                            then calls **RegCloseKey** to save the information in the database:

```
HKEY hkProtocol;

if (RegCreateKey(HKEY_CLASSES_ROOT,                /* root               */
    "NewAppDocument\\protocol\\StdFileEditing", /* protocol string */
    &hkProtocol) != ERROR_SUCCESS)                 /* protocol key handle */
        return FALSE;

RegSetValue(hkProtocol,              /* handle of protocol key      */
    "server",                        /* name of subkey              */
    REG_SZ,                          /* required                    */
    "newapp.exe",                    /* command to activate server  */
    10);                             /* text string size            */

RegSetValue(hkProtocol,              /* handle of protocol  key     */
    "verb\\0",                       /* name of subkey              */
    REG_SZ,                          /* required                    */
    "EDIT",                          /* server should edit object   */
    4);                              /* text string size            */

RegCloseKey(hkProtocol);       /* closes protocol key and subkeys   */
```

See Also   **RegCreateKey, RegDeleteKey, RegOpenKey, RegSetValue**

RegCreateKey   3.1

#include <shellapi.h>

LONG RegCreateKey(_hkey, lpszSubKey, lphkResult_**)**
HKEY _hkey_;   /* handle of an open key   */
LPCSTR _lpszSubKey_;   /* address of string for subkey to open   */
HKEY FAR* _lphkResult_;   /* address of handle of open key   */

The **RegCreateKey** function creates the specified key. If the key already exists in the registration database, **RegCreateKey** opens it.

Parameters

hkey
Identifies an open key (which can be HKEY_CLASSES_ROOT). The key opened or created by the **RegCreateKey** function is a subkey of the key identified by the *hkey* parameter. This value should not be NULL.

lpszSubKey
Points to a null-terminated string specifying the subkey to open or create.

lphkResult
Points to the handle of the key that is opened or created.

Return Value

The return value is ERROR_SUCCESS if the function is successful. Otherwise, it is an error value.

Comments

An application can create keys that are subordinate to the top level of the database by specifying HKEY_CLASSES_ROOT for the *hKey* parameter. An application can use the **RegCreateKey** function to create several keys at once. For example, an application could create a subkey four levels deep and the three preceding subkeys by specifying a string of the following form for the *lpszSubKey* parameter:

subkey1\subkey2\subkey3\subkey4

Example

The following example uses the **RegCreateKey** function to create the handle of a protocol, uses the **RegSetValue** function to set up the subkeys of the protocol, and then calls **RegCloseKey** to save the information in the database:

```
HKEY hkProtocol;

if (RegCreateKey(HKEY_CLASSES_ROOT,               /* root            */
    "NewAppDocument\\protocol\\StdFileEditing", /* protocol string */
    &hkProtocol) != ERROR_SUCCESS)              /* protocol key handle */
        return FALSE;

RegSetValue(hkProtocol,         /* handle of protocol key    */
    "server",                   /* name of subkey            */
    REG_SZ,                     /* required                  */
    "newapp.exe",               /* command to activate server */
    10);                        /* text string size          */

RegSetValue(hkProtocol,         /* handle of protocol key    */
    "verb\\0",                  /* name of subkey            */
    REG_SZ,                     /* required                  */
    "EDIT",                     /* server should edit object */
    4);                         /* text string size          */

RegCloseKey(hkProtocol);        /* closes protocol key and subkeys  */
```

See Also   **RegCloseKey**, **RegOpenKey**, **RegSetValue**

RegDeleteKey   3.1

#include <shellapi.h>

LONG RegDeleteKey(*hkey*, *lpszSubKey*)
HKEY *hkey*;   /* handle of an open key   */
LPCSTR *lpszSubKey*;   /* address of string for subkey to delete   */

The **RegDeleteKey** function deletes the specified key. When a key is deleted, its value and all of its subkeys are deleted.

Parameters   *hkey*
Identifies an open key (which can be HKEY_CLASSES_ROOT). The key deleted by the **RegDeleteKey** function is a subkey of this key.

lpszSubKey
Points to a null-terminated string specifying the subkey to delete. This value should not be NULL.

Return Value   The return value is ERROR_SUCCESS if the function is successful. Otherwise, it is an error value.

If the error value is ERROR_ACCESS_DENIED, either the application does not have delete privileges for the specified key or another application has opened the specified key.

Example   The following example uses the **RegQueryValue** function to retrieve the name of an object handler and then calls the **RegDeleteKey** function to delete the key if its value is nwappobj.dll:

```
char szBuff[80];
LONG cb;
HKEY hkStdFileEditing;

if (RegOpenKey(HKEY_CLASSES_ROOT,
        "NewAppDocument\\protocol\\StdFileEditing",
        &hkStdFileEditing) == ERROR_SUCCESS) {

    cb = sizeof(szBuff);
```

```
if (RegQueryValue(hkStdFileEditing,
            "handler",
            szBuff,
            &cb) == ERROR_SUCCESS
            && lstrcmpi("nwappobj.dll", szBuff) == 0)
        RegDeleteKey(hkStdFileEditing, "handler");
    RegCloseKey(hkStdFileEditing);
}
```

See Also   **RegCloseKey**

RegEnumKey   3.1

#include <shellapi.h>

LONG RegEnumKey(*hkey, iSubkey, lpszBuffer, cbBuffer*)
HKEY *hkey*;   /* handle of key to query   */
DWORD *iSubkey*;   /* index of subkey to query   */
LPSTR *lpszBuffer*;   /* address of buffer for subkey string */
DWORD *cbBuffer*;   /* size of subkey buffer   */

The **RegEnumKey** function enumerates the subkeys of a specified key.

Parameters   *hkey*
                       Identifies an open key (which can be HKEY_CLASSES_ROOT) for which sub-
                       key information is retrieved.

                       iSubkey
                       Specifies the index of the subkey to retrieve. This value should be zero for the
                       first call to the **RegEnumKey** function.

                       lpszBuffer
                       Points to a buffer that contains the name of the subkey when the function
                       returns. This function copies only the name of the subkey, not the full key
                       hierarchy, to the buffer.

                       cbBuffer
                       Specifies the size, in bytes, of the buffer pointed to by the *lpszBuffer* parameter.

Return Value   The return value is ERROR_SUCCESS if the function is successful. Otherwise, it
                       is an error value.

Comments   The first parameter of the **RegEnumKey** function must specify an open key. Ap-
                       plications typically precede the call to the **RegEnumKey** function with a call to
                       the **RegOpenKey** function and follow it with a call to the **RegCloseKey** function.

Calling **RegOpenKey** and **RegCloseKey** is not necessary when the first parameter is HKEY_CLASSES_ROOT, because this key is always open and available; however, calling **RegOpenKey** and **RegCloseKey** in this case is a time optimization. While an application is using the **RegEnumKey** function, it should not make calls to any registration functions that might change the key being queried.

To enumerate subkeys, an application should initially set the *iSubkey* parameter to zero and then increment it on successive calls.

Example

The following example uses the **RegEnumKey** function to put the values associated with top-level keys into a list box:

```
HKEY hkRoot;
char szBuff[80], szValue[80];
static DWORD dwIndex;
LONG cb;

if (RegOpenKey(HKEY_CLASSES_ROOT, NULL, &hkRoot) == ERROR_SUCCESS) {
    for (dwIndex = 0; RegEnumKey(hkRoot, dwIndex, szBuff,
            sizeof(szBuff)) == ERROR_SUCCESS; ++dwIndex) {
        if (*szBuff == '.')
            continue;
        cb = sizeof(szValue);
        if (RegQueryValue(hkRoot, (LPSTR) szBuff, szValue,
                &cb) == ERROR_SUCCESS)
            SendDlgItemMessage(hDlg, ID_ENUMLIST, LB_ADDSTRING, 0,
                (LONG) (LPSTR) szValue);
    }
    RegCloseKey(hkRoot);
}
```

See Also   **RegQueryValue**

RegisterClass   `2.x`

ATOM RegisterClass(*lpwc*)
const WNDCLASS FAR* *lpwc*;   /* address of structure with class data   */

The **RegisterClass** function registers a window class for subsequent use in calls to the **CreateWindow** or **CreateWindowEx** function.

Parameters

lpwc

Points to a **WNDCLASS** structure. The structure must be filled with the appropriate class attributes before being passed to the function. The **WNDCLASS** structure has the following form:

```
typedef struct tagWNDCLASS {      /* wc */
    UINT       style;
    WNDPROC    lpfnWndProc;
    int        cbClsExtra;
    int        cbWndExtra;
    HINSTANCE  hInstance;
    HICON      hIcon;
    HCURSOR    hCursor;
    HBRUSH     hbrBackground;
    LPCSTR     lpszMenuName;
    LPCSTR     lpszClassName;
} WNDCLASS;
```

For a full description of this structure, see the *Microsoft Windows Programmer's Reference, Volume 3*.

Return Value

The return value is an atom that uniquely identifies the class being registered. For Windows versions 3.0 and earlier, the return value is nonzero if the function is successful or zero if an error occurs.

Comments

An application cannot register a global class if either a global class or a task-specific class already exists with the given name.

An application can register a task-specific class with the same name as a global class. The task-specific class overrides the global class for the current task only. A task cannot register two local classes with the same name. However, two different tasks can register task-specific classes using the same name.

Example

The following example registers a window class, then creates a window of that class:

```
WNDCLASS wc;
HINSTANCE hinst;
char szMyClass[] = "MyClass";
HWND hwndMyWindow;

/* Register the window class. */

wc.style          = 0;
wc.lpfnWndProc    = MyWndProc;
wc.cbClsExtra     = 0;
wc.cbWndExtra     = 0;
wc.hInstance      = hinst;
wc.hIcon          = LoadIcon(hinst, "MyIcon");
wc.hCursor        = LoadCursor(NULL, IDC_ARROW);
wc.hbrBackground  = (HBRUSH) (COLOR_WINDOW + 1);
wc.lpszMenuName   = (LPCSTR) NULL;
wc.lpszClassName  = szMyClass;
```

```
if (!RegisterClass(&wc))
    return FALSE;

/* Create the window. */

hwndMyWindow = CreateWindow(szMyClass, "MyApp",
    WS_OVERLAPPED | WS_SYSMENU, CW_USEDEFAULT, 0,
    CW_USEDEFAULT, 0, NULL, NULL,
    hinst, NULL );
```

See Also   **CreateWindow, CreateWindowEx, GetClassInfo, GetClassName, Unregister-Class, WindowProc**

RegisterClipboardFormat   `2.x`

UINT RegisterClipboardFormat(*lpszFormatName***)**
LPCSTR *lpszFormatName*;   /* address of name string   */

The **RegisterClipboardFormat** function registers a new clipboard format. The registered format can be used in subsequent clipboard functions as a valid format in which to render data, and it will appear in the clipboard's list of formats.

Parameters   *lpszFormatName*
    Points to a null-terminated string that names the new format.

Return Value   The return value indicates the newly registered format. If the identical format name has been registered before, even by a different application, the format's reference count is incremented (increased by one) and the same value is returned as when the format was originally registered. The return value is zero if the format cannot be registered.

Comments   The format value returned by the **RegisterClipboardFormat** function is within the range 0xC000 through 0xFFFF.

See Also   **CountClipboardFormats, EnumClipboardFormats, GetClipboardFormat-Name, GetPriorityClipboardFormat, IsClipboardFormatAvailable**

RegisterWindowMessage

UINT RegisterWindowMessage(*lpsz*)
LPCSTR *lpsz*;   /* address of message string   */

The **RegisterWindowMessage** function defines a new window message that is guaranteed to be unique throughout the system. The returned message value can be used when calling the **SendMessage** or **PostMessage** function.

Parameters   *lpsz*
                  Points to a null-terminated string that specifies the message to be registered.

Return Value   The return value is an unsigned short integer in the range 0xC000 through 0xFFFF if the message is successfully registered. Otherwise, the return value is 0.

Comments   **RegisterWindowMessage** is typically used to register messages for communicating between two cooperating applications.

                  If two different applications register the same message string, the applications return the same message value. The message remains registered until the Windows session ends.

                  Use the **RegisterWindowMessage** function only when more than one application must process the same message. For sending private messages within a window class, an application can use any integer in the range WM_USER through 0x7FFF. (Messages in this range are private to a window class, not to an application. For example, such predefined control classes as BUTTON, EDIT, LISTBOX, and COMBOBOX may use values in this range.)

See Also   **PostAppMessage**, **PostMessage**, **SendMessage**

RegOpenKey

#include <shellapi.h>

LONG RegOpenKey(*hkey*, *lpszSubKey*, *lphkResult*)
HKEY *hkey*;   /* handle of an open key   */
LPCSTR *lpszSubKey*;   /* address of string for subkey to open */
HKEY FAR* *lphkResult*;   /* address of handle of open key   */

The **RegOpenKey** function opens the specified key.

Parameters	*hkey*
	Identifies an open key (which can be HKEY_CLASSES_ROOT). The key opened by the **RegOpenKey** function is a subkey of the key identified by this parameter. This value should not be NULL.
	lpszSubKey
	Points to a null-terminated string specifying the name of the subkey to open.
	lphkResult
	Points to the handle of the key that is opened.

Return Value   The return value is ERROR_SUCCESS if the function is successful. Otherwise, it is an error value.

Comments   Unlike the **RegCreateKey** function, the **RegOpenKey** function does not create the specified key if the key does not exist in the database.

Example   The following example uses the **RegOpenKey** function to retrieve the handle of the StdFileEditing subkey, calls the **RegQueryValue** function to retrieve the name of an object handler, and then calls the **RegDeleteKey** function to delete the key if its value is nwappobj.dll:

```
char szBuff[80];
LONG cb;
HKEY hkStdFileEditing;

if (RegOpenKey(HKEY_CLASSES_ROOT,
        "NewAppDocument\\protocol\\StdFileEditing",
        &hkStdFileEditing) == ERROR_SUCCESS) {

    cb = sizeof(szBuff);
    if (RegQueryValue(hkStdFileEditing,
            "handler",
            szBuff,
            &cb) == ERROR_SUCCESS
            && lstrcmpi("nwappobj.dll", szBuff) == 0)
        RegDeleteKey(hkStdFileEditing, "handler");
    RegCloseKey(hkStdFileEditing);
}
```

See Also   **RegCreateKey**

RegQueryValue

#include <shellapi.h>

LONG RegQueryValue(*hkey***,** *lpszSubKey***,** *lpszValue***,** *lpcb***)**
HKEY *hkey***;**   /* handle of key to query   */
LPCSTR *lpszSubKey***;**   /* address of string for subkey to query   */
LPSTR *lpszValue***;**   /* address of buffer for returned string   */
LONG FAR* *lpcb***;**   /* address of buffer for size of returned string */

The **RegQueryValue** function retrieves the text string associated with a specified key.

Parameters

hkey
Identifies a currently open key (which can be HKEY_CLASSES_ROOT). This value should not be NULL.

lpszSubKey
Points to a null-terminated string specifying the name of the subkey of the *hkey* parameter for which a text string is retrieved. If this parameter is NULL or points to an empty string, the function retrieves the value of the *hkey* parameter.

lpszValue
Points to a buffer that contains the text string when the function returns.

lpcb
Points to a variable specifying the size, in bytes, of the buffer pointed to by the *lpszValue* parameter. When the function returns, this variable contains the size of the string copied to *lpszValue*, including the null-terminating character.

Return Value

The return value is ERROR_SUCCESS if the function is successful. Otherwise, it is an error value.

Example

The following example uses the **RegOpenKey** function to retrieve the handle of the StdFileEditing subkey, calls the **RegQueryValue** function to retrieve the name of an object handler and then calls the **RegDeleteKey** function to delete the key if its value is nwappobj.dll:

```
char szBuff[80];
LONG cb;
HKEY hkStdFileEditing;

if (RegOpenKey(HKEY_CLASSES_ROOT,
        "NewAppDocument\\protocol\\StdFileEditing",
        &hkStdFileEditing) == ERROR_SUCCESS) {

    cb = sizeof(szBuff);
```

```
if (RegQueryValue(hkStdFileEditing,
        "handler",
        szBuff,
        &cb) == ERROR_SUCCESS
        && lstrcmpi("nwappobj.dll", szBuff) == 0)
    RegDeleteKey(hkStdFileEditing, "handler");
  RegCloseKey(hkStdFileEditing);                '
}
```

See Also   **RegEnumKey**

RegSetValue   `3.1`

#include <shellapi.h>

LONG RegSetValue(*hkey, lpszSubKey, fdwType, lpszValue, cb***)**
HKEY *hkey*;	/* handle of key	*/
LPCSTR *lpszSubKey*;	/* address of string for subkey	*/
DWORD *fdwType*;	/* must be REG_SZ	*/
LPCSTR *lpszValue*;	/* address of string for key	*/
DWORD *cb*;	/* ignored	*/

The **RegSetValue** function associates a text string with a specified key.

Parameters   *hkey*
Identifies a currently open key (which can be HKEY_CLASSES_ROOT). This
value should not be NULL.

lpszSubKey
Points to a null-terminated string specifying the subkey of the *hkey* parameter
with which a text string is associated. If this parameter is NULL or points to an
empty string, the function sets the value of the *hkey* parameter.

fdwType
Specifies the string type. For Windows version 3.1, this value must be REG_SZ.

lpszValue
Points to a null-terminated string specifying the text string to set for the given
key.

cb
Specifies the size, in bytes, of the string pointed to by the *lpszValue* parameter.
For Windows version 3.1, this value is ignored.

Return Value   The return value is ERROR_SUCCESS if the function is successful. Otherwise, it
is an error value.

Comments   If the key specified by the *lpszSubKey* parameter does not exist, the **RegSetValue** function creates it.

Example   The following example uses the **RegSetValue** function to register a filename extension and its associated class name:

```
RegSetValue(HKEY_CLASSES_ROOT,  /* root                          */
    ".XXX",                      /* string for filename extension */
    REG_SZ,                      /* required                      */
    "NewAppDocument",            /* class name for extension      */
    14);                         /* size of text string           */

RegSetValue(HKEY_CLASSES_ROOT,  /* root                          */
    "NewAppDocument",            /* string for class-definition key */
    REG_SZ,                      /* required                      */
    "New Application",           /* text description of class     */
    15);                         /* size of text string           */
```

See Also   **RegCreateKey**, **RegQueryValue**

ReleaseCapture   2.x

void ReleaseCapture(void)

The **ReleaseCapture** function releases the mouse capture and restores normal input processing. A window with the mouse capture receives all mouse input regardless of the position of the cursor.

Parameters   This function has no parameters.

Return Value   This function does not return a value.

Comments   An application calls this function after calling the **SetCapture** function.

See Also   **SetCapture**

ReleaseDC

int **ReleaseDC**(*hwnd*, *hdc*)
HWND *hwnd*;   /* handle of window with device context   */
HDC *hdc*;   /* handle of device context   */

> The **ReleaseDC** function releases the given device context, freeing it for use by other applications.

Parameters   *hwnd*
> Identifies the window whose device context is to be released.

hdc
> Identifies the device context to be released.

Return Value   The return value is 1 if the function is successful. Otherwise, it is 0.

Comments   The effect of **ReleaseDC** depends on the type of device context. It frees only common and window device contexts. It has no effect on class or private device contexts.

> The application must call the **ReleaseDC** function for each call to the **Get-WindowDC** function and for each call to the **GetDC** function that retrieves a common device context.

See Also   **BeginPaint**, **EndPaint**, **GetDC**, **GetWindowDC**

RemoveFontResource

BOOL RemoveFontResource(*lpszFile*)
LPCSTR *lpszFile*;   /* address of string for filename   */

> The **RemoveFontResource** function removes an added font resource from the specified file or from the Windows font table.

Parameters   *lpszFile*
> Points to a string that names the font resource file or contains a handle of a loaded module. If this parameter points to the font resource file, the string must be null-terminated and have the MS-DOS filename format. If the parameter contains a handle, the handle must be in the low-order word and the high-order word must be zero.

Return Value   The return value is nonzero if the function is successful. Otherwise, it is zero.

Comments   Any application that adds or removes fonts from the Windows font table should send a WM_FONTCHANGE message to all top-level windows in the system by using the **SendMessage** function with the *hwnd* parameter set to 0xFFFF.

In some cases, the **RemoveFontResource** function may not remove the font resource immediately. If there are outstanding references to the resource, it remains loaded until the last logical font using it has been removed (deleted) by using the **DeleteObject** function.

Example   The following example uses the **AddFontResource** function to add a font resource from a file, notifies other applications by using the **SendMessage** function, then removes the font resource by calling the **RemoveFontResource** function:

```
AddFontResource("fontres.fon");
SendMessage(HWND_BROADCAST, WM_FONTCHANGE, 0, 0);
    .
    . /* Work with the font. */
    .
if (RemoveFontResource("fontres.fon")) {
    SendMessage(HWND_BROADCAST, WM_FONTCHANGE, 0, 0);
    return TRUE;
}
else
    return FALSE;
```

See Also   **AddFontResource, DeleteObject, SendMessage**

RemoveMenu   3.0

BOOL RemoveMenu(*hmenu*, *idItem*, *fuFlags*)
HMENU *hmenu*;   /* handle of menu   */
UINT *idItem*;   /* menu item to delete   */
UINT *fuFlags*;   /* menu flags   */

The **RemoveMenu** function deletes a menu item with an associated pop-up menu from a menu but does not destroy the handle of the pop-up menu, allowing the menu to be reused. Before calling this function, an application should call the **Get-SubMenu** function to retrieve the pop-up menu handle.

Parameters   *hmenu*
    Identifies the menu to be changed.

idItem
Specifies the menu item to be removed, as determined by the *fuFlags* parameter.

fuFlags
Specifies how the *idItem* parameter is to be interpreted. This parameter can be one of the following values:

Value	Meaning
MF_BYCOMMAND	The *idItem* parameter specifies the menu-item identifier.
MF_BYPOSITION	The *idItem* parameter specifies the zero-based position of the menu item.

Return Value
The return value is nonzero if the function is successful. Otherwise it is zero.

Comments
Whenever a menu changes (whether or not it is in a window that is displayed), the application should call the **DrawMenuBar** function.

See Also
AppendMenu, **CreateMenu**, **DeleteMenu**, **DrawMenuBar**, **GetSubMenu**, **InsertMenu**

RemoveProp

2.x

HANDLE RemoveProp(*hwnd*, *lpsz*)
HWND *hwnd*;   /* handle of window   */
LPCSTR *lpsz*;   /* atom or address of string */

The **RemoveProp** function removes an entry from the property list of the given window. The **RemoveProp** function returns a data handle so that the application can free the data associated with the handle.

Parameters
hwnd
Identifies the window whose property list is to be changed.

lpsz
Points to a null-terminated string or an atom that identifies a string. If an atom is given, it must be a global atom created by a previous call to the **GlobalAdd-Atom** function. The atom, a 16-bit value, must be placed in the low-order word of this parameter; the high-order word must be zero.

Return Value
The return value is the handle of the given string if the function is successful. Otherwise, it is NULL—for example, if the string cannot be found in the given property list.

Comments	An application can remove only those properties it has added. It should not remove properties added by other applications or by Windows itself.

An application must free the data handles associated with entries removed from a property list. The application should remove only those properties it added to the property list.

See Also   **GetProp**, **GlobalAddAtom**

ReplaceText   3.1

#include <commdlg.h>

HWND ReplaceText(*lpfr***)**
FINDREPLACE FAR* *lpfr*;   /* address of structure with initialization data   */

The **ReplaceText** function creates a system-defined modeless dialog box that makes it possible for the user to find and replace text within a document. The application must perform the actual find and replace operations.

Parameters   *lpfr*
Points to a **FINDREPLACE** structure that contains information used to initialize the dialog box. When the user makes a selection in the dialog box, the system fills this structure with information about the user's selection and then sends a message to the application. This message contains a pointer to the **FINDREPLACE** structure.

The **FINDREPLACE** structure has the following form:

```
#include <commdlg.h>

typedef struct tagFINDREPLACE {      /* fr */
    DWORD     lStructSize;
    HWND      hwndOwner;
    HINSTANCE hInstance;
    DWORD     Flags;
    LPSTR     lpstrFindWhat;
    LPSTR     lpstrReplaceWith;
    UINT      wFindWhatLen;
    UINT      wReplaceWithLen;
    LPARAM    lCustData;
    UINT      (CALLBACK* lpfnHook)(HWND, UINT, WPARAM, LPARAM);
    LPCSTR    lpTemplateName;
} FINDREPLACE;
```

For a full description of this structure, see the *Microsoft Windows Programmer's Reference, Volume 3*.

Return Value The return value is the window handle of the dialog box, or it is NULL if an error occurs. An application can use this handle to communicate with or to close the dialog box.

Errors Use the **CommDlgExtendedError** function to retrieve the error value, which may be one of the following:

CDERR_FINDRESFAILURE
CDERR_INITIALIZATION
CDERR_LOADRESFAILURE
CDERR_LOADSTRFAILURE
CDERR_LOCKRESFAILURE
CDERR_MEMALLOCFAILURE
CDERR_MEMLOCKFAILURE
CDERR_NOHINSTANCE
CDERR_NOHOOK
CDERR_NOTEMPLATE
CDERR_STRUCTSIZE
FRERR_BUFFERLENGTHZERO

Comments The dialog box procedure for the **ReplaceText** function passes user requests to the application through special messages. The *lParam* parameter of each of these messages contains a pointer to a **FINDREPLACE** structure. The procedure sends the messages to the window identified by the **hwndOwner** member of the **FINDREPLACE** structure. An application can register the identifier for these messages by specifying the commdlg_FindReplace string in a call to the **RegisterWindowMessage** function.

For the TAB key to function correctly, any application that calls the **ReplaceText** function must also call the **IsDialogMessage** function in its main message loop. (The **IsDialogMessage** function returns a value that indicates whether messages are intended for the Replace dialog box.)

Example This example initializes a **FINDREPLACE** structure and calls the **ReplaceText** function to display the Replace dialog box:

```
static FINDREPLACE fr;
char szFindWhat[256] = "";      /* string to find    */
char szReplaceWith[256] = "";   /* string to replace */

/* Set all structure fields to zero. */

memset(&fr, 0, sizeof(FINDREPLACE));
```

```
                    fr.lStructSize = sizeof(FINDREPLACE);
                    fr.hwndOwner = hwnd;
                    fr.lpstrFindWhat = szFindWhat;
                    fr.wFindWhatLen = sizeof(szFindWhat);
                    fr.lpstrReplaceWith = szReplaceWith;
                    fr.wReplaceWithLen = sizeof(szReplaceWith);

                    hDlg = ReplaceText(&fr);
```

In addition to initializing the members of the **FINDREPLACE** structure and
calling the **ReplaceText** function, an application must register the special
FINDMSGSTRING message and process messages from the dialog box. Refer to
the description of the **FindText** function for an example that shows how an application registers and processes a message.

See Also   **FindText, IsDialogMessage, RegisterWindowMessage**

ReplyMessage   2.x

void ReplyMessage(*lResult***)**
LRESULT *lResult*;   /* message-dependent reply   */

The **ReplyMessage** function is used to reply to a message sent through the **Send-
Message** function without returning control to the function that called **Send-
Message**.

Parameters   *lResult*
                    Specifies the result of the message processing. The possible values depend on
                    the message sent.

Return Value   This function does not return a value.

Comments   By calling this function, the window procedure that receives the message allows
                    the task that called **SendMessage** to continue to run as though the task that re-
                    ceived the message had returned control. The task that calls **ReplyMessage** also
                    continues to run.

                    Usually, a task that calls **SendMessage** to send a message to another task will not
                    continue running until the window procedure that Windows calls to receive the
                    message returns. However, if a task that is called to receive a message must per-
                    form some type of operation that might yield control (such as calling the **Message-
                    Box** or **DialogBox** function), Windows could be deadlocked, as when the sending
                    task must run and process messages but cannot because it is waiting for

SendMessage to return. An application can avoid this problem if the task receiving the message calls **ReplyMessage** before performing any operation that could cause the task to yield.

The **ReplyMessage** function has no effect if the message was not sent through the **SendMessage** function or if the message was sent by the same task.

See Also   **DialogBox**, **MessageBox**, **SendMessage**

ResetDC   `3.1`

#include <print.h>

HDC ResetDC(*hdc*, *lpdm*)
HDC *hdc*;   /* handle of device context   */
const DEVMODE FAR* *lpdm*;   /* address of DEVMODE structure   */

The **ResetDC** function updates the given device context, based on the information in the specified **DEVMODE** structure.

Parameters   *hdc*
Identifies the device context to be updated.

lpdm
Points to a **DEVMODE** structure containing information about the new device context. The **DEVMODE** structure has the following form:

```
#include <print.h>

typedef struct tagDEVMODE {    /* dm */
    char  dmDeviceName[CCHDEVICENAME];
    UINT  dmSpecVersion;
    UINT  dmDriverVersion;
    UINT  dmSize;
    UINT  dmDriverExtra;
    DWORD dmFields;
    int   dmOrientation;
    int   dmPaperSize;
    int   dmPaperLength;
    int   dmPaperWidth;
    int   dmScale;
    int   dmCopies;
    int   dmDefaultSource;
    int   dmPrintQuality;
```

```
    int    dmColor;
    int    dmDuplex;
    int    dmYResolution;
    int    dmTTOption;
} DEVMODE;
```

For a full description of this structure, see the *Microsoft Windows Programmer's Reference, Volume 3*.

Return Value

The return value is the handle of the original device context if the function is successful. Otherwise, it is NULL.

Comments

An application will typically use the **ResetDC** function when a window receives a WM_DEVMODECHANGE message. **ResetDC** can also be used to change the paper orientation or paper bins while printing a document.

The **ResetDC** function cannot be used to change the driver name, device name or the output port. When the user changes the port connection or device name, the application must delete the original device context and create a new device context with the new information.

Before calling **ResetDC**, the application must ensure that all objects (other than stock objects) that had been selected into the device context have been selected out.

See Also

DeviceCapabilities, Escape, ExtDeviceMode

ResizePalette

3.0

BOOL ResizePalette(*hpal, cEntries***)**
HPALETTE *hpal*;   /* handle of palette   */
UINT *cEntries*;   /* number of palette entries after resizing   */

The **ResizePalette** function changes the size of the given logical palette.

Parameters

hpal
Identifies the palette to be changed.

cEntries
Specifies the number of entries in the palette after it has been resized.

Return Value

The return value is nonzero if the function is successful. Otherwise, it is zero.

Comments

If an application calls the **ResizePalette** function to reduce the size of the palette, the entries remaining in the resized palette are unchanged. If the application calls

ResizePalette to enlarge the palette, the additional palette entries are set to black (the red, green, and blue values are all zero) and the flags for all additional entries are set to zero.

RestoreDC

BOOL RestoreDC(*hdc***,** *nSavedDC***)**
HDC *hdc*;   /* handle of device context   */
int *nSavedDC*;   /* integer identifying device context to restore   */

The **RestoreDC** function restores the given device context to a previous state. The device context is restored by popping state information off a stack created by earlier calls to the **SaveDC** function.

Parameters   *hdc*
Identifies the device context.

nSavedDC
Specifies the device context to be restored. This parameter can be a value returned by a previous **SaveDC** function. If the parameter is −1, the most recently saved device context is restored.

Return Value   The return value is nonzero if the function is successful. Otherwise, it is zero.

Comments   The stack can contain the state information for several instances of the device context. If the context specified by the *nSavedDC* parameter is not at the top of the stack, **RestoreDC** deletes all state information between the instance specified by *nSavedDC* and the top of the stack.

Example   The following example uses the **GetMapMode** function to retrieve the mapping mode for the current device context, uses the **SaveDC** function to save the state of the device context, changes the mapping mode, restores the previous state of the device context by using the **RestoreDC** function, and retrieves the mapping mode again. The final mapping mode is the same as the mapping mode prior to the call to the **SaveDC** function.

```
HDC hdcLocal;
int MapMode;
char *aModes[] = {"ZERO", "MM_TEXT", "MM_LOMETRIC", "MM_HIMETRIC",
    "MM_LOENGLISH", "MM_HIENGLISH", "MM_TWIPS",
    "MM_ISOTROPIC", "MM_ANISOTROPIC" };

hdcLocal = GetDC(hwnd);
MapMode = GetMapMode(hdcLocal);
```

```
        TextOut(hdc, 100, 100, (LPSTR) aModes[MapMode],
            lstrlen(aModes[MapMode]));

        SaveDC(hdcLocal);

        SetMapMode(hdcLocal, MM_LOENGLISH);
        MapMode = GetMapMode(hdcLocal);
        TextOut(hdc, 100, 120, (LPSTR) aModes[MapMode],
            lstrlen(aModes[MapMode]));

        RestoreDC(hdcLocal, -1);

        MapMode = GetMapMode(hdcLocal);
        TextOut(hdc, 100, 140, (LPSTR) aModes[MapMode],
            lstrlen(aModes[MapMode]));

        ReleaseDC(hwnd, hdcLocal);
```

See Also   **SaveDC**

RoundRect   2.x

BOOL RoundRect(*hdc, nLeftRect, nTopRect, nRightRect, nBottomRect, nEllipseWidth, nEllipseHeight***)**
HDC *hdc*;   /* handle of device context   */
int *nLeftRect*;   /* x-coordinate upper-left corner   */
int *nTopRect*;   /* y-coordinate upper-left corner   */
int *nRightRect*;   /* x-coordinate lower-right corner   */
int *nBottomRect*;   /* y-coordinate lower-right corner   */
int *nEllipseWidth*; /* width of ellipse for rounded corners */
int *nEllipseHeight*; /* height of ellipse for rounded corners */

The **RoundRect** function draws a rectangle with rounded corners, using the current pen. The interior of the rectangle is filled by using the current brush.

Parameters   *hdc*
Identifies the device context.

nLeftRect
Specifies the logical x-coordinate of the upper-left corner of the rectangle.

nTopRect
Specifies the logical y-coordinate of the upper-left corner of the rectangle.

nRightRect
Specifies the logical x-coordinate of the lower-right corner of the rectangle.

nBottomRect
Specifies the logical y-coordinate of the lower-right corner of the rectangle.

nEllipseWidth
Specifies the width, in logical units, of the ellipse used to draw the rounded corners.

nEllipseHeight
Specifies the height, in logical units, of the ellipse used to draw the rounded corners.

Return Value   The return value is nonzero if the function is successful. Otherwise, it is zero.

Comments   The figure this function draws extends up to but does not include the right and bottom coordinates. This means that the height of the figure is *nBottomRect* – *nTopRect* and the width of the figure is *nRightRect* – *nLeftRect*.

Both the width and the height of a rectangle must be greater than 2 units and less than 32,767 units.

Example   The following example uses a **RECT** structure to store the coordinates used by the **RoundRect** function:

```
HDC hdc;

RECT rc = { 10, 10, 180, 140 };
int iEllipseWidth, iEllipseHeight;

iEllipseWidth = 20;
iEllipseHeight = 40;

RoundRect(hdc, rc.left, rc.top, rc.right, rc.bottom,
    iEllipseWidth, iEllipseHeight);
```

See Also   **Rectangle**

SaveDC

2.x

int SaveDC(*hdc***)**
HDC *hdc*;   /* handle of device context   */

The **SaveDC** function saves the current state of the given device context by copying state information (such as clipping region, selected objects, and mapping mode) to a context stack. The saved device context can later be restored by using the **RestoreDC** function.

Parameters	*hdc* Identifies the device context to be saved.
Return Value	The return value is an integer identifying the saved device context if the function is successful. This integer can be used to restore the device context by calling the **RestoreDC** function. The return value is zero if an error occurs.
Comments	The **SaveDC** function can be used any number of times to save any number of device-context states.
Example	The following example uses the **GetMapMode** function to retrieve the mapping mode for the current device context, uses the **SaveDC** function to save the state of the device context, changes the mapping mode, restores the previous state of the device context by using the **RestoreDC** function, and retrieves the mapping mode again. The final mapping mode is the same as the mapping mode prior to the call to the **SaveDC** function.

```
HDC hdcLocal;
int MapMode;
char *aModes[] = {"ZERO", "MM_TEXT", "MM_LOMETRIC", "MM_HIMETRIC",
    "MM_LOENGLISH", "MM_HIENGLISH", "MM_TWIPS",
    "MM_ISOTROPIC", "MM_ANISOTROPIC" };

hdcLocal = GetDC(hwnd);
MapMode = GetMapMode(hdcLocal);
TextOut(hdc, 100, 100, (LPSTR) aModes[MapMode],
    lstrlen(aModes[MapMode]));

SaveDC(hdcLocal);

SetMapMode(hdcLocal, MM_LOENGLISH);
MapMode = GetMapMode(hdcLocal);
TextOut(hdc, 100, 120, (LPSTR) aModes[MapMode],
    lstrlen(aModes[MapMode]));

RestoreDC(hdcLocal, -1);

MapMode = GetMapMode(hdcLocal);
TextOut(hdc, 100, 140, (LPSTR) aModes[MapMode],
    lstrlen(aModes[MapMode]));

ReleaseDC(hwnd, hdcLocal);
```

See Also	**RestoreDC**

ScaleViewportExt

DWORD ScaleViewportExt(*hdc, nXNum, nXDenom, nYNum, nYDenom*)
HDC *hdc*;   /* handle of device context   */
int *nXNum*;   /* amount by which current x-extent is multiplied   */
int *nXDenom*;   /* amount by which current x-extent is divided   */
int *nYNum*;   /* amount by which current y-extent is multiplied   */
int *nYDenom*;   /* amount by which current y-extent is divided   */

The **ScaleViewportExt** function modifies the viewport extents relative to the current values.

Parameters

hdc
　Identifies the device context.

nXNum
　Specifies the amount by which to multiply the current x-extent.

nXDenom
　Specifies the amount by which to divide the result of multiplying the current x-extent by the value of the *nXNum* parameter.

nYNum
　Specifies the amount by which to multiply the current y-extent.

nYDenom
　Specifies the amount by which to divide the result of multiplying the current y-extent by the value of the *nYNum* parameter.

Return Value

The low-order word of the return value contains the x-extent, in device units, of the previous viewport if the function is successful; the high-order word contains the y-extent.

Comments

The new viewport extents are calculated by multiplying the current extents by the given numerator and then dividing by the given denominator, as shown in the following formulas:

```
nXNewVE = (nXOldVE * nXNum) / nXDenom
nYNewVE = (nYOldVE * nYNum) / nYDenom
```

Example

The following example draws a rectangle that is 4 logical units high and 4 logical units wide. It then calls the **ScaleViewportExt** function and draws a rectangle that is 8 units by 8 units. Because of the viewport scaling, the second rectangle is the same size as the first.

```
HDC  hdc;
RECT rc;

GetClientRect(hwnd, &rc);
hdc = GetDC(hwnd);
SetMapMode(hdc, MM_ANISOTROPIC);

SetWindowExt(hdc, 10, 10);
SetViewportExt(hdc, rc.right, rc.bottom);
Rectangle(hdc, 3, 3, 7, 7);

ScaleViewportExt(hdc, 1, 2, 1, 2);
Rectangle(hdc, 6, 6, 14, 14);

ReleaseDC(hwnd, hdc);
```

See Also   **GetViewportExt**

ScaleViewportExtEx $\boxed{3.1}$

BOOL ScaleViewportExtEx(*hdc, nXnum, nXdenom, nYnum, nYdenom, lpSize***)**
HDC *hdc*;	/* handle of device context	*/
int *nXnum*;	/* amount by which current x-extent is multiplied	*/
int *nXdenom*;	/* amount by which current x-extent is divided	*/
int *nYnum*;	/* amount by which current y-extent is multiplied	*/
int *nYdenom*;	/* amount by which current y-extent is divided	*/
SIZE FAR* *lpSize*;	/* address of SIZE structure	*/

The **ScaleViewportExtEx** function modifies the viewport extents relative to the current values. The formulas are written as follows:

```
xNewVE = (xOldVE * Xnum) / Xdenom
yNewVE = (yOldVE * Ynum) / Ydenom
```

The new extent is calculated by multiplying the current extents by the given numerator and then dividing by the given denominator.

Parameters   *hdc*
     Identifies the device context.

     nXnum
     Specifies the amount by which to multiply the current x-extent.

     nXdenom
     Specifies the amount by which to divide the current x-extent.

nYnum
Specifies the amount by which to multiply the current y-extent.

nYdenom
Specifies the amount by which to divide the current y-extent.

lpSize
Points to a **SIZE** structure. The previous viewport extents, in device units, are placed in this structure. If *lpSize* is NULL, nothing is returned.

Return Value   The return value is nonzero if the function is successful. Otherwise, it is zero.

ScaleWindowExt   2.x

DWORD ScaleWindowExt(*hdc, nXNum, nXDenom, nYNum, nYDenom*)
HDC *hdc*;   /* handle of device context   */
int *nXNum*;   /* amount by which current x-extent is multiplied   */
int *nXDenom*;   /* amount by which current x-extent is divided   */
int *nYNum*;   /* amount by which current y-extent is multiplied   */
int *nYDenom*;   /* amount by which current y-extent is divided   */

The **ScaleWindowExt** function modifies the window extents relative to the current values.

Parameters   *hdc*
Identifies the device context.

nXNum
Specifies the amount by which to multiply the current x-extent.

nXDenom
Specifies the amount by which to divide the result of multiplying the current x-extent by the value of the *nXNum* parameter.

nYNum
Specifies the amount by which to multiply the current y-extent.

nYDenom
Specifies the amount by which to divide the result of multiplying the current y-extent by the value of the *nYNum* parameter.

Return Value   The low-order word of the return value contains the x-extent, in logical units, of the previous window, if the function is successful; the high-order word contains the y-extent.

Comments

The new window extents are calculated by multiplying the current extents by the given numerator and then dividing by the given denominator, as shown in the following formulas:

```
nXNewWE = (nXOldWE * nXNum) / nXDenom
nYNewWE = (nYOldWE * nYNum) / nYDenom
```

Example

The following example draws a rectangle that is 4 logical units high and 4 logical units wide. It then calls the **ScaleWindowExt** function and draws a rectangle that is 8 units by 8 units. Because of the window scaling, the second rectangle is the same size as the first.

```
HDC  hdc;
RECT rc;

GetClientRect(hwnd, &rc);
hdc = GetDC(hwnd);
SetMapMode(hdc, MM_ANISOTROPIC);

SetWindowExt(hdc, 10, 10);
SetViewportExt(hdc, rc.right, rc.bottom);
Rectangle(hdc, 3, 3, 7, 7);

ScaleWindowExt(hdc, 2, 1, 2, 1);
Rectangle(hdc, 6, 6, 14, 14);

ReleaseDC(hwnd, hdc);
```

See Also   **GetWindowExt**

ScaleWindowExtEx   3.1

BOOL ScaleWindowExtEx(*hdc, nXnum, nXdenom, nYnum, nYdenom, lpSize***)**
HDC *hdc*;   /* handle of device context   */
int *nXnum*;   /* amount by which current x-extent is multiplied */
int *nXdenom*;   /* amount by which current x-extent is divided   */
int *nYnum*;   /* amount by which current y-extent is multiplied */
int *nYdenom*;   /* amount by which current y-extent is divided   */
SIZE FAR* *lpSize*;   /* address of SIZE structure   */

The **ScaleWindowExtEx** function modifies the window extents relative to the current values. The formulas are written as follows:

```
xNewWE = (xOldWE * Xnum) / Xdenom
yNewWE = (yOldWE * Ynum) / Ydenom
```

The new extent is calculated by multiplying the current extents by the given numerator and then dividing by the given denominator.

Parameters

hdc
Identifies the device context.

nXnum
Specifies the amount by which to multiply the current x-extent.

nXdenom
Specifies the amount by which to divide the current x-extent.

nYnum
Specifies the amount by which to multiply the current y-extent.

nYdenom
Specifies the amount by which to divide the current y-extent.

lpSize
Points to a **SIZE** structure. The previous window extents, in logical units, are placed in this structure. If *lpSize* is NULL, nothing is returned.

Return Value

The return value is nonzero if the function is successful. Otherwise, it is zero.

ScreenToClient

2.x

void ScreenToClient(*hwnd*, *lppt*)
HWND *hwnd*;   /* window handle for source coordinates   */
POINT FAR* *lppt*;   /* address of structure with coordinates   */

The **ScreenToClient** function converts the screen coordinates of a given point on the screen to client coordinates.

Parameters

hwnd
Identifies the window whose client area is to be used for the conversion.

lppt
Points to a **POINT** structure that contains the screen coordinates to be converted. The **POINT** structure has the following form:

```
typedef struct tagPOINT {   /* pt */
    int x;
    int y;
} POINT;
```

For a full description of this structure, see the *Microsoft Windows Programmer's Reference, Volume 3*.

Return Value   This function does not return a value.

Comments   The **ScreenToClient** function replaces the screen coordinates in the **POINT** structure with client coordinates. The new coordinates are relative to the upper-left corner of the given window's client area.

Example   The following example uses the **GetWindowRect** function to retrieve the screen coordinates for a specified window, calls the **ScreenToClient** function to convert the upper-left and lower-right corners of the window rectangle to client coordinates, and then reports the results in a message box:

```
RECT  rc;            /* window's screen coordinates      */
POINT ptUpperLeft;   /* client coordinate of upper left  */
POINT ptLowerRight;  /* client coordinate of lower right */
char  szText[128];   /* char buffer for wsprintf         */

GetWindowRect(hwnd, &rc);

ptUpperLeft.x  = rc.left;
ptUpperLeft.y  = rc.top;
ptLowerRight.x = rc.right;
ptLowerRight.y = rc.bottom;

ScreenToClient(hwnd, &ptUpperLeft );
ScreenToClient(hwnd, &ptLowerRight);

wsprintf(szText,
    "S: (%d,%d)-(%d,%d) --> C: (%d,%d)-(%d,%d)",
    rc.left, rc.top, rc.right, rc.bottom,
    ptUpperLeft.x, ptUpperLeft.y, ptLowerRight.x, ptLowerRight.y);

MessageBox(hwnd, szText, "ScreenToClient", MB_OK);
```

See Also   **ClientToScreen, MapWindowPoints**

ScrollDC   2.x

BOOL ScrollDC(*hdc, dx, dy, lprcScroll, lprcClip, hrgnUpdate, lprcUpdate*)
HDC *hdc*;	/* handle of device context	*/
int *dx*;	/* horizontal scroll units	*/
int *dy*;	/* vertical scroll units	*/
const RECT FAR* *lprcScroll*;	/* address of scrolling rectangle	*/
const RECT FAR* *lprcClip*;	/* address of clipping rectangle	*/
HRGN *hrgnUpdate*;	/* handle of scrolling region	*/
RECT FAR* *lprcUpdate*;	/* address of structure for update rect.	*/

The **ScrollDC** function scrolls a rectangle of bits horizontally and vertically.

Parameters

hdc
Identifies the device context that contains the bits to be scrolled.

dx
Specifies the number of horizontal scroll units.

dy
Specifies the number of vertical scroll units.

lprcScroll
Points to the **RECT** structure that contains the coordinates of the scrolling rectangle. The **RECT** structure has the following form:

```
typedef struct tagRECT {    /* rc */
    int left;
    int top;
    int right;
    int bottom;
} RECT;
```

For a full description of this structure, see the *Microsoft Windows Programmer's Reference, Volume 3.*

lprcClip
Points to the **RECT** structure that contains the coordinates of the clipping rectangle. When this rectangle is smaller than the original one pointed to by the *lprcScroll* parameter, scrolling occurs only in the smaller rectangle.

hrgnUpdate
Identifies the region uncovered by the scrolling process. The **ScrollDC** function defines this region; it is not necessarily a rectangle.

lprcUpdate
Points to the **RECT** structure that receives the coordinates of the rectangle that bounds the scrolling update region. This is the largest rectangular area that requires repainting. The values in the structure when the function returns are in client coordinates, regardless of the mapping mode for the given device context.

Return Value

The return value is nonzero if the function is successful. Otherwise, it is zero.

Comments

If the *lprcUpdate* parameter is NULL, Windows does not compute the update rectangle. If both the *hrgnUpdate* and *lprcUpdate* parameters are NULL, Windows does not compute the update region. If *hrgnUpdate* is not NULL, Windows assumes that it contains a valid handle of the region uncovered by the scrolling process (defined by the **ScrollDC** function).

When the **ScrollDC** function returns, the values in the structure pointed to by the *lprcUpdate* parameter are in client coordinates. This allows applications to use the update region in a call to the **InvalidateRgn** function, if required.

An application should use the **ScrollWindow** function when it is necessary to scroll the entire client area of a window; otherwise, it should use **ScrollDC**.

See Also   **InvalidateRgn**, **ScrollWindow**, **ScrollWindowEx**

ScrollWindow
2.x

void ScrollWindow(*hwnd*, *dx*, *dy*, *lprcScroll*, *lprcClip*)
HWND *hwnd*;   /* handle of window to scroll   */
int *dx*;   /* amount of horizontal scrolling   */
int *dy*;   /* amount of vertical scrolling   */
const RECT FAR* *lprcScroll*;   /* address of structure with scroll rect. */
const RECT FAR* *lprcClip*;   /* address of structure with clip rect.   */

The **ScrollWindow** function scrolls the contents of a window's client area.

Parameters   *hwnd*
                     Identifies the window to be scrolled.

                     dx
                     Specifies the amount, in device units, of horizontal scrolling. This parameter must be a negative value to scroll to the left.

                     dy
                     Specifies the amount, in device units, of vertical scrolling. This parameter must be a negative value to scroll up.

                     lprcScroll
                     Points to a **RECT** structure that specifies the portion of the client area to be scrolled. If this parameter is NULL, the entire client area is scrolled. The caret is repositioned if the cursor rectangle intersects the scroll rectangle.

                     The **RECT** structure has the following form:

```
typedef struct tagRECT {    /* rc */
    int left;
    int top;
    int right;
    int bottom;
} RECT;
```

                     For a full description of this structure, see the *Microsoft Windows Programmer's Reference, Volume 3*.

                     lprcClip
                     Points to a **RECT** structure that specifies the clipping rectangle to scroll. This structure takes precedence over the rectangle pointed to by *lprcScroll*. Only bits

inside this rectangle are scrolled. Bits outside this rectangle are not scrolled, even if they are in the *lprcScroll* rectangle. If this parameter is NULL, no clipping is performed on the scroll rectangle.

Return Value

This function does not return a value.

Comments

If the caret is in the window being scrolled, **ScrollWindow** automatically hides the caret to prevent it from being erased, then restores the caret after the scroll is finished. The caret position is adjusted accordingly.

The area uncovered by the **ScrollWindow** function is not repainted, but it is combined into the window's update region. The application will eventually receive a WM_PAINT message notifying it that the region needs repainting. To repaint the uncovered area at the same time the scrolling is done, call the **UpdateWindow** function immediately after calling **ScrollWindow**.

If the *lprcScroll* parameter is NULL, the positions of any child windows in the window are offset by the amount specified by the *dx* and *dy* parameters, and any invalid (unpainted) areas in the window are also offset. **ScrollWindow** is faster when *lprcScroll* is NULL.

If the *lprcScroll* parameter is not NULL, the positions of child windows are not changed and invalid areas in the window are not offset. To prevent updating problems when *lprcScroll* is not NULL, call the **UpdateWindow** function to repaint the window before calling **ScrollWindow**.

See Also

ScrollDC, ScrollWindowEx, UpdateWindow

ScrollWindowEx

3.1

```
int ScrollWindowEx(hwnd, dx, dy, lprcScroll, lprcClip, hrgnUpdate, lprcUpdate, fuScroll)
HWND hwnd;                      /* handle of window to scroll            */
int dx;                         /* amount of horizontal scrolling        */
int dy;                         /* amount of vertical scrolling          */
const RECT FAR* lprcScroll;     /* address of structure with scroll rect. */
const RECT FAR* lprcClip;       /* address of structure with clip rect.  */
HRGN hrgnUpdate;                /* handle of update region               */
RECT FAR* lprcUpdate;           /* address of structure for update rect. */
UINT fuScroll;                  /* scrolling flags                       */
```

The **ScrollWindowEx** function scrolls the contents of a window's client area. This function is similar to the **ScrollWindow** function, with some additional features.

Parameters

hwnd
Identifies the window to be scrolled.

dx
Specifies the amount, in device units, of horizontal scrolling. This parameter must be a negative value to scroll to the left.

dy
Specifies the amount, in device units, of vertical scrolling. This parameter must be a negative value to scroll up.

lprcScroll
Points to a **RECT** structure that specifies the portion of the client area to be scrolled. If this parameter is NULL, the entire client area is scrolled. The **RECT** structure has the following form:

```
typedef struct tagRECT {     /* rc */
    int left;
    int top;
    int right;
    int bottom;
} RECT;
```

For a full description of this structure, see the *Microsoft Windows Programmer's Reference, Volume 3*.

lprcClip
Points to a **RECT** structure that specifies the clipping rectangle to scroll. This structure takes precedence over the rectangle pointed to by the *lprcScroll* parameter. Only bits inside this rectangle are scrolled. Bits outside this rectangle are not affected even if they are in the *lprcScroll* rectangle. If this parameter is NULL, no clipping is performed on the scroll rectangle.

hrgnUpdate
Identifies the region that is modified to hold the region invalidated by scrolling. This parameter may be NULL.

lprcUpdate
Points to a **RECT** structure that will receive the boundaries of the rectangle invalidated by scrolling. This parameter may be NULL.

fuScroll
Specifies flags that control scrolling. This parameter can be one of the following values:

Value	Meaning
SW_ERASE	When specified with SW_INVALIDATE, erases the newly invalidated region by sending a WM_ERASEBKGND message to the window.
SW_INVALIDATE	Invalidates the region identified by the *hrgnUpdate* parameter after scrolling.
SW_SCROLLCHILDREN	Scrolls all child windows that intersect the rectangle pointed to by *lprcScroll* by the number of pixels specified in the *dx* and *dy* parameters. Windows sends a WM_MOVE message to all child windows that intersect *lprcScroll*, even if they do not move. The caret is repositioned when a child window is scrolled and the cursor rectangle intersects the scroll rectangle.

Return Value

The return value is SIMPLEREGION (rectangular invalidated region), COMPLEXREGION (nonrectangular invalidated region; overlapping rectangles), or NULLREGION (no invalidated region), if the function is successful. Otherwise, the return value is ERROR.

Comments

If SW_INVALIDATE and SW_ERASE are not specified, **ScrollWindowEx** does not invalidate the area that is scrolled away from. If either of these flags is set, **ScrollWindowEx** invalidates this area. The area is not updated until the application calls the **UpdateWindow** function, calls the **RedrawWindow** function (specifying RDW_UPDATENOW or RDW_ERASENOW), or retrieves the WM_PAINT message from the application queue.

If the window has the WS_CLIPCHILDREN style, the returned areas specified by *hrgnUpdate* and *lprcUpdate* represent the total area of the scrolled window that must be updated, including any areas in child windows that need qpdating.

If the SW_SCROLLCHILDREN flag is specified, Windows will not properly update the screen if part of a child window is scrolled. The part of the scrolled child window that lies outside the source rectangle will not be erased and will not be redrawn properly in its new destination. Use the **DeferWindowPos** function to move child windows that do not lie completely within the *lprcScroll* rectangle.

All input and output coordinates (for *lprcScroll*, *lprcClip*, *lprcUpdate*, and *hrgnUpdate*) are assumed to be in client coordinates, regardless of whether the window has the CS_OWNDC or CS_CLASSDC class style. Use the **LPtoDP** and **DPtoLP** functions to convert to and from logical coordinates, if necessary.

See Also

RedrawWindow, ScrollDC, ScrollWindow, UpdateWindow

SelectClipRgn

`2.x`

int SelectClipRgn(*hdc*, *hrgn*)
HDC *hdc*;   /* handle of device context   */
HRGN *hrgn*;   /* handle of region   */

The **SelectClipRgn** function selects the given region as the current clipping region for the given device context.

Parameters

hdc
    Identifies the device context.

hrgn
    Identifies the region to be selected. If this value is NULL, the entire client area is selected and output is still clipped to the window.

Return Value

The return value is SIMPLEREGION (region has no overlapping borders), COMPLEXREGION (region has overlapping borders), or NULLREGION (region is empty), if the function is successful. Otherwise, the return value is ERROR.

Comments

The **SelectClipRgn** function selects only a copy of the specified region. Because **SelectClipRgn** uses only a copy, the region can be selected for any number of other device contexts or it can be deleted.

The coordinates for the specified region should be specified in device units.

Some printer devices support text output at a higher resolution than graphics output in order to retain the precision needed to express text metrics. These devices report device units at the higher resolution—that is, text units. These devices then scale coordinates for graphics so that several reported device units map to only one graphics unit. Applications should always call the **SelectClipRgn** function using the text unit. Applications that must take the scaling of graphics objects in the graphics device interface (GDI) can use the GETSCALINGFACTOR printer escape to determine the scaling factor. This scaling factor affects clipping. If a region is used to clip graphics, GDI divides the coordinates by the scaling factor. (If the region is used to clip text, however, GDI makes no scaling adjustment.) A scaling factor of 1 causes the coordinates to be divided by 2; a scaling factor of 2 causes the coordinates to be divided by 4; and so on.

Example

The following example uses the **GetClipBox** function to determine the size of the current clipping region and the **GetTextExtent** function to determine the width of a line of text. If the text will not fit in the clipping region, the **SelectClipRgn** is used to make the region wide enough for the text. The output is clipped to the window regardless of the size of the region specified in the second parameter of **SelectClipRegion**.

```
                    HRGN hrgnClip;
                    RECT rcClip;
                    LPSTR lpszTest = "Test of clipping region.";
                    DWORD dwStringLen;
                    WORD wExtent;

                    GetClipBox(hdc, &rcClip);
                    dwStringLen = GetTextExtent(hdc, lpszTest, lstrlen(lpszTest));
                    wExtent = LOWORD(dwStringLen);
                    if (rcClip.right < 50 + wExtent) {
                        hrgnClip = CreateRectRgn(50, 50, 50 + wExtent, 80);
                        SelectClipRgn(hdc, hrgnClip);
                    }

                    TextOut(hdc, 50, 60, lpszTest, lstrlen(lpszTest));

                    DeleteObject(hrgnClip);
```

See Also   **GetClipBox, GetTextExtent**

SelectObject   `2.x`

HGDIOBJ SelectObject(*hdc*, *hgdiobj*)
HDC *hdc*;   /* handle of device context   */
HGDIOBJ *hgdiobj*;   /* handle of object   */

The **SelectObject** function selects an object into the given device context. The new object replaces the previous object of the same type.

Parameters   *hdc*
                     Identifies the device context.

                     hgdiobj
                     Identifies the object to be selected. The object can be one of the following and must have been created by using one of the listed functions:

Object	Functions
Bitmap	**CreateBitmap, CreateBitmapIndirect, CreateCompatibleBitmap, CreateDIBitmap**
Brush	**CreateBrushIndirect, CreateDIBPatternBrush, CreateHatchBrush, CreatePatternBrush, CreateSolidBrush**
Font	**CreateFont, CreateFontIndirect**
Pen	**CreatePen, CreatePenIndirect**

Object	Functions
Region	**CreateEllipticRgn**, **CreateEllipticRgnIndirect**, **CreatePolygonRgn**, **CreateRoundRectRgn**, **CreateRectRgn**, **CreateRectRgnIndirect**

Return Value

The return value is the handle of the object being replaced, if the function is successful. Otherwise, it is NULL.

If the *hgdiobj* parameter identifies a region, this function performs the same task as the **SelectClipRgn** function and the return value is SIMPLEREGION (region has no overlapping borders), COMPLEXREGION (region has overlapping borders), or NULLREGION (region is empty). If an error occurs, the return value is ERROR and the previously selected object of the specified type remains selected in the device context.

Comments

When an application uses the **SelectObject** function to select a font, pen, or brush, the system allocates space for that object in its data segment. Because data-segment space is limited, an application should use the **DeleteObject** function to remove each drawing object that it no longer requires. Before removing the object, the application should select it out of the device context. To do this, the application can select a different object of the same type back into the device context; typically, this different object is the original object for the device context.

When the *hdc* parameter identifies a metafile device context, the **SelectObject** function does not return the handle of the previously selected object. When the device context is a metafile, calling **SelectObject** with the *hgdiobj* parameter set to a value returned by a previous call to **SelectObject** can cause unpredictable results. Because metafiles perform their own object cleanup, an application need not reselect default objects when recording a metafile.

Memory device contexts are the only device contexts into which an application can select a bitmap. A bitmap can be selected into only one memory device context at a time. The format of the bitmap must either be monochrome or be compatible with the given device; if it is not, **SelectObject** returns an error.

Example

The following example creates a pen, uses the **SelectObject** function to select it into a device context, uses the pen to draw a rectangle, selects the previous pen back into the device context, and uses the **DeleteObject** function to remove the pen that was just created:

```
HPEN hpen, hpenOld;

hpen = CreatePen(PS_SOLID, 6, RGB(0, 0, 255));
hpenOld = SelectObject(hdc, hpen);

Rectangle(hdc, 10, 10, 100, 100);
```

```
SelectObject(hdc, hpenOld);
DeleteObject(hpen);
```

See Also   **DeleteObject**, **SelectClipRgn**, **SelectPalette**

SelectPalette

3.0

HPALETTE SelectPalette(*hdc*, *hpal*, *fPalBack*)
HDC *hdc*;   /* handle of device context   */
HPALETTE *hpal*;   /* handle of palette   */
BOOL *fPalBack*;   /* flag for forcing palette to background */

The **SelectPalette** function selects the specified logical palette into the given device context. The selected palette replaces the previous palette for that device context.

Parameters   *hdc*
Identifies the device context.

hpal
Identifies the logical palette to be selected.

fPalBack
Specifies whether the logical palette is always to be a background palette. If this parameter is nonzero, the selected palette is always a background palette. If this parameter is zero and the device context is attached to a window, the logical palette is a foreground palette when the window has the input focus. (The device context is attached to a window if it was obtained by using the **GetDC** function or if the window-class style is CS_OWNDC.)

Return Value   The return value is the handle of the previous logical palette for the given device context, if the function is successful. Otherwise, it is NULL.

Comments   An application can select a logical palette into more than one device context. However, changes to a logical palette will affect all device contexts for which it is selected. If an application selects a palette into more than one device context, the device contexts must all belong to the same physical device.

Example   The following example calls the **SelectPalette** function to select a logical palette into a device context and then calls the **RealizePalette** function to change the palette size:

```
            HPALETTE hpal, hPalPrevious;

            hdc = GetDC(hwnd);

            hPalPrevious = SelectPalette(hdc, hpal, FALSE);
            if (RealizePalette(hdc) == NULL)
                MessageBox(hwnd, "Can't realize palette", "Error", MB_OK);

            ReleaseDC(hwnd, hdc);
```

See Also   **CreatePalette, GetDC, RealizePalette**

SendDlgItemMessage   2.x

LRESULT SendDlgItemMessage(*hwndDlg, idDlgItem, uMsg, wParam, lParam*)
HWND *hwndDlg*;   /* handle of dialog box   */
int *idDlgItem*;   /* identifier of dialog box item */
UINT *uMsg*;   /* message   */
WPARAM *wParam*;   /* first message parameter   */
LPARAM *lParam*;   /* second message parameter   */

The **SendDlgItemMessage** function sends a message to a control in a dialog box.

Parameters   *hwndDlg*
                  Identifies the dialog box that contains the control.

                  idDlgItem
                  Specifies the identifier of the dialog item that will receive the message.

                  uMsg
                  Specifies the message to be sent.

                  wParam
                  Specifies 16 bits of additional message-dependent information.

                  lParam
                  Specifies 32 bits of additional message-dependent information.

Return Value   The return value specifies the result of the message processing and depends on the
                  message sent.

Comments   The **SendDlgItemMessage** function does not return until the message has been
                  processed.

Using **SendDlgItemMessage** is identical to retrieving a handle of the given control and calling the **SendMessage** function.

See Also   **PostMessage**, **SendMessage**

SendDriverMessage

3.1

LRESULT **SendDriverMessage**(*hdrvr*, *msg*, *lParam1*, *lParam2*)
HDRVR *hdrvr*;   /* handle of installable driver   */
UINT *msg*;   /* message   */
LPARAM *lParam1*;   /* first message parameter   */
LPARAM *lParam2*;   /* second message parameter   */

The **SendDriverMessage** function sends the specified message to the given installable driver.

Parameters   *hdrvr*
Identifies the installable driver.

msg
Specifies the message that the driver must process. The following messages should never be sent by an application directly to the driver; they are sent only by the system:

DRV_CLOSE
DRV_DISABLE
DRV_ENABLE
DRV_EXITAPPLICATION
DRV_EXITSESSION
DRV_FREE
DRV_LOAD
DRV_OPEN

lParam1
Specifies 32 bits of additional message-dependent information.

lParam2
Specifies 32 bits of additional message-dependent information.

Return Value   The return value is nonzero if the function is successful. Otherwise, it is zero.

See Also   **DefDriverProc**

SendMessage

```
LRESULT SendMessage(hwnd, uMsg, wParam, lParam)
HWND hwnd;            /* handle of destination window      */
UINT uMsg;            /* message to send                   */
WPARAM wParam;        /* first message parameter           */
LPARAM lParam;        /* second message parameter          */
```

The **SendMessage** function sends the specified message to the given window or windows. The function calls the window procedure for the window and does not return until that window procedure has processed the message. This is in contrast to the **PostMessage** function, which places (posts) the message in the window's message queue and returns immediately.

Parameters

hwnd
Identifies the window to which the message will be sent. If this parameter is HWND_BROADCAST, the message will be sent to all top-level windows, including disabled or invisible unowned windows.

uMsg
Specifies the message to be sent.

wParam
Specifies 16 bits of additional message-dependent information.

lParam
Specifies 32 bits of additional message-dependent information.

Return Value

The return value specifies the result of the message processing and depends on the message sent.

Comments

If the message is being sent to another application and the *wParam* or *lParam* parameter is used to pass a handle or pointer to global memory, the memory should be allocated by the **GlobalAlloc** function using the GMEM_SHARE flag.

Example

The following example calls the **SendMessage** function to send an EM_SETSEL message to a multiline edit control, telling it to select all the text. It then calls **SendMessage** to send a WM_COPY message to copy the selected text to the clipboard.

```
SendMessage(hwndMle, EM_SETSEL, 0, MAKELONG(0, -1));
SendMessage(hwndMle, WM_COPY, 0, 0L);
```

See Also

InSendMessage, **PostMessage**, **SendDlgItemMessage**

SetAbortProc

int SetAbortProc(*hdc*, *abrtprc*)
HDC *hdc*;   /* handle of device context   */
ABORTPROC *abrtprc*;   /* instance address of abort function */

The **SetAbortProc** function sets the application-defined procedure that allows a print job to be canceled during spooling. This function replaces the SETABORTPROC printer escape for Windows version 3.1.

Parameters   *hdc*
Identifies the device context for the print job.

abrtprc
Specifies the procedure-instance address of the callback function. The address must have been created by using the **MakeProcInstance** function. For more information about the callback function, see the description of the **AbortProc** callback function.

Return Value   The return value is greater than zero if the function is successful. Otherwise, it is less than zero.

See Also   **AbortDoc**, **AbortProc**, **Escape**

SetActiveWindow

HWND SetActiveWindow(*hwnd*)
HWND *hwnd*;   /* handle of window to activate   */

The **SetActiveWindow** function makes the specified top-level window the active window.

Parameters   *hwnd*
Identifies the top-level window to be activated.

Return Value   The return value identifies the window that was previously active, if the function is successful.

Comments	The **SetActiveWindow** function should be used with care, since it allows an application to arbitrarily take over the active window and input focus. Normally, Windows takes care of all activation.

See Also	**GetActiveWindow**, **SetCapture**, **SetFocus**

SetBitmapBits   2.x

LONG SetBitmapBits(*hbmp*, *cBits*, *lpvBits*)
HBITMAP *hbmp*;   /* handle of bitmap   */
DWORD *cBits*;   /* number of bytes in bitmap array   */
const void FAR* *lpvBits*;   /* address of array with bitmap bits */

The **SetBitmapBits** function sets the bits of the given bitmap, to the specified bit values.

Parameters	*hbmp*
	Identifies the bitmap to be set.
	cBits
	Specifies the number of bytes pointed to by the *lpvBits* parameter.
	lpvBits
	Points to an array of bytes for the bitmap bits.

Return Value	The return value is the number of bytes used in setting the bitmap bits, if the function is successful. Otherwise, the return value is zero.

See Also	**GetBitmapBits**

SetBitmapDimension   2.x

DWORD SetBitmapDimension(*hbmp*, *nWidth*, *nHeight*)
HBITMAP *hbmp*;   /* handle of bitmap   */
int *nWidth*;   /* bitmap width   */
int *nHeight*;   /* bitmap height   */

The **SetBitmapDimension** function assigns a width and height to a bitmap, in 0.1-millimeter units. The graphics device interface (GDI) does not use these values except to return them when an application calls the **GetBitmapDimension** function.

Parameters

hbmp
Identifies the bitmap.

nWidth
Specifies the bitmap width, in 0.1-millimeter units.

nHeight
Specifies the bitmap height, in 0.1-millimeter units.

Return Value

The return value is the dimensions of the previous bitmap, in 0.1-millimeter units, if the function is successful. The low-order word contains the previous width; the high-order word contains the previous height.

See Also

GetBitmapDimension

SetBitmapDimensionEx

$\boxed{\text{3.1}}$

BOOL SetBitmapDimensionEx(*hbm*, *nX*, *nY*, *lpSize***)**
HBITMAP *hbm*;	/* handle of bitmap	*/
int *nX*;	/* bitmap width	*/
int *nY*;	/* bitmap height	*/
SIZE FAR* *lpSize*;	/* address of structure for prev. dimensions	*/

The **SetBitmapDimensionEx** function assigns the preferred size to a bitmap, in 0.1-millimeter units. The graphics device interface (GDI) does not use these values, except to return them when an application calls the **GetBitmap-DimensionEx** function.

Parameters

hbm
Identifies the bitmap.

nX
Specifies the width of the bitmap, in 0.1-millimeter units.

nY
Specifies the height of the bitmap, in 0.1-millimeter units.

lpSize
Points to a **SIZE** structure. The previous bitmap dimensions are placed in this structure. If *lpSize* is NULL, nothing is returned. The **SIZE** structure has the following form:

```
typedef struct tagSIZE {
    int cx;
    int cy;
} SIZE;
```

For a full description of this structure, see the *Microsoft Windows Programmer's Reference, Volume 3.*

Return Value   The return value is nonzero if the function is successful. Otherwise, it is zero.

SetBkColor   2.x

COLORREF SetBkColor(*hdc***,** *clrref***)**
HDC *hdc*;   /* handle of device context   */
COLORREF *clrref*;   /* color specification   */

The **SetBkColor** function sets the current background color to the specified color.

Parameters   *hdc*
Identifies the device context.

clrref
Specifies the new background color.

Return Value   The return value is the RGB value of the previous background color, if the function is successful. The return value is 0x80000000 if an error occurs.

Comments   If the background mode is OPAQUE, the system uses the background color to fill the gaps in styled lines, the gaps between hatched lines in brushes, and the background in character cells. The system also uses the background color when converting bitmaps between color and monochrome device contexts.

If the device cannot display the specified color, the system sets the background color to the nearest physical color.

For information about color-bitmap conversions, see the descriptions of the **BitBlt** and **StretchBlt** functions.

Example   The following example uses the **GetBkColor** function to determine whether the current background color is white. If it is, the **SetBkColor** function sets it to red.

```
DWORD dwBackColor;

dwBackColor = GetBkColor(hdc);
if (dwBackColor == RGB(255, 255, 255)) { /* if color is white */
    SetBkColor(hdc, RGB(255, 0, 0));      /* sets color to red */
    TextOut(hdc, 100, 200, "SetBkColor test.", 16);
}
```

See Also   **BitBlt, GetBkColor, GetBkMode, SetBkMode, StretchBlt**

SetBkMode

int SetBkMode(*hdc, fnBkMode*)
HDC *hdc*;   /* handle of device context   */
int *fnBkMode*;   /* background mode   */

The **SetBkMode** function sets the specified background mode. The background mode defines whether the system removes existing background colors on the drawing surface before drawing text, hatched brushes, or any pen style that is not a solid line.

Parameters   *hdc*
                        Identifies the device context.

                        fnBkMode
                        Specifies the background mode to be set. This parameter can be one of the following values:

Value	Meaning
OPAQUE	Background is filled with the current background color before the text, hatched brush, or pen is drawn. This is the default background mode.
TRANSPARENT	Background is not changed before drawing.

Return Value   The return value is the previous background mode, if the function is successful.

Example   The following example determines the current background mode by calling the **GetBkMode** function. If the mode is OPAQUE, the **SetBkMode** function sets it to TRANSPARENT.

```
int nBackMode;

nBackMode = GetBkMode(hdc);
if (nBackMode == OPAQUE) {
    TextOut(hdc, 90, 100, "This background mode is OPAQUE.", 31);
    SetBkMode(hdc, TRANSPARENT);
}
```

See Also   **GetBkColor, GetBkMode, SetBkColor**

SetBoundsRect

UINT SetBoundsRect(*hdc, lprcBounds, flags*)
HDC *hdc*;   /* handle of device context   */
const RECT FAR* *lprcBounds*;   /* address of structure for rectangle   */
UINT *flags*;   /* specifies information to return   */

The **SetBoundsRect** function controls the accumulation of bounding-rectangle information for the specified device context.

Parameters

hdc
Identifies the device context to accumulate bounding rectangles for.

lprcBounds
Points to a **RECT** structure that is used to set the bounding rectangle. Rectangle dimensions are given in logical coordinates. This parameter can be NULL. The **RECT** structure has the following form:

```
typedef struct tagRECT {    /* rc */
    int left;
    int top;
    int right;
    int bottom;
} RECT;
```

For a full description of this structure, see the *Microsoft Windows Programmer's Reference, Volume 3*.

flags
Specifies how the new rectangle will be combined with the accumulated rectangle. This parameter may be a combination of the following values:

Value	Meaning
DCB_ACCUMULATE	Add the rectangle specified by the *lprcBounds* parameter to the bounding rectangle (using a rectangle union operation).
DCB_DISABLE	Turn off bounds accumulation.
DCB_ENABLE	Turn on bounds accumulation. (The default setting for bounds accumulation is disabled.)

Return Value

The return value is the current state of the bounding rectangle, if the function is successful. Like the *flags* parameter, the return value can be a combination of the following values:

Value	Meaning
DCB_ACCUMULATE	The bounding rectangle is not empty. (This value will always be set.)

Value	Meaning
DCB_DISABLE	Bounds accumulation is off.
DCB_ENABLE	Bounds accumulation is on.

Comments   Windows can maintain a bounding rectangle for all drawing operations. This rectangle can be queried and reset by the application. The drawing bounds are useful for invalidating bitmap caches.

See Also   **GetBoundsRect**

SetBrushOrg

2.x

DWORD SetBrushOrg(*hdc***,** *nXOrg***,** *nYOrg***)**
HDC *hdc*;   /* handle of device context   */
int *nXOrg*;   /* x-coordinate of new origin   */
int *nYOrg*;   /* y-coordinate of new origin   */

The **SetBrushOrg** function specifies the origin that GDI will assign to the next brush an application selects into the specified device context.

Parameters   *hdc*
                   Identifies the device context.

                   nXOrg
                   Specifies the x-coordinate, in device units, of the new origin. This value must be in the range 0 through 7.

                   nYOrg
                   Specifies the y-coordinate, in device units, of the new origin. This value must be in the range 0 through 7.

Return Value   The return value is the coordinates, in device units, of the previous origin, if the function is successful. The low-order word contains the x-coordinate; the high-order word contains the y-coordinate.

Comments   The default coordinates for the brush origin are (0, 0).

                   To alter the origin of a brush, an application should call the **UnrealizeObject** function, specifying the handle of the brush for which the origin will be set; call **SetBrushOrg**; and then call the **SelectObject** function to select the brush into the device context.

                   The **SetBrushOrg** function should not be used with stock objects.

Example   The following example uses the **SetBrushOrg** function to shift the brush origin
                     vertically by 5 pixels:

```
HBRUSH hbr, hbrOld;
SetBkMode(hdc, TRANSPARENT);
hbr = CreateHatchBrush(HS_CROSS, RGB(0, 0, 0));

UnrealizeObject(hbr);
SetBrushOrg(hdc, 0, 0);
hbrOld = SelectObject(hdc, hbr);

Rectangle(hdc, 0, 0, 200, 200);

hbr = SelectObject(hdc, hbrOld);                  /* deselects hbr */
UnrealizeObject(hbr);  /* resets origin next time hbr selected */
SetBrushOrg(hdc, 3, 5);
hbrOld = SelectObject(hdc, hbr);              /* selects hbr again */

Rectangle(hdc, 0, 0, 200, 200);

SelectObject(hdc, hbrOld);
DeleteObject(hbr);
```

See Also   **GetBrushOrg, SelectObject, UnrealizeObject**

SetCapture   `2.x`

HWND SetCapture(*hwnd*)
HWND *hwnd*;   /* handle of window to receive all mouse messages   */

The **SetCapture** function sets the mouse capture to the specified window. With
the mouse capture set to a window, all mouse input is directed to that window, regardless of whether the cursor is over that window. Only one window can have the
mouse capture at a time.

Parameters   *hwnd*
                     Identifies the window that is to receive all mouse messages.

Return Value   The return value is the handle of the window that previously received all mouse
                     input, if the function is successful. It is NULL if there is no such window.

Comments   When the window no longer requires all mouse input, the application should call
                     the **ReleaseCapture** function so that other windows can receive mouse input.

See Also   **ReleaseCapture**

SetCaretBlinkTime   2.x

void SetCaretBlinkTime(*uMSeconds*)
UINT *uMSeconds*;   /* blink rate in milliseconds   */

The **SetCaretBlinkTime** function sets the caret blink rate. The blink rate is the elapsed time, in milliseconds, between caret flashes.

Parameters   *uMSeconds*
Specifies the new blink rate, in milliseconds.

Return Value   This function does not return a value.

Comments   The caret flashes on or off every *uMSeconds* milliseconds. One complete flash (off-on) takes twice *uMSeconds* milliseconds.

The caret is a shared resource. A window should set the caret blink rate only if it owns the caret. It should restore the previous rate before it loses the input focus or becomes inactive.

See Also   **GetCaretBlinkTime**

SetCaretPos   2.x

void SetCaretPos(*x*, *y*)
int *x*;   /* horizontal position   */
int *y*;   /* vertical position   */

The **SetCaretPos** function sets the position of the caret.

Parameters   *x*
Specifies the new x-coordinate, in client coordinates, of the caret.

y
Specifies the new y-coordinate, in client coordinates, of the caret.

Return Value   This function does not return a value.

Comments   The **SetCaretPos** function moves the caret only if it is owned by a window in the current task. **SetCaretPos** moves the caret whether or not the caret is hidden.

The caret is a shared resource. A window should not move the caret if it does not own the caret.

See Also   **GetCaretPos**

SetClassLong   2.x

LONG SetClassLong(*hwnd, nIndex, nVal*)
HWND *hwnd*;   /* handle of window   */
int *nIndex*;   /* index of value to change   */
LONG *nVal*;   /* new value   */

The **SetClassLong** function sets a long value at the specified offset into the extra class memory for the window class to which the specified window belongs. Extra class memory is reserved by specifying a nonzero value in the **cbClsExtra** member of the **WNDCLASS** structure used with the **RegisterClass** function.

Parameters   *hwnd*
Identifies the window.

nIndex
Specifies the zero-based byte offset of the long value to change. Valid values are in the range zero through the number of bytes of class memory, minus four. (For example, if 12 or more bytes of extra class memory were specified, a value of 8 would be an index to the third long integer.) This parameter can also be GCL_WNDPROC, which sets a new long pointer to the window procedure.

nVal
Specifies the replacement value.

Return Value   The return value is the previous value of the specified long integer, if the function is successful. Otherwise, it is zero.

Comments   If the **SetClassLong** function and GCL_WNDPROC index are used to set a window procedure, the specified window procedure must have the window-procedure form and be exported in the module-definition file. For more information, see the description of the **RegisterClass** function.

Calling **SetClassLong** with the GCL_WNDPROC index creates a subclass of the window class that affects all windows subsequently created by using the class.

Applications should not call **SetClassLong** with the GCL_MENUNAME value.

To access any extra 4-byte values allocated when the window-class structure was created, use a positive byte offset as the index specified by the *nIndex* parameter, starting at 0 for the first 4-byte value in the extra space, 4 for the next 4-byte value, and so on.

See Also   **GetClassLong**, **RegisterClass**, **SetClassWord**

SetClassWord

2.x

WORD SetClassWord(*hwnd*, *nIndex*, *wNewWord*)
HWND *hwnd*;   /* handle of window   */
int *nIndex*;   /* index of value to change   */
WORD *wNewWord*;   /* new value   */

The **SetClassWord** function sets a word value at the specified offset into the extra class memory for the window class to which the given window belongs. Extra class memory is reserved by specifying a nonzero value in the **cbClsExtra** member of the **WNDCLASS** structure used with the **RegisterClass** function.

Parameters   *hwnd*
Identifies the window.

nIndex
Specifies the zero-based byte offset of the word value to change. Valid values are in the range zero through the number of bytes of class memory, minus two (for example, if 10 or more bytes of extra class memory were specified, a value of 8 would be an index to the fifth integer), or one of the following values:

Value	Meaning
GCW_HBRBACKGROUND	Sets a new handle of a background brush.
GCW_HCURSOR	Sets a new handle of a cursor.
GCW_HICON	Sets a new handle of an icon.
GCW_STYLE	Sets a new style bit for the window class.

wNewWord
Specifies the replacement value.

Return Value   The return value is the previous value of the specified word, if the function is successful. Otherwise, it is zero.

Comments   The **SetClassWord** function should be used with care. For example, it is possible to change the background color for a class by using **SetClassWord**, but this change does not cause all windows belonging to the class to be repainted immediately. Applications should not attempt to set the class word values of any class attribute except those listed for the *nIndex* parameter.

To access any extra 2-byte values allocated when the window-class structure was created, use a positive byte offset as the index specified by the *nIndex* parameter, starting at 0 for the first 2-byte value in the extra space, 2 for the next 2-byte value, and so on.

See Also   **GetClassWord, RegisterClass, SetClassLong**

SetClipboardData $\boxed{2.x}$

HANDLE SetClipboardData(*uFormat*, *hData*)
UINT *uFormat*;   /* clipboard format   */
HANDLE *hData*;   /* data handle   */

The **SetClipboardData** function sets the data in the clipboard. The application must have called the **OpenClipboard** function before calling the **SetClipboardData** function.

Parameters   *uFormat*
    Specifies the format of the data. It can be any one of the system-defined formats or a format registered by the **RegisterClipboardFormat** function. For a list of system-defined formats, see the following Comments section.

hData
    Identifies the data to be placed in the clipboard. For all formats except CF_BITMAP and CF_PALETTE, this parameter must be a handle of the memory allocated by the **GlobalAlloc** function. For CF_BITMAP format, the *hData* parameter is a bitmap handle (see the description of the **LoadBitmap** function). For the CF_PALETTE format, *hData* is a palette handle (see the description of the **CreatePalette** function).

    If this parameter is NULL, the owner of the clipboard will be sent a WM_RENDERFORMAT message when it must supply the data.

Return Value   The return value is a handle of the data, if the function is successful. Otherwise, it is NULL.

Comments   If the *hData* parameter contains a handle of the memory allocated by the **GlobalAlloc** function, the application must not use this handle once it has called the **SetClipboardData** function.

Following are the system-defined clipboard formats:

Value	Meaning
CF_BITMAP	The data is a bitmap.
CF_DIB	The data is a memory object containing a **BITMAPINFO** structure followed by the bitmap data.
CF_DIF	The data is in Data Interchange Format (DIF).
CF_DSPBITMAP	The data is a bitmap representation of a private format. This data is displayed in bitmap format in lieu of the privately formatted data.
CF_DSPMETAFILEPICT	The data is a metafile representation of a private data format. This data is displayed in metafile-picture format in lieu of the privately formatted data.
CF_DSPTEXT	The data is a textual representation of a private data format. This data is displayed in text format in lieu of the privately formatted data.
CF_METAFILEPICT	The data is a metafile (see the description of the **META-FILEPICT** structure in the *Microsoft Windows Programmer's Reference*, *Volume 3*).
CF_OEMTEXT	The data is an array of text characters in the OEM character set. Each line ends with a carriage return–linefeed (CR–LF) combination. A null character signals the end of the data.
CF_OWNERDISPLAY	The data is in a private format that the clipboard owner must display.
CF_PALETTE	The data is a color palette.
CF_PENDATA	The data is for the pen extensions to the Windows operating system.
CF_RIFF	The data is in Resource Interchange File Format (RIFF).
CF_SYLK	The data is in Microsoft Symbolic Link (SYLK) format.
CF_TEXT	The data is an array of text characters. Each line ends with a carriage return–linefeed (CR–LF) combination. A null character signals the end of the data.
CF_TIFF	The data is in Tag Image File Format (TIFF).
CF_WAVE	The data describes a sound wave. This is a subset of the CF_RIFF data format; it can be used only for RIFF WAVE files.

Private data formats in the range CF_PRIVATEFIRST through CF_PRIVATELAST are not automatically freed when the data is removed from the clipboard. Data handles associated with these formats should be freed upon receiving a WM_DESTROYCLIPBOARD message.

Private data formats in the range CF_GDIOBJFIRST through CF_GDIOBJLAST will be automatically removed by a call to the **DeleteObject** function when the data is removed from the clipboard.

If Windows Clipboard is running, it will not update its window to show the data placed in the clipboard by the **SetClipboardData** until after the **CloseClipboard** function is called.

See Also   CloseClipboard, GetClipboardData, GlobalAlloc, OpenClipboard, RegisterClipboardFormat

---

SetClipboardViewer   2.x

HWND SetClipboardViewer(*hwnd*)
HWND *hwnd*;   /* handle of clipboard viewer   */

The **SetClipboardViewer** function adds the given window to the chain of windows that are notified (by means of the WM_DRAWCLIPBOARD message) whenever the contents of the clipboard are changed.

Parameters   *hwnd*
      Identifies the window to receive clipboard-viewer chain messages.

Return Value   The return value is the handle of the next window in the clipboard-viewer chain, if the function is successful.

Comments   Applications should save this handle in static memory and use it when responding to clipboard-viewer chain messages.

Windows that are part of the clipboard-viewer chain must respond to WM_CHANGECBCHAIN, WM_DRAWCLIPBOARD, and WM_DESTROY messages.

To remove itself from the clipboard-viewer chain, an application must call the **ChangeClipboardChain** function.

See Also   ChangeClipboardChain, GetClipboardViewer

SetCommBreak

int **SetCommBreak**(*idComDev*)
int *idComDev*;   /* device to suspend   */

The **SetCommBreak** function suspends character transmission and places the communications device in a break state.

Parameters   *idComDev*
Specifies the communications device to be suspended. The **OpenComm** function returns this value.

Return Value   The return value is zero if the function is successful. Otherwise, it is less than zero.

Comments   The communications device remains suspended until the application calls the **ClearCommBreak** function.

See Also   **ClearCommBreak, OpenComm**

SetCommEventMask

UINT FAR* SetCommEventMask(*idComDev*, *fuEvtMask*)
int *idComDev*;   /* device to enable   */
UINT *fuEvtMask*;   /* events to enable   */

The **SetCommEventMask** function enables events in the event word of the specified communications device.

Parameters   *idComDev*
Specifies the communications device to be enabled. The **OpenComm** function returns this value.

fuEvtMask
Specifies which events are to be enabled. This parameter can be any combination of the following values:

Value	Meaning
EV_BREAK	Set when a break is detected on input.
EV_CTS	Set when the CTS (clear-to-send) signal changes state.
EV_CTSS	Set to indicate the current state of the CTS signal.
EV_DSR	Set when the DSR (data-set-ready) signal changes state.

Value	Meaning
EV_ERR	Set when a line-status error occurs. Line-status errors are CE_FRAME, CE_OVERRUN, and CE_RXPARITY.
EV_PERR	Set when a printer error is detected on a parallel device. Errors are CE_DNS, CE_IOE, CE_LOOP, and CE_PTO.
EV_RING	Set to indicate the state of ring indicator during the last modem interrupt.
EV_RLSD	Set when the RLSD (receive-line-signal-detect) signal changes state.
EV_RLSDS	Set to indicate the current state of the RLSD signal.
EV_RXCHAR	Set when any character is received and placed in the receiving queue.
EV_RXFLAG	Set when the event character is received and placed in the receiving queue. The event character is specified in the device's control block.
EV_TXEMPTY	Set when the last character in the transmission queue is sent.

Return Value   The return value is a pointer to the event word for the specified communications device, if the function is successful. Each bit in the event word specifies whether a given event has occurred. A bit is 1 if the event has occurred.

Comments   Only enabled events are recorded. The **GetCommEventMask** function retrieves and clears the event word.

See Also   **GetCommEventMask**, **OpenComm**

SetCommState   2.x

int **SetCommState**(*lpdcb*)
const **DCB FAR*** *lpdcb*;   /* address of device control block   */

The **SetCommState** function sets a communications device to the state specified by a device control block.

Parameters   *lpdcb*
Points to a **DCB** structure that contains the desired communications settings for the device. The **Id** member of the **DCB** structure must identify the device. The **DCB** structure has the following form:

```
typedef struct tagDCB             /* dcb                          */
{
    BYTE Id;                      /* internal device identifier   */
    UINT BaudRate;                /* baud rate                    */
    BYTE ByteSize;                /* number of bits/byte, 4-8      */
    BYTE Parity;                  /* 0-4=none,odd,even,mark,space  */
    BYTE StopBits;                /* 0,1,2 = 1, 1.5, 2            */
    UINT RlsTimeout;              /* timeout for RLSD to be set    */
    UINT CtsTimeout;              /* timeout for CTS to be set     */
    UINT DsrTimeout;              /* timeout for DSR to be set     */

    UINT fBinary       :1;        /* binary mode (skip EOF check)  */
    UINT fRtsDisable   :1;        /* don't assert RTS at init time */
    UINT fParity       :1;        /* enable parity checking        */
    UINT fOutxCtsFlow  :1;        /* CTS handshaking on output     */
    UINT fOutxDsrFlow  :1;        /* DSR handshaking on output     */
    UINT fDummy        :2;        /* reserved                      */
    UINT fDtrDisable   :1;        /* don't assert DTR at init time */

    UINT fOutX         :1;        /* enable output XON/XOFF        */
    UINT fInX          :1;        /* enable input XON/XOFF         */
    UINT fPeChar       :1;        /* enable parity err replacement */
    UINT fNull         :1;        /* enable null stripping         */
    UINT fChEvt        :1;        /* enable Rx character event     */
    UINT fDtrflow      :1;        /* DTR handshake on input        */
    UINT fRtsflow      :1;        /* RTS handshake on input        */
    UINT fDummy2       :1;

    char XonChar;                 /* Tx and Rx XON character       */
    char XoffChar;                /* Tx and Rx XOFF character      */
    UINT XonLim;                  /* transmit XON threshold        */
    UINT XoffLim;                 /* transmit XOFF threshold       */
    char PeChar;                  /* parity error replacement char */
    char EofChar;                 /* end of Input character        */
    char EvtChar;                 /* received event character      */
    UINT TxDelay;                 /* amount of time between chars  */
} DCB;
```

For a full description of this structure, see the *Microsoft Windows Programmer's Reference, Volume 3.*

Return Value   The return value is zero if the function is successful. Otherwise, it is less than zero.

Example   The following example uses the **BuildCommDCB** and **SetCommState** functions to set up COM1 at 9600 baud, no parity, 8 data bits, and 1 stop bit:

```
idComDev = OpenComm("COM1", 1024, 128);
if (idComDev < 0) {
    ShowError(idComDev, "OpenComm");
    return 0;
}
err = BuildCommDCB("COM1:9600,n,8,1", &dcb);
if (err < 0) {
    ShowError(err, "BuildCommDCB");
    return 0;
}

err = SetCommState(&dcb);
if (err < 0) {
    ShowError(err, "SetCommState");
    return 0;
}
```

Comments   This function reinitializes all hardware and controls as defined by the **DCB** structure, but it does not empty transmission or receiving queues.

See Also   **GetCommState**

SetCursor   `2.x`

HCURSOR SetCursor(*hcur***)**
HCURSOR *hcur*;   /* handle of cursor   */

The **SetCursor** function changes the given cursor.

Parameters   *hcur*
Identifies the cursor resource. The resource must have been loaded by using the **LoadCursor** function. If this parameter is NULL, the cursor is removed from the screen.

Return Value   The return value is the handle of the previous cursor, if the function is successful. It is NULL if there is no previous cursor.

Comments   The cursor is set only if the new cursor is different from the previous cursor; otherwise, the function returns immediately. The function is quite fast if the new cursor is the same as the old.

The cursor is a shared resource. A window should set the cursor only when the cursor is in the window's client area or when the window is capturing all mouse input. In systems without a mouse, the window should restore the previous cursor before the cursor leaves the client area or before the window relinquishes control to another window.

Any application that must set the cursor while it is in a window must ensure that the class cursor for the given window's class is set to NULL. If the class cursor is not NULL, the system restores the previous shape each time the mouse is moved.

See Also   **GetCursor, LoadCursor, ShowCursor**

SetCursorPos

2.x

void SetCursorPos(*x, y*)
int *x*;   /* horizontal position   */
int *y*;   /* vertical position   */

The **SetCursorPos** function sets the position, in screen coordinates, of the cursor. If the new coordinates are not within the screen rectangle set by the most recent **ClipCursor** function, Windows automatically adjusts the coordinates so that the cursor stays within the rectangle.

Parameters   *x*
              Specifies the new x-coordinate, in screen coordinates, of the cursor.

              y
              Specifies the new y-coordinate, in screen coordinates, of the cursor.

Return Value   This function does not return a value.

Comments   The cursor is a shared resource. A window should move the cursor only when the cursor is in its client area.

See Also   **ClipCursor, GetCursorPos**

SetDIBits

int SetDIBits(*hdc*, *hbmp*, *uStartScan*, *cScanLines*, *lpvBits*, *lpbmi*, *fuColorUse*)
HDC *hdc*;   /* handle of device context   */
HBITMAP *hbmp*;   /* handle of bitmap   */
UINT *uStartScan*;   /* starting scan line   */
UINT *cScanLines*;   /* number of scan lines   */
const void FAR* *lpvBits*;   /* address of array with bitmap bits   */
BITMAPINFO FAR* *lpbmi*;   /* address of structure with bitmap data */
UINT *fuColorUse*;   /* type of color indices to use   */

The **SetDIBits** function sets the bits of a bitmap to the values given in a device-independent bitmap (DIB) specification.

Parameters

hdc
Identifies the device context.

hbmp
Identifies the bitmap to set the data in.

uStartScan
Specifies the zero-based scan number of the first scan line in the buffer pointed to by the *lpvBits* parameter.

cScanLines
Specifies the number of scan lines in the *lpvBits* buffer to copy into the bitmap identified by the *hbmp* parameter.

lpvBits
Points to the device-independent bitmap bits that are stored as an array of bytes. The format of the bitmap values depends on the **biBitCount** member of the **BITMAPINFOHEADER** structure, which is the first member of the **BITMAPINFO** structure pointed to by the *lpbmi* parameter.

The **BITMAPINFOHEADER** structure has the following form:

```
typedef struct tagBITMAPINFOHEADER {    /* bmih */
    DWORD   biSize;
    LONG    biWidth;
    LONG    biHeight;
    WORD    biPlanes;
    WORD    biBitCount;
    DWORD   biCompression;
    DWORD   biSizeImage;
    LONG    biXPelsPerMeter;
    LONG    biYPelsPerMeter;
    DWORD   biClrUsed;
    DWORD   biClrImportant;
} BITMAPINFOHEADER;
```

For a full description of this structure, see the *Microsoft Windows Programmer's Reference*, *Volume 3*.

lpbmi

Points to a **BITMAPINFO** structure that contains information about the device-independent bitmap. The **BITMAPINFO** structure has the following form:

```
typedef struct tagBITMAPINFO {   /* bmi */
    BITMAPINFOHEADER    bmiHeader;
    RGBQUAD             bmiColors[1];
} BITMAPINFO;
```

For a full description of this structure, see the *Microsoft Windows Programmer's Reference*, *Volume 3*.

fuColorUse

Specifies whether the **bmiColors** member of the **BITMAPINFO** structure contains explicit RGB values or indices into the currently realized logical palette. This parameter must be one of the following values:

Value	Meaning
DIB_PAL_COLORS	The color table consists of an array of 16-bit indices into the palette of the device context identified by the *hdc* parameter.
DIB_RGB_COLORS	The color table contains literal RGB values.

Return Value

The return value is the number of scan lines copied, if the function is successful. Otherwise, it is zero.

Comments

The bitmap identified by the *hbmp* parameter must not be selected into a device context when the application calls this function.

To reduce the amount of memory required to set bits from a large device-independent bitmap on a device surface, an application can band the output by repeatedly calling the **SetDIBitsToDevice** function, placing a different portion of the entire bitmap into the *lpvBits* buffer each time. The values of the *uStartScan* and *cScanLines* parameters identify the portion of the entire bitmap that is contained in the *lpvBits* buffer.

The origin of a device-independent bitmap is the bottom-left corner of the bitmap, not the top-left corner, which is the origin when the mapping mode is MM_TEXT. GDI performs the necessary transformation to display the image correctly.

See Also

SetDIBitsToDevice

SetDIBitsToDevice

int **SetDIBitsToDevice**(*hdc, XDest, YDest, cx, cy, XSrc, YSrc, uStartScan, cScanLines, lpvBits, lpbmi, fuColorUse*)

HDC *hdc*;	/* handle of device context */
int *XDest*;	/* x-coordinate origin of destination rect */
int *YDest*;	/* y-coordinate origin of destination rect */
int *cx*;	/* rectangle width */
int *cy*;	/* rectangle height */
int *XSrc*;	/* x-coordinate origin of source rect */
int *YSrc*;	/* y-coordinate origin of source rect */
UINT *uStartScan*;	/* number of first scan line in array */
UINT *cScanLines*;	/* number of scan lines */
void FAR* *lpvBits*;	/* address of array with DIB bits */
BITMAPINFO FAR* *lpbmi*;	/* address of structure with bitmap info */
UINT *fuColorUse*;	/* RGB or palette indices */

The **SetDIBitsToDevice** function sets bits from a device-independent bitmap (DIB) directly on a device surface. The device coordinates specified define a rectangle within the total bitmap. **SetDIBitsToDevice** sets the bits in this rectangle directly on the display surface of the output device associated with the given device context, at the specified logical coordinates.

Parameters

hdc
Identifies the device context.

XDest
Specifies the logical x-coordinate of the origin of the destination rectangle.

YDest
Specifies the logical y-coordinate of the origin of the destination rectangle.

cx
Specifies the x-extent, in device units, of the rectangle in the bitmap.

cy
Specifies the y-extent, in device units, of the rectangle in the bitmap.

XSrc
Specifies the x-coordinate, in device units, of the source rectangle in the bitmap.

YSrc
Specifies the y-coordinate, in device units, of the source rectangle in the bitmap.

uStartScan
Specifies the scan-line number of the device-independent bitmap that is contained in the first scan line of the buffer pointed to by the *lpvBits* parameter.

cScanLines
Specifies the number of scan lines in the *lpvBits* buffer to copy to the device.

lpvBits

Points to the DIB bits that are stored as an array of bytes.

lpbmi

Points to a **BITMAPINFO** structure that contains information about the bit-map. The **BITMAPINFO** structure has the following form:

```
typedef struct tagBITMAPINFO {  /* bmi */
    BITMAPINFOHEADER    bmiHeader;
    RGBQUAD             bmiColors[1];
} BITMAPINFO;
```

For a full description of this structure, see the *Microsoft Windows Programmer's Reference, Volume 3*.

fuColorUse

Specifies whether the **bmiColors** member of the *lpbmi* parameter contains explicit RGB values or indices into the currently realized logical palette. This parameter must be one of the following values:

Value	Meaning
DIB_PAL_COLORS	The color table consists of an array of 16-bit indices into the currently realized logical palette.
DIB_RGB_COLORS	The color table contains literal RGB values.

Return Value

The return value is the number of scan lines set, if the function is successful.

Comments

The origin of a device-independent bitmap is the bottom-left corner of the bitmap, not the top-left corner, which is the origin when the mapping mode is MM_TEXT. GDI performs the necessary transformation to display the image correctly.

To reduce the amount of memory required to set bits from a large device-independent bitmap on a device surface, an application can band the output by repeatedly calling **SetDIBitsToDevice**, placing a different portion of the entire bitmap into the *lpvBits* buffer each time. The values of the *uStartScan* and *cScanLines* parameters identify the portion of the entire bitmap that is contained in the *lpvBits* buffer.

See Also

SetDIBits

SetDlgItemInt

2.x

void SetDlgItemInt(*hwndDlg*, *idControl*, *uValue*, *fSigned*)
HWND *hwndDlg*;   /* handle of dialog box   */
int *idControl*;   /* identifier of control   */
UINT *uValue*;   /* value to set   */
BOOL *fSigned*;   /* signed or unsigned indicator   */

The **SetDlgItemInt** function sets the text of a given control in a dialog box to the string representation of a specified integer value.

Parameters   *hwndDlg*
          Identifies the dialog box that contains the control.

          idControl
          Specifies the control to be changed.

          uValue
          Specifies the integer value used to generate the item text.

          fSigned
          Specifies whether the *uValue* parameter is signed or unsigned. If this parameter is TRUE, *uValue* is signed. If this parameter is TRUE and *uValue* is less than zero, a minus sign is placed before the first digit in the string. If this parameter is FALSE, *uValue* is unsigned.

Return Value   This function does not return a value.

Comments   **SetDlgItemInt** sends a WM_SETTEXT message to the given control.

See Also   **GetDlgItemInt, SetDlgItemText**

SetDlgItemText

2.x

void SetDlgItemText(*hwndDlg*, *idControl*, *lpsz*)
HWND *hwndDlg*;   /* handle of dialog box   */
int *idControl*;   /* identifier of control   */
LPCSTR *lpsz*;   /* text to set   */

The **SetDlgItemText** function sets the title or text of a control in a dialog box.

Parameters   *hwndDlg*
          Identifies the dialog box that contains the control.

idControl
    Identifies the control whose text is to be set.

lpsz
    Points to the null-terminated string that contains the text to be copied to the control.

Return Value   This function does not return a value.

Comments   The **SetDlgItemText** function sends a WM_SETTEXT message to the given control.

See Also   **GetDlgItemText, SetDlgItemInt**

SetDoubleClickTime   2.x

void SetDoubleClickTime(*uInterval*)
UINT *uInterval*;   /* double-click interval   */

The **SetDoubleClickTime** function sets the double-click time for the mouse. A double-click is a series of two clicks of the mouse button, the second occurring within a specified time after the first. The double-click time is the maximum number of milliseconds that may occur between the first and second clicks of a double-click.

Parameters   *uInterval*
    Specifies the number of milliseconds that can occur between double-clicks.

Return Value   This function does not return a value.

Comments   If the *uInterval* parameter is zero, Windows uses the default double-click time of 500 milliseconds.

The **SetDoubleClickTime** function alters the double-click time for all windows in the system.

See Also   **GetDoubleClickTime**

SetErrorMode

2.x

UINT SetErrorMode(*fuErrorMode*)
UINT *fuErrorMode*;   /* specifies the error-mode flag   */

The **SetErrorMode** function controls whether Windows handles MS-DOS Interrupt 24h errors or allows the calling application to handle them.

Parameters   *fuErrorMode*
Specifies the error-mode flag. The flag can be a combination of the following values:

Value	Meaning
SEM_FAILCRITICALERRORS	Windows does not display the critical-error-handler message box and returns the error to the calling application.
SEM_NOGPFAULTERRORBOX	Windows does not display the general-protection-fault message box. This flag should be set *only* by debugging applications that handle GP faults themselves.
SEM_NOOPENFILEERRORBOX	Windows does not display a message box when it fails to find a file.

Return Value   The return value is the previous state of the error-mode flag, if the function is successful.

Example   The following example uses the **SetErrorMode** function to turn off the file-not-found message box (the application handles this error itself):

```
/* Turn off the "File not found" error box. */

SetErrorMode(SEM_NOOPENFILEERRORBOX);

/* Load the TOOLHELP.DLL library module. */

hinstToolHelp = LoadLibrary("TOOLHELP.DLL");

if (hinstToolHelp > HINSTANCE_ERROR) {    /* loaded successfully */

    .
    . /* Use the DLL here. */
    .

}
```

```
            else {
                strcpy(szBuf, "LoadLibrary failed");
            }

            MessageBox(NULL, szBuf, "Library Functions", MB_ICONHAND);
```

SetFocus

HWND SetFocus(*hwnd*)
HWND *hwnd*;   /* handle of window to receive focus   */

The **SetFocus** function sets the input focus to the given window. All subsequent keyboard input is directed to this window. The window, if any, that previously had the input focus loses it.

Parameters   *hwnd*
Identifies the window to receive the keyboard input. If this parameter is NULL, keystrokes are ignored.

Return Value   The return value identifies the window that previously had the input focus, if the function is successful. It is NULL if there is no such window or if the specified handle is invalid.

Comments   The **SetFocus** function sends a WM_KILLFOCUS message to the window that loses the input focus and a WM_SETFOCUS message to the window that receives the input focus. It also activates either the window that receives the focus or the parent of the window that receives the focus.

If a window is active but does not have the focus (that is, no window has the focus), any key pressed will produce the WM_SYSCHAR, WM_SYSKEYDOWN, or WM_SYSKEYUP message. If the VK_MENU key is also pressed, the *lParam* parameter of the message will have bit 30 set. Otherwise, the messages that are produced do *not* have this bit set.

See Also   **GetActiveWindow, GetFocus, SetActiveWindow, SetCapture**

SetHandleCount

UINT SetHandleCount(*cHandles*)
UINT *cHandles*;   /* number of file handles needed   */

> The **SetHandleCount** function changes the number of file handles available to a task.

Parameters   *cHandles*
> Specifies the number of file handles the application requires. This count cannot be greater than 255.

Return Value   The return value is the number of file handles available to the application, if the function is successful. This number may be less than the number of handles specified.

Comments   By default, the maximum number of file handles available to a task is 20.

Example   The following example uses the **SetHandleCount** function to set the number of available file handles to 30:

```
UINT cHandles;
char szBuf[80];

cHandles = SetHandleCount(30);

sprintf(szBuf, "%d handles available", cHandles);
MessageBox(hwnd, szBuf, "SetHandleCount", MB_OK);
```

SetKeyboardState

void SetKeyboardState(*lpbKeyState*)
BYTE FAR* *lpbKeyState*;   /* address of array with virtual-key codes   */

> The **SetKeyboardState** function copies a 256-byte array of keyboard key states into the Windows keyboard-state table.

Parameters   *lpbKeyState*
> Points to a 256-byte array that contains keyboard key states.

Return Value   This function does not return a value.

Comments   In many cases, an application should call the **GetKeyboardState** function first to
                        initialize the 256-byte array. The application should then change the desired bytes.

                        SetKeyboardState sets the LEDs and BIOS flags for the NUMLOCK, CAPSLOCK,
                        and SCROLL LOCK keys according to the toggle state of the VK_NUMLOCK,
                        VK_CAPITAL, and VK_SCROLL entries of the array.

                        For more information, see the description of the **GetKeyboardState** function.

Example   The following example simulates the pressing of the CTRL key:

```
BYTE pbKeyState[256];

GetKeyboardState((LPBYTE) &pbKeyState);
pbKeyState[VK_CONTROL] |= 0x80;
SetKeyboardState((LPBYTE) &pbKeyState);
```

See Also   **GetKeyboardState**

SetMapMode   2.x

int SetMapMode(*hdc*, *fnMapMode*)
HDC *hdc*;   /* handle of device context   */
int *fnMapMode*;   /* mapping mode to set   */

                        The **SetMapMode** function sets the mapping mode of the given device context.
                        The mapping mode defines the unit of measure used to convert logical units to
                        device units; it also defines the orientation of the device's x- and y-axes. GDI uses
                        the mapping mode to convert logical coordinates into the appropriate device
                        coordinates.

Parameters   *hdc*
                            Identifies the device context.

                        fnMapMode
                            Specifies the new mapping mode. This parameter can be any one of the follow-
                            ing values:

Value	Meaning
MM_ANISOTROPIC	Logical units are converted to arbitrary units with arbitrarily scaled axes. Setting the mapping mode to MM_ANISOTROPIC does not change the current window or viewport settings. To change the units, orientation, and scaling, an application should use the **SetWindowExt** and **SetViewportExt** functions.
MM_HIENGLISH	Each logical unit is converted to 0.001 inch. Positive x is to the right; positive y is up.
MM_HIMETRIC	Each logical unit is converted to 0.01 millimeter. Positive x is to the right; positive y is up.
MM_ISOTROPIC	Logical units are converted to arbitrary units with equally scaled axes; that is, one unit along the x-axis is equal to one unit along the y-axis. The **SetWindowExt** and **SetViewportExt** functions must be used to specify the desired units and the orientation of the axes. GDI makes adjustments as necessary to ensure that the x and y units remain the same size.
MM_LOENGLISH	Each logical unit is converted to 0.01 inch. Positive x is to the right; positive y is up.
MM_LOMETRIC	Each logical unit is converted to 0.1 millimeter. Positive x is to the right; positive y is up.
MM_TEXT	Each logical unit is converted to one device pixel. Positive x is to the right; positive y is down.
MM_TWIPS	Each logical unit is converted to 1/20 of a point. (Because a point is 1/72 inch, a twip is 1/1440 inch). Positive x is to the right; positive y is up.

Return Value   The return value is the previous mapping mode, if the function is successful.

Comments   The MM_TEXT mode allows applications to work in device pixels, where one unit is equal to one pixel. The physical size of a pixel varies from device to device.

The MM_HIENGLISH, MM_HIMETRIC, MM_LOENGLISH, MM_LOMETRIC, and MM_TWIPS modes are useful for applications that must draw in physically meaningful units (such as inches or millimeters).

The MM_ISOTROPIC mode ensures a 1:1 aspect ratio, which is useful when it is important to preserve the exact shape of an image.

The MM_ANISOTROPIC mode allows the x- and y-coordinates to be adjusted independently.

Example   The following example uses the **SetMapMode** function to set the mapping mode to MM_TWIPS and then uses the **CreateFont** function to create an 18-point logical font:

```
HFONT hfont, hfontOld;
int MapModePrevious, iPtSize = 18;
PSTR pszFace = "MS Serif";

MapModePrevious = SetMapMode(hdc, MM_TWIPS);
hfont = CreateFont(-iPtSize * 20, 0, 0, 0, 0, /* specify pt size    */
    0, 0, 0, 0, 0, 0, 0, 0, pszFace);          /* and face name only */

hfontOld = SelectObject(hdc, hfont);

TextOut(hdc, 100, -500, pszFace, strlen(pszFace));
SetMapMode(hdc, MapModePrevious);
SelectObject(hdc, hfontOld);
DeleteObject(hfont);
```

See Also   **GetMapMode, SetViewportExt, SetWindowExt**

SetMapperFlags   2.x

DWORD SetMapperFlags(*hdc, fdwMatch*)
HDC *hdc*;   /* handle of device context   */
DWORD *fdwMatch*;   /* mapper flag   */

The **SetMapperFlags** function changes the method used by the font mapper when
it converts a logical font to a physical font. An application can use **SetMapper-
Flags** to cause the font mapper to attempt to choose only a physical font that exactly matches the aspect ratio of the specified device.

Parameters   *hdc*
Identifies a device context.

fdwMatch
Specifies whether the font mapper attempts to match a font's aspect height and
width to the device. When this value is ASPECT_FILTERING, the mapper
selects only fonts whose x-aspect and y-aspect exactly match those of the
specified device, and the remaining bits are ignored.

Return Value   The return value is the previous value of the font-mapper flag, if the function is
successful.

Comments   An application that uses only raster fonts can use the **SetMapperFlags** function to
ensure that the font selected by the font mapper is attractive and readable on the
specified device. Applications that use scalable (TrueType) fonts typically do not
use **SetMapperFlags**.

If no physical font has an aspect ratio that matches the specifications in the logical font, GDI chooses a new aspect ratio and selects a font that matches this new aspect ratio.

SetMenu

2.x

BOOL SetMenu(*hwnd*, *hmenu*)
HWND *hwnd*;   /* handle of window   */
HMENU *hmenu*;   /* handle of menu   */

The **SetMenu** function sets the given window's menu to the specified menu.

Parameters
hwnd
Identifies the window whose menu is to be changed.

hmenu
Identifies the new menu. If this parameter is NULL, the window's current menu is removed.

Return Value
The return value is nonzero if the function is successful. Otherwise, it is zero.

Comments
The **SetMenu** function causes the window to be redrawn to reflect the menu change.

SetMenu will not destroy a previous menu. An application should call the **DestroyMenu** function to accomplish this task.

Example
```
HMENU hmenu;

hmenu = LoadMenu(hinst, "My Menu");
SetMenu(hwnd, hmenu);
```

See Also
DestroyMenu, LoadMenu, LoadMenuIndirect

SetMenuItemBitmaps

BOOL SetMenuItemBitmaps(*hmenu, idItem, fuFlags, hbmUnchecked, hbmChecked*)
HMENU *hmenu*;   /* handle of menu   */
UINT *idItem*;   /* menu-item identifier   */
UINT *fuFlags*;   /* menu-item flags   */
HBITMAP *hbmUnchecked*;   /* handle of unchecked bitmap   */
HBITMAP *hbmChecked*;   /* handle of checked bitmap   */

The **SetMenuItemBitmaps** function associates the given bitmaps with a menu item. Whether the menu item is checked or unchecked, Windows displays the appropriate check-mark bitmap next to the menu item.

Parameters

hmenu
Identifies the menu.

idItem
Specifies the menu item to be changed, as determined by the *fuFlags* parameter.

fuFlags
Specifies how the *idItem* parameter is interpreted. This parameter can be one of the following values:

Value	Meaning
MF_BYCOMMAND	The *idItem* parameter specifies the menu-item identifier (default value).
MF_BYPOSITION	The *idItem* parameter specifies the zero-based position of the menu item.

hbmUnchecked
Identifies the check-mark bitmap to display when the menu item is not checked.

hbmChecked
Identifies the check-mark bitmap to display when the menu item is checked.

Return Value

The return value is nonzero if the function is successful. Otherwise, it is zero.

Comments

If either the *hbmUnchecked* or the *hbmChecked* parameter is NULL, Windows displays nothing next to the menu item for the corresponding attribute. If both parameters are NULL, Windows uses the default check mark when the item is checked and removes the check mark when the item is unchecked.

When the menu is destroyed, these bitmaps are not destroyed; the application must destroy them.

The **GetMenuCheckMarkDimensions** function retrieves the dimensions of the default check mark used for menu items. The application should use these values to determine the appropriate size for the bitmaps supplied with this function.

See Also   **GetMenuCheckMarkDimensions**

SetMessageQueue

2.x

BOOL SetMessageQueue(*cMsg*)
int *cMsg*;   /* size of message queue   */

The **SetMessageQueue** function creates a new message queue. It is particularly useful in applications that require a queue that contains more than eight messages (the maximum size of the default queue).

Parameters   *cMsg*
Specifies the maximum number of messages that the new queue may contain. This value must not be larger than 120.

Return Value   The return value is nonzero if the function is successful. If the value specified in the *cMsg* parameter is larger than 120, the return value is nonzero but the message queue is not created. The return value is zero if an error occurs.

Comments   The function must be called from an application's **WinMain** function before any windows are created and before any messages are sent. The **SetMessageQueue** function destroys the old queue, along with messages it might contain.

If the return value is zero, the application has no queue, because the **Set-MessageQueue** function deletes the original queue before attempting to create a new one. The application must continue calling **SetMessageQueue** with a smaller queue size until the function returns nonzero.

See Also   **GetMessage**, **PeekMessage**

SetMetaFileBits

2.x

HGLOBAL SetMetaFileBits(*hmf*)
HMETAFILE *hmf*;   /* handle of metafile   */

The **SetMetaFileBits** function creates a memory metafile from the data in the given global memory object.

Parameters
    hmf
        Identifies the global memory object that contains the metafile data. The object must have been created by a previous call to the **GetMetaFileBits** function.

Return Value
    The return value is the handle of a memory metafile, if the function is successful. Otherwise, it is NULL.

Comments
    After the **SetMetaFileBits** function returns, the metafile handle it returns must be used instead of the *hmf* handle to refer to the metafile. If **SetMetaFileBits** is successful, the application should not use or free the memory handle specified by the *hmf* parameter, because that handle is reused by Windows.

    When the application no longer needs the metafile header, it should free the handle by calling the **DeleteMetaFile** function.

See Also
    GetMetaFileBits, GlobalFree

SetMetaFileBitsBetter

3.1

HGLOBAL SetMetaFileBitsBetter(*hmf*)
HMETAFILE *hmf*;   /* handle of the metafile   */

The **SetMetaFileBitsBetter** function creates a memory metafile from the data in the specified global-memory object.

Parameters
    hmf
        Identifies the global-memory object that contains the metafile data. The object must have been created by a previous call to the **GetMetaFileBits** function.

Return Value
    The return value is the handle of a memory metafile, if the function is successful. Otherwise, the return value is NULL.

Comments   The global-memory handle returned by **SetMetaFileBitsBetter** is owned by GDI, not by the application. This enables applications that use metafiles to support object linking and embedding (OLE) to use metafiles that persist beyond the termination of the application. An OLE application should always use **SetMeta-FileBitsBetter** instead of the **SetMetaFileBits** function.

After the **SetMetaFileBitsBetter** function returns, the metafile handle returned by the function should be used to refer to the metafile, instead of the handle identified by the *hmf* parameter.

See Also   **GetMetaFileBits**, **SetMetaFileBits**

SetPaletteEntries   [3.0]

UINT SetPaletteEntries(*hpal*, *iStart*, *cEntries*, *lppe***)**
HPALETTE *hpal*;   /* handle of palette   */
UINT *iStart*;   /* index of first entry to set   */
UINT *cEntries*;   /* number of entries to set   */
const PALETTEENTRY FAR* *lppe*;   /* address of array of structures   */

The **SetPaletteEntries** function sets RGB color values and flags in a range of entries in the given logical palette.

Parameters   *hpal*
                    Identifies the logical palette.

iStart
    Specifies the first logical-palette entry to be set.

cEntries
    Specifies the number of logical-palette entries to be set.

lppe
    Points to the first member of an array of **PALETTEENTRY** structures containing the RGB values and flags. The **PALETTEENTRY** structure has the following form:

```
typedef struct tagPALETTEENTRY {      /* pe */
    BYTE   peRed;
    BYTE   peGreen;
    BYTE   peBlue;
    BYTE   peFlags;
} PALETTEENTRY;
```

For a full description of this structure, see the *Microsoft Windows Programmer's Reference, Volume 3.*

Return Value   The return value is the number of entries set in the logical palette, if the function is successful. Otherwise, it is zero.

Comments   If the logical palette is selected into a device context when the application calls the **SetPaletteEntries** function, the changes will not take effect until the application calls the **RealizePalette** function.

See Also   **RealizePalette**

SetParent   2.x

HWND SetParent(*hwndChild*, *hwndNewParent*)
HWND *hwndChild*;   /* handle of window whose parent is changing   */
HWND *hwndNewParent*;   /* handle of new parent window   */

The **SetParent** function changes the parent window of the given child window.

Parameters   *hwndChild*
Identifies the child window.

hwndNewParent
Identifies the new parent window.

Return Value   The return value is the handle of the previous parent window, if the function is successful.

Comments   If the window identified by the *hwndChild* parameter is visible, Windows performs the appropriate redrawing and repainting.

See Also   **GetParent, IsChild**

SetPixel   2.x

COLORREF SetPixel(*hdc*, *nXPos*, *nYPos*, *clrref*)
HDC *hdc*;   /* handle of device context   */
int *nXPos*;   /* x-coordinate of pixel to set   */
int *nYPos*;   /* y-coordinate of pixel to set   */
COLORREF *clrref*;   /* color of set pixel   */

The **SetPixel** function sets the pixel at the specified coordinates to the closest approximation of the given color. The point must be in the clipping region; if it is not, the function does nothing.

Parameters

hdc
Identifies the device context.

nXPos
Specifies the logical x-coordinate of the point to be set.

nYPos
Specifies the logical y-coordinate of the point to be set.

clrref
Specifies the color to be used to paint the point.

Return Value

The return value is the RGB value for the color the point is painted, if the function is successful. This value can be different from the specified value if an approximation of that color is used. The return value is −1 if the function fails (if the point is outside the clipping region).

Comments

Not all devices support the **SetPixel** function. To discover whether a device supports raster operations, an application can call the **GetDeviceCaps** function using the RC_BITBLT index.

See Also

GetDeviceCaps, **GetPixel**

SetPolyFillMode   2.x

int SetPolyFillMode(*hdc*, *fnMode*)
HDC *hdc*;   /* handle of device context   */
int *fnMode*;   /* polygon-filling mode   */

The **SetPolyFillMode** function sets the specified polygon-filling mode.

Parameters

hdc
Identifies the device context.

fnMode
Specifies the new filling mode. This value may be either ALTERNATE or WINDING. The default mode is ALTERNATE.

Return Value

The return value specifies the previous filling mode, if the function is successful. Otherwise, it is zero.

Comments

When the polygon-filling mode is ALTERNATE, the system fills the area between odd-numbered and even-numbered polygon sides on each scan line. That is, the system fills the area between the first and second side, between the third and fourth side, and so on.

When the polygon-filling mode is WINDING, the system uses the direction in which a figure was drawn to determine whether to fill an area. Each line segment in a polygon is drawn in either a clockwise or a counterclockwise direction. Whenever an imaginary line drawn from an enclosed area to the outside of a figure passes through a clockwise line segment, a count is incremented (increased by one); when the line passes through a counterclockwise line segment, the count is decremented (decreased by one). The area is filled if the count is nonzero when the line reaches the outside of the figure.

Example

The following example uses winding mode to draw the same figure twice. The figure is a rectangle that completely encloses a triangle. The first time the figure is drawn, both the rectangle and the triangle are drawn clockwise, and both the rectangle and the triangle are filled. The second time, the rectangle is drawn clockwise, but the triangle is drawn counterclockwise; the rectangle is filled, but the triangle is not. (If the figures had been drawn using alternate mode, the rectangle would have been filled and the triangle would not have been filled, in both cases.)

```
HBRUSH hbrGray, hbrPrevious;

/*
 * Define the points for a clockwise triangle in a clockwise
 * rectangle.
 */

POINT aPolyPoints[9] = {{  50,  60 }, { 250,  60 }, { 250, 260 },
    {  50, 260 }, {  50,  60 }, { 150,  80 },
    { 230, 240 }, {  70, 240 }, { 150,  80 }};

int aPolyCount[] = { 5, 4 };
int cValues, i;

hbrGray = GetStockObject(GRAY_BRUSH);
hbrPrevious = SelectObject(hdc, hbrGray);

cValues = sizeof(aPolyCount) / sizeof(int);

SetPolyFillMode(hdc, WINDING);      /* sets winding mode */
PolyPolygon(hdc, aPolyPoints, aPolyCount, cValues);

/* Define the triangle counter-clockwise */

aPolyPoints[6].x = 70;  aPolyPoints[6].y = 240;
aPolyPoints[7].x = 230; aPolyPoints[7].y = 240;
```

```
for (i = 0; i < sizeof(aPolyPoints) / sizeof(POINT); i++)
    aPolyPoints[i].x += 300;   /* moves figure 300 units right */

PolyPolygon(hdc, aPolyPoints, aPolyCount, cValues);

SelectObject(hdc, hbrPrevious);
```

See Also   **GetPolyFillMode, PolyPolygon**

SetProp   2.x

BOOL SetProp(*hwnd*, *lpsz*, *hData*)
HWND *hwnd*;   /* handle of window   */
LPCSTR *lpsz*;   /* atom or address of string   */
HANDLE *hData*;   /* handle of data   */

The **SetProp** function adds a new entry or changes an existing entry in the property list of the given window. The function adds a new entry to the list if the given character string does not exist already in the list. The new entry contains the string and the handle. Otherwise, the function replaces the string's current handle with the given handle.

Parameters   *hwnd*
Identifies the window whose property list receives the new entry.

lpsz
Points to a null-terminated string or an atom that identifies a string. If this parameter is an atom, it must be a global atom created by a previous call to the **GlobalAddAtom** function. The atom, a 16-bit value, must be placed in the low-order word of *lpsz*; the high-order word must be zero.

hData
Identifies data to be copied to the property list. The data handle can identify any 16-bit value useful to the application.

Return Value   The return value is nonzero if the data handle and string are added to the property list. Otherwise, it is zero.

Comments   Before destroying a window (that is, before processing the WM_DESTROY message), an application must remove all entries it has added to the property list. The **RemoveProp** function must be used to remove entries from a property list.

See Also   **GetProp, GlobalAddAtom, RemoveProp**

SetRect

void SetRect(*lprc, nLeft, nTop, nRight, nBottom*)
RECT FAR* *lprc*;   /* address of structure with rectangle to set   */
int *nLeft*;   /* left side   */
int *nTop*;   /* top side   */
int *nRight*;   /* right side   */
int *nBottom*;   /* bottom side   */

The **SetRect** function sets rectangle coordinates. The action of this function is equivalent to assigning the left, top, right, and bottom arguments to the appropriate members of the **RECT** structure.

Parameters

lprc
Points to the **RECT** structure that contains the rectangle to be set. The **RECT** structure has the following form:

```
typedef struct tagRECT {    /* rc */
    int left;
    int top;
    int right;
    int bottom;
} RECT;
```

For a full description of this structure, see the *Microsoft Windows Programmer's Reference, Volume 3*.

nLeft
Specifies the x-coordinate of the upper-left corner.

nTop
Specifies the y-coordinate of the upper-left corner.

nRight
Specifies the x-coordinate of the lower-right corner.

nBottom
Specifies the y-coordinate of the lower-right corner.

Return Value

This function does not return a value.

Comments

The width of the rectangle, specified by the absolute value of *nRight* – *nLeft*, must not exceed 32,767 units. This limit also applies to the height of the rectangle.

See Also

CopyRect, SetRectEmpty

SetRectEmpty

void SetRectEmpty(*lprc***)**
RECT FAR* *lprc*;   /* address of struct. with rectangle to set to empty   */

The **SetRectEmpty** function creates an empty rectangle (all coordinates set to zero).

Parameters   *lprc*
Points to the **RECT** structure that contains the rectangle to be set to empty. The **RECT** structure has the following form:

```
typedef struct tagRECT {    /* rc */
    int left;
    int top;
    int right;
    int bottom;
} RECT;
```

For a full description of this structure, see the *Microsoft Windows Programmer's Reference, Volume 3.*

Return Value   This function does not return a value.

See Also   **CopyRect, SetRect**

SetRectRgn

void SetRectRgn(*hrgn, nLeftRect, nTopRect, nRightRect, nBottomRect***)**
HRGN *hrgn*;   /* handle of region   */
int *nLeftRect*;   /* x-coordinate top-left corner of rectangle   */
int *nTopRect*;   /* y-coordinate top-left corner of rectangle   */
int *nRightRect*;   /* x-coordinate bottom-right corner of rectangle   */
int *nBottomRect*;   /* y-coordinate bottom-right corner of rectangle   */

The **SetRectRgn** function changes the given region into a rectangular region with the specified coordinates.

Parameters   *hrgn*
Identifies the region.

nLeftRect
Specifies the x-coordinate of the upper-left corner of the rectangular region.

nTopRect
Specifies the y-coordinate of the upper-left corner of the rectangular region.

nRightRect
Specifies the x-coordinate of the lower-right corner of the rectangular region.

nBottomRect
Specifies the y-coordinate of the lower-right corner of the rectangular region.

Return Value   This function does not return a value.

Comments   Applications can use this function instead of the **CreateRectRgn** function to avoid allocating more memory from the GDI heap. Because the memory allocated for the *hrgn* parameter is reused, no new allocation is performed.

Example   The following example uses the **CreateRectRgn** function to create a rectangular region and then calls the **SetRectRgn** function to change the region coordinates:

```
HRGN hrgn;

hrgn = CreateRectRgn(10, 10, 30, 30);
PaintRgn(hdc, hrgn);

SetRectRgn(hrgn, 50, 50, 150, 200);
PaintRgn(hdc, hrgn);

DeleteObject(hrgn);
```

See Also   **CreateRectRgn**

SetResourceHandler

2.x

RSRCHDLRPROC SetResourceHandler(*hinst, lpszType, lpLoadProc*)
HINSTANCE *hinst*;   /* handle of application instance   */
LPCSTR *lpszType*;   /* address of resource-type identifier   */
RSRCHDLRPROC *lpLoadProc*;   /* callback procedure-instance address   */

The **SetResourceHandler** function installs a callback function that loads resources.

Parameters   *hinst*
Identifies the instance of the module whose executable file contains the resource.

lpszType
Points to a null-terminated string that specifies a resource type. For predefined resource types, the high-order word should be zero and the low-order word should indicate the resource type.

lpLoadProc
Specifies the procedure-instance address of the application-supplied callback function. For more information, see the description of the **LoadProc** callback function.

Return Value
The return value is a pointer to the previously installed resource handler, if the function is successful. If no resource handler has been explicitly installed, the return value is a pointer to the default resource handler.

Comments
An application may find this function useful for handling its own resource types, but the use of this function is not required.

The address passed as the *lpLoadProc* parameter must be created by using the **MakeProcInstance** function.

See Also
FindResource, LoadProc, LockResource, MakeProcInstance

SetROP2

`2.x`

int **SetROP2**(*hdc, fnDrawMode*)
HDC *hdc*;   /* handle of device context   */
int *fnDrawMode*;   /* new drawing mode   */

The **SetROP2** function sets the current drawing mode. The drawing mode specifies how the colors of the pen and the interior of filled objects are combined with the color already on the screen surface.

Parameters
hdc
Identifies the device context.

fnDrawMode
Specifies the new drawing mode. This parameter can be one of the following values:

Value	Meaning
R2_BLACK	Pixel is always black.
R2_WHITE	Pixel is always white.
R2_NOP	Pixel remains unchanged.
R2_NOT	Pixel is the inverse of the screen color.
R2_COPYPEN	Pixel is the pen color.
R2_NOTCOPYPEN	Pixel is the inverse of the pen color.
R2_MERGEPENNOT	Pixel is a combination of the pen color and the inverse of the screen color (final pixel = (~screen pixel) | pen).
R2_MASKPENNOT	Pixel is a combination of the colors common to both the pen and the inverse of the screen (final pixel = (~screen pixel) & pen).
R2_MERGENOTPEN	Pixel is a combination of the screen color and the inverse of the pen color (final pixel = (~pen) | screen pixel).
R2_MASKNOTPEN	Pixel is a combination of the colors common to both the screen and the inverse of the pen (final pixel = (~pen) & screen pixel).
R2_MERGEPEN	Pixel is a combination of the pen color and the screen color (final pixel = pen | screen pixel).
R2_NOTMERGEPEN	Pixel is the inverse of the R2_MERGEPEN color (final pixel = ~(pen | screen pixel)).
R2_MASKPEN	Pixel is a combination of the colors common to both the pen and the screen (final pixel = pen & screen pixel).
R2_NOTMASKPEN	Pixel is the inverse of the R2_MASKPEN color (final pixel = ~(pen & screen pixel)).
R2_XORPEN	Pixel is a combination of the colors that are in the pen and in the screen, but not in both (final pixel = pen ^ screen pixel).
R2_NOTXORPEN	Pixel is the inverse of the R2_XORPEN color (final pixel = ~(pen ^ screen pixel)).

Return Value   The return value specifies the previous drawing mode, if the function is successful.

Comments   The drawing mode is for raster devices only; it does not apply to vector devices.

Drawing modes are binary raster-operation codes representing all possible Boolean combinations of two variables. These values are created by using the binary operations AND, OR, and XOR (exclusive OR) and the unary operation NOT.

See Also   **GetDeviceCaps, GetROP2**

SetScrollPos

$\boxed{\text{2.x}}$

int SetScrollPos(_hwnd, fnBar, nPos, fRepaint_**)**
HWND _hwnd_;   /* handle of window with scroll bar   */
int _fnBar_;   /* scroll bar flag   */
int _nPos_;   /* new position of scroll box   */
BOOL _fRepaint_;   /* redraw flag   */

The **SetScrollPos** function sets the position of a scroll box (thumb) and, if requested, redraws the scroll bar to reflect the new position of the scroll box.

Parameters

hwnd
Identifies the window whose scroll bar is to be set.

fnBar
Specifies the scroll bar to be set. This parameter can be one of the following values:

Value	Meaning
SB_CTL	Sets the position of the scroll box in a scroll bar. In this case, the _hwnd_ parameter must be the handle of a scroll bar.
SB_HORZ	Sets the position of the scroll box in a window's horizontal scroll bar.
SB_VERT	Sets the position of the scroll box in a window's vertical scroll bar.

nPos
Specifies the new position of the scroll box. It must be within the scrolling range.

fRepaint
Specifies whether the scroll bar should be repainted to reflect the new scroll box position. If this parameter is TRUE, the scroll bar is repainted. If it is FALSE, the scroll bar is not repainted.

Return Value

The return value is the previous position of the scroll box, if the function is successful. Otherwise, it is zero.

Comments

Setting the _fRepaint_ parameter to FALSE is useful whenever the scroll bar will be redrawn by a subsequent call to another function.

See Also

GetScrollPos, **GetScrollRange**, **ScrollWindow**, **SetScrollRange**

SetScrollRange

void SetScrollRange(*hwnd, fnBar, nMin, nMax, fRedraw*)
HWND *hwnd*;   /* handle of window with scroll bar   */
int *fnBar*;   /* scroll bar flag   */
int *nMin*;   /* minimum scrolling position   */
int *nMax*;   /* maximum scrolling position   */
BOOL *fRedraw*;   /* redraw flag   */

The **SetScrollRange** function sets minimum and maximum position values for the given scroll bar. It can also be used to hide or show standard scroll bars.

Parameters

hwnd
Identifies a window or a scroll bar, depending on the value of *fnBar*.

fnBar
Specifies the scroll bar to be set. This parameter can be one of the following values:

Value	Meaning
SB_CTL	Sets the range of a scroll bar. In this case, the *hwnd* parameter must be the handle of a scroll bar.
SB_HORZ	Sets the range of a window's horizontal scroll bar.
SB_VERT	Sets the range of a window's vertical scroll bar.

nMin
Specifies the minimum scrolling position.

nMax
Specifies the maximum scrolling position.

fRedraw
Specifies whether the scroll bar should be redrawn to reflect the change. If this parameter is TRUE, the scroll bar is redrawn. If it is FALSE, the scroll bar is not redrawn.

Return Value

This function does not return a value.

Comments

An application should not call this function to hide a scroll bar while processing a scroll-bar notification message.

If the call to **SetScrollRange** immediately follows the call to the **SetScrollPos** function, the *fRedraw* parameter in **SetScrollPos** should be zero, to prevent the scroll bar from being drawn twice.

The default range for a standard scroll bar is 0 through 100. The default range for a scroll bar control is empty (both the *nMin* and *nMax* values are zero). The difference between the values specified by the *nMin* and *nMax* parameters must not be greater than 32,767.

See Also   **GetScrollPos, GetScrollRange, ScrollWindow, SetScrollPos**

SetSelectorBase   3.1

UINT SetSelectorBase(*selector*, *dwBase*)
UINT *selector*;   /* new selector   */
DWORD *dwBase*;   /* new base   */

The **SetSelectorBase** function sets the base and limit of a selector.

Parameters   *selector*
        Specifies the selector value to modify.

        dwBase
        Specifies the new base value. This value is the starting linear address that selector will reference.

Return Value   The return value is the selector value, or zero if an error occurs.

See Also   **GetSelectorBase, GetSelectorLimit, SetSelectorLimit**

SetSelectorLimit   3.1

UINT SetSelectorLimit(*selector*, *dwBase*)
UINT *selector*;   /* new selector   */
DWORD *dwBase*;   /* current base   */

The **SetSelectorLimit** function sets the limit of a selector.

Parameters   *selector*
        Specifies the selector to modify.

        dwBase
        Specifies the new limit value for *selector*. For an 80286 processor, this value must be less than 0x10000.

Return Value   The return value is always zero.

See Also   GetSelectorBase, GetSelectorLimit, SetSelectorBase

---

SetSoundNoise   `2.x`

int **SetSoundNoise**(*fnSource*, *nDuration*)
int *fnSource*;   /* source of noise   */
int *nDuration*;   /* duration of noise   */

This function is obsolete. Use the Microsoft Windows multimedia audio functions instead. For information about audio functions, see the *Microsoft Windows Multimedia Programmer's Reference.*

SetStretchBltMode   `2.x`

int **SetStretchBltMode**(*hdc*, *fnStretchMode*)
HDC *hdc*;   /* handle of device context   */
int *fnStretchMode*;   /* bitmap-stretching mode   */

The **SetStretchBltMode** function sets the bitmap-stretching mode. The bitmap-stretching mode defines how information is removed from bitmaps that are compressed by using the **StretchBlt** function.

Parameters   *hdc*
Identifies the device context.

fnStretchMode
Specifies the new bitmap-stretching mode. This parameter can be one of the following values:

Value	Meaning
STRETCH_ANDSCANS	Uses the AND operator to combine eliminated lines with the remaining lines. This mode preserves black pixels at the expense of colored or white pixels. It is the default mode.
STRETCH_DELETESCANS	Deletes the eliminated lines. Information in the eliminated lines is not preserved.
STRETCH_ORSCANS	Uses the OR operator to combine eliminated lines with the remaining lines. This mode preserves colored or white pixels at the expense of black pixels.

Return Value   The return value is the previous stretching mode, if the function is successful. It can be STRETCH_ANDSCANS, STRETCH_DELETESCANS, or STRETCH_ORSCANS.

Comments   The STRETCH_ANDSCANS and STRETCH_ORSCANS modes are typically used to preserve foreground pixels in monochrome bitmaps. The STRETCH_DELETESCANS mode is typically used to preserve color in color bitmaps.

See Also   **GetStretchBltMode, StretchBlt, StretchDIBits**

SetSwapAreaSize   2.x

LONG SetSwapAreaSize(*cCodeParagraphs*)
UINT *cCodeParagraphs*;   /* number of paragraphs for code   */

The **SetSwapAreaSize** function sets the amount of memory that an application uses for its code segments.

Parameters   *cCodeParagraphs*
Specifies the number of 16-byte paragraphs requested by the application for use as code segments. If this parameter is zero, the return value specifies the current size of the code-segment space.

Return Value   The return value is the amount of space available for the code segment, if the function is successful. The low-order word specifies the number of paragraphs obtained for use as a code-segment space (or the current size if the *cCodeParagraphs* parameter is zero); the high-order word specifies the maximum size available.

Comments   If *cCodeParagraphs* specifies a size larger than is available, this function sets the size to the available amount. The maximum amount of memory available is one half the space remaining after Windows is loaded.

Calling this function can improve an application's performance by preventing Windows from swapping code segments to the hard disk. However, increasing the code-segment space reduces the amount of memory available for data objects and can reduce the performance of other applications.

See Also   **GetNumTasks, GlobalAlloc**

SetSysColors

2.x

void SetSysColors(*cDspElements*, *lpnDspElements*, *lpdwRgbValues*)
int *cDspElements*;   /* number of elements to change   */
const int FAR* *lpnDspElements*;   /* address of array of elements   */
const COLORREF FAR* *lpdwRgbValues*;   /* address of array of RGB values   */

The **SetSysColors** function sets the system colors for one or more display elements. Display elements are the various parts of a window and the Windows background that appear on the screen.

The **SetSysColors** function sends a WM_SYSCOLORCHANGE message to all windows to inform them of the change in color. It also directs Windows to repaint the affected portions of all currently visible windows.

Parameters

cDspElements
Specifies the number of display elements in the array pointed to by the *lpnDspElements* parameter.

lpnDspElements
Points to an array of integers that specify the display elements to be changed. For a list of possible display elements, see the following Comments section.

lpdwRgbValues
Points to an array of unsigned long integers that contains the new RGB (red-green-blue) color value for each display element in the array pointed to by the *lpnDspElements* parameter.

Return Value

This function does not return a value.

Comments

The **SetSysColors** function changes the current Windows session only. The new colors are not saved when Windows terminates.

Following are the display elements that may be used in the *lpnDspElements* array:

Value	Meaning
COLOR_ACTIVEBORDER	Active window border.
COLOR_ACTIVECAPTION	Active window title.
COLOR_APPWORKSPACE	Background color of multiple document interface (MDI) applications.
COLOR_BACKGROUND	Desktop.
COLOR_BTNFACE	Face shading on push buttons.
COLOR_BTNHIGHLIGHT	Selected button in a control.
COLOR_BTNSHADOW	Edge shading on push buttons.
COLOR_BTNTEXT	Text on push buttons.

Value	Meaning
COLOR_CAPTIONTEXT	Text in title bar, size button, scroll-bar arrow button.
COLOR_GRAYTEXT	Grayed (dimmed) text. This color is zero if the current display driver does not support a solid gray color.
COLOR_HIGHLIGHT	Background of selected item in a control.
COLOR_HIGHLIGHTTEXT	Text of selected item in a control.
COLOR_INACTIVEBORDER	Inactive window border.
COLOR_INACTIVECAPTION	Inactive window title.
COLOR_INACTIVECAPTIONTEXT	Color of text in an inactive title.
COLOR_MENU	Menu background.
COLOR_MENUTEXT	Text in menus.
COLOR_SCROLLBAR	Scroll-bar gray area.
COLOR_WINDOW	Window background.
COLOR_WINDOWFRAME	Window frame.
COLOR_WINDOWTEXT	Text in windows.

Example   The following example changes the window background to black and the text in the window to green:

```
int aiDspElements[2];
DWORD aRgbValues[2];

aiDspElements[0] = COLOR_WINDOW;
aRgbValues[0] = RGB(
    0x00,    /* red   */
    0x00,    /* green */
    0x00);   /* blue  */
aiDspElements[1] = COLOR_WINDOWTEXT;
aRgbValues[1] = RGB(
    0x00,    /* red   */
    0xff,    /* green */
    0x00);   /* blue  */
SetSysColors(2, aiDspElements, aRgbValues);
```

See Also   **GetSysColor**

SetSysModalWindow

HWND SetSysModalWindow(*hwnd*)
HWND *hwnd*;   /* handle of window to become system modal   */

The **SetSysModalWindow** function makes the given window the system-modal window.

Parameters   *hwnd*
Identifies the window to be made system modal.

Return Value   The return value is the handle of the window that was previously the system-modal window, if the function is successful.

Comments   If another window is made the active window (for example, the system-modal window creates a dialog box that becomes the active window), the active window becomes the system-modal window. When the original window becomes active again, it is once again the system-modal window. To end the system-modal state, destroy the system-modal window.

If a WH_JOURNALRECORD hook is in place when **SetSysModalWindow** is called, the hook is called with a hook code of HC_SYSMODALON (for turning on the system-modal window) or HC_SYSMODALOFF (for turning off the system-modal window).

See Also   **GetSysModalWindow**

SetSystemPaletteUse

UINT SetSystemPaletteUse(*hdc*, *fuStatic*)
HDC *hdc*;   /* handle of device context   */
UINT *fuStatic*;   /* system-palette contents   */

The **SetSystemPaletteUse** function sets the use of static colors in the system palette. The default system palette contains 20 static colors, which are not changed when an application realizes its logical palette. An application can use **SetSystemPaletteUse** to change this to two static colors (black and white).

Parameters   *hdc*
Identifies the device context. This device context must support color palettes.

fuStatic

Specifies the new use of the system palette. This parameter can be either of the following values:

Value	Meaning
SYSPAL_NOSTATIC	System palette contains no static colors except black and white.
SYSPAL_STATIC	System palette contains static colors that will not change when an application realizes its logical palette.

Return Value

The return value is the previous setting for the static colors in the system palette, if the function is successful. This setting is either SYSPAL_NOSTATIC or SYSPAL_STATIC.

Comments

An application must call this function only when its window is maximized and has the input focus.

If an application calls **SetSystemPaletteUse** with *fuStatic* set to SYSPAL_NOSTATIC, Windows continues to set aside two entries in the system palette for pure white and pure black, respectively.

After calling this function with *fuStatic* set to SYSPAL_NOSTATIC, an application must follow these steps:

1. Call the **UnrealizeObject** function to force the graphics device interface (GDI) to remap the logical palette completely when it is realized.

2. Realize the logical palette.

3. Call the **GetSysColor** function to save the current system-color settings.

4. Call the **SetSysColors** function to set the system colors to reasonable values using black and white. For example, adjacent or overlapping items (such as window frames and borders) should be set to black and white, respectively.

5. Send the WM_SYSCOLORCHANGE message to other top-level windows to allow them to be redrawn with the new system colors.

When the application's window loses focus or closes, the application must perform the following steps:

1. Call **SetSystemPaletteUse** with the *fuStatic* parameter set to SYSPAL_STATIC.

2. Call **UnrealizeObject** to force GDI to remap the logical palette completely when it is realized.

3. Realize the logical palette.

4. Restore the system colors to their previous values.

5. Send the WM_SYSCOLORCHANGE message.

See Also   GetSysColor, SetSysColors, SetSystemPaletteUse, UnrealizeObject

SetTextAlign   `2.x`

UINT SetTextAlign(*hdc, fuAlign*)
HDC *hdc*;   /* handle of device context   */
UINT *fuAlign*;   /* text-alignment flags   */

The **SetTextAlign** function sets the text-alignment flags for the given device context.

Parameters   *hdc*
Identifies the device context.

fuAlign
Specifies text-alignment flags. The flags specify the relationship between a point and a rectangle that bounds the text. The point can be either the current position or coordinates specified by a text-output function (such as the **Ext-TextOut** function). The rectangle that bounds the text is defined by the adjacent character cells in the text string.

The *fuAlign* parameter can be one or more flags from the following three categories. Choose only one flag from each category.

The first category affects text alignment in the x-direction:

Value	Meaning
TA_CENTER	Aligns the point with the horizontal center of the bounding rectangle.
TA_LEFT	Aligns the point with the left side of the bounding rectangle. This is the default setting.
TA_RIGHT	Aligns the point with the right side of the bounding rectangle.

The second category affects text alignment in the y-direction:

Value	Meaning
TA_BASELINE	Aligns the point with the base line of the chosen font.
TA_BOTTOM	Aligns the point with the bottom of the bounding rectangle.
TA_TOP	Aligns the point with the top of the bounding rectangle. This is the default setting.

The third category determines whether the current position is updated when text is written:

Value	Meaning
TA_NOUPDATECP	Does not update the current position after each call to a text-output function. This is the default setting.
TA_UPDATECP	Updates the current x-position after each call to a text-output function. The new position is at the right side of the bounding rectangle for the text. When this flag is set, the coordinates specified in calls to the **TextOut** function are ignored.

Return Value

The return value is the previous text-alignment settings, if the function is successful. The low-order byte contains the horizontal setting; the high-order byte contains the vertical setting. Otherwise, the return value is zero.

Comments

The text-alignment flags set by **SetTextAlign** are used by the **TextOut** and **Ext-TextOut** functions.

Example

The following example uses the **GetTextFace** function to retrieve the name of the current typeface, calls **SetTextAlign** so that the current position is updated when the **TextOut** function is called, and then writes some introductory text and the name of the typeface by calling **TextOut**:

```
int nFaceNameLen;
char aFaceName[80];

nFaceNameLen = GetTextFace(hdc, /* returns length of string */
    sizeof(aFaceName),        /* size of face-name buffer   */
    (LPSTR) aFaceName);       /* address of face-name buffer */

SetTextAlign(hdc,
    TA_UPDATECP);             /* updates current position    */
MoveTo(hdc, 100, 100);       /* sets current position       */
TextOut(hdc, 0, 0,           /* uses current position for text */
    "This is the current face name: ", 31);
TextOut(hdc, 0, 0, aFaceName, nFaceNameLen);
```

See Also

ExtTextOut, GetTextAlign, TextOut

SetTextCharacterExtra

2.x

```
int SetTextCharacterExtra(hdc, nExtraSpace)
HDC hdc;            /* handle of device context   */
int nExtraSpace;   /* extra character spacing    */
```

The **SetTextCharacterExtra** function sets the amount of intercharacter spacing. The graphics device interface (GDI) adds this spacing to each character, including break characters, when it writes a line of text to the device context.

Parameters   *hdc*
Identifies the device context.

nExtraSpace
Specifies the amount of extra space, in logical units, to be added to each character. If the current mapping mode is not MM_TEXT, this parameter is transformed and rounded to the nearest pixel.

Return Value   The return value is the previous intercharacter spacing, if the function is successful.

Comments   The default value for the amount of intercharacter spacing is zero.

See Also   **GetTextCharacterExtra**

SetTextColor   `2.x`

COLORREF SetTextColor(*hdc, clrref*)
HDC *hdc*;   /* handle of device context   */
COLORREF *clrref*;   /* new color for text   */

The **SetTextColor** function sets the text color to the specified color. The system uses the text color when writing text to a device context and also when converting bitmaps between color and monochrome device contexts.

Parameters   *hdc*
Identifies the device context.

clrref
Specifies the color of the text.

Return Value   The return value is the RGB (red-green-blue) value for the previous text color, if the function is successful.

Comments   If the device cannot represent the specified color, the system sets the text color to the nearest physical color.

The background color for a character is specified by the **SetBkColor** and **SetBkMode** functions.

Example

The following example sets the text color to red if the **GetTextColor** function determines that the current text color is black. The text color is specified by using the **RGB** macro.

```
DWORD dwColor;

dwColor = GetTextColor(hdc);
if (dwColor == RGB(0, 0, 0))    /* if current color is black */
    SetTextColor(hdc, RGB(255, 0, 0)); /* sets color to red  */
```

See Also

GetTextColor, BitBlt, SetBkColor, SetBkMode

SetTextJustification

2.x

int SetTextJustification(*hdc*, *nExtraSpace*, *cBreakChars*)
HDC *hdc*;   /* handle of device context   */
int *nExtraSpace*;   /* space to add to string   */
int *cBreakChars*;   /* number of break characters in the string */

The **SetTextJustification** function adds space to the break characters in a string. An application can use the **GetTextMetrics** function to retrieve a font's break character.

Parameters

hdc
Identifies the device context.

nExtraSpace
Specifies the total extra space, in logical units, to be added to the line of text. If the current mapping mode is not MM_TEXT, the value given by this parameter is converted to the current mapping mode and rounded to the nearest device unit.

cBreakChars
Specifies the number of break characters in the line.

Return Value

The return value is 1 if the function is successful. Otherwise, it is zero.

Comments

After the **SetTextJustification** function is called, a call to a text-output function (for example, **TextOut**) distributes the specified extra space evenly among the specified number of break characters. The break character is usually the space character (ASCII 32), but it may be defined by a font as some other character.

The **GetTextExtent** function is typically used with **SetTextJustification**. The **GetTextExtent** function computes the width of a given line before alignment. An application can determine how much space to specify in the *nExtraSpace* parameter by subtracting the value returned by **GetTextExtent** from the width of the string after alignment.

The **SetTextJustification** function can be used to align a line that contains multiple runs in different fonts. In this case, the line must be created piecemeal by aligning and writing each run separately.

Because rounding errors can occur during alignment, the system keeps a running error term that defines the current error. When aligning a line that contains multiple runs, **GetTextExtent** automatically uses this error term when it computes the extent of the next run, allowing the text-output function to blend the error into the new run. After each line has been aligned, this error term must be cleared to prevent it from being incorporated into the next line. The term can be cleared by calling **SetTextJustification** with the *nExtraSpace* parameter set to zero.

Example

The following example writes two lines of text inside a box; one of the lines is aligned, and the other is not. The **GetTextExtent** function determines the width of the unaligned string. The **GetTextMetrics** function determines the break character that is used by the current font; this information is then used to determine how many break characters the string contains. The **SetTextJustification** function specifies the total amount of extra space and the number of break characters to distribute it among. After writing a line of aligned text, **SetTextJustification** is called again, to set the error term to zero.

```
POINT aPoints[5];
int iLMargin = 10, iRMargin = 10, iBoxWidth;
int cchString;
LPSTR lpszJustified = "Text to be justified in this test.";
DWORD dwExtent;
WORD wTextWidth;
TEXTMETRIC tm;
int j, cBreakChars;

aPoints[0].x = 100; aPoints[0].y =  50;
aPoints[1].x = 600; aPoints[1].y =  50;
aPoints[2].x = 600; aPoints[2].y = 200;
aPoints[3].x = 100; aPoints[3].y = 200;
aPoints[4].x = 100; aPoints[4].y =  50;

Polyline(hdc, aPoints, sizeof(aPoints) / sizeof(POINT));

TextOut(hdc, 100 + iLMargin, 100, "Unjustified text.", 17);
cchString = lstrlen(lpszJustified);
dwExtent = GetTextExtent(hdc, lpszJustified, cchString);
wTextWidth = LOWORD(dwExtent);

iBoxWidth = aPoints[1].x - aPoints[0].x;
GetTextMetrics(hdc, &tm);
```

```
for (cBreakChars = 0, j = 0; j < cchString; j++)
    if (*(lpszJustified + j) == (char) tm.tmBreakChar)
        cBreakChars++;

SetTextJustification(hdc,
    iBoxWidth - wTextWidth - (iLMargin + iRMargin),
    cBreakChars);

TextOut(hdc, 100 + iLMargin, 150, lpszJustified, cchString);

SetTextJustification(hdc, 0, 0);      /* clears error term */
```

See Also   **GetMapMode**, **GetTextExtent**, **GetTextMetrics**, **SetMapMode**, **TextOut**

SetTimer
2.x

UINT SetTimer(*hwnd*, *idTimer*, *uTimeout*, *tmprc*)
HWND *hwnd*;   /* handle of window for timer messages   */
UINT *idTimer*;   /* timer identifier   */
UINT *uTimeout*;   /* time-out duration   */
TIMERPROC *tmprc*;   /* instance address of timer procedure   */

The **SetTimer** function installs a system timer. A time-out value is specified, and every time a time-out occurs, the system posts a WM_TIMER message to the installing application's message queue or passes the message to an application-defined **TimerProc** callback function.

Parameters   *hwnd*
Identifies the window to be associated with the timer. If the *tmprc* parameter is NULL, the window procedure associated with this window receives the WM_TIMER messages generated by the timer. If this parameter is NULL, no window is associated with the timer.

idTimer
Specifies a nonzero timer identifier. If the *hwnd* parameter is NULL, this parameter is ignored.

uTimeout
Specifies the time-out value, in milliseconds.

tmprc

Specifies the procedure-instance address of the callback function that processes the WM_TIMER messages. If this parameter is NULL, the WM_TIMER messages are placed in the application's message queue and the **hwnd** member of the **MSG** structure contains the window handle specified in *hwnd*. For more information, see the description of the **TimerProc** callback function.

The **MSG** structure has the following form:

```
typedef struct tagMSG {      /* msg */
    HWND    hwnd;
    UINT    message;
    WPARAM  wParam;
    LPARAM  lParam;
    DWORD   time;
    POINT   pt;
} MSG;
```

For a full description of this structure, see the *Microsoft Windows Programmer's Reference, Volume 3*.

Return Value

The return value is the identifier of the new timer if *hwnd* is NULL and the function is successful. An application passes this value to the **KillTimer** function to kill the timer. The return value is nonzero if *hwnd* is a valid window handle and the function is successful. Otherwise, the return value is zero.

Comments

Timers are a limited global resource; therefore, it is important that an application check the value returned by the **SetTimer** function to verify that a timer is available.

The *tmprc* parameter must specify a procedure-instance address of the callback function, and the callback function must be exported in the application's module-definition file. A procedure-instance address can be created by using the **MakeProcInstance** function. The callback function must use the Pascal calling convention and must be declared as **FAR**.

Example

The following example installs a system timer. The system will pass WM_TIMER messages generated by the timer to the "MyTimerProc" callback function.

```
TIMERPROC lpfnMyTimerProc;

lpfnMyTimerProc = (TIMERPROC) MakeProcInstance(MyTimerProc, hinst);
SetTimer(hwnd, ID_MYTIMER, 5000, lpfnMyTimerProc);
```

See Also

KillTimer, MakeProcInstance, TimerProc

SetViewportExt

DWORD SetViewportExt(*hdc*, *nXExtent*, *nYExtent*)
HDC *hdc*;   /* handle of device context   */
int *nXExtent*;   /* x-extent of viewport   */
int *nYExtent*;   /* y-extent of viewport   */

The **SetViewportExt** function sets the x- and y-extents of the viewport of the given device context. The viewport, along with the window, defines how points are converted from logical coordinates to device coordinates.

Parameters

hdc
Identifies the device context.

nXExtent
Specifies the x-extent, in device units, of the viewport.

nYExtent
Specifies the y-extent, in device units, of the viewport.

Return Value

The return value is the previous viewport extents, in device units, if the function is successful. The low-order word contains the previous x-extent; the high-order word contains the previous y-extent. Otherwise, the return value is zero.

Comments

When the following mapping modes are set, calls to the **SetWindowExt** and **SetViewportExt** functions are ignored:

MM_HIENGLISH
MM_HIMETRIC
MM_LOENGLISH
MM_LOMETRIC
MM_TEXT
MM_TWIPS

When the mapping mode is MM_ISOTROPIC, an application must call the **SetWindowExt** function before calling **SetViewportExt**.

The x- and y-extents of the viewport define how much the graphics device interface (GDI) must stretch or compress units in the logical coordinate system to fit units in the device coordinate system. For example, if the x-extent of the window is 2 and the x-extent of the viewport is 4, GDI converts two logical units (measured from the x-axis) into four device units. Similarly, if the y-extent of the window is 2 and the y-extent of the viewport is −1, GDI converts two logical units (measured from the y-axis) into one device unit.

The extents also define the relative orientation of the x- and y-axes in both coordinate systems. If the signs of matching window and viewport extents are the same, the axes have the same orientation. If the signs are different, the orientation is reversed. For example, if the y-extent of the window is 2 and the y-extent of the viewport is −1, GDI converts the positive y-axis in the logical coordinate system to the negative y-axis in the device coordinate system. If the x-extents are 2 and 4, GDI converts the positive x-axis in the logical coordinate system to the positive x-axis in the device coordinate system.

Example

The following example uses the **SetMapMode**, **SetWindowExt**, and **SetViewportExt** functions to create a client area that is 10 logical units wide and 10 logical units high, and then draws a rectangle that is 4 logical units wide and 4 logical units high:

```
HDC   hdc;
RECT  rc;

GetClientRect(hwnd, &rc);
hdc = GetDC(hwnd);
SetMapMode(hdc, MM_ANISOTROPIC);
SetWindowExt(hdc, 10, 10);
SetViewportExt(hdc, rc.right, rc.bottom);
Rectangle(hdc, 3, 3, 7, 7);
ReleaseDC(hwnd, hdc);
```

See Also

GetViewportExt, SetWindowExt

SetViewportExtEx

3.1

BOOL SetViewportExtEx(*hdc, nX, nY, lpSize***)**
HDC *hdc*;	/* handle of device context	*/
int *nX*;	/* x-extent of viewport	*/
int *nY*;	/* y-extent of viewport	*/
SIZE FAR* *lpSize*;	/* address of struct. with prev. extents	*/

The **SetViewportExtEx** function sets the x- and y-extents of the viewport of the specified device context. The viewport, along with the window, defines how points are mapped from logical coordinates to device coordinates.

Parameters

hdc
Identifies the device context.

nX
Specifies the x-extent of the viewport, in device units.

nY
Specifies the y-extent of the viewport, in device units.

lpSize
> Points to a **SIZE** structure. The previous extents of the viewport, in device units, are placed in this structure. If *lpSize* is NULL, nothing is returned. The **SIZE** structure has the following form:

```
typedef struct tagSIZE {
    int cx;
    int cy;
} SIZE;
```

> For a full description of this structure, see the *Microsoft Windows Programmer's Reference, Volume 3.*

Return Value
> The return value is nonzero if the function is successful. Otherwise, it is zero.

Comments
> When the following mapping modes are set, calls to the **SetWindowExtEx** and **SetViewportExtEx** functions are ignored:

> MM_HIENGLISH
> MM_HIMETRIC
> MM_LOENGLISH
> MM_LOMETRIC
> MM_TEXT
> MM_TWIPS

> When MM_ISOTROPIC mode is set, an application must call the **SetWindowExtEx** function before it calls **SetViewportExtEx**.

See Also
> **SetWindowExtEx**

SetViewportOrg   `2.x`

DWORD SetViewportOrg(*hdc, nXOrigin, nYOrigin***)**
HDC *hdc*;   /* handle of device context   */
int *nXOrigin*;   /* x-coordinate of new origin   */
int *nYOrigin*;   /* y-coordinate of new origin   */

> The **SetViewportOrg** function sets the viewport origin of the specified device context. The viewport, along with the window, defines how points are converted from logical coordinates to device coordinates.

Parameters
> *hdc*
>> Identifies the device context.

nXOrigin

Specifies the x-coordinate, in device coordinates, of the origin of the viewport. This value must be within the range of the device coordinate system.

nYOrigin

Specifies the y-coordinate, in device coordinates, of the origin of the viewport. This value must be within the range of the device coordinate system.

Return Value

The return value is the coordinates of the previous viewport origin, in device units, if the function is successful. The low-order word contains the previous x-coordinate; the high-order word contains the previous y-coordinate. Otherwise, the return value is zero.

Comments

The viewport origin is the origin of the device coordinate system. The graphics device interface (GDI) converts points from the logical coordinate system to device coordinates. (An application can specify the origin of the logical coordinate system by using the **SetWindowOrg** function.) GDI converts all points in the logical coordinate system to device coordinates in the same way as it converts the origin.

Example

The following example uses the **SetViewportOrg** function to set the viewport origin to the center of the client area and then draws a rectangle centered over the origin:

```
HDC  hdc;
RECT rc;

GetClientRect(hwnd, &rc);
hdc = GetDC(hwnd);
SetViewportOrg(hdc, rc.right/2, rc.bottom/2);
Rectangle(hdc, -100, -100, 100, 100);
ReleaseDC(hwnd, hdc);
```

See Also   **SetWindowOrg**

SetViewportOrgEx   3.1

BOOL SetViewportOrgEx(*hdc, nX, nY, lpPoint*)
HDC *hdc*;   /* handle of device context   */
int *nX*;   /* x-coordinate of new origin   */
int *nY*;   /* y-coordinate of new origin   */
POINT FAR* *lpPoint*;   /* address of struct. with prev. origin */

The **SetViewportOrgEx** function sets the viewport origin of the specified device context. The viewport, along with the window, defines how points are mapped from logical coordinates to device coordinates.

Parameters   *hdc*
Identifies the device context.

nX
Specifies the x-coordinate, in device units, of the origin of the viewport.

nY
Specifies the y-coordinate, in device units, of the origin of the viewport.

lpPoint
Points to a **POINT** structure. The previous origin of the viewport, in device coordinates, is placed in this structure. If *lpPoint* is NULL, nothing is returned. The **POINT** structure has the following form:

```
typedef struct tagPOINT {    /* pt */
    int x;
    int y;
} POINT;
```

For a full description of this structure, see the *Microsoft Windows Programmer's Reference, Volume 3*.

Return Value   The return value is nonzero if the function is successful. Otherwise, it is zero.

See Also   **SetWindowOrgEx**

SetVoiceAccent

2.x

int SetVoiceAccent(*nVoice***,** *nTempo***,** *nVolume***,** *fnMode***,** *nPitch***)**
int *nVoice***;**   /* voice queue   */
int *nTempo***;**   /* number of quarter notes per minute   */
int *nVolume***;**   /* volume level   */
int *fnMode***;**   /* how notes are to be played   */
int *nPitch***;**   /* pitch   */

This function is obsolete. Use the Microsoft Windows multimedia audio functions instead. For information about these functions, see the *Microsoft Windows Multimedia Programmer's Reference*.

SetVoiceEnvelope

int **SetVoiceEnvelope**(*nVoice*, *nShape*, *nRepeat*)
int *nVoice*;   /* voice queue   */
int *nShape*;   /* index into an OEM wave-shape table   */
int *nRepeat*;   /* repetition count   */

This function is obsolete. Use the Microsoft Windows multimedia audio functions instead. For information about these functions, see the *Microsoft Windows Multimedia Programmer's Reference*.

SetVoiceNote

int **SetVoiceNote**(*voice*, *value*, *length*, *cdots*)
int *voice*;   /* voice queue   */
int *value*;   /* note   */
int *length*;   /* length of note   */
int *cdots*;   /* duration of note */

This function is obsolete. Use the Microsoft Windows multimedia audio functions instead. For information about these functions, see the *Microsoft Windows Multimedia Programmer's Reference*.

SetVoiceQueueSize

int **SetVoiceQueueSize**(*nVoice*, *cbQueue*)
int *nVoice*;   /* voice queue   */
int *cbQueue*;   /* size of queue */

This function is obsolete. Use the Microsoft Windows multimedia audio functions instead. For information about these functions, see the *Microsoft Windows Multimedia Programmer's Reference*.

SetVoiceSound

int **SetVoiceSound**(*nVoice, dwFrequency, nDuration*)
int *nVoice*;   /* voice queue   */
DWORD *dwFrequency*;   /* frequency   */
int *nDuration*;   /* duration of sound   */

> This function is obsolete. Use the Microsoft Windows multimedia audio functions instead. For information about these functions, see the *Microsoft Windows Multimedia Programmer's Reference*.

SetVoiceThreshold

int **SetVoiceThreshold**(*voice, cNotesThreshold*)
int *voice*;   /* voice queue   */
int *cNotesThreshold*;   /* threshold level   */

> This function is obsolete. Use the Microsoft Windows multimedia audio functions instead. For information about these functions, see the *Microsoft Windows Multimedia Programmer's Reference*.

SetWinDebugInfo

BOOL SetWinDebugInfo(*lpwdi*)
const WINDEBUGINFO FAR* *lpwdi*;   /* address of **WINDEBUGINFO structure**   */

> The **SetWinDebugInfo** function sets current system-debugging information for the debugging version of the Windows 3.1 operating system.

Parameters   *lpwdi*
> Points to a **WINDEBUGINFO** structure that specifies the type of debugging information to be set. The **WINDEBUGINFO** structure has the following form:

```
typedef struct tagWINDEBUGINFO {
    UINT    flags;
    DWORD   dwOptions;
    DWORD   dwFilter;
```

```
    char    achAllocModule[8];
    DWORD   dwAllocBreak;
    DWORD   dwAllocCount;
} WINDEBUGINFO;
```

For a full description of this structure, see the *Microsoft Windows Programmer's Reference, Volume 3.*

Return Value

The return value is nonzero if the function is successful. It is zero if the pointer specified in the *lpwdi* parameter is invalid, the **flags** member of the **WINDEBUGINFO** structure is invalid, or the function is not called in the debugging version of Windows 3.1.

Comments

The **flags** member of the **WINDEBUGINFO** structure specifies which debugging information should be set. Applications need initialize only those members of the **WINDEBUGINFO** structure that correspond to the flags set in the **flags** member.

Changes to debugging information made by calling **SetWinDebugInfo** apply only until you exit the system or restart your computer.

See Also

GetWinDebugInfo

SetWindowExt

2.x

DWORD SetWindowExt(*hdc*, *nXExtent*, *nYExtent***)**
HDC *hdc*;   /* handle of device context   */
int *nXExtent*;   /* x-extent of window   */
int *nYExtent*;   /* y-extent of window   */

The **SetWindowExt** function sets the x- and y-extents of the window associated with the given device context. The window, along with the viewport, defines how logical coordinates are converted to device coordinates.

Parameters

hdc
Identifies the device context.

nXExtent
Specifies the x-extent, in logical units, of the window.

nYExtent
Specifies the y-extent, in logical units, of the window.

Return Value

The return value is the window's previous extents, in logical units, if the function is successful. The low-order word contains the previous x-extent; the high-order word contains the previous y-extent. Otherwise, the return value is zero.

Comments

When the following mapping modes are set, calls to the **SetWindowExt** and **SetViewportExt** functions are ignored:

MM_HIENGLISH
MM_HIMETRIC
MM_LOENGLISH
MM_LOMETRIC
MM_TEXT
MM_TWIPS

When MM_ISOTROPIC mode is set, an application must call the **SetWindowExt** function before calling **SetViewportExt**.

The x- and y-extents of the window define how much the graphics device interface (GDI) must stretch or compress units in the logical coordinate system to fit units in the device coordinate system. For example, if the x-extent of the window is 2 and the x-extent of the viewport is 4, GDI converts two logical units (measured from the x-axis) into four device units. Similarly, if the y-extent of the window is 2 and the y-extent of the viewport is −1, GDI converts two logical units (measured from the y-axis) into one device unit.

The extents also define the relative orientation of the x- and y-axes in both coordinate systems. If the signs of matching window and viewport extents are the same, the axes have the same orientation. If the signs are different, the orientation is reversed. For example, if the y-extent of the window is 2 and the y-extent of the viewport is −1, GDI converts the positive y-axis in the logical coordinate system to the negative y-axis in the device coordinate system. If the x-extents are 2 and 4, GDI converts the positive x-axis in the logical coordinate system to the positive x-axis in the device coordinate system.

Example

The following example uses the **SetMapMode**, **SetWindowExt**, and **Set-ViewportExt** functions to create a client area that is 10 logical units wide and 10 logical units high and then draws a rectangle that is 4 units wide and 4 units high:

```
HDC   hdc;
RECT  rc;

GetClientRect(hwnd, &rc);
hdc = GetDC(hwnd);
SetMapMode(hdc, MM_ANISOTROPIC);
SetWindowExt(hdc, 10, 10);
SetViewportExt(hdc, rc.right, rc.bottom);
Rectangle(hdc, 3, 3, 7, 7);
ReleaseDC(hwnd, hdc);
```

See Also   **GetWindowExt, SetViewportExt**

SetWindowExtEx

BOOL SetWindowExtEx(*hdc, nX, nY, lpSize***)**
HDC *hdc*;   /* handle of device context   */
int *nX*;   /* x-extent of window   */
int *nY*;   /* y-extent of window   */
SIZE FAR* *lpSize*;   /* address of struct. with prev. extents */

The **SetWindowExtEx** function sets the x- and y-extents of the window associated with the specified device context. The window, along with the viewport, defines how points are mapped from logical coordinates to device coordinates.

Parameters   *hdc*
Identifies the device context.

nX
Specifies the x-extent, in logical units, of the window.

nY
Specifies the y-extent, in logical units, of the window.

lpSize
Points to a **SIZE** structure. The previous extents of the window (in logical units) are placed in this structure. If *lpSize* is NULL nothing is returned. The **SIZE** structure has the following form:

```
typedef struct tagSIZE {
    int cx;
    int cy;
} SIZE;
```

For a full description of this structure, see the *Microsoft Windows Programmer's Reference, Volume 3.*

Return Value   The return value is nonzero if the function is successful. Otherwise, it is zero.

Comments   When the following mapping modes are set, calls to the **SetWindowExtEx** and **SetViewportExt** functions are ignored:

MM_HIENGLISH
MM_HIMETRIC
MM_LOENGLISH

MM_LOMETRIC
MM_TEXT
MM_TWIPS

When MM_ISOTROPIC mode is set, an application must call the **SetWindow-ExtEx** function before calling **SetViewportExt**.

See Also   **SetViewportExtEx**

SetWindowLong   `2.x`

LONG SetWindowLong(_hwnd_, _nOffset_, _nVal_**)**
HWND _hwnd_;   /* handle of window   */
int _nOffset_;   /* offset of value to set   */
LONG _nVal_;   /* new value   */

The **SetWindowLong** function places a long value at the specified offset into the extra window memory of the given window. Extra window memory is reserved by specifying a nonzero value in the **cbWndExtra** member of the **WNDCLASS** structure used with the **RegisterClass** function.

Parameters   _hwnd_
                        Identifies the window.

                        nOffset
                        Specifies the zero-based byte offset of the value to change. Valid values are in the range zero through the number of bytes of extra window memory, minus four (for example, if 12 or more bytes of extra memory were specified, a value of 8 would be an index to the third long integer), or one of the following values:

Value	Meaning
GWL_EXSTYLE	Extended window style
GWL_STYLE	Window style
GWL_WNDPROC	Long pointer to the window procedure

The following values are also available when the _hwnd_ parameter identifies a dialog box:

Value	Meaning
DWL_DLGPROC	Specifies the address of the dialog box procedure.
DWL_MSGRESULT	Specifies the return value of a message processed in the dialog box procedure.

Value	Meaning
DWL_USER	Specifies extra information that is private to the application, such as handles or pointers.

nVal
Specifies the long value to place in the window's reserved memory.

Return Value

The return value is the previous value of the specified long integer, if the function is successful. Otherwise, it is zero.

Comments

If the **SetWindowLong** function and the GWL_WNDPROC index are used to set a new window procedure, that procedure must have the window-procedure form and be exported in the module-definition file of the application. For more information, see the description of the **RegisterClass** function.

Calling **SetWindowLong** with the GCL_WNDPROC index creates a subclass of the window class used to create the window. An application should not attempt to create a window subclass for standard Windows controls such as combo boxes and buttons.

An application should not use this function to set the WS_DISABLE style for a window. Instead, the application should use the **EnableWindow** function.

To access any extra 4-byte values allocated when the window-class structure was created, use a positive byte offset as the index specified by the *nOffset* parameter, starting at 0 for the first 4-byte value in the extra space, 4 for the next 4-byte value, and so on.

An application can use the DWL_MSGRESULT value to return values from a dialog box procedure's window procedure. Typically, a dialog box procedure must return TRUE in order for a value to be returned to the sender of the message. Some messages, however, return a value in the Boolean return value of the dialog box procedure. The following messages return values in the return value of the dialog box procedure:

WM_CHARTOITEM
WM_COMPAREITEM
WM_CTLCOLOR
WM_INITDIALOG
WM_QUERYDRAGICON
WM_VKEYTOITEM

Example

The following example shows how to use the **SetWindowLong** function with the DWL_MSGRESULT value to return a value from a dialog box procedure. Applications often include a **switch** statement to handle the messages that return values in the Boolean return value of the dialog box procedure, even when the dialog box procedure does not process these messages. This practice makes it easy to revise the dialog box procedure to handle the message and has a negligible effect on speed and memory.

```
BOOL CALLBACK MyDlgProc(hwndDlg, msg, wParam, lParam)
HWND hwndDlg;
UINT msg;
WPARAM wParam;
LPARAM lParam;
{
    BOOL fProcessed = FALSE;
    LRESULT lResult;

    /*
     * To return a value for a specific message, set lResult to the
     * return value and fProcessed to TRUE.
     */

    switch (msg) {
        .
        .  /* process messages */
        .

    case WM_QUERYENDSESSION:

        /*
         * Example: Do not allow the system to terminate
         * while the dialog box is displayed.
         */

        fProcessed = TRUE;
        lResult = (LRESULT) (UINT) FALSE;
        break;

    default:
        break;
    }

    if (fProcessed) {
        switch (msg) {
        case WM_CTLCOLOR:
        case WM_COMPAREITEM:
        case WM_VKEYTOITEM:
        case WM_CHARTOITEM:
        case WM_QUERYDRAGICON:
        case WM_INITDIALOG:
            return (BOOL) LOWORD(lResult);
```

```
                       default:
                           SetWindowLong(hwndDlg, DWL_MSGRESULT, (LPARAM) lResult);
                       }
                   }
                   return fProcessed;
               }
```

See Also   **EnableWindow**, **GetWindowLong**, **RegisterClass**, **SetWindowWord**

SetWindowOrg   2.x

DWORD SetWindowOrg(*hdc*, *nXOrigin*, *nYOrigin*)
HDC *hdc*;   /* handle of device context   */
int *nXOrigin*;   /* x-coordinate to map to upper-left window corner   */
int *nYOrigin*;   /* y-coordinate to map to upper-left window corner   */

The **SetWindowOrg** function sets the window origin for the given device context.

Parameters   *hdc*
                        Identifies the device context.

                        nXOrigin
                        Specifies the logical x-coordinate to map to the upper-left corner of the window.

                        nYOrigin
                        Specifies the logical y-coordinate to map to the upper-left corner of the window.

Return Value   The return value is the coordinates of the previous window origin, in logical units,
                        if the function is successful. The low-order word contains the x-coordinate of the
                        previous window origin; the high-order word contains the y-coordinate. Other-
                        wise, the return value is zero.

Comments   The window origin is the origin of the logical coordinate system for a window.
                        By changing the window origin, an application can change the way the graphics
                        device interface (GDI) converts logical coordinates to device coordinates (the
                        viewport). GDI converts logical coordinates to the device coordinates of the view-
                        port in the same way as it converts the origin.

                        To convert points to the right, an application can specify a negative value for the
                        nXOrigin parameter. Similarly, to convert points down (in the MM_TEXT map-
                        ping mode), the *nYOrigin* parameter can be negative.

Example   The following example uses the **CopyMetaFile** function to copy a metafile to a
                        specified file, plays the copied metafile, uses the **GetMetaFile** function to retrieve

a handle of the copied metafile, uses the **SetWindowOrg** function to change the position at which the metafile is played 200 logical units to the right, and then plays the metafile at the new location:

```
HANDLE hmf, hmfSource, hmfOld;
LPSTR lpszFile1 = "MFTest";

hmf = CopyMetaFile(hmfSource, lpszFile1);
PlayMetaFile(hdc, hmf);
DeleteMetaFile(hmf);

hmfOld = GetMetaFile(lpszFile1);
SetWindowOrg(hdc, -200, 0);
PlayMetaFile(hdc, hmfOld);

DeleteMetaFile(hmfSource);
DeleteMetaFile(hmfOld);
```

See Also   **CopyMetaFile, GetMetaFile, GetWindowOrg, PlayMetaFile, SetViewportOrg**

SetWindowOrgEx   3.1

BOOL SetWindowOrgEx(*hdc, nX, nY, lpPoint***)**
HDC *hdc*;   /* handle of device context   */
int *nX*;   /* x-coordinate of window   */
int *nY*;   /* y-coordinate of window   */
POINT FAR* *lpPoint*;   /* address of struct. with prev. origin */

The **SetWindowOrgEx** function sets the window origin of the specified device context. The window, along with the viewport, defines how points are mapped from logical coordinates to device coordinates.

Parameters   *hdc*
Identifies the device context.

nX
Specifies the logical x-coordinate of the new origin of the window.

nY
Specifies the logical y-coordinate of the new origin of the window.

lpPoint
Points to a **POINT** structure. The previous origin of the window is placed in this structure. If *lpPoint* is NULL nothing is returned. The **POINT** structure has the following form:

```
typedef struct tagPOINT {    /* pt */
    int x;              .
    int y;
} POINT;
```

For a full description of this structure, see the *Microsoft Windows Program-mer's Reference, Volume 3*.

Return Value   The return value is nonzero if the function is successful. Otherwise, it is zero.

See Also   **SetViewportOrgEx**

SetWindowPlacement   3.1

BOOL SetWindowPlacement(*hwnd*, *lpwndpl*)
HWND *hwnd*;   /* handle of the window   */
const WINDOWPLACEMENT FAR* *lpwndpl*;   /* address of structure with position data */

The **SetWindowPlacement** function sets the show state and the normal (restored), minimized, and maximized positions for a window.

Parameters   *hwnd*
                        Identifies the window.

                        lpwndpl
                        Points to a **WINDOWPLACEMENT** structure that specifies the new show state and positions. The **WINDOWPLACEMENT** structure has the following form:

```
typedef struct tagWINDOWPLACEMENT {     /* wndpl */
    UINT  length;
    UINT  flags;
    UINT  showCmd;
    POINT ptMinPosition;
    POINT ptMaxPosition;
    RECT  rcNormalPosition;
} WINDOWPLACEMENT;
```

For a full description of this structure, see the *Microsoft Windows Program-mer's Reference, Volume 3*.

Return Value   The return value is nonzero if the function is successful. Otherwise, it is zero.

See Also   **GetWindowPlacement**

SetWindowPos

BOOL SetWindowPos(*hwnd, hwndInsertAfter, x, y, cx, cy, fuFlags*)
HWND *hwnd*;   /* handle of window   */
HWND *hwndInsertAfter*;   /* placement-order handle   */
int *x*;   /* horizontal position   */
int *y*;   /* vertical position   */
int *cx*;   /* width   */
int *cy*;   /* height   */
UINT *fuFlags*;   /* window-positioning flags   */

The **SetWindowPos** function changes the size, position, and Z-order of child, pop-up, and top-level windows. These windows are ordered according to their appearance on the screen; the window on top receives the highest rank and is the first window in the Z-order.

Parameters

hwnd
Identifies the window to be positioned.

hwndInsertAfter
Identifies the window to precede the positioned window in the Z-order. This parameter must be a window handle or one of the following values:

Value	Meaning
HWND_BOTTOM	Places the window at the bottom of the Z-order. If *hwnd* identifies a topmost window, the window loses its topmost status; the system places the window at the bottom of all other windows.
HWND_TOP	Places the window at the top of the Z-order.
HWND_TOPMOST	Places the window above all non-topmost windows. The window maintains its topmost position even when it is deactivated.
HWND_NOTOPMOST	Repositions the window to the top of all non-topmost windows (that is, behind all topmost windows). This flag has no effect if the window is already a non-topmost window.

For rules about how this parameter is used, see the following Comments section.

x
Specifies the new position of the left side of the window.

y
Specifies the new position of the top of the window.

cx
Specifies the new width of the window.

cx

Specifies the new width of the window.

cy

Specifies the new height of the window.

fuFlags

Specifies the window sizing and positioning options. This parameter can be a combination of the following values:

Value	Meaning
SWP_DRAWFRAME	Draws a frame (defined in the window's class description) around the window.
SWP_HIDEWINDOW	Hides the window.
SWP_NOACTIVATE	Does not activate the window. If this flag is not set, the window is activated and moved to the top of either the topmost or non-topmost group (depending on the setting of the *hwndInsertAfter* parameter).
SWP_NOMOVE	Retains the current position (ignores the *x* and *y* parameters).
SWP_NOSIZE	Retains the current size (ignores the *cx* and *cy* parameters).
SWP_NOREDRAW	Does not redraw changes. If this flag is set, no repainting of any kind occurs. This applies to the client area, the non-client area (including the title and scroll bars), and any part of the parent window uncovered as a result of the moved window. When this flag is set, the application must explicitly invalidate or redraw any parts of the window and parent window that must be redrawn.
SWP_NOZORDER	Retains the current ordering (ignores the *hwndInsertAfter* parameter).
SWP_SHOWWINDOW	Displays the window.

Return Value

The return value is nonzero if the function is successful. Otherwise, it is zero.

Comments

If the SWP_SHOWWINDOW or the SWP_HIDEWINDOW flags are set, the window cannot be moved or sized.

All coordinates for child windows are client coordinates (relative to the upper-left corner of the parent window's client area).

A window can be made a topmost window either by setting the *hwndInsertAfter* parameter to HWND_TOPMOST and ensuring that the SWP_NOZORDER flag is not set, or by setting a window's Z-order so that it is above any existing topmost windows. When a non-topmost window is made topmost, its owned windows are also made topmost. Its owners are not changed.

If neither SWP_NOACTIVATE nor SWP_NOZORDER is specified (that is, when the application requests that a window be simultaneously activated and placed in the specified Z-order), the value specified in *hwndInsertAfter* is used only in the following circumstances:

- Neither HWND_TOPMOST or HWND_NOTOPMOST is specified in the *hwndInsertAfter* parameter.
- The window specified in the *hwnd* parameter is not the active window.

An application cannot activate an inactive window without also bringing it to the top of the Z-order. Applications can change the Z-order of an activated window without restrictions or activate a window and then move it to the top of the topmost or non-topmost windows.

A topmost window is no longer topmost if it is repositioned to the bottom (HWND_BOTTOM) of the Z-order or after any non-topmost window. When a topmost window is made non-topmost, all of its owners and its owned windows are also made non-topmost windows.

A non-topmost window may own a topmost window, but not vice versa. Any window (for example, a dialog box) owned by a topmost window is itself made a topmost window, to ensure that all owned windows stay above their owner.

Example   The following example sets the size of a window equal to one-fourth the size of the desktop and then positions the window in the upper-left corner of the desktop:

```
RECT rect;

GetWindowRect(GetDesktopWindow(), &rect);
SetWindowPos(hwnd, (HWND) NULL, 0, 0,
    rect.right / 2, rect.bottom / 2,
    SWP_NOZORDER | SWP_NOACTIVATE);
```

See Also   **BringWindowToTop**, **GetWindowRect**, **MoveWindow**

SetWindowsHook   2.x

HHOOK SetWindowsHook(*idHook***, ***hkprc***)**
int *idHook*;   /* type of hook to install   */
HOOKPROC *hkprc*;   /* filter function procedure-instance address   */

The **SetWindowsHook** function is obsolete but has been retained for backward compatibility with Windows versions 3.0 and earlier. Applications written for Windows version 3.1 should use the **SetWindowsHookEx** function.

The **SetWindowsHook** function installs an application-defined hook function into a hook chain.

Parameters

idHook

Specifies the type of hook to be installed. This parameter can be one of the following values:

Value	Meaning
WH_CALLWNDPROC	Installs a window-procedure filter. For more information, see the description of the **CallWnd-Proc** callback function.
WH_CBT	Installs a computer-based training (CBT) filter. For more information, see the description of the **CBTProc** callback function.
WH_DEBUG	Installs a debugging filter. For more information, see the description of the **DebugProc** callback function.
WH_GETMESSAGE	Installs a message filter. For more information, see the description of the **GetMsgProc** callback function.
WH_HARDWARE	Installs a nonstandard hardware-message filter. For more information, see the description of the **HardwareProc** callback function.
WH_JOURNALPLAYBACK	Installs a journaling playback filter. For more information, see the description of the **Journal-PlaybackProc** callback function.
WH_JOURNALRECORD	Installs a journaling record filter. For more information, see the description of the **Journal-RecordProc** callback function.
WH_KEYBOARD	Installs a keyboard filter. For more information, see the description of the **KeyboardProc** callback function.
WH_MOUSE	Installs a mouse-message filter. For more information, see the description of the **MouseProc** callback function.
WH_MSGFILTER	Installs a message filter. For more information, see the description of the **MessageProc** callback function.
WH_SHELL	Installs a shell-application filter. For more information, see the description of the **ShellProc** callback function.
WH_SYSMSGFILTER	Installs a system-wide message filter. For more information, see the description of the **SysMsg-Proc** callback function.

hkprc
Specifies the procedure-instance address of the application-defined hook procedure to be installed.

Return Value   The return value is a handle of the installed hook, if the function is successful. Otherwise, it is NULL.

Comments   Before terminating, an application must call the **UnhookWindowsHook** function to free system resources associated with the hook.

The WH_CALLWNDPROC hook affects system performance. It is supplied for debugging purposes only.

The system hooks are a shared resource. Installing a hook affects all applications. Most hook functions must be in libraries. The only exception is WH_MSGFILTER, which is task-specific. System hooks should be restricted to special-purpose applications or to use as a development aid during debugging of an application. Libraries that no longer need the hook should remove the filter function.

To install a filter function, the **SetWindowsHook** function must receive a procedure-instance address of the function and the function must be exported in the library's module-definition file. A task must use the **MakeProcInstance** function to get a procedure-instance address. A dynamic-link library can pass the procedure address directly.

See Also   **DefHookProc, GetProcAddress, MakeProcInstance, MessageBox, PeekMessage, PostMessage, SendMessage, SetWindowsHookEx, UnhookWindowsHook**

SetWindowsHookEx   3.1

HHOOK SetWindowsHookEx(*idHook***,** *hkprc***,** *hinst***,** *htask***)**
int *idHook***;**   /* type of hook to install   */
HOOKPROC *hkprc***;**   /* procedure-instance address of filter function   */
HINSTANCE *hinst***;**   /* handle of application instance   */
HTASK *htask***;**   /* task to install the hook for   */

The **SetWindowsHookEx** function installs an application-defined hook function into a hook chain. This function is an extended version of the **SetWindowsHook** function.

Parameters

idHook

Specifies the type of hook to be installed. This parameter can be one of the following values:

Value	Meaning
WH_CALLWNDPROC	Installs a window-procedure filter. For more information, see the description of the **CallWndProc** callback function.
WH_CBT	Installs a computer-based training (CBT) filter. For more information, see the description of the **CBTProc** callback function.
WH_DEBUG	Installs a debugging filter. For more information, see the description of the **DebugProc** callback function.
WH_GETMESSAGE	Installs a message filter. For more information, see the description of the **GetMsgProc** callback function.
WH_HARDWARE	Installs a nonstandard hardware-message filter. For more information, see the description of the **HardwareProc** callback function.
WH_JOURNALPLAYBACK	Installs a journaling playback filter. For more information, see the description of the **JournalPlaybackProc** callback function.
WH_JOURNALRECORD	Installs a journaling record filter. For more information, see the description of the **JournalRecordProc** callback function.
WH_KEYBOARD	Installs a keyboard filter. For more information, see the description of the **KeyboardProc** callback function.
WH_MOUSE	Installs a mouse-message filter. For more information, see the description of the **MouseProc** callback function.
WH_MSGFILTER	Installs a message filter. For more information, see the description of the **MessageProc** callback function.
WH_SYSMSGFILTER	Installs a system-wide message filter. For more information, see the description of the **SysMsgProc** callback function.

hkprc

Specifies the procedure-instance address of the application-defined hook procedure to be installed.

hinst

Identifies the instance of the module containing the hook function.

htask

Identifies the task for which the hook is to be installed. If this parameter is NULL, the installed hook function has system scope and may be called in the context of any process or task in the system.

Return Value

The return value is a handle of the installed hook, if the function is successful. The application or library must use this handle to identify the hook when it calls the **CallNextHookEx** and **UnhookWindowsHookEx** functions. The return value is NULL if an error occurs.

Comments

An application or library can use the **GetCurrentTask** or **GetWindowTask** function to obtain task handles for use in hooking a particular task.

Hook procedures used with **SetWindowsHookEx** must be declared as follows:

```
DWORD CALLBACK HookProc(code, wParam, lParam)
int code;
WPARAM wParam;
LPARAM lParam;
{
    if (...)
        return CallNextHookEx(hhook, code, wParam, lParam);
}
```

Chaining to the next hook procedure (that is, calling the **CallNextHookProc** function) is optional. An application or library can call the next hook procedure either before or after any processing in its own hook procedure.

Before terminating, an application must call the **UnhookWindowsHookEx** function to free system resources associated with the hook.

Some hooks may be set with system scope only, and others may be set only for a specific task, as shown in the following list:

Hook	Scope
WH_CALLWNDPROC	Task or system
WH_CBT	Task or system
WH_DEBUG	Task or system
WH_GETMESSAGE	Task or system
WH_HARDWARE	Task or system
WH_JOURNALRECORD	System only
WH_JOURNALPLAYBACK	System only
WH_KEYBOARD	Task or system
WH_MOUSE	Task or system
WH_MSGFILTER	Task or system

Hook	Scope
WH_SYSMSGFILTER	System only

For a given hook type, task hooks are called first, then system hooks.

The WH_CALLWNDPROC hook affects system performance. It is supplied for debugging purposes only.

The system hooks are a shared resource. Installing one affects all applications. All system hook functions must be in libraries. System hooks should be restricted to special-purpose applications or to use as a development aid during debugging of an application. Libraries that no longer need the hook should remove the filter function.

It is a good idea for several reasons to use task hooks rather than system hooks: They do not incur a system-wide overhead in applications that are not affected by the call (or that ignore the call); they do not require packaging the hook-procedure implementation in a separate dynamic-link library; they will continue to work even when future versions of Windows prevent applications from installing system-wide hooks for security reasons.

To install a filter function, the **SetWindowsHookEx** function must receive a procedure-instance address of the function and the function must be exported in the library's module-definition file. Libraries can pass the procedure address directly. Tasks must use the **MakeProcInstance** function to get a procedure-instance address. Dynamic-link libraries must use the **GetProcAddress** function to get a procedure-instance address.

For a given hook type, task hooks are called first, then system hooks.

The WH_SYSMSGFILTER hooks are called before the WH_MSGFILTER hooks. If any of the WH_SYSMSGFILTER hook functions return TRUE, the WH_MSGFILTER hooks are not called.

See Also

CallNextHookEx, GetProcAddress, MakeProcInstance, MessageBox, PeekMessage, PostMessage, SendMessage, UnhookWindowsHookEx

SetWindowText

2.x

```
void SetWindowText(hwnd, lpsz)
HWND hwnd;       /* handle of window    */
LPCSTR lpsz;     /* address of string   */
```

The **SetWindowText** function sets the given window's title to the specified text.

Parameters   *hwnd*
     Identifies the window or control whose text is to be set.

lpsz
     Points to a null-terminated string to be used as the new title or control text.

Return Value   This function does not return a value.

Comments   This function causes a WM_SETTEXT message to be sent to the given window or control.

If the window specified by the *hwnd* parameter is a control, the text within the control is set. If the specified window is a list-box control created with WS_CAPTION style, however, **SetWindowText** will set the caption for the control, not for the list-box entries.

Example   The following example sets a window title:

```
char szBuf[64];
char szFileName[64];

wsprintf((LPSTR) szBuf, "PrntFile - %s", (LPSTR) szFileName);
SetWindowText(hwnd, (LPSTR) szBuf);
```

See Also   **GetWindowText**

SetWindowWord   2.x

WORD SetWindowWord(*hwnd*, *nOffset*, *nVal*)
HWND *hwnd*;   /* handle of window   */
int *nOffset*;   /* offset of value to set   */
WORD *nVal*;   /* new value   */

The **SetWindowWord** function places a word value at the specified offset into the extra window memory of the given window. Extra window memory is reserved by specifying a nonzero value in the **cbWndExtra** member of the **WNDCLASS** structure used with the **RegisterClass** function.

Parameters   *hwnd*
     Identifies the window.

nOffset

Specifies the zero-based byte offset of the value to change. Valid values are in the range zero through the number of bytes of extra window memory, minus two (for example, if 10 or more bytes of extra memory were specified, a value of 8 would be an index to the fifth integer), or one of the following values:

Value	Meaning
GWW_HINSTANCE	Specifies the instance handle of the module that owns the window.
GWW_ID	Specifies the identifier of the child window.

nVal

Specifies the word value to be placed in the window's reserved memory.

Return Value

The return value is the previous value of the specified word, if the function is successful. Otherwise, it is zero.

Comments

To access any extra 2-byte values allocated when the window-class structure was created, use a positive byte offset as the index specified by the *nOffset* parameter, starting at 0 for the first 2-byte value in the extra space, 2 for the next 2-byte value, and so on.

An application should call the **SetParent** function, not the **SetWindowWord** function, to change a value in the parent of a child window.

See Also

GetWindowWord, **RegisterClass**, **SetParent**, **SetWindowLong**

ShellExecute

3.1

#include <shellapi.h>

HINSTANCE ShellExecute(*hwnd*, *lpszOp*, *lpszFile*, *lpszParams*, *lpszDir*, *fsShowCmd*)
HWND *hwnd*;   /* handle of parent window   */
LPCSTR *lpszOp*;   /* address of string for operation to perform   */
LPCSTR *lpszFile*;   /* address of string for filename   */
LPCSTR *lpszParams*;   /* address of string for executable-file parameters */
LPCSTR *lpszDir*;   /* address of string for default directory   */
int *fsShowCmd*;   /* whether file is shown when opened   */

The **ShellExecute** function opens or prints the specified file.

Parameters   *hwnd*

Identifies the parent window. This window receives any message boxes an application produces (for example, for error reporting).

lpszOp

Points to a null-terminated string specifying the operation to perform. This string can be "open" or "print". If this parameter is NULL, "open" is the default value.

lpszFile

Points to a null-terminated string specifying the file to open.

lpszParams

Points to a null-terminated string specifying parameters passed to the application when the *lpszFile* parameter specifies an executable file. If *lpszFile* points to a string specifying a document file, this parameter is NULL.

lpszDir

Points to a null-terminated string specifying the default directory.

fsShowCmd

Specifies whether the application window is to be shown when the application is opened. This parameter can be one of the following values:

Value	Meaning
SW_HIDE	Hides the window and passes activation to another window.
SW_MINIMIZE	Minimizes the specified window and activates the top-level window in the system's list.
SW_RESTORE	Activates and displays a window. If the window is minimized or maximized, Windows restores it to its original size and position (same as SW_SHOWNORMAL).
SW_SHOW	Activates a window and displays it in its current size and position.
SW_SHOWMAXIMIZED	Activates a window and displays it as a maximized window.
SW_SHOWMINIMIZED	Activates a window and displays it as an icon.
SW_SHOWMINNOACTIVE	Displays a window as an icon. The window that is currently active remains active.
SW_SHOWNA	Displays a window in its current state. The window that is currently active remains active.
SW_SHOWNOACTIVATE	Displays a window in its most recent size and position. The window that is currently active remains active.

Value	Meaning
SW_SHOWNORMAL	Activates and displays a window. If the window is minimized or maximized, Windows restores it to its original size and position (same as SW_RESTORE).

Return Value

The return value is the instance handle of the application that was opened or printed, if the function is successful. (This handle could also be the handle of a DDE server application.) A return value less than or equal to 32 specifies an error. The possible error values are listed in the following Comments section.

Errors

The **ShellExecute** function returns the value 31 if there is no association for the specified file type or if there is no association for the specified action within the file type. The other possible error values are as follows:

Value	Meaning
0	System was out of memory, executable file was corrupt, or relocations were invalid.
2	File was not found.
3	Path was not found.
5	Attempt was made to dynamically link to a task, or there was a sharing or network-protection error.
6	Library required separate data segments for each task.
8	There was insufficient memory to start the application.
10	Windows version was incorrect.
11	Executable file was invalid. Either it was not a Windows application or there was an error in the .EXE image.
12	Application was designed for a different operating system.
13	Application was designed for MS-DOS 4.0.
14	Type of executable file was unknown.
15	Attempt was made to load a real-mode application (developed for an earlier version of Windows).
16	Attempt was made to load a second instance of an executable file containing multiple data segments that were not marked read-only.
19	Attempt was made to load a compressed executable file. The file must be decompressed before it can be loaded.
20	Dynamic-link library (DLL) file was invalid. One of the DLLs required to run this application was corrupt.
21	Application requires Microsoft Windows 32-bit extensions.

Comments

The file specified by the *lpszFile* parameter can be a document file or an executable file. If it is a document file, this function opens or prints it, depending on the value of the *lpszOp* parameter. If it is an executable file, this function opens it, even if the string "print" is pointed to by *lpszOp*.

See Also   **FindExecutable**

ShellProc   3.1

LRESULT CALLBACK ShellProc(*code*, *wParam*, *lParam*)
int *code*;   /* process-message flag   */
WPARAM *wParam*;   /* current-task flag   */
LPARAM *lParam*;   /* undefined   */

The **ShellProc** function is a library-defined callback function that a shell application can use to receive useful notifications from the system.

Parameters   *code*
Specifies a shell-notification code. This parameter can be one of the following values:

Value	Meaning
HSHELL_ACTIVATESHELLWINDOW	The shell application should activate its main window.
HSHELL_WINDOWCREATED	A top-level, unowned window was created. The window exists when the system calls a **ShellProc** function.
HSHELL_WINDOWDESTROYED	A top-level, unowned window is about to be destroyed. The window still exists when the system calls a **ShellProc** function.

wParam
Specifies additional information the shell application may need. The interpretation of this parameter depends on the value of the *code* parameter, as follows:

code	wParam
HSHELL_ACTIVATESHELLWINDOW	Not used.
HSHELL_WINDOWCREATED	Specifies the handle of the window being created.
HSHELL_WINDOWDESTROYED	Specifies the handle of the window being destroyed.

lParam
Reserved; not used.

Return Value   The return value should be zero.

Comments   An application must install this callback function by specifying the WH_SHELL filter type and the procedure-instance address of the callback function in a call to the **SetWindowsHook** function.

ShellProc is a placeholder for the library-defined function name. The actual name must be exported by including it in an **EXPORTS** statement in the library's module-definition file.

See Also   **DefHookProc, SendMessage, SetWindowsHook**

ShowCaret   2.x

void ShowCaret(*hwnd*)
HWND *hwnd*;   /* handle of window with caret   */

The **ShowCaret** function shows the caret on the screen at the caret's current position. Once shown, the caret begins flashing automatically.

Parameters   *hwnd*
Identifies the window that owns the caret. This parameter can be set to NULL to indirectly specify the window in the current task that owns the caret.

Return Value   This function does not return a value.

Comments   The **ShowCaret** function shows the caret only if it has a current shape and has not been hidden two or more times consecutively. If the given window does not own the caret, the caret is not shown. If the *hwnd* parameter is NULL, the **ShowCaret** function shows the caret only if it is owned by a window in the current task.

Hiding the caret is cumulative. If the **HideCaret** function has been called five times consecutively, **ShowCaret** must be called five times to show the caret.

The caret is a shared resource. A window should show the caret only when it has the input focus or is active.

See Also   **CreateCaret, GetActiveWindow, GetFocus, HideCaret**

ShowCursor

2.x

int ShowCursor(*fShow*)
BOOL *fShow*;   /* cursor visibility flag   */

The **ShowCursor** function shows or hides the cursor.

Parameters   *fShow*
Specifies whether the display count is incremented or decremented (increased or decreased by one). If this parameter is TRUE, the display count is incremented; otherwise, it is decremented.

Return Value   The return value specifies the new display count, if the function is successful.

Comments   A cursor show-level count is kept internally. It is incremented by a show operation and decremented by a hide operation. The cursor is visible only if the count is greater than or equal to zero. If a mouse exists, the initial setting of the cursor show level is zero; otherwise, it is −1.

The cursor is a shared resource. A window that hides the cursor should show it before the cursor leaves its client area or before the window relinquishes control to another window.

See Also   **SetCursor**

ShowOwnedPopups

2.x

void ShowOwnedPopups(*hwnd, fShow*)
HWND *hwnd*;   /* handle of window   */
BOOL *fShow*;   /* window visibility flag   */

The **ShowOwnedPopups** function shows or hides all pop-up windows owned by the given window.

Parameters   *hwnd*
Identifies the window that owns the pop-up windows to be shown or hidden.

fShow

Specifies whether pop-up windows are to be shown or hidden. If this parameter is TRUE, all hidden pop-up windows are shown. If this parameter is FALSE, all visible pop-up windows are hidden.

Return Value   This function does not return a value.

See Also   **IsWindowVisible, ShowWindow**

ShowScrollBar   2.x

void ShowScrollBar(*hwnd, fnBar, fShow*)
HWND *hwnd*;   /* handle of window with scroll bar   */
int *fnBar*;   /* scroll-bar flag   */
BOOL *fShow*;   /* scroll-bar visibility flag   */

The **ShowScrollBar** function shows or hides a scroll bar.

Parameters   *hwnd*

Identifies a scroll bar or a window that contains a scroll bar in its nonclient area, depending on the value of the *fnBar* parameter. If *fnBar* is SB_CTL, *hwnd* identifies a scroll bar. If *fnBar* is SB_HORZ, SB_VERT, or SB_BOTH, *hwnd* identifies a window that has a scroll bar in its nonclient area.

fnBar

Specifies whether the scroll bar is a control or part of a window's nonclient area. If the scroll bar is part of the nonclient area, *fnBar* also indicates whether the scroll bar is positioned horizontally, vertically, or both. This parameter can be one of the following values:

Value	Meaning
SB_BOTH	Specifies the window's horizontal and vertical scroll bars.
SB_CTL	Specifies that the *hwnd* parameter identifies a scroll bar control.
SB_HORZ	Specifies the window's horizontal scroll bar.
SB_VERT	Specifies the window's vertical scroll bar.

fShow

Specifies whether the scroll bar is shown or hidden. If this parameter is TRUE, the scroll bar is shown; otherwise, it is hidden.

Return Value   This function does not return a value.

Comments   An application should not call this function to hide a scroll bar while processing a scroll-bar notification message.

See Also   **GetScrollPos, GetScrollRange, ScrollWindow, SetScrollPos, SetScrollRange**

ShowWindow

2.x

BOOL ShowWindow(*hwnd*, *nCmdShow*)
HWND *hwnd*;   /* handle of window   */
int *nCmdShow*;   /* window visibility flag   */

The **ShowWindow** function sets the given window's visibility state.

Parameters   *hwnd*
Identifies the window.

nCmdShow
Specifies how the window is to be shown. This parameter can be one of the following values:

Value	Meaning
SW_HIDE	Hides the window and passes activation to another window.
SW_MINIMIZE	Minimizes the specified window and activates the top-level window in the system's list.
SW_RESTORE	Activates and displays a window. If the window is minimized or maximized, Windows restores it to its original size and position (same as SW_SHOWNORMAL).
SW_SHOW	Activates a window and displays it in its current size and position.
SW_SHOWMAXIMIZED	Activates a window and displays it as a maximized window.
SW_SHOWMINIMIZED	Activates a window and displays it as an icon.
SW_SHOWMINNOACTIVE	Displays a window as an icon. The window that is currently active remains active.
SW_SHOWNA	Displays a window in its current state. The window that is currently active remains active.

Value	Meaning
SW_SHOWNOACTIVATE	Displays a window in its most recent size and position. The window that is currently active remains active.
SW_SHOWNORMAL	Activates and displays a window. If the window is minimized or maximized, Windows restores it to its original size and position (same as SW_RESTORE).

Return Value   The return value is nonzero if the window was previously visible. It is zero if the window was previously hidden.

Comments   The **ShowWindow** function must be called only once per application using the *nCmdShow* parameter from the **WinMain** function. Subsequent calls to **Show-Window** must use one of the values listed in the preceding list, instead of the one specified by the *nCmdShow* parameter from **WinMain**.

See Also   **IsWindowVisible, ShowOwnedPopups**

SizeofResource $\boxed{\text{2.x}}$

DWORD SizeofResource(*hinst, hrsrc*)
HINSTANCE *hinst*;   /* handle of module with resource   */
HRSRC *hrsrc*;   /* handle of resource   */

The **SizeofResource** function returns the size, in bytes, of the given resource.

Parameters   *hinst*
          Identifies the instance of the module whose executable file contains the resource.

hrsrc
          Identifies the resource. This handle must have been created by using the **FindResource** function.

Return Value   The return value specifies the number of bytes in the resource, if the function is successful. It is zero if the resource cannot be found.

Comments   The value returned may be larger than the resource due to alignment. An application should not rely upon this value for the exact size of a resource.

See Also   **AccessResource, FindResource**

SpoolFile

HANDLE SpoolFile(*lpszPrinter,* *lpszPort,* *lpszJob,* *lpszFile*)
LPSTR *lpszPrinter*;   /* printer name   */
LPSTR *lpszPort*;   /* port name   */
LPSTR *lpszJob*;   /* job name   */
LPSTR *lpszFile*;   /* file name   */

The **SpoolFile** function puts a file into the spooler queue. This function is typically used by device drivers.

Parameters

lpszPrinter
Points to a null-terminated string specifying the printer name—for example, "HP LasterJet IIP".

lpszPort
Points to a null-terminated string specifying the local name—for example, "LPT1:". This must be a local port.

lpszJob
Points to a null-terminated string specifying the name of the print job for the spooler. This string cannot be longer than 32 characters, including the null-terminating character.

lpszFile
Points to a null-terminated string specifying the path and filename of the file to put in the spooler queue. This file contains raw printer data.

Return Value

The return value is the global handle that is passed to the spooler, if the function is successful. Otherwise, it is an error value, which can be one of the following:

SP_APPABORT
SP_ERROR
SP_NOTREPORTED
SP_OUTOFDISK
SP_OUTOFMEMORY
SP_USERABORT

Comments

Applications should ensure that the spooler is enabled before calling the **SpoolFile** function.

StackTraceCSIPFirst

#include <toolhelp.h>

BOOL StackTraceCSIPFirst(*lpste*, *wSS*, *wCS*, *wIP*, *wBP*)
STACKTRACEENTRY FAR* *lpste*;   /* address of stack-frame structure   */
WORD *wSS*;   /* value of SS register   */
WORD *wCS*;   /* value of CS register   */
WORD *wIP*;   /* value of IP register   */
WORD *wBP*;   /* value of BP register   */

The **StackTraceCSIPFirst** function fills the specified structure with information that describes the specified stack frame.

Parameters

lpste
Points to a **STACKTRACEENTRY** structure to receive information about the stack. The **STACKTRACEENTRY** structure has the following form:

```
#include <toolhelp.h>

typedef struct tagSTACKTRACEENTRY {  /* ste */
    DWORD   dwSize;
    HTASK   hTask;
    WORD    wSS;
    WORD    wBP;
    WORD    wCS;
    WORD    wIP;
    HMODULE hModule;
    WORD    wSegment;
    WORD    wFlags;
} STACKTRACEENTRY;
```

For a full description of this structure, see the *Microsoft Windows Programmer's Reference, Volume 3.*

wSS
Contains the value in the SS register. This value is used with the *wBP* value to determine the next entry in the stack trace.

wCS
Contains the value in the CS register of the first stack frame.

wIP
Contains the value in the IP register of the first stack frame.

wBP
Contains the value in the BP register. This value is used with the *wSS* value to determine the next entry in the stack trace.

Return Value

The return value is nonzero if the function is successful. Otherwise, it is zero.

Comments   The **StackTraceFirst** function can be used to begin a stack trace of any task except the current task. When a task is inactive, the kernel maintains its state, including its current stack, stack pointer, CS and IP values, and BP value. The kernel does not maintain these values for the current task. Therefore, when a stack trace is done on the current task, the application must use **StackTraceCSIPFirst** to begin a stack trace. An application can continue to trace through the stack by using the **StackTraceNext** function.

Before calling **StackTraceCSIPFirst**, an application must initialize the **STACK-TRACEENTRY** structure and specify its size, in bytes, in the **dwSize** member.

See Also   **StackTraceNext, StackTraceFirst**

StackTraceFirst

3.1

#include <toolhelp.h>

BOOL StackTraceFirst(*lpste*, *htask*)
STACKTRACEENTRY FAR* *lpste*;   /* address of stack-frame structure   */
HTASK *htask*;   /* handle of task   */

The **StackTraceFirst** function fills the specified structure with information that describes the first stack frame for the given task.

Parameters   *lpste*
Points to a **STACKTRACEENTRY** structure to receive information about the task's first stack frame. The **STACKTRACEENTRY** structure has the following form:

```
#include <toolhelp.h>

typedef struct tagSTACKTRACEENTRY {  /* ste */
    DWORD    dwSize;
    HTASK    hTask;
    WORD     wSS;
    WORD     wBP;
    WORD     wCS;
    WORD     wIP;
    HMODULE  hModule;
    WORD     wSegment;
    WORD     wFlags;
} STACKTRACEENTRY;
```

For a full description of this structure, see the *Microsoft Windows Programmer's Reference, Volume 3*.

htask
Identifies the task whose stack information is to be described.

Return Value   The return value is nonzero if the function is successful. Otherwise, it is zero.

Comments   The **StackTraceFirst** function can be used to begin a stack trace of any task except the current task. When a task is inactive, the kernel maintains its state, including its current stack, stack pointer, CS and IP values, and BP value. The kernel does not maintain these values for the current task. Therefore, when a stack trace is done on the current task, the application must use the **StackTraceCSIPFirst** function to begin a stack trace. An application can continue to trace through the stack by using the **StackTraceNext** function.

Before calling **StackTraceFirst**, an application must initialize the **STACK-TRACEENTRY** structure and specify its size, in bytes, in the **dwSize** member.

See Also   **StackTraceCSIPFirst**, **StackTraceNext**

StackTraceNext   3.1

#include <toolhelp.h>

BOOL StackTraceNext(*lpste***)**
STACKTRACEENTRY FAR* *lpste*;   /* address of stack-frame structure   */

The **StackTraceNext** function fills the specified structure with information that describes the next stack frame in a stack trace.

Parameters   *lpste*
Points to a **STACKTRACEENTRY** structure to receive information about the next stack frame. The **STACKTRACEENTRY** structure has the following form:

```
#include <toolhelp.h>

typedef struct tagSTACKTRACEENTRY {  /* ste */
    DWORD   dwSize;
    HTASK   hTask;
    WORD    wSS;
    WORD    wBP;
    WORD    wCS;
```

```
    WORD    wIP;
    HMODULE hModule;
    WORD    wSegment;
    WORD    wFlags;
} STACKTRACEENTRY;
```

For a full description of this structure, see the *Microsoft Windows Programmer's Reference*, *Volume 3*.

Return Value   The return value is nonzero if the function is successful. Otherwise, it is zero.

Comments   The **StackTraceNext** function can be used to continue a stack trace started by using the **StackTraceFirst** or **StackTraceCSIPFirst** function.

See Also   **StackTraceCSIPFirst, StackTraceFirst, STACKTRACEENTRY**

StackDoc   3.1

int StartDoc(*hdc*, *lpdi*)
HDC *hdc*;   /* handle of device context   */
DOCINFO FAR* *lpdi*;   /* pointer to DOCINFO structure   */

The **StartDoc** function starts a print job. For Windows version 3.1, this function replaces the STARTDOC printer escape.

Parameters   *hdc*
Identifies the device context for the print job.

lpdi
Points to a **DOCINFO** structure containing the name of the document file and the name of the output file. The **DOCINFO** structure has the following form:

```
typedef struct {    /* di */
    int    cbSize;
    LPCSTR lpszDocName;
    LPCSTR lpszOutput;
} DOCINFO;
```

For a full description of this structure, see the *Microsoft Windows Programmer's Reference*, *Volume 3*.

Return Value   The return value is positive if the function is successful. Otherwise, it is SP_ERROR.

Comments	Applications should call the **StartDoc** function immediately before beginning a print job. Using this function ensures that documents containing more than one page are not interspersed with other print jobs.
	The **StartDoc** function should not be used inside metafiles.
See Also	**EndDoc**, **Escape**

StartPage

int **StartPage**(*hdc*)
HDC *hdc*;   /* handle of device context   */

The **StartPage** function prepares the printer driver to accept data.

Parameters	*hdc* Identifies the device context for the print job.
Return Value	The return value is greater than zero if the function is successful. It is less than or equal to zero if an error occurs.
Comments	The system disables the **ResetDC** function between calls to the **StartPage** and **EndPage** functions. This means that applications cannot change the device mode except at page boundaries.
See Also	**EndPage**, **Escape**, **ResetDC**

StartSound

int **StartSound**(void)

This function is obsolete. Use the Microsoft Windows multimedia audio functions instead. For information about these functions, see the *Microsoft Windows Multimedia Programmer's Reference*.

StopSound

int StopSound(void)

> This function is obsolete. Use the Microsoft Windows multimedia audio functions instead. For information about these functions, see the *Microsoft Windows Multimedia Programmer's Reference*.

StretchBlt

BOOL StretchBlt(*hdcDest, nXOriginDest, nYOriginDest, nWidthDest, nHeightDest, hdcSrc,
nXOriginSrc, nYOriginSrc, nWidthSrc, nHeightSrc, fdwRop***)**

HDC *hdcDest*;	/* destination device-context handle	*/
int *nXOriginDest*;	/* x-coordinate of origin of destination rectangle	*/
int *nYOriginDest*;	/* y-coordinate of origin of destination rectangle	*/
int *nWidthDest*;	/* width of destination rectangle	*/
int *nHeightDest*;	/* height of destination rectangle	*/
HDC *hdcSrc*;	/* source device-context handle	*/
int *nXOriginSrc*;	/* x-coordinate of origin of source rectangle	*/
int *nYOriginSrc*;	/* y-coordinate of origin of source rectangle	*/
int *nWidthSrc*;	/* width of source rectangle	*/
int *nHeightSrc*;	/* height of source rectangle	*/
DWORD *fdwRop*;	/* raster operation	*/

> The **StretchBlt** function copies a bitmap from a source rectangle into a destination rectangle, stretching or compressing the bitmap if necessary to fit the dimensions of the destination rectangle. The **StretchBlt** function uses the stretching mode of the destination device context (set by the **SetStretchBltMode** function) to determine how to stretch or compress the bitmap.

Parameters

hdcDest
Identifies the device context to receive the bitmap.

nXOriginDest
Specifies the logical x-coordinate of the upper-left corner of the destination rectangle.

nYOriginDest
Specifies the logical y-coordinate of the upper-left corner of the destination rectangle.

nWidthDest
Specifies the width, in logical units, of the destination rectangle.

nHeightDest
Specifies the height, in logical units, of the destination rectangle.

hdcSrc
Identifies the device context that contains the source bitmap.

nXOriginSrc
Specifies the logical x-coordinate of the upper-left corner of the source rectangle.

nYOriginSrc
Specifies the logical y-coordinate of the upper-left corner of the source rectangle.

nWidthSrc
Specifies the width, in logical units, of the source rectangle.

nHeightSrc
Specifies the height, in logical units, of the source rectangle.

fdwRop
Specifies the raster operation to be performed. Raster-operation codes define how the graphics device interface (GDI) combines colors in output operations that involve a current brush, a possible source bitmap, and a destination bitmap. This parameter can be one of the following values:

Code	Description
BLACKNESS	Turns all output black.
DSTINVERT	Inverts the destination bitmap.
MERGECOPY	Combines the pattern and the source bitmap by using the Boolean AND operator.
MERGEPAINT	Combines the inverted source bitmap with the destination bitmap by using the Boolean OR operator.
NOTSRCCOPY	Copies the inverted source bitmap to the destination.
NOTSRCERASE	Inverts the result of combining the destination and source bitmaps by using the Boolean OR operator.
PATCOPY	Copies the pattern to the destination bitmap.
PATINVERT	Combines the destination bitmap with the pattern by using the Boolean XOR operator.
PATPAINT	Combines the inverted source bitmap with the pattern by using the Boolean OR operator. Combines the result of this operation with the destination bitmap by using the Boolean OR operator.
SRCAND	Combines pixels of the destination and source bitmaps by using the Boolean AND operator.
SRCCOPY	Copies the source bitmap to the destination bitmap.
SRCERASE	Inverts the destination bitmap and combines the result with the source bitmap by using the Boolean AND operator.

Code	Description
SRCINVERT	Combines pixels of the destination and source bitmaps by using the Boolean XOR operator.
SRCPAINT	Combines pixels of the destination and source bitmaps by using the Boolean OR operator.
WHITENESS	Turns all output white.

Return Value

The return value is nonzero if the function is successful. Otherwise, it is zero.

Comments

The **StretchBlt** function stretches or compresses the source bitmap in memory and then copies the result to the destination. If a pattern is to be merged with the result, it is not merged until the stretched source bitmap is copied to the destination.

If a brush is used, it is the selected brush in the destination device context.

The destination coordinates are transformed according to the destination device context; the source coordinates are transformed according to the source device context.

If the destination, source, and pattern bitmaps do not have the same color format, **StretchBlt** converts the source and pattern bitmaps to match the destination bitmaps. The foreground and background colors of the destination device context are used in the conversion.

If **StretchBlt** must convert a monochrome bitmap to color, it sets white bits (1) to the background color and black bits (0) to the foreground color. To convert color to monochrome, it sets pixels that match the background color to white (1) and sets all other pixels to black (0). The foreground and background colors of the device context with color are used.

StretchBlt creates a mirror image of a bitmap if the signs of the *nWidthSrc* and *nWidthDest* or *nHeightSrc* and *nHeightDest* parameters differ. If *nWidthSrc* and *nWidthDest* have different signs, the function creates a mirror image of the bitmap along the x-axis. If *nHeightSrc* and *nHeightDest* have different signs, the function creates a mirror image of the bitmap along the y-axis.

Not all devices support the **StretchBlt** function. Applications can discover whether a device supports **StretchBlt** by calling the **GetDeviceCaps** function and specifying the RASTERCAPS index.

Example

The following example retrieves the handle of the desktop window and uses it to create a device context. After retrieving the dimensions of the desktop window, the example calls the **StretchBlt** function to copy the desktop bitmap into a smaller rectangle in the destination device context.

```
HWND hwndDesktop;
HDC hdcLocal;
RECT rc;

hwndDesktop = GetDesktopWindow();
hdcLocal = GetDC(hwndDesktop);
GetWindowRect(GetDesktopWindow(), &rc);

StretchBlt(hdc, 10, 10, 138, 106,
    hdcLocal, 0, 0, rc.right, rc.bottom, SRCCOPY);

ReleaseDC(hwndDesktop, hdcLocal);
```

See Also   **BitBlt, GetDeviceCaps, SetStretchBltMode, StretchDIBits**

StretchDIBits   3.0

int **StretchDIBits**(*hdc, XDest, YDest, cxDest, cyDest, XSrc, YSrc, cxSrc, cySrc, lpvBits, lpbmi,
    fuColorUse, fdwRop*)

HDC *hdc*;	/* handle of device context	*/
int *XDest*;	/* x-coordinate of destination rectangle	*/
int *YDest*;	/* y-coordinate of destination rectangle	*/
int *cxDest*;	/* width of destination rectangle	*/
int *cyDest*;	/* height of destination rectangle	*/
int *XSrc*;	/* x-coordinate of source rectangle	*/
int *YSrc*;	/* y-coordinate of source rectangle	*/
int *cxSrc*;	/* width of source rectangle	*/
int *cySrc*;	/* height of source rectangle	*/
const void FAR* *lpvBits*;	/* address of buffer with DIB bits	*/
LPBITMAPINFO *lpbmi*;	/* address of structure with bitmap data	*/
UINT *fuColorUse*;	/* RGB or palette indices	*/
DWORD *fdwRop*;	/* raster operation	*/

The **StretchDIBits** function moves a device-independent bitmap (DIB) from a
source rectangle into a destination rectangle, stretching or compressing the bitmap
if necessary to fit the dimensions of the destination rectangle.

Parameters   *hdc*
            Identifies the destination device context for a screen surface or memory bitmap.

        XDest
            Specifies the logical x-coordinate of the destination rectangle.

        YDest
            Specifies the logical y-coordinate of the destination rectangle.

cxDest
    Specifies the logical x-extent of the destination rectangle.

cyDest
    Specifies the logical y-extent of the destination rectangle.

XSrc
    Specifies the x-coordinate, in pixels, of the source rectangle in the DIB.

YSrc
    Specifies the y-coordinate, in pixels, of the source rectangle in the DIB.

cxSrc
    Specifies the width, in pixels, of the source rectangle in the DIB.

cySrc
    Specifies the height, in pixels, of the source rectangle in the DIB.

lpvBits
    Points to the DIB bits that are stored as an array of bytes.

lpbmi
    Points to a **BITMAPINFO** structure that contains information about the DIB.
    The **BITMAPINFO** structure has the following form:

```
typedef struct tagBITMAPINFO {  /* bmi */
    BITMAPINFOHEADER    bmiHeader;
    RGBQUAD             bmiColors[1];
} BITMAPINFO;
```

    For a full description of this structure, see the *Microsoft Windows Program-
    mer's Reference, Volume 3*.

fuColorUse
    Specifies whether the **bmiColors** member of the *lpbmi* parameter contains ex-
    plicit RGB (red-green-blue) values or indices into the currently realized logical
    palette. The *fuColorUse* parameter can be one of the following values:

Value	Meaning
DIB_PAL_COLORS	The color table consists of an array of 16-bit indices into the currently realized logical palette.
DIB_RGB_COLORS	The color table contains literal RGB values.

fdwRop
    Specifies the raster operation to be performed. Raster-operation codes define
    how the graphics device interface (GDI) combines colors in output operations
    that involve a current brush, a possible source bitmap, and a destination bitmap.
    For a list of raster-operation codes, see the description of the **BitBlt** function.
    For a complete list of the raster operations, see the *Microsoft Windows Pro-
    grammer's Reference, Volume 4*.

Return Value   The return value is the number of scan lines copied, if the function is successful.

Comments

The **StretchDIBits** function uses the stretching mode of the destination device context (set by the **SetStretchBltMode** function) to determine how to stretch or compress the bitmap.

The origin of the coordinate system for a device-independent bitmap is the lower-left corner. The origin of the coordinates of the destination rectangle depends on the current mapping mode of the device context.

StretchDIBits creates a mirror image of a bitmap if the signs of the *cxSrc* and *cxDest* parameters or the *cySrc* and *cyDest* parameters differ. If *cxSrc* and *cxDest* have different signs, the function creates a mirror image of the bitmap along the x-axis. If *cySrc* and *cyDest* have different signs, the function creates a mirror image of the bitmap along the y-axis.

See Also

SetMapMode, **SetStretchBltMode**

SubtractRect

3.1

BOOL SubtractRect(*lprcDest***,** *lprcSource1***,** *lprcSource2***)**
RECT FAR* *lprcDest***;**   /* pointer to destination rectangle   */
const RECT FAR* *lprcSource1***;**   /* pointer to rect. to subtract from   */
const RECT FAR* *lprcSource2***;**   /* pointer to rect. to subtract   */

The **SubtractRect** function retrieves the coordinates of a rectangle by subtracting one rectangle from another.

Parameters

lprcDest
Points to the **RECT** structure to receive the dimensions of the new rectangle. The **RECT** structure has the following form:

```
typedef struct tagRECT {    /* rc */
    int left;
    int top;
    int right;
    int bottom;
} RECT;
```

For a full description of this structure, see the *Microsoft Windows Programmer's Reference, Volume 3*.

lprcSource1
Points to the **RECT** structure from which a rectangle is to be subtracted.

lprcSource2
>   Points to the **RECT** structure that is to be subtracted from the rectangle pointed to by the *lprcSource1* parameter.

Return Value   The return value is nonzero if the function is successful. Otherwise, it is zero.

Comments   The rectangle specified by the *lprcSource2* parameter is subtracted from the rectangle specified by *lprcSource1* only when the rectangles intersect completely in either the x- or y-direction. For example, if *lprcSource1* were (10,10, 100,100) and *lprcSource2* were (50,50, 150,150), the rectangle pointed to by *lprcDest* would contain the same coordinates as *lprcSource1* when the function returned. If *lprcSource1* were (10,10, 100,100) and *lprcSource2* were (50,10, 150,150), however, the rectangle pointed to by *lprcDest* would contain the coordinates (10,10, 50,100) when the function returned.

See Also   **IntersectRect**, **UnionRect**

SwapMouseButton   2.x

BOOL SwapMouseButton(*fSwap*)
BOOL *fSwap*;   /* reverse or restore buttons   */

>   The **SwapMouseButton** function reverses the meaning of left and right mouse buttons.

Parameters   *fSwap*
>   Specifies whether the button meanings are reversed or restored. If this parameter is TRUE, the left button generates right-button mouse messages and the right button generates left-button messages. If this parameter is FALSE, the buttons are restored to their original meanings.

Return Value   The return value specifies the meaning of the mouse buttons immediately before the function is called. It is nonzero if the meaning was reversed. Otherwise, it is zero.

Comments   Button swapping is provided as a convenience to people who use the mouse with their left hands. The **SwapMouseButton** function is usually called by Control Panel only. Although an application is free to call the function, the mouse is a shared resource and reversing the meaning of the mouse button affects all applications.

Example   The following example swaps the mouse buttons, depending on the check state of
                     a check box:

```
BOOL fSwap;

fSwap = (BOOL) SendDlgItemMessage(hdlg, IDD_SWAP,
    BM_GETCHECK, 0, 0L);
SwapMouseButton(fSwap);
```

SwapRecording   3.0

void SwapRecording(*fuFlag*)
UINT *fuFlag*;   /* whether to start or stop swap recording   */

The **SwapRecording** function starts or stops recording data about memory swapping. Because this function can be used only in real mode, it cannot be used with
Windows 3.1.

SwitchStackBack   3.0

void SwitchStackBack(void)

The **SwitchStackBack** function restores the stack of the current task, canceling
the effect of the **SwitchStackTo** function.

Parameters   This function has no parameters.

Return Value   This function does not return a value.

Comments   **SwitchStackBack** preserves the contents of the AX:DX registers when it returns.

See Also   **SwitchStackTo**

SwitchStackTo

void SwitchStackTo(*uStackSegment, uStackPointer, uStackTop*)
UINT *uStackSegment*;   /* new stack data segment   */
UINT *uStackPointer*;   /* offset of beginning of stack   */
UINT *uStackTop*;   /* offset of top of stack   */

The **SwitchStackTo** function changes the stack of the current task to the specified data segment.

Parameters   *uStackSegment*
Specifies the data segment to contain the stack.

uStackPointer
Specifies the offset to the beginning of the stack in the data segment.

uStackTop
Specifies the offset to the top of the stack from the beginning of the stack.

Return Value   This function does not return a value.

Comments   Dynamic-link libraries (DLLs) do not have private stacks; instead, a DLL uses the stack of the task that calls the library. As a result, a DLL function fails if it treats the contents of the data-segment (DS) and stack-segment (SS) registers as equal. A task can call **SwitchStackTo** before calling a function in a DLL that treats the SS and DS registers as equal. When the DLL function returns, the task must then call the **SwitchStackBack** function to redirect its stack to its own data segment.

A DLL can also call **SwitchStackTo** before calling a function that assumes SS and DS to be equal and then call **SwitchStackBack** before returning to the task that called the DLL function.

Calls to **SwitchStackTo** and **SwitchStackBack** cannot be nested. That is, after calling **SwitchStackTo**, an application must call **SwitchStackBack** before calling **SwitchStackTo** again.

See Also   **SwitchStackBack**

SyncAllVoices

2.x

int SyncAllVoices(void)

> This function is obsolete. Use the Microsoft Windows multimedia audio functions instead. For information about these functions, see the *Microsoft Windows Multimedia Programmer's Reference.*

SysMsgProc

3.1

LRESULT CALLBACK SysMsgProc(*code***,** *wParam***,** *lParam***)**
int *code*;   /* message type   */
WPARAM *wParam*;   /* undefined   */
LPARAM *lParam*;   /* pointer to an MSG structure   */

> The **SysMsgProc** function is a library-defined callback function that the system calls after a dialog box, message box, or menu has retrieved a message, but before the message is processed. The callback function can process or modify messages for any application in the system.

Parameters

code
> Specifies the type of message being processed. This parameter can be one of the following values:

Value	Meaning
MSGF_DIALOGBOX	Messages inside a dialog box or message box procedure are being processed.
MSGF_MENU	Keyboard and mouse messages in a menu are being processed.

> If the *code* parameter is less than zero, the callback function must pass the message to the **CallNextHookEx** function without further processing and return the value returned by **CallNextHookEx**.

wParam
> Must be NULL.

lParam
> Points to the **MSG** structure to contain the message. The **MSG** structure has the following form:

```
typedef struct tagMSG {      /* msg */
    HWND    hwnd;
    UINT    message;
    WPARAM  wParam;
    LPARAM  lParam;
    DWORD   time;
    POINT   pt;
} MSG;
```

For a full description of this structure, see the *Microsoft Windows Programmer's Reference*, *Volume 3*.

Return Value   The return value should be nonzero if the function processes the message. Otherwise, it should be zero.

Comments   This callback function must be in a dynamic-link library (DLL).

An application must install this callback function by specifying the WH_SYSMSGFILTER filter type and the procedure-instance address of the callback function in a call to the **SetWindowsHookEx** function.

SysMsgProc is a placeholder for the library-defined function name. The actual name must be exported by including it in an **EXPORTS** statement in the library's module-definition file.

See Also   **CallNextHookEx**, **MessageBox**, **SetWindowsHookEx**

SystemHeapInfo   3.1

#include <toolhelp.h>

BOOL SystemHeapInfo(*lpshi*)
SYSHEAPINFO FAR* *lpshi*;   /* address of heap-info structure   */

The **SystemHeapInfo** function fills the specified structure with information that describes the USER.EXE and GDI.EXE heaps.

Parameters   *lpshi*
Points to a **SYSHEAPINFO** structure to receive information about the USER and GDI heaps. The **SYSHEAPINFO** structure has the following form:

```
#include <toolhelp.h>

typedef struct tagSYSHEAPINFO {  /* shi */
    DWORD    dwSize;
    WORD     wUserFreePercent;
    WORD     wGDIFreePercent;
    HGLOBAL  hUserSegment;
    HGLOBAL  hGDISegment;
} SYSHEAPINFO;
```

For a full description of this structure, see the *Microsoft Windows Programmer's Reference, Volume 3*.

Return Value   The return value is nonzero if the function is successful. Otherwise, it is zero.

Comments   This function is included for advisory purposes. Before calling **SystemHeapInfo**, an application must initialize the **SYSHEAPINFO** structure and specify its size, in bytes, in the **dwSize** member.

SystemParametersInfo   3.1

BOOL SystemParametersInfo(*uAction, uParam, lpvParam, fuWinIni***)**
UINT *uAction*;   /* system parameter to query or set   */
UINT *uParam*;   /* depends on system parameter   */
void FAR* *lpvParam*;   /* depends on system parameter   */
UINT *fuWinIni*;   /* WIN.INI update flag   */

The **SystemParametersInfo** function queries or sets system-wide parameters. This function can also update the WIN.INI file while setting a parameter.

Parameters   *uAction*
Specifies the system-wide parameter to query or set. This parameter can be one of the following values:

Value	Meaning
SPI_GETBEEP	Retrieves a **BOOL** value that indicates whether the warning beep is on or off.
SPI_GETBORDER	Retrieves the border multiplying factor that determines the width of a window's sizing border.
SPI_GETFASTTASKSWITCH	Determines whether fast task switching is on or off.

Value	Meaning
SPI_GETGRIDGRANULARITY	Retrieves the current granularity value of the desktop sizing grid.
SPI_GETICONTITLELOGFONT	Retrieves the logical-font information for the current icon-title font.
SPI_GETICONTITLEWRAP	Determines whether icon-title wrapping is on or off.
SPI_GETKEYBOARDDELAY	Retrieves the keyboard repeat-delay setting.
SPI_GETKEYBOARDSPEED	Retrieves the keyboard repeat-speed setting.
SPI_GETMENUDROPALIGNMENT	Determines whether pop-up menus are left-aligned or right-aligned relative to the corresponding menu-bar item.
SPI_GETMOUSE	Retrieves the mouse speed and the mouse threshold values, which Windows uses to calculate mouse acceleration.
SPI_GETSCREENSAVEACTIVE	Retrieves a **BOOL** value that indicates whether screen saving is on or off.
SPI_GETSCREENSAVETIMEOUT	Retrieves the screen-saver time-out value.
SPI_ICONHORIZONTALSPACING	Sets the width, in pixels, of an icon cell.
SPI_ICONVERTICALSPACING	Sets the height, in pixels, of an icon cell.
SPI_LANGDRIVER	Forces the user to load a new language driver.
SPI_SETBEEP	Turns the warning beep on or off.
SPI_SETBORDER	Sets the border multiplying factor that determines the width of a window's sizing border.
SPI_SETDESKPATTERN	Sets the current desktop pattern to the value specified in the Pattern entry in the WIN.INI file or to the pattern specified by the *lpvParam* parameter.
SPI_SETDESKWALLPAPER	Specifies the filename that contains the bitmap to be used as the desktop wallpaper.
SPI_SETDOUBLECLKHEIGHT	Sets the height of the rectangle within which the second click of a double-click must fall for it to be registered as a double-click.
SPI_SETDOUBLECLICKTIME	Sets the double-click time for the mouse. The double-click time is the maximum number of milliseconds that may occur between the first and second clicks of a double-click.

Value	Meaning
SPI_SETDOUBLECLKWIDTH	Sets the width of the rectangle in which the second click of a double-click must fall to be registered as a double-click.
SPI_SETFASTTASKSWITCH	Turns fast task switching on or off.
SPI_SETGRIDGRANULARITY	Sets the granularity of the desktop sizing grid.
SPI_SETICONTITLELOGFONT	Sets the font that is used for icon titles.
SPI_SETICONTITLEWRAP	Turns icon-title wrapping on or off.
SPI_SETKEYBOARDDELAY	Sets the keyboard repeat-delay setting.
SPI_SETKEYBOARDSPEED	Sets the keyboard repeat-speed setting.
SPI_SETMENUDROPALIGNMENT	Sets the alignment value of pop-up menus.
SPI_SETMOUSE	Sets the mouse speed and the x and y mouse-threshold values.
SPI_SETMOUSEBUTTONSWAP	Swaps or restores the meaning of the left and right mouse buttons.
SPI_SETSCREENSAVEACTIVE	Sets the state of the screen saver.
SPI_SETSCREENSAVETIMEOUT	Sets the screen-saver time-out value.

uParam

Depends on the *uAction* parameter. For more information, see the following Comments section.

lpvParam

Depends on the *uAction* parameter. For more information, see the following Comments section.

fuWinIni

If a system parameter is being set, specifies whether the WIN.INI file is updated, and if so, whether the WM_WININICHANGE message is broadcast to all top-level windows to notify them of the change. This parameter can be a combination of the following values:

Value	Meaning
SPIF_UPDATEINIFILE	Writes the new system-wide parameter setting to the WIN.INI file.
SPIF_SENDWININICHANGE	Broadcasts a WM_WININICHANGE message after WIN.INI is updated. This flag has no effect if SPIF_UPDATEINIFILE is not specified.

Return Value

The return value is nonzero if the function is successful. Otherwise, it is zero.

Comments

The **SystemParameterInfo** function is intended for applications, such as Control Panel, that allow the user to customize the Windows environment.

The following table describes the *uParam* and *lpvParam* parameters for each SPI_ constant:

Constant	uParam	lpvParam
SPI_GETBEEP	0	Points to a **BOOL** variable that receives TRUE if the beep is on, FALSE if it is off.
SPI_GETBORDER	0	Points to an integer variable that receives the border multiplying factor.
SPI_GETFASTTASKSWITCH	0	Points to a **BOOL** variable that receives TRUE if fast task switching is on, FALSE if it is off.
SPI_GETGRIDGRANULARITY	0	Points to an integer variable that receives the grid-granularity value.
SPI_GETICONTITLELOGFONT	Size of **LOGFONT** structure	Points to a **LOGFONT** structure that receives the logical-font information.
SPI_GETICONTITLEWRAP	0	Points to a **BOOL** variable that receives TRUE if wrapping is on, FALSE if wrapping is off.
SPI_GETKEYBOARDDELAY	0	Points to an integer variable that receives the keyboard repeat-delay setting.
SPI_GETKEYBOARDSPEED	0	Points to a **WORD** variable that receives the current keyboard repeat-speed setting.
SPI_GETMENUDROPALIGNMENT	0	Points to a **BOOL** variable that receives TRUE if pop-up menus are right-aligned, FALSE if they are left-aligned.
SPI_GETMOUSE	0	Points to an integer array name lpiMouse, where lpiMouse[0] receives the WIN.INI entry **MouseThreshold1**, lpiMouse[1] receives the entry **MouseThreshold2**, and lpiMouse[2] receives the entry **MouseSpeed**.
SPI_GETSCREENSAVEACTIVE	0	Points to a **BOOL** variable that receives TRUE if the screen saver is active, FALSE if it is not.
SPI_GETSCREENSAVETIMEOUT	0	Points to an integer variable that receives the screen-saver time-out value, in milliseconds.
SPI_ICONHORIZONTALSPACING	New width, in pixels, for horizontal spacing of icons	Is NULL if the icon cell width, in pixels, is returned in *uParam*. If this value is a pointer to an integer, the current horizontal spacing is returned in that variable and *uParam* is ignored.
SPI_ICONVERTICALSPACING	New height, in pixels, for vertical spacing of icons	Is NULL if the icon cell height, in pixels, is returned in *uParam*. If this value is a pointer to an integer, the current vertical spacing is returned in that variable and *uParam* is ignored.

Constant	*uParam*	*lpvParam*
SPI_LANGDRIVER	0	Points to a string containing the new language driver filename. The application should make sure that all other international settings remain consistent when changing the language driver.
SPI_SETBEEP	TRUE = turn the beep on; FALSE = turn the beep off	Is NULL.
SPI_SETBORDER	Border multiplying factor	Is NULL.
SPI_SETDESKPATTERN	0 or −1	Specifies the desktop pattern. If this value is NULL and the *uParam* parameter is −1, the value is reread from the WIN.INI file. This value can also be a null-terminated string (**LPSTR**) containing a sequence of 8 numbers that represent the new desktop pattern; for example, "170 85 170 85 170 85 170 85" represents a 50% gray pattern.
SPI_SETDESKWALLPAPER	0	Points to a string that specifies the name of the bitmap file.
SPI_SETDOUBLECLKHEIGHT	Double-click height, in pixels	Is NULL.
SPI_SETDOUBLECLICKTIME	Double-click time, in milliseconds	Is NULL.
SPI_SETDOUBLECLKWIDTH	Double-click width, in pixels	Is NULL.
SPI_SETFASTTASKSWITCH	TRUE = turn on fast task switching; FALSE = turn it off	Is NULL.
SPI_SETGRIDGRANULARITY	Grid granularity,	
SPI_SETICONTITLELOGFONT	Size of the **LOGFONT** structure	Points to a **LOGFONT** structure that defines the font to use for icon titles. If *uParam* is set to zero and *lParam* is set to NULL, Windows uses the icon-title font and spacings that were in effect when Windows was started.
SPI_SETICONTITLEWRAP	TRUE = turn wrapping on; FALSE = turn wrapping off	Is NULL.
SPI_SETKEYBOARDDELAY	Keyboard-delay setting	Is NULL.
SPI_SETKEYBOARDSPEED	Repeat-speed setting	Is NULL.

Constant	uParam	lpvParam
SPI_SETMENUDROPALIGNMENT	TRUE = right-alignment; FALSE = left-alignment	Is NULL.
SPI_SETMOUSE	0	Points to an integer array named lpiMouse, where lpiMouse[0] receives the WIN.INI entry **xMouseThreshold**, lpiMouse[1] receives the entry **yMouseThreshold**, and lpiMouse[2] receives the entry **MouseSpeed**.
SPI_SETMOUSEBUTTONSWAP	TRUE = reverse the meaning of the left and right mouse buttons; FALSE = restore the buttons to their original meanings	Is NULL.
SPI_SETSCREENSAVEACTIVE	TRUE = activate screen saving; FALSE = deactivate screen saving	Is NULL.
SPI_SETSCREENSAVETIMEOUT	Idle time-out duration, in seconds, before screen is saved	Is NULL.

Example   The following example retrieves the value for the DoubleClickSpeed entry from the WIN.INI file and uses the value to initialize an edit control. In this example, while the WM_COMMAND message is being processed, the user-specified value is retrieved from the edit control and used to set the double-click time.

```
char szBuf[32];
int iResult;

case WM_INITDIALOG:

    /* Initialize edit control to the current double-click time. */

    iResult = GetProfileInt("windows",
        "DoubleClickSpeed", 550);
    itoa(iResult, szBuf, 10);
    SendDlgItemMessage(hdlg, IDD_DCLKTIME, WM_SETTEXT, 0,
        (DWORD) (LPSTR) szBuf);

    .
    . /* Initialize any other controls. */
    .

    return FALSE;
```

```
case WM_COMMAND:
    switch(wParam) {

        case IDOK:

            /* Set double-click time to a user-specified value. */

            SendDlgItemMessage(hdlg, IDD_DCLKTIME, WM_GETTEXT,
                sizeof(szBuf), (DWORD) (LPSTR) szBuf);
            SystemParametersInfo(SPI_SETDOUBLECLICKTIME, atoi(szBuf),
                (LPVOID) NULL, SPIF_UPDATEINIFILE |
                SPIF_SENDWININICHANGE);

            .
            . /* Set any other system-wide parameters. */
            .

            EndDialog(hdlg, TRUE);
            return TRUE;
    }
```

TabbedTextOut

LONG TabbedTextOut(*hdc, xPosStart, yPosStart, lpszString, cbString, cTabStops, lpnTabPositions,*
   *nTabOrigin***)**

HDC *hdc*;	/* handle of device context	*/
int *xPosStart*;	/* x-coordinate of starting position	*/
int *yPosStart*;	/* y-coordinate of starting position	*/
LPCSTR *lpszString*;	/* address of string	*/
int *cbString*;	/* number of characters in string	*/
int *cTabStops*;	/* number of tabs in array	*/
int FAR* *lpnTabPositions*;	/* address of array with tab positions	*/
int *nTabOrigin*;	/* x-coordinate for tab expansion	*/

The **TabbedTextOut** function writes a character string at the specified location, expanding tabs to the values specified in the array of tab-stop positions. The function writes text in the currently selected font.

Parameters

hdc
    Identifies the device context.

xPosStart
    Specifies the logical x-coordinate of the starting point of the string.

yPosStart
    Specifies the logical y-coordinate of the starting point of the string.

lpszString
Points to the character string to be drawn.

cbString
Specifies the number of characters in the string.

cTabStops
Specifies the number of values in the array of tab-stop positions.

lpnTabPositions
Points to an array containing the tab-stop positions, in device units. The tab stops must be sorted in increasing order; the smallest x-value should be the first item in the array.

nTabOrigin
Specifies the logical x-coordinate of the starting position from which tabs are expanded.

Return Value   The return value is the dimensions of the string, in logical units, if the function is successful. The low-order word contains the string width; the high-order word contains the string height. Otherwise, the return value is zero.

Comments   If the *cTabStops* parameter is zero and the *lpnTabPositions* parameter is NULL, tabs are expanded to eight times the average character width.

If *cTabStops* is 1, the tab stops are separated by the distance specified by the first value in the *lpnTabPositions* array.

If the *lpnTabPositions* array contains more than one value, a tab stop is set for each value in the array, up to the number specified by *cTabStops*.

The *nTabOrigin* parameter allows an application to call the **TabbedTextOut** function several times for a single line. If the application calls **TabbedTextOut** more than once with the *nTabOrigin* set to the same value each time, the function expands all tabs relative to the position specified by *nTabOrigin*.

By default, the current position is not used or updated by the **TabbedTextOut** function. If an application must update the current position when calling **TabbedTextOut**, it can call the **SetTextAlign** function with the *wFlags* parameter set to TA_UPDATECP. When this flag is set, Windows ignores the *xPosStart* and *yPosStart* parameters on subsequent calls to the **TabbedTextOut** function, using the current position instead.

Example   The following example expands tabs from the same x-coordinate as the string's starting point:

```
LPSTR lpszTabbedText = "Column 1\tColumn 2\tTest of TabbedTextOut";
int aTabs[2] = { 150, 300 };
int iStartXPos = 100;
int iStartYPos = 100;
```

```
TabbedTextOut(hdc,                    /* handle of device context   */
    iStartXPos, iStartYPos,           /* starting coordinates        */
    lpszTabbedText,                   /* address of text             */
    lstrlen(lpszTabbedText),          /* number of characters        */
    sizeof(aTabs) / sizeof(int),      /* number of tabs in array     */
    aTabs,                            /* array for tab positions     */
    iStartXPos);                      /* x-coord. for tab expanding  */
```

See Also   **GetTabbedTextExtent, SetTextAlign, SetTextColor, TextOut**

TaskFindHandle   3.1

#include <toolhelp.h>

BOOL TaskFindHandle(*lpte*, *htask*)
TASKENTRY FAR* *lpte*;   /* address of **TASKENTRY structure**   */
HTASK *htask*;   /* handle of task   */

The **TaskFindHandle** function fills the specified structure with information that describes the given task.

Parameters   *lpte*
Points to a **TASKENTRY** structure to receive information about the task. The **TASKENTRY** structure has the following form:

```
#include <toolhelp.h>

typedef struct tagTASKENTRY {  /* te */
    DWORD       dwSize;
    HTASK       hTask;
    HTASK       hTaskParent;
    HINSTANCE   hInst;
    HMODULE     hModule;
    WORD        wSS;
    WORD        wSP;
    WORD        wStackTop;
    WORD        wStackMinimum;
    WORD        wStackBottom;
    WORD        wcEvents;
    HGLOBAL     hQueue;
    char        szModule[MAX_MODULE_NAME + 1];
    WORD        wPSPOffset;
    HANDLE      hNext;
} TASKENTRY;
```

For a full description of this structure, see the *Microsoft Windows Programmer's Reference, Volume 3*.

htask
Identifies the task to be described.

Return Value   The return value is nonzero if the function is successful. Otherwise, it is zero.

Comments   The **TaskFindHandle** function can be used to begin a walk through the task queue. An application can examine subsequent entries in the task queue by using the **TaskNext** function.

Before calling **TaskFindHandle**, an application must initialize the **TASKENTRY** structure and specify its size, in bytes, in the **dwSize** member.

See Also   **TaskFirst, TaskNext**

TaskFirst   3.1

#include <toolhelp.h>

BOOL TaskFirst(*lpte***)**
TASKENTRY FAR* *lpte*;   /* address of TASKENTRY structure   */

The **TaskFirst** function fills the specified structure with information about the first task on the task queue.

Parameters   *lpte*
Points to a **TASKENTRY** structure to receive information about the first task. The **TASKENTRY** structure has the following form:

```
#include <toolhelp.h>

typedef struct tagTASKENTRY {  /* te */
    DWORD       dwSize;
    HTASK       hTask;
    HTASK       hTaskParent;
    HINSTANCE   hInst;
    HMODULE     hModule;
    WORD        wSS;
    WORD        wSP;
    WORD        wStackTop;
    WORD        wStackMinimum;
    WORD        wStackBottom;
    WORD        wcEvents;
```

```
            HGLOBAL    hQueue;
            char       szModule[MAX_MODULE_NAME + 1];
            WORD       wPSPOffset;
            HANDLE     hNext;
        } TASKENTRY;
```

For a full description of this structure, see the *Microsoft Windows Programmer's Reference, Volume 3.*

Return Value   The return value is nonzero if the function is successful. Otherwise, it is zero.

Comments   The **TaskFirst** function can be used to begin a walk through the task queue. An application can examine subsequent entries in the task queue by using the **TaskNext** function.

Before calling **TaskFirst**, an application must initialize the **TASKENTRY** structure and specify its size, in bytes, in the **dwSize** member.

See Also   **TaskFindHandle**, **TaskNext**

TaskGetCSIP

3.1

#include <toolhelp.h>

DWORD TaskGetCSIP(*htask*)
HTASK *htask*;   /* handle of task   */

The **TaskGetCSIP** function returns the next CS:IP value of a sleeping task. This function is useful for applications that must "know" where a sleeping task will begin execution upon awakening.

Parameters   *htask*
Identifies the task whose CS:IP value is being examined. This task must be sleeping when the application calls **TaskGetCSIP**.

Return Value   The return value is the next CS:IP value, if the function is successful. If the *htask* parameter is invalid, the return value is NULL.

Comments   **TaskGetCSIP** should not be called if *htask* identifies the current task.

See Also   **DirectedYield**, **TaskSetCSIP**, **TaskSwitch**

TaskNext

3.1

#include <toolhelp.h>

BOOL TaskNext(*lpte***)**
TASKENTRY FAR* *lpte*;   /* address of **TASKENTRY structure**   */

> The **TaskNext** function fills the specified structure with information about the next task on the task queue.

Parameters   *lpte*

> Points to a **TASKENTRY** structure to receive information about the next task. The **TASKENTRY** structure has the following form:

```
#include <toolhelp.h>

typedef struct tagTASKENTRY {  /* te */
    DWORD     dwSize;
    HTASK     hTask;
    HTASK     hTaskParent;
    HINSTANCE hInst;
    HMODULE   hModule;
    WORD      wSS;
    WORD      wSP;
    WORD      wStackTop;
    WORD      wStackMinimum;
    WORD      wStackBottom;
    WORD      wcEvents;
    HGLOBAL   hQueue;
    char      szModule[MAX_MODULE_NAME + 1];
    WORD      wPSPOffset;
    HANDLE    hNext;
} TASKENTRY;
```

> For a full description of this structure, see the *Microsoft Windows Programmer's Reference, Volume 3*.

Return Value   The return value is nonzero if the function is successful. Otherwise, it is zero.

Comments   The **TaskNext** function can be used to continue a walk through the task queue. The walk must have been started by the **TaskFirst** or **TaskFindHandle** function.

See Also   **TaskFindHandle, TaskFirst**

TaskSetCSIP

3.1

#include <toolhelp.h>

DWORD TaskSetCSIP(*htask*, *wCS*, *wIP*)
HTASK *htask*;   /* handle of task   */
WORD *wCS*;   /* value in CS register   */
WORD *wIP*;   /* value in IP register   */

The **TaskSetCSIP** function sets the CS:IP value of a sleeping task. When the task is yielded to, it will begin execution at the specified address.

Parameters   *htask*
Identifies the task to be assigned the new CS:IP value.

wCS
Contains the new value of the CS register.

wIP
Contains the new value of the IP register.

Return Value   The return value is the previous CS:IP value for the task. The **TaskSwitch** function uses this value. The return value is NULL if the *htask* parameter is invalid.

Comments   **TaskSetCSIP** should not be called if *htask* identifies the current task.

See Also   **DirectedYield, TaskGetCSIP, TaskSwitch**

TaskSwitch

3.1

#include <toolhelp.h>

BOOL TaskSwitch(*htask*, *dwNewCSIP*)
HTASK *htask*;   /* handle of task   */
DWORD *dwNewCSIP*;   /* execution address within task */

The **TaskSwitch** function switches to the given task. The task begins executing at the specified address.

Parameters   *htask*
Identifies the new task.

dwNewCSIP
> Identifies the address within the given task at which to begin execution. Be very careful that this address is not in a code segment owned by the given task.

Return Value   The return value is nonzero if the task switch is successful. Otherwise, it is zero.

Comments   When the task identified by the *htask* parameter yields, **TaskSwitch** returns to the calling application.

> **TaskSwitch** changes the CS:IP value of the task's stack frame to the value specified by the *dwNewCSIP* parameter and then calls the **DirectedYield** function.

See Also   **DirectedYield, TaskSetCSIP, TaskGetCSIP**

TerminateApp   3.1

#include <toolhelp.h>

void TerminateApp(*htask*, *wFlags*)
HTASK *htask*;   /* handle of task   */
WORD *wFlags*;   /* termination flags   */

> The **TerminateApp** function ends the given application instance (task).

Parameters   *htask*
> Identifies the task to be ended. If this parameter is NULL, it identifies the current task.

wFlags
> Indicates how to end the task. This parameter can be one of the following values:

Value	Meaning
UAE_BOX	Calls the Windows kernel to display the Application Error message box and then ends the task.
NO_UAE_BOX	Calls the Windows kernel to end the task but does not display the Application Error message box. The application's interrupt or notification callback function should have displayed an error message, a warning, or both.

Return Value   This function returns only if *htask* is not NULL and does not identify the current task.

Comments   The **TerminateApp** function unregisters all callback functions registered with the Tool Help functions and then ends the application as if the given task had produced a general-protection (GP) fault or other error.

TerminateApp should be used only by debugging applications, because the function may not free not all objects owned by the ended application.

See Also   **InterruptRegister**, **InterruptUnRegister**, **NotifyRegister**, **NotifyUnRegister**

TextOut
`2.x`

```
BOOL TextOut(hdc, nXStart, nYStart, lpszString, cbString)
HDC hdc;              /* handle of device context        */
int nXStart;          /* x-coordinate of starting position */
int nYStart;          /* y-coordinate of starting position */
LPCSTR lpszString;    /* address of string               */
int cbString;         /* number of bytes in string       */
```

The **TextOut** function writes a character string at the specified location, using the currently selected font.

Parameters
hdc
  Identifies the device context.

nXStart
  Specifies the logical x-coordinate of the starting point of the string.

nYStart
  Specifies the logical y-coordinate of the starting point of the string.

lpszString
  Points to the character string to be drawn.

cbString
  Specifies the number of bytes in the string.

Return Value   The return value is nonzero if the function is successful. Otherwise, it is zero.

Comments   Character origins are at the upper-left corner of the character cell.

By default, the **TextOut** function does not use or update the current position. If an application must update the current position when calling **TextOut**, it can call the **SetTextAlign** function with the *wFlags* parameter set to TA_UPDATECP. When this flag is set, Windows ignores the *nXStart* and *nYStart* parameters on subsequent calls to the **TextOut** function, using the current position instead.

Example

The following example uses the **GetTextFace** function to retrieve the face name of the current font, calls **SetTextAlign** so that the current position is updated when the **TextOut** function is called, and then writes some introductory text and the face name by calling **TextOut**:

```
int nFaceNameLen;
char aFaceName[80];

nFaceNameLen = GetTextFace(hdc, /* returns length of string */
    sizeof(aFaceName),          /* size of face-name buffer   */
    (LPSTR) aFaceName);         /* address of face-name buffer */

SetTextAlign(hdc,
    TA_UPDATECP);              /* updates current position    */
MoveTo(hdc, 100, 100);        /* sets current position       */
TextOut(hdc, 0, 0,            /* uses current position for text */
    "This is the current face name: ", 31);
TextOut(hdc, 0, 0, aFaceName, nFaceNameLen);
```

See Also

ExtTextOut, GetTextExtent, SetTextAlign, SetTextColor, TabbedTextOut

---

Throw

2.x

void Throw(*lpCatchBuf*, *nErrorReturn***)**
const int FAR* *lpCatchBuf*;   /* address of CATCHBUF saved by Catch   */
int *nErrorReturn*;   /* value to return from Catch function   */

The **Throw** function restores the execution environment to the values saved in the specified array. Execution then transfers to the **Catch** function that copied the environment to the array.

Parameters

lpCatchBuf
Points to a **CATCHBUF** array that contains the execution environment. This array must have been set by a previous call to the **Catch** function.

nErrorReturn
Specifies the value to be returned to the **Catch** function. The meaning of the value is determined by the application. The value should be nonzero, so that the call to the **Catch** function can distinguish between a return from **Catch** (which returns zero) and a return from **Throw**.

Return Value

This function does not return a value.

Comments

The **Throw** function is similar to the C run-time function **longjmp**.

The function that calls **Catch** must free any resources allocated between the time **Catch** was called and the time **Throw** was called.

Do not use the **Throw** function across messages. For example, if an application calls **Catch** while processing a WM_CREATE message and then calls **Throw** while processing a WM_PAINT message, the application will terminate.

Example

The following example calls the **Catch** function to save the current execution environment before calling a recursive sort function. The first return from **Catch** is zero. If the doSort function calls the **Throw** function, execution will again return to the **Catch** function. This time, **Catch** returns the STACKOVERFLOW error passed by the doSort function. The doSort function is recursive—that is, it calls itself. It maintains a variable, wStackCheck, that is used to check the amount of stack space used. If more than 3K of the stack has been used, doSort calls **Throw** to drop out of all the nested function calls back into the function that called **Catch**.

```
#define STACKOVERFLOW 1

UINT uStackCheck;
CATCHBUF catchbuf;

{
    int iReturn;
    char szBuf[80];

    if ((iReturn = Catch((int FAR*) catchbuf)) != 0) {
        .
        . /* Error processing goes here. */
        .
    }
    else {
        uStackCheck = 0;        /* initializes stack-usage count */
        doSort(1, 100);         /* calls sorting function        */
    }
    break;
}

void doSort(int sLeft, int sRight)
{
    int sLast;

    /*
     * Determine whether more than 3K of the stack has been
     * used, and if so, call Throw to drop back into the
     * original calling application.
     *
     * The stack is incremented by the size of the two parameters,
     * the two local variables, and the return value (2 for a near
     * function call).
     */
```

```
uStackCheck += (sizeof(int) * 4) + 2;

if (uStackCheck > (3 * 1024))
    Throw((int FAR*) catchbuf, STACKOVERFLOW);
.
. /* A sorting algorithm goes here. */
.

doSort(sLeft, sLast - 1);   /* note recursive call       */
uStackCheck -= 10;          /* updates stack-check variable */
}
```

See Also   **Catch**

TimerCount

#include <toolhelp.h>

BOOL TimerCount(*lpti*)
TIMERINFO FAR* *lpti*;   /* address of structure for execution times   */

The **TimerCount** function fills the specified structure with the execution times of the current task and VM (virtual machine).

Parameters   *lpti*

Points to the **TIMERINFO** structure that will receive the execution times. The **TIMERINFO** structure has the following form:

```
#include <toolhelp.h>

typedef struct tagTIMERINFO {  /* ti */
    DWORD dwSize;
    DWORD dwmsSinceStart;
    DWORD dwmsThisVM;
} TIMERINFO;
```

For a full description of this structure, see the *Microsoft Windows Programmer's Reference, Volume 3.*

Return Value   The return value is nonzero if the function is successful. Otherwise, it is zero.

Comments   The **TimerCount** function provides a consistent source of timing information, accurate to the millisecond. In enhanced mode, **TimerCount** uses the VTD (virtual timer device) to obtain accurate execution times.

In standard mode, **TimerCount** calls the **GetTickCount** function, which returns information accurate to one clock tick (approximately 55 ms). **TimerCount** then reads the hardware timer to estimate how many milliseconds remain until the next clock tick. The resulting time is accurate to 1 ms.

Before calling **TimerCount**, an application must initialize the **TIMERINFO** structure and specify its size, in bytes, in the **dwSize** member.

See Also   **GetTickCount**

TimerProc

2.x

void CALLBACK **TimerProc**(*hwnd*, *msg*, *idTimer*, *dwTime*)
HWND *hwnd*;   /* handle of window for timer messages   */
UINT *msg*;   /* WM_TIMER message   */
UINT *idTimer*;   /* timer identifier   */
DWORD *dwTime*;   /* current system time   */

The **TimerProc** function is an application-defined callback function that processes WM_TIMER messages.

Parameters   *hwnd*
Identifies the window associated with the timer.

msg
Specifies the WM_TIMER message.

idTimer
Specifies the timer's identifier.

dwTime
Specifies the current system time.

Return Value   This function does not return a value.

Comments   **TimerProc** is a placeholder for the application-defined function name. The actual name must be exported by including it in an **EXPORTS** statement in the application's module-definition file.

See Also   **KillTimer, SetTimer**

ToAscii

int **ToAscii**(*uVirtKey, uScanCode, lpbKeyState, lpdwTransKey, fuState*)
UINT *uVirtKey*;   /* virtual-key code   */
UINT *uScanCode*;   /* scan code   */
BYTE FAR* *lpbKeyState*;   /* address of key-state array   */
DWORD FAR* *lpdwTransKey*;   /* 32-bit buffer for translated key   */
UINT *fuState*;   /* active-menu flag   */

The **ToAscii** function translates the specified virtual-key code and keyboard state to the corresponding Windows character or characters.

Parameters   *uVirtKey*
Specifies the virtual-key code to be translated.

uScanCode
Specifies the hardware scan code of the key to be translated. The high-order bit of this value is set if the key is not pressed (is up).

lpbKeyState
Points to a 256-byte array that contains the current keyboard state. Each element (byte) in the array contains the state of one key. If the high-order bit of a byte is set, the key is pressed (is down).

lpdwTransKey
Points to a doubleword buffer to receive the translated Windows character or characters.

fuState
Specifies whether a menu is active. This parameter must be 1 if a menu is active, or zero otherwise.

Return Value   The return value is a negative value if the specified key is a dead key. Otherwise, it is one of the following values:

Value	Meaning
2	Two characters were copied to the buffer. This is usually an accent and a dead-key character, when the dead key cannot be translated otherwise.
1	One Windows character was copied to the buffer.
0	The specified virtual key has no translation for the current state of the keyboard.

Comments   If a previous dead key is stored in the keyboard driver, the parameters supplied to the **ToAscii** function might not be sufficient to translate the virtual-key code.

Typically, **ToAscii** performs the translation based on the virtual-key code. In some cases, however, the *uScanCode* parameter may be used to distinguish between a key press and a key release. The scan code is used for translating ALT+*number* key combinations.

See Also   **OemKeyScan**, **VkKeyScan**

TrackPopupMenu

3.0

BOOL TrackPopupMenu(*hmenu*, *fuFlags*, *x*, *y*, *nReserved*, *hwnd*, *lprc*)
HMENU *hmenu*;	/* handle of menu	*/
UINT *fuFlags*;	/* screen-position and mouse-button flags	*/
int *x*;	/* horizontal screen position	*/
int *y*;	/* vertical screen position	*/
int *nReserved*;	/* reserved	*/
HWND *hwnd*;	/* handle of owner window	*/
const RECT FAR* *lprc*;	/* address of structure with rectangle	*/

The **TrackPopupMenu** function displays the given floating pop-up menu at the specified location and tracks the selection of items on the pop-up menu. A floating pop-up menu can appear anywhere on the screen.

Parameters   *hmenu*
Identifies the pop-up menu to be displayed. The application retrieves this handle by calling the **CreatePopupMenu** function to create a new pop-up menu or by calling the **GetSubMenu** function to retrieve the handle of a pop-up menu associated with an existing menu item.

fuFlags
Specifies the screen-position and mouse-button flags. The screen-position flag can be one of the following:

Value	Meaning
TPM_CENTERALIGN	Centers the pop-up menu horizontally relative to the coordinate specified by the *x* parameter.
TPM_LEFTALIGN	Positions the pop-up menu so that its left side is aligned with the coordinate specified by the *x* parameter.
TPM_RIGHTALIGN	Positions the pop-up menu so that its right side is aligned with the coordinate specified by the *x* parameter.

The mouse-button flag can be one of the following:

Value	Meaning
TPM_LEFTBUTTON	Causes the pop-up menu to track the left mouse button.
TPM_RIGHTBUTTON	Causes the pop-up menu to track the right mouse button instead of the left.

x

Specifies the horizontal position, in screen coordinates, of the pop-up menu. Depending on the value of the *fuFlags* parameter, the menu can be left-aligned, right-aligned, or centered relative to this position.

y

Specifies the vertical position, in screen coordinates, of the top of the menu on the screen.

nReserved

Reserved; must be zero.

hwnd

Identifies the window that owns the pop-up menu. This window receives all WM_COMMAND messages from the menu. The window will not receive WM_COMMAND messages until **TrackPopupMenu** returns.

lprc

Points to a **RECT** structure that contains the screen coordinates of a rectangle in which the user can click without dismissing the pop-up menu. If this parameter is NULL, the pop-up menu is dismissed if the user clicks outside the pop-up menu. The **RECT** structure has the following form:

```
typedef struct tagRECT {      /* rc */
    int left;
    int top;
    int right;
    int bottom;
} RECT;
```

For a full description of this structure, see the *Microsoft Windows Programmer's Reference, Volume 3*.

Return Value

The return value is nonzero if the function is successful. Otherwise, it is zero.

Example

The following example creates and tracks a pop-up menu when the user clicks the left mouse button:

```
POINT ptCurrent;
HMENU hmenu;

ptCurrent = MAKEPOINT(lParam);
hmenu = CreatePopupMenu();
```

```
AppendMenu(hmenu, MF_ENABLED, IDM_ELLIPSE, "Ellipse");
AppendMenu(hmenu, MF_ENABLED, IDM_SQUARE, "Square");
AppendMenu(hmenu, MF_ENABLED, IDM_TRIANGLE, "Triangle");
ClientToScreen(hwnd, &ptCurrent);
TrackPopupMenu(hmenu, TPM_LEFTALIGN, ptCurrent.x,
    ptCurrent.y, 0, hwnd, NULL);
```

See Also   **CreatePopupMenu, GetSubMenu**

TranslateAccelerator   2.x

int TranslateAccelerator(*hwnd*, *haccl*, *lpmsg*)
HWND *hwnd*;   /* handle of window   */
HACCEL *haccl*;   /* handle of accelerator table   */
MSG FAR* *lpmsg*;   /* address of structure with message information */

The **TranslateAccelerator** function processes accelerator keys for menu commands. The function translates WM_KEYUP and WM_KEYDOWN messages to WM_COMMAND or WM_SYSCOMMAND messages if there is an entry for the accelerator key in the application's accelerator table.

Parameters   *hwnd*
               Identifies the window whose messages are to be translated.

               haccl
               Identifies an accelerator table (loaded by using the **LoadAccelerators** function).

               lpmsg
               Points to an **MSG** structure retrieved by a call to the **GetMessage** or **Peek-Message** function. The structure contains message information from the application's message queue. The **MSG** structure has the following form:

```
typedef struct tagMSG {      /* msg */
    HWND    hwnd;
    UINT    message;
    WPARAM  wParam;
    LPARAM  lParam;
    DWORD   time;
    POINT   pt;
} MSG;
```

               For a full description of this structure, see the *Microsoft Windows Programmer's Reference, Volume 3*.

Return Value   The return value is nonzero if the message is translated. Otherwise, it is zero.

Comments

The high-order word of the *lParam* parameter of the WM_COMMAND or WM_SYSCOMMAND message contains the value 1, to differentiate the message from messages sent by menus or controls.

WM_COMMAND or WM_SYSCOMMAND messages are sent directly to the window, rather than being posted to the application queue. The **Translate-Accelerator** function does not return until the message is processed.

Accelerator keystrokes that are defined to select items from the System menu are translated into WM_SYSCOMMAND messages; all other accelerator keystrokes are translated into WM_COMMAND messages.

When **TranslateAccelerator** returns a nonzero value (meaning that the message is translated), the application should *not* process the message again by using the **TranslateMessage** function.

Keystrokes in accelerator tables need not correspond to menu items.

If the accelerator keystroke does correspond to a menu item, the application is sent WM_INITMENU and WM_INITMENUPOPUP messages, just as if the user were trying to display the menu. However, these messages are not sent if any of the following conditions are present:

- The window is disabled.
- The menu item is disabled.
- The accelerator keystroke does not correspond to an item on the System menu and the window is minimized.
- A mouse capture is in effect (for more information, see the description of the **SetCapture** function).

If the window is the active window and there is no keyboard focus (generally the case if the window is minimized), WM_SYSKEYUP and WM_SYSKEYDOWN messages are translated instead of WM_KEYUP and WM_KEYDOWN messages.

If an accelerator keystroke that corresponds to a menu item occurs when the window that owns the menu is minimized, no WM_COMMAND message is sent. However, if an accelerator keystroke that does not match any of the items on the window's menu or the System menu occurs, a WM_COMMAND message is sent, even if the window is minimized.

See Also

GetMessage, LoadAccelerators, PeekMessage, SetCapture

TranslateMDISysAccel

BOOL TranslateMDISysAccel(*hwndClient, lpmsg*)
HWND *hwndClient*;   /* handle of parent MDI client window   */
MSG FAR* *lpmsg*;   /* address of structure with message data   */

The **TranslateMDISysAccel** function processes accelerator keystrokes for the given multiple document interface (MDI) child window. The function translates WM_KEYUP and WM_KEYDOWN messages to WM_SYSCOMMAND messages.

Parameters   *hwndClient*
Identifies the parent MDI client window.

lpmsg
Points to an **MSG** structure retrieved by a call to the **GetMessage** or **Peek-Message** function. The structure contains message information from the application's message queue. The **MSG** structure has the following form:

```
typedef struct tagMSG {      /* msg */
    HWND    hwnd;
    UINT    message;
    WPARAM  wParam;
    LPARAM  lParam;
    DWORD   time;
    POINT   pt;
} MSG;
```

For a full description of this structure, see the *Microsoft Windows Programmer's Reference, Volume 3*.

Return Value   The return value is nonzero if the function is successful. Otherwise, it is zero.

Comments   The high-order word of the *lParam* parameter of the WM_SYSCOMMAND message contains the value 1, to differentiate the message from messages sent by menus or controls.

See Also   **GetMessage, PeekMessage**

TranslateMessage

BOOL TranslateMessage(*lpmsg***)**
const MSG FAR* *lpmsg*;   /* address of MSG structure   */

The **TranslateMessage** function translates virtual-key messages into character messages, as follows:

- WM_KEYDOWN/WM_KEYUP combinations produce a WM_CHAR or WM_DEADCHAR message.

- WM_SYSKEYDOWN/WM_SYSKEYUP combinations produce a WM_SYSCHAR or WM_SYSDEADCHAR message.

The character messages are posted to the application's message queue, to be read the next time the application calls the **GetMessage** or **PeekMessage** function.

Parameters   *lpmsg*
Points to an **MSG** structure retrieved by a call to the **GetMessage** or **Peek-Message** function. The structure contains message information from the application's message queue. The **MSG** structure has the following form:

```
typedef struct tagMSG {        /* msg */
    HWND    hwnd;
    UINT    message;
    WPARAM  wParam;
    LPARAM  lParam;
    DWORD   time;
    POINT   pt;
} MSG;
```

For a full description of this structure, see the *Microsoft Windows Programmer's Reference, Volume 3*.

Return Value   The return value is nonzero if the message is WM_KEYDOWN, WM_KEYUP, WM_SYSKEYDOWN, or WM_SYSKEYUP, regardless of whether the key that was pressed or released generates a WM_CHAR message. Otherwise, the return value is zero.

Comments   The **TranslateMessage** function does not modify the message pointed to by the *lpmsg* parameter.

TranslateMessage produces WM_CHAR messages only for keys that are mapped to ASCII characters by the keyboard driver.

An application should not call **TranslateMessage** if the application processes virtual-key messages for some other purpose. For instance, an application should not call **TranslateMessage** if the **TranslateAccelerator** function returns nonzero.

See Also   **GetMessage**, **PeekMessage**, **TranslateAccelerator**

TransmitCommChar   2.x

int TransmitCommChar(*idComDev*, *chTransmit*)
int *idComDev*;   /* communications device   */
char *chTransmit*;   /* character to transmit   */

The **TransmitCommChar** function places the specified character at the head of the transmission queue for the specified device.

Parameters   *idComDev*
                        Specifies the communications device to transmit the character. The **Open-Comm** function returns this value.

                        chTransmit
                        Specifies the character to be transmitted.

Return Value   The return value is zero if the function is successful. It is less than zero if the character cannot be transmitted.

Comments   The **TransmitCommChar** function cannot be called repeatedly if the device is not transmitting. Once **TransmitCommChar** places a character in the transmission queue, the character must be transmitted before the function can be called again. **TransmitCommChar** returns an error if the previous character has not yet been sent.

Example   The following example uses the **TransmitCommChar** function to send characters from the keyboard to the communications port:

```
case WM_CHAR:

    ch = (char)wParam;
    TransmitCommChar(idComDev, ch);

    /* Add a linefeed for every carriage return. */

    if (ch == 0x0d)
        TransmitCommChar(idComDev, 0x0a);

    break;
```

See Also   **OpenComm**, **WriteComm**

UnAllocDiskSpace

#include <stress.h>

void UnAllocDiskSpace(*drive*)
UINT *drive*;

> The **UnAllocDiskSpace** function deletes the STRESS.EAT file from the root directory of the specified drive. This frees the disk space previously consumed by the **AllocDiskSpace** function.

Parameters

drive
> Specifies the disk partition on which to delete the STRESS.EAT file. This can be one of the following values:

Value	Meaning
EDS_WIN	Deletes the file on the Windows partition.
EDS_CUR	Deletes the file on the current partition.
EDS_TEMP	Deletes the file on the partition that contains the TEMP directory.

Return Value

This function does not return a value.

See Also

AllocDiskSpace

UnAllocFileHandles

#include <stress.h>

void UnAllocFileHandles(void)

> The **UnAllocFileHandles** function frees all file handles allocated by the **AllocFileHandles** function.

Parameters

This function has no parameters.

Return Value

This function does not return a value.

See Also

AllocFileHandles

UndeleteFile

#include <wfext.h>

int FAR PASCAL UndeleteFile(*hwndParent*, *lpszDir*)
HWND *hwndParent*;   /* handle of File Manager window   */
LPSTR *lpszDir*;   /* address of name of initial directory   */

The **UndeleteFile** function is an application-defined callback function that File Manager calls when the user chooses the Undelete command from the File Manager File menu.

Parameters   *hwndParent*
Identifies the File Manager window. An "undelete" dynamic-link library (DLL) should use this handle to specify the parent window for any dialog box or message box the DLL may display.

lpszDir
Points to a null-terminated string that contains the name of the initial directory.

Return Value   The return value is one of the following, if the function is successful:

Value	Meaning
–1	An error occurred.
IDOK	A file was undeleted. File Manager will repaint its windows.
IDCANCEL	No file was undeleted.

UngetCommChar   2.x

int UngetCommChar(*idComDev*, *chUnget*)
int *idComDev*;   /* communications device   */
char *chUnget*;   /* character to place in queue   */

The **UngetCommChar** function places the specified character back in the receiving queue. The next read operation will return this character first.

Parameters   *idComDev*
Specifies the communications device that will receive the character. The **Open-Comm** function returns this value.

chUnget
Specifies the character to be placed in the receiving queue.

Return Value   The return value is zero if the function is successful. Otherwise, it is less than zero.

Comments   Consecutive calls to the **UngetCommChar** function are not permitted. The character placed in the queue must be read before this function can be called again.

UnhookWindowsHook

`2.x`

BOOL UnhookWindowsHook(*idHook*, *hkprc*)
int *idHook*;   /* type of hook function to remove   */
HOOKPROC *hkprc*;   /* hook function procedure-instance address   */

The **UnhookWindowsHook** function is obsolete but has been retained for backward compatibility with Windows versions 3.0 and earlier. Applications written for Windows version 3.1 should use the **UnhookWindowsHookEx** function.

The **UnhookWindowsHook** function removes an application-defined hook function from a chain of hook functions. A hook function processes events before they are sent to an application's message loop in the **WinMain** function.

Parameters   *idHook*
Specifies the type of function to be removed. This parameter can be one of the following values:

Value	Meaning
WH_CALLWNDPROC	Removes a window-procedure filter. For more information, see the description of the **CallWnd-Proc** callback function.
WH_CBT	Removes a computer-based training (CBT) filter. For more information, see the description of the **CBTProc** callback function.
WH_DEBUG	Removes a debugging filter. For more information, see the description of the **DebugProc** callback function.
WH_GETMESSAGE	Removes a message filter. For more information, see the description of the **GetMsgProc** callback function.
WH_HARDWARE	Removes a nonstandard hardware-message filter. For more information, see the description of the **HardwareProc** callback function.
WH_JOURNALPLAYBACK	Removes a journaling playback filter. For more information, see the description of the **Journal-PlaybackProc** callback function.

Value	Meaning
WH_JOURNALRECORD	Removes a journaling record filter. For more information, see the description of the **Journal-RecordProc** callback function.
WH_KEYBOARD	Removes a keyboard filter. For more information, see the description of the **KeyboardProc** callback function.
WH_MOUSE	Removes a mouse-message filter. For more information, see the description of the **MouseProc** callback function.
WH_MSGFILTER	Removes a message filter. For more information, see the description of the **MessageProc** callback function.
WH_SYSMSGFILTER	Removes a system-wide message filter. For more information, see the description of the **SysMsg-Proc** callback function.

hkprc
Specifies the procedure-instance address of the application-defined filter function to remove.

Return Value   The return value is nonzero if the function is successful. Otherwise, it is zero.

Comments   The **UnhookWindowsHook** function calls the hook chain, causing the hook function to receive a negative value for the *idHook* parameter. The hook function must then call the **DefHookProc** function, which removes the hook function from the chain.

See Also   **SetWindowsHook**

UnhookWindowsHookEx   3.1

BOOL UnhookWindowsHookEx(*hhook***)**
HHOOK *hhook*;   /* handle of hook function to remove   */

The **UnhookWindowsHookEx** function removes an application-defined hook function from a chain of hook functions. A hook function processes events before they are sent to an application's message loop in the **WinMain** function.

Parameters   *hhook*
Identifies the hook function to be removed. This is the value returned by the **SetWindowsHookEx** function when the hook was installed.

Return Value   The return value is nonzero if the function is successful. It is zero if the hook cannot be found.

Comments   The **UnhookWindowsHookEx** function must be used in combination with the **SetWindowsHookEx** function.

Example   The following example uses the **UnhookWindowsHookEx** function to remove a message filter that was used to provide context-sensitive help for a dialog box:

```
DLGPROC lpfnAboutProc;
HOOKPROC lpfnFilterProc;
HHOOK    hhook;

case IDM_ABOUT:
    lpfnAboutProc = (DLGPROC) MakeProcInstance(About, hinst);
    lpfnFilterProc = (HOOKPROC) MakeProcInstance(FilterFunc, hinst);
    hhook = SetWindowsHookEx(WH_MSGFILTER, lpfnFilterProc,
        hinst, (HTASK) NULL);

    DialogBox(hinst, "AboutBox", hwnd, lpfnAboutProc);

    UnhookWindowsHookEx(hhook);
    FreeProcInstance((FARPROC) lpfnFilterProc);
    FreeProcInstance((FARPROC) lpfnAboutProc);

    break;
```

See Also   **CallNextHookEx, SetWindowsHookEx**

UnionRect   `2.x`

BOOL UnionRect(*lprcDst, lprcSrc1, lprcSrc2***)**
RECT FAR* *lprcDst*;   /* address of structure for union   */
const RECT FAR* *lprcSrc1*;   /* address of structure with 1st rect.   */
const RECT FAR* *lprcSrc2*;   /* address of structure with 2nd rect.   */

The **UnionRect** function creates the union of two rectangles. The union is the smallest rectangle that contains both source rectangles.

Parameters   *lprcDst*
        Points to a **RECT** structure to receive a rectangle containing the rectangles pointed to by the *lprcSrc1* and *lprcSrc2* parameters. The **RECT** structure has the following form:

```
typedef struct tagRECT {     /* rc */
    int left;
    int top;
    int right;
    int bottom;
} RECT;
```

For a full description of this structure, see the *Microsoft Windows Programmer's Reference, Volume 3*.

lprcSrc1
Points to a **RECT** structure that contains the first source rectangle.

lprcSrc2
Points to a **RECT** structure that contains the second source rectangle.

Return Value   The return value is nonzero if the function is successful—that is, if the *lprcDst* parameter contains a nonempty rectangle. It is zero if the rectangle is empty or an error occurs.

Comments   Windows ignores the dimensions of an empty rectangle—that is, a rectangle that has no height or no width.

See Also   **InflateRect, IntersectRect, OffsetRect, SubtractRect**

UnlockSegment   2.x

void UnlockSegment(*uSegment*)
UINT *uSegment*;   /* specifies segment to unlock   */

The **UnlockSegment** function unlocks the specified discardable memory segment. The function decrements (decreases by one) the segment's lock count. The segment is completely unlocked and subject to discarding when the lock count reaches zero.

Parameters   *uSegment*
Specifies the segment address of the segment to be unlocked. If this parameter is −1, the **UnlockSegment** function unlocks the current data segment.

Return Value   The return value is the lock count for the segment, if the function is successful. This function returns its result in the CX register. When the CX register contains zero, the segment is completely unlocked.

The value returned when the function is called in C should be ignored, because the return value can be checked only in assembly language.

Comments   An application should not rely on the return value to determine the number of times it must subsequently call **UnlockSegment** for the segment.

Other functions also can affect the lock count of a memory object. For a list of these functions, see the description of the **GlobalFlags** function.

Each time an application calls **LockSegment** for a segment, it must eventually call **UnlockSeg:nent** for the segment.

See Also   **GlobalFlags, LockSegment, UnlockData**

UnrealizeObject   2.x

BOOL UnrealizeObject(*hgdiobj*)
HGDIOBJ *hgdiobj*;   /* handle of brush or palette   */

The **UnrealizeObject** function resets the origin of a brush or resets a logical palette. If the *hgdiobj* parameter identifies a brush, **UnrealizeObject** directs the system to reset the origin of the brush the next time it is selected. If the *hgdiobj* parameter identifies a logical palette, **UnrealizeObject** directs the system to realize the palette as though it had not previously been realized. The next time the application calls the **RealizePalette** function for the specified palette, the system completely remaps the logical palette to the system palette.

Parameters   *hgdiobj*
        Identifies the object to be reset.

Return Value   The return value is nonzero if the function is successful. Otherwise, it is zero.

Comments   The **UnrealizeObject** function should not be used with stock objects.

The **UnrealizeObject** function must be called whenever a new brush origin is set (by using the **SetBrushOrg** function).

A brush identified by the *hgdiobj* parameter must not be the currently selected brush of any device context.

A palette identified by *hgdiobj* can be the currently selected palette of a device context.

Example

The following example uses the **SetBrushOrg** function to set the origin coordinates of the current brush to (3,5), uses the **SelectObject** function to remove that brush from the device context, uses the **UnrealizeObject** function to force the system to reset the origin of the specified brush, and then calls **SelectObject** again to select the brush into the device context with the new brush origin:

```
HBRUSH hbr, hbrOld;
SetBkMode(hdc, TRANSPARENT);
hbr = CreateHatchBrush(HS_CROSS, RGB(0, 0, 0));

UnrealizeObject(hbr);
SetBrushOrg(hdc, 0, 0);
hbrOld = SelectObject(hdc, hbr);

Rectangle(hdc, 0, 0, 200, 200);

hbr = SelectObject(hdc, hbrOld);          /* deselects hbr */
UnrealizeObject(hbr);  /* resets origin next time hbr selected */
SetBrushOrg(hdc, 3, 5);
hbrOld = SelectObject(hdc, hbr);          /* selects hbr again */

Rectangle(hdc, 0, 0, 200, 200);

SelectObject(hdc, hbrOld);
DeleteObject(hbr);
```

See Also

RealizePalette, SelectObject, SetBrushOrg

UnregisterClass

3.0

BOOL UnregisterClass(*lpszClassName*, *hinst*)
LPCSTR *lpszClassName*;   /* address of class-name string   */
HINSTANCE *hinst*;   /* handle of application instance   */

The **UnregisterClass** function removes a window class, freeing the storage required for the class.

Parameters

lpszClassName
Points to a null-terminated string containing the class name. This class name must have been registered by a previous call to the **RegisterClass** function with a valid **hinstance** member of the **WNDCLASS** structure. Predefined classes, such as dialog box controls, cannot be unregistered. The **WNDCLASS** structure has the following form:

```
typedef struct tagWNDCLASS {     /* wc */
    UINT       style;
    WNDPROC    lpfnWndProc;
    int        cbClsExtra;
    int        cbWndExtra;
    HINSTANCE  hInstance;
    HICON      hIcon;
    HCURSOR    hCursor;
    HBRUSH     hbrBackground;
    LPCSTR     lpszMenuName;
    LPCSTR     lpszClassName;
} WNDCLASS;
```

For a full description of this structure, see the *Microsoft Windows Programmer's Reference, Volume 3.*

hinst
    Identifies the instance of the module that created the class.

Return Value   The return value is nonzero if the function successful. It is zero if the class could not be found or if a window exists that was created with the class.

Comments   Before calling this function, an application should destroy all windows that were created with the specified class.

See Also   **RegisterClass**

UpdateColors

3.0

int UpdateColors(*hdc*)
HDC *hdc*;   /* handle of device context   */

The **UpdateColors** function updates the client area of the given device context by matching the current colors in the client area, pixel by pixel, to the system palette. An inactive window with a realized logical palette may call **UpdateColors** as an alternative to redrawing its client area when the system palette changes.

Parameters   *hdc*
    Identifies the device context.

Return Value   The return value is not used.

Comments

Using **UpdateColors** to update a client area is typically faster than redrawing the area. However, because **UpdateColors** performs the color translation based on the color of each pixel before the system palette changed, each call to this function results in the loss of some color accuracy.

UpdateWindow

2.x

void UpdateWindow(*hwnd***)**
HWND *hwnd*;   /* handle of window   */

The **UpdateWindow** function updates the client area of the given window by sending a WM_PAINT message to the window if the update region for the window is not empty. The function sends a WM_PAINT message directly to the window procedure of the given window, bypassing the application queue. If the update region is empty, no message is sent.

Parameters

hwnd
Identifies the window to be updated.

Return Value

This function does not return a value.

See Also

ExcludeUpdateRgn, GetUpdateRect, GetUpdateRgn, InvalidateRect, InvalidateRgn

ValidateCodeSegments

3.0

void ValidateCodeSegments(void)

The **ValidateCodeSegments** function tests all code segments for random memory overwrites. The function works only in real mode (for Windows versions earlier than 3.1) and only with the debugging version of Windows.

Parameters

This function has no parameters.

Return Value

This function does not return a value.

Comments   Because code segments are not writable in protected mode (standard or enhanced), this function does nothing in Windows 3.1.

See Also   **ValidateFreeSpaces**

ValidateFreeSpaces   `2.x`

void ValidateFreeSpaces(void)

The **ValidateFreeSpaces** function checks free segments in memory for valid contents. This function is available only in the debugging version of Windows.

Parameters   This function has no parameters.

Return Value   This function does not return a value.

Comments   In the debugging version of Windows, the kernel fills all the bytes in free segments with the hexadecimal value 0x0CC. This function begins checking for valid contents in the free segment with the lowest address; it continues checking until it finds an invalid byte or until it has determined that all free space contains valid contents. Before calling this function, put the following lines in the WIN.INI file:

```
[KERNEL]
EnableFreeChecking=1
EnableHeapChecking=1
```

Windows sends debugging information to the debugging terminal if an invalid byte is encountered, and then it performs a fatal exit.

The [KERNEL] entries in WIN.INI cause automatic checking of free memory. Before returning a memory object to the application in response to a call to the **GlobalAlloc** function, Windows checks that memory to make sure it is filled with 0x0CC. Before a call to the **GlobalCompact** function, all free memory is checked. Note that using this function slows Windows system-wide by about twenty percent.

See Also   **GlobalAlloc, GlobalCompact, ValidateCodeSegments**

ValidateRect

$\boxed{\text{2.x}}$

void ValidateRect(*hwnd*, *lprc*)
HWND *hwnd*;   /* handle of window   */
const RECT FAR* *lprc*;   /* address of structure with validation rect.   */

The **ValidateRect** function validates the client area within the given rectangle by removing the rectangle from the update region of the given window.

Parameters

hwnd
Identifies the window whose update region is to be modified.

lprc
Points to a **RECT** structure that contains the client coordinates of the rectangle to be removed from the update region. If this parameter is NULL, the entire client area is removed. The **RECT** structure has the following form:

```
typedef struct tagRECT {    /* rc */
    int left;
    int top;
    int right;
    int bottom;
} RECT;
```

For a full description of this structure, see the *Microsoft Windows Programmer's Reference, Volume 3*.

Return Value

This function does not return a value.

Comments

The **BeginPaint** function automatically validates the entire client area. Neither the **ValidateRect** nor the **ValidateRgn** function should be called if a portion of the update region needs to be validated before the next WM_PAINT message is generated.

Windows continues to generate WM_PAINT messages until the current update region is validated.

See Also

BeginPaint, InvalidateRect, InvalidateRgn, ValidateRgn

ValidateRgn

void ValidateRgn(*hwnd***,** *hrgn***)**
HWND *hwnd*;   /* handle of window   */
HRGN *hrgn*;   /* handle of valid region   */

The **ValidateRgn** function validates the client area within the given region by removing the region from the current update region of the specified window.

Parameters

hwnd
Identifies the window whose update region is to be modified.

hrgn
Identifies a region that defines the area to be removed from the update region. If this parameter is NULL, the entire client area is removed.

Return Value

This function does not return a value.

Comments

The given region must have been created by a region function. The region coordinates are assumed to be client coordinates.

The **BeginPaint** function automatically validates the entire client area. Neither the **ValidateRect** nor the **ValidateRgn** function should be called if a portion of the update region must be validated before the next WM_PAINT message is generated.

See Also

BeginPaint, InvalidateRect, InvalidateRgn, ValidateRect

VerFindFile

#include <ver.h>

UINT VerFindFile(*flags***,** *lpszFilename***,** *lpszWinDir***,** *lpszAppDir***,** *lpszCurDir***,** *lpuCurDirLen***,**
    *lpszDestDir***,** *lpuDestDirLen***)**
UINT *flags*;   /* source-file flags   */
LPCSTR *lpszFilename*;   /* address of buffer for file   */
LPCSTR *lpszWinDir*;   /* address of Windows directory   */
LPCSTR *lpszAppDir*;   /* address of application directory   */
LPSTR *lpszCurDir*;   /* address of buffer for current directory */
UINT FAR* *lpuCurDirLen*;   /* address of buffer size for directory   */
LPSTR *lpszDestDir*;   /* address of buffer for dest. directory   */
UINT FAR* *lpuDestDirLen*;   /* address of size for dest. directory   */

The **VerFindFile** function determines where to install a file based on whether it locates another version of the file in the system. The values **VerFindFile** returns are used in a subsequent call to the **VerInstallFile** function.

Parameters

flags

Contains a bitmask of flags. This parameter can be VFFF_ISSHAREDFILE, which indicates that the source file may be shared by multiple applications. **VerFindFile** uses this information to determine where the file should be copied. All other values are reserved for future use.

lpszFilename

Points to a null-terminated string specifying the name of the file to be installed. This name should include only the filename and extension, not a path.

lpszWinDir

Points to a null-terminated string specifying the Windows directory. This string is returned by the **GetWindowsDir** function. The dynamic-link library (DLL) version of **VerFindFile** ignores this parameter.

lpszAppDir

Points to a null-terminated string specifying the drive letter and directory where the installation program is installing a set of related files. If the installation program is installing an application, this is the directory where the application will reside. This directory will also be the application's working directory unless you specify otherwise.

lpszCurDir

Points to a buffer that receives the path to a current version of the file being installed. The path is a null-terminated string. If a current version is not installed, the buffer will contain the source directory of the file being installed. The buffer must be at least _MAX_PATH bytes long.

lpuCurDirLen

Points to a null-terminated string specifying the length, in bytes, of the buffer pointed to by *lpszCurDir*. On return, *lpuCurDirLen* contains the size, in bytes, of the data returned in *lpszCurDir*, including the terminating null character. If the buffer is too small to contain all the data, *lpuCurDirLen* will be greater than the actual size of the buffer.

lpszDestDir

Points to a buffer that receives the path to the installation directory recommended by **VerFindFile**. The path is a null-terminated string. The buffer must be at least _MAX_PATH bytes long.

lpuDestDirLen

Points to the length, in bytes, of the buffer pointed to by *lpszDestDir*. On return, *lpuDestDirLen* contains the size, in bytes, of the data returned in *lpszDestDir*, including the terminating null character. If the buffer is too small to contain all the data, *lpuDestDirLen* will be greater than the actual size of the buffer.

Return Value   The return value is a bitmask that indicates the status of the file, if the function is successful. This value may be one or more of the following:

Error	Meaning
VFF_CURNEDEST	Indicates that the currently installed version of the file is not in the recommended destination.
VFF_FILEINUSE	Indicates that Windows is using the currently installed version of the file; therefore, the file cannot be overwritten or deleted.
VFF_BUFFTOOSMALL	Indicates that at least one of the buffers was too small to contain the corresponding string. An application should check the *lpuCurDirLen* and *lpuDestDirLen* parameters to determine which buffer was too small.

All other values are reserved for future use.

Comments   The dynamic-link library (DLL) version of **VerFindFile** searches for a copy of the specified file by using the **OpenFile** function. In the LIB version, the function searches for the file in the Windows directory, the system directory, and then the directories specified by the PATH environment variable.

VerFindFile determines the system directory from the specified Windows directory, or it searches the path.

If the *flags* parameter indicates that the file is private to this application (not VFFF_ISSHAREDFILE), **VerFindFile** recommends installing the file in the application's directory. Otherwise, if the system is running a shared copy of Windows, the function recommends installing the file in the Windows directory. If the system is running a private copy of Windows, the function recommends installing the file in the system directory.

See Also   **VerInstallFile**

VerInstallFile

#include <ver.h>

DWORD VerInstallFile(*flags*, *lpszSrcFilename*, *lpszDestFilename*, *lpszSrcDir*, *lpszDestDir*,
   lpszCurDir, *lpszTmpFile*, *lpwTmpFileLen*)

UINT *flags*;	/* source-file flags	*/
LPCSTR *lpszSrcFilename*;	/* address of source filename	*/
LPCSTR *lpszDestFilename*;	/* address of destination filename	*/
LPCSTR *lpszSrcDir*;	/* address of buffer for source dir. name	*/
LPCSTR *lpszDestDir*;	/* address of buffer for dest. dir. name	*/
LPCSTR *lpszCurDir*;	/* address of buffer for preexisting dir.	*/
LPSTR *lpszTmpFile*;	/* address of buffer for temp. filename	*/
UINT FAR* *lpwTmpFileLen*;	/* address of buffer for temp. file size	*/

The **VerInstallFile** function attempts to install a file based on information returned from the **VerFindFile** function. **VerInstallFile** decompresses the file with the **LZCopy** function and checks for errors, such as outdated files.

Parameters   *flags*

Contains a bitmask of flags. This parameter can be a combination of the following values:

Value	Meaning
VIFF_FORCEINSTALL	Installs the file regardless of mismatched version numbers. The function will check only for physical errors during installation.
	If *flags* includes VIFF_FORCEINSTALL and *lpszTmpFileLen* is not a pointer to zero, **VerInstall-File** will skip all version checks of the temporary file and the destination file and rename the temporary file to the name specified by *lpszSrcFilename*, as long as the temporary file exists in the destination directory, the destination file is not in use, and the user has privileges to delete the destination file and rename the temporary file. The return value from **VerInstallFile** should be checked for any errors.
VIFF_DONTDELETEOLD	Installs the file without deleting the previously installed file, if the previously installed file is not in the destination directory. If the previously installed file is in the destination directory, **VerInstallFile** replaces it with the new file upon successful installation.

All other values are reserved for future use.

lpszSrcFilename

Points to the name of the file to be installed. This is the filename in the directory pointed to by *lpszSrcDir*; the filename should include only the filename and extension, not a path. **VerInstallFile** opens the source file by using the **LZOpenFile** function. This means it can handle both files as specified and files that have been compressed and renamed by using the /**r** option with COMPRESS.EXE.

lpszDestFilename

Points to the name **VerInstallFile** will give the new file upon installation. This filename may be different than the filename in the directory pointed to by *lpszSrcFilename*. The new name should include only the filename and extension, not a path.

lpszSrcDir

Points to a buffer that contains the directory name where the new file is found.

lpszDestDir

Points to a buffer that contains the directory name where the new file should be installed. The **VerFindFile** function returns this value in the *lpszDestDir* parameter.

lpszCurDir

Points to a buffer that contains the directory name where the preexisting version of this file is found. **VerFindFile** returns this value in the *lpszCurDir* parameter. If the filename specified in *lpszDestFilename* already exists in the *lpszCurDir* directory and *flags* does not include VIFF_DONTDELETEOLD, the existing file will be deleted. If *lpszCurDir* is a pointer to NULL, a previous version of the file does not exist on the system.

lpszTmpFile

Points to a buffer that should be empty upon the initial call to **VerInstallFile**. The function fills the buffer with the name of a temporary copy of the source file. The buffer must be at least _MAX_PATH bytes long.

lpwTmpFileLen

Points to the length of the buffer pointed to by *lpszTmpFile*. On return, *lpwTmpFileLen* contains the size, in bytes, of the data returned in *lpszTmpFile*, including the terminating null character. If the buffer is too small to contain all the data, *lpwTmpFileLen* will be greater than the actual size of the buffer.

If *flags* includes VIFF_FORCEINSTALL and *lpwTmpFileLen* is not a pointer to zero, **VerInstallFile** will rename the temporary file to the name specified by *lpszSrcFilename*.

Return Value   The return value is a bitmask that indicates exceptions, if the function is successful. This value may be one or more of the following:

Value	Meaning
VIF_TEMPFILE	Indicates that the temporary copy of the new file is in the destination directory. The cause of failure is reflected in other flags. Applications should always check whether this bit is set and delete the temporary file, if required.
VIF_MISMATCH	Indicates that the new and preexisting files differ in one or more attributes. This error can be overridden by calling **VerInstallFile** again with the VIFF_FORCEINSTALL flag.
VIF_SRCOLD	Indicates that the file to install is older than the preexisting file. This error can be overridden by calling **VerInstallFile** again with the VIFF_FORCEINSTALL flag.
VIF_DIFFLANG	Indicates that the new and preexisting files have different language or code-page values. This error can be overridden by calling **VerInstallFile** again with the VIFF_FORCEINSTALL flag.
VIF_DIFFCODEPG	Indicates that the new file requires a code page that cannot be displayed by the currently running version of Windows. This error can be overridden by calling **VerInstallFile** with the VIFF_FORCEINSTALL flag.
VIF_DIFFTYPE	Indicates that the new file has a different type, subtype, or operating system than the preexisting file. This error can be overridden by calling **VerInstallFile** again with the VIFF_FORCEINSTALL flag.
VIF_WRITEPROT	Indicates that the preexisting file is write-protected. The installation program should reset the read-only bit in the destination file before proceeding with the installation.
VIF_FILEINUSE	Indicates that the preexisting file is in use by Windows and cannot be deleted.
VIF_OUTOFSPACE	Indicates that the function cannot create the temporary file due to insufficient disk space on the destination drive.
VIF_ACCESSVIOLATION	Indicates that a create, delete, or rename operation failed due to an access violation.
VIF_SHARINGVIOLATION	Indicates that a create, delete, or rename operation failed due to a sharing violation.
VIF_CANNOTCREATE	Indicates that the function cannot create the temporary file. The specific error may be described by another flag.

Value	Meaning
VIF_CANNOTDELETE	Indicates that the function cannot delete the destination file or cannot delete the existing version of the file located in another directory. If the VIF_TEMPFILE bit is set, the installation failed and the destination file probably cannot be deleted.
VIF_CANNOTRENAME	Indicates that the function cannot rename the temporary file but already deleted the destination file.
VIF_OUTOFMEMORY	Indicates that the function cannot complete the requested operation due to insufficient memory. Generally, this means the application ran out of memory attempting to expand a compressed file.
VIF_CANNOTREADSRC	Indicates that the function cannot read the source file. This could mean that the path was not specified properly, that the file does not exist, or that the file is a compressed file that has been corrupted. To distinguish these conditions, use **LZOpenFile** to determine whether the file exists. (Do not use the **OpenFile** function, because it does not correctly translate filenames of compressed files.) Note that VIF_CANNOTREADSRC does not cause either the VIF_ACCESSVIOLATION or VIF_SHARINGVIOLATION bit to be set.
VIF_CANNOTREADDST	Indicates that the function cannot read the destination (existing) files. This prevents the function from examining the file's attributes.
VIF_BUFFTOOSMALL	Indicates that the *lpszTmpFile* buffer was too small to contain the name of the temporary source file. On return, *lpwTmpFileLen* contains the size of the buffer required to hold the filename.

All other values are reserved for future use.

Comments   **VerInstallFile** is designed for use in an installation program. This function copies a file (specified by *lpszSrcFilename*) from the installation disk to a temporary file in the destination directory. If necessary, **VerInstallFile** expands the file by using the functions in LZEXPAND.DLL.

If a preexisting copy of the file exists in the destination directory, **VerInstallFile** compares the version information of the temporary file to that of the preexisting file. If the preexisting file is more recent than the new version, or if the files' attributes are significantly different, **VerInstallFile** returns one or more error values. For example, files with different languages would cause **VerInstallFile** to return VIF_DIFFLANG.

VerInstallFile leaves the temporary file in the destination directory. If all of the errors are recoverable, the installation program can override them by calling **Ver-**

InstallFile again with the VIFF_FORCEINSTALL flag. In this case, *lpszSrcFilename* should point to the name of the temporary file. Then, **VerInstall-File** deletes the preexisting file and renames the temporary file to the name specified by *lpszSrcFilename*. If the VIF_TEMPFILE bit indicates that a temporary file exists and the application does not force the installation by using the VIFF_FORCEINSTALL flag, the application must delete the temporary file.

If an installation program attempts to force installation after a nonrecoverable error, such as VIF_CANNOTREADSRC, **VerInstallFile** will not install the file.

See Also   **VerFindFile**

VerLanguageName   ˌ   ⎡3.1⎤

#include <ver.h>

UINT VerLanguageName(*uLang*, *lpszLang*, *cbLang*)
UINT *uLang*;   /* Microsoft language identifier   */
LPSTR *lpszLang*;   /* address of buffer for language string */
UINT *cbLang*;   /* size of buffer   */

The **VerLanguageName** function converts the specified binary Microsoft language identifier into a text representation of the language.

Parameters   *uLang*
Specifies the binary Microsoft language identifier. For example, **VerLanguageName** translates 0x040A into Castilian Spanish. If **Ver-LanguageName** does not recognize the identifier, the *lpszLang* parameter will point to a default string, such as "Unknown language". For a complete list of the language identifiers supported by Windows, see the following Comments section.

lpszLang
Points to the buffer to receive the null-terminated string representing the language specified by the *uLang* parameter.

cbLang
Indicates the size of the buffer, in bytes, pointed to by *lpszLang*.

Return Value   The return value is the length of the string that represents the language identifier, if the function is successful. This value does not include the null character at the end of the string. If this value is greater than *cbLang*, the string was truncated to *cbLang*. The return value is zero if an error occurs. Unknown *uLang* values do not produce errors.

Comments   Typically, an installation application uses this function to translate a language identifier returned by the **VerQueryValue** function. The text string may be used in a
dialog box that asks the user how to proceed in the event of a language conflict.

Windows supports the following language identifiers:

Value	Language
0x0401	Arabic
0x0402	Bulgarian
0x0403	Catalan
0x0404	Traditional Chinese
0x0405	Czech
0x0406	Danish
0x0407	German
0x0408	Greek
0x0409	U.S. English
0x040A	Castilian Spanish
0x040B	Finnish
0x040C	French
0x040D	Hebrew
0x040E	Hungarian
0x040F	Icelandic
0x0410	Italian
0x0411	Japanese
0x0412	Korean
0x0413	Dutch
0x0414	Norwegian – Bokmål
0x0415	Polish
0x0416	Brazilian Portuguese
0x0417	Rhaeto-Romanic
0x0418	Romanian
0x0419	Russian
0x041A	Croato-Serbian (Latin)
0x041B	Slovak
0x041C	Albanian
0x041D	Swedish
0x041E	Thai
0x041F	Turkish
0x0420	Urdu
0x0421	Bahasa

Value	Language
0x0804	Simplified Chinese
0x0807	Swiss German
0x0809	U.K. English
0x080A	Mexican Spanish
0x080C	Belgian French
0x0810	Swiss Italian
0x0813	Belgian Dutch
0x0814	Norwegian – Nynorsk
0x0816	Portuguese
0x081A	Serbo-Croatian (Cyrillic)
0x0C0C	Canadian French
0x100C	Swiss French

VerQueryValue

3.1

#include <ver.h>

BOOL VerQueryValue(*lpvBlock*, *lpszSubBlock*, *lplpBuffer*, *lpcb***)**
const void FAR* *lpvBlock*;   /* address of buffer for version resource   */
LPCSTR *lpszSubBlock*;   /* address of value to retrieve   */
VOID FAR* FAR* *lplpBuffer*;   /* address of buffer for version pointer   */
UINT FAR* *lpcb*;   /* address of buffer for version-value length   */

The **VerQueryValue** function returns selected version information from the specified version-information resource. To obtain the appropriate resource, the **GetFileVersionInfo** function must be called before **VerQueryValue**.

Parameters

lpvBlock
Points to the buffer containing the version-information resource returned by the **GetFileVersionInfo** function.

lpszSubBlock
Points to a zero-terminated string specifying which version-information value to retrieve. The string consists of names separated by backslashes (\) and can have one of the following forms:

Form	Description
\	Specifies the root block. The function retrieves a pointer to the **VS_FIXEDFILEINFO** structure for the version-information resource.
\VarFileInfo\Translation	Specifies the translation table in the variable information block. The function retrieves a pointer to an array of language and character-set identifiers. An application uses these identifiers to create the name of an language-specific block in the version-information resource.
\StringFileInfo\lang-charset\\string-name	Specifies a value in a language-specific block. The *lang-charset* name is a concatenation of a language and character-set identifier pair found in the translation table for the resource. The *lang-charset* name must be specified as a hexadecimal string. The *string-name* name is one of the predefined strings described in the following Comments section.

lplpBuffer
   Points to a buffer that receives a pointer to the version-information value.

lpcb
   Points to a buffer that receives the length, in bytes, of the version-information value.

Return Value   The return value is nonzero if the specified block exists and version information is available. If *lpcb* is zero, no value is available for the specified version-information name. The return value is zero if the specified name does not exist or the resource pointed to by *lpvBlock* is not valid.

Comments   The *string-name* in the *lpszSubBlock* parameter can be one of the following predefined names:

Name	Value
Comments	Specifies additional information that should be displayed for diagnostic purposes.
CompanyName	Specifies the company that produced the file—for example, "Microsoft Corporation" or "Standard Microsystems Corporation, Inc.". This string is required.

Name	Value
FileDescription	Specifies a file description to be presented to users. This string may be displayed in a list box when the user is choosing files to install—for example, "Keyboard Driver for AT-Style Keyboards" or "Microsoft Word for Windows". This string is required.
FileVersion	Specifies the version number of the file—for example, "3.10" or "5.00.RC2". This string is required.
InternalName	Specifies the internal name of the file, if one exists—for example, a module name if the file is a dynamic-link library. If the file has no internal name, this string should be the original filename, without extension. This string is required.
LegalCopyright	Specifies all copyright notices that apply to the file. This should include the full text of all notices, legal symbols, copyright dates, and so on—for example, "Copyright Microsoft Corporation 1990–1991". This string is optional.
LegalTrademarks	Specifies all trademarks and registered trademarks that apply to the file. This should include the full text of all notices, legal symbols, trademark numbers, and so on—for example, "Windows(TM) is a trademark of Microsoft Corporation". This string is optional.
OriginalFilename	Specifies the original name of the file, not including a path. This information enables an application to determine whether a file has been renamed by a user. The format of the name depends on the file system for which the file was created. This string is required.
PrivateBuild	Specifies information about a private version of the file—for example, "Built by TESTER1 on \TESTBED". This string should be present only if the VS_FF_PRIVATEBUILD flag is set in the **dwFileFlags** member of the **VS_FIXEDFILEINFO** structure of the root block.
ProductName	Specifies the name of the product with which the file is distributed—for example, "Microsoft Windows". This string is required.
ProductVersion	Specifies the version of the product with which the file is distributed—for example, "3.10" or "5.00.RC2". This string is required.
SpecialBuild	Specifies how this version of the file differs from the standard version—for example, "Private build for TESTER1 solving mouse problems on M250 and M250E computers". This string should be present only if the VS_FF_SPECIALBUILD flag is set in the **dwFileFlags** member of the **VS_FIXEDFILEINFO** structure in the root block.

Example

The following example loads the version information for a dynamic-link library and retrieves the company name:

```
BYTE    abData[512];
DWORD   handle;
DWORD   dwSize;
LPBYTE  lpBuffer;
char    szName[512];

dwSize = GetFileVersionInfoSize("c:\\dll\\sample.dll", &handle));

GetFileVersionInfo("c:\\dll\\sample.dll", handle, dwSize, abData));

VerQueryValue(abData, "\\VarFileInfo\\Translation", &lpBuffer,
&dwSize));

if (dwSize!=0) {
    wsprintf(szName, "\\StringFileInfo\\%8lx\\CompanyName", &lpBuffer);
    VerQueryValue(abData, szName, &lpBuffer, &dwSize);
}
```

See Also   **GetFileVersionInfo**

VkKeyScan

2.x

UINT VkKeyScan(*uChar*)
UINT *uChar*;   /* character to translate   */

The **VkKeyScan** function translates a Windows character to the corresponding virtual-key code and shift state for the current keyboard.

Parameters   *uChar*
                 Specifies the character to be translated to a virtual-key code.

Return Value   The return value is the virtual-key code and shift state, if the function is successful. The low-order byte contains the virtual-key code; the high-order byte contains the shift state, which can be one of the following:

Value	Meaning
1	Character is shifted.
2	Character is a control character.
3–5	Shift-key combination that is not used for characters.
6	Character is generated by the CTRL+ALT key combination.
7	Character is generated by the SHIFT+CTRL+ALT key combination.

If no key is found that translates to the passed Windows code, the return value is –1.

Comments   Translations for the numeric keypad (VK_NUMPAD0 through VK_DIVIDE) are ignored. This function is intended to force a translation for the main keyboard only.

Applications that send characters by using the WM_KEYUP and WM_KEYDOWN messages use this function.

See Also   **OemKeyScan**

WaitMessage   2.x

void WaitMessage(void)

The **WaitMessage** function yields control to other applications when an application has no other tasks to perform. The **WaitMessage** function suspends the application and does not return until a new message is placed in the application's queue.

Parameters   This function has no parameters.

Return Value   This function does not return a value.

Comments   The **WaitMessage** function normally returns immediately if there is a message in the queue. If an application has used the **PeekMessage** function but not removed the message, however, **WaitMessage** does not return until the message is received. Applications that use the **PeekMessage** function should remove any retrieved messages from the queue before calling **WaitMessage**.

The **GetMessage**, **PeekMessage**, and **WaitMessage** functions yield control to other applications. Using these functions is the only way to allow other applications to run. Applications that do not call any of these functions for long periods prevent other applications from running.

See Also   **GetMessage, PeekMessage**

WaitSoundState

int WaitSoundState(*fnState*)
int *fnState*;   /* state to wait for   */

> This function is obsolete. Use the Microsoft Windows multimedia audio functions instead. For information about these functions, see the *Microsoft Windows Multimedia Programmer's Reference*.

WEP

int CALLBACK WEP(*nExitType*)
int *nExitType*;   /* type of exit   */

> The **WEP** (Windows exit procedure) callback function performs cleanup for a dynamic-link library (DLL) before the library is unloaded. This function is called by Windows. Although a **WEP** function was required for every dynamic-link library in previous versions of the Windows operating system, for version 3.1 the **WEP** function is optional. Most dynamic-link libraries use the **WEP** function.

Parameters   *nExitType*
> Specifies whether all of Windows is shutting down or only the individual library. This parameter can be either WEP_FREE_DLL or WEP_SYSTEM_EXIT.

Return Value   The return value should be 1 if the function is successful.

Comments   For Windows version 3.1, **WEP** is called on the stack of the application that is terminating. This enables **WEP** to call Windows functions. In Windows version 3.0, however, **WEP** is called on a KERNEL stack that is too small to process most calls to Windows functions. These calls, including calls to global-memory functions, should be avoided in a **WEP** function for Windows 3.0. Calls to MS-DOS functions go through a KERNEL intercept and can also overflow the stack in Windows 3.0. There is no general reason to free memory from the global heap in a **WEP** function, because the kernel frees this kind of memory automatically.

> In some low-memory conditions, **WEP** can be called before the library initialization function is called and before the library's DGROUP data-segment group has been created. A **WEP** function that relies on the library initialization function should verify that the initialization function has been called. Also, **WEP** functions that rely on the validity of DGROUP should check for this. The following

procedure is recommended for dynamic-link libraries in Windows 3.0; for Windows 3.1, only step 3 is necessary.

1. Verify that the data segment is present by using a **lar** instruction and checking the present bit. This will indicate whether DS has been loaded. (The DS register always contains a valid selector.)

2. Set a flag in the data segment when the library initialization is performed. Once the **WEP** function has verified that the data segment exists, it should test this flag to determine whether initialization has occurred.

3. Declare **WEP** in the **EXPORTS** section of the module-definition file for the DLL. Following is an example declaration:

```
WEP  @1  RESIDENTNAME
```

The keyword **RESIDENTNAME** makes the name of the function (**WEP**) resident at all times. (It is not necessary to use the ordinal reference 1.) The name listed in the **LIBRARY** statement of the module-definition file must be in uppercase letters and must match the name of the DLL file.

Windows calls the **WEP** function by name when it is ready to remove the DLL. Under low-memory conditions, it is possible for the DLL's nonresident-name table to be discarded from memory. If this occurs, Windows must load the table to determine whether a **WEP** function was declared for the DLL. Under low-memory conditions, this method could fail, causing a fatal exit. Using the **RESIDENTNAME** option forces Windows to keep the name entry for **WEP** in memory whenever the DLL is in use.

In Windows 3.0, **WEP** must be placed in a fixed code segment. If it is placed instead in a discardable segment, under low-memory conditions Windows must load the **WEP** segment from disk so that the **WEP** function can be called before the DLL is discarded. Under certain low-memory conditions, attempting to load the segment containing **WEP** can cause a fatal exit. When **WEP** is in a fixed segment, this situation cannot occur. (Because fixed DLL code is also page-locked, you should minimize the amount of fixed code.)

If a DLL is explicitly loaded by calling the **LoadLibrary** function, its **WEP** function is called when the DLL is freed by a call to the **FreeLibrary** function. (The **FreeLibrary** function should not be called from within a **WEP** function.) If the DLL is implicitly loaded, **WEP** is also called, but some debugging applications will indicate that the application has been terminated before **WEP** is called.

The **WEP** functions of dependent DLLs can be called in any order. This order depends on the order in which the usage counts for the DLLs reach zero.

See Also   **FreeLibrary, LibMain, RegisterClass, UnRegisterClass**

WindowFromPoint

HWND WindowFromPoint(*pt*)
POINT *pt*;   /* structure with point   */

The **WindowFromPoint** function retrieves the handle of the window that contains the specified point.

Parameters   *pt*
Specifies a **POINT** structure that defines the screen coordinates of the point to be checked. The **POINT** structure has the following form:

```
typedef struct tagPOINT {    /* pt */
    int x;
    int y;
} POINT;
```

For a full description of this structure, see the *Microsoft Windows Programmer's Reference, Volume 3*.

Return Value   The return value is the handle of the window in which the point lies, if the function is successful. The return value is NULL if no window exists at the specified point.

Comments   The **WindowFromPoint** function does not retrieve the handle of a hidden, disabled, or transparent window, even if the point is within the window. An application should use the **ChildWindowFromPoint** function for a nonrestrictive search.

See Also   **ChildWindowFromPoint**

WindowProc

LRESULT CALLBACK WindowProc(*hwnd*, *msg*, *wParam*, *lParam*)
HWND *hwnd*;   /* handle of window   */
UINT *msg*;   /* message   */
WPARAM *wParam*;   /* first message parameter   */
LPARAM *lParam*;   /* second message parameter */

The **WindowProc** function is an application-defined callback function that processes messages sent to a window.

Parameters   *hwnd*
Identifies the window.

msg
Specifies the message.

wParam
Specifies 16 bits of additional message-dependent information.

lParam
Specifies 32 bits of additional message-dependent information.

Return Value   The return value is the result of the message processing. The value depends on the message being processed.

Comments   The **WindowProc** name is a placeholder for the application-defined function name. The actual name must be exported by including it in an **EXPORTS** statement in the application's module-definition file.

See Also   **DefWindowProc**, **RegisterClass**

WinExec   3.0

UINT **WinExec**(*lpszCmdLine, fuCmdShow*)
LPCSTR *lpszCmdLine*;   /* address of command line   */
UINT *fuCmdShow*;   /* window style for new app.   */

The **WinExec** function runs the specified application.

Parameters   *lpszCmdLine*
Points to a null-terminated Windows character string that contains the command line (filename plus optional parameters) for the application to be run. If the string does not contain a path, Windows searches the directories in this order:

1. The current directory.
2. The Windows directory (the directory containing WIN.COM); the **GetWindowsDirectory** function retrieves the path of this directory.
3. The Windows system directory (the directory containing such system files as GDI.EXE); the **GetSystemDirectory** function retrieves the path of this directory.
4. The directory containing the executable file for the current task; the **GetModuleFileName** function retrieves the path of this directory.

5. The directories listed in the PATH environment variable.

6. The directories mapped in a network.

fuCmdShow

Specifies how a Windows application window is to be shown. See the description of the **ShowWindow** function for a list of the acceptable values for the *fuCmdShow* parameter. For a non-Windows application, the program-information file (PIF), if any, for the application determines the window state.

Return Value

The return value identifies the instance of the loaded module, if the function is successful. Otherwise, the return value is an error value less than 32.

Errors

The error value may be one of the following:

Value	Meaning
0	System was out of memory, executable file was corrupt, or relocations were invalid.
2	File was not found.
3	Path was not found.
5	Attempt was made to dynamically link to a task, or there was a sharing or network-protection error.
6	Library required separate data segments for each task.
8	There was insufficient memory to start the application.
10	Windows version was incorrect.
11	Executable file was invalid. Either it was not a Windows application or there was an error in the .EXE image.
12	Application was designed for a different operating system.
13	Application was designed for MS-DOS 4.0.
14	Type of executable file was unknown.
15	Attempt was made to load a real-mode application (developed for an earlier version of Windows).
16	Attempt was made to load a second instance of an executable file containing multiple data segments that were not marked read-only.
19	Attempt was made to load a compressed executable file. The file must be decompressed before it can be loaded.
20	Dynamic-link library (DLL) file was invalid. One of the DLLs required to run this application was corrupt.
21	Application requires Microsoft Windows 32-bit extensions.

Comments

The **LoadModule** function provides an alternative method for running an application.

Example

The following example uses the **WinExec** function to run DRAW.EXE:

```
                    WORD wReturn;
                    char szMsg[80];

                    wReturn = WinExec("draw", SW_SHOW);

                    if (wReturn < 32) {
                        sprintf(szMsg, "WinExec failed; error code = %d", wReturn);
                        MessageBox(hwnd, szMsg, "Error", MB_ICONSTOP);
                    }
                    else {
                        sprintf(szMsg, "WinExec returned %d", wReturn);
                        MessageBox(hwnd, szMsg, "", MB_OK);
                    }
```

See Also   **GetModuleFileName, GetSystemDirectory, GetWindowsDirectory, Load-
                      Module, ShowWindow**

WinHelp   3.0

BOOL WinHelp(_hwnd_**,** _lpszHelpFile_**,** _fuCommand_**,** _dwData_**)**
HWND _hwnd_**;**   /* handle of window requesting help   */
LPCSTR _lpszHelpFile_**;**   /* address of directory-path string   */
UINT _fuCommand_**;**   /* type of help   */
DWORD _dwData_**;**   /* additional data   */

The **WinHelp** function starts Windows Help (WINHELP.EXE) and passes optional data indicating the nature of the help requested by the application. The application specifies the name and, where required, the path of the help file that the
Help application is to display. For information about creating and using help files,
see _Microsoft Windows Programming Tools._

Parameters   _hwnd_
                        Identifies the window requesting Help. The **WinHelp** function uses this handle
                        to keep track of which applications have requested Help.

                        lpszHelpFile
                        Points to a null-terminated string containing the path, if necessary, and the
                        name of the help file that the Help application is to display.

                        The filename may be followed by an angle bracket (>) and the name of a sec-
                        ondary window if the topic is to be displayed in a secondary window rather
                        than in the primary window. The name of the secondary window must have
                        been defined in the [WINDOWS] section of the Help project (.HPJ) file.

fuCommand
>Specifies the type of help requested. For a list of possible values and how they affect the value to place in the *dwData* parameter, see the following Comments section.

dwData
>Specifies additional data. The value used depends on the value of the *fuCommand* parameter. For a list of possible values, see the following Comments section.

Return Value   The return value is nonzero if the function is successful. Otherwise, it is zero.

Comments   Before closing the window that requested the help, the application must call **Win-Help** with *fuCommand* set to HELP_QUIT. Until all applications have done this, Windows Help does not terminate.

The following table shows the possible values for the *fuCommand* parameter and the corresponding formats of the *dwData* parameter:

fuCommand	*dwData*	Action
HELP_CONTEXT	An unsigned long integer containing the context number for the topic.	Displays Help for a particular topic identified by a context number that has been defined in the [MAP] section of the .HPJ file.
HELP_CONTENTS	Ignored; applications should set to 0L.	Displays the Help contents topic as defined by the Contents option in the [OPTIONS] section of the .HPJ file.
HELP_SETCONTENTS	An unsigned long integer containing the context number for the topic the application wants to designate as the Contents topic.	Determines which Contents topic Help should display when a user presses the F1 key.
HELP_CONTEXTPOPUP	An unsigned long integer containing the context number for a topic.	Displays in a pop-up window a particular Help topic identified by a context number that has been defined in the [MAP] section of the .HPJ file.
HELP_KEY	A long pointer to a string that contains a keyword for the desired topic.	Displays the topic found in the keyword list that matches the keyword passed in the *dwData* parameter if there is one exact match. If there is more than one match, displays the Search dialog box with the topics listed in the Go To list box. If there is no match, displays the Search dialog box.

fuCommand	*dwData*	**Action**
HELP_PARTIALKEY	A long pointer to a string that contains a keyword for the desired topic.	Displays the topic found in the keyword list that matches the keyword passed in the *dwData* parameter if there is one exact match. If there is more than one match, displays the Search dialog box with the topics found listed in the Go To list box. If there is no match, displays the Search dialog box. If you just want to bring up the Search dialog box without passing a keyword (the third result), you should use a long pointer to an empty string.
HELP_MULTIKEY	A long pointer to the **MULTI-KEYHELP** structure, as defined in WINDOWS.H. This structure specifies the table footnote character and the keyword.	Displays the Help topic identified by a keyword in an alternate key word table.
HELP_COMMAND	A long pointer to a string that contains a Help macro to be executed.	Executes a Help macro.
HELP_SETWINPOS	A long pointer to the **HELPWININFO** structure, as defined in WINDOWS.H. This structure specifies the size and position of the primary Help window or a secondary window to be displayed.	Displays the Help window if it is minimized or in memory, and positions it according to the data passed.
HELP_FORCEFILE	Ignored; applications should set to 0L.	Ensures that WinHelp is displaying the correct Help file. If the correct Help file is currently displayed, there is no action. If the incorrect Help file is displayed, WinHelp opens the correct file.
HELP_HELPONHELP	Ignored; applications should set to 0L.	Displays the Contents topic of the designated Using Help file.
HELP_QUIT	Ignored; applications should set to 0L.	Informs the Help application that Help is no longer needed. If no other applications have asked for Help, Windows closes the Help application.

The **MULTIKEYHELP** structure has the following form:

```
typedef struct tagMULTIKEYHELP {    /* mkh */
    UINT  mkSize;
    BYTE  mkKeylist;
    BYTE  szKeyphrase[1];
} MULTIKEYHELP;
```

For a full description of this structure, see the *Microsoft Windows Programmer's Reference, Volume 3*.

WinMain

int PASCAL **WinMain**(*hinstCurrent*, *hinstPrevious*, *lpszCmdLine*, *nCmdShow*)
HINSTANCE *hinstCurrent*;   /* handle of current instance   */
HINSTANCE *hinstPrevious*;   /* handle of previous instance   */
LPSTR *lpszCmdLine*;   /* address of command line   */
int *nCmdShow*;   /* show-window type (open/icon)   */

The **WinMain** function is called by the system as the initial entry point for a Windows application.

Parameters   *hinstCurrent*
Identifies the current instance of the application.

hinstPrevious
Identifies the previous instance of the application.

lpszCmdLine
Points to a null-terminated string specifying the command line for the application.

nCmdShow
Specifies how the window is to be shown. This parameter can be one of the following values:

Value	Meaning
SW_HIDE	Hides the window and passes activation to another window.
SW_MINIMIZE	Minimizes the specified window and activates the top-level window in the system's list.
SW_RESTORE	Activates and displays a window. If the window is minimized or maximized, Windows restores it to its original size and position (same as SW_SHOWNORMAL).
SW_SHOW	Activates a window and displays it in its current size and position.
SW_SHOWMAXIMIZED	Activates a window and displays it as a maximized window.

Value	Meaning
SW_SHOWMINIMIZED	Activates a window and displays it as an icon.
SW_SHOWMINNOACTIVE	Displays a window as an icon. The window that is currently active remains active.
SW_SHOWNA	Displays a window in its current state. The window that is currently active remains active.
SW_SHOWNOACTIVATE	Displays a window in its most recent size and position. The window that is currently active remains active.
SW_SHOWNORMAL	Activates and displays a window. If the window is minimized or maximized, Windows restores it to its original size and position (same as SW_RESTORE).

Return Value   The return value is the return value of the **PostQuitMessage** function if the function is successful. This function returns NULL if it terminates before entering the message loop.

Comments   The **WinMain** function calls the instance-initialization function and, if no other instance of the program is running, the application-initialization function. It then performs a message retrieval-and-dispatch loop that is the top-level control structure for the remainder of the application's execution. The loop is terminated when a WM_QUIT message is received, at which time this function exits the application instance by returning the value passed by the **PostQuitMessage** function.

Example   The following example uses the **WinMain** function to initialize the application (if necessary), initialize the instance, and establish a message loop:

```
int PASCAL WinMain(HINSTANCE hinstCurrent, HINSTANCE hinstPrevious,
    LPSTR lpszCmdLine, int nCmdShow)
{
    MSG msg;

    if (hinstPrevious == NULL)              /* other instances?      */
        if (!InitApplication(hinstCurrent)) /* shared items          */
            return FALSE;                   /* initialization failed */

    /* Perform initializations for this instance. */

    if (!InitInstance(hinstCurrent, nCmdShow))
        return FALSE;
```

```
                 /* Get and dispatch messages until WM_QUIT message. */

                 while (GetMessage(&msg, NULL, 0, 0)) {
                     TranslateMessage(&msg); /* translates virtual key codes */
                     DispatchMessage(&msg);  /* dispatches message to window */
                 }
                 return ((int) msg.wParam);       /* return value of PostQuitMessage */
             }
```

See Also   **DispatchMessage, GetMessage, PostQuitMessage, TranslateMessage**

WNetAddConnection   3.1

UINT WNetAddConnection(*lpszNetPath*, *lpszPassword*, *lpszLocalName*)
LPSTR *lpszNetPath*;   /* address of network device   */
LPSTR *lpszPassword*;   /* address of password   */
LPSTR *lpszLocalName*;   /* address of local device   */

The **WNetAddConnection** function redirects the specified local device (either a
disk drive or a printer port) to the given shared device or remote server.

Parameters   *lpszNetPath*
                    Points to a null-terminated string specifying the shared device or remote server.

                    lpszPassword
                    Points to a null-terminated string specifying the network password for the given
                    device or server.

                    lpszLocalName
                    Points to a null-terminated string specifying the local drive or device to be re-
                    directed. All *lpszLocalName* strings (such as LPT1) are case-independent. Only
                    the drive names A through Z and the device names LPT1 through LPT3 are
                    used.

Return Value   The return value is one of the following:

Value	Meaning
WN_SUCCESS	The function was successful.
WN_NOT_SUPPORTED	The function was not supported.
WN_OUT_OF_MEMORY	The system was out of memory.
WN_NET_ERROR	An error occurred on the network.
WN_BAD_POINTER	The pointer was invalid.
WN_BAD_NETNAME	The network resource name was invalid.

Value	Meaning
WN_BAD_LOCALNAME	The local device name was invalid.
WN_BAD_PASSWORD	The password was invalid.
WN_ACCESS_DENIED	A security violation occurred.
WN_ALREADY_CONNECTED	The local device was already connected to a remote resource.

See Also   **WNetCancelConnection, WNetGetConnection**

WNetCancelConnection

3.1

UINT WNetCancelConnection(*lpszName, fForce*)
LPSTR *lpszName*;   /* address of device or resource   */
BOOL *fForce*;   /* forced closure flag   */

The **WNetCancelConnection** function cancels a network connection.

Parameters   *lpszName*
Points to the name of the redirected local device (such as LPT1 or D:).

fForce
Specifies whether any open files or open print jobs on the device should be closed before the connection is canceled. If this parameter is FALSE and there are open files or jobs, the connection should not be canceled and the function should return the WN_OPEN_FILES error value.

Return Value   The return value is one of the following:

Value	Meaning
WN_SUCCESS	The function was successful.
WN_NOT_SUPPORTED	The function was not supported.
WN_OUT_OF_MEMORY	The system was out of memory.
WN_NET_ERROR	An error occurred on the network.
WN_BAD_POINTER	The pointer was invalid.
WN_BAD_VALUE	The *lpszName* parameter was not a valid local device or network name.

Value	Meaning
WN_NOT_CONNECTED	The *lpszName* parameter was not a redirected local device or currently accessed network resource.
WN_OPEN_FILES	Files were open and the *fForce* parameter was FALSE. The connection was not canceled.

See Also   **WNetAddConnection, WNetGetConnection**

WNetGetConnection

3.1

UINT WNetGetConnection(*lpszLocalName, lpszRemoteName, cbRemoteName***)**
LPSTR *lpszLocalName*;   /* address of local device name   */
LPSTR *lpszRemoteName*;   /* address of remote device name   */
UINT FAR* *cbRemoteName*;   /* max. number of bytes in buffer   */

The **WNetGetConnection** function returns the name of the network resource associated with the specified redirected local device.

Parameters   *lpszLocalName*
Points to a null-terminated string specifying the name of the redirected local device.

lpszRemoteName
Points to the buffer to receive the null-terminated name of the remote network resource.

cbRemoteName
Points to a variable specifying the maximum number of bytes the buffer pointed to by *lpszRemoteName* can hold. The function sets this variable to the number of bytes copied to the buffer.

Return Value   The return value is one of the following:

Value	Meaning
WN_SUCCESS	The function was successful.
WN_NOT_SUPPORTED	The function was not supported.
WN_OUT_OF_MEMORY	The system was out of memory.
WN_NET_ERROR	An error occurred on the network.
WN_BAD_POINTER	The pointer was invalid.
WN_BAD_VALUE	The *szLocalName* parameter was not a valid local device.

Value	Meaning
WN_NOT_CONNECTED	The *szLocalName* parameter was not a redirected local device.
WN_MORE_DATA	The buffer was too small.

See Also   **WNetAddConnection, WNetCancelConnection**

WordBreakProc

3.1

int CALLBACK WordBreakProc(*lpszEditText*, *ichCurrentWord*, *cbEditText*, *action*)
LPSTR *lpszEditText*;   /* address of edit text   */
int *ichCurrentWord*;   /* index of starting point   */
int *cbEditText*;   /* length of edit text   */
int *action*;   /* action to take   */

The **WordBreakProc** function is an application-defined callback function that the system calls whenever a line of text in a multiline edit control must be broken.

Parameters   *lpszEditText*
Points to the text of the edit control.

ichCurrentWord
Specifies an index to a word in the buffer of text that identifies the point at which the function should begin checking for a word break.

cbEditText
Specifies the number of bytes in the text.

action
Specifies the action to be taken by the callback function. This parameter can be one of the following values:

Value	Action
WB_LEFT	Look for the beginning of a word to the left of the current position.
WB_RIGHT	Look for the beginning of a word to the right of the current position.
WB_ISDELIMITER	Check whether the character at the current position is a delimiter.

Return Value   If the *action* parameter specifies WB_ISDELIMITER, the return value is non-zero (TRUE) if the character at the current position is a delimiter, or zero if it is not.

Otherwise, the return value is an index to the begining of a word in the buffer of text.

Comments

A carriage return (CR) followed by a linefeed (LF) must be treated as a single word by the callback function. Two carriage returns followed by a linefeed also must be treated as a single word.

An application must install the callback function by specifying the procedure-instance address of the callback function in a EM_SETWORDBREAKPROC message.

WordBreakProc is a placeholder for the library-defined function name. The actual name must be exported by including it in an **EXPORTS** statement in the library's module-definition file.

See Also

SendMessage

WriteComm

2.x

int **WriteComm**(*idComDev*, *lpvBuf*, *cbWrite*)
int *idComDev*;   /* identifier of comm. device   */
const void FAR* *lpvBuf*;   /* address of data buffer   */
int *cbWrite*;   /* number of bytes to write   */

The **WriteComm** function writes to the specified communications device.

Parameters

idComDev
Specifies the device to receive the bytes. The **OpenComm** function returns this value.

lpvBuf
Points to the buffer that contains the bytes to be written.

cbWrite
Specifies the number of bytes to be written.

Return Value

The return value specifies the number of bytes written, if the function is successful. The return value is less than zero if an error occurs, making the absolute value of the return value the number of bytes written.

Comments

To determine what caused an error, use the **GetCommError** function to retrieve the error value and status.

For serial ports, the **WriteComm** function deletes data in the transmission queue if there is not enough room in the queue for the additional bytes. Before calling **WriteComm**, applications should check the available space in the transmission queue by using the **GetCommError** function. Also, applications should use the **OpenComm** function to set the size of the transmission queue to an amount no smaller than the size of the largest expected output string.

See Also   **GetCommError, OpenComm, TransmitCommChar**

WritePrivateProfileString   3.0

BOOL WritePrivateProfileString(*lpszSection*, *lpszEntry*, *lpszString*, *lpszFilename*)
LPCSTR *lpszSection*;   /* address of section   */
LPCSTR *lpszEntry*;   /* address of entry   */
LPCSTR *lpszString*;   /* address of string to add   */
LPCSTR *lpszFilename*;   /* address of initialization filename   */

The **WritePrivateProfileString** function copies a character string into the specified section of the specified initialization file.

Parameters   *lpszSection*
Points to a null-terminated string that specifies the section to which the string will be copied. If the section does not exist, it is created. The name of the section is case-independent; the string may be any combination of uppercase and lowercase letters.

lpszEntry
Points to the null-terminated string containing the entry to be associated with the string. If the entry does not exist in the specified section, it is created. If this parameter is NULL, the entire section, including all entries within the section, is deleted.

lpszString
Points to the null-terminated string to be written to the file. If this parameter is NULL, the entry specified by the *lpszEntry* parameter is deleted.

lpszFilename
Points to a null-terminated string that names the initialization file.

Return Value   The return value is nonzero if the function is successful. Otherwise, it is zero.

Comments   To improve performance, Windows keeps a cached version of the most-recently accessed initialization file. If that filename is specified and the other three parameters are NULL, Windows flushes the cache.

Sections in the initialization file have the following form:

[*section*]
entry=string
.
.
.

If *lpszFilename* does not contain a fully qualified path and filename for the file, **WritePrivateProfileString** searches the Windows directory for the file. If the file does not exist, this function creates the file in the Windows directory.

If *lpszFilename* contains a fully qualified path and filename and the file does not exist, this function creates the file. The specified directory must already exist.

An application should use a private (application-specific) initialization file to record information that affects only that application. This improves the performance of both the application and Windows itself by reducing the amount of information that Windows must read when it accesses the initialization file. The exception to this is that device drivers should use the SYSTEM.INI file, to reduce the number of initialization files Windows must open and read during the startup process.

An application can use the **WriteProfileString** function to add a string to the WIN.INI file.

Example

The following example uses the **WritePrivateProfileString** function to add the string "testcode.c" to the LastFile entry in the [MyApp] section of the TESTCODE.INI initialization file:

```
BOOL fSuccess;

DebugBreak();

fSuccess = WritePrivateProfileString("MyApp",
    "LastFile", "testcode.c", "testcode.ini");

if (fSuccess)
    MessageBox(hwnd, "String added successfully",
            "WritePrivateProfileString", MB_OK);
else
    MessageBox(hwnd, "String could not be added",
            "WritePrivateProfileString", MB_ICONSTOP);
```

See Also   **WriteProfileString**

WriteProfileString

BOOL WriteProfileString(*lpszSection*, *lpszEntry*, *lpszString*)
LPCSTR *lpszSection*;   /* address of section   */
LPCSTR *lpszEntry*;   /* address of entry   */
LPCSTR *lpszString*;   /* address of string to write */

The **WriteProfileString** function copies a string into the specified section of the Windows initialization file, WIN.INI.

Parameters

lpszSection
> Points to a null-terminated string that specifies the section to which the string is to be copied. If the section does not exist, it is created. The name of the section is case-independent; the string may be any combination of uppercase and lowercase letters.

lpszEntry
> Points to the null-terminated string containing the entry to be associated with the string. If the entry does not exist in the specified section, it is created. If this parameter is NULL, the entire section, including all entries within the section, is deleted.

lpszString
> Points to the null-terminated string to be written to the file. If this parameter is NULL, the entry specified by the *lpszEntry* parameter is deleted.

Return Value

The return value is nonzero if the function is successful. Otherwise, it is zero.

Comments

Windows keeps a cached version of WIN.INI to improve performance. If all three parameters are NULL, Windows flushes the cache.

Sections in the WIN.INI initialization file have the following form:

[*section*]
entry=string
> .
> .
> .

Example

The following example calls the **GetWindowRect** function to retrieve the dimensions of the current window, converts the dimensions of a string, and writes the string to WIN.INI by using the **WriteProfileString** function. The next time the application is run, it could call the **GetProfileString** function to read the string, convert it to numbers, and pass the numbers as parameters to the **CreateWindow** function, thereby creating the window again with the same dimensions it had when the application terminated.

```
RECT rect;
BOOL fSuccess;
char szBuf[20];

GetWindowRect(hwnd, &rect);

sprintf(szBuf, "%u %u %u %u",
    rect.left, rect.right - rect.left,
    rect.top, rect.bottom - rect.top);

fSuccess = WriteProfileString("MySection",
        "Window dimensions", szBuf);

if (fSuccess)
    MessageBox(hwnd, "String added successfully",
            "WriteProfileString", MB_OK);
else
    MessageBox(hwnd, "String could not be added",
            "WriteProfileString", MB_ICONSTOP);
```

See Also   **GetProfileString, WritePrivateProfileString**

wsprintf

3.0

int _cdecl wsprintf(*lpszOutput, lpszFormat, ...*)
LPSTR *lpszOutput*;   /* address of string for output   */
LPSTR *lpszFormat*;   /* address of format-control string   */

The **wsprintf** function formats and stores a series of characters and values in a buffer. Each argument (if any) is converted according to the corresponding format specified in the format string.

Parameters   *lpszOutput*

Points to a null-terminated string to receive the string formatted as specified in the *lpszFormat* parameter.

lpszFormat

Points to a null-terminated string that contains the format-control string. In addition to the standard ASCII characters, a format specification for each argument appears in this string. For more information about the format specification, see the following Comments section.

. . .

Specifies zero or more optional arguments. The number and type of the optional arguments depend on the corresponding format-control character sequences specified in the *lpszFormat* parameter.

Return Value

The return value is the number of bytes stored in the *lpszOutput* string, not counting the terminating null character, if the function is successful.

Comments

The largest buffer that **wsprintf** can create is 1K.

Unlike most Windows functions, **wsprintf** uses the C calling convention (_**cdecl**) rather than the Pascal calling convention. As a result, the calling function must pop arguments off the stack. Also, arguments must be pushed on the stack from right to left. In C-language modules, the C compiler performs this task. (The **wvsprintf** function uses the Pascal calling convention.)

The format-control string contains format specifications that determine the output format for the arguments that follow the *lpszFormat* parameter. Format specifications always begin with a percent sign (%). If a percent sign is followed by a character that has no meaning as a format field, the character is not formatted. For example, %% produces a single percent-sign character.

The format-control string is read from left to right. When the first format specification is encountered, it causes the value of the first argument after the format-control string to be converted according to the format specification. The second format specification causes the second argument to be converted, and so on. If there are more arguments than there are format specifications, the extra arguments are ignored. The results are undefined if there are not enough arguments for all of the format specifications.

A format specification has the following form:

%[-][#][**0**][*width*][*.precision*]*type*

Each field of the format specification is a single character or number signifying a particular format option. The *type* characters, for example, determine whether the associated argument is interpreted as a character, a string, or a number. The simplest format specification contains only the percent sign and a *type* character (for example, %s). The optional fields (in brackets) control other aspects of the formatting. Following are the optional and required fields and their meanings:

Field	Meaning
-	Pad the output value with blanks or zeros to the right to fill the field width, aligning the output value to the left. If this field is omitted, the output value is padded to the left, aligning it to the right.
#	Prefix hexadecimal values with 0x (lowercase) or 0X (uppercase).
0	Pad the output value with zeros to fill the field width. If this field is omitted, the output value is padded with blank spaces.

Field	Meaning
width	Convert the specified minimum number of characters. The *width* field is a nonnegative integer. The width specification never causes a value to be truncated; if the number of characters in the output value is greater than the specified width, or if the *width* field is not present, all characters of the value are printed, subject to the value of the *precision* field.
precision	Convert the specified minimum number of digits. If there are fewer digits in the argument than the specified value, the output value is padded on the left with zeros. The value is not truncated when the number of digits exceeds the specified precision. If the specified precision is zero or omitted entirely, or if the period (.) appears without a number following it, the precision is set to 1.
	For strings, convert the specified maximum number of characters.
type	Format the corresponding argument as a character, a string, or a number. This field may be any of the following character sequences:

Sequence	Meaning
c	Insert a single character argument. The **wsprintf** function ignores character arguments with a numeric value of zero.
d, i	Insert a signed decimal integer argument.
ld, li	Insert a long signed decimal integer argument.
u	Insert an unsigned integer argument.
lu	Insert a long unsigned integer argument.
lx, lX	Insert a long unsigned hexadecimal integer argument in lowercase or uppercase.
s	Insert a string.

See Also   **wvsprintf**

---

wvsprintf   `3.0`

int wvsprintf(*lpszOutput, lpszFormat, lpvArglist*)
LPSTR *lpszOutput*;   /* address of output destination   */
LPCSTR *lpszFormat*;   /* address of format string   */
const void FAR* *lpvArglist*;   /* address of array of arguments   */

The **wvsprintf** function formats and stores a series of characters and values in a buffer. The items pointed to by the argument list are converted according to the corresponding format specification in the format string.

Parameters   *lpszOutput*
     Points to a null-terminated string to receive the string formatted as specified in the *lpszFormat* parameter.

lpszFormat
     Points to a null-terminated string that contains the format-control string. In addition to the standard ASCII characters, a format specification for each argument appears in this string. For more information about the format specification, see the description of the **wsprintf** function.

lpvArglist
     Points to an array of 16-bit values, each of which specifies an argument for the format-control string. The number, type, and interpretation of the arguments depend on the corresponding format-control character sequences specified in the *lpszFormat* parameter. Each character or 16-bit integer (**%c**, **%d**, **%x**, **%i**) requires one word in *lpvArglist*. Long integers (**%ld**, **%li**, **%lx**) require two words, the low-order word of the integer followed by the high-order word. A string (**%s**) requires two words, the offset followed by the segment (which together make up a far pointer).

Return Value   The return value is the number of bytes stored in the *lpszOutput* string, not counting the terminating null character, if the function is successful.

See Also   **wsprintf**

Yield   2.x

void Yield(void)

     The **Yield** function stops the current task and starts any waiting task.

Parameters   This function has no parameters.

Return Value   This function does not return a value.

Comments   Use the **Yield** function only when the application will not receive any messages.

     Applications that contain windows should use a **DispatchMessage**, **PeekMessage**, or **TranslateMessage** loop rather than call the **Yield** function directly. The message-loop functions handle message synchronization properly and yield at the appropriate times.

See Also   **DispatchMessage, PeekMessage, TranslateMessage**